Five Screenplays
by
Preston Sturges

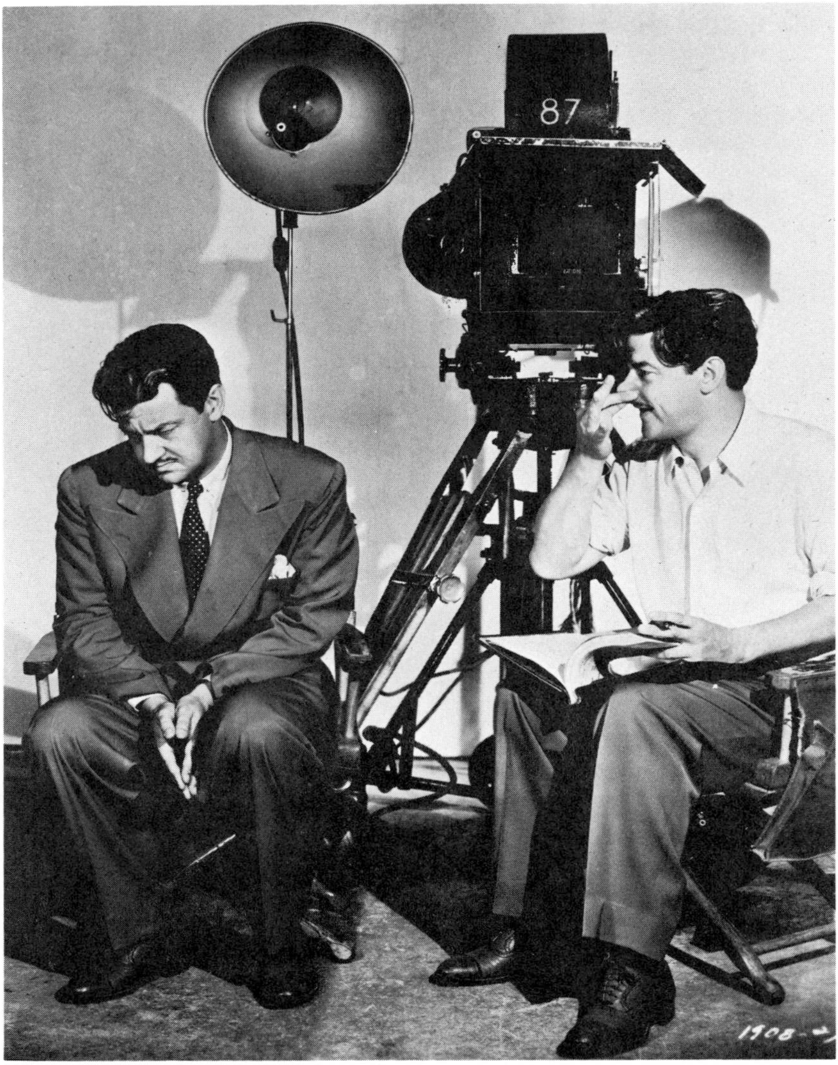

Being a writer-director is not easy: Sturges the director tells Sturges the writer what he thinks of his script.

Five Screenplays by Preston Sturges

Edited with an Introduction
by
BRIAN HENDERSON

UNIVERSITY OF CALIFORNIA PRESS
Berkeley Los Angeles London

The illustrations in this volume
were provided through the courtesy of
Sandy Sturges, the UCLA Special Collections,
and the Museum of Modern Art.

University of California Press
Berkeley and Los Angeles

University of California Press, Ltd.
London, England

Library of Congress Cataloging in Publication Data:
Sturges, Preston.
Five screenplays.
Contents: The great McGinty—Christmas in July—The Lady Eve—[etc.]
1. Moving-picture plays. I. Henderson, Brian.
II. Title.
PN1997.A1S84 1985 791.43'75 85–1020
ISBN 0–520–05442–3
Printed in the United States of America
1 2 3 4 5 6 7 8 9

Contents

Foreword

I have been struggling for weeks now to write some sort of foreword for this collection of my father's screenplays.

I've tried any number of glib, witty, sincerely playful and fascinating essays on everything from Humor in American Film in the Forties to The Responsibilities of Those with Screwball Comic Wherewithal. My wastebasket is overflowing with futile attempts at poetry, verse, haiku, soliloquy, and one ill-fated stab at finger painting. It's no use.

These screenplays were written to be enjoyed more than forewordeded or anything else they'll be subjected to in this form.

So let the bells peal, let the studious study, let those who look for meaning and import in every word do just that. The rest of you are in for a great read . . .

. . . thanks to the efforts of Nancy Cushing-Jones and Annette Wells, Lilace Hatayama, David Stewart Hull and Ernest Callenbach. And a very special thank you to my mother, Sandy.

Tom Sturges

Los Angeles, California
28 December 1984

Introduction

Preston Sturges was "by far the wittiest scriptwriter the English-speaking cinema has known" (Andrew Sarris).[1] He was "probably the most spectacular manipulator of sheer humor since Mark Twain" (Manny Farber).[2] He "restored to American film a sense of social satire . . . equalled only in Chaplin's films" (André Bazin).[3] "He was Hollywood's greatest writer-director, with emphasis on the former. He created a racy, malapropriate idiom whose deceptive ease would prove inimitable" (Richard Corliss).[4]

Sturges wrote and directed twelve films. The first eight were made for Paramount Pictures between 1939 and 1944: *The Great McGinty* (1940), *Christmas in July* (1940), *The Lady Eve* (1941), *Sullivan's Travels* (1942), *The Palm Beach Story* (1942), *The Great Moment* (1944), *The Miracle of Morgan's Creek* (1944), and *Hail the Conquering Hero* (1944). In partnership with Howard Hughes, Sturges wrote and directed *The Sin of Harold Diddlebock* in 1946; it was cut by Hughes and released as *Mad Wednesday* in 1947. For Twentieth Century–Fox, Sturges wrote and directed *Unfaithfully Yours* (1948) and *The Beautiful Blonde from Bashful Bend* (1949). In Paris he wrote and directed (in French and English versions) *Les Carnets du Major Thompson* [*The French They Are a Funny Race*] (1955).

Critics and other viewers generally agree that Sturges's last two films were failures. His extremely high reputation as a writer-director thus rests on ten films. This volume collects Sturges's shooting scripts for five of those films: the first four that he made for Paramount—*The Great McGinty, Christmas in July, The Lady Eve,* and *Sullivan's Travels*—and the eighth and last, *Hail the Conquering Hero.* The selection of these five for inclusion in the present volume was determined by the availability of publication rights. The grouping, although arbitrary, nevertheless has a certain logic. It allows the reader to trace Sturges's development as a writer-director in an unbroken line through his first four films, then skips to his final film in the Paramount series—which is to many, including Sturges, his finest.

Despite the time it has taken for these five scripts to be published, they are still, of course, not enough. At a minimum, *The Palm Beach Story* (1942), *The*

Great Moment (1944), *The Miracle of Morgan's Creek* (1944), *The Sin of Harold Diddlebock* (1946), and *Unfaithfully Yours* (1948) should also be published. Among the scripts that Sturges wrote in the 1930s for other directors, at least *The Power and the Glory* (1933), *Diamond Jim* (1935), *Easy Living* (1937), and *Remember the Night* (1940) should be made available. In addition, there are a number of interesting Sturges scripts that were never filmed, among them a version of *Roman Holiday* (1953) Sturges wrote for William Wyler that is decidedly less sweet than the filmed version.

The five scripts printed in this volume appear exactly as Sturges wrote them, photocopied from the last version of each before shooting began.[5] As studio production scripts, they follow a prescribed form—they were designed to be used not only by the director and the actors but by budget personnel, set designers, the costume department, the camera and sound crews, and so on. Among other divisions, the scripts are broken down by "sequences" that are marked "A," "B," "C," "D," "E," "F," "G," "H," "J," "K," etc. (There are no sequences designated "I," perhaps to avoid confusion with the Roman numeral.) The studio script's use of the term "sequence" is not susceptible to rigorous definition. A new sequence heading usually marks a shift in time and/or in setting, but other temporal and/or spatial shifts may take place within a sequence. Considered overall, the sequence is simply a convenient division of the script, and hence of the film-to-be, into large sections. Of the scripts in this volume, *Down Went McGinty* (*The Great McGinty*) has nine sequences, *The New Yorkers* (*Christmas in July*) six, *The Lady Eve* ten, *Sullivan's Travels* ten, and *The Little Marine* (*Hail the Conquering Hero*) five. The number of sequences in a script does not correspond to its overall number of pages or to the running time of the finished film, as the following table indicates:

	Number of pages	Number of sequences	Running time of film
Down Went McGinty	134	9	81 min.
The New Yorkers	111	6	70 min.
The Lady Eve	155	10	97 min.
Sullivan's Travels	145	10	90 min.
The Little Marine	137	5	101 min.

A studio production script contains a good deal of information besides scene-setting descriptions and dialogue. For instance, each page of a script bears the date on which it was completed or, more precisely, on which it was typed at the studio. This date is placed at the bottom left of the page in all the scripts printed below except *The Little Marine* (*Hail the Conquering Hero*), in which it is printed at the upper right of the page. *Down Went McGinty* (*The Great McGinty*), *The New Yorkers* (*Christmas in July*), and *The Lady Eve* have the same date marking on each page; the pages of *Sullivan's Travels* and *The Little Marine* (*Hail the Conquering Hero*) do not all have the same date markings. Each page of the scripts printed below is also designated by the letter of the sequence in which it is located. The pages of Sequence A are designated "A-1," "A-2," etc. The pages of the sequences after Sequence A are marked both by the sequence in which they occur and by their place in the overall script. Thus the first page of Sequence B of *The Lady Eve* is marked "B-1 (8)," indicating that it is the first page of Sequence B and the eighth page of the script as a whole; the last page of the script is marked "K-9 (155)." (In addition, of course, each script page in this volume is paginated consecutively by numbers placed at the bottom of the page.) In the introductions to the five scripts, page references are always to the overall numbering of the script in question, thus "(page A-1)" for the first page of *The Lady Eve,* "(page 155)" for its last page, etc. It should also be noted that, for better or for worse, the terms "screenplay" and "script" are used interchangeably throughout this introduction and the individual introductions to the five scripts.

Finally, like all studio production scripts, the screenplays printed here are organized according to the successive shots of the film-to-be. These shots are numbered according to the sequence in which they occur—"A-1," "A-2," etc. (Needless to say, there is a possibility for confusion between such shot designations and the sequence page numbers. In the introductions below, references are always to page numbers unless otherwise specified.) Following the shot number, Sturges describes the subject of the shot in capital letters. At the beginning of a sequence—or of a new scene within the sequence—this description always includes the setting of the shot, which appears in underlined capital letters, presumably for the benefit of production staff members. If the setting is clear from the description of the first shot of a sequence or scene, it is not repeated in the subsequent shots of that passage. If the shot includes camera movement or character action or if a particular demeanor of actors or quality of objects, etc., is desired, that is specified in lower case below the shot designation. ("Dialogue continuities," which are transcripts of a film's dialogue taken down after a film has been shot, omit all such information, everything indeed except dialogue.)

Preserving the notation of studio production scripts makes for a somewhat cluttered page, but it has its advantages. The general reader will find them highly readable and will have immediate access to Sturges's superb dialogue. In smoothed-over, continuous scripts—those published without the original page numbers or breakdowns into shots—it is often hard to find things. For critics, teachers, and students, reproduction of an original script preserves its value as a research document, whereas an adapted script becomes an additional puzzle to be solved and thereby compounds the problems of interpretation. In any case, Sturges did not adapt or otherwise prepare his screenplays for publication in his lifetime; to attempt to do so for him would be presumptuous in the extreme.

In addition to the obvious benefits of having Sturges's screenplays in print, there are a number of delightful surprises. The scripts provide access to Sturges's work process, including notes to himself and other items that do not appear on the screen. For instance, the second shot of *The Lady Eve* is described thus on page A-1:

> CHARLES PIKE, PROF. JONES, MUGGSY, TWO YOUNG SCIENTISTS, SEVEN INDIANS AND THE BRAZILIAN PILOT OF THE MOTOR LAUNCH—IN THE SELVA AT THE EDGE OF THE JUTAHY
>
> In other words, the bank of a tropical river.

Even Sturges's censor-dodging strategies show up occasionally in his scripts. In *Sullivan's Travels:*

> THE GIRL
> Then don't get Ritzie. And I'll tell you some other things I haven't got; I haven't got a yacht, or a pearl necklace, or a fur coat, or a country seat or even a winter seat . . . and I could use a new girdle too.
> (Protection: stockings) (page 52)

"Girdle" got by in this case, but elsewhere in his scripts many words, phrases, lines, and situations—whose censorship problems were unforeseen by Sturges or which were not so readily sacrificed by him—did not. Numerous instances of Sturges's censorship problems are discussed in the introductions to the individual scripts.

Some of Sturges's notes take us to the heart of the directing process itself and hence to relations between Sturges the writer and Sturges the director (see the frontispiece). Toward the beginning of a large group dialogue in *Hail the Conquering Hero*, Judge Dennis, Doc Bissell, and the other town fathers confront Woodrow, his mother, Libby, her aunt, and the six Marines. Sturges has duly indicated cutting back and forth between the two groups:

> C-39 THE JUDGE AND THE OTHERS . . .
> C-40 WOODROW AND HIS GROUP . . .
> C-41 THE JUDGE AND HIS GROUP . . .
> C-42 WOODROW AND HIS GROUP (pages 58–59)

Then he writes:

> NOTE: I am tired of cutting back and forth. The rest of this will be written as a master scene. (page 59)

Sturges does write it that way until the scene concludes, or merges into another scene, two pages later. In the filmed passage, however, he continues to cut between the two groups and among closer shots within each group.

Sturges the writer and Sturges the director have had their respective partisans. Andrew Sarris said of Sturges that "all his screenwriting efforts in the Thirties would now be of only the most esoteric concern if he had not made the decisive leap from the writer's cubicle to the director's chair."[6] Evidently responding to Sarris, Richard Corliss wrote a few years later in his book on Hollywood screenwriters: "While his direction, especially of extended dialogue scenes, shows far more control than contemporary critics were willing to grant it, Sturges's direction would be of only the most esoteric concern today if he had not written eight or ten of Hollywood's best screenplays."[7] This opposition at first glance resembles a Kantian antinomy—each proposition appears to be necessarily true yet both cannot be true. The opposition itself, however, may be questioned, arising as it does in a dispute about the relative importance of directors and screenwriters generally. Perhaps Sturges is not a good example for such disputes—he was hardly a typical screenwriter or a typical director.

Sturges was the sole major Hollywood director who filmed only his own original screenplays. *The Great Moment* draws its facts from a published biography, but otherwise Sturges—his last two films aside—never adapted his screenplays from someone else's story, novel, or play. The exceptions of *Easy Living* and *The Lady Eve*, based on stories by Vera Caspary and Monckton

Sturges the busy screenwriter–typing, smoking, and telephoning at the same time. (He was also interested in yachts–note the hull models on the wall.)

Hoffe respectively, only prove the rule. The stories are so completely transformed by Sturges that screen credit to the "original authors" seems ludicrous. As a screenwriter, moreover, Sturges never, as far as I know, collaborated with another writer. He was sometimes assigned, especially in the 1930s, to improve or rewrite the scripts of a prior writer or writers who had departed a project. Even then Sturges preferred, as often as possible, to discard the prior work and start all over again. It is perhaps not surprising that Sturges as writer-director was not able to meet such exacting standards for much more than a decade—no one else was able to sustain them for even that long. (Billy Wilder has functioned as a successful writer-director for an astonishing five decades, but he has always collaborated with other writers and has frequently adapted novels and plays.)

Separate introductions follow for each of the screenplays collected in this volume, detailing their genesis and development. For the most part, these introductions treat Sturges's direction as, in effect, the final stage of script revision. This perspective leaves out most of what is usually defined as direction, but the fact that Sturges directed his own scripts is enormously important in itself. Negatively speaking, it means that no other person altered the script in question by adding or subtracting things, however small, by imposing a questionable pace, by selecting the wrong cast members, or by guiding them incorrectly. The most common—and bitter—complaint of Hollywood writers of all eras is that their work has been distorted by other writers and/or by the director. Sturges had the opportunity to alter his dialogue, even to omit scenes or to change the order of scenes if he chose to, during shooting or in the editing. His own brilliance and his tireless revising aside, this opportunity resulted in a final polish and perfection that few scripts have ever enjoyed. It is for these reasons that the introductions below venture frequently forward from the early versions of Sturges's screenplays, to the final versions printed here, to the actual film versions—for they constitute a single continuous process of revision.

It should be pointed out, finally, that there are many differences in dialogue, most of them minor, between the final scripts and the films, and that the majority of these are not noted in the introductions. There simply was not space to do so. (Note, however, that the passages of dialogue quoted in the introductions have been corrected to accord with the film version.) An excellent activity for prospective screenwriters, students, or anyone else interested in Sturges's work is to see one of his films with script in hand and to make notations of differences.

* * *

Mary Dempsey, who later called herself Mary Desmond, Mary d'Este, and finally Mary Desti, was born in Chicago in 1871. At some point she married

Edmund P. Biden, about whom little is known. Their son Edmund Preston Biden was born on August 29, 1898. In late 1900 or early 1901 Mary d'Este left Biden for Europe and a singing career, taking her infant son; she called him Preston because she disliked the name Edmund.

In Paris she met Isadora Duncan (the famous modern dancer), a few years younger than she, and soon moved into her studio; Preston was taken to Giverny to live with Isadora's mother. At the request of her mother, Mary returned to Chicago after a year with Isadora. On October 3, 1901, she married an old sweetheart, Solomon Sturges, a stockbroker from a Chicago banking family, who legally adopted Preston in January 1902.

One of the liberties that Solomon allowed Mary was her annual visit to Europe, up to six months a year. (When Mary wanted to extend her license to eleven months a year, the marriage was over.) Mary returned to Europe nearly every year, and she always took young Preston with her. In 1903 Mary left Preston with a family named Rousseau in Joinville-le-Pont long enough for him to regard the adults as *maman* and *papa* and their son as a brother; during this period, Preston's English almost disappeared. Once in a while, Mary would return, a beautiful lady in a cloud of perfume, arriving in a shining conveyance with presents for everyone.

In 1904 Mary spent six months with Isadora at Bayreuth under the sponsorship of Cosima Wagner. A photo from this stay shows Preston in breastplate, accompanied by Temple Duncan, Isadora's niece, whom he later called his first love. "She kept me broke for years buying her highly perfumed soap and doll-sized Singer sewing machines," he remembered.[8] The children were left at an inn with a governess while Mary and Isadora shared a peasant's villa close by. The party eventually moved on to Berlin, Hanover, Florence, and Venice and was then met by Solomon; he put Isadora on a train to Berlin and returned to Chicago with Mary and Preston.

Sturges, who never thought of Solomon as a stepfather, later remembered a night in 1907 after he and Mary had returned to Chicago following a long absence. His parents argued at length, decided to separate, and at last asked Preston to choose Paris with his mother or Chicago with his father. He chose to stay with his father, but Solomon said, "I am not your father," after which the boy cried inconsolably. He was taken to Paris despite his wishes and in the following years was enrolled at a series of schools—the Lycée Janson (Paris), 1907–11; L'École des Roches (Normandy), 1911–13; La Villa (Lausanne), 1913–14.

One of Mary's later husbands, a Turk whose father had been personal physician to the sultan, gave Mary a skin cream that she decided to market as "Le Secret du Harem." Thus was born Maison Desti, a cosmetics emporium opened in Paris with the aid of Paris Singer, sewing machine heir and father of a child by Isadora. A shop in London and then in New York followed; there was also a seashore branch in Deauville, open for one summer, which Preston managed. With the declaration of war in 1914 Mary sent Preston home, and Solomon enrolled him at Irving Preparatory School, which regularly sent students on to Columbia University. But when Mary fired the head of her New York shop, Preston left school to manage it. He remained with Maison Desti until 1916, then worked as a runner for the brokerage firm F. B. Keech, and finally enrolled in pilot training in the Army Signal Corps. He learned to fly, but the war ended before he saw active service.

After the war Preston discussed possible careers with his father, but after returning briefly to F. B. Keech, he ended up once more running his mother's business in New York when she returned to Paris and Isadora. Finding management of a retail beauty shop less than a manly occupation, Preston closed the New York shop in 1920 and moved the operation to Brooklyn to run it as a manufacturing and wholesale concern. For several years he made a modest living and also saw many plays and read, among other things, H. L. Mencken's *The American Language.* In 1922 Sturges lived with Estelle De Wolfe Mudge Godfrey, whom he had wooed away from an older husband, in an apartment he designed and helped build behind the Desti plant, now at another location in Brooklyn. They married in December 1923, when Estelle's divorce was final. The business did fairly well for a while and became even more successful when Preston landed a contract to supply $1,000 worth of products a month to another company.

When Isadora returned to Russia with her husband in late 1923, Mary was stranded in Paris, her fifth marriage at an end; she returned to New York and reclaimed the business from Preston. He was appalled and argued that the business had been his responsibility since 1915, that he had made it profitable, and above all that she had given it to him. However, Mary was adamant; although the action estranged her from her son for some years, she took over the business in November 1924. Preston retained the rights to Kiss-Proof, the lipstick that he had developed, which brought him some income for another year or so. He and Estelle took an apartment on 39th Street in Manhattan and spent the warm months of the year at an unheated estate that Estelle purchased in Westchester County. Supported mainly by her trust income, the couple lived happily for about two years. Preston continued sales of his kiss-proof lipstick and worked on a series of inventions that, however ingenious, he never promoted successfully. In January 1927, when Sturges suggested they go to Paris to promote a possible new venture, Estelle stunned Preston by telling him she no longer loved him. He responded that it would be immoral for her to continue to occupy the bed of a man she did not love. This was an even greater shock, he later said, than Solomon's denial of his fatherhood twenty years earlier. Wounded deeply but apparently too proud to argue, Sturges packed his bag and left for Chicago.

Not until the first night at his father's apartment did the pain of the separation hit Preston. He sat on the floor by his father's bed all night, holding his father's hand. Solomon assured him that he would get over his loss, but as the pain grew worse, Preston seriously considered suicide. Only his witnessing the death of a construction worker in a fall from a scaffold decided him against the idea. He left for New York immediately to find Estelle. She was not at their apartment, and for three despairing weeks he could find no trace of her. When she did appear—she had been at Solomon's apartment in Chicago but had sworn him to secrecy—she was not interested in continuing the marriage. Unable to imagine life without his most cherished companion, Preston then suggested that they stay together for a time so he could accustom himself to the idea of their being apart forever. Estelle laughed. Sturges later said that this taught him that when a woman is finished with a man, she is finished.

Preston and his mother reconciled at this time, each promising the other that nothing would come between them again. (Nothing did.) Seriously worried about him, his mother and father agreed that Mary would give Maison Desti back to Preston and that Solomon would provide $1,000 a month to refurbish it and get it back on its feet. A guaranteed $1,000 a month gave enough financial security to put Mary on the next boat to Europe and Isadora. Shortly thereafter, Isadora was killed in a car accident, which Mary witnessed.

During this time Preston began his second song-writing career. (His first song had been published when he was a schoolboy.) Ted Snyder, quite famous in his day, taught him the concept of the "wedding of the words and music." (Years later when Ted was broke, Preston opened Snyder's restaurant for him to repay his kindness.) However, no songs from this collaboration were published.

At Christmas of 1927, during a visit to his father's tailor to be measured for some new suits, Preston had an attack of acute appendicitis. He almost died before medical advice was sought, and he spent six weeks in the hospital. There he wrote an operetta based on Irvin S. Cobb's *Speaking of Operations*, Solomon bringing him books on drama to help in his writing. Most useful was Brander Matthews's *A Study of the Drama*, which emphasized audience response rather than formal values for their own sake. He soon decided that his hospital play was worthless, a product of anesthesia and drugs.

Recuperating at his father's apartment, he was also going out with a successful actress, who taunted him with his failures and his lack of money. One night, after he had assessed her failings in retaliation, she responded that she was writing a play about a bore and that he was the model. Stung, he derisively announced that if she could write a play, he could write one too and, furthermore, that his would be produced first and run longer. He went home and wrote Act III of *The Guinea Pig* that night. The play concerns a young woman novelist who has written a romantic bestseller and is hired by a New York producer to turn it into a play. She is unable, however, to write a convincing seduction scene. A young man she meets in the producer's outer office becomes her way of finding out "exactly what does a young man say to a young woman to make her surrender herself instantly." The girl, not surprisingly, eventually falls in love with the young man. The play's funniest lines, the critics later agreed, belonged not to the leads but to Sam Small, the fur dealer-turned-producer who commissions the girl's play; Sturges had apparently based the character on the thickly accented professors he had known in Europe. Sturges convinced the Wharf Players of Provincetown to put on the play, gathered some good notices, and set out to seek a Broadway production.

Through an actor friend he got a job as assistant stage manager for a play produced by the successful director Brock Pemberton. When no one was interested in *The Guinea Pig*, Sturges produced the play himself on $2,500 donated by the hostess of a dinner party he attended. With the advice of Charles H. Abramson a low-budget production was staged, its opening timed for the return of the major critics from the Christmas holidays. Sturges was fortunate to get Alexander Carr, a well-known stage and screen actor, who brought Sam Small vividly to life. Carr also showed Sturges how to "point" his dialogue. In one scene Sturges had Small correct the girl's opinion of a third party: "No, dearie. He was a damn fool. Excuse me to contradict you." Carr turned the line around: "Excuse me to contradict you . . . but he was a damn fool."[9] (Sturges later summoned Carr from New York to play Mr. Schindel in *Christmas in July*.) The "uncertain little comedy" was praised by George S. Kaufman in the *New York Times* for having "quite a little simple and entertaining humor," and it ran sixty-four performances.

Sturges then joined a touring company of *Frankie and Johnnie* as assistant stage manager and actor. After *Frankie and Johnnie*, he was assistant stage manager for *Goin' Home* and then for a road company of *Hot Bed*, which he left in Chicago when it was closed by the police.

At his father's house Sturges wrote (in six days, as he later boasted) *Strictly Dishonorable*, a speakeasy comedy in which the sophisticated, foreign-born opera singer wins the girl from the clean-cut American boy. The most comic parts were Judge Dempsey, a chronic patron, and Patrolman Mulligan, neither of whom was a stickler for the rulebook. Sturges sent it to Pemberton, who wrote back immediately that, with work on the second and third acts, he would direct an August production. In stormy rehearsals and previews Pemberton forced Sturges to rewrite much of the play and made changes of his own in his work with the actors. Sturges acknowledges the collaboration of all concerned in the published version of the play: "A play, as produced, is rarely the work of one individual. During the rehearsal period, suggestions are accepted from everyone within shouting distance. Many of these suggestions are excellent, and all of them are used. It is impossible to list here the names of all the people responsible for *Strictly Dishonorable* as it stands; I thank them all, and spend my royalties to their good health."[10] At the time, however, Sturges resented the rewrites, feeling that Pemberton was undermining his work; often the two did not speak. The play was a great success, running 557 performances in New York alone. Sturges enjoyed the fame and the money but seems to have had a strong desire to succeed thenceforth without Pemberton's interference.

Sturges next wrote *Recapture* (1930), a comedy-drama with a tragic ending evidently based on his relationship with Estelle. An ex-husband seeks to recapture the love of his ex-wife and succeeds in Act I, both have doubts in Act II, she dies in an elevator accident in Act III. The venture was opposed by Pemberton and Abramson, who now shared an apartment with Sturges. Both of them urged him to write another comedy. The play opened in January 1930, was deplored by the critics, and ran twenty-four performances. (When Noël Coward's *Private Lives* opened later, Sturges noted that it was *Recapture* with a happy ending.)

By the time *Recapture* opened, Sturges was involved in another project considered by his theater friends to be even more dubious. H. Maurice Jacquet, a friend from his songwriting days, had written an operetta that had been produced expensively and had flopped. But he had saved the scenery and costumes and wanted to try again. Sturges agreed to write a new book and lyrics and some new songs to go with the sets and costumes on hand. To escape Abramson's outrage and the skepticism of others, Sturges left New York on February 10, 1930 (the same night that *Strictly Dishonorable* opened in Chicago), for the Palm Beach home of Paris Singer.

On the train he met heiress Eleanor Post Hutton, then twenty. They were married, despite her family's opposition, on April 12, 1930. Soon after, Sturges's mother returned from Europe in ill health, which she attributed to the shock of Isadora's death in 1927, and as a result, a honeymoon trip on Sturges's yacht, *Recapture*, was postponed. Then, backed by all of Sturges's available money, the operetta, retitled *The Well of Romance*, opened in November 1930, but it failed to excite critical or popular interest and folded after eight performances. Mary Desti died in April 1931; Eleanor left for Europe in June the same year—to continue her singing lessons. Sturges had apparently dominated Eleanor, had not taken her seriously, and had been depressed at his two failures and his mother's illness.

Sturges then worked on a bedroom farce called *Unfaithfully Yours* and wrote *A Cup of Coffee*, a three-act play about a slogan-contest winner. He gained weight and wore a flowing moustache that made him look much older than he was. He patronized a number of dime-a-dance halls and eventually wrote *Child of Manhattan*, which opened March 1, 1932, about a millionaire who falls in love with a dance-hall girl. The critics found it coarse on the one hand and trite on the other; although it ran eighty-seven performances, audiences also seemed to find it distasteful. While writing the play, Sturges asked Eleanor to return and, when she did not, he sailed for Paris to tell her of his resolve to be a better husband. But she had been enjoying her independence and the attentions of many titled suitors and was cool to Sturges. He wrote Abramson from Paris, "I'm terribly in love . . . but if you could only see her, Charley, she is unbelievably beautiful and smart."[11] She declined to return but apparently renewed her commitment to the marriage. When *Child of Manhattan* failed, he borrowed money to go to Paris again, angering the producer by leaving the show when it needed work. Eleanor asked how much he would accept for a divorce; insulted, he overlooked $100,000 he figured she owed him and said,

"It will cost you one courteous request, madame, and a polite thank-you when it is all over." Back in New York, however, he discovered that he could communicate with her only through her lawyers.

Before he met Eleanor, Sturges had done two filmscript rewrites for the Paramount Astoria studio on Long Island—*The Big Pond,* a Maurice Chevalier vehicle, in 1929 and *Fast and Loose* in 1930. He received only "dialogue" credit on these films, but he earned twelve thousand dollars for less than a month's work. *Strictly Dishonorable* was filmed in 1931 and *Child of Manhattan* in 1932, both under previously negotiated contracts. On the basis of the former, Carl Laemmle of Universal Pictures offered Sturges a contract, which he accepted. Never intending to stay, he went to Hollywood in 1932 in order to repair his fortunes. He kept his Manhattan apartment and his boat but took with him his secretary, Bianca Gilchrist, the estranged wife of a songwriter friend, and two cronies who followed in his Lincoln. In fact, he stayed in Hollywood for twenty years. For Laemmle he wrote an adaptation of H. G. Wells's *The Invisible Man*—ignoring, as was to become his habit, the eight previous attempts in the studio's file. In the end his version, like the others, was not used.

He stayed on in the studio bungalow and did three weeks' complimentary work on a comedy released later as *They Just Had to Get Married* (1933). "I hope that this bread cast upon the waters will return as ham sandwiches," he remarked.[12] He then wrote *The Power and the Glory,* which bore some relation to the life of Eleanor's grandfather, C. W. Post, a self-made millionaire who had killed himself at age fifty-five for unknown reasons. From time to time Eleanor had told him stories about her grandfather's life, and although nonchronological, they had a certain cohesiveness. Sturges thought he could successfully use that nonchronological structure to tell a story on film. *The Power and the Glory* may well have been the first use of "voice-under" in film. Sturges was hailed for inventing "narratage," and the script was displayed under glass in the lobby of the New York theater in which the film opened. Narratage included the voice of Tom Garner's old secretary remembering long-past conversations while the screen depicted the players mouthing the words we hear in the secretary's voice. With its tycoon subject and its nonchronological flashback structure, *The Power and the Glory* is a striking anticipation of the theme and method of *Citizen Kane* (1941). It differs most from the later work perhaps in its lugubrious direction by William K. Howard, who flattens the potential variety of its scenes into monotony and the bold complexity of its structure into sheer anticlimax.

Sturges wrote *The Power and the Glory* on speculation, as he was accustomed to do at this period, reasoning that no playwright gets better terms. (Later he was to decry "the Hollywood disease" of being unable to write unless on salary.) Jesse L. Lasky admired the script and agreed to film it exactly as written, offering Sturges a percentage of the profits against a $17,500 advance. This arrangement frightened many producers; B. P. Schulberg of Paramount wrote in *The Hollywood Reporter* against the percentage deal, the nonrevision clause, and particularly the use of a single screenwriter. Sturges wrote in defense of the arrangement; he also broke precedent by being present on the set during shooting. Indeed, several performers averred that they had never seen a writer before. Ostensibly serving as dialogue director, Sturges sought to learn as much about filmmaking as possible. *The Power and the Glory* was admired by critics and did well at first in the large city theaters but it was not commercially successful.

Sturges rented a house in the Hollywood hills, built a schooner, and developed a number of friendships among writers and humorists of the time. He wrote a political comedy, *The Vagrant,* in 1933, but after the failure of the much-touted *The Power and the Glory,* no studio was interested. He wrote a screenplay based on *The Green Hat* in eight weeks at MGM, but his contract was not renewed. Harry Cohn hired him on a comparable basis for Columbia and soon also fired him. He did some work on *Imitation of Life* (1934), then wrote the screenplays for *Thirty Day Princess* and *We Live Again* (1934), the latter an adaptation of Tolstoy's *Resurrection* for Rouben Mamoulian and Samuel Goldwyn. On the basis of that film, typecast for the moment as a specialist in literary adaptations, he was rehired at Universal for $1,500 a week.

Sturges wrote the script for *The Good Fairy* (1934), based on a Molnar play, for William Wyler and wrote a new screenplay for *Diamond Jim* (1935), another tycoon story, thought to be one of his best scripts. On both films Sturges was often on the set, observing and rewriting to some degree. A. Edward Sutherland, the director of *Diamond Jim,* often conferred with him on the nuances of scenes about to be shot. They fought the producer for their ending—Jim commits suicide by overeating—and won. Sturges received sole screen credit for *The Good Fairy* for the first time since *The Power and the Glory;* two prior writers received an adaptation credit on *Diamond Jim,* although Sturges had characteristically abandoned their script, and even the biography of Brady on which it was based, to begin again from scratch.

Sturges's salary was now $2,500 a week, and he had several offers. He did two rewrites for Universal, *Next Time We Love* (1935) and *Love Before Breakfast* (1935), vehicles for Margaret Sullavan and Carole Lombard respectively. Songs that he co-wrote appeared in *The Gay Deception* (1935) and *One Rainy Afternoon* (1936). Around this time Sturges also wrote a story and screenplay called *Song of Joy,* about a studio that has hired an opera singer for $19,000 a week and has to invent a picture for her in four weeks. Although Universal bought the story and screenplay, Sturges's stinging satire of producers, yes-men, writers, and directors did not appeal to his friend Sutherland or to anyone else, apparently to Sturges's genuine surprise. (See the introduction to *Sullivan's Travels* below.)

In March 1936 Sturges was hired by Paramount to write *Hotel Haywire* (1937), a vehicle for Burns and Allen that was eventually rewritten and made with other players. This led to a two-year contract with Paramount at $2,500 a week, Sturges's first regular employment by a studio, beginning September 29, 1936.

Sturges's first Paramount assignment was to Arthur Hornblow, Jr., who asked him to turn *Easy Living,* a Vera Caspary story owned by the studio, into a screenplay. The story concerned a poor cosmetician who impulsively steals a sable coat from one of her clients. Deception piles on deception, and she eventually loses both the man she loves and the coat itself. In Sturges's version, the coat is thrown from a high-rise by a millionaire banker (Edward Arnold) trying to teach his wife a lesson. It lands on Mary Smith (Jean Arthur), who is passing by on a bus. She tries to return the coat, but the banker insists she keep it and buys her a new hat. She loses her job but because everyone (falsely) thinks she is having an affair with the banker, she gets a luxurious hotel suite, room service, and beautiful clothes free.

Easy Living is Sturges's most explicit satire on the irrationality of the stock market, capitalism, and the lives lived under it. In one day a millionaire's son (Ray Milland) can be reduced to working in the Automat and a poor clerk can rise to living in a posh hotel. A coat that costs $58,000 is worth so little to a banker that he can throw it away, and worth so much to a clerk that she cannot grasp that it will utterly change her life. The stock market fluctuates on the unthinking words of a clerk, and fortunes are thereby made and lost. The son's silly buy-and-sell formulas for the stock market make millions, and he goes from total failure to total success in one day. A girl's notoriety makes her a walking advertisement for expensive goods; money flows toward her in expectation of a market break-through and a hotel's fortunes depend on her.

Sturges had given his father $15,000 of the proceeds of *Strictly Dishonorable* to invest—just before the crash of 1929. This was lost, as was most of Solomon's business. Perhaps as a consequence, Sturges did not invest the money he earned as a screenwriter in the thirties and as a writer-director in the forties, a decision that cost him dearly in the long run. (With the large sums he earned, Sturges built boats, opened and continually supplied capital to restaurants—first Snyder's, then The Players—bought and remodeled a house, opened and continually supplied capital for the Sturges Engineering Company, paid salaries for household staff, paid alimony and child support, and so on. By the time of World War II, he was in the 96 percent tax bracket.) *Easy Living* is Sturges's light-hearted revenge on Wall Street or, as it is called in the film, Broad Street. J. B. Ball is "the bull of Broad Street," which becomes, in one marvelous transposition, "the Ball of Bull Street."

After *Easy Living,* Sturges worked on *Port of Seven Seas* (1937), *College Swing* (1937), and *Never Say Die* (1938). *If I Were King* (1938), a film about François Villon directed by Frank Lloyd, with Ronald Colman and Basil Rathbone, engaged his interest far more than these. Sturges entirely rewrote the forty-year-old play on which the film was based, translated Villon's poetry himself, and in some cases invented his own.

Bianca Gilchrist, who was living with Sturges and supervising reconstruction of his house, left him when he seemed to have little time for her amidst an engineering company he set up to develop his inventions, a restaurant he was establishing, and other activities. During this time Sturges met Louise Tevis, who was separated from her husband, a man Sturges knew slightly. They fell in

A determined restaurateur, Sturges liked to cook at home too.

love and were married in Reno, when her divorce was final, on November 7, 1938. In Reno Sturges worked on *Two Bad Hats* from a Monckton Hoffe story of the same name, finishing a draft on November 30, 1938; it was later revised and directed by Sturges himself as *The Lady Eve.* This project was developed for the Paramount producer Albert Lewin, with whom Sturges enjoyed working but who left Paramount in 1939. (See the introduction to *The Lady Eve* below.)

Another project for Lewin was *Beyond These Tears,* which became *The Amazing Marriage* and finally *Remember the Night* (1940). Lewin's memos helped shape the plot of this film and, to some degree, of *Eve. Remember the Night* is an unusual Sturges script—sentimental, romantic, gentle. In it a district attorney (Fred MacMurray) prosecutes a shoplifter (Barbara Stanwyck) just before Christmas. He wins a continuance over the holidays, undercutting her lawyer's lachrymose work on the jury. Feeling guilty, he arranges her bail; she is dropped at his door by mistake and he ends up taking her to his Indiana home for Christmas, where everyone likes her and he falls in love. He has told his mother

(Beulah Bondi) that Stanwyck is a criminal. Separately, she asks Stanwyck not to undermine her son's hard-won career. Back in New York, MacMurray is mean to Stanwyck on the stand in order to turn the jury in her favor; to foil this strategy, she confesses to the crime. Once she is convicted, she tells him that things have worked out for the best, and he agrees to wait for her.

Lewin's departure and that of Arthur Hornblow, Jr., another Paramount producer congenial to Sturges, meant that Mitchell Leisen, now his own producer, had a free hand with the film. He preferred his own cuts to rewrites with the writer. Sturges felt that such cuts were unnecessary and that they interfered with his pacing, but because Leisen had been successful in recent years, the head of production, William LeBaron, let him make them. On the other hand, LeBaron wanted to keep Sturges, who was talking of leaving Paramount for another studio where he might have more control of his scripts. He gave Sturges permission to proceed with a favorite project, *Triumph over Pain,* which later became *The Great Moment,* but Sturges was still unhappy.

LeBaron then agreed, apparently with considerable misgiving, to let him direct a low-budget film of his earlier script *The Vagrant.* Sturges went over the script, revising it extensively; the shooting script, printed below, was finished on November 28, 1939. Shooting began on December 11 and continued until January 1940; the film was retitled *The Great McGinty.* (See the introduction to *The Great McGinty* below.)

* * *

However brief his sojourn as a Hollywood director, Sturges has been blessed with some of the best American film criticism ever devoted to a single director. It began, of course, with James Agee. Although I take exception to certain of Agee's strictures on Sturges in what follows, his writing on the director is deeply felt, perceptive, and lively; he never doubted Sturges's value and importance. Now that we know more about Agee, moreover, his writing on Sturges may be read as much in relation to himself as to Sturges. He seems at times to be projecting himself rather directly onto Sturges, which may account for the intensity of the passages quoted below and is arguably the highest tribute that a writer of Agee's stature may pay to another artist.

Manny Farber's 1954 essay on Preston Sturges (written with W. S. Poster)[13] is, in my judgment, the most brilliant piece ever written on Sturges and one of the finest pieces of film criticism in any language. It is virtually an anthropology of Sturges's cinematic world—akin, all differences aside, to Roland Barthes's Racinian anthropology in *On Racine.*[14]

Andrew Sarris has written a number of fine pieces on Sturges, among them a rare interview with Sturges in 1957 and an expert survey of Sturges's scriptwriting work in the 1930s.[15] Richard Corliss's essay on ten of Sturges's best scripts in *Talking Pictures* is perhaps the best chapter in that accomplished book.[16] Stanley Cavell's chapter on *The Lady Eve* in *Pursuits of Happiness* has a number of remarkable insights into that film.[17] Elliot Rubenstein's essay on

Sullivan's Travels in *Sight and Sound* is the most complete analysis of that work's meta-filmic aspects.[18]

Outside of American film criticism the most important work is undoubtedly that of André Bazin, who wrote on Sturges between 1948 and 1951, when Sturges's Paramount films and *Mad Wednesday* were first being shown in Europe.[19] Bazin wrote only four brief pieces on Sturges, barely totaling fifteen pages, but they are as assured, far-reaching, and valuable as Bazin's most highly regarded work.

The foundations of Sturges criticism were laid during his career, indeed at its high point, by James Agee. In a series of essays written in 1944, Agee developed a biographical-psychological interpretation of Sturges and his work that has proven astonishingly durable. In one variant or another, Agee's interpretation has turned up in most later writing on Sturges. There are important instances of the Agee position in writings on Sturges in the 1950s, 1960s, 1970s, and 1980s.

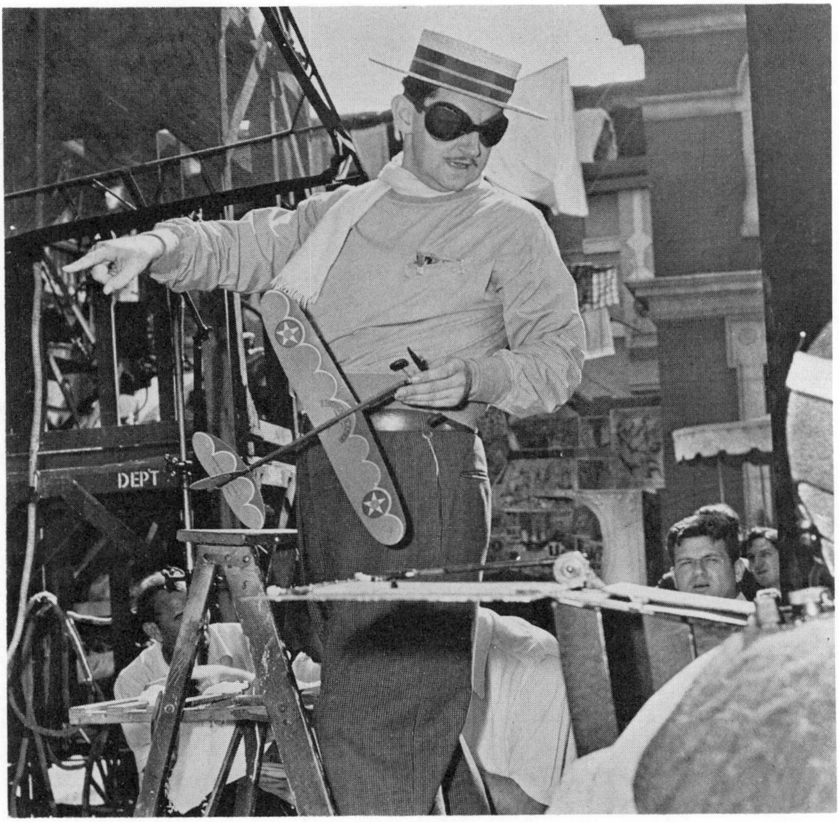

Sturges on the set—directing the "street festival," with children's toys, in CHRISTMAS IN JULY.

Agee wrote regularly about film for *Time* and *The Nation* and occasionally for *Partisan Review*. Needless to say, these journals represented different echelons of intellectual sophistication and had distinct audiences. In the 1940s, it is worth remembering, the sophistication of an audience was directly proportional to its hostility to what were then called "the movies."

Agee wrote in different styles, made different points, and sometimes came to different conclusions for his various audiences. Manny Farber once noted that *Agee on Film* (New York: McDowell, Obolensky, 1958), the posthumous collection of Agee's film essays, showed "no evidence of his conflicting reviews on the same picture for the power (*Time*) and the glory (*The Nation*)."[20]

Agee's review of Sturges's *The Miracle of Morgan's Creek* (1944) appeared in the February 5, 1944, issue of *The Nation*. He begins: "*The Miracle of Morgan's Creek,* the new Preston Sturges film, seems to me funnier, more adventurous, more abundant, more intelligent, and more encouraging than anything that has been made in Hollywood for years. Yet the more I think of it, the less I esteem it. I have, then, both to praise and defend it, and to attack it."[21] Here, in his first words on the subject, is that striking ambivalence toward Sturges that characterizes all of Agee's writing on him.

Agee goes on to praise the film for its audacity and its effective mixing of tender pathos and nihilistic farce. He defends the film against those who have dismissed it as mere comedy, for its frantic, rough character, for its bad taste, or for its multiplicity of attack and shiftiness of style.

> Yet the more I think about the film, the less I like it. There are too many things that Sturges, once he had won all the victories and set all the things moving which he managed to here, should have achieved unhindered, purely as a good artist; and he has not even attempted them. . . . The whole tone of the dialogue, funny and bright as it often is, rests too safely within the pseudo-cute, pseudo-authentic, patronizing diction perfected by Booth Tarkington. And in the stylization of action as well as language it seems to me clear that Sturges holds his characters, and the people they comically represent, and their predicament, and his audience, and the best potentialities of his own work, essentially in contempt. His emotions, his intelligence, his aesthetic ability never fully commit themselves; all the playfulness becomes rather an avoidance of commitment than an extension of means for it . . . nearly every central and final responsibility is shirked.[22]

Agee concludes the review with an unfavorable comparison of Sturges to René Clair, whom Agee calls "one of the few great artists of this century"[23]—a judgment that few critics, if any, would share today. Agee concludes: "Sturges, in his middle forties, is still just the most gifted American working in films, vividly successful in the kind of artful-dodging which frustrates Clair; hollow and evasive at those centers in which Clair is so firm. I suspect that Sturges feels that conscience and comedy are incompatible. It would be hard for a man of talent to make a more self-destructive mistake."[24]

In this review, the framework of Agee's ultimate position on Sturges is already in place, although no biographical fact has been adduced as yet. Agee feels that Sturges has remarkable talent, intelligence, and inventiveness but lacks moral and aesthetic seriousness, what Agee calls "commitment." This imbalance (which in fact is generated by Agee's own premises) seems to baffle and disturb him—it constitutes a gap in his argument and in his understanding. That gap will soon be filled by a psychological-biographical analysis of Sturges himself, perhaps already suggested in the previous quotation by Agee's speculation about what Sturges feels and his attribution of self-destructiveness to him.

The *Time* review of February 14 pursues the same line of argument in a more colloquial style, but it substitutes biographical data for the moral-aesthetic judgments of his review in *The Nation:*

> Chief credit for *The Miracle* must go to Sturges. . . . The chief failures are his, too. Some of the film is painfully unfunny, because it is like a joker who outroars his audience's reaction. Some of the pity is pitiful because it is smashed before it has a chance to crystallize. Most of the finest human and comic potentialities of the story are lost because Sturges is so much less interested in his characters than in using them as hobby-horses for his own wit.[25]

Then, as though to illuminate his own criticisms, Agee quotes a remark by René Clair that Sturges should slow down, be a little more selfish, and worry about his reputation; then he launches into a summary of Sturges's life story:

> The life of Preston Sturges might read as dizzily as one of his own comedies if it were not, in essence, so intensely bitter. On his first day at school in Chicago, Preston rode a bicycle and wore a Greek chiton. The bicycle was his stepfather's influence—Solomon Sturges, stockbroker and socialite, was a champion cyclist and a good amateur baseball player. The Attic haberdashery was his mother's idea. . . . Preston's mother was determined that he should be a genius. "I was never allowed," Sturges says, "to play with other kids. They wedged art into me from every side. I was dragged into every goddamn museum in the world." There were gay moments, but they usually stank of culture.
>
> The effect of such training was predictable. "They did everything they could," he says, "to make me an artist, but I didn't want to be an artist. I wanted to be a good businessman like my father". . . .
>
> Sturges' brilliant, successful yet always deeply self-absorbing films suggest a warring blend of the things he picked up through respect for his solid stepfather, contact with his strange mother, and the intense need to enjoy himself and to succeed which came from 30 years of misery and failure. . . . The combination might explain his matchless skill in producing some of the most intoxicating bits of nihilism the screen has known, but always at the expense of a larger excellence.[26]

Agee's views on Sturges also emerged in his writing for *Partisan Review.* In Spring 1944 he wrote a rather despairing essay on folk art, which concludes, "Preston Sturges' latest film reaches the great audience if only through its vivacity, but it is hardly a work of art, popular or unpopular; it fails through snobbery, cynicism, cowardice and a radical lack of love."[27]

Agee's final piece on Sturges is a September 23, 1944, review of *Hail the Conquering Hero* for *The Nation.* Agee used the occasion to formulate definitively his overall position on Sturges. Indeed, at least for those who admire the film, it is almost as though Agee did not see *Hail the Conquering Hero* at all; he merely subsumed it under a file he had opened earlier.

> Any adequate review of this remarkable movie would devote at least as much space to its unqualified praise as I have to qualifying the praise; it would have to spend more space than that, I think, getting at even a tentative explanation of why Sturges functions as he does. "Hollywood" is no explanation, surely; "Hollywood" was made for Sturges and he in turn is its apotheosis; but why? It seems to me that Sturges had reason, through his mother, to develop, as they caromed around high-Bohemian Europe during his childhood, from opera to opera and gallery to gallery, not only his singular mercurialism and resourcefulness, which come especially natural to some miserably unhappy children, but also a retching, permanently incurable loathing for everything that stank of "culture," of "art." I gather further that through his stepfather, a stable and charming Chicago sportsman and business man, he developed an all but desperate respect and hunger for success, enhanced by a sickening string of failures as a business man and inventor up to the age of about thirty; and that this again assumed the dimensions of a complex. I believe that in his curious career as a never-quite-artist of not-quite-genius he has managed to release and guide the energies of these influences in the only way open to him.
>
> I hesitate to write this sort of thing, drawn only from such superficialities as have appeared in print and from some remarkable photographs of Sturges as a child and young man which appeared in the *Saturday Evening Post;* but I risk the worse than questionable taste because I see no other way to understand what Sturges' films are about. They are wonderful as comedies and they are wonderfully complex and ingenious; they seem to me also wonderfully, uncontrollably, almost proudly corrupt, vengeful, fearful of intactness and self-commitment; most essentially, they are paradoxical marvels of self-perpetuation and self-destruction; their mastering object, aside from success, seems to be to sail as steep into the wind as possible without for an instant incurring the disaster of becoming seriously, wholly acceptable as art. They seem to me, indeed, in much of their twisting, the elaborately counterpointed image of a neurosis. It is an especially interesting neurosis, not only because Sturges is a man of such talent and not only because it expresses itself in such fecund and in themselves suggestive images, but also because, in relation to art, it seems the definitive expression of this country at present—the stranglehold wedlock of the American female tradition of "culture," the male tradition of "success."[28]

Manny Farber and W. S. Poster's 1954 essay on Sturges reflects Agee's biographical-psychological interpretation of Sturges and his work. It does so, however, in the context of a critical approach to its subject which is very different from Agee's, whose criticism Farber questions as well as praises in another essay. In the ten years that separate Agee's essays from Farber's, Sturges's Hollywood career had ended. It was perhaps no longer possible to speak, as Agee had, of Sturges's "all but desperate respect and hunger for success." In any case, Farber sees Sturges's mother/father, artist/businessman conflicts as a positive force, which led to the distinctive, indeed unique qualities of his films. Farber celebrates Sturges with only minor reservations. He uses Agee's biographical-psychological scheme to account for Sturges's successes as a filmmaker, not for his failures:

> One of his characters calls society a "cockeyed caravan," and Sturges, himself, is less a settled, bona fide resident of America than a hurried, Argus-eyed traveler through

its shifting scenes, a nomad in space observing a society nomadic in time and projecting his sensations in uniquely computed terms.

This modern cinematic perspective of mobility seen by a mobile observer comes easily to Sturges because of his strange family background and broken-up youth. He was the son of a normal, sports-loving, successful father and a fantastic culture-bug mother who wanted him to be a genius and kept him in Paris from the age of eight to about fifteen. "She dragged me through every goddam museum on the continent," he has rancorously remarked. Glutted at an early age, by an overrich diet of esthetic dancing, high-hatted opera audiences, and impressionist painting, Sturges still shows the marks of his youthful trauma.

The most obvious result of his experience has been a violent reaction against all estheticism. He has also expressed fervent admiration for his father's business ability and a desire to emulate him. The fact that he did not, however, indicates that his early training provoked more than a merely negative reaction in him and made him a logical candidate for Hollywood, whose entire importance in the history of culture resides in its unprecedented effort to merge art and big business.

As a moviemaker, the businessman side of Sturges was superficially dominant. He seems to have begun his career with the intention of giving Hollywood a lesson in turning out quick, cheap, popular pictures. He whipped together his scripts in record-breaking time, cast his pictures with unknowns, and shot them faster than anyone dreamed possible. . . .

What made Sturges a viciously alive artist capable of discovering new means of expressiveness in a convention-ridden medium was the frenetic, split sensibility that kept him reacting to and away from the opposite sides of his heredity. These two sides are, in fact, the magnetic poles of American society. Accepting, in exaggerated fashion, the businessman approach to films, he nevertheless brought to his work intelligence, taste, and a careful study of the more estimable movies of the past. He also took care to disappoint rigid-minded esthetes and reviewers.[29]

The last line may be a reference to Agee's reservations about Sturges. The piece as a whole in effect counters Agee's charges of aesthetic and moral failure in Sturges's work. In a later review of *Agee on Film,* Farber criticized "the growing Agee legend" in addition to praising him on Farber's own grounds: "His criticism had an excessive richness that came from a fine writing ear as well as cautious hesitancy, ganglia, guilt. The sentences are swamps that are filled with a suspicious number of right-sounding insights. Actually, Agee's appreciations stick pretty close to what the middle-brow wants to hear."[30]

In *The American Cinema* (1968), Andrew Sarris wrote in his Sturges entry:

Sturges was criticized at his peak by James Agee and Manny Farber for an ambivalence in his work derived from a childhood conflict between a culturally demanding mother and an admired businessman foster father. This unusually Freudian analysis of the director's work, unusual, that is, for its time, sought to explain the incongruity of continental sophistication being challenged by American pragmatism. Sturges himself was seen as an uneasy mixture of savant and wise guy. On the one hand, his extreme literacy, rare among Hollywood screenwriters, enabled him to drop words like "ribaldry" and "vestal" into their proper contexts without a pretentious thud. On the other, he seemed unwilling to develop the implications of his serious ideas. His flair for props and gags suited the popularly recalled image of the young inventor of kissproof lipstick.[31]

By attributing the biographical-psychological criticism of Sturges to other critics, Sarris himself managed to straddle the issue. By recounting the Agee view of Sturges, however, his work served to pass it on to a younger generation of film critics, just as his indirect discourse of attribution allowed it to pass into the texture of his own argument.

It is interesting that at least one younger critic has returned to the Agee position in its undiluted state. In *Talking Pictures,* Richard Corliss discusses Sturges's screenwriting for other directors and for himself. In his discussion of *The Great Moment* (1944), Corliss says:

> Endings in Sturges films tend to be schizophrenic showdowns between the two sides of the writer-director. On one side is Preston the Pride of Paramount, laughgetter and moneymaker, stepson of millionaire stockbroker Solomon Sturges; this is the Sturges who gave audiences the endings they wanted, in *Sullivan's Travels, The Palm Beach Story, The Miracle of Morgan's Creek,* and *Hail the Conquering Hero.* On the other side, frowning at his alter ego like Jekyll at Hyde, is Sturges the artist, adapter of Tolstoy, Molnar, and Pagnol, joy and despair of James Agee, only son of the notorious aesthete and adventuress Mary Desti; this is the Sturges who sent Tom Garner and Jim Brady to their lonely deaths, who dazzled the Hays Office with *The Lady Eve*'s double-lutz plot turns, whose studio advertised his pictures as the works of a genius.
>
> Too often, Sturges's artistry would carry a film until the last reel, when the happy hack would take over, turning the fade-out into a cop-out. Too rarely does a Sturges film possess any consistency of tone, and when it does it is often somber and monotonous like *The Power and the Glory,* or easy and impersonal like *If I Were King.* The only important Sturges films with sustained, affecting moods are *Diamond Jim, Remember the Night,* and (precariously) *The Lady Eve.* The characters are developed with as much sense as affection; the dialogue serves the situation instead of tyrannizing it; the climaxes have an aura of inevitability about them, whether dirgelike, teary, or wry. In only one other (very uneven) film did an ending exalt both Sturges and the viewer, and not demean them. This was *The Great Moment,* the last Sturges film Paramount was to release before he left the studio for Howard Hughes and one of the most precipitous pratfalls in screen history.[32]

Corliss's essay on Sturges marks a resurgence of the Agee position—not only because he adheres to Agee's biographical-psychological approach but also because he uses it to account for what he perceives as an aesthetic failure in Sturges's films. Corliss suggests also, if not as explicitly as Agee does, that this is a moral failure too—a kind of selling out.

James Curtis's *Between Flops: A Biography of Preston Sturges* is not a critical biography, but Curtis endorses—or at least perpetuates—the Agee position by quoting the long passage from Agee's September 23, 1944, *Nation* review of *Hail the Conquering Hero* quoted above. Curtis omits only the first, qualifying sentence of each paragraph—Agee's profession of esteem for the film in the first and his acknowledgment of the superficiality of his biographical information in the second. The fact that Curtis cites this passage without disagreement or qualification is surprising, since his own findings tend to undermine Agee's position. This is perhaps the ultimate triumph of Agee's view of Sturges—that it has survived the establishment of directly countervailing facts.

That Sturges compromised particular scripts or films in order to achieve success or, in general, that he had insufficient artistic ambition is not in keeping with the facts as we now know them. Sturges persisted with *The Great*

Moment, even though it cost him the enmity of his studio and finally undid him, simply because he believed in the project. Even before *The Great Moment,* Sturges had not had a box-office success since *The Lady Eve* in 1941—and was not to have another until *The Miracle of Morgan's Creek* in 1944. *Sullivan's Travels* was not expected to be popular and it wasn't; *The Palm Beach Story* was expected to bring in large audiences but it did not. For Sturges to insist on making *The Great Moment* under these conditions and despite the opposition of Paramount chief of production, Buddy DeSylva, was to court disaster.

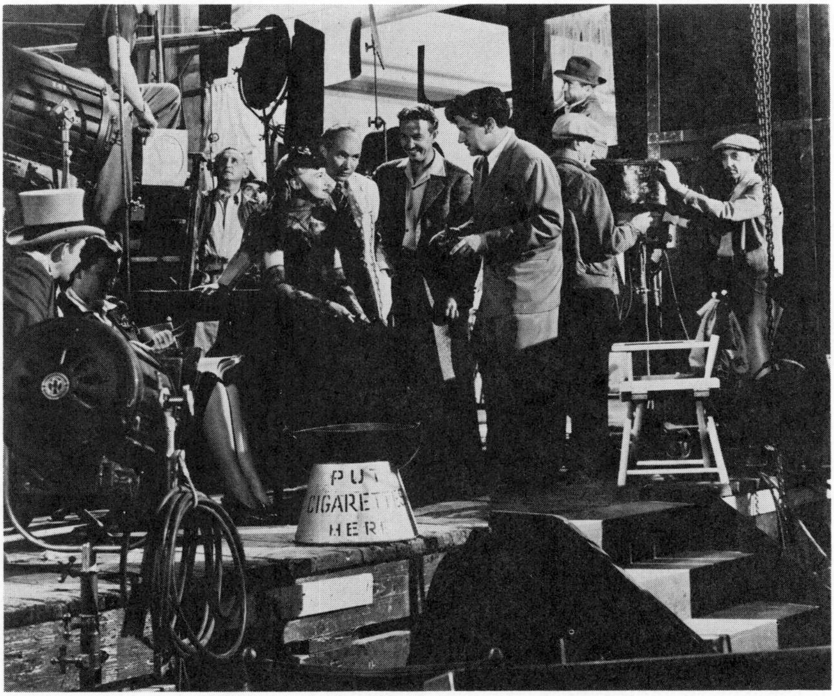

Sturges directing Veronica Lake in SULLIVAN'S TRAVELS*–on the set of a film herself, her character is about to hear that Sullivan is alive after all.*

Sturges's Paramount trials merely repeated his experience in the theater a decade earlier. *Strictly Dishonorable* (1929) had been one of the great comedy successes of the twenties. His colleagues urged Sturges to write another frothy comedy, but instead he wrote *Recapture* (1930), a comedy-drama with a tragic ending, then *The Well of Romance* (1930), an operetta that had already failed with a book by someone else, and finally *Child of Manhattan* (1932), a comedy-drama about a dance-hall girl and a millionaire that audiences found distasteful. These three flops quickly ended what had been a most promising Broadway career.

Moving to Agee's own ground, we might ask where Agee obtained the facts on which his interpretation is based. His sources, by his own admission, were "superficialities"—popular magazine accounts of Sturges. But such "celebrity profiles" were a blend of studio promotion, audience expectation, and Sturges's own willing presentation of self. By most accounts, Sturges played the role of flamboyant movie director with relish and attracted publicity of all sorts; "spell my name right" was his attitude, according to Louise Sturges.[33] That he did this in good part to buoy his position at Paramount—in order to make films as much as possible on his own terms—seems likely. His position at the studio was shakier than anyone, including Agee, could have known at the time. Sturges's childhood was good copy—when interviewed, he told anecdotes about it for hours on end.[34] What Agee took as the Sturges facts were at least partly a self-made myth, whose central "conflicts" between artist and businessman had as much to do with his current situation in the industry as with Sturges's actual early life. The public Sturges played the "genius" that Paramount publicity billed him as but also rejected the "artist" label of his mother's side in favor of the "businessman" label of his father's side. But this is obligatory Hollywood-speak, as any reader of interviews of directors knows. Direction was "just a job of work" for John Ford; Don Siegel plays down his degree from Cambridge University; and so on. Peer pressure, the tough-director image, and above all, perhaps, producers' unease at artistic talk—which they equate with business loss—account for this persistent phenomenon. The directors who spoke like artists or conspicuously acted like them or even looked the part did not last long in Hollywood: Erich von Stroheim, Joseph von Sternberg, and Orson Welles are only the best known.

Agee's analysis of Sturges's "especially interesting neurosis" is too general to belong to any identifiable school of psychiatry. But what sort of psychoanalysis, even of a generalized sort, bases itself entirely on the self-conscious statements of the subject, indeed on public interviews and press releases? If there is no notion of a hidden truth, that is, of repression, hence of interpretation in some sense against the conscious statements of the subject, can we speak of psychoanalysis at all?

So deeply entrenched is Agee's reading of Sturges, however, that no mere statement of facts or counter-argument is likely to prevail against it. It has become that most insiduous of critical phenomena—an interpretation that is later taken as fact. It is mythic in the Barthesian sense that it is not perceived as such—it operates beneath the awareness of those who invoke it, manipulating even those who think they manipulate it. Dissent from the Agee view of Sturges may therefore not succeed on the rational terms that that dissent proposes. Perhaps a myth can finally be displaced, or its stranglehold loosened, only by counter-myths.

There are, after all, other ways in which Sturges's films might be related to his life, even if no one has suggested any since Agee's time. The new biographical and textual information on Sturges and his work might suggest ways to oppose the still prevailing myth. The point is not to propose a counter-myth for its own sake but to question the authority of the Agee myth by posing alternatives that are at least equally plausible.

For instance, the saga of Mary Desti and young Preston might be read differently from the way the official myth has it. Was the child's psychic wound caused by compulsory attendance at art events or, on the contrary, by his mother's abandoning him again and again with strange people in strange places? Sturges never spoke publicly of this as far as I know, but such vulnerability was less acceptable in 1940s America than a dismissal of art and artiness. That his mother always left him in the name of art might have led the child to hate art. It might also have led him to model himself on and compete with what carried his mother away, that is, to become an artist. This same scenario of rejection followed by resort to artistic creation was enacted—or reenacted—in the actress's insults that led Sturges to write his first produced play, *The Guinea Pig* (1928). (This pattern seems also to have been involved, more generally speaking, in Sturges's turning from inventing to songwriting and playwriting after Estelle left him.) *Strictly Dishonorable* (1929) was based upon a characteristic Sturges switch—the girl is won by the suave Italian opera singer away from the clean-cut American boy, who turns out to be a rotter. (The American was played by Louis Jean Heydt, a specialist in the type, which he repeated for Sturges in *The Great McGinty* and *The Great Moment.*) Europe stole his mother away from him again and again—why shouldn't Sturges identify with it?

Recapture was the title of Sturges's failed play of 1930. (He named his first yacht *Recapture* before he knew the play had failed.) His experience with Estelle was evidently the immediate point of departure for the play. Perhaps the extremity of his reaction to Estelle's rejection was due in part to the incident's reactivation of old wounds, notably his mother's abandoning him initially and her subsequent repetitions of the trauma. In *Recapture* the husband wins back his ex-wife's love—she realizes that she will never love so rapturously again—but she dies in an elevator accident in the third act. Psychoanalytically speaking, the play arguably fuses the fantasy of recapture with the fantasy of revenge. (Of course the Oedipus complex itself may be understood as a recapture fantasy—the child wishes to recapture the exclusive bond with the mother enjoyed in infancy.) The notion of recapture, in any case, is fundamental to Sturges's work in many periods.

Before she rejected him, at least, Sturges's relationship with Eleanor seems to have been more complex in psychological terms, if less emotionally intense, than that with Estelle or, of course, his mother. He was the author of a still-running hit and a more recent flop when he met her. In asking for Eleanor's hand of her father, founder of E. F. Hutton and Company and chairman of the board of General Foods, he boasted an income of $1,500 a week. "For her that's pin money," her father replied. During his marriage to Eleanor, Sturges worked on *The Well of Romance.* ("Well" suggests a source one can return to again and again for sustenance and renewal, which Sturges's romances proved to be throughout his life. A well is the place for wishes of unlimited happiness but also for plunges to bottomless despair.) When Sturges had encountered difficulty finding backers, Eleanor agreed to back *The Well of Romance* entirely with part of the inheritance she would receive on the occasion of her birthday (in December 1930). On this basis Sturges put all the money he had—$64,000—into the production, which opened on November 7. Its failure plunged Sturges down a financial well—Eleanor never made good on her promise—as well as a romantic one; she sailed for Paris in June 1931. (Perhaps significantly, around this time Sturges wrote the bedroom farce *Unfaithfully Yours* and also *A Cup of Coffee,* which concerned the mistaken winner of a slogan contest.)

Sturges's lack of money after the *Well of Romance* fiasco sent him to Hollywood in 1932. An "existential psychoanalysis" might stress Sturges's unconscious complicity in accepting the destiny apparently imposed upon him by Eleanor's actions—as by Estelle's and his actress friend's before that. It might also suggest the larger pattern of his coming to accept Mary Desti's destiny for him: to become an artist. The schooner he had built in 1933, after he had decided to stay on in Hollywood, was called *The Destiny.* (It was named after his mother and his first home port: Desti—New York.)

Among Sturges's films, critics have usually found *Sullivan's Travels* to be, as Andrew Sarris says, "the most profound expression of the director's personality."[35] Richard Corliss calls the film autobiographical and believes that Sturges identifies with his hero. The film's defense of comedy does seem to relate to Sturges's experience. He tried serious plays and screenplays before accepting his destiny as a writer-director of comedies, although *The Great Moment* indicates that he did not entirely accept the earlier film's conclusion. In psychoanalytic terms, however, *Sullivan's Travels* is utterly "secondary," that is, remote from highly charged instinctual and emotional conflicts. The film's central dilemma is a conscious one—should a comedy director attempt to do something serious in a time of crisis? Its method of resolving the question brings the film close to rationalization in both a psychoanalytic and a popular sense. In addition, the love relations presented in the film are rather affectless. Sullivan seems to feel no strong emotion about his estranged wife or about "the Girl" (Veronica Lake). One could argue indeed that the too-evident identifiability of Sturges and Sullivan almost guaranteed a detached handling of the material.

I would argue that it is instead his "frivolous" films, notably the screwball comedies *The Lady Eve* and *The Palm Beach Story,* that pose issues and situations highly charged for Sturges. (That these are the most genre-typed films that he made provides, besides their lightness itself, a built-in defense structure. No director is responsible for the subject or even the plot of a genre film—they are taken as given.) Perhaps Sturges identifies more with Jean in *The Lady Eve* than with Sullivan, or at least at a deeper level. She is smart and street-smart, witty yet still able to feel, indeed to be carried away by emotion. Charles Pike, like Sturges's wife Eleanor, is the pampered product of wealth, who has never had to struggle or live by his wits. He is also retarded emotion-

Henry Fonda, Preston Sturges, and Barbara Stanwyck on the set of THE LADY EVE.

ally—uneasy with his sexual feelings and spitefully cutting off his emotions when he feels betrayed. One might speculate further that Eleanor's many suitors once she had left Sturges are displaced forward in the film to the fortune-hunters who seek to attract Charles before he meets Jean—after which they disappear, an obvious fantasy.

The second half of *The Lady Eve* fuses the revenge drive with the recapture quest. Jean both punishes Charles and wins him back. Her means is to impersonate a titled foreigner, thereby asserting her social superiority to the rejecting lover, disparaging the notion of titles generally, and asserting her own worth. She then, in the guise of the high-born Eve, torments Charles with stories of her sexual promiscuity, with the result that Charles appreciates what he had in Jean. To suggest that Sturges may have fantasized impersonating one of Eleanor's titled suitors in Paris in order to expose them, prove his own worth, and win her back would be speculative, not to say presumptuous, but it seems to me as plausible as Agee's reading. When Charles wants a divorce from Jean, she refuses to take any money—insisting, as did Sturges, only that he ask her. Charles, like Eleanor, refuses to do so and even refuses to speak to her in person or by telephone.

The Palm Beach Story is wilder, crazier, and far less well organized than *The Lady Eve* but, perhaps for this reason, is even closer to Sturges's romantic experience than is the earlier film. In it Tom Jeffers is a failed inventor, a total business flop who cannot pay his rent or other bills. Nevertheless, he is charming and well dressed, and he lives on Park Avenue. His wife, Gerry, walks out on him but not before paying all the bills—shades of Estelle on both counts. That she is doing so in part to raise money for a project of Tom's is a fantasy

Sturges on the set of HAIL THE CONQUERING HERO.

element, as is her receiving money from a kindly old (symbolically impotent) man, the "Weenie King," who also gives Tom money to follow her. Penniless on a train to Palm Beach, Gerry is given a ticket and escort by the members of "The Ale and Quail Society." She is then picked up by a millionaire, who buys her clothes, finally finances Tom's project, and is also in effect sexless. The symbolic impotence of all of these men is a fantasy element that avoids the pain of cuckoldry. The film as a whole thus concerns Tom's ultimately successful recapture quest.

It might be said, finally, that *Unfaithfully Yours* (1948) is a psychological version of the recapture motif. Sir Alfred de Carter suspects his wife of infidelity, fantasizes revenge, then discovers that she has been faithful after all—a kind of armchair recapture.

The difficulty with psychoanalytic explanations is not that they are wrong, but that there can be too many of them—what Freud called overdetermination. For any problem there is a multiplicity of satisfactory explanations, and no single explanation can be proven to be uniquely correct. This difficulty does not, however, hinder the present purpose—which is merely to break the exclusivity of a reigning single explanation.

* * *

All who are interested in Preston Sturges's work have cause to thank Tom Sturges, Preston's son, for initiating this project and seeing it through to its conclusion. I am especially grateful to Ernest Callenbach for asking me to write the introductions and for his helpful comments throughout. Sandy Sturges, Preston's widow, was most helpful in providing detailed corrections of the biographical summary and other passages and in facilitating my research in a variety of ways. I hope that she will share with his countless admirers her immense knowledge of Preston Sturges's life and work by writing a book about him. I wish to thank the UCLA Special Collections staff for their assistance on my research in the Sturges Archive. My thanks also to Diane Jacobs for her helpful comments on an early draft of the general introduction and to Albert LaValley for his comments on an early draft of the whole. Sarah Ulen Henderson went through the entire manuscript carefully, making countless stylistic and other suggestions that improved it greatly. Errors and shortcomings that remain are, of course, my responsibility alone.

NOTES

1. Andrew Sarris, "Preston Sturges," in Stuart Byron and Elizabeth Weis (eds.), *Movie Comedy* (New York: Penguin, 1977), pages 83, 86.

2. Manny Farber, *Negative Space* (New York: Praeger, 1971), page 91.

3. André Bazin, *The Cinema of Cruelty: From Buñuel to Hitchcock,* ed. François Truffaut (New York: Seaver, 1982), page 44.

4. Richard Corliss, *Talking Pictures: Screenwriters in the American Cinema* (New York: Penguin, 1974), page 26.

5. There is a copy of *The Great McGinty* dated December 5, 1939, that is dated eight days later than the November 28, 1939, script printed below. There is only one known copy of this script, which is in private hands, and it is, unfortunately, too delicate to photocopy or to work with. This is the only instance among the five scripts

printed below in which a later script is known to exist. In March 1944 Sturges wrote a new ending to the June 21, 1943, script (itself finished on July 12, 1943) of *Hail the Conquering Hero,* which new ending he filmed in April 1944. This revised ending, which was page-numbered and shot-numbered by Sturges to fit exactly into the earlier script, appears as the conclusion to the script printed below (pages 131–137).

6. Andrew Sarris, "Preston Sturges," in Richard Corliss (ed.), *The Hollywood Screenwriters* (New York: Avon, 1972), page 93.

7. Corliss, *Talking Pictures,* page 26.

8. James Curtis, *Between Flops: A Biography of Preston Sturges* (New York: Harcourt Brace Jovanovich, 1982), page 11. This book is a signal contribution to film scholarship. My account of Sturges's life is much indebted to Curtis's extensive research. Abundant material on all periods of Sturges's life and career was also furnished to me by Sandy Sturges, his widow. I found further information in the UCLA Sturges Archive.

9. Ibid., page 46.

10. Preston Sturges, *Strictly Dishonorable: A Comedy in Three Acts* (New York: Liveright, 1929), page 5.

11. Curtis, op. cit., page 69.

12. Ibid., page 78.

13. Farber, op. cit., page 89.

14. Roland Barthes, *On Racine* (New York: Hill and Wang, 1964).

15. Sarris's writings on Sturges include those in Byron and Weis, op. cit., and in Corliss, *The Hollywood Screenwriters;* his entry on Sturges in *The American Cinema* (New York: Dutton, 1968), page 112; and his interview with Sturges in Andrew Sarris (ed.), *Hollywood Voices: Interviews with Hollywood Directors* (Indianapolis: Bobbs-Merrill, 1971), page 85.

16. Corliss, *Talking Pictures,* page 25.

17. Stanley Cavell, *Pursuits of Happiness: The Hollywood Comedy of Remarriage* (Cambridge: Harvard, 1981), page 45.

18. Elliot Rubenstein, "Hollywood Travels: Sturges and Sullivan," *Sight and Sound,* Volume 47, No. 1 (Winter 1977–78), pages 50–52.

19. Bazin, op. cit., pages 33–47.

20. Farber, op. cit., page 87.

21. James Agee, *Agee on Film* (New York: McDowell, Obolensky, 1958), page 73.

22. Ibid., pages 75–76.

23. Ibid., page 76.

24. Ibid.

25. Ibid., page 343.

26. Ibid., pages 344–345.

27. Ibid., page 410.

28. Ibid., pages 116–117.

29. Farber, op. cit., pages 94–96.

30. Ibid., page 85.

31. Sarris, *The American Cinema,* page 114.

32. Corliss, *Talking Pictures,* pages 52–53.

33. Curtis, op. cit., pages 194–197.

34. Ibid., page 194.

35. Sarris, *The American Cinema,* page 115.

The Great McGinty

The first draft of *The Great McGinty* was "completed" on August 14, 1933, and "refinished" on September 1 of that year, according to a note on its last page.[1] It was called *The Vagrant;* Sturges had worked on it nights during the shooting of *The Power and the Glory* (1933), hoping to show it to producers once the success of that film was assured. His contract for *The Power and the Glory* had an unprecedented percentage provision and a nonrevision clause that was equally unheard of. He planned to sell *The Vagrant* on condition that he also direct it, a provision he apparently saw as an extension of the earlier nonrevision clause. How better to protect the author's intentions than for the author himself to direct? Sturges was willing to forego a percentage arrangement for this opportunity and, indeed, to work for much less than the usual screenwriter's fee.

There was some interest in the project, but it evaporated when *The Power and the Glory* turned out to be a commercial failure. Despite the film's good reviews, Sturges found himself at the bottom of the screenwriter's ladder. While working on innumerable other projects over the next six years, he tried repeatedly to sell *The Vagrant,* always insisting that he direct it. Sturges did not work on the script during this time, except occasionally to try new titles like *The Story of a Man, The Biography of a Bum,* and, finally, *Down Went McGinty,* under which title it was submitted to Paramount on April 28, 1939.[2] This time, for reasons discussed in the Introduction, Paramount bought the script—reputedly for one dollar—and acceded to Sturges's demand to direct. Contracts were signed on August 18 and 23; shooting was set for December 11.

Exactly when Paramount gave *Down Went McGinty* the go-ahead and just when Sturges began to revise his six-year-old script are unclear. The rewrites of *Remember the Night* occupied him at least through July 1939; what he did in August and most of September of that year is uncertain. However, we do know, from extant notes and discard pages, that from September 28 to November 28, 1939, the date of the script printed below, he completely rewrote *The Vagrant* and that he retained for the new work the latest title he had given to the old one—*Down Went McGinty.* We also know, from the finished film, that Sturges revised the November 28 script extensively, at least up until the start of shooting on December 11 and almost certainly during shooting as well.[3]

Filming was completed in mid-January 1940; a rough cut was assembled and previewed to delighted audiences. Paramount salespeople suggested the title *The Great McGinty,* Sturges agreed, and the film premiered at the Paramount Theater in Times Square on August 14, 1940. Critics praised it to the skies, and its box-office performance was solid. In February 1941, by which time Sturges had completed *Christmas in July* and *The Lady Eve, The Great McGinty* received the first Academy Award ever given for Best Original Screenplay.

The Vagrant is a sort of comic version of *The Power and the Glory.* In each film, a man rises to wealth and prominence from poverty and obscurity and then loses everything. Tom Garner in *The Power and the Glory* starts out as an honest workman whereas John O'Hara, called Dan McGinty in the revised script and film, begins and ends as a bum. Garner has a son of his own; O'Hara acquires a son and daughter by marriage. Garner kills himself when he loses everything; O'Hara leaves the country. According to James Curtis, Sturges considered doing a number of films, even a classical trilogy, treating the American success syndrome—a string of prestigious films that would bridge Hollywood and Broadway. It never happened, but the notion itself has striking similarities to Eugene O'Neill's projected play cycle "A Tale of Possessors Self-Dispossessed," of which only *A Touch of the Poet* and the unfinished *More Stately Mansions* were realized.[4]

The Vagrant was based on stories Sturges had heard in Chicago, like those about Tammany-style politician William "Old Bill" Sulzer, who had been elected governor of Illinois but was impeached when his concern for the people's welfare interfered with the workings of the Democratic machine. Another source was Andy McCrery, Sturges's neighbor in Westchester County, who had been killed in 1929 when he failed to make payments on a city magistracy that he had purchased. McCrery had told Sturges about Tammany procedures—how they got out the vote in bad weather, how repeat voters were used, how influence was routinely bought and sold.

The Vagrant turns this material into a narrative, adding a romance to motivate the main character's defection from graft to virtue and also a corrupt Boss to dump him when he does. The result is the comic epic of John O'Hara's rise and fall, with detailed emphasis upon the procedures and stages by which they are accomplished.

Like *The Power and the Glory, The Vagrant* is enclosed by a framing story, set in the present, which tells the hero's story in retrospect. In the earlier film, Garner's friend Henry and Henry's wife review the hero's life and its meaning after Garner's funeral; in *The Vagrant* O'Hara tells his own story and leaves its meaning up to his listener. But before he tells his story, there is a sunny, midday scene between O'Hara, now a bartender on a Caribbean island, and Joe, the owner of the bar, in which Joe tries to persuade O'Hara (whom he calls "Juan") to help clean up the bar from the night before. That evening Joe asks

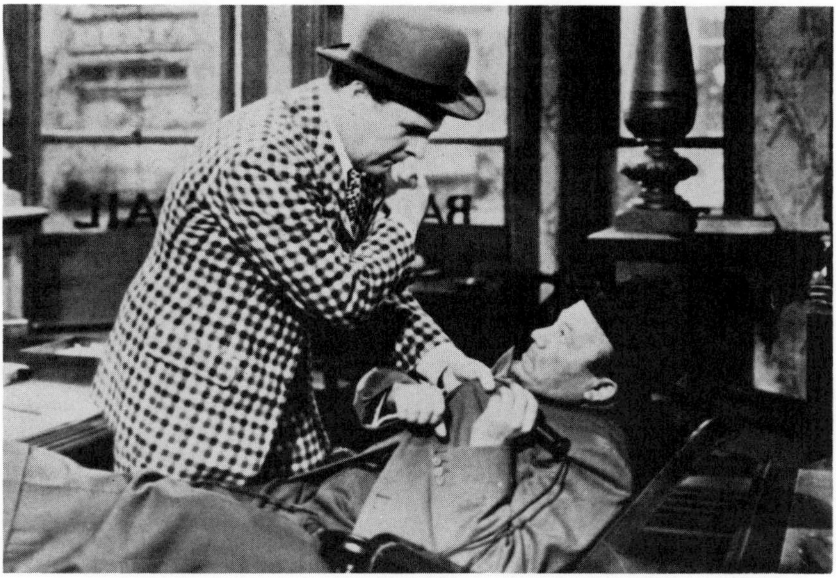

McGinty on his way to the top in city politics–
collecting protection money in THE GREAT MCGINTY.

O'Hara why he gave money to one of the bar girls; O'Hara replies that she needed it. A former bank cashier, identified in the script as "The American," then enters the bar and speaks to O'Hara as though he were an old friend. He tells him that he robbed the bank where he worked and then fled the country, leaving his wife and children. He talks of killing himself, and O'Hara tries to dissuade him. When the American says that he ruined his life in "one crazy minute" of dishonesty, O'Hara replies that *he* was the governor of a state and launches into his story.

In the flashback that follows, O'Hara begins as a bum in front of a restaurant window, as a policeman is telling him to move on—a scene cut from the revised script and film. Standing in a soup line, he is offered two dollars to vote for the machine candidate for mayor. Seeing a way to make some money, O'Hara votes twenty-four times—thirty-seven in the revised script; three examples show us how it is done. His feat draws the attention of the Politician, who gives him a job collecting protection money from clients who refuse to pay; again three examples are given. Eventually O'Hara is appointed alderman and expertly shakes down a Mr. Maxwell, who has been seeking a bus franchise from the city. At this point in the script the character of the Boss is introduced.

DISSOLVE TO:
OFFICE OF THE BIG BOSS

He is a huge, fat old man, bent over a desk writing, in a very small hand, figures and names in a small account book. We hear the voice of O'Hara booming:

O'HARA

Hello, boss.

The boss speaks with an Irish brogue.

BOSS

Hello, bhoy. How are they after treatin' ye?

O'HARA

Hotsy Totsy. Everything's fine.

BOSS

Good. Now. I forgot to tell ye this morning there would be a feller called Maxwell comin' to see ye about some bus franchises.

O'HARA

Is that so?

BOSS

Sure, and he needs them bad. They ought to be worth two fifty to 'im, if you handle 'im with skill.

O'HARA

Is that so?

BOSS

That's so. So be on the lookout and keep a sharp eye out for 'im.

O'HARA

I just left 'im. We agreed on five hundred thousand.

The Boss looks at him longly, then returns to his book and picks up his pen. He speaks very mildly.

THE BOSS

You're doin' nicely, bhoy . . . you're doin' nicely.

FADE OUT.

A graft scandal that discredits the machine-controlled mayor leads to O'Hara's running as the mayoral candidate of the Reform party—which the

A publicity still of Mr. and Mrs. McGinty–Brian Donlevy and Muriel Angelus–from THE GREAT MCGINTY.

Boss also controls. Victorious, Mayor O'Hara reluctantly attends a Purity League tea and, while hiding from some questioners, meets "a pretty woman, about twenty-eight," who has been required to attend by her fiancé George, a wealthy philanthropist. The next day the Boss, himself married twenty-seven years, casually suggests that O'Hara get married. O'Hara protests, but after he lunches with his new acquaintance and her two children from a former marriage, there is a dissolve to a wedding picture of the couple in the newspaper.

Next there is a montage of city improvements followed by a dissolve to O'Hara reading a story to his sleepy children. (The revised script inserts a gag here: McGinty, rapt, reads to the end of the story even though the children have fallen asleep.) In the same scene his wife tells him that he is an honest man, who, if he could, would eliminate graft, tenements, sweatshops, and child labor. O'Hara says that he has not thought about those things but that some day he will do something for her sake if he becomes strong enough. He later proposes the reforms to the Boss, who happily foresees a new round of shakedowns to prevent their passage.

Later O'Hara runs for and wins the governorship, the campaign shown by an ironic montage of speeches by the Politician and a spokesman for the opposition. During his inaugural parade O'Hara's wife tells him that he is now strong enough to keep his promises; he pessimistically agrees to try. In the governor's office the Boss discloses new plans for graft; O'Hara rejects them and proposes reform legislation instead. When he sees that O'Hara is serious, the Boss says simply:

> You were a nice boy, John . . . It's going to be too bad.
> So long.

Some time later five angry businessmen tell the Boss to stop O'Hara's attempts at reform, but a headline—"Assembly Passes Child Labor Act"—and a happy scene between O'Hara and his wife indicate that the Boss has not been able to block him. The Boss and a cohort then plan O'Hara's fall; they have him arrested at home on graft charges. O'Hara says good-bye to his wife and children and leaves with the detectives. The Boss and his backers read of O'Hara's arrest in the newspaper and arrange to have bail set at $50,000. Next we see the judge instructing the jury, which returns a guilty verdict, and sentencing O'Hara to two years in prison.

In jail O'Hara receives a letter from his wife telling him that her old fiancé George has been helpful to her and that the children are now attending a school where they are not known. Later George tells O'Hara that parole has been arranged and offers him money, while admitting that he is still in love with O'Hara's wife. When O'Hara is released, she meets him at the prison gate and drives him to the small home she has bought. There he sees the sleeping children and tells her abruptly that he must go downtown. Sensing that he is leaving for good, she begins to cry. By telephone O'Hara asks George to tell her it will be better for her if he goes away and she files for divorce. There is a dissolve to O'Hara, who has become a bum again. At a bar he asks for a drink on credit and is thrown out. He is next seen looking at the plaque on a building that he erected and is told by a policeman to move on, just as in the first scene. Then there is a return to the framing story.

> O'HARA
> That sure was a funny one . . . Right there in bronze, starin' me in the face.
>
> THE AMERICAN
> You're not kiddin' me?
>
> O'HARA
> Kiddin' hell! You can go see it for yourself when you get home.
>
> THE AMERICAN (Falteringly)
> Do you think maybe I CAN go home some day?
>
> O'HARA
> Why sure you can . . .

While they talk about the American's chances of getting home, O'Hara pockets the dollar the American pays for his drink, rather than putting it in the till. Here, unlike the revised script and film, there is no Boss to catch him—Joe is looking the other way—since O'Hara has taken the rap by himself and gone into exile alone.

Sturges's revision of *The Vagrant* in late September, October, and November 1939 was apparently the first instance of his returning to a project begun much earlier. The revised script and film allow us to gauge Sturges's remarkable development as a screenwriter in the six years between the project's drafts. This advance has been overshadowed by his even more astonishing performance as an assured director on his first try and as unquestionably the best interpreter of his own scripts. As a script alone, however, *Down Went McGinty* is greatly superior to *The Vagrant* in almost every way.

The most conspicuous changes from *The Vagrant* to *Down Went McGinty* are in the figures of the Boss and the wife. These entail in turn a changed McGinty, and the three altered characters lead to an altered narrative construction. The latter part of *The Vagrant,* which traces O'Hara's fall in meticulous detail, is greatly abbreviated in *Down Went McGinty,* and the framing story becomes much more important—serving, as it does, to tie up some of the loose ends in the story that McGinty tells.

In the revised script Sturges introduces the Boss much earlier; he and McGinty meet on the first election night. The Boss's accent is changed from Irish to Russian and his age from tired seniority to vigorous middle age. The benign remoteness of the earlier Boss becomes the later Boss's passionate, pugnacious involvement in every aspect of McGinty's political career. The apparent mildness of the earlier Boss, however, masks his ruthlessness when crossed, just as the bombast of the later Boss masks his loyalty to his friends, even those who defect. Whether or not Sturges specifically rewrote the part for Akim Tamiroff, whom it fits like a glove, I have not been able to determine.

The revised script has the Politician (William Demarest) bring McGinty to the mayor's victory party to get him his money; the Boss is amused by McGinty's prodigious voting but is genuinely fascinated by his insolence. McGinty is unimpressed with the bigwigs, talks back to the mayor and the Boss, and hits back when the Boss slaps him. Hovering between anger and delight, the Boss says finally with a laugh: "He thinks he's me!" This mirror equivalence explains the Boss's interest in someone who seems to be just another hobo. The Boss's exclamation is of course reversible: I think I'm him—either the bum armed only with moxie that he himself used to be or the bum he expects to be when his empire collapses.[5] It also illuminates his interest in McGinty's fate, which will turn out to be his fate as well. Later the Boss says: "You're a card you are . . . Yesterday you was a hobo on the breadline . . . today you got a thousand berries and a new suit. I wonder where you'll be tomorrow" (page 38).

McGinty's success as a protection collector gets him an appointment as alderman, and his success in that capacity, with the aid of a graft scandal involving the incumbent, leads to his running for mayor. All of this remains unchanged from *The Vagrant.* In *Down Went McGinty,* however, the Boss, now a bachelor himself, insists that McGinty marry before he runs for mayor. "Women got the vote now . . . maybe you didn't hear about it . . . they don't like bachelors." Since it is McGinty's marriage that will eventually bring down his political career—and with it the Boss's—this directive is another link between the two men and their destinies.

The closer intertwining of the Boss and McGinty in the revised script requires a different conclusion. So in the revised version the Boss tries to shoot McGinty when he learns of his reform plans, and this attempt lands him in jail. As before, McGinty is implicated by the Boss for his past graft activities and is arrested at home, but he makes his good-byes to his wife and children then and there. Cut are the trial scenes, the scenes in which McGinty receives his wife's letter in jail, talks to George, returns home with his wife only to leave again, and the scenes in which he reverts to bumhood. Instead, with the aid of the Politician, McGinty and the Boss escape from jail the night of the day they are arrested. McGinty telephones his wife to tell her to divorce and forget him. We see him rejoin the Boss in their getaway car, and then the film returns to the framing story.

The revised script's expansion of the character of the Boss requires an expansion of the character of the wife also since her influence over McGinty must balance and, for a time, prevail over his. If the Boss is sketchy in *The Vagrant,* so is the romance, which develops late and is not sufficient to motivate O'Hara's about-face. The introduction of McGinty's wife, like that of the Boss, is necessarily moved forward in the revised screenplay. McGinty hurriedly marries his secretary in preparation for the mayoral race. Her two children, he discovers later, are a political asset—as a dissolve to a photo of the candidate and his family shows. The eventual transformation of their show marriage into a love match allows her to influence McGinty between his elections as mayor and as governor—at the same point as she does in the original, but now with more than adequate preparation and motivation.

Perhaps alone among Sturges's scripts, *Down Went McGinty* calls to mind Leslie Fiedler's *Love and Death in the American Novel:* it is a kind of love story between two men. Ishmael flees to the sea and Huck and Jim to the Mississippi River in order to escape women, domesticity, and the responsibilities of civic life. McGinty and the Boss roam an urban wilderness of graft and illegality that is, however, no less their haven. The script's lineage may also be traced to John Gay's *The Beggar's Opera* (1728), called by its author "a Newgate pastoral." *McGinty,* like Nelson Algren's works—especially *The Man with the Golden Arm*—might be called Chicago pastoral.

Into this male Eden comes Woman with her repressive notions of virtue and civilization. The young woman in *The Vagrant,* though not greatly developed, is at least introduced as a renegade from the Purity League—even if she later applies herself to McGinty's reform. Catherine of the revised script, particularly as played by English-accented Muriel Angelus(!), seems, from the beginning, a schoolmarm type. One may even feel a sense of relief when McGinty is forced to leave her and a sense of crocodile tears on both sides when they say good-bye, Catherine presumably rejoining the refined George, McGinty rejoining the Boss in terminal flight from domestic womanhood—to a "banana republic" indeed!

This reunion comes too late, however, to revive fully the high spirits of the earlier part of the film. The scene between the Boss and McGinty in the governor's office on McGinty's first and last day in office is lively, but it is not enough to regain the momentum of their early battling. Strategically speaking, Sturges has built up the romance to motivate McGinty's turn to virtue: the heightened rapport between McGinty and the Boss requires more romantic emphasis to counter it. But as a result, the Boss is missing from pages 74 to 110, far longer than in *The Vagrant*.

Sturges wisely eliminates from *Down Went McGinty* the earlier script's overdetailed treatment of O'Hara's decline. But he may have overcorrected, for the revised script seems to wrap up too quickly. McGinty announces an intention to reform, but he has no chance to act because the Boss loses his composure so quickly, totally, and disastrously as to take a shot at him. Power sometimes evaporates in an instant, but more often it does not—unless wrapping up a plot requires it. One might have said that *Down Went McGinty* has Act II problems—the long romance and family scenes, with cute children and dachshund—but they also spill over into Act III, which seems to conclude before it begins.

In *Between Flops,* James Curtis speculates provocatively that "Sturges found himself intrigued by men like Sulzer and McCrery, men who achieved their position through cooperation and obedience and then suddenly began to see themselves as being beyond the circumstances that made them what they were."[6]

Considered as a plot, this is traditionally a comic one and, of course, becomes overtly so in Sturges's treatment. His serious dramas, whether or not they are tragedies, follow another mold; in them the men who fall from prominence—Tom Garner in *The Power and the Glory,* Diamond Jim in the film of that name, Dr. Morton in *The Great Moment*—were once solid successes. They had actually achieved autonomy and freedom—not just aspired to it—but are cut down by an inner flaw, by circumstances, or by noble self-sacrifice. The man who imagines himself bigger or more powerful than he actually is is an appropriate figure for comedy. There is inevitability, if not justice, in his fall; by classical standards he is restored to his proper place. In modern society, however, the individual has no predetermined place, and no firm traditions say where he or she ought to be. No filmmaker reflects this situation better than Sturges, which may be why traditional genres become so mixed in his work, never again to be disentangled with assurance. At the same time Sturges also has the most thorough awareness of classical comic forms among modern directors, at least the American ones—another Sturges paradox.

If the plot of *Down Went McGinty* recalls classical comedy, its framing story bears some relation to the shaggy dog story. A man starts to tell his life story to a bartender, then the bartender interrupts him and tells the man *his* life story as the former governor of a state. According to Eric Partridge: "The 'shaggy dog' story . . . demands a wittily unexpected and sudden ending, all the more unexpected in that the 'lead-in' and the 'lead-up' have had to be deceptively leisurely and almost diffuse."[7] The spoken shaggy dog story most often consists of a very long lead-up followed by a punch line. In *The Great McGinty* the punch line is McGinty's story itself, which is much longer than the lead-in, but the principle of the unexpected twist remains the same. In cinematic terms, at least, the lead-in to McGinty's story is indeed leisurely in both script versions and in the film itself, although the mechanics differ in each.

In the revised script and film the framing story begins with a rumba dancer, designated in the script as the Girl, who dances with the band and then asks "Tommy" Thompson—who corresponds to "the American" in *The Vagrant*—to buy her a drink. While Thompson, who is already drunk, starts to tell her his story, we see McGinty, standing to one side, take their order—"Two Maiden's Prayers"—and mix their drinks. Thompson's apparent sickness and his suicide attempt in the washroom bring McGinty reluctantly into it. McGinty grabs Thompson's gun and after a struggle takes it away. Thompson pleads to be allowed to kill himself—he is not a crook like the other fugitives in the bar; he was cashier of the First National Bank. McGinty pushes him outside and onto a bar stool and tells the Girl laughingly: "Guy wants to burn his brains 'cause he was cashier in a bank. No foolin'." She replies: "And I suppose you was the president of a bank!" As he pours them two drinks, he says: "Who me? . . . No. I was the Governor of a State, baby."

Only the revised opening resembles a shaggy dog story because McGinty is introduced as a side character in what seems to be Thompson's story, which sets up the twist. In *The Vagrant,* the cashier knows O'Hara well enough to talk to him of suicide but knows nothing of O'Hara's own background. The revised script more plausibly makes them strangers and introduces the rumba dancer so that Thompson can talk to someone. It is only his suicide attempt that brings Thompson and McGinty together.

McGinty, moreover, is now a hard-boiled character—not the philanthropist he was in *The Vagrant,* which is far more consistent with the story he is about to tell. The scene also gives us his tough-minded views on suicide. He has more reason than Thompson to kill himself since he fell from a greater height. But he prefers to survive as a bum rather than perish as an idealist—in pointed contrast to Sturges's dramatic heroes Tom Garner, Diamond Jim, and Dr. Morton. McGinty is a Sancho Panza, not a Don Quixote; tragedy is utterly alien to his view of the world. In this light the film's foreword, discussed below, may suggest that "one crazy minute" of honesty in the life of a crook is more easily and totally repented than a minute of dishonesty for an honest man; perhaps even that dishonesty is a better preparation for survival than honesty.

The framing story sets up the main story as a flashback. McGinty does not propose to tell a story; he merely says that he was the governor of a state in a situation in which a story and its telling are implied. The film takes over and, as it were, amplifies his remark by telling his story for him. In the revised script, there are three returns to the framing story before the final return that concludes the film—in the finished film there are only two.

The first return to the framing story follows the scenes of McGinty's collecting protection money; the Boss has let McGinty keep the money, but they fight anyway, tumbling out of the limousine they are in as it pulls up to a hotel.

DISSOLVE TO:
McGINTY—PAST THOMPSON AND THE GIRL—IN THE BANANA CAFE

McGINTY
(Laughing)
He was always a little muscle-bound, see, and I could beat him to the punch. Boy we had some Brannigans!
(He chuckles in pleasant reminiscence)

THOMPSON
(A little drunkenly and very sourly)
Thought you said you were the Governor of a state.

THE GIRL
Yes, you was just a cheap crook.

McGINTY
Well, you gotta crawl before you creep, don't ya?
(Now he proceeds with enjoyment)
I collect the chicken-feed for a while, see? Then the guy makes me an alderman and I move in on the second floor. You know: bus franchises, garbage disposal . . nice stuff. (page 40)

In this scene McGinty is commenting on the action we have just seen and is thus tied into the narration more explicitly than he had been in the opening sequence. Thompson and the Girl speak for the impatient viewer: when will he get to the governorship? Was he indeed the governor of a state? All that he has told so far is that he was a cheap crook, something they had already surmised. Thompson and the Girl, perhaps like the audience, think that being governor and being a cheap crook are mutually exclusive. McGinty links them; being a cheap crook prepares one to be an expensive crook—in this case, a governor. McGinty then moves beyond mere commentary on the action and begins to narrate the next part of his story. The ensuing scenes in effect illustrate his narration by showing him as an alderman negotiating a bus franchise.

In the revised script, the main story recommences as we see headlines about graft exposure and then the Boss suggesting that McGinty run for mayor, followed by a long scene of McGinty's negotiating the bus franchise. The film here improves on the revised script, in which McGinty's narration veers into an irrelevant gag about "turning on the heat" (page 41), and he tells Thompson to explain that expression to the Girl. The film eliminates the "heat" gag and cuts from the bus franchise line to the scene illustrating it. This relates the framing story to the main story far more smoothly and lucidly and shows us this stage of McGinty's rise to power in its proper order: voter, collector, alderman, mayor, governor. To proceed, as *Down Went McGinty* did, from McGinty as collector to the Boss's considering him for mayor and then back to the alderman scene would have been confusing to the viewer. The film's return to the framing story at this point makes clear McGinty's role in the narration, and the reversion to the main story is accomplished without missing a beat. The film now briefly illustrates McGinty's career as an alderman—the scene with Mr. Maxwell is condensed from five script pages to one—before moving him along to the next stage.

The next long section of the film shows McGinty's candidacy for mayor, the Boss's requirement that he marry, and then the many scenes with Catherine, her children, their dog, and their servants. After we see McGinty reading to the children and then Catherine urging him to buck the political machine, the film returns again to the framing story. Placing the return here requires McGinty, as narrator, to respond to Catherine's point. But first there is the following exchange:

THE GIRL
You liked the kids, huh?

THOMPSON
Why shouldn't he like 'em?

McGINTY
Sure I liked 'em. (page 103)

Then there is some business about McGinty's bartending—a waiter relays a customer's complaint and McGinty tells him off. All of this delays McGinty's reaction to Catherine's speech and creates suspense. Thompson and the Girl, again as stand-ins for the audience, "watch McGinty fixedly." They are responding, in motivational terms, to the very heart of the story: why did McGinty fall? How did he get to Latin America? Equally at stake is a hard-boiled character's admission that he loved his family, indeed gave up everything for love, which—by American film convention—such a character cannot say directly. (In the revised script, the suspense and McGinty's toughness are somewhat dispelled by a paragraph about what has become of his adopted children, which the film wisely cuts.) After a pause McGinty says:

McGINTY
She kept sayin': "You'll be strong enough some day" . . . I knew it was wrong, see, but I liked the way it made me look in her eyes . . . and the kids' . . . so one day I said: "All right, I'm strong enough now."
(He chuckles, then adds)
In a pig's ear I was strong enough. (page 103)

At this point the film returns to the main story with a "MONTAGE OF THE GUBERNATORIAL RACE," just as the revised script indicates. Then we see the inaugural parade, McGinty's agreeing to attempt some reforms, and his first-day meeting with the Boss and its disastrous results.

The revised script specifies a return to the framing story just following the headline shot, "Governor Arrested: McGinty Spends Night in Jail" (page 121). In that scene, missing from the film, McGinty explains to Thompson and the Girl that he and the Boss might have "squashed" the matter except that the

Boss had already had him indicted and a federal income tax investigation was also under way. The scene is consistent with the rest of the revised screenplay in that the two men's political careers are destroyed because the investigation quickly outgrows the feuding pals' ability to control it. But it also seems a holdover from the 1933 script's elaborate detailing of O'Hara's decline. The film perhaps does better without it, not to mention one more gag on the Girl's misunderstanding American slang (page 122).

The revised script returns to the framing story for its conclusion following McGinty's final phone call to his wife and his speedy getaway with the Boss. In the film's version of the scene, the part in which McGinty antagonizes Thompson to make him sore enough to take the ship home (pages 132–134)—a residue from *The Vagrant* of O'Hara the philanthropist—is cut. The film retains, of course, the revelation of the people around the bar, whom we have seen thus far only from behind, as the Boss, the Politician, and two minor characters from the main story, Dr. Jarvis and Louis. Then McGinty pockets Thompson's two dollars, the Boss catches him at it, and the two fight as the film ends. In the revised script their fight is over a different issue. McGinty has told Thompson and the Girl to "get outta here" (page 133); the Boss says: "Since when are you chasing the customers?" (page 134), and they fight. The film's conclusion, which is more appropriate for a film about thieving and thieves, skillfully adapts the conclusion of *The Vagrant* to the context of *The Great McGinty.*

There are many such instances in Sturges's scripts and films: he was a most effective reviser and a brilliant editor of his own material. The available drafts

"Boy we had some Brannigans!" –McGinty and the Boss fighting in THE GREAT McGINTY.

of Sturges's scripts for other directors provide glimpses of this ability, but *The Great McGinty* opens up yet another dimension. The filming process now becomes the final revision of the script, and the film itself the final script version.

Sturges may not have intended it—it may just be the structural effect of the various revisions—but there is a *Cabinet of Dr. Caligari* aspect to the concluding scene. Perhaps, after all, McGinty has spun out an elaborate fiction, to distract and console a would-be suicide or simply to pass the time. Perhaps, looking around the room, he has just made up a story about the bar owner, the waiter, the card players, and himself and how they got there. When the story is over, Thompson asks: "Why didn't he [the Boss] kill you?" McGinty admits that he could never figure that out, which can be read as an inconsistency in McGinty's story or as a denial of the emotional bond between the Boss and himself. The Girl says to Thompson: "I know why . . . Because he's a big liar . . . about the whole thing." (In the film she says this to McGinty; so "he's a big liar" is changed to "you're a big liar.") McGinty laughs and says: "Okay, sister, have it your way," as though speaking to the viewer. He then says to Thompson: "That'll be two bucks, you," as though demanding payment for his story/film.

This issue is illuminated by the film's opening title, which we have not considered yet. In fact, the 1933 and 1939 script versions and the film itself each have a distinct headnote. *The Vagrant* has the following "Foreword":

> Too much has been said of the virtues of honesty. Practically everyone has a kind word for it, although, like exercise, fresh air, or parting the hair in the middle, it agrees with certain people only.
>
> Meat is not good for cows, whiskey is terrible for gold fish, and I purpose to show that honesty is as disastrous for a crook as is knavery for the cashier of a bank.
>
> A man is what he is. So he was made. So will he be.

Whether or not this passage was to appear in the film is unclear. It is presented, like a note to the reader, before and outside the script, yet who but producers would read it there? In *Down Went McGinty,* by contrast, Sturges makes it explicit that the headnote is to be printed over the first shot:

> This story has no moral,
> This story has no end,
> This story only goes to show
> There is no good in men.

The finished film, of course, has the following note:

> This is the story of two men who met in a banana republic. One of them was honest all his life except one crazy minute. The other was dishonest all his life except one crazy minute. They both had to get out of the country.

As modern criticism tells us, forewords, prefaces, epigraphs, and headnotes are ambiguously situated both inside the text and outside it. They purport to tell us how to read the text but most often serve to compound the problem of reading. The film's note seems to validate, from inside-outside the film, the story that McGinty tells. The implied director of the film has placed this title for us to read, creating an implied narrator—and interpreter—of the fiction that is about to unfold; both lend their authority to McGinty's story. On the other hand, Thompson—the honest man referred to in the headnote—himself uses the expression "one crazy minute," early in the film, to describe his life-changing thievery. Is he quoting the headnote, as if he has privileged access to the narration itself? Or does the headnote quote him, which seems to privilege his perspective, including his skepticism about McGinty's story later on?

Theory aside, there is something puzzling about works that have gone through a series of different forewords or headnotes. It is as though there were in such cases not only doubt that the work would stand on its own but also doubt as to the meaning to be conveyed; hence the trail of discarded formulations. We see a comparable process in only one other Sturges work—*Sullivan's Travels,* in which the final headnote was originally part of Sullivan's concluding speech. Aside from this, Sturges never used such a formulation again, except for the quotation from *Twelfth Night* that concludes, or simply stops, the ungovernable madness of *The Miracle of Morgan's Creek* (1944), but this is quite a different thing.[8]

What may be the most important aspect of *The Great McGinty* does not emerge from a consideration of its genesis. The genre identification of a film presumably draws its audience to the theater and, once they are inside, governs their experience of the film itself. *The Great McGinty,* like most Sturges films, confounds audience expectations by belonging to no single genre and by outmaneuvering, with remarkably sustained invention, modes of response inherited from other films.[9]

What most countered audience expectations of *The Great McGinty,* one supposes, was the film's cynical presentation of politics. Frank Capra's films are only the best-known opposing instances. Capra's films, written by various screenwriters, pile up obstacles to the central character's virtue—Deeds, Smith, Doe, George Bailey[10]—but in the end he always triumphs and thereby redeems the American system. His hero's struggles also remind all but the most villainous of their own natural, if misplaced, goodness of heart. Sturges, one need hardly add, offers no such solace. The viewer may be engaged by the political person—McGinty or the Boss—but politics itself is corrupt. Furthermore, the individual's will to reform is by no means sufficient to change things; human affairs have a logic and a structure that are supra-individual. There is a tide in the affairs of men, but it usually drowns the individual who opposes it.

This runs fundamentally counter to American ideology, especially as found in commercial films, according to which the self's moral resolve eventually sweeps away obstacles, including the most ingrained social structures. This is the legacy of American Transcendentalism; Capra is closer to Emerson than is usually realized. From the end of *It Happened One Night* forward in Capra's work, the walls of Jericho keep falling. In Sturges's films they are pointed to and ridiculed, but they do not fall.

NOTES

1. The note reads: COMPLETED 11:45 P.M.
August fourteenth
1 9 3 3

Preston Sturges spoke
Bianca Gilchrist wrote

Refinished September
1st, 1933.

2. James Curtis reports this succession of titles in *Between Flops: A Biography of Preston Sturges* (New York: Harcourt Brace Jovanovich, 1982), page 127. The only copy of the 1933 script that I found in the UCLA Special Collections Department has *Down Went McGinty* on the cover page and a note at the bottom, "Copied April 18, 1939." Beneath this is an earlier cover page: "*Biography of a Bum, An original screenplay by Preston Sturges*" with "Copyright by the author, 1933" at the bottom. Beneath this is the "Foreword," quoted above, with "The Author" written under it and "Hollywood, July nineteenth, 1933" at the bottom. This date indicates that Sturges wrote the foreword at or near the beginning of his work on the project rather than at the end. Within the script itself, Sequence A has "The Vagrant" typed above it; Sequences B, D, E, and F have "Biography of a Bum" typed above them; Sequence C has no designation at its top or elsewhere.

3. As mentioned above, there is a copy of *The Great McGinty* dated December 5, 1939, that is, eight days later than the November 28, 1939, script printed below and six days before the beginning of shooting on December 11. There is only one known copy of this script, which is in private hands, and it is, unfortunately, too delicate to photocopy or even to work with. A very quick perusal of this document indicated to me that it includes some of the revisions evident in the film, but by no means all. Sturges revised all of his scripts in the process of shooting them, including *The Great McGinty.* This is the only instance among the five scripts reproduced here in which a later script is known to exist.

4. See *Eugene O'Neill at Work: Newly Released Ideas for Plays,* ed. and annotated by Virginia Floyd (New York: Ungar, 1981), pages 215–222. The contrasts between O'Neill and Sturges are so great that no one, as far as I know, has considered parallels between them. Both did their most successful work on the Broadway stage in the twenties, and both had left it by the mid-thirties. Sturges never parodied O'Neill, as did Ring Lardner, perhaps because some of his themes were close to some of O'Neill's.

5. Because he manipulates McGinty and his image, the Boss is a director figure. Like another director, Sullivan in *Sullivan's Travels,* he is fascinated with hobos and hobohood, perhaps from anxiety at himself falling to such low estate.

6. Curtis, op. cit., page 91.

7. Eric Partridge, *The "Shaggy Dog" Story: Its Origin, Development, and Nature (with a Few Seemly Examples)* (London: Faber and Faber, 1953), page 52.

8. "Some are born great, some achieve greatness, and some have greatness thrust upon them" (Act II, scene 5).

9. Pare Lorentz said in a review of the film: "All during the showing of *The Great McGinty* I expected the writer-director to fall into old movie clichés, but at each turn of

the story he came up with an amusing or inventive scene, and finally, when there seemed no way he could end his picture except with a standard, implausible happy ending, he wound up with a logical, but novel and gay finale that gave the picture a final fillip—accurate, in exactly the right mood, unexpected, and really funny" (*Lorentz on Film, Movies 1927 to 1941* [New York: Hopkinson and Blake, 1975], page 194).

10. Robert Riskin wrote the scripts of *Mr. Deeds Goes to Town* (1936) and *Meet John Doe* (1941); Sidney Buchman wrote *Mr. Smith Goes to Washington* (1939); Frances Goodrich and Albert Hackett wrote *It's a Wonderful Life* (1946).

SF 8387

~~DOWN WENT McGINTY~~

The Great McGinty

November 28, 1939

SEQUENCE "A"

During the Main Titles we see a succession of shots of the harbor and waterfront of a banana republic. The last title is imposed over a NIGHT SHOT of a drinking establishment. Now we HEAR some rumba music and we TRUCK FORWARD SLOWLY TOWARD THE CAFE. At this point the following is imposed over the shot:

This story has no moral,
This story has no end,
This story only goes to show
There is no good in men.

DISSOLVE TO:

A-1 A PRETTY RUMBA DANCER PERFORMING IN FRONT OF A BAND

We see a few customers IN THE FOREGROUND but they are not particularly interested. In other words, they give one look then turn away. Noticing the lack of interest she bends over and grabs her skirt.

A-2 THE RUMBA DANCER FROM THE WAIST DOWN

Slowly she starts to pull up her skirt. The CAMERA FOLLOWS her as she dances.

A-3 LOW CAMERA SHOT UP AT A TABLE OF MEN

They are not paying any attention. One of them is lighting a pipe. As he turns his head away to escape the cloud of smoke his eye catches the legs on the floor. There is a slight double-take, then he gives the legs his undivided attention. A second later the other men at his table follow his gaze. Now the whole table looks on stonily. In the BACKGROUND we see McGinty working at the bar but he is OUT OF FOCUS

A-4 THE GIRL'S LEGS AS SHE DANCES

A-5 THE GIRL'S UPPER HALF

She looks around and is amused at the effect her legs are having.

A-6 TRUCKING SHOT - PAST THE TABLES AT RINGSIDE

The CAMERA represents the girl's eyes and sees what she sees as she dances by. In this way we pass the

11-28-39 (Continued)

A-6 (Cont'd)

rest of the ringside tables, with all the occupants looking down under us. Be sure to have some bald heads here. The heads turn slowly as we pass. A waiter is circulating between the tables serving drinks but we do not see his face. The last table we see is back a little from the dance floor. Here seven men are playing poker. With their BACKS TO US and unrecognizable, are The Boss and Dr. Jarvis, the latter in a green eyeshade. Directly across the table in a strong light is a pale drunken young American, Thompson. Two Americans and two Spanish types complete the game. Behind Thompson stands Louie twiddling a toothpick. The top of the frame cuts him off at the necktie. (NOTE: This is the exact shot we use at the end of the picture except for Thompson who will have left the game.) A second after we come in on the SHOT Thompson throws down his cards disgustedly and gets to his feet unsteadily.

A-7 THE RUMBA DANCER

Without stopping her dance she calls out.

THE GIRL
You buy me a drink, Tommy?

A-8 THOMPSON - WALKING AWAY

He stops and looks back a second before answering.

THOMPSON
Okay.

His eyes fix on a table and he starts for it.

A-9 THE GIRL DANCER IN FRONT OF THE BAND

She looks back over her shoulder and gives a signal. The music comes to a quick stop and there is a spatter of applause. The girl pulls her skirts down and star for the table at which Thompson is waiting. The CAMERA PANS her to the table. As she sits --

A-10 CLOSER SHOT - THE GIRL AND THOMPSON

THE GIRL
(Finishing sitting)
Thank you, Tommy, is hot work.
(She wipes her brow
with a handkerchief)
You lose much?

11-28-39 (Continued)

A-10 (Cont'd)

THOMPSON
(Thickly)
No...don't matter anyway.

THE GIRL
(Yelling over her shoulder)
Two Maiden's Prayer.

A-11 CLOSE SHOT - THE BAR

McGINTY
(Raising up from a beer box)
On the fire.

He breaks an egg into a glass cocktail shaker.

A-12 CLOSE SHOT - THE GIRL AND THOMPSON

THE GIRL
You don't feel so good tonight, Tommy, hunh?

THOMPSON
(Vaguely)
I'll be all right...tell 'em to play "Blue Heaven" will you?

THE GIRL
(Calling to the orchestra in Spanish)
Play him the "Blue Heaven," Manuel.
(Then putting her hand on Thompson's arm)
I'm sorry, Tommy.

THOMPSON
(Quietly)
I had a wife and a couple o' kids, see, and the house was almost paid for, it's what they call half-timbered.

The orchestra starts to play "Blue Heaven."

A-13 SHOT OF THE ORCHESTRA - PLAYING

A-14 CLOSE SHOT - THE GIRL AND THOMPSON

Thompson looks distantly at the musicians.

THE GIRL
My father live in a big house, too... with many butlers and...

11-28-39 (Continued)

A-14 (Cont'd)

THOMPSON
(Vaguely)
What? Oh! It doesn't matter. People used to say, "You watch that Thompson boy...he'll go a long way in this world."
(He chuckles bitterly)
I came a long way all right...
(He holds up his forefinger)
...one crazy minute...one crazy minute.

McGINTY'S VOICE
Hey!

A-15 McGINTY - BEHIND THE BAR

The completed drinks are in front of him.

McGINTY
(Yelling over, with a bottle of Tabasco in his hand)
You want the Tabasco in it?

A-16 THE GIRL AND THOMPSON

Thompson is still far away.

THE GIRL
(Repeating)
You want the Tabasco in it?

THOMPSON
Yeah.

THE GIRL
(Yelling over her shoulder)
Yeah.

A-17 McGINTY - BEHIND THE BAR

McGINTY
Oke.

He puts three strong shakes of Tabasco in each drink, then turns behind him and hits the bell for the waiter. The waiter's shoulder moves INTO THE SHOT.

McGINTY
(Sliding the drinks over)
For Concepcion and the kid.

The waiter's hands put the drinks on a little tray.

11-28-39

A-18 THE GIRL AND THOMPSON

THE GIRL
What you do back home, Tommy?

THOMPSON
(Without looking at her)
Bank.
(Now he turns and looks at her a little suspiciously)
What'da you care what I did?

THE GIRL
(Innocently)
I was just talking, Tommy.
(She looks hurt. Now she sees the waiter)
Thank you.

The waiter puts the drinks down but we must not recognize him. Seeing the waiter, Thompson throws some bills on the table. One bill falls to the floor and the girl picks it up quickly.

THOMPSON
That's right...don't lose any of it...s'wonderful stuff.

The waiter takes a bill off the table and goes OUT OF THE SHOT.

THOMPSON
(Jerking his thumb toward the band)
She used to play that.
(Now he picks up the drink)
Here's to you.

The girl clinks glasses with him but keeps looking down. Thompson tosses off half the drink, then the rest of it. Now he points to one of the bills on the table.

THOMPSON
Give that to the band.

He feels of his pocket, then with difficulty starts to get to his feet.

THE GIRL
You goin' home so soon, Tommy?

THOMPSON
(Pointing vaguely)
No, I'm goin' in there.

He gets unsteadily to his feet and the CAMERA DRAWS BACK. The girl gets up and steadies him.

11-28-39 (Continued)

A-18 (Cont'd)

THE GIRL
You feel bad?

THOMPSON
You ask a lotta questions, don't you?

He smiles a slightly insane smile.

THE GIRL
I'll help you.

She reaches back for the money on the table and they start through the tables and the CAMERA PANS after them which brings McGinty INTO VIEW IN THE BACKGROUND. There are a couple of snickers from adjoining tables. The music ends. We HEAR only conversation and the sound of chips from the poker game.

A-19 McGINTY - BEHIND THE BAR

He pauses in the act of wiping up the bar to watch disapprovingly the approach of Thompson.

A-20 THOMPSON AND THE GIRL - OVER McGINTY'S RIGHT SHOULDER

The poker game is going strong IN THE BACKGROUND. The girl steadies Thompson. As they get close to the bar the girl falls behind Thompson so that she can make motions to McGinty without Thompson seeing her. (This means that she must be between McGinty and Thompson.)

THE GIRL
(Mouthing the word)
Sick.

She points to her stomach then motions to McGinty that he is to take Thompson into the washroom.

McGINTY
What's that got to do with me?

The CAMERA TRUCKS AHEAD with the girl and Thompson. The girl again signals to McGinty, who has been left behind.

McGINTY
All right.

He throws down his bar-cloth and moves along behind the bar till he comes to the end. He comes out from behind the bar, puts his hand on Thompson's shoulder and starts to pilot him. The girl drops back.

THE GIRL
Thank you.

11-28-39

A-21 INT. OF THE WASHROOM

The door is kicked open and Thompson comes in, piloted by McGinty.

McGINTY
(Pushing him
OUTSIDE THE SHOT)
Go ahead. Come on - heave ho!

McGinty walks into the corner and starts examining a cheap perfume machine which has a mirror on the face of it. Suddenly he becomes rigid and stares at the mirror.

A-22 SHOT IN THE WAVY MIRROR - PAST McGINTY'S HEAD

We see Thompson draw a revolver. McGinty's head disappears from the SHOT and now we see McGinty also in the mirror as he reaches the boy's side. We HEAR a shot.

A-23 McGINTY - WRESTLING WITH THOMPSON IN THE SMOKE-FILLED WASHROOM

He holds Thompson's wrist in an iron grip.

THOMPSON
(Hysterically)
Gimme that gun, Dan...Give it to me...
Let me have it willya?

The gun clanks to the floor.

McGINTY
(Roughly)
What are you tryin' to do, give
this place a bad name?

A-24 THE GIRL - NEAR THE BAR

The Band is playing the "Rancho Grande." The Girl is frowning as if she has just heard something. Now she comes PAST THE CAMERA.

A-25 THOMPSON AND McGINTY

THOMPSON
(Starting to cry)
What are you butting in for,
you lousy...

McGinty bats him against the wall.

A-26 THE DOOR OF THE WASHROOM

The girl runs in.

THE GIRL
(After sniffing)
What happened? What you doing
to him, you big bull?

A-27 McGINTY AND THOMPSON

McGINTY
(Looking around)
What are you doing in the gents'
room? Get outta here !

A-28 THE GIRL

THE GIRL
(Pointing)
What's that smoke?

A-29 McGINTY AND THOMPSON - PAST THE GIRL

McGINTY
Somebody lit a firecracker. Come
on, get outta here. I'll bring
him out.

The girl turns slowly and goes PAST THE CAMERA.
McGinty watches her go, then turns back to Thompson.

THOMPSON
(Pleadingly)
Give it to me, willya? What do
you care? Lemme do it while I
still got the guts. Come on, Dan.
I'm not like the rest of the trash
around here. I don't fit, see. I'm
not a crook.

McGINTY
Come on, now.

He stoops, picks up the gun and puts it in his pocket.

THOMPSON
I was...I was the cashier of the
First National Bank.

A-30 McGINTY - PAST THOMPSON

McGINTY
(Not believing his ears)
The what?

11-28-39 (Continued)

A-30 (Cont'd)

A smile comes around his mouth.

THOMPSON
The cashier of the First National Bank.

McGinty snorts and breaks into a guffaw. Now he roars. Now he stops laughing as suddenly as he started.

McGINTY
Come on outside.

He forces Thompson forward.

A-31 THE WASHROOM DOOR - FROM THE MAIN DOOR

The girl is waiting nervously. The music is playing gaily. Now the door opens and McGinty shoves Thompson out ahead of him, but holds onto his arm. Suddenly Thompson tries to break loose. McGinty tightens his grip till the boy cringes.

McGINTY
(Roughly)
Don't get fresh, lug, you're giving away too much weight.

The girl rushes to the other side of Thompson.

THE GIRL
(Excitedly)
What's the matter, Tommy, what happened?

McGINTY
(Amused)
Guy wants to burn his brains 'cause he was cashier in a bank.
(He starts to laugh again)
No foolin'.

He pulls the gun out a little so the girl can see it.

THOMPSON
(Angrily)
I suppose you were the president of a bank! It strikes you so funny!

McGINTY
(Innocently)
Who, me?...No. Come on behave yourself and I'll buy you a drink.

11-28-39 (Continued)

A-31 (Cont'd)

He shoves Thompson and the girl onto stools. The girl puts her arm around Thompson as McGinty goes behind the bar.

THE GIRL
Don't feel bad, Tommy.

McGinty fills two glasses with bar whisky, slides them across the bar and speaks very quietly.

McGINTY
I was the Governor of a State, baby.

A-32 THOMPSON AND THE GIRL - PAST McGINTY

Behind them the cafe life goes on as usual. Thompson looks at McGinty in astonisment.

THE GIRL
(Frowning)
What you were?

A-33 McGINTY - PAST THE GIRL AND THOMPSON

McGINTY
Oh, yes.

He chuckles.

We HEAR the clang of a streetcar bell and faintly the voices of newsboys.

DISSOLVE TO:

END OF SEQUENCE "A"

11-28-39

SEQUENCE "B"

DISSOLVE INTO:

B-1 A SMALL CITY SQUARE - (NIGHT SHOT) - SNOWING

The ghost of a streetcar glides in OVER McGinty and Thompson. McGinty opens the door of the washroom and we see him lead Thompson out into the room beyond. The streetcar bell RINGS loudly now. On the side of the car there is a banner which reads:

VOTE FOR MAYOR TILLINGHAST
HE'D DO THE SAME FOR YOU

The bell RINGS again and the streetcar moves OUT OF THE SHOT. We start TRUCKING ACROSS the street toward a SOUP KITCHEN. This bears a placard which says:

FREE SOUP KITCHEN NO. 11
DONATED BY MAYOR WILFRED H. TILLINGHAST
Don't forget your friend.

The soup kitchen has a hinged front and is brilliantly lighted inside. A cook doles out the soup and bread while a policeman stands in authority outside. A queue of hungry men trails into the darkness. As we get near we hear the policeman more clearly.

THE POLICEMAN
One at a time, now, one at a time...
There's plenty for everybody... and
don't forget who give it to you.

The bum at the head of the line gets his cup of soup and starts dunking his bread in it.

THE POLICEMAN
Step ahead, now, and give your friends
a chanst... and don't forget the mayor
who didn't forget to remember the less
fortunate than himself... on this
election night.

The bum moves on and McGinty steps into the light. He is younger and leaner. His cap is pulled down over his eyes and his coat collar turned up. He stares at the soup and the bread, then massages his hands and blows on them so they will work better, but even so, when he is given the bread and the soup he holds them stiffly. Now the cook leans forward and speaks in his ear.

11-28-39

B-2 CLOSEUP - HEADS OF McGINTY AND THE COOK

THE COOK
Could you use a couple of bucks?

McGINTY
(Viciously)
Who do you think you're kiddin'?

THE COOK
I ain't kiddin'..., soon as you're finished mosey around to the shack behind this one...they'll tell you how to do it.

B-3 THE POLICEMAN

THE POLICEMAN
Keep moving, please. Step ahead and give your friends a chanst, and don't forget to remember who give you the soup.

B-4 McGINTY AND THE COOK

McGinty downs the soup in one gulp and starts forward. The CAMERA PANS him up to the policeman who bars his way with an outstretched arm.

THE POLICEMAN
(Confidentially)
It's just around in back... there's a cop standing outside.

McGinty looks at him then disappears into the shadows.

THE POLICEMAN
One at a time, boys. There's plenty for everybody, and don't forget to remember the man...

B-5 CLOSE SHOT - A LITTLE TOOL HOUSE

A cop stands outside. Two tramps come out of the tool house as McGinty comes INTO THE PICTURE.

B-6 THE POLITICIAN INSIDE THE TOOL HOUSE

It is lit by a gasoline lantern. It contains a table with a drawer that locks, and a chair. The Politician

B-6 (Cont'd)

is a cheap looking gent of thirty-five. Through the open door we see the cop. McGinty comes in slowly, holding his piece of bread.

THE POLITICIAN
You lookin' for somebody, big boy?

McGINTY
The soup guy sent me over.

THE POLITICIAN
Some soup, ain't it? Certainly kind of the Mayor to think of the less fortunate on a night like this, ain't it?

McGINTY
Never mind the applesauce, how do I get the two bucks?

THE POLITICIAN
(A little taken aback)
Very simple, my boy, you just go down and vote for Mayor Tillinghast and come right back here and collect.

McGINTY
How do I know you'll be here?

THE POLITICIAN
(Indignantly)
How do you know I'll be here! How do you like that!
(He calls to the cop outside)
Listen to this guy: we fill him full of soup and now he don't trust nobody!
(He swings on McGinty)
You got your soup, dintcha? Well, you'll get your two bucks!

McGINTY
Where do I vote?

THE POLITICIAN
The nerve some guys got!

He opens the drawer and takes out a list of polling places.

11-28-39 (Continued)

B-6 (Cont'd)

THE POLITICIAN
(Reading the list)
"How do I know you'll be here!" Go around the corner to the barber shop on Van Buren. Twenty-one twenty-one. Did you register?

McGINTY
No.

THE POLITICIAN
It's all the same. When the guy asks your name, that's the watcher, see? You say "Hello, Bill," then he'll call out the right name for you. You vote and that's all there is to it...twenty-one twenty-one Van Buren.

McGINTY
What's the sentence for repeatin'?

THE POLITICIAN
(Scandalized)
Who said anything about repeatin'? Where do you think this is, Hicks Corners? Some people is too lazy to vote, that's all... They don't like this kind of weather. Some of them is sick in bed and can't vote! Maybe a couple of 'em croaked recently!... That ain't no reason why Mayor Tillinghast should be cheated outta their support. All we're doin' is gettin' out the vote.

McGINTY
How will you know I voted?

THE POLITICIAN
First of all I ain't like you, see? I'll trust you....And besides, the watcher'll give you a ticket.

McGINTY
(After a pause)
Suppose I bring you two tickets?

THE POLITICIAN
Two tickets is four fish.

McGINTY
And three is six?

11-28-39 (Continued)

B-6 (Cont'd)

THE POLITICIAN
And four is eight...You can't get away from arithmetic...but you better watch your step.

McGINTY
(Reaching into the drawer)
Gimme one of them lists.

He crumples it and starts out.

DISSOLVE TO:

B-7 EXT. A BARBER SHOP

This is below the street level and reached by steps. There is snow on the ground. Through the glass front we see that the barber shop is arranged for voting. McGinty comes INTO THE PICTURE, looks at the place, then straightens his cap, turns down his coat collar, arranges his tie, throws back his shoulders and descends.

B-8 INT. OF THE BARBER SHOP

Outside of its regular fixtures it has a table and a ballot box. Outside of the barbers there are several examiners, a policeman, a bootblack and a man getting a haircut. A bell jangles as McGinty enters. The watcher, with a large badge on his lapel and papers in his hand, turns and looks at McGinty suspiciously.

THE WATCHER
Your name, please.

McGINTY
(Stiffly)
Why uh...hello, Bill.

THE WATCHER
(Relaxing)
Why hello, there, hello, hello, hello.

He consults a list in his hand, gives McGinty a ticket, then placing a hand on McGinty's shoulder, announces:

THE WATCHER
Rufus J. Widdicombe, 165 North Clark Street.
(He smiles at McGinty)
Glad ta seen you, Rufe.

11-28-39 (Continued)

B-8 (Cont'd)

McGinty goes to the proper place, receives and marks his ballot, folds it, drops it in the ballot box, then starts out.

McGINTY
So long...Bill.

THE WATCHER
So long...Rufe.

McGINTY
Give my love to Minnie.

THE WATCHER
(Blankly)
Thanks, I'll...tell her you...asked about her.

He watches McGinty leave.

B-9 EXT. OF BARBER SHOP

We are SHOOTING DOWN at the DOOR as McGinty comes out. He chuckles, then takes the list out of his pocket, runs his finger down it, decides on the nearest place, then hurries up PAST THE CAMERA.

DISSOLVE TO:

B-10 A PUBLIC SCHOOL ROOM

Geometrical examples on the blackboard help to identify it. Some spinsterish ladies handle the lists at a table and a most respectable looking bearded gentleman of the professor type wears the watcher's badge. McGinty comes in and stops a little sheepishly.

THE PROFESSOR
What is your name please, sir?

McGINTY
(After looking around to see if there could be someone else)
Why uh..uh...hello there uh....
(In a very small voice he questions)
...Bill?

11-28-39 (Continued)

B-10 (Cont'd)

THE PROFESSOR
(Delighted at finding his old friend)
Why certainly...heh-heh-heh.

From his inside pocket he whips out a list, consults it and announces:

THE PROFESSOR
Dr. Heindrich L. Schutzendorf, 20 East Goethe Street...thank you, Heindrich.

He presses a ticket in his hand.

THE FIRST LADY
(Writing in her book)
Dr. Heindrich L. Schutzendorf.

THE SECOND LADY
(Suddenly)
Why, I could have sworn Dr. Schutzendorf was dead!

She bends a suspicious look on McGinty.

McGINTY
(Pleasantly)
Not yet, lady...not quite.

DISSOLVE TO:

B-11 INT. OF A LAUNDRY

This is also rigged up for voting.

THE WATCHER
(In a loud voice)
Emanuel J. Goldberg, 1117 North Division Street.
(Now he indicates a place)
Right this way, Mr. Goldberg.

B-12 McGINTY COMING FORWARD

He passes his hand over his nose.

B-13 EXT. OF A LAUNDRY

McGinty hurries out of it and PAST US.

B-14 A BROWNSTONE HOUSE

McGinty hurries AWAY FROM US and up the steps.

11-28-39

B-15 EXT. OF A PUBLIC SCHOOL

McGinty emerges and hurries PAST US.

B-16 EXT. OF A LIBRARY

McGinty hurries in.

B-17 EXT. OF A FIRE STATION

McGinty hurries out.

B-18 EXT. OF A TURKISH BATH

McGinty hurries in.

B-19 EXT. OF A POLICE STATION

McGinty hurries out.

DISSOLVE TO:

B-20 THE POLITICIAN IN THE TOOL HOUSE

He stands, watch in hand, talking indignantly to the cop outside.

THE POLITICIAN
Well, I ain't goin' to wait here all night...I got a right to eat, ain't I? The guy's had time to vote ten times! I'm goin' to eat. If you see him, you tell him I got somethin' better to do than...

McGINTY'S VOICE
Than what?

B-21 McGINTY - PAST THE COP

The cop finishes turning around to look at him. Now McGinty goes PAST THE CAMERA.

B-22 THE POLITICIAN IN THE TOOLHOUSE

McGinty comes in, reaches into his right pants pocket, and chucks five tickets on the table.

11-28-39 (Continued)

B-22 (Cont'd)

THE POLITICIAN
(Counting them with his hand)
From the time you took anybody'd think....

From his left pants pocket McGinty throws ten more tickets on the table. This stops the Politician right in the middle of his sentence. He watches goggle-eyed as McGinty throws ten more from his right coat pocket. He watches stupefied as McGinty extracts another ten from his left coat pocket.

THE POLITICIAN
(In an awe-struck voice)
Is that all?

McGINTY
Wait a minute.
(He pulls two more tickets from his breast pocket)
That's it.

THE POLITICIAN
(Muttering to himself as he counts the tickets)
Thirty-five, thirty-six, thirty-seven....sixty-four bucks!

McGINTY
Seventy-four bucks.

THE POLITICIAN
Come in here a minute, Mike, you might never see anything like this again.
(Now he notices that Mike has left)
He's gone. Well look....
(He pulls a few bills out of his pants pocket)
I been payin' off a little heavier than I figured....How would you like to meet me some place.....tomorrow?

McGinty looks at him stonily.

THE POLITICIAN
You wouldn't care for that? Well...
(Then loudly)
You'll get your dough. You don't have to look sidewise at everybody...

11-28-39 (Continued)

B-22 (Cont'd)

THE POLITICIAN (Cont'd)
come on, we'll go down to the club
and you'll get your dough.

McGINTY
You said it.

The Politician reaches for the gasoline lamp.

DISSOLVE TO:

B-23 EXT. THE LOCAL HEADQUARTERS

It is draped with Tillinghast banners. We HEAR the SOUND of much gaiety.

B-24 THE MAIN HALL

Actually this is a series of parlors opening into each other. Some men are playing pool, others are eating, drinking and talking. The CAMERA PANS OVER all this and COMES TO REST on McGinty who stands near a champagne and food table. He looks wolfishly at the food, reaches out for a piece of something, then thinks better of it, pulls his hand back and looks around the room. Now he thinks of the whole matter from a different standpoint. Suddenly he glares at the room as if it were filled with his enemies, squares his shoulders, grabs two enormous pieces of bread and covers them with about two pounds of assorted food. He squeezes the two halves together into a fantastic sandwich, grabs the sandwich in his big mitts and chews the corner off it.

B-25 THE POLITICIAN - IN AN INNER ROOM

He stands before a table at which sits a suspicious looking cashier with a money box. Ten or fifteen men move around in the background.

THE CASHIER
(Incredulously)
What do you mean, he voted thirty-seven times?

THE POLITICIAN
(Crossly)
He voted thirty-seven times and I
need the dough to pay him off....

11-28-39 (Continued)

B-25 (Cont'd)

THE CASHIER
I don't believe a man can vote thirty-seven times.

B-26 A DOORWAY ON THE OTHER SIDE OF THE ROOM

It opens quickly and six men come in: first two bodyguards, then the Boss and Mayor Tillinghast, then two more bodyguards. As they start across the room toward the Boss' private quarters, we HEAR:

THE POLITICIAN'S VOICE
(Very loud)
I TELL YOU HE VOTED THIRTY-SEVEN TIMES!

The Boss and the Mayor stop and exchange an amused look.

THE BOSS
(Quietly)
Who voted thirty-seven times?

B-27 THE POLITICIAN AND THE CASHIER - PAST THE BOSS

THE POLITICIAN
Oh, evening, Boss....Good evening, Mr. Mayor....A lug I got outside here. He voted thirty-seven times but Charlie won't give me the dough for him.

CHARLIE
(Indignantly)
All I say is.....

B-29 THE BOSS, THE MAYOR AND THE BODYGUARDS

THE BOSS
Pay him off.
(He turns and chuckles to the Mayor)
You see what kind of service we're giving you, Wilfred.
(He turns back to the Politician)
Bring the guy in,...we want to look at him.

THE MAYOR
(Chuckling)
We certainly do.

They move on.

B-29 THE POLITICIAN AND THE CASHIER

THE POLITICIAN
(Astonished)
You mean the....lug?
(He jerks his thumb over his shoulder)

B-30 McGINTY WOLFING HIS SANDWICH

THE POLITICIAN'S VOICE
Hey!

McGinty turns slowly.

B-31 THE POLITICIAN - IN THE DOORWAY

THE POLITICIAN
(Sourly)
Come in here.

B-32 McGINTY - IN FRONT OF THE FOOD

He turns from the Politician and considers the food regretfully. Now he sticks a wedge of cheese into the already full sandwich and leaves.

B-33 THE BOSS' INSIDE OFFICE

This is a splendid, large room with mahogony paneling, a piano and a private bar. There is a large desk with some 'phones on it. The Mayor sits on the edge of the desk, the Boss behind it. Four of the telephones have been unhooked and election results are coming in from the various precincts. There are about twenty men in the room.

THE BOSS
(Quietly, into a telephone)
Okay...
(He turns to the Mayor)
Everything coming in very nice on the south side.

He picks up another telephone.

THE BOSS
(Into telephone)
Yes, Touhey, yes...two to one, hunh?..

11-28-39 (Continued)

B-33 (Cont'd)

THE BOSS (Cont'd)
(He looks at the Mayor)
Stockyards precinct.
(He puts the phone down
and picks up another one)
Okay....
(He puts the phone down)
They ain't got the figures yet but
we should worry. You want a little
nip o' something?

THE MAYOR
Just a little whiskey and soda.....
These elections always make me
nervous.

THE BOSS
What would you do in a real elec-
tion?
(He yells across the
room)
One whiskey and soda....one orangeade.

THE BARTENDER'S VOICE
Yes, sir.

THE BOSS
(Looking PAST THE CAMERA)
This is the lug, hunh?

B-34 McGINTY AND THE POLITICIAN - PAST THE BOSS AND THE MAYOR

McGinty holds the enormous sandwich in one hand and a wad of bills in the other.

THE POLITICIAN
Yeah, this is him.

B-35 THE BOSS AND THE MAYOR - PAST McGINTY AND THE POLITICIAN

THE BOSS
(Amused)
Don't you know you ain't supposed
to vote more than wunst?

B-36 McGINTY AND THE POLITICIAN - PAST THE BOSS AND THE MAYOR

McGINTY
(Hard)
Who ast <u>you</u> anything?

(Continued)

B-36 (Cont'd)

The Politician makes a helpless gesture.

B-37 THE BOSS AND THE MAYOR - PAST McGINTY AND THE POLITICIAN

THE BOSS
(Amused)
A tough guy, hunh?
(He picks up a phone;
into the telephone:)
You got 'em now?.... Phew! A land-
slide!....
(He looks up at the
Mayor)
A landslide.
(Into phone)
Thanks, Yiffney.

He puts down the telephone and notices McGinty again.

THE BOSS
A tough guy, hunh?

He gets up and walks around the desk and addresses the Mayor.

THE BOSS
Come over to the bar, Wilfred....
you too, tough guy.

The Boss and the Mayor move OUT OF THE SHOT. The CAMERA PANS with McGinty and the Politician as they follow.

B-38 THE ROOM - OVER THE BAR

The Bartender is TIPPED INTO THE CORNER OF THE SHOT. We see the Boss, the Mayor, McGinty and the Politician approaching. A whiskey and soda and an orange juice stand ready on the bar.

THE BOSS
Set 'em up. What'll you have, boys?

THE POLITICIAN
(Looking at the orange
juice)
Orange juice.

11-28-39 (Continued)

B-38 (Cont'd)

McGINTY
(Nudging the Mayor)
Orange juice! How's my back-hair, Flossie?
(He turns to the Bartender)
Gimme a double fudge pecan twist with an extra cherry on the top of it. And if you're out of that gimme a slug o' whisky and a glass o' beer.

THE BOSS
(Coldly)
A funny guy, hunh? I guess you don't know where you are.

McGINTY
That's right....and I don't care neither.

THE BOSS
(Almost admiringly)
It's a wonderful feeling....anyway, the gentleman on your right happens to be the mayor of this city, the Honorable W. H. Tillinghast...

McGINTY
(Looking at the Mayor disbelievingly)
This gink?

THE BOSS
And me, I happen to be somebody you'd better not forget the next time you see me....so just to help you remember..

He gives McGinty a terrific slap across his face. McGinty gives it back to him so fast that we hardly see the blow. The Boss staggers against the bar.

B-39 LOUIE - THE BODYGUARD

He reaches quietly into his coat pocket.

B-40 THE POLITICIAN, McGINTY, THE BOSS AND THE MAYOR - <u>IN FRONT OF THE BAR</u>

THE BOSS
(Seeing Louie)
Cut it! The guy don't know no better...I'll take care of him later.

(Continued)

B-40 (Cont'd)

A 'phone bell rings piercingly.

B-41 LOUIE - THE BODYGUARD

He takes his hand out of his coat pocket, takes a toothpick from his breast pocket and starts to pick his teeth.

B-42 ANOTHER BODYGUARD - AT THE DESK

He is listening to the telephone.

THE BODYGUARD
(Into telephone)
Okay.
(He hangs up and calls across the room)
Mayor Tillinghast just win de election!

B-43 THE BOSS, THE MAYOR, THE POLITICIAN AND McGINTY - IN FRONT OF THE BAR

The Boss is walking toward McGinty.

THE BOSS
(Over his shoulder)
Congratulations, Wilfred.
(Now he points a finger at McGinty)
Now listen, you.

McGINTY
(Roughly)
Take your finger outta my face.

The Boss looks at him in astonishment for a moment then slaps the bar and bursts out laughing.

THE BOSS
(To the Mayor)
This guy kills me...he thinks he's me!

McGinty looks at him blankly.

FADE OUT:

END OF SEQUENCE "B"

SEQUENCE "C"

FADE IN:

C-1 INT. OF A BARBER SHOP - CLOSE SHOT ON A NEWSPAPER BEING MANICURED

That is to say, we see only the pretty manicurist, one of McGinty's hands and the spread newspaper with the headline:

TILLINGHAST WINS
IN LANDSLIDE

Another manicurist COMES INTO THE SHOT and leans on the first manicurist's shoulder.

THE NEW MANICURIST
You seem to be making quite a hit, dear.

THE FIRST MANICURIST
(Putting on final polish on McGinty's nail)
That's all, Romeo.

The newspaper is thrown to the ground, McGinty is revealed in a brand new and rather loud outfit.

McGINTY
(Examining his nails)
Okay, kid, all you need is a lot of practice.

He chucks her a dollar and starts out.

DISSOLVE TO:

C-2 THE BOSS - AT THE TELEPHONE - AT POLITICAL HEADQUARTE

This is at the big desk with the many telephones. He has an open notebook at his hand.

THE BOSS
(Purring amiably)
Hello, Nicky? ... This is your pal speaking...you know who it is?... That's right, Nicky. Now I'll tell you why I'm calling, Nicky. I see in the book here...
(He taps the book before him)
...you ain't paid up for last week or the week before that or even the

C-2 (Cont'd)

THE BOSS (Cont'd)
week before that...Is restaurant business so terrible?...It is, hunh? Tt,tt,tt...Well, tell me something, Nicky, if it's so terrible why did you have two extra deliveries yesterday afternoon?...It isn't just you and the waiters drinking up all that stuff, is it? That would be bad for your health, Nicky. And I'll tell you something else that would be bad for your health... that's if I send somebody down to see you, Nicky...Yes, I think you better. Thank you, Nicky, and my regards to the Mrs.

He hangs up gently and makes a cross in the book. A buzzer sounds and he picks up the telephone again.

THE BOSS
(Into the telephone)
Oh...Send him in.

He looks up.

C-3 THE DOOR

McGinty enters, followed by Louie who closes the door after him.

McGINTY
Got a new suit.

He comes forward and his left shoe squeaks at each step. Louie hangs himself against the wall and starts to work on his teeth.

C-4 THE BOSS - PAST McGINTY

He watches McGinty's approach, first with a sneer, then with a chuckle.

THE BOSS
It looks more like the suit got you.

C-5 McGINTY

McGINTY
(Narrowing his eyes)
11-28-39 Listen, you.

C-6 THE BOSS - PAST McGINTY

THE BOSS
(Raspingly)
Suppose you listen for a change! The reason you're alive and walkin' around in that horse blanket isn't because I like to be slugged by a crummy in front of everybody, see? It's because I can use some moxie in my business. Not moxie behind a rod, see? Anybody's got that ... but moxie with the bare mitts... like I got. There's been too much rod play in this city and it's very unhealthy. It introduces the bad element...like Louie, see?
(He points to Louie)

C-7 CLOSE SHOT - LOUIE

He takes his toothpick out of his mouth and looks at us very sourly.

THE BOSS' VOICE
You take away his rod and what you got left?...a violet!

Louie looks profoundly wounded.

C-8 THE BOSS AND McGINTY

THE BOSS
What I'm in is a business and a business has to be run businesslike. When a customer is late and a rod like Louie handles him he discontinues to be a customer.
(He gets up and faces McGinty)
Now you think you're tough, hunh?

McGINTY
(Quietly)
Tough enough.

THE BOSS
(Dismissing the matter)
I could slap you down with one hand. Anyway...

11-28-39

C-9 McGINTY - PAST THE BOSS

McGINTY
(Amiably)
You and who else?

C-10 THE BOSS - PAST McGINTY

THE BOSS
(Shrugging)
All right...I haven't got time now...You'll find out. In the meantime if you want to do some collecting you got a job. I'll give you a few names that are way behind and if you can collect I give you twenty percent.
(He smiles faintly)
I pay hospital bills too.

McGINTY
I get it. What is it, protection?

THE BOSS
(Sincerely)
And good protection, too. If it wasn't for me, everybody'd pick on 'em. They'd be at the mercy.

McGINTY
They oughta be grateful, hunh?

THE BOSS
(Not knowing how McGinty means this)
Yeah. So here's what you do.
(He picks up a list)
Here's a little list of where they live and what they owe. You start at Madam Jusso's... she owes two fifty, see? And you tell that old...harpie, that...

McGINTY
What does she run?

THE BOSS
A wax works...a kind of a living wax works...Two fifty or the wax works gets the works.

DISSOLVE TO:

11-28-39

C-11 A GROUP OF WAX FIGURINES UNDER GLASS

This sample of her manufacture sits on a Louis XV stand.

MADAM JUSSO'S VOICE
(Angrily)
It's an outrage, that's what it is! I work and slave and give the best years of my life...

C-12 THE OFFICE OF MADAM JUSSO'S WAXWORKS

It contains a handsome Louis XV desk, some chairs and some wax samples under glass. McGinty sits stonily in a small chair twirling the brim of his hat.

MADAM JUSSO
(Pacing up and down)
...to put away a few miserable bucks with the sweat of my brow and then you bloodsuckers suck it away from me! You ought to be ashamed of yourself to gouge a poor honest old woman.

McGINTY
You got the wrong slant on it altogether, Mrs. uh...

MADAM JUSSO
Just call me Mamie.

McGINTY
Mamie. You gotta pay protection. You want to be at the mercy of every slug who wears a uniform? You want fire inspectors telling you your joint is a trap? You want plumbing inspectors telling you your pipes stink and health inspectors saying your air is vicious?
(He leans back)
Well...Somebody's gotta cooperate all those guys and protect you from human greed! You'd have to pay anyway...but when you buy from us it's like getting club rates.

MADAM JUSSO
(Almost in tears)
Well..,I'm just a poor old woman...
(She sniffs)
but you explain everything so nice.

She pulls up her skirt and goes into her stocking.

11-28-39 (Continued)

C-12 (Cont'd)

MADAM JUSSO
You're a nice looking boy ...
to be doing this kind of work.
(She starts counting
out the money)
You want to go upstairs and
look around before you go?

McGINTY
No thanks, Mamie, this is
strictly business today.

MADAM JUSSO
(Handing him the money)
Well...You know where it is.

DISSOLVE TO:

C-13 A SIGN OUTSIDE OF A CHEAP BUILDING

It says:

B. FELGMAN & CO.
Interior Decorators

C-14 McGINTY - FRAMED IN THE DOORWAY

He finishes reading the sign, refers to his paper, then enters the building and goes PAST THE CAMERA. We HEAR him pounding up the steps.

C-15 McGINTY - ARRIVING ON THE FIRST LANDING

The CAMERA PANS him around to a door which also bears the sign:

B. FELGMAN & CO.
Interior Decorators

McGinty raps on the door which contains a speakeasy sliding panel.

C-16 A CHEAP, EMPTY SPEAKEASY

The bar extends IN THE BACKGROUND. At a table we see the rough Benny Felgman in his shirt sleeves playing solitaire. The Hophead is just rising and starting for the door.

THE HOPHEAD
(Pausing and looking back)
But you c-can't p-put that b-black
k-king on the b-black queen, B-Benny.

11-28-39 (Continued)

C-16 (Cont'd)

BENNY
(Giving him a look)
Who says I can't?

He puts the black king on the black queen.

C-17 THE HOPHEAD - AT THE DOOR

He looks through the slide at McGinty.

THE HOPHEAD
(Calling back to Benny)
'Sa guy alone.

BENNY'S VOICE
Well, let him in.

The Hophead opens the door and McGinty enters quietly. The Hophead closes the door.

McGINTY
(Looking over)
You Benny Felgman?

C-18 FELGMAN - SHOT OVER THE TABLE

BENNY
(Looking around slowly)
What about it?

McGinty comes INTO THE SHOT and looks down at the cards.

McGINTY
(Pointing)
You can't put a black king
on a black queen.

BENNY
Who are you?

McGINTY
The Boss sent me over...he says
you're late again.

BENNY
(Pushing his chair back)
He got a grudge against you?

McGINTY
No, he's just startin' me out
with the easy work.

BENNY
(Rising to his full magnificence)
Oh, yeah. Now look...
(He taps McGinty on the chest)

11-28-39 (Continued)

C-18 (Cont'd)

THE HOPHEAD
(Coming to the other side of Benny)
D-don't slug him, B-Benny... he's green.

BENNY
I'm goin' to let you off easy, see? Go back and tell him I'm through, see? I don't need protection from him or nobody else and if he don't like it he knows where I live.

McGINTY
(Amiably)
What's the use o' takin' that... attitude? We're tryin' to run everything smooth and brotherly. Why don't you just fork up the five hundred and save yourself a shellacking?

BENNY
(Moving around into position)
What?

THE HOPHEAD
D-don't p-paste him, Benny.

McGINTY
Suppose they send some big rough guy down here instead o' me.... What'll you do then?

BENNY
I'll show you.

He shoots a right. McGinty ducks under it and brings up a tremendous body punch.

BENNY
Oof!

He drops to his hands and knees. McGinty starts to take off his coat.

McGINTY
If that's your Sunday punch, baby, you're in for a lotta trouble.

He puts the coat over the back of a chair. Now Benny staggers to his feet and McGinty starts for him.

11/28/39 (Continued)

C-18 (Cont'd)

THE HOPHEAD
D-don't s-slug him, p-pal!

McGINTY
(Shoving him aside)
Out of the way, flea bag!

C-19 THE HOPHEAD - WATCHING

Suddenly he slaps his hands over his eyes and we HEAR half a ton of furniture hit the floor. Now he looks and closes his eyes again. Now he opens his eyes, picks up a bottle by the neck, hefts it, then puts it down again.

THE HOPHEAD
(After another moment's watching)
Wh-what did he ever do to you, p-pal?

C-20 BENNY - PROPPED IN A CORNER WITH McGINTY FINISHING HIM OFF

Benny keeps falling forward and each time McGinty knocks him back with a punch to the solar plexus. Now Benny's knees start to buckle. At this McGinty props him up and stops hitting him.

McGINTY
(Panting)
Ya had enough?

BENNY
(Weakly)
Yeah.

McGINTY
Ya need protection?

BENNY
Yeah.

McGINTY
(Turning around and speaking to the Hophead)
Now the guy's gettin' wise to himself.

Benny starts to fall forward and McGinty catches him just in time. As he guides him to a chair --

DISSOLVE TO:

11-28-39

C-21 McGINTY - COMING DOWN THE STAIRS TOWARD US

He is counting Benny's money slowly. As he reaches the street level he puts the big roll in his pocket, consults a list, then goes BY US.

DISSOLVE TO:

C-22 DOOR - ON WHICH IS PAINTED (Not too well.):

INTERNATIONAL BONDING CO.
State -- Federal
Immigration
BAIL BONDS
Night or Day Service.

C-23 REVERSE SHOT - AN ENORMOUS MAN SLEEPING AT HIS DESK

He is tilted back in the chair, his feet are on the desk and his derby is tipped forward over his eyes. The door flies open, McGinty strides in, grabs th big man by the back of the collar and yanks back so that the man's feet fall on the floor as does his hat.

McGINTY
(Roughly)
Listen, you fat slob, I don't feel like arguin', see? I just showed a guy whether he needed protection or not and I got enough left to show you.

He gives him a shake in the chair like you shake a carpet.

McGINTY
Now what's it goin' to be?

THE FAT MAN
(Almost whimpering)
Well I got a right to be a little late, don't I?
(He feels for his bankroll)

McGINTY
You'd think you guys was doin' us a favor or somethin'.

He swings the man around in the chair, then picks a cigarette out of his breast pocket, sticks it in his mouth, lights the match with his thumbnail and gets the cigarette going.

DISSOLVE TO:

11-28-39

C-24 THE DOOR OF THE INTERNATIONAL BONDING CO.

McGinty comes out with a wad of bills. He goes down a couple of steps. Now he stuffs a big wad of bills in his left pants pocket, his right pants pocket being already full. This done, he starts down the stairs.

C-25 A HUGE AUTOMOBILE - AT THE CURB - (DUSK)

This is supposed to be built of armored steel and shatterproof glass. Looking through the open door we see the Boss. Next to the chauffeur sits Louie.

THE BOSS
Jump in, I'll take you for a ride.
(He chuckles at his little joke)

C-26 McGINTY - IN THE DOORWAY OF A CHEAP BUILDING

He comes forward. As he goes BY THE CAMERA we HEAR the heavy door close, and the car zip away from the curb.

C-27 INT. OF THE MOVING CAR

THE BOSS
(Faintly amused)
You collect anything except a black eye?

In reply McGinty starts pulling money from his pockets.

McGINTY
Two fifty and five and four hundred... that's eleven fifty...Count it.

The Boss looks at the money but does not take it.

THE BOSS
I guess you think you're kinda hot stuff, hunh?...All right, keep the change!

McGINTY
(Not understanding)
Keep what change? I got twenty percent comin'!

THE BOSS
I said keep the whole wad... I never expected to collect it anyway.

11-28-39 (Continued)

C-27 (Cont'd)

McGINTY
(Indignantly)
Then what's the big idea in sending me out?

After a stupefied moment the Boss laughs.

THE BOSS
I'm glad you didn't disappoint me... For a minute I was afraid you were going to say "thank you."
(He looks at McGinty and chuckles again)
You're a card you are...Yesterday you was a 'bo on the breadline...today you got a thousand berries and a new suit. If you can keep on like you've started today there's no telling where you'll be tomorrow. This is a land of great opportunity...You take me: Where I come from is very poor, see? All the richness....

McGINTY
(Interrupting)
What makes this bus so quiet? You don't hear nothing in here.

THE BOSS
(Very matter-of-fact)
It's armored...All the richness is gone a long time ago...so everybody lives...

McGINTY
(Interrupting)
What's it armored for?

THE BOSS
So people shouldn't interrupt me... So everybody lives by chiseling everybody else...It come to me very natural. If I live five hundred years ago I guess I be a baron maybe, a robber baron...I live on a rock and chisel the city down below and everybody call me "baron"....Now I live on a penthouse and everybody call me "Boss"...everybody except you.
(He chuckles)

McGINTY
(Suddenly knocking on the glass)
I get it: bullet-proof, hunh?

11-28-39

(Continued)

C-27 (Cont'd)

THE BOSS
(Purring)
That's right, and if you think I'm not the Boss, you try and cross me up sometime.

McGINTY
You got me all atremble. I bet you're scared to death of yourself.

THE BOSS
All right, you asked for it.

He takes a swipe at McGinty who counters. In a seconc both men have slipped off the seat and we see only their legs and hear the grunts and thuddings.

C-28 LOUIE AND THE CHAUFFEUR

During this scene an occasional fist or foot appears above the partition and once the Boss emerges apparently to stamp on McGinty's face. During the scene Louie picks his teeth and examines his findings with some pleasure.

THE CHAUFFEUR
And then she says "you and who else?" and I says "Oh, yea," and she says "Yeah is right," and I says "So what?" and she says "So when?" and I says "You and me both," and she says "And that goes double for me," and I says "Oh, yeah!" and then the operator says, "Deposit another twenty-fie cents for three minutes," so I hang up on her. You ever let 'em get an angle on you you're a goner.

LOUIE
You said it.

CHAUFFEUR
You're telling me.

At this point the Boss' feet appear over the back of the seat.

C-29 INT. OF THE CAR

The Boss and McGinty are sitting on the floor nearly u conscious. Now they take careful aim and land on eacl other simultaneously.

11-28-39 DISSOLVE TO:

C-30 SHOT THROUGH WINDSHIELD - PAST CHAUFFEUR AND LOUIE

We see an APARTMENT HOTEL, with Doorman standing on the sidewalk. As we swerve to the curb the Doorman steps forward and a pretty girl and a young man come out of the hotel.

C-31 THE DOORMAN - AT THE CURB

The big car slides INTO THE SHOT and Louie starts to get out. The Doorman opens the rear door and steps back in surprise as a fighting mass starts to fall out. The young girl screams.

DISSOLVE TO:

C-32 McGINTY - PAST THOMPSON AND THE GIRL - IN THE BANANA CAFE

McGINTY
(Laughing)
He was always a little muscle-bound, see, and I could beat him to the punch. Boy we had some Brannigans!
(He chuckles in pleasant reminiscence)

C-33 THOMPSON AND THE GIRL - PAST McGINTY

THOMPSON
(A little drunkenly and very sourly)
Thought you said you were the Governor of a state.

THE GIRL
You was just a cheap crook.

C-34 McGINTY - PAST THOMPSON AND THE GIRL

McGINTY
Well, you gotta crawl before you walk don't ya?
(Now he proceeds with enjoyment)
I collect the chicken-feed for a while, see? Then the guy makes me alderman and I move in on the second floor. You know: bus franchises, garbage disposal...nice stuff. He was goin' to make me Superior Court

11-28-39 (Continued)

C-34 (Cont'd)

McGINTY (Cont'd)
Judge just for the laugh except they pick that time to turn on the heat...

C-35 THE GIRL AND THOMPSON - PAST McGINTY

THE GIRL
(Not understanding)
It was cold?

C-36 McGINTY - PAST THE GIRL AND THOMPSON

McGINTY
(Irritatedly)
Tell her what "the heat" means, willya?

DISSOLVE TO:

END OF SEQUENCE "C"

11-28-39

SEQUENCE "D"

D-1 MONTAGE OF NEWSPAPER HEADLINES

The following items come through:

42 INDICTED IN CITY HALL SHAKEUP

SCHOOL SUPERINTENDENT SURRENDERS

GRAFT BLANKETS CITY

"TISSUE OF LIES" --
AVERS TILLINGHAST

CLEANUP OF CITY PLEDGED BY VOTERS

CITIZENS THREATEN RECALL

CONSPIRACY CHARGES MAYOR

CIVIC PURITY LEAGUE TO ACT

Dr. Jonas J. Jarvis, chairman of the Federation of Civic Purity, in a statement to the press...

DISSOLVE TO:

D-2 THE BOSS - IN HIS OFFICE AT POLITICAL HEADQUARTERS

He is sitting back against the edge of a table looking at the newspapers which have been spread fan-wise on the floor. About eight of the Boss's assistants including the other bodyguard and Charlie, the cashier, stand around also looking at the papers. Louie hovers in the background picking his teeth.

THE BOSS
(Mournfully)
What a racket!

THE OTHER BODYGUARD
Yeah, that's what I al...

THE BOSS
Shut up!

11-28-39 (Continued)

D-2 (Cont'd)

Louie makes a sucking noise and the Boss turns on him savagely.

THE BOSS
QUIT SUCKING YOUR CLACKERS, YOU!

The startled Louie drops the toothpick behind him.

THE BOSS
AND DON'T DROP YOUR TRUCK ON THE CARPET!

Poor Louie picks up the toothpick and puts it in his pocket.

THE BOSS
Now get outta here!

Louie moves away and the Boss picks up a telephone.

THE BOSS
Get me Jarvis.

D-3 A PRETTY SWITCHBOARD OPERATOR - IN THE LOBBY OF THE CIVIC PURITY LEAGUE

THE OPERATOR
(Answering the buzz)
Peace be with you... Civic Purity League, good afternoon...he's on the other line, will you wait? Thank you.

D-4 DR. JARVIS - AT THE TELEPHONE IN HIS OFFICE

He is a bald-headed saintly looking man who looks like an old faker.

DR. JARVIS
(Into the telephone)
That was highway robbery!
(He shakes his head then consults his paper)
And twenty on Armadillo in the seventh, that goat has to come in sometime. Thank you, Eddy...Peace be with you.

He hangs up, picks up a pencil, then gives the phone a dirty look as it rings again.

11-28-39 (Continued)

D-4 (Cont'd)

DR. JARVIS
Peace be with you... Oh!
(He looks all around
the room)
Hello.

D-5 THE BOSS AT THE TELEPHONE - IN HIS OFFICE AT HEAD-QUARTERS

THE BOSS
I suppose you saw the afternoon papers...They cut down good trees to print stuff like that on 'em... Tillinghast? Dead as a doornail! I don't even want him around me... he gives me the creeps... Look, Jonas, we need a new face...clean... typical American...upright... dependable...somebody they don't know too much about...what do you think of McGinty?...the Alderman... never heard of him, hunh?...WELL THAT'S JUST WHAT I'M TALKING ABOUT!

DISSOLVE TO:

D-6 MR. MAXWELL - PAST McGINTY - IN McGINTY'S PRIVATE OFFICE

They are both smoking cigars.

MR. MAXWELL
(Screaming)
A hundred thousand dollars!

McGINTY
That's what they tell me.

MR. MAXWELL
But that's a confounded outrage, Mr. Alderman!
(He shakes an angry
finger)
Even in the days of Boss Herman we didn't have to pay that much for franchises! Even in the days of Bathhouse Jake!... Those boys were pikers compared to this mob!

11-28-39

D-7 McGINTY - PAST MAXWELL

McGINTY
(Soothingly)
You don't mean that, Mr. Maxwell. You gotta remember everything's gone up. Living expenses is higher, there's an income tax now, you're dealing with a better class of men...Bathhouse Jake.

D-8 TWO SHOT - McGINTY AND MR. MAXWELL

MR. MAXWELL
I will not pay graft! Millions for defense but not one cent for tribute!

McGINTY
(Gently)
You could call it advertising.

MR. MAXWELL
No, sir.

McGINTY
(Philosophically)
If there were more people like you...

MR. MAXWELL
(Sourly)
What is the rock bottom price for those three franchises?

McGINTY
Look, Mr. Maxwell, I'm only one of the aldermen. If it was up to me I'd make you a present of all the franchises you wanted. I think you run a beautiful bus. I travel on them myself and I want you to know I get a real kick every morning when I climb on that big, safe, shiny, silver...

MR. MAXWELL
(Coldly)
You mean green...my buses are green.

McGINTY
Green!
(He licks his lips)
Aren't you the president of the Silver Arrow Bus Company?

11-28-39 (Continued)

D-8 (Cont'd)

MR. MAXWELL
(Infuriated)
Silver Arrow! I wouldn't be found dead in one of their cheap jallopies! I'm the president of the Metropolitan Bus Company... "Go Green For Comfort!"

McGINTY
(Greatly embarrassed)
Mr. Maxwell, I...
(He passes his hand over his eyes)
... I don't know what to say. This is the first time anything like this has ever happened to me and... I wasn't supposed to see you at all... I've got a note on my desk that says: "If Maxwell calls don't see him"...and now I've let the cat out of the bag.

He puts his arm around Maxwell and urges him toward the door.

McGINTY
Imagine lousing up a deal by switching Maxwell for Silverbeck! I oughta have my nut examined. They don't even sound alike.

They reach the door.

McGINTY
You'll just have to forget about it, Mr. Maxwell. Charge it up to a dumb guy. No hard feelin's.

MR. MAXWELL
(Refusing to move any further)
Now you wait a minute! Is that cheesy Silver Arrow Company bidding for the same franchises I want?

McGINTY
(Pleadingly)
Mr. Maxwell, you're just going to get me in a lot of trouble. Forget about it, will you? Things are tough enough as it is... I suppose you saw the papers this afternoon.

D-8 (Cont'd)

MR. MAXWELL
Never mind the papers. Did they offer a hundred thousand for those franchises?

McGINTY
(Putting his arm around Maxwell's shoulder)
Look, Mr. Maxwell, you're just embarrassing me. Nobody wants anything from you at all. It's a well known fact that Maxwell does not do business....and I had to mix you up with Silverbeck! You don't think I'd be sucker enough to ask you...

MR. MAXWELL
(Decisively)
I'll pay a hundred and twenty-five thousand and not a bus ride more!

McGINTY
(Helplessly)
Mr. Maxwell, I'm....you're trying to open the door and I'm trying to tell you the horse has gone. You may not think much of practical politics but when they give their word....that's it.

The phone rings. McGinty goes back and picks up the phone.

McGINTY
(Into the telephone)
Yeah?

D-9 THE BOSS AT THE TELEPHONE - IN HIS OFFICE

THE BOSS
Come over here, I want to talk to you.

D-10 McGINTY AT THE TELEPHONE - IN McGINTY'S OFFICE

McGINTY
Well I was just talking to Maxwell... I know I shouldn't have but...

MR. MAXWELL
(Coming INTO THE SHOT)
Is that that Silverbeck?

11-28-39

D-11 THE BOSS AT THE TELEPHONE - IN HIS OFFICE

THE BOSS
I got something more important than that. Anyway, Maxwell is a cheap skinflint and Silverbeck will pay sixty. So come over.

He hangs up.

D-12 McGINTY AND MAXWELL AT THE TELEPHONE - IN McGINTY'S OFFICE

McGINTY
Of course that's an awful lot of money, Mr. uh...

MR. MAXWELL
Now listen, McGinty.

McGINTY
Of course there is this other party here, but if you feel I gave you my word...

MAXWELL
(Desperately)
Give me a chance to talk, will you?

McGINTY
(Resignedly)
Well, if that's the way you feel about it...I'll be right over.

He hangs up, shrugs to Maxwell and reaches for his hat. As he starts across the room -

MR. MAXWELL
(With a break in the middle)
You know those franchises aren't worth more than...a hundred and fifty thousand.

McGINTY
(Pleasantly)
I agree with you...but he don't. So long.

He starts for the door. Maxwell starts after him, then returns for his hat and hurries out.

11-28-39

D-13 McGINTY'S OUTER OFFICE

It contains some handsome furniture, a political poster of McGinty in a typical pose, and a handsome young woman of twenty-eight. McGinty is coming from his office. Maxwell appears a moment later.

McGINTY
(To Catherine)
Be back in a little while.

CATHERINE
Yes, Mr. McGinty.

MR. MAXWELL
(Hurrying to overtake McGinty)
Now look here, McGinty...

They go PAST THE CAMERA WHICH MOVES ONTO Catherine. Catherine chuckles at Maxwell's anxiety, then rises, picks up some letters and crosses to McGinty's office. The CAMERA PANS with her.

D-14 McGINTY'S OFFICE

It is full of smoke. Catherine enters, makes a face at the smoke, opens the window, then crosses and puts the papers on McGinty's desk. She straightens up the desk, empties the ashtrays and replaces the chair. Now she starts out of the room. The phone rings. She picks it up at McGinty's desk.

CATHERINE
(Into telephone)
No he isn't, I'm sorry...he'll be back after while...I'll be glad to...
(While writing)
Hamilton one six, six, six...what was that again? Miss Lucy Dangerfield...I certainly will, Miss Dangerfield.

She hangs up, tears off the sheet, then starts toward the door.

D-15 THE OUTER OFFICE

Catherine comes in. As she reaches her desk the door opens.

CATHERINE
Hello, Skeeters.

11-28-39

D-16 THE POLITICIAN ENTERING

THE POLITICIAN
Hello, Sweets, how's about puttin' on the feed bag tonight?

D-17 CATHERINE - PAST THE POLITICIAN

CATHERINE
I'm sorry, Skeeters, I've got a date.

D-18 THE POLITICIAN AND CATHERINE

THE POLITICIAN
(Resentfully)
You always got a date! Why don't you marry that guy and teach him a lesson?

CATHERINE
Because I've already learned my lesson.

THE POLITICIAN
Oh.
(Now the thought begins to take hold and he looks at Catherine)
You mean you already been married?

CATHERINE
(Quietly)
I have.

THE POLITICIAN
(Delightedly)
Well for heaven sake! That puts everything on an entirely different basis.

CATHERINE
(Amused)
No it doesn't, Skeeters. Everything's exactly where it was before.

THE POLITICIAN
(Depressed)
Oh.
(Now he adds gloomily)
I suppose you saw the papers.

CATHERINE
I saw them at lunch time.

THE POLITICIAN
It's gone up. Seventeen counts of

D-19 (Cont'd)

THE POLITICIAN (Cont'd)
bribery, thirteen of mal...fee...
aysance, whatever that is, and twelve
of imitation...imitidation.

CATHERINE
Intimidation.

THE POLITICIAN
That's it. They're always throwin'
guys out that's already got theirs
to put in a bunch that needs every-
thing from the socks up...you'd think
they'd learn.

CATHERINE
Especially since you can't rob the
people anyway.

THE POLITICIAN
(With a double-take)
Sure...how was that?

CATHERINE
Because what you rob you spend, and
what you spend goes right back to the
people, so where's the robbery?

THE POLITICIAN
(Rough-eyed)
Say, where'd you get that?

CATHERINE
In a book on politico something-or-
other...it's what you call a sophistry.

THE POLITICIAN
That book should be in every home.
(Then after a pause)
Do you think he'll need me any more
tonight?

CATHERINE
I don't think so, Skeeters.

THE POLITICIAN
Then I think I'll take a powder...I
gotta promote myself a date somehow.

CATHERINE
Good luck.

The Politician starts to go, then turns back.

THE POLITICIAN
How was that again? What you rob
you spend, and what you spend...

11-28-39 (Continued)

D-18 (Cont'd) CATHERINE
...goes back to the people, so where's the robbery?

THE POLITICIAN
How do you know so much about politics, anyway?

CATHERINE
My father was a judge.

THE POLITICIAN
(In two stages)
Oh...is that so? Well don't the practical end of politics seem kinda...I mean bein' a judge's daughter and all...or was he a practical judge?

CATHERINE
I'm afraid he wasn't, Skeeters. He didn't even leave any insurance money, the poor old sap.

THE POLITICIAN
Well, for heaven sake. And with all that opportunity!...you'd think a man'd think of his wife and children, wouldn't you? Well, so long. Don't take no wooden Indians.

He exits.

D-19. INT. OF THE BOSS'S OFFICE AT POLITICAL HEADQUARTERS

McGINTY
(Coming in)
Hello.

D-20 THE BOSS - BEHIND HIS DESK

THE BOSS
Hello. Listen:

D-21 McGINTY - PAST THE BOSS

McGINTY
That guy'll pay two and a quarter. That Maxwell.

11-28-39 (Continued)

D-22 THE BOSS - PAST McGINTY

THE BOSS
No.
(Now he busts out laughing)
That's the only good news I heard all day.
(He picks up a pencil and plays with it)
Listen: you want to be reform mayor?

D-23 McGINTY - PAST THE BOSS

McGINTY
What do you mean, reform mayor?

D-24 TWO SHOT - THE BOSS AND McGINTY

THE BOSS
(With irritation)
What do _you_ think it means? Don't make me say everything twice, will you. I said, do you want to be reform mayor... MAYOR of this city?

McGINTY
(Suspicious of a joke)
Whata you got to do with the reform party?

THE BOSS
I _am_ the reform party, who do you _think_?

McGINTY
Since when?

THE BOSS
Since a long time. In this town I'm _all_ the parties. You think I'm _goin'_ to starve every time they change administrations?

McGINTY
Then where does Jarvis come in and the Purity League?

11-28-39 (Continued)

D-24 (Cont'd)

THE BOSS
They come in the back door...
every Wednesday. Don't ask so
many questions, will you? I
ask you if you want to be reform
mayor. You can give me a plain
answer.

McGINTY
(Slightly flabbergasted)
Well...sure...I guess so.

THE BOSS
All right, you're in. You'll
have to kiss a lotta babies and
mitt a lotta guys but...oh, and
wear your old clothes, they don't
want no doods after Tillinghast,
and oh! You'll have to get
married right away.

McGINTY
(Galvanized)
What do you mean, get married
right away?

THE BOSS
(Yelling)
What do you think it means?
Do I have to start saying every-
thing twice again? Women got
the vote now...maybe you didn't
hear about it...they don't like
bachalors.

McGINTY
(Hard)
Oh, they don't hunh? Well if
they don't like 'em they know what
they can do with 'em.

THE BOSS
(Getting up and coming
around his desk)
What's the matter with you, are
you nuts?

McGINTY
(With heavy sarcasm)
No, I'm just playing hard-to-get.

11-28-39 (Continued)

D-24 (Cont'd)

THE BOSS
(Pretending to be astounded)
Don't you know what marriage is? Don't you know that marriage has always been the most beautiful... the most beautiful set-up between the sexes? Don't you know that a man without a wife is like a...a coat without the pants, like a.. like a pig without a poke? Marriage is the most..the most.....

McGINTY
Then why don't you try it?

THE BOSS
Because I ain't running for mayor.

McGINTY
(Indignantly)
Yeah? Well I ain't neither. Poke that in your pig!

He turns and leaves an astonished Boss behind him.

DISSOLVE TO:

D-25 CATHERINE - AT HER DESK - IN McGINTY'S OFFICE

She is reading a book. Now she looks at her wrist watch, puts a marker in the book, then rises, goes to a little mirror and starts to do her hair. Behind her the door crashes open and McGinty comes in.

McGINTY
(Indignantly)
Now the guy wants me to get married right away! How do you like that one?

Catherine turns with her arms still up in the air.

CATHERINE
(Astonished)
What for? Who?

McGINTY
Because the women have got the vote and they don't vote for single men.

CATHERINE
But what are you running for?

11-28-39 (Continued)

D-25 (Cont'd)

McGINTY
(As if he had already told her)
For mayor!

CATHERINE
(Breaking into a slow smile)
Oh, but that's wonderful, Mr. McGinty. I suppose it's as reform mayor.

McGINTY
Yeah.

CATHERINE
I'm so happy for you, Mr. McGinty. We'll have more fun than a barrel of monkeys....that is if you take me with you.

McGINTY
(Scowling)
What are you talking about? I told him to go fly a kite. Can you see me telling some rib where I been till two o'clock in the morning and "how did you get that lip rouge on your hat, Oscar?"

CATHERINE
I don't think it's so bad as all that, Mr. McGinty.

McGINTY
Look: my parents was married...I know all about it. Catch me walkin' the floor all night with an armload o' little muzzlers yellin' in my face!

CATHERINE
(Looking away)
You mightn't have any.

McGINTY
What do you mean, I mightn't have any? They never had less than eight on either side of my family.

CATHERINE
(Still looking away)
I don't want to go into that, of course...but they don't yell so much...anyway, it sounds like music to the father.

11-28-39 (Continued)

D-25 (Cont'd)

McGINTY
(Slightly mollified)
Well I don't care for music neither.

CATHERINE
(In faint embarrassment)
Of course it's entirely up to you, Mr. McGinty. As a matter of fact I don't care any more about marriage than you do, but...I'd certainly think twice before I'd turn down an opportunity like you have... even with the drawback...you'd ride in all the parades, you'd welcome all the potentates...you'd lay all the corner stones...

McGINTY
In a silk hat! The municipal brick-layer!

CATHERINE
(After a chuckle)
Oh, I suppose it just seems so wonderful to me because it's so far beyond anything I could ever hope for and...because I'm so interested in your career, Mr. McGinty...you're a sort of a favorite of mine.

McGINTY
Well, thanks, but if you think I'm going to get hitched to some Jane I don't even know or give a whoopdeedee about...

CATHERINE
How about...Miss Lucy Dangerfield? She called and wanted you...

McGINTY
(Vehemently)
In spades!

CATHERINE
Well...

She shrugs and turns away. Suddenly she turns back and speaks rapidly.

CATHERINE
I'd be willing to do it for you, Mr. McGinty.

11-38-39 (Continued)

D-25 (Cont'd)

McGINTY
(Not understanding)
Hunh?

CATHERINE
You see I don't want to get married either...I feel the same way you do about it...this way we'd both be protected...because there's always somebody who wants her to marry them. We'd never have to see each other except to be photographed on the steps of the city hall, and I could run your house for you and make speeches for you at women's clubs...and be your lawful wedded wife in everything except...when we were alone...you see I've already been married...and you'd get the women's vote...which is the really important thing.

D-26 McGINTY - PAST CATHERINE

He looks slowly up from her feet to the top of her head.

CATHERINE
(Bearing the inspection as long as she can)
What's that got to do with it?

The phone rings. Catherine turns to answer.

McGINTY
If that's Lucy tell her I'll be a little late...I gotta think this over.

CATHERINE
(Quietly)
Yes, sir.

She turns to the telephone.

FADE OUT:

END OF SEQUENCE "D"

11-28-39

SEQUENCE "E"

FADE IN:

E-1 CLOSE SHOT - LOUIE - (DAY)

He leans against some gray masonry, picking his teeth. He wears a cutaway, a little too long, and a derby hat. Behind him we see a small Gothic window and a black and gold sign which reads:

THE WEE KIRK AROUND THE KORNER

Hours: weekdays 9 to 6
Sundays: open all day
Night calls: Cicero 3985

We hear FAINT ORGAN MUSIC. The CAMERA PANS TO THE RIGHT as we

DISSOLVE TO:

E-2 THE DOOR OF THE WEE KIRK AROUND THE KORNER

The silk-hatted wedding party comes out hurriedly. Louie springs to attention.

THE BOSS
(To Louie)
Well?

LOUIE
(Suddenly remembering)
Oh ... yeah.

He throws a handful of rice in the Boss' face and the CAMERA PANS the party across the sidewalk and into the armored car, the door of which booms shut like the bulkhead of a battleship. We hear the roar of the engine, the scream of a siren and the car thunders away. The CAMERA PANS after it and we see for the first time that the rear of the car is festooned with white satin ribbons, shoes, tin cans and cowbells.

E-3 INT. OF THE ARMORED CAR

It is still on an angle from taking the turn. Catherine sits on the back seat with the Boss on one side and McGinty on the other. The Politician sits on a folding seat.

11-28-39 (Continued)

E-3 (Cont'd)

CATHERINE
(Frightened)
Does he have to drive like that?

THE BOSS
(Chuckling)
He's kinda nervous...He don't want the boys to eat everything up before he gets there. I ordered a swell feed for you... a big blowout.

CATHERINE
(Worried)
Oh...but...

THE BOSS
You like caviar?

CATHERINE
Yes, of course, but...

THE BOSS
And bortch with sour cream and bleenies and shash-lik and more booze than you ever seen in your life?...This is going to be some smear.

CATHERINE
(Genuinely contrite)
I'm terribly sorry...It was wonderfully kind of you...but I can't come. You see I...

McGINTY
Why not?

CATHERINE
Well you see I'm...expected home. I didn't have time to explain everything to you and...

THE BOSS
(Thoroughly displeased)
What kind of a wedding _is_ this?

McGINTY
(Somewhat crestfallen)
Can't you come even for a little while?

11-28-39 (Continued)

E-3 (Cont'd)

CATHERINE
(Looking at her watch)
I really can't. You see it's almost six o'clock and uh...

THE BOSS
(Roughly)
All right, send her home in a taxi...there's plenty o' dames...

McGINTY
(Bristling)
She'll go home in any kind of a rig she likes...and keep your trap shut!

THE BOSS
(Leaning across Catherine)
Listen, you...

McGINTY
(Leaning across Catherine)
Any time, see?

CATHERINE
(Putting a hand on each of them)
Please.

THE BOSS
What a wedding.

DISSOLVE TO:

E-4 THE SIDEWALK - IN FRONT OF A MODEST APARTMENT HOUSE

A taxicab is approaching. It stops at the curb. McGinty gets out and helps Catherine to the sidewalk.

McGINTY
(Sheepishly)
Well, I'll see you tomorrow at the office.

CATHERINE
Thank you very much for bringing me home...Would you like to come up and have a drink...and see where I live?

11-28-39 (Continued)

E-4 (Cont'd)

McGINTY
(Jerking a thumb over his shoulder)
I really...outta be gettin' down there...one of us ought to be there.

CATHERINE
(Resigned)
Well...

McGINTY
(Suddenly, as if he were telling the Boss where to get off)
Certainly I'll come and have a drink!
(He calls over his shoulder to the driver)
Wait there, buddy.
(He takes Catherine's arm)
Come on.

The CAMERA PANS them across the sidewalk. As they enter the apartment building.

E-5 THE VERY SMALL BATHROOM IN CATHERINE'S FLAT

This is occupied by a very large colored woman drying a little boy of four, a little girl of six in a long white nightgown brushing her teeth, and a Dachshund puppy getting in the way.

BESSY
(The colored woman)
Lanksakes alive will you quit wigglin'!

THE LITTLE BOY
Want wagadog.

He reaches for the puppy

BESSY
You lay off dat dawg when you's all clean and sweet.
(She scowls at the puppy)
Bath wouldn't hurt him none neither.

11-28-39 (Continued)

E-5 (Cont'd)

She picks the pup up by the slack on its back and inhales it.

BESSY
Pew!

She plops it in the bathtub.

BESSY
There!...Dunk yourself in that!

The children scream with glee as the puppy splatters around in the soapy water. Bessy reaches for the little boy's pajamas with feet.

E-6 THE HALLWAY OUTSIDE CATHERINE'S FLAT

Catherine and McGinty come up the stairs.

CATHERINE
(Puffing)
There.

The CAMERA PANS them to a door. She opens her bag and starts looking for her key.

CATHERINE
(Nervously)
Mr. McGinty.

McGINTY
Yeah?

CATHERINE
(A little more nervously)
I uh...I told you I was married before, didn't I...Of course I did.

McGINTY
(With gruff amiability)
Sure, what about it?

CATHERINE
Nothing,..I uh I never can find this key, I divorced him on grounds of desertion. I don't know where he is and I don't care either.

11-28-39 (Continued)

E-6 (Cont'd)

McGINTY
You outa put it on a little
chain hooked to the bag.

CATHERINE
(Nervously)
That would be a good idea,
wouldn't it? There's some-
thing else I probably should
have told you before...but I
don't really see that it makes
the slightest difference.

McGINTY
(Pointing)
There it is.

CATHERINE
Oh, yes, thank you.

She takes out the key and opens the door.

E-7 THE SITTING ROOM OF CATHERINE'S APARTMENT

CATHERINE
(Leading McGinty in)
Do you like gin or...well that's
all I've got. Let me take your
hat.

McGINTY
(Handing it over)
That was his idea .

CATHERINE
You look very well in it.

McGINTY
Yeah, like a coalstove.

CATHERINE
(Smoothing the hat)
I suppose we're really married,
aren't we...I mean legally.

McGINTY
That's what the guy said.

11-29-39 (Continued)

E-7 (Cont'd)

CATHERINE
(Very nervously)
I don't want you to think I've been concealing anything from you. There's no reason why I should. It's just that in the excitement...

McGINTY
What?

CATHERINE
Sit down, Mr. McGinty.

Now she walks up and down rubbing the hat the wrong way.

McGINTY
(Indicating politely)
Rub it the other way, willya?

CATHERINE
(Distressed)
I'm so sorry.
(Now she starts to blurt it out)
You see, Mr. McGinty...

We hear a joyous shout from the two children.

E-8 A SHOT DOWN THE LONG HALL

The little boy and the little girl are galloping toward us, screaming gleefully. Now Bessy hurries into the hall and after them.

BESSY
You come back heah, you little monkeys! All hot from your bath an' all. You' catch your...

E-9 CLOSE SHOT - THE PUPPY IN THE BATHTUB

It is splashing up and down to get out. Now it succeeds, shakes itself once on the floor, then hurries out into the hall.

E-10 CLOSE SHOT - McGINTY IN A CHAIR

His jaw hangs open in astonishment. His eyes wander from right to left.

11-28-39

E-11 CATHERINE AND THE CHILDREN - PAST McGINTY

Bessy is hanging onto the door jamb. The two children are hanging onto their mother's skirt and she has her arms on their shoulders.

CATHERINE
That's what I wanted to tell you...they're mine! Now you know!

At this point the puppy comes sprinting into the room and makes straight for McGinty (we hope).

E-12 CLOSE SHOT - McGINTY IN THE CHAIR

The puppy is thrown into his lap and he starts to smooth it instinctively.

McGINTY
(Looking from right to left)
Well...well.

Now he discovers that his right hand is covered with soap and water. He examines it dully for a second then reaches for his handkerchief.

E-13 THE OTHERS - PAST McGINTY

The children start to laugh; Catherine laughs against her will, and Bessy joins in with enthusiasm.

E-14 McGINTY - PAST THE LAUGHING GROUP

He grins a little wolfishly, then puts his finger inside his collar to loosen it. The collar flies open.

McGINTY
Yeah!

The other side of his collar flies open.

DISSOLVE TO:

11-28-39

E-15 THE FRONT DOOR OF THE VACANT APARTMENT - (NIGHT)

We HEAR the key in the lock. Catherine and McGinty enter.

CATHERINE
I'm sorry it's a little bit dark, the current won't be on until tomorrow.

McGINTY
I got some matches.

CATHERINE
Good.

They walk PAST THE CAMERA and their footsteps and voices become fainter and fainter.

CATHERINE'S VOICE
This is the foyer which leads into the living room through double doors here, they're not up yet. There's a powder room behind you, a big closet here, and a door to the pantry.

DISSOLVE TO:

E-16 A VERY LARGE LIVING ROOM

Catherine and McGinty appear at the far end of it and come down three steps. McGinty's match goes out and he strikes another.

E-17 CLOSE SHOT - McGINTY AND CATHERINE

McGINTY
Say, this is some joint! What's the damage on it?

CATHERINE
They make a very special rate for Mayors. Of course, if you shouldn't be elected...

11-28-39 (Continued)

E-17 (Cont'd)

McGINTY
That would be their hard luck...
I like that room for the kids...
Fix that up with all sorts of
stuff they like. You know: A
doll house and a slide and some
railroading for the little fellow
and uh...the whole works.

CATHERINE
That's very kind of you, Mr. McGinty.

McGINTY
Y'only live once.

CATHERINE
Thank you. Now if you could just
give me some idea of how you'd
like the other furniture, in here,
I could get that too.

McGINTY
Well I'd uh...sort of uh...put a
piano or something over there...
or maybe over here, and then I'd
uh...kind of put something to sit
on or something over on that side
and then uh,..I guess that takes
care of that.

CATHERINE
Would you like curtains at the
windows?

McGINTY
That's a good idea. Sure.

CATHERINE
And maybe a rug on the floor?

McGINTY
Why not?...Or maybe a bear skin.

CATHINE
Possibly, yes. I think I have
your general thought. Here's the
balcony.

E-18 REVERSE SHOT FROM THE BALCONY

Catherine opens the windows, and she and McGinty
come out to us.

11-28-39 (Continued)

E-18 (Cont'd)

McGINTY
Pretty, ain't it?
(Now he squints into the darkness)
What's that across the street, a church?

CATHARINE
Yes, it is.

McGINTY
(Scowling)
Ring a lotta bells?

CATHERINE
(Mildly)
I don't think so.

We HEAR a deep "bong". McGinty gives Catherine a look.

McGINTY
(After a moment)
Well, I guess we seen everything.

He turns to enter the apartment.

CATHERINE
Mr. McGinty.

McGINTY
Yes, ma'am.

CATHERINE
I...
(She takes his hand diffidently)
I just wanted to tell you that... even though our...our...marriage is a...a peculiar one..to say the least...it's made me very happy.

McGINTY
It's a cinch we ain't got nothin' to fight about...
(He chuckles)
...like people that's in love with each other.

CATHERINE
How right you are.

He starts to follow her in. Now he cocks his head to listen. Very faintly we HEAR the strains of a band.

11-28-39 (Continued)

D-18 (Cont'd)

McGINTY
Wait a minute.

Catherine turns back.

CATHERINE
What's the matter?

McGINTY
(After a second's listening)
THEY'RE HAVING THE PARADE TONIGHT!...I ALMOST FORGOT.

CATHERINE
So did I, Your Honor.

McGINTY
Come on! I gotta see that.

They hurry into the apartment.

DISSOLVE TO:

E-19 A TORCHLIGHT PARADE - (NIGHT)

A brass band goes by playing "There'll Be A Hot Time in The Old Town Tonight." Now a succession of illuminated signs is borne PAST US.

SIGNS:
1. McGINTY AND A SQUARE DEAL
2. DOWN TO EARTH - McGINTY
3. McGINTY FOR MAYOR
4. DOWN WITH THE INTERESTS -- McGINTY THE PEOPLE'S CHOICE

Another band goes by playing the "Battle Hymn of the Republic".

E-20 McGINTY AND CATHERINE - IN THE CROWD AT THE EDGE OF THE SIDEWALK

The lights flicker on their faces. They wave and shout with the others and purchase two little McGinty banners from an old peddler.

E-21 THE PASSING PARADE

The signs read:
1. McGINTY THE TRUST BUSTER
2. A NEW BROOM SWEEPS CLEAN

11-28-39 (Continued)

E-21 (Cont'd)

3. CLEAN UP THE CROOKS WITH McGINTY
4. OF THE PEOPLE, FOR THE PEOPLE - McGINTY
5. McGINTY vs. McGRAFT
6. THE IRON FIST vs. THE IRON RING
7. DOWN WITH McBOODLE - UP WITH McGINTY

A band goes by playing "The Stars and Stripes Forever."

E-22 McGINTY, CATHERINE AND THE PEOPLE AROUND THEM.

waving their banners, they fall in after the band.

E-23 MOVING SHOT - AHEAD OF McGINTY AND CATHERINE

We watch them for a few moments as they march in time to the music.

DISSOLVE TO:

E-24 MONTAGE OF ELECTION NIGHT:

The music of "The Stars and Stripes" continues full blast.

(1-5)
ASSORTED SHOTS OF PEOPLE VOTING

(6)
A NEWSPAPER BOY YELLING HIS EXTRA

The headline reads:

"TILLINGHAST TRAILS"

(7)
A LINE OF TOUGH LOOKING CUSTOMERS WAITING TO GET INTO A VOTING PLACE

(8-11)
MEN AND WOMEN VOTING

(12)
THE SAME NEWSPAPER BOY

The headline says:

"McGINTY IN LEAD"

11-28-39 (Continued)

E-24 (Cont'd)

(13)
McGINTY, THE BOSS, THE POLITICIAN, LOUIE AND OTHERS IN THE BACKGROUND - AT THE BOSS' DESK - IN POLITICAL HEADQUARTERS.

The Boss is listening to a 'phone. Now he grins and picks up another 'phone.

(14)
ANOTHER NEWSPAPER BOY

The headline reads:

"McGINTY IN LANDSLIDE"

(15)
A HALF-FINISHED BEDROOM IN THE McGINTY APARTMENT

The children are playing on the floor and Catherine is on a step ladder attaching some glass curtains to a window. Catherine turns her head sharply.

(16)
HIGH CAMERA SHOT DOWN ON THE ROOM FROM CATHERINE'S POSITION

Bessy is running in with a newspaper. As she gets to the foot of the ladder she stretches it up for us to see. It says:

"McGINTY ELECTED"

The CAMERA MOVES IN to a VERY CLOSE SHOT OF THIS.

DISSOLVE TO:

E-25 THE BIG ROOM AT POLITICAL HEADQUARTERS

In one corner a jazz band is going full blast. At the same time as the PHOTOGRAPHIC DISSOLVE, the MONTAGE MUSIC DISSOLVES INTO THE JAZZ BAND MUSIC. The party is a shambles, drunken ladies and gentlemen weave back and forth, dance and yell jokes at each other. Paper hats, horns, bells and razzberry noise-makers are much in evidence. The CAMERA MOVES THROUGH all this then comes TO REST on the DOORS LEADING TO THE PRIVATE ROOM.

The doors open and the Boss appears. He raises a hand for silence. The noise dribbles off.

11-28-39 (Continued)

E-25 (Cont'd)

THE BOSS
(Pompously)
Ladies and gentlemen: THE MAYOR!

McGinty appears, supported on one side by Louie and on the other by the Politician. He wears an enormous paper hat in the shape of a cock's comb. His tie is undone and his pockets are stuffed with a couple of hundred cigars which he sows like wheat on his triumphal march across the room. The CAMERA PRECEDES him and the noise is deafening.

DISSOLVE TO:

E-26 REVERSE SHOT

McGinty comes in, feels for the light button without success, then closes the door after him. We are now in complete darkness. McGinty scratches a match and holds it high over his head. Vaguely we see some large objects of furniture still covered with sheets or wrapping paper. McGinty starts forward and the match goes out. We HEAR a couple of footsteps, then an exclamation and a deafening crash followed by a second one which sounds like crockery.

E-27 CATHERINE - IN BED

Some light streams through the windows onto the counterpane. She sits up in bed and puts on the bed-light. We HEAR a distant bumping and a tinkle of glassware. She hops out of bed, puts on a very lovely satin dressing gown and slippers, and hurries toward the door.

E-28 THE PITCH-BLACK HALLWAY

We HEAR a bumping and scraping and the fall of some more crockery. Now a light goes on in the background, Catherine appears in silhouette against it, then pushes another switch which lights up the scene. She looks in horror at McGinty on the floor. He is tangled up in a step ladder. About nine hundred dollars' worth of dishes and several boxes of glassware are littered around him on the floor. A sideboard has also been tipped over. On a table we see some piles of dishes intact.

CATHERINE
(Hurrying to McGinty)
I'm terribly sorry, Mr. McGinty. It was stupid of me to leave all this here without even a night light or a...a...

E-28 (Cont'd)

McGINTY
Red lantern.
(He chuckles, then picks up half a plate)
Very pretty.

CATHERINE
I'm awfully sorry it happened.
(She helps him to his feet)
I think it's covered by the insurance though.

McGINTY
(Wisely)
Collison.
(He chuckles again)

CATHERINE
It's awfully nice of you to take it so good-naturedly. Many men would...oh!

McGINTY
(Startled)
What'sa matter?

CATHERINE
I forgot to congratulate you.

McGINTY
(Pointing to the detritus)
On this?

CATHERINE
On being mayor, silly....I mean, Your Honor.

McGINTY
(Suspiciously)
Now don't you start!

CATHERINE
What?

McGINTY
(With dignity)
I can take a rib as well as the next guy but a little bit goes a long way.

Catherine looks at him without understanding.

McGINTY
(With still more dignity)
Now if you'd be kind enough to

E-28 (Cont'd)

McGINTY (Cont'd)
show me where I live in this...
boneyard...

CATHERINE
I'd be very glad to show you,
Mr. McGinty.
(Suddenly)
Be careful where you step.

McGINTY
(Offended)
I can take care of myself,
thank you.

With which he steps onto a carpet sweeper and falls flat on his face.

CATHERINE
(Getting to her
knees beside him)
I'm terribly sorry, Mr. McGinty.

She helps him to his feet again and props him up.

McGINTY
(Confidentially)
Had it coming to me.

CATHERINE
Now you just let me show you
the way...
(She puts her arm
around his waist)
and I'll have you in bed before
you can say British constitution.

McGINTY
That might take quite a while.

They walk away from us down the hall. As they reach the light switch, Catherine puts out the light.

E-29 McGINTY'S BEDROOM

We see the light in the hall outside. Catherine leads McGinty in, switches on the light, then sits him on the bed.

CATHERINE
Do you think you'll be all right now?

McGINTY
Never felt better...in my life.

He puts his feet up on the bed, stretches out and says:

11-28-39 (Continued)

E-29 (Cont'd)

McGINTY
Good night.

CATHERINE
Don't you think you'd better take
your shoes off?

McGINTY
(Settling himself)
I'll take 'em off after while.

Catherine smiles at him as at a child. Then loosens the laces and pulls his shoes off. After this she looks at him for a moment, then removes his tie and unbuttons his vest. After this she takes the watch out of his vest, winds it and puts it on the night table. Now she notices that there is an enormous lump in the right hand pocket of his trousers. She reaches into the pocket and starts to pull it out, when McGinty seizes her hand as in a vise.

McGINTY
(Roughly)
Oh no you don't!...That's been
tried before.

CATHERINE
(Shocked)
Why Mr. McGinty.

McGINTY
(Coming to)
Hunh? I'm sorry.

He sits up in bed and hangs his feet over the side. Now he pulls a roll out of his pocket that would choke a horse.

McGINTY
(Handing it to her)
Here...Get yourself a hat.

CATHERINE
(Distressed)
I don't want your money, Mr.
McGinty...I just want to make
you more comfortable.

She puts the money on the side-table, then tries to get him out of his coat. This presents quite a problem. In the middle of the effort McGinty stops.

McGINTY
I'll tell you a little secret...
I'm as drunk as a skunk.

11-28-39 (Continued)

E-29 (Cont'd)

CATHERINE
(Loyally)
Why of course you're not, Mr. McGinty.

McGINTY
I don't want to argue with you, but
I can tell you from past experience...

Suddenly he stiffens and looks at the door. Now he nudges Catherine and draws her attention to it.

E-30 THE TWO CHILDREN - IN THE DOORWAY

They wear pajamas with feet. The little boy holds the Dachshund under his arm. The children are round-eyed as they watch McGinty.

E-31 CATHERINE AND McGINTY

CATHERINE
(With fire)
Now you go right straight to
bed! What do you mean by
getting up and coming in here
at this hour of the night?
I'll be in in one minute and
if you're not in bed...

E-32 THE CHILDREN - IN THE DOORWAY

They hurry away.

E-33 CATHERINE AND McGINTY

McGinty is the picture of dejection.

CATHERINE
(Turning to him)
I'm terribly sorry, Mr. McGinty.
They have no business coming to
this part of the house in the
first place and...

McGINTY
(Waving for silence)
Only thing I'm sorry about is
that they had to see me like this.

His lip curls in disgust. Catherine puts her hand on his shoulder and takes it off again.

FADE OUT:

END OF SEQUENCE "E"

SEQUENCE "F"

FADE IN:

F-1 MR. MAXWELL - PAST McGINTY - IN THE MAYOR'S PRIVATE OFFICE

MR. MAXWELL
(Screaming)
How can the city contemplate a municipal bus line when it has a minety-nine year contract with me? A uh...contract you may even remember something about.

F-2 McGINTY - PAST MR. MAXWELL

McGINTY
I don't know what you're talking about, Mr. Maxwell, but as far as your contract is concerned there's a flaw in it.

MR. MAXWELL
(Screeching)
A flaw!

McGINTY
A flaw.

MR. MAXWELL
(Miserably)
How big a flaw?

McGINTY
Just big enough to drive a bus through. Goodbye, Mr. Maxwell.

F-3 MR. MAXWELL - PAST McGINTY

MR. MAXWELL
(Almost in tears)
Don't start goodbyeing me right away, Mr. Mayor, give me a chance to express myself. I won't mention the millions we have invested, the thousands of buses, the tens of thousands of employees....

F-4 McGINTY - PAST MAXWELL

McGINTY
(Quietly)
Of the people, by the people, for the people. Give 'em their own bus line. It's a great idea.

11-28-39

F-5 MAXWELL - PAST McGINTY

MAXWELL
(Screeching)
But municipal ownership has invariably proved disasterous, Mr. Mayor! You sow millions and what do you reap? Dimes! Thin dimes!

F-6 McGINTY-- PAST MAXWELL

He rises and Maxwell does likewise.

McGINTY
Look, Mr. Maxwell, I'm only the Mayor, see? If it was up to me I'd give you the bus rights of this city as a free gift.

F-7 MR. MAXWELL - PAST McGINTY

He looks far from persuaded.

McGINTY
I think you run a beautiful bus. I travel on them myself and I'll be genuinely sorry to see them disappear from our streets.

He drops a consoling hand on Maxwell's shoulder.

MR. MAXWELL
(In cold horror)
But Mr. Mayor, there must be some way, some solution of mutual satisfaction... I don't know just how to talk with a Mayor, but if I could just persuade you...

F-8 McGINTY - PAST MAXWELL

McGINTY
You can't persuade me, Mr. Maxwell, because it's entirely out of my hands, but I'll tell you what I'll do for old times sake: I'll send the chairman of the bus committee up and if you can persuade <u>him</u> it's all right with me.

MR. MAXWELL
Is he...difficult to persuade?

11-28-39 (Continued)

F-8 (Cont'd)

McGINTY
Well, he probably ain't impossible.

F-9 MR. MAXWELL - PAST McGINTY

MAXWELL
Because you see, Mr. Mayor, I have got a contract with the city and...

F-10 McGINTY - PAST MAXWELL

McGINTY
I wouldn't mention that if I was you...,you're just liable to irritate him. Just treat him nice.

F-11 MR. MAXWELL - PAST McGINTY

MR. MAXWELL
You couldn't give me a rough idea of about how nice, could you?

F-12 TRUCKING SHOT - AHEAD OF McGINTY AND MAXWELL

McGinty claps Maxwell on the back and shoves him forward.

McGINTY
I don't know what you're talking about, Mr. Maxwell. Glad to see you looking so well. Drop in again some afternoon and we'll take in a ball game. Do you like baseball?

MR. MAXWELL
Well I'm not a uh...fan I believe you call it...by any means.

McGINTY
That's where you fellows make your big mistake. You worry too much about business...and contracts... and flaws in them and things like that. You ought to get out in the open, fill your lungs with air and forget your troubles. Look at that crowd!

He points to a large picture on the wall near the door.

F-12 (Cont'd)

McGINTY
How many people do you think were at that game?

MR. MAXWELL
(After a vague look at the photograph)
I'm sure I haven't the faintest idea.

McGINTY
Look again. How many people do you think there are in that photograph?

F-13 McGINTY AND MAXWELL - IN FRONT OF THE BIG PHOTOGRAPH

MR. MAXWELL
I don't know...ten thousand?

McGINTY
Guess again.

MR. MAXWELL
Twenty thousand?

McGINTY
(Coldly)
You're not even warm, Mr. Maxwell

MR. MAXWELL
(Who doesn't really give a dam about baseball)
Well I...Oh!
(The groan escapes him as McGinty's diabolical scheme dawns upon him)
You mean...it's more like forty thousand?

McGINTY
It's more like it but that ain't it.

MR. MAXWELL
But Mr. Mayor, that flaw you mentioned...

McGINTY
(Coldly)
There's no flaw in that photograph, Mr. Maxwell, it's perfect. What was your last guess?

MR. MAXWELL
(After a hard swallow)
Fifty thousand?

F-13 (Cont'd)

McGINTY
(Pointing)
There were seventy-five thousand people in that stadium, Mr. Maxwell, seventy-five thousand! Wonderful, isn't it? Goodbye, Mr. Maxwell, I'll send the guy up to see you. Goodbye.

He waves and returns to his desk.

McGINTY
(Into telephone)
Who else is waiting?...well, make it tomorrow...I've seen enough for today and, by the way, see if you can get me a big picture of the Dempsey-Carpentier fight, willya? Yeah, that's right, the frog.

DISSOLVE TO:

F-14 THE NURSERY OF McGINTY'S NEW APARTMENT

It is a lovely room with a shiny linoleum floor. In the floor are inlaid, and on the walls are painted, Mother Goose figures. The room contains a nice slide with a mat to land on, a playhouse for the children against one wall, the usual collection of rocking horses, wheeled sheep, lions, elephants, blocks, etc. Catherine, in a lovely dressing gown, is sitting on the edge of a bed. The two children are at her knees saying their prayers. The Dachsund puppy is chained to a little dog-house.

THE CHILDREN
...I pray the Lord my soul to take. Amen.

CATHERINE
(Prompting)
And God bless...

THE CHILDREN
Papa who's in heaven and Mama and Uncle George and Bessy and Brownie...

There is a yip from the puppy.

THE CHILDREN
...and...and....

11-28-39 (Continued)

F-14 (Cont'd)

CATHERINE
And Mr. McGinty.

THE CHILDREN
And Mr. McGinty.

CATHERINE
Who has been so kind and generous to us all.

THE CHILDREN
Who has been so kinda generous to us all. Amen.

The little boy now leaps to his feet, scampers up to the top of the slide and shoots down onto the pad with a happy yell. As the little girl starts to do the same thing her mother catches her.

THE LITTLE GIRL
Please, Mummy.

CATHERINE
Now you're going right to bed.

THE LITTLE GIRL
Please play one more game.

THE LITTLE BOY
(Jumping up and down)
Blindman's buff!

CATHERINE
You've got to go to bed and Mother hasn't time anyway. She's going out to dinner and....

THE CHILDREN
Please, Mummy!

CATHERINE
....and she has to dress and... Well, this is absolutely the last one.

The children yell gleefully and the puppy bounces up and down. The little girl brings Catherine a handkerchief.

F-14 (Cont'd)

CATHERINE
(Tying on the handkerchief)
All right: one, two, three, four, five, six, seven, eight, nine, ten! Here I come and don't you dare to move.

She starts straight for the little boy who tiptoes toward the door.

CATHERINE
Now don't you move.

She starts for the little girl who also tiptoes toward the door.

CATHERINE
Fee, fie, fo, fum, I smell the blood of an Englishmun...now you're moving, children.

The children slip out into the hall and the little dog starts to yip.

CATHERINE
Be he alive or be he dead, I'll grind his bones to make my bread...I can hear you over there.

As this brings forth no squeals, she lifts a corner of the handkerchief and cheats a little. Now she pulls the handkerchief up a little further and looks around the whole room. She ends up by looking at the playhouse.

CATHERINE
Now you come out of there! You know perfectly well it's cheating to hide in the house. Now hurry out...All right, we'll see about that.

She goes to the playhouse and opens the door.

CATHERINE
I'll give you up to three and then... one, two, three. All right.

She gets on her knees and sticks her head in the playhouse. A second later she pulls her head out again and looks around the room. Suddenly she frowns.

F-15 CLOSE SHOT - THE DOOR

It is open a few inches.

11-28-39

F-16 CATHERINE - ON HER KNEES IN FRONT OF THE PLAYHOUSE

She gets to her feet.

CATHERINE
Oh! Will you be sorry when I catch you.

She hurries PAST THE CAMERA.

F-17 GEORGE - IN THE LIVING ROOM

He is a quiet looking, amiable man of about thirty-five. He wears a dinner jacket. He is sitting in a very large chair, and the children are standing between his back and the back of the chair.

GEORGE
(Nervously)
Now you're just going to get me in wrong.

THE LITTLE GIRL
No we won't, Uncle George.

THE LITTLE BOY
No we won't.

THE LITTLE GIRL
You just sit quiet and...
(In a whisper)
Here she comes!

The children duck behind George's shoulders. George spreads himself but looks uneasy.

F-18 CATHERINE - IN THE FOYER OUTSIDE THE LIVING ROOM

CATHERINE
(Looking around)
I'm sorry I'm not dressed yet, George...Those little brats...
(Now she frowns a little suspiciously)
You haven't seen them, have you?

F-19 GEORGE - IN THE CHAIR

GEORGE
(Who is a rotten actor)
Well uh...heh,heh...just how do you mean that?

11-28-39

F-20 CATHERINE

CATHERINE
(Frowning slightly)
What do you mean, "How do I mean that?" You're not in court, you know...YOU HAVE SEEN THEM!
(She starts forward)
Where are they?

F-21 GEORGE - IN THE CHAIR

The little boy pokes an eye over George's shoulder then squeals and disappears, as he sees his mother.

F-22 CATHERINE - PAST GEORGE'S CHAIR

CATHERINE
You come out of there, you little monkey.
(She reaches for him)
And you too, you little vixen. You're going to get a good spanking for this.

F-23 GEORGE AND THE CHILDREN - PAST CATHERINE WHO IS REACHING FOR THEM

GEORGE
I don't think they meant any harm, Honey.

CATHERINE
You save your "Honey" for somebody else. Now give me those children.

The little boy starts to wail.

GEORGE
They were just playing. They didn't mean any wrong.

Now the little girl adds her wails to the symphony. At this point the puppy comes in dragging its doghouse behind it. It adds its yapping to the general turmoil.

F-24 THE FRONT DOOR - IN THE FOYER

McGinty enters cheerfully and turns in surprise at the noise. Now he hangs up his hat, closes the door after him and the CAMERA PANS him across the foyer so he can see into the living room.

F-25 GEORGE - STANDING WITH THE TWO CHILDREN IN HIS ARMS - AND CATHERINE - PAST McGINTY

George looks miserable and the children are crying.

CATHERINE
Now you stop it. Stop it at once
or I'll tell Mr. McGinty on you
and then you'll see.

The children wail at this.

F-26 McGINTY - IN THE DOORWAY OF THE LIVING ROOM

McGINTY
They'll see what?

F-27 CATHERINE, GEORGE AND THE CHILDREN - PAST McGINTY

CATHERINE
(Faintly distressed)
Oh, good evening, Mr. McGinty.
I'm sorry you had to walk in on
this. I seem to be always
apologizing for them. I just
used your name to f-r-i-g-h-t-e-n
them.

F-28 CLOSE SHOT - McGINTY

McGINTY
Oh.

He turns and gives George an unpleasant look.

F-29 THE GROUP - PAST McGINTY

GEORGE
(Perfunctorily)
Good evening.

Without a word, McGinty turns and exits.

CATHERINE
I think you could be a little
more polite, George.

GEORGE
Why should I be polite, I don't
like him.

11-28-39 (Continued)

F-29 (Cont'd)

CATHERINE
Well, put the children to bed for me, I'll get ready as soon as I can.

DISSOLVE TO:

F-30 McGINTY - IN HIS BEDROOM

He is in his shirtsleeves, brushing his hair. A colored man comes from the dressing room with his coat and vest.

THE COLORED MAN
You playin' pool tonight, Your Honor?

McGinty does not answer.

THE COLORED MAN
Funny thing happened to me the other day...I'm playin' the twelve for the side pocket and the eight is right over....

McGinty throws down the hairbrush and walks out of the room.

F-31 THE CORRIDOR OUTSIDE OF CATHERINE'S ROOM

McGinty comes toward us and seems to be looking for the right door. Now he raps smartly on the door.

CATHERINE'S VOICE
Come in.

McGinty pulls the door open and walks into a clothes closet. As he backs out again --

F-32 CATHERINE - IN FRONT OF HER MAKEUP TABLE

This is in an alcove off her bedroom. She is in her underwear, making up her lips. There is a knock on the door.

CATHERINE
Come in.

We HEAR a door open and we see McGinty's reflection in the mirror.

11-28-39 (Continued)

F-32 (Cont'd)

CATHERINE
Put it on the bed, Bessy.

She finishes her lips and stands up.

F-33 McGINTY - LOOKING TOWARD THE ALCOVE

We see Catherine's reflection in a mirror.

CATHERINE'S VOICE
Did you wash out those other stockings?

McGINTY
Not yet.

F-34 CATHERINE - IN FRONT OF HER DRESSING TABLE

She whirls, then pulls on the dressing gown from the chair.

CATHERINE
Why, Mr. McGinty...What are you doing in my room?

F-35 McGINTY - PAST CATHERINE

McGINTY
Who's this lug who gives me the "good evening" every night when I get here?

CATHERINE
Just George.

McGINTY
What does he do...room here?

CATHERINE
Why, of course he doesn't, Mr. McGinty. He always wanted to marry me, that's all...And since I'm still...free...in a way...he just takes me out to dinner, that's all.
(Now she adds hastily)
Oh, we go to very quiet places where I won't be seen...or up to his flat.

11-28-39

(Continued)

F-35 (Cont'd)

McGINTY
Oh, yeah!

He looks displeased and rather nonplussed at this.

McGINTY
(Continuing)
Well you tell him to hand me one more "good evening" like he give me tonight and I'll hand him something that will take his mind off marriage for quite some time.
(Suddenly he gets still angrier)
Where does this bozo get off to be propositioning my wife anyway?
(He glares toward the living room)

CATHERINE
You mean "proposing", Mr. McGinty, and he doesn't any more anyway. He just takes me out to dinner.

McGINTY
(Roughly)
Why don't you eat home once in a while? Is there anything the matter with the grub around here?

CATHERINE
(Who has had about enough of this)
Well if there was, Mr. McGinty, you wouldn't know it.

McGINTY
(Stopped in his tracks)
Hunh?
(Then after thinking it over)
What have I got to do with it?

CATHERINE
(Quietly)
I don't think you have anything to do with it, Mr. McGinty. I'm running your house as best I can; I go to all sorts of clubs and meetings; I'm photographed all the time, I...I...You've already got the women's vote...and if I want to go out quietly with an old friend instead of sitting alone in the evening I don't really see that...that...

(Continued)

F-35 (Cont'd)

McGINTY
I'm sorry.

CATHERINE
That's quite all right, Mr. McGinty.

McGINTY
No hard feelin's.

He puts his hand out slowly and she takes it.

CATHERINE
(Smiling)
Of course not.

As McGinty does not release her hand she looks at it in surprise.

McGINTY
(With great hesitancy)
Why don't you...Why don't _we_ have dinner together sometime?

CATHERINE
(Politely)
I'd be very glad to, Mr. McGinty.

She takes another look at her hand.

CATHERINE
...Any time except tonight.

McGINTY
(Hanging onto her hand)
Ya know...if ya told anybody that we been living here like this... just down the hall...for six months ...and neither one of us ever give the other one a thought....they wouldn't believe it.
(He bends forward a little)

CATHERINE
(A little nervously)
That's right.
(She moves a little closer to him now)
Even if it was true, they wouldn't believe it.

McGINTY
(Astonished)
Well, fork....
(He grabs her to him.)

11-28-39 (Continued)

F-35 (Cont'd)

She is a little tense during the early part of the kiss but presently relaxes.

F-36 THE HALL - OUTSIDE THE BEDROOM

Bessy hurries toward us carrying a lovely evening gown on a hanger. She knocks, opens the door and speaks simultaneously.

BESSY
Here 'tis, Miss Catherine, it...

F-37 THE DOOR - PAST McGINTY AND CATHERINE

Bessy is just coming in.

BESSY
...taken a little longer...

Her voice slips off to one side.

F-38 CLOSE SHOT - BESSY

Her expression tells us she does not believe what she is seeing. She licks her lips nervously, then suddenly lets out a whoop of laughter. Immediately afterward she claps her hand over her mouth.

F-39 McGINTY AND CATHERINE - PAST BESSY

McGinty turns slowly and gives Bessy a chilling look.

McGINTY
(After a pause)
Put it on the bed.

BESSY
(Wilting)
Y-y-yassuh, Mista Mayor.

She crosses to the bed and lays the lovely dress on it, then gives McGinty a frightened look and starts for the door.

McGINTY
And ya know that John squattin'
in the front parlor?

11-28-39 (Continued)

F-39 (Cont'd)

BESSY
Yassuh, Mista Mayor.

CATHERINE
(Coming to life)
But, Mr. McGinty.

McGINTY
(Ignoring her)
Tell him he's barking up the
wrong tree!

BESSY
Y-yassuh, Mista Mayor.

She rolls her eyes up to heaven and hurries out.

CATHERINE
But...Daniel.

McGinty turns slowly and a ghost of a smile comes over his face.

McGINTY
Say that again.

CATHERINE
(Softly)
Daniel.

McGINTY
(Angrily)
I musta been blind.

He takes her in his arms once more.

FADE OUT:

END OF SEQUENCE "F"

11-28-39

SEQUENCE "G"

FADE IN:

G-1 A HUGE EXCAVATION

The usual group of loafers is watching the work go on. A farm boy type, in a Montgomery Ward suit, forces his way up to the fence and gapes, then he turns to one of the railbirds.

FARM BOY
What's that agoin' to be when she's through, Mister?

RAILBIRD
That's a hole to put the taxpayers money in.

FARM BOY
She's agoin' to be big, ain't she.

RAILBIRD
Big! They're puttin' up a warehouse over there for the rest of it.

FARM BOY
No foolin'!

He walks out of the picture.

G-2 SHOT OF BUILDING IN CONSTRUCTION

The Farm Boy walks into the picture, taps one of the watchers in the foreground on the shoulder.

FARM BOY
Is this the warehouse they put the money in, Mister?

ONLOOKER
You said it!

FARM BOY
Gosh all hemlock!

G-3 A HIGH FENCE

The farm Boy comes into the picture, looks all over, then finally glues his eyes to a little crack about four feet from the sidewalk. After looking for a moment, he straightens up, looks around for somebody to pester, sees somebody, and walks out of the picture.

G-4 POLICEMAN - FANNING HIS STICK - IN FRONT OF ANOTHER SECTION OF THE FENCE

The Farm Boy hurries into the picture. He points to the fence.

FARM BOY
What's agoin' on behind that fence, Mister?

POLICEMAN
They're working on the new city bathing beach.

FARM BOY
What for?

POLICEMAN
So that you and the other tax-payers can go for a swim when it's hot, see? It'll be just like the ocean -- only nicer.

FARM BOY
(Sadly)
I don't live here. I'm just on an excursion.

POLICEMAN
That's your hard luck.

G-5 CLOSE SHOT - A RIVETEER

The noise of his airgun is deafening. The noise continues as we:

DISSOLVE TO:

G-6 A HUGE SIGN - PAST THE BOSS' ARMORED CAR

The sign painter is putting the finishing touches to the signature. On the left side of the sign there is a bad likeness of McGinty flanked by American flags. The message reads:

"FELLOW CITIZENS
The improvements in this district cost the city $18,000,000. As a result of these improvements the real estate values have gone up $140,000,000. Your profit is $122,000,000.
Sincerely,
Your Mayor, Dan McGinty"

11-28-39 (Continued)

G-6 (Cont'd)

The riveting sound is pretty low by now.

G-7 THE BOSS AND McGINTY - LOOKING THROUGH THE WINDOW OF THE ARMORED CAR

We do not hear the dialogue but we see them speaking:

THE BOSS
(Proudly)
Is that swell?

McGINTY
(Scowling)
Swell, he's got me cross-eyed.

He crosses his fingers and jabs them toward his eyes.

DISSOLVE TO:

G-8 CLOSE SHOT - THE DACHSHUND PUPPY ASLEEP (OR WAGGING ITS TAIL) IN FRONT OF THE FIREPLACE - IN McGINTY'S LIVING ROOM

McGinty's voice comes in simultaneously and the CAMERA STARTS PANNING SLOWLY.

McGINTY'S VOICE
But they had to get up pretty early to be smarter than Peter Rabbit because he was as full of brains as a dog is full of fleas.

(Possibility of dog scratching itself on this cue.)

The CAMERA PASSES OVER a doll lying on the floor, and sweeps onto Catherine from the waist down. She wears a very lovely negligee. We see her hands busy knitting. Now the CAMERA ANGLES UP ONTO her.

McGINTY'S VOICE
Our old friend didn't even stop to think. He took a hop, skip and a jump....

Catherine looks up from her work and smiles across the room.

G-9 McGINTY - IN A BIG CHAIR UNDER A READING LIGHT

He wears a flowery dressing gown and slippers. On one arm of his chair sits the little girl, Mary. On the

G-9 (Cont'd)

other arm sits the little boy, Bill. The children are having trouble keeping their eyes open.

McGINTY
....and started across the clover field as fast as his little fat legs would carry him.

The little boy blinks once more, then closes his eyes.

McGINTY
Just as he got to the edge of the field by the old split rail fence, a shadow fell across his path and who do you suppose it was?

The little girl's eyes close.

McGINTY
I'll give you three guesses and then three more and three other ones, but you could try all night without guessing who it really was because it was none other than....

CATHERINE'S VOICE
(Very gently)
Darling.

McGINTY
(Looking up)
Hunh?

G-10 CATHERINE

In pantomime she indicates that the children are asleep.

G-11 McGINTY AND THE CHILDREN

He looks down at them.

McGINTY
Oh.
(Now he looks back at the book)
Just a minute....
(Reading)
....none other than our friend Muggledy-Wump the Tor-toys....
that's who I thought it was.
(He chuckles, then looks down at the children)

11-28-39 (Continued)

G-11 (Cont'd)

The little boy's head is resting on his shoulder; the little girl's hand is on his arm.

G-12 CATHERINE - PAST McGINTY

She puts her knitting in a bag then crosses to McGinty's chair and smiles down gently on the little group.

CATHERINE
They love you so...and to think, I used to use you as the boogieman!

McGinty chuckles.

McGINTY
I don't feel no different toward 'em than...if they was mine.

CATHERINE
Do you love them?

McGINTY
You bet.

CATHERINE
They're so proud of you...it hurts sometimes. They think you're George Washington and Abraham Lincoln rolled together...only finer. Billy had a fight on your account today.

McGINTY
(Beaming)
He did, hunh? The little son-of-a-gun.
(Now he frowns slightly)
What about?

CATHERINE
Another boy heard his father say you were a grafter and he yelled it out at recess. Billy didn't know just what it meant but he hit him anyway.

McGinty almost chuckles as he looks at the little boy.

CATHERINE
Too bad, isn't it?

She looks away a little bit unhappily.

McGINTY
I thought you didn't care about that stuff....what's your slogan? You can't rob the people because what you rob you spend and what you spend you something-or-other.

G-12 (Cont'd)

CATHERINE
(Looking up at him)
I wasn't married to you then.

She sits on the chair and smooths the little boy's hair.

CATHERINE
I think you're a fine man, Dan.

McGINTY
Who, me?

CATHERINE
(Looking him right in the eye)
Yes, you. I think you're a fine honest man with decent impulses and everything else. I couldn't have been as close to you as I have been... and be mistaken. I don't think I could love you so much...I know I couldn't admire you so much.

McGINTY
What you been drinkin', catnip?

Catherine plays with his hair and chuckles, then resumes.

CATHERINE
You're just a tough guy, McGinty... You're not a wrong guy. If you were on the other side of the fence, you'd play just as hard the other way.

McGINTY
(Horrified)
You mean a dick?

CATHERINE
I don't mean anything in particular, I just mean that to have all the power you have and all the opportunities you have to do things for people and never to do anything but... shake them down a little... it seems like a waste of something... It doesn't balance. Do you understand?

McGINTY
(With perfect simplicity)
No.

11-28-39 (Continued)

G-12 (Cont'd)

CATHERINE
As if somebody left you an opening and you didn't cross your right.

McGINTY
What are you trying to do, reform me?

CATHERINE
I guess I'm just being dull... I guess I went to one reform lunch too many this week.
(She smiles)
I've heard so much about child labor and sweatshops and the fire-traps poor people live in, I just...
(She smiles sheepishly)

McGINTY
(Seriously)
I couldn't do anything about those things if I wanted to. Those are the people he works with... Those are the people who put me in. You gotta understand how these things work.

CATHERINE
(Leaning forward happily)
You mean you would...if you could?

McGINTY
(Suspiciously)
What?

CATHERINE
Oh...do something about the tenements, maybe.

McGINTY
Why, you got some relatives down there?

CATHERINE
You know I haven't.

McGINTY
You like all that stuff, hunh... You know those people like to be let alone...they like to be dirty. They don't like people foolin' around with 'em... You give 'em a bathtub and they keep the coal in it.

11-28-39 (Continued)

G-12 (Cont'd)

Catherine doesn't say anything. After a moment McGinty picks up a telephone.

McGINTY
(Into the telephone)
Riverside one six, six, six.

CATHERINE
What are you going to do?

McGINTY
Hello.

G-13 THE BOSS - AT THE TELEPHONE IN HIS OFFICE AT HEAD-QUARTERS

THE BOSS
(Delighted)
Hello, there, Mr. Newlywed... You comin' over? I got a coupla dames that's...

G-14 McGINTY - AT THE TELEPHONE

McGinty looks at his wife for a moment as the Boss keeps on talking.

McGINTY
Listen: I happen to come home through the poor district, see?
(He winks at his wife)
And I was wonderin', while we're cleanin' up the rest of the city, how about a tenement house bill? You know, make 'em clean 'em up... and put in some windows and some plumbing...stuff like that?......
(Now he smiles with surprise)
Ya do, hunh?

He puts his hand over the telephone and says to his wife:

McGINTY
He thinks it's a marvelous idea.

CATHERINE
(In an awestruck voice)
No.

11-28-39 (Continued)

G-14 (Cont'd)

McGINTY
(Into the telephone)
Hunh?

G-15 THE BOSS - AT THE TELEPHONE

THE BOSS
Your mind is really beginning to circulate. I don't know why I didn't think of it. This is going to ring the bell and how. Give it to the newspapers first thing in the morning. Tenements must go! The city without a slum! They'll be coming in around two o'clock and I'll get Jarvis to send you down the list and how much they're good for by noon.

G-16 McGINTY - AT THE TELEPHONE

McGINTY
(Scowling a little)
What list?

He gives his wife a sidewise look.

G-17 THE BOSS - AT THE TELEPHONE

THE BOSS
(Happily)
The landlords! Who they are and how much they'll pay to kill the bill! You're doing all right, baby... You keep on like this and you'll be surprised where you'll wind up... yes, sir.

He hangs up the receiver.

G-18 McGINTY - AT THE TELEPHONE

McGinty hangs up slowly.

CATHERINE
What did he say?

McGINTY
(Shrugging)
It's just what I told you...I didn't understand him at first.

11-28-39 (Continued)

G-18 (Cont'd)

CATHERINE
(Quietly)
You'll be strong enough some day, Dan..
and then you'll wash clean of graft
and crooks and thieving politicians
and really deserve your title: The
Honorable.

McGinty looks at her.

DISSOLVE TO:

G-19 THE GIRL AND THOMPSON - PAST McGINTY - IN THE BANANA CAFE

McGinty is finishing with a cocktail. He fills three glasses. The girl and Thompson watch McGinty fixedly.

THE GIRL
You liked the kids, hunh?

THOMPSON
Why shouldn't he?

G-20 McGINTY - PAST THOMPSON AND THE GIRL

McGINTY
Sure I liked 'em.
(Then to the waiter)
Take 'em away.

The waiter's arm comes INTO THE SHOT and removes the three cocktails.

McGINTY
She's goin' to be married this fall...
she must be a beautiful girl....the
kid's at West Point....don't know what
their ma's goin' to do now...I told
her to divorce me....but she never did..
anyway, nobody ever told me.
(He wipes up the bar a
little, then continues)
She kept sayin': "You'll be strong
enough some day"...I knew it was wrong,
see, but I liked the way it made me
look in her eyes....and the kids'...
so one day I said: "All right, I'm strong
enough now."
(He chuckles, then adds)
In a pig's nose I was strong enough.

FADE OUT:

END OF SEQUENCE "G"

SEQUENCE "H"

FADE IN:

H-1 MONTAGE OF THE GUBERNATORIAL RACE

(1)
TORCHLIGHT PARADE WITH APPROPRIATE SIGNS

(2)
THE POLITICIAN STANDING ON THE BACK OF A CAR

He is lit by torches. A banner reads:

McGINTY FOR GOVERNOR

THE POLITICIAN
(With very little voice left)
Look what he done to our lake front! Look what he done to our city -- for our city! Look what he done for YOU... and you...and you. The least you can do, friends, the smallest token of gratitude that you can show, is to send him to the capitol. I'm giving it to you straight, friends ... You owe him that.

(3)
AN OPPOSITION SPEAKER

He also stands in THE TONNEAU OF A CAR flanked with torches. His banner reads:

HONEYWELL FOR GOVERNOR

Honeywell & Honesty

OPPOSITION SPEAKER
...the worst crook we've had since the year of the big wind! Senator Honeywell, on the other hand, my friends...

(4)
THE POLITICIAN

THE POLITICIAN
You won't be makin' no mistake, friends, and I'll tell you somethin' else...

11-28-39 (Continued)

H-1 (Cont'd)

(5)
THE OPPOSITION SPEAKER

THE OPPOSITION SPEAKER
Just compare them coolly and without prejudice. On the one hand we have virture, on the other...

(6)
THE POLITICIAN

THE POLITICIAN
...year alone he put forty thousand men to work...forty thousand lunch pails, my friends...forty thousand happy families...money in circulation...prosperity!

(7)
THE OPPOSITION SPEAKER

THE OPPOSITION SPEAKER
He gutted the treasury...he raided the city...he raised the taxes... he built miles of useless buildings, bridges, beaches...eyesores, my friends, each and every one a monument, a testimonial, to graft.

(8)
THE POLITICIAN

THE POLITICIAN
(Reaching his highspot)
...and gave you the most beautiful city in the world!

(9)
THE TORCHLIGHT PARADE GOING BY

(10)
NEWSPAPER HEADINGS FLASH IN AND OUT OVER THE PARADE

HONEYWELL LEADS BY 10,000

HONEYWELL LEADS BY 30,000

BOTH PARTIES CLAIM VICTORY

McGINTY LEADS BY 6,000

H-1 (Cont'd)

(10 Cont'd)

McGINTY PLURALITY 70,000

McGINTY BY 400,000

BOTH PARTIES CLAIM VICTORY

A BAND goes by, playing "The Stars and Stripes Forever".

Now a very big HEADLINE:

McGINTY WINS -- HONEYWELL DEMANDS RECOUNT

The MUSIC gets very loud.

DISSOLVE TO:

(11)
STOCK SHOT - A BIG CITY PARADE - (DAYLIGHT)

(12)
A DIFFERENT ANGLE OF THE PARADE

(13)
A SECTION OF THE CROWD ON THE SIDEWALK

(14)
LOW CAMERA SHOT - THE CHILDREN AND BESSY - ON A BALCONY

The children are five years older than when we saw them last. They wave little flags. Now they get very much excited and lean far out. Bessy makes a grab for them.

(15)
HIGH CAMERA SHOT - DOWN ON THE STREET

It is empty for a second, then a flag-decked shiny automobile rolls slowly into view. Governor and Mrs. McGinty sit on the back seat acknowledging the salutes of the crowd. Catherine carries a big bunch of flowers. Suddenly she looks up, nudges the Governor, then throws a kiss to the children.

(16)
LOW CAMERA SHOT - UP AT THE BALCONY

The children, Bessy and the colored man behind them are going wild with excitement.

11-28-39

H-2 THE GOVERNOR & MRS. McGINTY

The NOISE from the band, and the yelling, is quite loud. They wave once more to the children, then look down again. McGinty doffs his silk hat to some of the crowd.

CATHERINE
I'm so proud of you, Dan.

McGINTY
(Leaning closer)
What?

CATHERINE
I'm so proud of you.

McGINTY
Oh.
(He smiles and tips his hat again)

CATHERINE
You're strong enough for anything now.

McGINTY
What?

CATHERINE
I said you're strong enough.

McGINTY
(Realizing what she means)
Oh.

CATHERINE
You can keep your promise now.

McGINTY
(With a trace of irritation)
Look: I'm the Governor of the state, you're the governor's lady. Everybody don't get to be governor. Isn't that enough for you? Why don't we leave well enough alone?

CATHERINE
(Hurt)
But, Dan...

McGINTY
(Shrugging his shoulders)
All right.

He looks ahead glumly for a moment then forces a smile and tips his hat from right to left.

DISSOLVE TO:

11-28-39

H-3 LONG SHOT - A STATE CAPITOL

DISSOLVE TO:

H-4 McGINTY - TAKING THE OATH OF OFFICE

This takes place in a sort of CHAPEL. The Chief Justice administers it. There are flags and we see about twenty people of those present.

McGINTY
I, Daniel McGinty, do solemnly swear that I will faithfully discharge all duties incumbent upon me as Governor, that I will do equal right to the poor and to the rich, and that I will, to the best of my ability, preserve, protect, and defend the Constitution and the Laws of this sovereign state. So help me, God.

McGinty turns slowly and meets his wife's gaze. The band begins to play "The Star Spangled Banner."

DISSOLVE TO:

H-5 THE GOVERNOR'S OUTER OFFICE

It contains quite a few cranks, whackpots, and old political fogies. It also contains Louie who leans against the wall picking his teeth. We do not see Louie, however. We HEAR the "Star Spangled Banner" some distance off.

SOME VOICES
Here he comes.
Here he comes now.
Get off my foot, will you?

Now McGinty's secretary leads McGinty, Catherine and George into the office.

THE SECRETARY
Make way, please make way...
Right this way, Mr. Governor.

AN OLD GENTLEMAN
Mr. Governor, as Senior State Senator...

THE SECRETARY
If you'll be kind enough to make an appointment, Senator.

11-28-39 (Continued)

H-5 (Cont'd)

ANOTHER OLD CRACKPOT
Governor McGinty, I am here on behalf...

McGINTY
(Pointing to the Secretary)
You heard what the guy said, didn't you?

The Old Crackpot pulls up in surprise.

THE SECRETARY
(Indicating the door)
Just through here, Mr. Governor.

McGinty starts forward with Catherine and stops as he sees somebody.

H-6 LOUIE - LEANING AGAINST THE WALL

He is examining his toothpick at the moment. He does not look at McGinty.

H-7 McGINTY, CATHERINE AND THE SECRETARY - IN THE CROWD

McGINTY
(To the Secretary)
Have I got another room someplace?

THE SECRETARY
(Amused and astounded)
Well I should say you have, Mr. Governor. You have the west conference room, the east conference room, the small reception room, the green reception room...

McGINTY
(Shutting him off)
Well take my wife some place where she'll be comfortable...
(He points toward his office)
I got something to attend to.

THE SECRETARY
Certainly, Mr. Governor.

McGINTY
I'll just be a couple of minutes.

He turns toward his office and Catherine smiles after him.

11-28-39

H-8 FULL SHOT - THE GOVERNOR'S OFFICE - PAST THE GREAT CHAIR WHICH IS TIPPED IN

The afternoon sun streams in through the high windows and the old-fashioned mahogany furniture gleams cheerfully. Portraits of former governors adorn the walls. McGinty comes through the door at the far end, looks straight TOWARDS US for a moment, then comes across the big room, leans on the desk and looks PAST THE CAMERA into the chair.

H-9 THE BOSS - PAST McGINTY

He is comfortably ensconsed in the GOVERNOR'S CHAIR.

THE BOSS
(Cheerfully)
Well, here we are. It took a little doing but it's worth it.

McGINTY
That's right.

THE BOSS
(Perplexed)
You don't look as happy as you should. Don't you feel good?

He gets up and comes around the desk.

McGINTY
I feel all right.

THE BOSS
You should feel all right...with this staring you in the face.
(He shakes his head)
What a wonderful opportunity: This state needs everything! They had honest governors so long the whole place is in wrack and ruin!

McGINTY
(Nervously)
Is that so.

THE BOSS
It's fantastic.

He takes a little book out of his pocket and enumerates a few items.

11-28-39 (Continued)

H-9 (Cont'd)

THE BOSS
The roads, for instance. They're in terrible condition. In case of war we'd be at the mercy. We need a whole new highway system.

McGINTY
How would an enemy ever get to here?

THE BOSS
How do I know, am I a general?
(He looks at his book again)
Then we'll need a new water works system, a state canal and...
(He looks up)
You'll kiss me for this one... A new dam!

McGINTY
(Strangely)
We do, hunh?

THE BOSS
(Disappointed)
I can see from your expression you don't know what a dam is. You think a dam is something you put a lot of water in... A dam is something you put a lotta concrete in...and it doesn't matter how much you put in there's always room for a lot more...and any time you're afraid it's finished there's always a crack in it and you put some more concrete. And in the third place it's always behind a mountain somewhere at the top of the state where nobody could find it in the first place.

McGINTY
What's the matter with the old dam?

THE BOSS
(Giving him a look)
It's got a crack in it.

McGINTY
Oh.

11-28-39 (Continued)

H-9 (Cont'd)

McGINTY (Cont'd)
(Now he speaks with a little harshness in his voice)
What are ya thinking of starting with, the dam?

THE BOSS
No. You start small and get goin' afterwards. Right now while the farmers are looking on we could start off with a nice little state capitol building. Maybe white marble...or do you like pink?

McGINTY
What do we need a state capitol building for?

THE BOSS
(In hurt surprise)
What do we need it for?
(He points to the walls)
This one is falling apart.

He goes over and pounds on the solid wall, then stamps on the floor.

THE BOSS
It ain't safe.

McGINTY
Looks safe enough to me...I'm the guy that's got to live here.

The Boss looks quietly at McGinty a moment before speaking.

THE BOSS
You're kinda dumb this morning, aintcha, Dan?

McGINTY
(Looking him in the eye)
Yeah.

The Boss looks at him blankly for a moment, then his eyes narrow and he speaks savagely.

THE BOSS
What are you trying to pull, lug?

11-28-39 (Continued)

H-9 (Cont'd)

McGINTY
There ain't going to be no dams
and no bridges and no buildings
the people don't need...from now
on.

THE BOSS
(Stupefied)
The people!
(Now he gives McGinty
a searching look)
Say, are you sick or something?

McGINTY
I feel fine.

THE BOSS
(Savagely, stepping
forward)
Then what are you trying to put
over, you lousy double-crossing
rat after I spend four hundred
grand to put you in here!

McGINTY
I got that all figured out...

He takes a key out of his vest pocket and chucks it on the desk.

McGINTY
Here's the key to my box... I'll
pay you the rest out of my salary.

The Boss picks up the key and looks at it.

THE BOSS
Out of what salary? You know
how long you're going to be here?

McGINTY
Yeah, I know exactly how long I'm
going to be here.

THE BOSS
You think you know. You poor
sucker! I'll put you in the jug
so long you'll splash when you
come out!

McGINTY
Yeah! Well you'll be splashin'
right along with me! And maybe
you'll be splashin' by yourself!

11-28-39. (Continued)

H-9 (Cont'd)

THE BOSS
You think so? Listen: Anything ever happens to me you'll be in the clink ten minutes later. You think I'm an amatoor or something? I can pin so much on you you'll look like a Christmas tree.

McGINTY
What are you goin' to pin on me when I only started this mornin'? I know what I'm doin'. I been hatchin' it a long time. I'm goin' to put in a child labor bill and then I'm goin' to stamp out the sweatshops and then I'm goin' to banish the tenements and then...

THE BOSS
(Enraged and mystified)
What do you know about child labor? You never even seen a sweatshop! What's this tenement business... Who've you been talking to anyway?
(His eyes narrow)
...You're spouting like a woman!
(Suddenly he points an accusing finger)
Aha! Your wife! That cheesecake you married!...

McGINTY
(Stepping forward)
Listen, you make one crack about her...

THE BOSS
(Desperately)
Don't you know nothing? Don't you know a rib started all the trouble? Didn't you never hear of Sampson and Delilah? or Sodom and Gomorrah....?

McGINTY
(Starting forward)
I told you to leave her out of it.

He drives a terrific smash to the Boss' face. The Boss staggers back toward the desk.

11-28-39

H-10 THE BOSS - LEANING AGAINST THE DESK

THE BOSS
(Panting)
All right.

He pulls a gun out of an arm holster.

H-11 McGINTY

He ducks behind a heavy chair. We hear a shot.

H-12 THE BOSS

He fires again.

H-13 McGINTY

He hurls the heavy chair straight AT US.

H-14 THE BOSS

As he fires again the chair crashes on him and he falls backward on the desk.

H-15 McGINTY

He takes a flying leap straight AT US.

H-16 McGINTY AND THE BOSS - STRUGGLING ON THE DESK

The smashed chair is in the background. McGinty is holding the Boss' right wrist with his left hand. With his right he swings a heavy bronze lamp in an effort to knock the Boss' brains out.

H-17 CLOSE SHOT - THE BOSS' HAND WITH THE REVOLVER AND McGINTY'S HAND HOLDING THE WRIST

The Boss' hand goes down on a push-button.

H-18 THE GOVERNOR'S OUTER OFFICE

The Secretary smiles, gathers some papers and goes sedately toward the Governor's door. As he opens it -

11-28-39

H-19 REVERSE SHOT - THE SECRETARY COMING IN

The smile freezes on his face.

THE SECRETARY
Help!

He rushes out.

H-20 McGINTY AND THE BOSS - FIGHTING ON THE DESK

They roll off it onto the floor.

H-21 THE SECRETARY - ARRIVING AT HIS DESK ON THE RUN

He pushes about ten buttons and we hear alarm bells going off all over the building.

THE SECRETARY
(Pointing to the Governor's office)
In there!

He runs toward the office and everybody follows.

H-22 CLOSE SHOT - LOUIE

He looks toward the Governor's office for a moment, then throws his gun in a waste paper basket, pulls his hat lower over his eyes and starts for the exit.

H-23 THE GOVERNOR'S OFFICE

The Boss and McGinty are pulled to their feet by the people from the outside office. The bells are clanging merrily.

H-24 THE DOORWAY OF THE GOVERNOR'S OFFICE

Catherine and George appear, pause a second, then Catherine runs forward. The bells are still RINGING loudly.

H-25 THE BOSS AND McGINTY - FACING EACH OTHER IN THE GROUP

Catherine comes INTO THE SHOT and tries to put her

11-28-39 (Continued)

H-25 (Cont'd)

arms around McGinty but he is so busy exchanging insults with the Boss that he puts her to one side.

DISSOLVE TO:

H-26 NEWSPAPER HEADLINE:

GOVERNOR ESCAPES ASSASSIN'S BULLETS

GANG CHIEF JAILED

* * *

Governor McGinty narrowly escaped with his life late this afternoon when the spitting bullets from the automatic of......

THE CAMERA DRAWS BACK and we see McGinty and Catherine in the GOVERNOR'S UPSTAIRS SITTING ROOM. We see the BEDROOM beyond.

Catherine sits on the arm of his chair and they are both reading the inside story.

CATHERINE
(Indignantly)
It serves him right, too. I hope he gets twenty years for it.

McGinty lowers the paper and speaks with some irritation.

McGINTY
I'm not goin' to press the charges. He ain't a bad guy, honey...according to his way of lookin' at things. You gotta remember he took me off a breadline and....

CATHERINE
But he tried to kill you!

McGINTY
(Getting to his feet)
Why shouldn't he? Don't you think I'd take a pop at a guy who gimme the triple-cross?

CATHERINE
Well you gave him back the money.

11-28-39 (Continued)

H-26 (Cont'd)

McGINTY
(With fresh irritation)
Sure, and if anything should slip up we'd be up the creek and no foolin'.

Catherine gets up and comes over to him.

CATHERINE
(Soothingly, putting her arms on his shoulders)
You're just tired and irritated, darling. Nothing is going to slip up. Nothing can go wrong. You're going to do your best for everybody! You're going to be the finest Governor this state ever had.

McGINTY
There's no money in it, you understand. Just a salary.

CATHERINE
There are some things finer than money, dear.

McGINTY
(Not having any of this)
Yeah, well I feel leery about the whole setup. Sweatshops and tenements are very hot stuff to handle and child labor is plain dynamite.

CATHERINE
(Courageously)
Suppose it is! It's worth the effort, isn't it?

McGINTY
Maybe.

CATHERINE
(Indignantly)
Maybe! Doesn't it mean anything to you to stop little children from being exploited in dark airless factories when they ought to be out playing in the sunshine?

McGINTY
Did you ever work in a factory?

CATHERINE
(Levelly)
I did not.

11-28-39 (Continued)

H-26 (Cont'd)

McGINTY
Well, I did, see? When I was seven years old. Instead of playing on the street and learning dirty words I earned four dollars a week for my mother and it wasn't dark and airless, it was very neat and clean. We'd fold the boxes and then....
(He demonstrates with his hands)
....twist the oil paper around the taffy ....what we didn't eat. And I want to tell you something: We liked it!

CATHERINE
(Angrily)
Sometimes, Dan, you're simply impossible.

McGinty shrugs. Catherine starts out of the room. We hear a DOORBELL in the distance. Catherine stops and looks around.

CATHERINE
Who can that be at this hour?

McGINTY
I don't know....Maybe it's George.

CATHERINE
Why should George call at this hour?

McGINTY
Maybe it isn't George.

He goes out of the room and slams the door after him. Catherine looks after him a little disapprovingly.

H-27 THE DARK FRONT HALL

We see McGinty coming down the last of the steps and the CAMERA PANS WITH HIM as he crosses to the FRONT DOOR.

A hastily dressed colored man appears and opens the door, revealing two big men of the Hibernian type.

ONE OF THE MEN
Governor McGinty?

McGINTY
That's right.

H-27 (Cont'd)

THE MAN
I'm afraid I got bad news for
you Governor McGinty....

DISSOLVE TO:

H-28 THE CHILDREN'S BEDROOM UPSTAIRS IN THE GOVERNOR'S HOUSE

The room is dark. We are SHOOTING FROM A SPOT BETWEEN THE BEDS toward Catherine who is just inside the room silhouetted against the upstairs sitting room. Catherine comes forward quietly and pulls the blanket up a little higher on the boy's bed. As she starts toward the girl's bed McGinty appears in the BACKGROUND. He looks around for his wife, then comes into the children's room. He watches her pull the cover up over the little girl's bed before speaking.

McGINTY
(Quietly)
Catherine.

CATHERINE
(Turning suddenly)
Yes, Dan, I'm sorry, you frightened me.

McGINTY
I'm sorry I got sore just now.

CATHERINE
(Going near him)
It didn't mean anything. You're
just tired and nervous.

McGinty puts his arm around her and pats her.

McGINTY
I'm uh...I gotta go away for a little
while tonight. I uh...it may even
take a few days...

CATHERINE
(Alarmed)
Why Dan, what are you talking about?

McGINTY
Well, there's some kind o' trouble
about a bridge or something I built
as mayor and I'll have to go down
home and explain it, that's all.

H-29 CLOSE SHOT - THE LITTLE BOY IN THE BED

THE LITTLE BOY
Where ya going, Dada?

11-28-39

H-30 McGINTY AND CATHERINE

McGINTY
By golly, I went and talked too loud.

The CAMERA PANS him over to the little boy.

McGINTY
I got to go away for a few days.
You take good care of your mother
while I'm gone.

THE LITTLE BOY
Yes, sir.

McGINTY
That's the idea. And you take
good care of your sister too.

He pats the boy's head, and looks over toward the sleeping girl.

McGINTY
She's goin' to break a lotta
hearts when she grows up.

He chuckles, then walks with Catherine toward the door.

H-31 REVERSE SHOT - SHOOTING INTO THE CHILDREN'S ROOM FROM THE UPSTAIRS SITTING ROOM

McGinty and his wife come out. McGinty closes the door.

CATHERINE
(Levelly)
What's the matter, Dan?

McGINTY
(Embarrassed)
It's a little hard to yell ya,
honey...it sounds kinda foolish...
The guys are waiting downstairs...

DISSOLVE TO:

H-32 NEWSPAPER HEADLINE:

GOVERNOR ARRESTED

McGinty Spends
Night in Jail
* * *
City Looted While Mayor
is in Charge.

DISSOLVE TO:

11-28-39

H-33 McGINTY - IN THE BANANA REPUBLIC - PAST THOMPSON AND THE GIRL DANCER

McGINTY
(Laughing)
Oh boy! That turned out to be some smear. They confronted us in court: I said he tried to kill me and he said I tried to kill him, then he said I was a crook and I said he was a crook, and it looked like a stand-off and we coulda squashed the whole thing with nobody hurt, see, but when Jarvis had me indicted he went too far. And the first thing you know the Federal Government got ahold of our boxes and wanted to know about our income tax for those years, see, then everybody started leaving town. Everybody except us 'cause they had us right in the basket.

H-34 THOMPSON AND THE GIRL - PAST McGINTY

THE GIRL
(Round-eyed)
What kind of a basket?

THOMPSON
He means the penitentiary.

H-35 McGINTY - PAST THE GIRL AND THOMPSON

McGINTY
Not the pen, the jail! There's a h.... quite a difference.

DISSOLVE TO:

H-36 THE VISITING ROOM IN THE CITY JAIL

McGinty stands behind some bars in a sort of cell with a metal door in the back. In front of the bars stand Catherine and George.

CATHERINE
(Vehemently)
They can't do this to you, Dan. I'll go to the Supreme Court, I'll see the President, I'll get up a petition signed by every citizen of the state! They can't put a man in jail for doing something honest.

11-28-39 (Continued)

H-36 (Cont'd)

McGINTY
(With a trace of asperity)
Maybe they can't, honey, but they're puttin' up a good bluff.
(He turns to George)
Did you get that habeas corpus?

GEORGE
The judge was out for dinner. I'll locate him later.

McGINTY
Why don't you find out where he eats?

CATHERINE
How long are they....hoping to.... sentence you for?

McGINTY
They're hoping for ten years.

CATHERINE
(Fervently)
I'll stand by you, Dan. I'll fight for you night and day. We'll lick them if it takes twenty years.

McGINTY
(With irritation)
Well never mind about that part of it. Just get me out of here on bail and I'll take care of the rest of it.

GEORGE
(Hesitantly)
As a matter of fact, Dan, I did find the judge. He won't issue the writ.

McGINTY
Oh.

CATHERINE
(Who knew about this)
But don't you worry about it, dear, we'll do everything humanly possible.

GEORGE
Yes.

McGINTY
Well, I guess that's that.

CATHERINE
(Beginning to weep)
Good night, Dan.

11-28-39 (Continued)

H-36 (Cont'd)

McGINTY
Good night, honey.
(Then to George)
Take her home and see that she gets some rest.

CATHERINE
(Putting her arms around McGinty's neck)
I'm terribly sorry, dear.

McGINTY
(Not too amiably)
That's all right.

Catherine turns away and George takes her arm.

H-37 THE BOSS - IN A CELL IN THE CITY JAIL

He holds onto the bars and looks as though he would like to chew his way out. Now he looks down the hall in the direction from which McGinty is approaching.

H-38 SHOT PARTLY DOWN THE HALL

A Guard brings McGinty to the cell next to the Boss' and locks him in.

THE GUARD
(Cheerfully after looking at his watch)
Well, good night, boys.

A general growl is heard in reply and the guard departs.

THE BOSS
Well, I see you're still here.

McGINTY
Who ast you anything?

THE BOSS
(Happily)
You know how long you're going to get? You're going to get ten to twenty and not in no country club neither....you get Leavenworth or the Beach.

McGINTY
And what do you get, thirty days?

THE BOSS
I hope you're satisfied, you rat! The first time I catch you alone I'll bat your brains all over the yard!

11-28-39 (Continued)

H-36 (Cont'd)

McGINTY
Yeah, you and your little brother.

H-39 AN ADJOINING CELL

THE UGLY PRISONER
How about a little quiet down there?
Why don't you shut up.

H-40 McGINTY AND THE BOSS

THE BOSS
(Toward the Ugly
Prisoner)
How about shutting your own trap.

McGINTY
Stick a cork in it.

H-41 THE UGLY PRISONER

THE UGLY PRISONER
You're pretty brave behind them bars.

H-42 McGINTY AND THE BOSS

THE BOSS
Listen, you cockeyed cockroach....

McGINTY
(Seeing the Guard
approaching)
Cheese it!

A uniformed Guard hurries INTO THE SHOT.

THE GUARD
(Pounding the bars
with a nightclub)
Here, here, here! Quiet!

The Boss and McGinty watch him pop-eyed.

THE GUARD
Who do you think you are anyway?

H-43 THE GUARD - PAST McGINTY

We recognize the Politician.

THE GUARD
Just because I'm new here don't think
you're going to get away with anything.

11-28-39 (Continued)

H-43 (Cont'd)

THE GUARD (Cont'd)
Any more rumpus and I'll put you both in solitary.
(He shakes the keys before their eyes)
I got all the keys right here and it will be very simple....
(Now he shouts toward the Ugly Prisoner)
And that goes for you too, Baby Face.

He gives the Boss and McGinty one solemn wink then turns to go.

H-44 McGINTY AND THE BOSS - PAST THE GUARD

The Guard moves away. McGinty and the Boss watch him go.

DISSOLVE TO:

H-45 THE FOYER OF McGINTY'S CITY APARTMENT

Some of the furniture is covered with sheets and we gather that the apartment is somewhat dismantled. Now we HEAR a key in the lock and the door opens, revealing Catherine and George. Catherine enters and turns to say goodnight.

CATHERINE
Thank you, George, you've been very kind.

GEORGE
(Sympathetically)
I'm awfully sorry, Catherine. I wish there was something I could say that...you know how I've always felt about you...you know how I always will feel about you...I'll stand by you.

CATHERINE
(Taking his hand)
Thank you, George.
(Now she smiles bravely)
But tomorrow's a new day and with a new day comes new courage. We know we're right and we'll draw strength from that knowledge. Goodnight, dear.

She closes the door softly, leans against it for a moment, then starts down the hall. The CAMERA TRUCKS AHEAD of her. Suddenly from the recess of a chair a large object springs up and we hear two screams.

11-28-39

H-46 BESSY - PAST CATHERINE

BESSY
I'm sorry, Miss Catherine, I was waitin' up for you and I musta drapt off.

CATHERINE
That's all right, Bessy. Are the children asleep?

BESSY
Yassum.

CATHERINE
They don't know anything?

BESSY
No, mam. I just told them the boss was very sick in the hospital so they wouldn't worry none.

CATHERINE
(After chuckling reluctantly)
Go to bed now, Bessy. I'll explain to them tomorrow. Good night.

BESSY
Good night. Don't you want me to rub you with alcohol or somethin'?

CATHERINE
(Turning away)
No thank you.

Bessy shakes her head.

H-47 CATHERINE'S BEDROOM

The door is open and we see the lighted hall beyond, Catherine comes in, switches on the room light, turns off the hall light and closes the door. She walks dejectedly toward the bed. Suddenly she throws herself on her face. After a moment we hear a single sob.

FADE OUT:

END OF SEQUENCE "H"

FADE IN:

J-1 THE DOWNSTAIRS GUARD IN THE CITY JAIL - (NIGHT)

He is half asleep in a chair which is tilted way back against the wall. A night special extra lies on his lap. On the front of the paper is printed:

McGINTY JAILED FOR TAX EVASIONS

J-2 DOORWAY OF THE ROOM

Very slowly the Politician's head comes around and peeks.

J-3 THE GUARD - SLEEPING AGAINST THE WALL

The shadow of the Politician goes by on tiptoes. The shadow of the Boss follows. A few feet behind comes the shadow of McGinty. Instead of passing the Guard, however, the shadow pauses.

J-4 McGINTY - TRYING TO READ THE HEADLINE ON THE GUARD'S PAPER

After nearly twisting his neck off, he reaches down quietly and picks up the paper.

J-5 THE GUARD - SLEEPING AGAINST THE WALL

McGinty passes OUT OF THE SHOT with the paper. A second later we hear a soft clang. The Guard opens his eyes, sighs, then reaches for his newspaper. Not finding it on his lap he looks first at the floor on his right, then at the floor on his left. An expression of stupefaction comes over his face. Suddenly he tries to leap to his feet but unfortunately the chair slips out from under him.

DISSOLVE TO:

J-6 A COUNTRY ROAD - (NIGHT)

Far away we see the lights of a car. Now the big armored car speeds toward us at a hundred miles an hour. As it roars PAST THE CAMERA -

11-28-39

J-7 THE COUNTRY ROAD

The big car roars away from us. As the NOISE of its motor dies out we HEAR only the SOUND of tree toads.

DISSOLVE TO:

J-8 A TELEPHONE BOX ON THE WALL OF CATHERINE'S ROOM - (NIGHT)

This is near the baseboard. It starts to ring.

J-9 CATHERINE - STILL LYING FACE DOWN ON HER BED

The 'phone continues to ring but she has fallen asleep. Suddenly she wakes up and reaches wildly for the telephone.

CATHERINE
(Into the telephone)
Hello? What? I can't hear you.
Can you speak a little louder, please.

J-10 McGINTY - AT THE TELEPHONE - IN A COUNTRY GAS STATION

Through the window we see the big car being filled with gasoline by the sleepy attendant. The chauffeur is out of the car. In the interior we see the shadows of the Boss and the Politician.

McGINTY
(Into the pay
telephone)
I can't talk too loud, honey, and
I've only got a minute anyway.

J-11 CATHERINE - AT THE TELEPHONE

CATHERINE
Dan! Where are you? How can you
be telephoning?

J-12 McGINTY - AT THE TELEPHONE

McGINTY
(Rapidly)
Listen, honey, you won't like what
I've done, see, but I only got one
life to live and I ain't goin' to
live it in the ice box...not a

11-28-39 (Continued)

J-12 (Cont'd)

McGINTY (Cont'd)
chance, they got me dead to rights. Now listen: I know you'd come along with me but that ain't right, see. You gotta think about the little guy and the little lady...It wouldn't do them no good to have their old man in stir or on the lam and the other kids razzin' 'em. So this is what you do, see. It's a little hard to say, honey, because I love ya and I love the kids and I always will, but you get George to get you a divorce, see, and then...

He makes a helpless gesture as Catherine begins to remonstrate, then interrupts:

McGINTY
Look, honey, I ain't got time to argue, see. There's some friends waitin' outside. It ain't as if we married like other people, though it isn't goin' to make it any easier, but we did it because we had a special reason, see, and that reason's all gone now.

The big engine roars out and the Politician leans out of the car and says:

THE POLITICIAN
Hey!

McGINTY
(Rapidly)
Look, honey, there's just one more thing. You know the dresser in my room? You pull out the left top drawer, see, and there's a key fastened between the drawers with court plaster. It's got a number on it and the name of the safe deposit company. They won't ask you any questions. It's a little something I held out on ya. It'll keep you goin' and put the kids through college...without selling magazines. So long, honey. I'm sorry it didn't work out, but you can't make a silk purse out of a pig's ear... Pat the little guy for me.

He starts to hang up.

11-28-39

J-13 CATHERINE - AT THE TELEPHONE

CATHERINE
(Almost hysterically)
But Dan...Don't talk like a fool.
Wherever you go...Dan!...Operator!

She jiggles the receiver.

CATHERINE
Oh, Dan.

She bursts out crying and buries her head in her arms.

J-14 THE BIG CAR AT THE GAS STATION

McGinty is just stepping into it. The door slams and the car roars away, scattering pebbles.

J-15 McGINTY, THE BOSS AND THE POLITICIAN - IN THE BACK SEAT OF THE CAR

McGINTY
(After a moment)
Thanks.

THE BOSS
(Roughly)
Why don't you shut up for a change?

McGinty gives him a look.

J-16 AUTOMOBILE SHOT - BEHIND THE BIG CAR

It pulls rapidly away from us. When it is almost gone -

DISSOLVE TO:

J-17 THE GIRL AND THOMPSON - PAST McGINTY - IN THE BANANA CAFE

The girl wipes a tear off her nose, then looks at McGinty quizzically.

THOMPSON
Why didn't he kill you?

McGINTY
I never could figure that out.

THE GIRL
(To Thompson)
I know why...Because he's a big
liar...about the whole thing.

11-28-39

J-18 McGINTY - PAST THE GIRL AND THOMPSON

McGINTY
(Laughing)
Okay, sister, you have it your way.
(Now he looks
at Thompson)
That'll be two bucks.

J-19 THE GIRL AND THOMPSON - PAST McGINTY

Still a little drunkenly Thompson puts two cartwheels on the bar.

THE GIRL
Why don't you go home, Tommy?

THOMPSON
All right.

THE GIRL
I mean really home where you belong. You ain't a tramp like him...
(She nods toward McGinty)
...anybody would be glad to get rid of. You could go home and in a little while everything would be forgotten...and there you are. All you need is a little courage.

J-20 McGINTY - PAST THOMPSON AND THE GIRL

McGINTY
(Chuckling)
That's all...but where's he goin' to find it?

J-21 THOMPSON AND THE GIRL - PAST McGINTY

THOMPSON
(Savagely)
Listen, you lousy hooligan, come on out here and I'll show you whether I got any courage or not.

THE GIRL
(Trying to subdue him)
Keep quiet, Tommy, quiet before he kill you.

11-28-39 (Continued)

J-21 (Cont'd)

THOMPSON
He isn't goin' to kill anybody,
I'll take one sock at him...

J-22 McGINTY - PAST THOMPSON AND THE GIRL

He is laughing cheerfully at the change in Thompson.

McGINTY
Come on, yellowbelly, you got
me all in a perspiration.

McGinty passes Thompson's gun over to the girl.

McGINTY
If you can keep him sore till
ship time tomorrow there may be
some hope...If he goes yellow
again give him his gun. NOW GET
OUTTA HERE!

J-23 THE POKER GAME

The Boss turns and looks toward McGinty.

McGINTY'S VOICE
Go on, get out!

The Boss throws down his cards and rises.

THE BOSS
He thinks he owns this place.

J-24 THOMPSON AND THE GIRL - WALKING AWAY FROM US DOWN THE BAR

McGinty follows them on the other side of the bar.

McGINTY
And if you're still here by noon
I'll beat the pulp outta you!
And if you're still here by the
next noon I'll beat you worse than
the first time and like that every
day, see.

The girl turns and looks at McGinty indignantly.
McGinty winks at her cheerfully, then roars.

McGINTY
Now get outta here!

The Boss walks INTO THE SHOT and grabs his arm.

11-28-39 (Continued)

J-24 (Cont'd)

THE BOSS
Since when are you chasing the customers?

McGINTY
Since when do you tell me where to get off?

THE BOSS
Listen, you cheapskate...

McGINTY
You listen, you fat fourflusher...

J-25 THE POLITICIAN DRESSED AS A WAITER

He is rapping on the bar with a coin.

THE POLITICIAN
(Wearily)
Come on, willya? Two Bombas and quit horsing around.

We hear the crack of a punch, the crash of a bottle and the tinkling of a mirror.

THE POLITICIAN
(Yelling across the room)
Hang on, boys, here we go again!

J-26 THE POKER TABLE

JARVIS
(Pushing back his eyeshade)
Peace, gentlemen, peace be with you.

LOUIE
(Flopping into a chair and INTO THE SHOT)
What's the use?

He removes his toothpick, examines the end of it, then looks over at the fight and picks his teeth peacefully.

FADE OUT:

THE END

Christmas in July

Christmas in July (1940) bridges a longer gap in Sturges's development as a writer than any of his other films. It was based upon his unproduced play of 1931, *A Cup of Coffee,* subtitled "An Alleged Comedy in Three Acts."[1] The biographical context in which the play was written is recounted in the Introduction: Sturges's play *Recapture* had opened in January 1930 and closed the next month; *The Well of Romance,* in which he had invested all his available money, had opened and closed in November 1930; his mother had died in April 1931; and his wife Eleanor had left him to study in Paris in June of that year. *Strictly Dishonorable* had opened in September 1929 and was still playing in June 1931, but its run was drawing to a close. Around this time, Sturges wrote a draft of a bedroom farce, which he called *Unfaithfully Yours,* and then turned to *A Cup of Coffee,* a comedy about a coffee salesman, James Macdonald, who wins a slogan contest sponsored by a rival company. Jimmy's affection for the company secretary, Tulip, provides the romance, and the blusterings of the firm's founder and two sons provide some characteristic Sturges satire of business.

We know exactly when Sturges began *A Cup of Coffee* and, to some degree, what he was feeling while writing it because of his "odd autobiographical habit" (James Joyce's phrase), which crops up in odd places. Here, for example, is a character list and action outline like no other.

CHARACTERS

1.	Ephraim Baxter	The founder of the firm
2.	Oliver Baxter	His son
3.	J. Bloodgood Baxter	His other son
4.	Julius Snaith	His male nurse
5.	Lomax Whortleberry	His bookkeeper
6.	Tulip Jones	His secretary
7.	James Macdonald	His youngest salesman
8.	Mr. Rasmussen	From Maxwell House
9.	John the Whitewing	From outside

10. Postman
11. Sign Painter
12. The Youth

ACT I

11:30 in the morning of October 16th, 1931. The scene is laid on the ground floor of the small wholesale coffee house of E. BAXTER & SONS, Coffee merchants, manufacturers of BAXTER'S BEST . . . "You'll like it!"

Upstage center hangs a large sliding door with a small door in it. The big door will accommodate a full sized two horse truck. The warehouse floor level is about 30 inches above the stage everywhere except for a sort of channel, the width of the door, coming straight down stage for the truck to back into and a clear space full across stage about seven feet deep. Two inclined runways lead from the platforms down to the stage. To Hell with all this anyway: See the plan.

ACT II

The interior of an old-fashioned office with a pot-bellied stove. Victorian furniture and spitoons. 2 o'clock that afternoon.

ACT III

Same as Act I. It is now five o'clock less a few minutes. The whistles will blow at five and pretty soon my play will be ended . . . except that it isn't even written yet. This page and a few pencilled notes being the sum total of my labor up 'til now, 3 A.M., June 23rd, 1931. If I think of a good title this will be a fairly successful play. Maybe six months. It will be carefully constructed, will appeal to the simplest emotions and be very conscientiously (?) written. It will not be a smash because it is not going to SHOCK either the proprieties or the sense of justice. All great plays are SHOCKERS.

No less surprising to a reader of *A Cup of Coffee* is Sturges's description of his main character's entrance, late in Act I.

JIMMY MACDONALD

(steps in. In his right hand he carries the sort of brief case preferred by gentlemen who travel in coffee and under his left arm he carries a small, very pink, and very cheap portable phonograph. TULIP doesn't hear him, goes back to the shelf again to get some napkins and some spoons which she polishes on the napkins and he, seizing the opportunity, opens the portable phonograph, starts the disc spinning and blatantly it begins to play the popular air of the moment, whatever that is by the time this play goes into rehearsal if it ever gets written, and if it's ever accepted for production, because God knows I'm through putting money in my own turkeys. So help me.

The parenthesis in which this paragraph is lodged is not closed and, one supposes, could not be.

We know, then, that *A Cup of Coffee* was begun on June 22, 1931, or early on June 23. A handwritten note on the last page of Act I tells us that it was finished on July 9 and had a reading time of forty-five minutes. A similar note at the end of Act II indicates that it was completed on July 31 and had a reading time of forty-three and one-half minutes. There is no note at the end of Act III, the shortest of the three, but Sturges had apparently finished it by mid-August. He wrote to his father on September 9:

> I have been working very hard and have completed *Consider the Lily*. I sent out the other play, *A Cup of Coffee*, but I can't say it caused any particular stir as no one has yet come forth who wanted to produce it. However, that doesn't really matter because it was an excellent exercise in writing and in discipline. I worked very hard on it and dug up so many ideas that by the time I came to *Consider the Lily* I was in full swing. The latter play took sixteen days to write and has "stood on his ear" everyone who has read it.[2]

Consider the Lily became *Child of Manhattan* and opened in March 1932 to become Sturges's third straight flop, ending his Broadway career and, in effect, sending him to Hollywood. In 1933 he wrote *The Power and the Glory*, which was filmed immediately, and *The Vagrant*, which was not. *A Cup of Coffee* and *The Vagrant*, perpetually unsalable properties, became Sturges's principal "trunk items." They were trotted out again and again in his various attempts to regain independence as a screenwriter—lost when *The Power and the Glory* failed—and to direct.

The next year, Sturges showed *A Cup of Coffee* to Universal producer Henry Henigson, for whom he was working on *The Good Fairy* (1934). Henigson advocated that Universal make the film and that Sturges direct it. Evidently heartened, Sturges wrote to Charles Abramson on June 15, 1934:

> Things are going pretty well here and with a little luck I should be all right. You always said I would get something sooner or later for the effort I put into *A Cup of Coffee*, and you seem to be right as Universal have already paid me $4000 on account with $5000 to come when the script is finished and $6000 to come for directing it, not counting the chance it gives me to direct, which is worth a great deal of money.[3]

However, work on *The Good Fairy* (1934) occupied Sturges until the end of 1934. Director William Wyler, with whom Sturges had become good friends, wanted him on the set for rewrites and as dialogue director. Thus *A Cup of Coffee* was postponed, and before Sturges could revive the project, he was asked to improve the script for *Diamond Jim* (1935), for which he characteristically wrote an entirely new screenplay.[4] Henigson left Universal to go to Paramount in April 1935, and with his departure plans to film *A Cup of Coffee* were dropped. But in September 1936, Sturges too signed with Paramount. Henigson was still enthusiastic about *A Cup of Coffee* but assigned Sturges to *Hotel Haywire* (1937), a film of his that was in trouble. After that, Sturges was assigned to Arthur Hornblow, Jr., for *Easy Living* (1937), then to Albert Lewin for *Two Bad Hats*—which ultimately became *The Lady Eve* (1941)—and *Remember the Night* (1940). Within the next few years, Henigson, Hornblow, and Lewin all left Paramount, leaving production chief William LeBaron to deal with Sturges's demands to direct.

In early January 1940, LeBaron had seen enough of *The Great McGinty*, still in production, to authorize another film. He asked what Sturges wanted to do, and the answer was *A Cup of Coffee*. The rights were bought from Universal for little more than the $6000 it had paid for it in 1934.[5] When the shooting and editing of *The Great McGinty* were finished, Sturges rewrote his 1931 play for the screen—a virtual transformation. Having begun in mid-February, he finished a complete draft by May 9, 1940, and a revised script, the one printed below, by May 23. Both bore the title *The New Yorkers*. Shooting began on June 3 and was completed in twenty-seven days. Editing continued through July, and the film was released in November 1940 as *Christmas in July*.

A Cup of Coffee takes place entirely at E. Baxter & Sons, a New York coffee company, in the course of one working day. There are three continuous acts and only two sets, one the interior of an office, the other showing the same office seen from the outside. (Sturges kept the scale of the play modest to increase its chances for production.) The play begins with a scene—a kind of surrealist minstrel show—between Julius, who is black, and Mr. Whortleberry, the firm's nervous Scottish bookkeeper. Their exchange is broken up harshly by J. Bloodgood Baxter while his milder brother Oliver attempts to mediate. It is only with the brothers' discussion of the company's failure to advertise (on page 11) and Jimmy's entrance (on page 14) that the plot we recognize from *Christmas in July* is set in motion.

Jimmy has been selling Baxter coffee for only a few weeks, but he and Tulip, a secretary for the firm, have struck up a romance. She wants to get married, but Jimmy thinks they are too poor. "What chance has a fellow got if he marries? For that matter, what chance has the girl got? I mean, unless they're rich." The play's Jimmy thinks first of himself and seems leery of marriage; the film's Jimmy genuinely wants to marry Betty, Tulip's name in the film, from the first, but thinks they are too poor to make a go of it.

Even though Jimmy has had a good morning, he is in an ill humor when he enters. He then makes a phone call to a customer that reveals his sales technique: he plays up how bad the times are, how badly he is doing, and how little business the customer's competitors are doing. The last cheers up the customer, who then places an order for coffee. Tulip dubs this method "ten cents worth of purple crepe," and she contrasts it favorably to the Horatio Alger techniques of the day—the "grip that gets 'em," the "voice that vibrates," and the "smile that stimulates."

Next, Jimmy tells Tulip about his entry in the Maxwell House new slogan contest: "If you can't sleep at night, it isn't the coffee, it's the bunk." There follows some humorous byplay about the slogan, though not as much as in the film. Tulip proposes to send out for lunch, and Jimmy agrees to stay. They are joined by Julius, Mr. Whortleberry, and the aged founder of the company, Ephraim Baxter, whom Tulip urges to listen to Jimmy's ideas about the company but who keeps falling asleep. In the midst of all this Jimmy puts a record on the phonograph he had bought for Tulip. Bloodgood comes in and is furious to find a party going on in the office; he fires Tulip because she is the owner of the phonograph. Jimmy says that he bought the machine and then insults Bloodgood, who reinstates Tulip and fires him. A messenger enters at this moment and announces that Jimmy has won the Maxwell House $25,000 prize. He and Tulip embrace as the curtain falls.

Act II opens in Bloodgood's office. He and Oliver are bickering over who is at fault for having dismissed Jimmy while a sign painter puts Jimmy's name on the door of the adjacent office. Since the Maxwell House prize includes a two-year job in sales promotion, they have decided to offer Jimmy $100 a week to stay at Baxter Brothers as sales promotion manager and thereby get free publicity from his prize. Their discussion continues until Tulip returns from lunch (on page 16), and when Jimmy returns (on page 21), they offer him the job. Act II, like Act I, takes a long time to crank up and then ends with a bang. Jimmy vacillates about the offer, but in the course of the discussion he suggests a new slogan for Baxter's—"The blueblood coffee, it's bred in the bean." Everyone is awestruck at the slogan, and Jimmy agrees to stay at Baxter's. He then calls Mrs. Schwartz, who has the only telephone in his apartment house, and asks to speak to his mother, who weeps at hearing his good news. Jimmy tells Tulip that nothing now prevents their marriage. She tells him she wants a more romantic proposal, he complies, and she accepts. Just then there enters a representative from Maxwell House, who tells Jimmy, after some build-up, that the true winner of the contest was a James Macdonald of Utica, New York. Jimmy walks out of the office in a daze as the curtain falls.

Act III begins at close to five o'clock the same day. Jimmy's new office, his contract, the Baxter brothers, and the entire staff await him, but Jimmy is not there. He enters quietly and talks with Julius, then with Mr. Whortleberry, who has paid for the packages that Jimmy had had sent when he was out earlier—presents for everyone in the office. When Bloodgood presents his contract, Jimmy confesses that he has not won the contest. (Sturges has penciled in a stage direction here—"The five o'clock whistle five o'clock whistles," with a little drawing of a whistle blowing over the final "s.") Bloodgood's offer is withdrawn, and the brothers retire to consider whether or not to offer Jimmy his old job back. Jimmy tells Tulip that he loves her but that they are back where they started. Marriage is again impossible because, for one thing, he will have to pay for the $227.50 worth of presents he has bought out of his salary.

Old Ephraim emerges "from the darkness," and Tulip urges him to take up Jimmy's cause. He is agreeable but starts to fall asleep, so Tulip sends Jimmy out for a cup of coffee to perk him up. Rousing himself, the old man insists that Jimmy get his contract after all, but Bloodgood threatens to resign if he does. On the last full page of the script, Tulip emotionally proposes a compromise: Jimmy gets the job but without the contract—he will have to prove himself to keep it. At this point the Maxwell House representative of Act II returns with the news that Jimmy has won the contest after all, and the final curtain falls.

There were, as mentioned, two versions of the screenplay that became *Christmas in July,* both called *The New Yorkers.* The May 23 script makes many small changes in the dialogue and action of its May 9 predecessor but not in its structure. Thus, for purposes of simplification, all further references to *The New Yorkers* will have to do with the May 23 screenplay, the one printed below.

Besides its refinement of the May 9 script, the May 23 version also responds to a May 13 "interoffice communication" to Sturges from Luigi Luraschi, Paramount's man in charge of censorship. The letter summarizes "different points" raised by the Hays Office regarding the May 9 script, almost entirely matters of language. The words "bum" and "punk" will never get by the British censors; the word "God" must be removed from two lines of dialogue; "mouthings" which suggest "hell" or "damn" must be avoided; and the line "Yeah, the old b . . ." "should be completed inoffensively." Sturges incorporated the majority of the urged changes in the May 23 script; others that he carried over were dropped at some later point because they do not appear in the film. Sturges did hold out successfully for jury member Bildocker's line, "It stinks," for that character says it twice in the film. (Luraschi admits in his letter: "If it is not used too often, the Censor Boards are inclined to pass it nowadays.")

In addition to censorship points, there were also "legal points," having to do in this case with Sturges's use of the name "Parkerhouse" for the coffee company that sponsors the slogan contest. The Paramount attorney consulted by Luraschi suggested "a play on the word 'Parker' which would retain the benefit of suggesting the title, yet not actually using the word." The May 23 script retains "Parker House" and "Dr. Parker," but the film, of course, changes these to "Maxford House" and "Dr. Maxford." Since the company's old slogan is "Grand to the last gulp," the suggestion of Maxwell House is, in any case, more appropriate. (To avoid needless confusion, we will refer to Maxford House and Dr. Maxford, even when speaking of the *The New Yorkers.)*

As was his usual practice, Sturges made important changes in the script in the process of shooting *Christmas in July*—more than in the May 23 rewrite. We mention some of the most notable of these below.

The script *The New Yorkers,* printed here, retains little more than *A Cup of Coffee*'s outline of events. A young man falsely believes that he has won a slogan contest, on which basis he gets a promotion and a raise and plans to marry. When the truth is revealed, he loses everything, but his fiancée negotiates a compromise whereby he will get a chance to prove himself without guarantees, whereupon it is revealed that he has won the contest after all. A number of the surrounding circumstances of the play's plot are also retained, among them the rival coffee companies, the main character's name, and the slogan itself: "If you can't sleep at night, it isn't the coffee, it's the bunk." The changes that were made from play to screenplay and film are, most important, the character of Jimmy, the events of the plot and their order, and the themes that derive from these elements.

Jimmy is the most important character in *A Cup of Coffee;* the others are sheer stereotypes. He is not, however, a consistent figure. In Act I, at least, he is something of a 1920s wise guy, bearing gimcracks, such as his cheap phono-

Sturges directing Dick Powell and Ellen Drew–
Jimmy gets the phony telegram in CHRISTMAS IN JULY.

graph when he enters, and boasting of his smart ways to con customers. He appears to want no part of marriage at this point—his pleading poverty seems a dodge. His young salesman's cynicism appears genuine and may be abiding. With booze and further disappointments in work and love, he could become a Eugene O'Neill character. When he hits it big, however, he suddenly becomes a sweet guy—he buys presents for everyone in the office and wants to marry Tulip immediately. And he remains sweet even when he loses everything. Here O'Neill gives way to Horatio Alger or, more correctly, to a kind of parody-critique of the Alger stories.

The play pursues its themes, none too steadily, largely through Jimmy's dialogue. For instance, when he first enters, Jimmy tells Tulip somewhat despondently:

> Well, it won't be long now, I guess . . . With things going the way they are now, pretty soon there'll be a sort of general bankruptcy and then the working man will come into his own.

"You mean a revolution?" asks Tulip. Jimmy replies:

> No . . . uh . . . just a sort of a readjustment . . . of course I haven't got it all figured out yet.

About the contest, Jimmy says later: "Aw, I won't win it. These contests are all fixed anyway," an expression of cynicism the film's Jimmy would never allow himself. Indeed, in the film when Betty complains that there were boxes under the peanuts in a "How many peanuts in the window?" contest, Jimmy says: "They had a right to do that" (page 11).

When Jimmy spouts his ideas to the assembled company in Act II of the play, he suggests a Baxter ad parodying the old Maxwell House slogan. Oliver calls this unfair competition, and Jimmy responds:

> For myself, I don't care for these namby-pamby methods that they call fair competition. As a matter of fact, Mr. Baxter, every great fortune in this country was founded with methods that the word "unfair" doesn't begin to describe. Big business was a hard game and a man's game. Look at Johnny Rockefeller, the elder Morgan, Hill, Fisk, Vanderbilt, Astor, and the rest of them—what a fine upstanding bunch of pirates those babies were!

Having hinted at revolutionism in Act I, in Act II Jimmy tells of his enthusiasm for the rampaging capitalism of the robber baron era. He does this, it is true, in utterly cynical terms; capitalism is not idealized as it is by the new conservatives of our day. Yet another contradiction is that Sturges places Jimmy's speech in the context of a Horatio Alger scene. The aged founder of the company responds spiritedly to the young man's words.

> EPHRAIM BAXTER
> Hooray! That's the way I like to hear a fellow talk. Listen, Oliver, if you knew what I did to get a start in this business, you couldn't sleep at night.
>
> OLIVER
> Don't tell me.
>
> EPHRAIM BAXTER
> I won't. Now go on, Jimmy.

Jimmy then walks up and down, thinking out loud about a new Baxter Brothers' slogan.

> Baxter's Best . . . Who are the best people? . . . the high-bred people? . . . the aristocrats? . . . AH! Baxter's Best, The Blueblood Coffee . . . It's Bred in the Bean.

This wows the Baxters, father and sons, although the latter drop Jimmy when they find he did not win the contest. Ephraim stands by Jimmy, but he cannot fulfill his Horatio Alger role because he no longer controls the company. Yet his championing of Jimmy against his sons leads to the compromise of Act III that will give Jimmy his chance to prove himself. In posing a de facto alliance between the rapacious old capitalist and the ambitious young upstart, against the inherited wealth and the stuffiness of the second generation, *A Cup of Coffee* follows Philip Barry's successful *Holiday* (1927).

In both the script and the film Jimmy accepts and identifies with the world as it is. All he wants is a way into that world, and since that seems impossible, he is despondent. Unlike the Jimmy in the play, he is not concerned with the world as it should be (revolution) or as it was in the era of early capitalism. That era, in any case, has disappeared without a trace by the time of *Christmas in July.* Its Mr. Baxter is resolutely of the second generation; in fact he refers to having inherited his father's money. There is no Ephraim Baxter in the film to champion the young man for his ideas and spirit alone. The film's Baxter wants "commercial insurance," here in the form of a won slogan contest.

The play attempts to speak its themes through explicit dialogue. The film dramatizes its themes by placing actions first and character response to them second. In the play revelatory speeches tend to pile on top of one another, only indirectly proceeding from prior events and leading to subsequent events. Jimmy's speeches and those by others in the film are not gratuitous unburdenings; they are wrenched out of the characters by the pressure of specific circumstances.

The script and film place less emphasis on Jimmy's ideas than on his situation and his likely prospects. In both the script and film Jimmy is a lowly clerk who walks to his desk with droves of others and sits in a long row of desks; he also wears a uniform office coat, just like all the other anonymous clerks. While allegedly bubbling with ideas, Jimmy is sincere and polite with everyone—even when his contest dreams are dashed. At the same time he is, like most of the characters in the film, beaten down, without plausible hopes—only fantastic ones. It is the late depression, and everyone seems ground down by years of struggling; those who have jobs cling to them. No one in this film would find the 1933 song "We're in the Money" amusing; the bravado of the early depression is long over.

Sturges's use of Dick Powell for the film's Jimmy is uncannily right, as his casting often is; indeed, it is an aspect of the film's structure. Powell brings with him the Horatio Alger aura of his thirties parts, especially in musicals. Ever the bouncy, ineffably confident juvenile lead, he always got the job, got the girl, and was a big hit in the show. Sturges places this familiar figure in a different kind of story, set in a different era. Powell himself is older in 1940 and slower—he doesn't bounce any more, and he seems not completely sure of himself, just as Jimmy is unsure that his dreams will be realized. Powell was, in fact, at a tentative point in his career, no longer the fresh, young singer, not yet the middle-aged private detective and director. An aging young man with boyish dreams fits perfectly into Sturges's late-depression world of long-deferred hope.

To turn from character to narrative construction, *The New Yorker* has six sequences: A, B, C, D, E, and F. In contrast to the play's three continuous acts in two sets, the film takes place in many locales, with much cutting back and forth among them. It also has many distinct time intervals, even though its overall time span, from evening of one day to evening of the next, is only slightly longer than the play's.

The script's Sequence A, which does not appear in the play, takes place in Jimmy and Betty's neighborhood on the night before the single working day that comprises Sequences B through F. In it, Jimmy and Betty listen to the radio program that will announce the winners of the slogan contest. There is a cut to the backstage conflicts at Maxford House that are preventing the selection of a winner, and this is followed by a long dialogue scene between Jimmy and Betty. Sequence B corresponds to the play's Act I and all but the very end of Act II. In that sequence Jimmy "learns" (through a phony telegram sent by office tricksters) that he has won the slogan contest, as a result of which Mr. Baxter listens to his ideas, offers him a promotion, a raise, and a secretary, and Jimmy plans to marry Betty.

Sequences C, D, and E present events that do not appear in the play. In Sequence C, a confused Dr. Maxford gives Jimmy the contest winner's check that he claims, then dismisses him and tries to reach the previously deadlocked jury for an explanation. Sequence D takes place at Schindel Brothers department store—where Jimmy and Betty buy a wedding ring, a davenport for Jimmy's mother, and presents for everyone in the neighborhood—and concludes in a cab on the couple's way home. Sequence E is the street festival in which the children and adults of Jimmy and Betty's neighborhood enjoy their presents. A cutback to Maxford shows him learning that Jimmy has not won the contest. Mr. Schindel arrives and demands the return of his merchandise, and he is followed by Maxford, who tricks Jimmy into returning the check and tears it up. The office tricksters come by and explain the phony telegram. Sequence F corresponds to Act III of the play. Mr. Baxter learns the truth and withdraws his offers to Jimmy, but Betty's plea wins Jimmy a chance to prove himself, and, at the last, it turns out that he has won the contest after all.

Sturges has essentially opened up a gap between the play's Acts II and III, into which he drops Sequences C, D, and E. This means that the revelation that closes Act II—that Jimmy has not won the contest—is postponed by the film for three sequences, which amount to nearly half the film. It is that revelation, of course, in both the play and the film that leads directly to the last act or sequence. Thus, to forestall the news that Jimmy has not won the contest is to forestall the ending of the film.

To postpone Jimmy's discovery that he has not won the contest is also to prolong his illusionary state, and at its ripest point—when Jimmy has won not only the contest but a new job, a raise, an office, a secretary, and marriage to Betty. The film strings Jimmy along for an extended period wherein, it is true, he proves himself by his loyalty to Betty, his generosity to his neighbors, and so on. The play's audience knows only what Jimmy knows and at the exact time that he knows it; it shares his adventures—victory, defeat, modified victory—on the same basis that he lives them. The film's audience, however, knows even before Jimmy receives it about the phony telegram sent by the office tricksters—their later reactions to the snowballing effects of their gag become one more element in the film's complex drama. Audience experience is thus split—the viewer simultaneously knows that Jimmy is heading for a fall and identifies with his illusion-based exultation. This excruciating tension, expertly prolonged and intensified by Sturges, carries Jimmy and Betty's dreams and the audience's pleasure/unpleasure to their furthest extent.

This makes *Christmas in July,* among other things, a precursor of Sturges's later *Hail the Conquering Hero,* in which Woodrow's (and the audience's) dreams of heroism are carried to their limits and beyond—the fantasy gets out of hand even as it is occurring. There too the dreaded exposure, which is more ignominious than Jimmy's loss of the contest and reversion to clerkhood, is postponed by a series of increasingly manic scenes. (Woodrow, unlike Jimmy,

Three vaudevillians–Sturges balances a stick on his cane as Ellen Drew and Ernest Truex look on during the shooting of CHRISTMAS IN JULY.

knows that he is involved in a falsehood, which makes his burden of guilt and fear—and the audience's—far greater.)

Delusions sustained until the end of the play are, of course, a trope of classical comedy, but Sturges adds a dimension of anxiety to the classical formula. We know, for instance, that Rosalind's impersonation of a boy will end at some point in *As You Like It,* but there is no dread at the coming revelation, no fear that Rosalind's charade will suddenly collapse or be exposed. Sturges's adaptation of the classical formula and the audience participation it implies perhaps resemble the modern notion of mania depression. The inevitable fall into depression is postponed as long as possible, and, in anticipation of this plunge, to forestall and supplant it in advance, the subject enters a spiraling state of increasingly frantic actions and/or mental activity. In *Christmas in July* and *Hail the Conquering Hero,* in any case, the audience's combined enjoyment and dread provide a guilty, anxious pleasure that is not in the least classical.

A closer look at the script and film, sequence by sequence, will reveal further the excellence of its construction and the intricacies of its themes.

The play's Jimmy does not mention the slogan contest until page 19 of Act I; Sequence A of the script poses it immediately—the sequence begins with the Maxford House radio program that will announce the winner. Of course, there can be no contest winner at this point or there would be no film, so Sturges gives us an aborted awards announcement and makes up conflicts within Maxford House to explain it. Never mind whether a large corporation would go on the air without the names of the winners, whether the announcer and the president of the company would not know that the jury was deadlocked, and whether indeed a contest jury would have to decide a winner unanimously, as though it were a criminal case. The logic of comic drama need not be referential; it need only be consistent—and in *The New Yorkers* it is. Everything follows from a few premises: the postponed announcement and Jimmy's desperation to win increase his preoccupation with the contest. This sets him up for the telegram ruse, just as his overanxious phoning from work tells his practical-joking office mates where he is vulnerable. The conflicts within the Maxford House organization also explain why Jimmy later gets his check even though he has not won—Maxford is so eager to upbraid Bildocker for not telling him of the alleged decision that he hands Jimmy the check and hurries him out of his office.

The script indicates a cut from the sign-off of the radio program to Jimmy (the Boy) and Betty (the Girl) listening to it on "a cheap little radio—on the parapet of a roof." Their ensuing exchange—about the contest, about the difficulty of marriage on their small salaries, etc.—takes up twelve script pages and is perhaps Sturges's finest achievement in sustained dialogue to that time. Jimmy and Betty ramble from topic to topic and are frequently irritated with one another. Both the flavor of their interaction and the essential points of their background, characters, and dreams are effectively conveyed. Brief exchanges with Jimmy's mother, Mrs. MacDonald, and with Mr. Zimmerman, a neighbor attempting to sleep, set up the return to the neighborhood in Sequence E.

The film makes a small but crucial change in the order of events of Sequence A. It begins with Jimmy and Betty listening to the radio on their roof, then cuts to the Maxford House scenes when the Maxford House program comes on the air. Sturges invented some characteristic if inconsequential dialogue for this brief opening—Betty reads an ad for a versatile one-room apartment that allows a young couple to live cheaply; Jimmy questions the workability of the scheme and asks: "Who wants to live cheaply?" They stop talking and listen to the program, after which their dialogue proceeds as the script indicates (pages 9–20). What Jimmy and Betty say in their brief opening is far less important than the fact that they begin the film. They are thus made the center of the film, in relation to whom all subsequently introduced forces and characters are to be evaluated and understood. To pick them up after the contest announcement is to make them a function of it, rather than the contest a function of their situation. Dramatically speaking, introducing Jimmy and Betty after the contest is anticlimactic after the fanfare, the aborted awards announcement, and the eruption of conflicts within Maxford House—particularly since their conversation is subdued, even somewhat depressed. Seeing Jimmy and Betty first, the viewer, at least unconsciously, awaits their reaction to the contest news. The script also calls for a "montage of various types listening to radios" (page 2), among whom, in the film, is a straw-hatted Sturges getting a shoeshine. In the script, this widens the focus of the contest—and of the film-to-be—without yet including Jimmy and Betty. The film's revised opening establishes them at the center first and then widens the focus.

The romance between Jimmy and Betty is a settled one, presumably of long duration, since we see them argue for twelve pages and barely peck at scene's end. A long-deferred sexual fulfillment may be suggested by the scene, accounting in part for Jimmy's irritability and adding a sexual dimension to his contest hopes and (false) victory—it is his potency too that he wants to win, does win, and loses. This is made more poignant because Betty, despite their poverty, is ready and willing to get married. Jimmy has to convince her of their need for more money before marrying, which seems to increase his frustration. Her acceptance of him seems to irritate him, perhaps because he cannot accept himself. To its credit, the film makes this a social point rather than a psychological one—there is nothing wrong with Jimmy that a better salary would not cure, and indeed winning the prize seems to make everything all right.

Sequence B begins with a breakfast scene between Jimmy, dressed in a dark suit for work, and his mother. We have seen her leaning out a window the night before, and that glimpse has prepared us for this scene, just as this scene prepares us for Jimmy's telephone call to her later in Sequence B and for Jimmy and Betty's return to the neighborhood in Sequence E. Mrs. MacDonald speaks in a decided Irish brogue and holds some vaguely Irish superstitions—"What falls to the floor comes to the door" (when Jimmy drops a quarter) and "Jimmy . . . There's money in your cup." Dr. Maxford later mentions his Scot-

Sturges's friend Jose Iturbi visits the set—probably that of CHRISTMAS IN JULY.

tish grandmother to Jimmy and on another occasion refers to him as McTavish, a remnant of Ephraim Baxter's series of Scottish misnomers for Jimmy in the play. This unresolved ethnic confusion reinforces Jimmy's doubtful status as an anonymous urban clerk. His mother's superstitions are also manifestations of a generalized folklore of capitalism, a pervasive mythology of luck as the key to success or in any case as the poor person's only chance to rise.[6] (The other premise of the folklore—that hard work results in success—is opposed to this one, but the contradiction allows the unsuccessful person to vacillate perpetually between the two premises.) The cup Mrs. MacDonald sees money in, by the way, is a cup of coffee. Sturges cuts to a close-up of the cup ("The surface is covered with bubbles" [page 23])—twenty-six years later Godard did the same thing in *Two or Three Things I Know About Her* (1966)—and dissolves from that shot to one of the Baxter Brothers' coffee sign in front of Jimmy's building. It is a nice irony that Mrs. MacDonald's superstitions and intuitions seem to be wrong; we're used to signs that come true in films of all eras. Here they serve only to set Jimmy up for the phony telegram and to set the audience up for the enjoyment of fantasies that it knows are ill-gotten but would like to think inevitable—the deserving young person will succeed, the young couple in love will prosper, etc.

At Baxter Brothers, Tom, Dick, and Harry, Jimmy's office mates, talk of gags they have pulled in the past as they put on their office coats. Pranks seem to be their protest against their faceless, automaton-like work, just as contests are for Jimmy. (The film's Baxter Brothers is a vastly larger concern than the play's, and its work space is conceived visually along the lines of *The Crowd,* King Vidor's 1928 study of urban mechanization and anonymity.) Still dressed in his suit, Jimmy calls Maxford House to find out if there is a winner in the slogan contest—it is as though he is forestalling the anonymity of his office coat. Tom, Dick, and Harry overhear and set about concocting their phony telegram.

Once at his desk, Jimmy is called to see Mr. Waterbury, the office manager. Jimmy's sums have been off, and, to find out why, Waterbury runs through the list of usual afflictions: drink, playing the races, a broken heart, henpecking at home, or just incompetence? The scene as a whole suggests that aspiring to higher things may jeopardize what one already has, that downward mobility is at least as likely under capitalism as upward mobility. When Jimmy admits to preoccupation with the Maxford House contest, Waterbury makes a speech, crucial to the film's themes, about his own realization one day that he would never have $25,000: "You see, ambition is all right if it works, but no system could be right where only half of one percent were successes and all the rest were failures. That wouldn't be right. I'm not a failure, I'm a success, and so are you, if you earn your own living and pay your bills and look the world in the eye" (page 28).

Waterbury's formula accurately states a contradiction, then denies it with an assertion ("I'm a success"), but he changes his definition of "success" between his major premise and his conclusion in order to avoid the implication, logically necessary, that the system is not right. He also thereby suppresses his minor premise that he and millions like him are not successes by prevailing standards. Through Waterbury's "illogic," Sturges brilliantly exposes a sociohistorical logic: where the integrity of the personality depends upon imposed, unattainable social values—here, financial success—psychological mechanisms such as denial and foreclosure may be activated, possibly on a mass scale.[7]

Jimmy finds the phony telegram when he comes out of Waterbury's office, an instance of what might be called Sturges's casual dramatic skill—his careful coordination of the small elements of the drama as well as the large ones. Jimmy's absence from his desk is necessary for the telegram to appear, just as the scene with Waterbury stresses his preoccupation with the contest. That scene also poses the issue of acceptance of one's lot versus striving for something better, which is correlated in the film with the questions that preoccupy Jimmy: Are my ideas good? Am I average or am I special? Will I succeed or am I daydreaming?

When Jimmy opens the telegram, he "lets out a war whoop," gets up on his desk to tell the rest of the office, and then calls his mother. There is a cut to Mrs. Schwartz, who answers the telephone, and another to Mrs. MacDonald, who says: "You're not hurt?" After this, the scene plays as it would have on the stage, the camera holding on Jimmy without further cuts to Mrs. MacDonald. The call is interrupted by Mr. Baxter's entry on the scene—Jimmy hangs up without having said good-bye to his mother. This is a small point, but a revealing one—Sturges's dramatic build-ups pile climax on climax in a way that sweeps the audience along.

Baxter is furious at the commotion in the office and fires Jimmy before he has a chance to explain. In the film Baxter is a combination of the play's two brothers and, indeed, of their temperaments. He is by turns savage like Bloodgood and gentle like Oliver. In the play, Jimmy is fired before he gets the contest news; in the film he gets the contest news and then is fired, but only briefly, because Baxter is impressed with Jimmy's victory and, once he has heard his ideas, offers him a promotion, raise, office, and secretary. It is Waterbury who intercedes with the angry Baxter and conveys the news that Jimmy has won the contest. He says: "These children are part of your family, Mr. Baxter, and anything that happens to them is happening to you" (page 36). Baxter clearly does not feel this way. Is Waterbury idealizing management-employee relations at the firm out of delusion, or is he citing a moral principle that should, but does not, govern those relations? (This conflation—and confusion—of what is and what ought to be is an abiding tendency of one strand of American idealism, ultimately religious.)

The scenes that follow between Jimmy, Baxter, and the advertising department play like the Alger stories they parody. Jimmy has been down to the department "about a thousand times" (persistence), but only now is everyone dazzled by his ideas (success). What sustains the parody is our awareness that it's all based on a mistaken premise, and, as the script later makes clear, Baxter, his staff, and indeed the world do not really believe in ideas but only in success. Jimmy and Betty sail out of the office to pick up his check from Maxford House and, as Baxter suggests, to visit a jewelry store for a wedding ring.

Sequence C switches to Maxford House as Maxford and his announcer discuss the debacle of the night before, for which they hold the contest jury responsible. Their conversation reminds the audience of the earlier scene, reintroduces its characters in a less formal setting, and makes it clear that a winner has not been selected. Jimmy's claim to be the winner fits right into Maxford's fulminations against the jury because he assumes they have chosen and notified a winner without telling him, and that gives him something more to complain about. He hurries Jimmy out of his office as soon as he gives him the check because he can't wait to get Bildocker on the intercom.

At this point the film departs from the script. The film ends Sequence C with C-11 (page 53), a shot of Maxford irate that Bildocker is not in his office. The script includes an additional scene in the jury room (C-12), which shows that Bildocker is, in fact, still there, that the jury is still deadlocked, and that it is Bildocker who is holding out against the other eleven jurors. The film places this scene just before E-18 (page 74), Maxford's second attempt to reach Bildocker, following which he goes to the jury room himself (E-19) to find out. This arrangement has the advantage of moving the action from Jimmy's receiving the check directly to Sequence D at the department store, with only a brief glimpse of Maxford's pique at Bildocker and his first attempt to reach him. The scene in the jury room, which shows the ongoing deadlock and identifies Bildocker as its cause, would have been anticlimactic at the end of Sequence C. Placing it there would also have made it too remote from the scene in which Maxford goes to the jury room himself twenty-two script pages later. The film's placement of these elements solves both problems and means also that the first cut away from the street festival in Sequence E is to the jury still deadlocked rather than to an irate Maxford. This is a more subtle and dramatic arrangement—we see the cause of Maxford's pique first and watch it build, rather than beginning with his pique full-blown. (The film also changes the slogan preferred by the majority of the jury from "Parker's Peps the Palate" to "Maxford's—Magnificent and Mellow." Bildocker's "It's putrid" no longer continues the "p" alliteration of the first slogan, but it is more surprising for that reason and applies even better to the mediocrity of the second slogan than to the outright badness of the first. The first slogan is a joke in itself, the second a good setup for the funnier gag that follows it, which also illuminates Bildocker's character.)

Sequence D takes place in Schindel Brothers department store and introduces a number of new characters—Mr. Hillbeiner, the jewelry salesman; Mr. Schmidt, the furniture salesman; and, above all, Mr. Schindel, played by Alexander Carr, whom Sturges sought for the part.[8] Jimmy and Betty's list of the neighbors to buy presents for grows, giving way to the decision to "just work down one side of the street and then up the other . . . that way we won't forget anybody" (page 61). Their cab ride to the neighborhood, loaded down with presents, recalls their earlier conversation, now recast in a more optimistic tone. A passage in which they discuss the blood test necessary for marriage (pages 66–67)—Girl: "I'll never pass it." Boy: "Hunh?"—is cut by the film.

Sequence E begins with Mrs. MacDonald, Mrs. Schwartz, and Mr. Zimmerman, all expecting the worst as a result of Jimmy's ravings on the telephone. Ethnic humor—Irish superstition, Jewish pessimism—gives way here to a social point: There can be no good news in these late-depression days; therefore, Jimmy, who does not drink, must be injured. Jimmy and Betty arrive and begin passing out presents to the neighborhood children.

It is at this point that Sturges cuts to the sequence of Maxford House scenes discussed above. The scene that follows these (E-20) shows Maxford frantically telling his secretary to call the bank. Scene E-21 shows Schindel, who has evidently just heard the news, slam down the phone and rush out. These scenes, of course, set up the arrival of Schindel and Maxford in Jimmy's neighborhood with the news that Jimmy has not won the contest. They also permit Sturges to cut, in effect, from the beginning of the street festival (Jimmy and Betty starting to hand out presents) to its climax, in which the street is jammed with neighbors enjoying their presents, with kids playing with their toys, eating ice cream, making noise, colliding with each other, etc. This climax is then interrupted, that is, topped, by Schindel's entrance with his salesmen in the back of a delivery truck and their futile efforts to recover their merchandise. This is topped in turn by the arrival of Maxford, who tricks the check away from Jimmy and tears it up, argues with Schindel about who will

Dick Powell, Sturges, Ellen Drew, the producer Paul Jones, and an unidentified crew member—shooting the rooftop sequence that opens CHRISTMAS IN JULY.

pay for the presents, and is pelted with fish by the neighborhood children. This last is not indicated in the script but was evidently felt necessary by Sturges to give the scene a fitting conclusion. A brief scene follows showing the reactions of Jimmy and Betty and the arrival of Tom, Dick, and Harry, with a davenport for Jimmy's mother and a confession. This concludes Sequence E.

Sequence F, a brief fifteen pages, is written and directed in a muted tone, unlike the tumultuous Act III of the play. The film, unlike the play, has just had its big scene in the neighborhood, and there is no way to top it for spectacle or frenzy. At the beginning of Sequence F, Jimmy and Betty show up at the office after hours. He is anxious to tell Mr. Baxter that he did not win the contest even though she wants to wait until morning. Some conversational byplay with Sam, the night porter—a remnant of Julius in the play—tells them that Mr. Baxter is still there. When a black cat crosses their path, Betty asks Sam if it's good luck or bad. "That all depends on what happens afterwards," he says. This deflation of superstition is appropriate to Jimmy's lost faith in luck as the answer to his problems, but it also sets up his good luck to come in getting his new job and office after all and, later, in winning the contest, with which the black cat is specifically associated. The cat in fact gets the film's last shot.

The film cuts the bantering exchange with the sign painter (pages 98–99)—it would have destroyed the elegiac mood of this sequence, just as the blood test exchange would have destroyed the romantic mood of the cab ride in Sequence D. There is instead a polite exchange of "Good evening," "It's lovely," and "Thank you," which is also a better preparation for the scene of regret, with Betty sobbing, which follows (pages 99–100).

Mr. Baxter finds them in the office, and the final scene with him ensues. Betty works out the compromise—Jimmy gets his chance, without guarantees—just as Tulip did in the play. They walk out of the office to the sad strains of "Penthouse Serenade," which sets the tone of this sequence just as it did when Jimmy and Betty were saying good-night in Sequence A. Jimmy notices the cat again, they say good-night to Sam, and, while they wait for the elevator, Betty looks out the window and points to the Maxford House sign. According to the script (page 108), at this point "We see the Maxford House tower in the distance and the head gulping its never-ending last gulp."

Sturges cuts to a zoom shot to, and into, the Maxford House tower, coming to rest on Maxford sitting at his desk, all "accompanied by the wail of a high siren," as the script specifies. Maxford's telephone conversation with his lawyer is discarded by the film in favor of a dialogue with his valet, as he brushes Maxford's fish-spattered coat: "Were you to a fish fry, Dr. Maxford?" Then Bildocker comes in with the name of the contest winner—Jimmy—and the scene plays as written, except that Sturges starts up the final theme music at the crash of the telephone that Maxford hurls at Bildocker. Thus the cut back to Betty and Jimmy is "silent"—their dialogue on pages 110–111 is cut completely. Also cut is the cat's "Meow!" and, indeed, the presence of the cat as Betty and Jimmy wait for the elevator. Instead of having the camera follow the elevator and end on a shot of the cat, in the film the cat appears on top of the descending elevator itself, staring into the camera. This is more imaginative, less realistic than the scripted version, and oddly parallels the animated snake that opens Sturges's next film, *The Lady Eve.* In both instances the director seems to be winking at the audience through a droll animal while at the same time making fun of the wink itself. The cat, which Jimmy and Betty do not see, signifies—in a reversal of the conventional superstition of the black cat—the good news that they have not yet heard. This validates Sam's point that a thing is lucky or not depending on what happens afterward, that is, that luck has no meaning or effect at all.

The scene between Jimmy, Betty, and Baxter in Sequence F is the culmination of the film's themes. Jimmy said to Maxford when he picked up his check at Maxford House:

> . . . to know I won this contest because I thought up a better slogan than anyone else means more to me than anything else on earth . . . and I'll tell you why: You see, I used to THINK maybe I had good ideas and was going to get somewhere in the world . . . but NOW I KNOW it . . . and that's what I want to thank you for, Dr. Maxford . . . even more than the money. (page 51)

Jimmy's effusive declaration at this pinnacle, entirely appropriate under the circumstances, is undercut by Maxford's total lack of interest in the ceremony, which is consistent with his character and is an instance of Sturges's dramatic irony. By evening Jimmy knows that he has not won the contest. Standing in his new office, he says to Mr. Baxter: "If you thought the ideas were good this afternoon, you think they're good now, don't you?" But, after a few more lines between them, Baxter replies:

> I didn't hang onto my father's money by backing my own judgment, you know. I make mistakes every day . . . You see, I THINK your ideas are good because they sound good to me. But I KNOW your ideas are good because you won this contest . . . over millions of aspirants. (page 102)

Baxter flies into a rage when he learns that Jimmy has not won the contest, and, while he rants, Jimmy is oddly silent. When he finishes, it is Betty who speaks up—as did Tulip in the play:

> He belongs in here because he THINKS he belongs in here . . . He belongs in here because he thinks he has ideas. He belongs in here until he proves himself or fails, and then somebody else belongs in here until he proves himself or fails . . . Oh, I know they're not going to succeed . . . at least most of them aren't . . . they'll all be like Mr. Waterbury soon enough . . . most of them, anyway . . . but they won't mind it . . . they'll find something else, and they'll be happy because they had their chance . . . because it's one thing to muff a chance when you get it . . . but it's another thing never to have had a chance. (pages 104–105)

Betty's mention of Waterbury undercuts his earlier speech in which he declared himself a success. She and Jimmy want real, not sophistic, success. Betty stresses opportunity, which has been a remarkably consistent theme in American politics and political theory in all eras and along a wide spectrum of ideological orientations. How opportunity is defined, of course, makes all the difference—opportunity for what, for whom, and under what restrictions and qualifications, whether explicit or implicit. In *Christmas in July,* as in all but a relatively few films of any era (American or European), opportunity is for white males. Betty's plea concerns neither herself (except as Jimmy's wife-to-be) nor Sam, the black night porter.

However, other aspects of the notion of "opportunity" are questioned by the film. When they are alone again, Jimmy tells Betty that she is wonderful but that he is leery of himself. She says that this is the chance of a lifetime and that he knows he's got what it takes. In response, Jimmy says:

> I DON'T know. I never DID know until I got that telegram. And now I don't know any more. I'm like Mr. Baxter, that's why I understood him and didn't say anything, see?
>
> (page 107)

Thanks to a practical joke, Jimmy has been able to finesse his "thinking" that he had good ideas into an actual opportunity. It took, however, both his and others' falsely believing that he had received an external validation of those ideas. Without the telegram, Jimmy would never have voiced his ideas to his boss and the staff, and, even if he had, no one would have listened to him. Faced with the promotion, without the external validation, Jimmy wonders whether he can perform as expected. Interestingly, his remarks to Betty on this point are his last speech, aside from a remark or two about the cat. The film leaves him stranded on his island of self-doubt, indeed so much so that the twist that he's won the contest after all seems only the film's final gag, necessary to tie up some plot ends but not a resolution of its themes.

The film's treatment of Jimmy's problems and its ambiguous resolution of them point to ambiguities in American film generally. The American film hero is usually simultaneously both ordinary and extraordinary, with suggestions that "the ordinary is extraordinary" or that "everyone is extraordinary in some respect, or has the potential to be." So also American stars are characteristically both ordinary types and extraordinarily handsome or charismatic. The ordinary aspects of stars and the characters they play are meant to ensure that the issues involved are of interest to most people, even that the success of the hero could plausibly be that of anyone in the audience. Since this is not possible, there is a continual play with mirrors regarding the ordinary and the extraordinary. The interest of *Christmas in July* in this respect is that it builds this ambiguity openly into its structure and theme, thereby treating it explicitly.

Finally, an autobiographical reading of *Christmas in July* easily presents itself. When Sturges wrote the script of the film from February to May 1940 and when he shot it in June of that year, *The Great McGinty* had not yet been released. Betty's plea that Jimmy be given the chance to prove himself until he failed is Sturges's plea, to his studio and to Hollywood generally, that he be given the chance to write and direct. He was already working on the final script for *The Lady Eve* when *The Great McGinty* was released in August 1940.

Notes

1. Some undated, unidentified stills of a theatrical production that appears to be *A Cup of Coffee* are lodged in a file under *Christmas in July* in the Sturges archive. In addition, the second page of the text of the play has a notice of registration with the Pasadena Community Playhouse Association dated January 5, 1940. This may have been a move on Sturges's part to establish his ownership of rights to the play. The possibility exists, however, that the play was produced somewhere between the time it was written and its conversion into a film script.

2. James Curtis, *Between Flops: A Biography of Preston Sturges* (New York: Harcourt Brace Jovanovich, 1982), page 68.

3. Ibid., page 99.

4. As far as I have been able to determine, Sturges never worked with other writers, even, as it were, when they had already departed the scene. He preferred, wherever possible, to start all over again.

5. See Sturges's letter to Charles Abramson, quoted in Curtis, op. cit., page 99. There is a discrepancy in Curtis, or rather in his sources, regarding the figure Universal actually paid Sturges for *A Cup of Coffee*—"$4000 on account with $5000 to come when the script is finished and $6000 to come for directing it," according to Sturges. But, on page 140, Curtis reports that Paramount bought it back from Universal for "little more than what the Laemmles [of Universal] had put into it—$6000."

6. André Bazin said of the film: "In *Christmas in July,* for example, the main protagonist is not shown on the screen. It is invisible and all-powerful luck, like God in *Athalie* (Albert Capellani, 1910)" (André Bazin, *The Cinema of Cruelty: From Buñuel to Hitchcock*, ed. François Truffaut [New York: Seaver, 1982]).

7. See J. Laplanche and J.-B. Pontalis, *The Language of Psychoanalysis,* tr. Donald Nicholson-Smith (New York: Norton, 1973): "Disavowal (Denial): Term used by Freud in the specific sense of a mode of defense which consists in the subject's refusing to recognize the reality of a traumatic perception . . ." (page 118). "Foreclosure (Repudiation): Term introduced by Jacques Lacan denoting a specific mechanism held to lie at the origin of the psychotic phenomenon and to consist in a primordial expulsion of a fundamental 'signifier' from the subject's symbolic universe. Foreclosure is deemed to be distinct from repression in two senses: (a) Foreclosed signifiers are not integrated into the subject's unconscious; (b) They do not return 'from the inside'—they re-emerge, rather, in 'the Real,' particularly through the phenomenon of hallucination" (page 166).

8. Carr, a well-known Broadway actor of the time, had greatly aided Sturges's first produced hit, *The Guinea Pig,* by taking the role of Sam Small, a Jewish fur-dealer-turned-producer who wanted a play, getting most of the laughs. Curtis reports that Carr also instructed Sturges in how to "point" his lines, a lesson he learned well (Curtis, op. cit., page 46).

SF 8413

THE NEW YORKERS

May 23, 1940

THE NEW YORKERS

PRELIMINARY CASTING

JIMMY MacDONALD..............................Dick Powell

BETTY CASEY..................................Ellen Drew

DR. PARKER...................................Ray Walburn

MR. BAXTER...................................Ernest Truex

MR. SCHINDEL.................................Alexander Carr

MR. BILDOCKER................................Bill Demarest

MR. WATERBURY................................

THE ANNOUNCER................................

TOM..

DICK...

HARRY..

MRS. MacDONALD...............................

MR. SCHMIDT..................................

MR. HILLBEINER...............................

MR. JENKINS..................................

PATROLMAN MURPHY.............................

MR. ZIMMERMAN................................

MRS. SCHWARTZ................................

BITS:

Furniture Salesman (Schindel's).............
Hat Salesman (Schindel's)...................
Sophie (Cripple Girl).......................
Sophie's Mother.............................
Porter (Baxter's)...........................
Sign Painter (Baxter's).....................
11 Judges for Parker House Contest..........
Night Elevator Man (Baxter's)..............
Secretary to Dr. Baxter.....................
Cashier (Dr. Parker's)......................

* * *

SEQUENCE "A"

The Main Titles take the form of electric signs against the night sky over New York. Some of them are flashing signs, some of them are animated, and some of them the traveling-message type. The last title DISSOLVES TO:

A-1 THE PARKER HOUSE TOWER - (NIGHT)

It is covered with an enormous four-stage electric sign which represents a man gulping a cup of coffee in four jerks. The main title music continues full blast. The CAMERA MOVES SLOWLY DOWN the facade of the tower and we read:

PARKER HOUSE COFFEE

"Grand to the last gulp"

All the windows are lit on the floor below the sign. The CAMERA STARTS for one of these windows. As we get near the building -

DISSOLVE TO:

A-2 THE PARKER HOUSE PRIVATE BROADCASTING STUDIO

We see the usual assortment of microphones and control men peering through the sides of their aquarium. A good-sized orchestra is playing the title music. Now it comes to a climax and holds an organ point. An announcer adjusts his microphone and elocutes throatily.

THE ANNOUNCER
I give you COFFEE, ladies and gentlemen...the end of the perfect dinner, the beginning of the perfect day.

Two little girls in white appear and go down to the audience with trays full of very small coffee cups.

THE ANNOUNCER
(Continued)
The friend of the poor man AND the rich man, the solace of the

5-23-40 (Continued)

A-2 (Cont'd)

THE ANNOUNCER (Cont'd)
unhappy and the ally of the merry-maker. To what do we turn in times of stress and national extremity? What is called for first in any disaster, be it a flood, a blizzard, a war, or any other human crisis? To what do we turn as naturally and instinctively as we turn to prayer... and sometimes, with more immediate results...Ladies and gentlemen? I GIVE YOU COFFEE!

The orchestra blares into: "A Cup of Coffee, A Sandwich, and Yoo-hoo." There is a spatter of applause from the little theatre full of spectators and the announcer receives a small cup of coffee which he discusses with visible gusto, toasting the audience between sips. The music ceases abruptly and there is a fanfare of trumpets.

THE ANNOUNCER
And now, ladies and gentlemen, the moment we have all been waiting for: we are about to give you the result of the $50,000 Parker House New Slogan Contest...

A-3 MONTAGE OF VARIOUS TYPES LISTENING TO RADIOS:

A poor family in a tenement; an old priest; a spinster dressmaker in a garret; a family in the kitchen of a farmhouse; a radio operator at sea; a colored boot-black in a barbershop; a masseur pausing in the midst of a massage; a cab driver listening to his auto radio, and the broadcast spectators.

THE ANNOUNCER'S VOICE
(Over all these)
...with a first prize of $25,000, a second prize of $5,000, a third prize of $2,500, a fourth prize of $1,500, a fifth prize of $1,000, and ninety-five other prizes totaling $15,000. Are some folks going to be delirious in a few minutes! As you may well imagine, ladies and gentlemen, all that sugar draws a lot of flies and the jury here has

5-23-40 (Continued)

A-3 (Cont'd)

THE ANNOUNCER'S VOICE (Cont'd)
been struggling for a week to try to pick the winnahs from a little snowdrift of two million, nine hundred and forty-seven thousand, five hundred and eighty-two answers.

A-4 THE ANNOUNCER - AT HIS MICROPHONE

THE ANNOUNCER
And that, laides and gentlemen, is a lot of answers in any language... including the Scandinavian, heh-heh-heh. Dr. Parker, our founder and president, is here by my side...

Dr. Parker steps into the SHOT and smiles toothily to the audience. He is an irritated-looking gentleman of sixty.

THE ANNOUNCER
(Continued)
...and I know that it will be only a matter of a few moments until the jury ceases wrestling with itself, hands Dr. Parker the verdict and he will himself, in that well known voice, read you the names of the winnahs, heh-heh-heh, oh boy!

In the meantime Dr. Parker is motioning violently to someone off-stage.

A-5 A MAN APPROACHING CARRYING A TELEPHONE

A long wire trails out behind him. The CAMERA PANS him INTO THE SHOT with Dr. Parker and the announcer. Dr. Parker moves away from the mike and mouths silently but furiously: "What the hell is the matter now?" The Radio Announcer gives them a worried look but continues to speak unctuously.

THE ANNOUNCER
We seem to have run into a little contretemps, fox pass or what have you, ladies and gentlemen, but I am sure that it will be only a

5-23-40 (Continued)

A-5 (Cont'd)

THE ANNOUNCER (Cont'd)
matter of a few moments until we
are handed the verdict and...

He mouths furiously and silently to the man with the telephone.

A-6 CLOSE SHOT - DR. PARKER AND THE MAN WITH THE TELEPHONE

DR. PARKER
(Silently but
furiously)
What's the matter?

THE MAN WITH THE TELEPHONE
(In a whisper)
The jury is deadlocked...eleven to
one.

DR. PARKER
(Clutching his
head)
Deadlocked!
(He turns toward
the announcer)

A-7 THE ANNOUNCER

He looks very jittery but his voice does not betray him.

THE ANNOUNCER
As I say, it will be only a
matter of a few moments until
the jury untangles itself and
the happy winners hear their
names broadcasted throughout
the world.

Dr. Parker ENTERS THE SHOT and whispers in his ear.

THE ANNOUNCER
(Silently but with
horror)
Deadlocked!...Then do something!

Dr. Parker frowns and hurries OUT OF THE PICTURE. The Announcer stares after him in dismay, then suddenly remembers that he is doomed to talk continuously.

5-23-40 (Continued)

A-7 (Cont'd)

THE ANNOUNCER
Just a little patience, ladies and gentlemen...perhaps the maestro would oblige....

He motions wildly: "For Pete sake, play something!"

THE ANNOUNCER
...with a little chamber music while the good old jury...
(He looks at his wristwatch)
...makes up what it humorously calls its mind, heh-heh-heh.

The music starts and he mops his head.

A-8 THE MARBLE STEPS LEADING TO THE FLOOR BELOW

We hear staccato footsteps and Dr. Parker comes tearing around and down to us. He nearly misses the last two, skids around the corner and runs down a long hall. The CAMERA PANS with him. As he bursts through a door --

A-9 REVERSE SHOT - DR. PARKER ENTERING THE CONFERENCE ROOM OF THE PARKER HOUSE COFFEE COMPANY

DR. PARKER
What's all this hogwash about being deadlocked? Where's that verdict?

A-10 THE JURY AS SEEN BY DR. PARKER

We SHOOT DOWN a long table at which sit twelve exasperated-looking men. On the table are piled millions of papers, in boxes and baskets and bales. More millions of papers are piled around the sides of the room. Down at the end of the table sits a small angry-looking man, He is somewhat detached from the others. A thin sour gentleman gets up from the position nearest us.

THIN SOUR GENTLEMAN
You'd better ask Bildocker.

5-23-40 (Continued)

A-10 (Cont'd)

BILDOCKER
(At the head of
the table)
Yes, and you'll get an answer
too. If you birds had the brains
of a rooster...

A large gentleman next to Bildocker slaps the table.

LARGE GENTLEMAN
I resent that, Bildocker...You
may know a little something about
the shipping department, but when
the eleven of us are agreed, I
say you have a fine crust to...

BILDOCKER
(Leaping to his
feet)
Yeah? Well let me tell you some-
thing, Mr. Fancy Pants...

A LARGE ROUGH GENTLEMAN
Why don't you shut up, Bildocker?
You've been trying to browbeat this
jury since ten o'clock last night
and all I got to say is...

A MILD GENTLEMAN
It seems more like last week.

BILDOCKER
Yes, and it will be ten o'clock
next week and then some before
I give in to a bunch of fat-
headed, mealy-mouthed lamebrains
that wouldn't know enough to...

Since the argument began, Dr. Parker's voice has been
heard saying: "Gentlemen, stop it!"

DR. PARKER'S VOICE
(Roaring)
QUIET! QUIET!

A-11 REVERSE SHOT - DR. PARKER

He is pounding on the end of the table, scattering
some of the answers.

5-23-40 (Continued)

A-11 (Cont'd)

DR. PARKER
QUIET! Jumping Johoshaphat! Do you happen to realize that we're on the air? Mr. Bildocker, do you happen to realize that the whole of America is awaiting your verdict? That a hundred and twenty million people are suspended from your lips? That you're giving heart failure to the Western Hemisphere?...What do you know about picking slogans anyway. You wouldn't know a slogan if you slipped on one. If you had the brains of an amoeba...

A WEARY GENTLEMAN
(Near him)
But we're all agreed, Dr. Parker. It's only Bildocker who's holding out.

DR. PARKER
(Virulently)
Oh, it is, is it? Well let me tell you something, Mr. Bildocker, you've been getting in my hair for the last twenty years and I meant to mention it before. I'm going to give you four seconds flat...

A-12 BILDOCKER

He narrows his eyes and speaks with deep conviction.

BILDOCKER
Oh, no you're not, Dr. Parker! I'm a member of this jury and I'm going to vote the way I think is right if it takes ten years! You can fire me out of the shipping department, but you aren't going to fire me off this jury because I don't work for you on this jury. I'm giving my services free...
(He points to all the papers)
...to the bunch of suckers who fell for this --

5-23-40 (Continued)

A-13 DR. PARKER

DR. PARKER
Who said anything about firing you, you lunk-head? All I said was...

A phone in front of him rings and he answers it.

DR. PARKER
(After listening a moment)
Oh, we are, are we...well that's just lovely.
(He hangs up)
We're going off the air, gentlemen, that includes you, Mr. Bildocker, so just take your time. You can stay here till next Wednesday or till Hoboken freezes over. We have failed in our promise to the public, we have muffed the most dramatic advertising moment in the annals of commerce, and you've made a fathead out of me. The next halfwit who talks to me about a contest had better duck before I swing on him. In conclusion, gentlemen, and especially you, Mr. Bildocker, let me say that I have seen far, far better heads on umbrellas!

He stamps out of the room and slams the door after him.

A-14 THE ANNOUNCER AT THE MICROPHONE

He is mopping his head. He waves to the musicians to start the signature music.

THE ANNOUNCER
And so, ladies and gentlemen, another broadcast slips into posterity as we bring to a close the four hundred and forty-ninth Parker House program. When and if the jury reaches a decision,

5-23-40 (Continued)

A-14 (Cont'd)

THE ANNOUNCER (Cont'd)
the winners will be notified by post, telegraph, pony express or what have you. I wish I could have given you the news you were so anxious to hear, but since I could not, I will conclude with what the prisoner said when the hangman couldn't find the rope: "No noose is good noose," heh-heh-heh. This is Don Hartman, heh-heh-heh, wishing you all... goodnight.

The music changes into "A CUP OF COFFEE, A SANDWICH AND YOO-HOO." The Announcer mops his head, switches off his microphone, looks to the nearest sympathetic person and says: "Phooey!"

A-15 A CHEAP LITTLE RADIO - ON THE PARAPET OF A ROOF - (NIGHT)

We hear the end of the broadcast music of "A CUP OF COFFEE, A SANDWICH AND YOO-HOO."

A-16 THE BOY AND THE GIRL - AGAINST THE NIGHT SKY

The Parker House sign is blinking in the distance.

THE BOY
(Indignantly)
Well, how do you like that one? They build you up for a big finish, then leave you hanging on the meat hook.

THE GIRL
Well, you heard what he said: "No news is good news."

5-23-40 (Continued)

A-16 (Cont'd)

THE BOY
(Almost crossly)
He said: "No noose is good noose."

THE GIRL
What's the difference?

THE BOY
...it doesn't matter, but I wish it were over one way or the other.
(He snaps off the radio)
You start thinking about that twenty-five thousand dollars... or even the five thousand dollars...

THE GIRL
Or even anything.

THE BOY
And then when you've practically got it in your mitts...they just leave you there with your tongue hanging out. There ought to be a law against things like that.

THE GIRL
Did you really think you were going to win it, Jimmy?

THE BOY
(Indignantly)
I haven't lost it yet, have I?

THE GIRL
How many have you lost?

THE BOY
(Crossly)
I don't know. But I do know every time I've lost a contest I've doubled my chances on the next one. It's what you call the law of averages...like I lost the "How many peanuts in the window?" contest, well that just doubled my chances on the...

5-23-40 (Continued)

A-16 (Cont'd)

THE GIRL
They put boxes under the peanuts.

THE BOY
They have a right to do that. They didn't say there weren't any boxes under the peanuts.... all they said was....

THE GIRL
"How many peanuts are there in the window?"

THE BOY
(With satisfaction)
All right, I lost. That doubled my chances on the "You fill in the missing words" contest.

THE GIRL
But you lost that one too.

THE BOY
Fine. So I was eight to one when I went into the limerick contest.

THE GIRL
(Almost crossly)
But you didn't win it, Jimmy.

THE BOY
(With satisfaction)
That's what makes me such a cinch in this one.
(He points to the Parker House tower)
Can't you just see it over there in lights? The guy swallows his coffee and it says: "It isn't the coffee... it's the bunk." You got to admit, that's some slogan.

THE GIRL
Unhunh.

THE BOY
(Looking at her suspiciously)
Well, you get the point, don't you? You understand what it means.

THE GIRL
Well -- yes -

5-23-40 (Continued)

A-16 (Cont'd)

THE BOY
What do you mean, well...yes? It's as clear as crystal. "It isn't the coffee, it's the bunk"...If you don't sleep at night, it means it isn't the coffee, it's the bunk...THE BUNK...when you don't sleep at night.

THE GIRL
(Impatiently)
I know what it says...I've heard it a thousand times...I just don't understand it.

THE BOY
Maybe you're not trying to understand.

THE GIRL
Well, maybe I'm not.

THE BOY
I should think a child of two could understand it. This Viennese doctor in the Sunday paper says the old idea is just a superstition, and instead of keeping you awake...COFFEE MAKES YOU SLEEP. That's simple enough, isn't it? It - makes - you - sleep.

THE GIRL
It doesn't make me sleep.

THE BOY
(Loudly)
He's a Viennese doctor. If he says it makes you sleep...

THE GIRL
(Interrupting)
Coffee keeps you awake, Jimmy. It's a well known fact. Why are you so pig-headed about it? I'm not just trying to contradict you...

THE BOY
I tell you it's the new scientific theory. It's the basis of my slogan! People think coffee keeps them awake, but people like that are nervous wrecks who can't sleep anyway, so why blame it on the coffee? So I say: "If you don't sleep at night, it isn't the coffee, it's the bunk." Do you get it?

5-23-40 (Continued)

A-16 (Cont'd)

THE GIRL
(Wearily)
I guess so.

THE BOY
(Suspiciously)
Then what does it mean?

THE GIRL
It's the bunk.

THE BOY
But do you get the play on words?

THE GIRL
(Sadly)
You don't need a play on words, Jimmy. Any time anybody tells you coffee makes you sleep you don't need a play on words to know it's the bunk.

THE BOY
(Grimly)
Don't you understand, it's funny.... people are going to laugh when they hear it...it means if you don't sleep at night, it isn't the coffee that's keeping you awake...it's the bed.

THE GIRL
With me, it's the coffee.

The boy throws his hands wide and leans back against the parapet and almost falls into the street. The girl catches him just in time.

THE GIRL
(Holding him tight)
You know I want you to win, Jimmy. I'm just as anxious as you are. You know that...and when you lose this one just think how much better your chances will be on the next one.

THE BOY
(Muttering)
Fine chance anybody's got o' winning anything with everybody going around yelling coffee keeps you awake.

THE GIRL
All right, let's go downstairs and drink a gallon of coffee and see which one sleeps the longest.

5-23-40 (Continued)

A-16 (Cont'd)

THE BOY
Oh, shut up!

The Girl snuggles up to him.

MRS. MacDONALD'S VOICE
Jimmy.

THE BOY
Yes, ma'am.

He leans over the parapet.

A-17 MRS. MacDONALD - LEANING OUT ON THE FIRE ESCAPE

MRS. MacDONALD
Mr. Zimmerman says would you please not talk so loud...he's trying to go to sleep.

A-18 THE BOY AND THE GIRL - ON THE ROOFTOP

THE BOY
(Leaning over the parapet)
Yes, ma'am.

THE GIRL
(Not too loud)
Tell him to drink a cup of coffee.

The Boy turns and gives the Girl a look.

A-19 MRS. MacDONALD - IN HER WINDOW

MRS. MacDONALD
And don't catch cold up there... Is Betty warm enough?

A-20 VERTICAL SHOT - UP AT THE PARAPET

The Boy's head is looking down at us. Now the Girl pokes her head over the edge.

THE GIRL
Yes, thank you, Mrs. MacDonald.

5-23-40

A-21 VERTICAL SHOT - DOWN ON MRS. MacDONALD - PAST THE TWO HEADS

MRS. MacDONALD
All right, dear -- Mrs. Schwartz says they didn't give out the winners yet in the contest.

THE BOY
I know, mamma, we've got a radio up here.

MRS. MacDONALD
All right, dear.

She disappears. After a moment, the Girl puts her arm around the Boy's neck.

THE GIRL
I'd like you just as much even if you didn't win the old contest.

THE BOY
That's because you're a sap.

THE GIRL
Well...maybe I am, but if I am, I'm glad of it. You know how we feel about each other.

THE BOY
Nix.

THE GIRL
Well it's true, isn't it? You can't say I'm being forward.

THE BOY
Not much.

THE GIRL
Well I'm not. Time is slipping by and we're not getting any younger.

THE BOY
Nix.

THE GIRL
Two can live as cheaply as one.

THE BOY
Who wants to live cheaply?

5-23-40 (Continued)

A-21 (Cont'd)

She reaches up and fondles his hair.

THE BOY
Cut it out, will you?

THE GIRL
(Langorously)
What would you do if you won $25,000?

THE BOY
Stick it in the bank.

THE GIRL
Wouldn't you even buy a little ring or something?

THE BOY
(Suppressing a smile)
I don't like rings on a man.

THE GIRL
Oh, you!

The Boy looks at her a moment, then squeezes her to him.

THE BOY
What's the use of talking, honey? You know I'd spend it all on you...and Mom. I'd get you a big shiny car and a swell apartment or maybe one of those little dream houses in the suburbs and some hired help and maybe a trip to Europe or maybe the Grand Canyon would be better these days and...we'd be happy all right.

THE GIRL
We could be happy anyway.

THE BOY
That's where you're wrong. Everything that means happiness costs money and...

THE GIRL
How much was your dad making when he married your mom?

THE BOY
Eighteen bucks a week.

THE GIRL
Well?

5-23-40 (Continued)

A-21 (Cont'd)

THE BOY

Well what? You think that proves something? She's never been to the country for more than a day. She's never had a nice piece of furniture. The dream of her life is a davenport that turns into a bed with a crank. She never had a pretty dress except what she made herself. I wore the old man's stuff cut down till I got my first job and he was worn out at forty-eight and croaked because he couldn't afford a decent doctor. Where do you get that eighteen bucks a week stuff?

THE GIRL

Well, I earn eighteen and you earn twenty-two and that's forty and...

THE BOY

Sure. And you got your ma and I got mine and then you get a kid and you have to quit work and we're right back to twenty-two again except there's you AND the kid AND the two old ladies and me.

THE GIRL

But Jimmy...

THE BOY

Nix. They didn't give you wrists like that and hands like that to spoil 'em in a washtub for some sap like me.

THE GIRL

But Jimmy...

THE BOY

(Wound up)

You got to look out for yourself in this world. You got to see the main chance and grab it...a chance with plenty of money. Men look out for themselves. They don't think of anything but money. A girl's got to do the same instead of fooling away her time on a guy...like me...unless, he crashes through.

THE GIRL

You make me tired.

5-23-40 (Continued)

A-21 (Cont'd)

THE BOY
Then why don't you go to bed?

THE GIRL
(Indignantly)
That's a nice thing to say. You invite a girl over on your roof and then yell at her. If I wanted to be insulted I could have gone out with the credit manager.

THE BOY
Who's stopping you?

THE GIRL
(Sitting up)
Thank you very much, Mr. MacDonald. It's nice to know where you stand.

THE BOY
I'm sorry.

THE GIRL
(Getting to her feet)
Maybe I will go out with the credit manager. Good night.

She turns away.

THE BOY
(Getting up)
I'll help you.

THE GIRL
I don't need any help, thank you.

She trips on a vent pipe and almost falls.

A-22 MR. ZIMMERMAN

in his room.

MR. ZIMMERMAN
(Looking up)
They got a horse up there yet?

A-23 THE GIRL AND THE BOY - ON THE ROOF

THE BOY
(Taking her arm)
Here.

5-23-40 (Continued)

A-23 (Cont'd)

THE GIRL
Kindly let go of my arm.

She pulls up her skirts, steps over a parapet and onto a cat. There is a wild yeowl and spitting.

THE BOY
Why don't you watch your step?

THE GIRL
Why don't you mind your own business?

THE BOY
Oh, shut up.

THE GIRL
Why don't you shut up?

A-24 HIGH CAMERA SHOT - DOWN ON AREAWAY

Mr. Zimmerman scowls up at us out of the top-story window.

MR. ZIMMERMAN
Why don't you both shut up?

A-25 THE GIRL AND THE BOY - ON THE ROOF

THE GIRL
You see?

They cross over onto the next roof and the Boy opens a trap revealing a ladder.

THE BOY
Try not to fall down the ladder.

THE GIRL
I've been down the ladder before.

She starts down it.

THE BOY
You fell down it before too.

THE GIRL
(After a pause)
Good night.

THE BOY
I'll see you at the office.

5-23-40 (Continued)

A-25 (Cont'd)

THE GIRL
Won't you take me?

THE BOY
All right.

THE GIRL
(Without moving)
Good night, Jimmy.

THE BOY
Good night.

THE GIRL
(Still without moving)
Good night.

After a moment The Boy bends over and kisses her on the lips.

THE BOY
Good night, honey.

THE GIRL
Good night, darling.

A-26 THE BALD-HEADED MAN IN THE AREAWAY

He cups his hands and hollers through this improvised megaphone.

MR. ZIMMERMAN
GOOD - NIGHT!

FADE OUT:

END OF SEQUENCE "A"

5-23-40

SEQUENCE "B"

FADE IN:

B-1 THE MacDONALD KITCHEN - (DAY)

The Boy is eating his breakfast. His mother is putting some egg shells into a coffee pot.

THE BOY
(Looking up)
I tell you it makes you sleep.

MRS. MacDONALD
All right, it makes you sleep, and water runs up hill and cats bark and dogs meow and water gets red hot in the winter and freezes over in the summer time. You're a dreamer...just like your father. With him it was always an auti-mo-bile where the wind it scooped up in the front blew out the back to make it go or some such wildness.

THE BOY
Yeah, well there's no wind blowing outa my ideas.

MRS. MacDONALD
You're windy enough...you got your carfare?

THE BOY
I think so.

He feels in his pocket and pulls a handkerchief out. A quarter falls to the floor. As he reaches to pick it up Mrs. MacDonald grabs his arm.

MRS. MacDONALD
Make a wish, first.

THE BOY
(Laughing)
All right.

MRS. MacDONALD
What falls to the floor comes to the door. You got nothing to laugh about. I mind the time your father, may his soul be

5-23-40 (Continued)

B-1 (Cont'd)

MRS. MacDONALD (Cont'd)
peaceful, dropped a quarter down a crack and it wasn't an hour till a near-sighted man give him a five dollar gold-piece instead of a nickel in paying his fare.
(She chuckles)
We went to Coney that night.

THE BOY
What was the matter with Pa's eyes?

MRS. MacDONALD
(Defiantly)
He happened to be looking somewhere else at the time. There was nothin' the matter with his eyes or any of the rest of him. He was the finest lookin' conductor on Third Avenue.

THE BOY
(Diplomatically)
Sure he was.

MRS. MacDONALD
You'd look like a shrimp beside him.

THE BOY
I sure would.

MRS. MacDONALD
Then don't be saying things against your father.

THE BOY
(Laughing)
I wasn't saying anything against him, Mom.

MRS. MacDONALD
(Severely)
Well, watch your step.

She pours him a cup of coffee and puts the pot back on the stove. Now she comes with some cream. Suddenly she grabs his shoulder.

MRS. MacDONALD
Jimmy.

5-23-40 (Continued)

B-1 (Cont'd)

THE BOY
Yes, m'am.

MRS. MacDONALD
(Strangely)
There's money on your cup.

The Boy looks down at it.

B-2 CLOSEUP - A CUP OF COFFEE

The surface is covered with bubbles.

DISSOLVE TO:

B-3 BRASS DOWNSTAIRS SIGN

It reads:

"E. BAXTER & SONS
COFFEE
Since 1887"

A lot of people hurry by and into the building, among them the Boy and the Girl.

DISSOLVE TO:

B-4 CLOSE SHOT - A TIME CLOCK

It is two minutes to nine. Hands appear and stamp cards rapidly.

B-5 THE MEN'S LOCKER ROOM

Here we see Tom, Dick and Harry cracking jokes as they change into their linen office coats. Behind them on the wall there is a pay telephone.

DICK
... and the sucker says, "Is Mr. Fish there?" and the guy at the other end says, "Which one do you want, this is the New York Aquarium."

During the laughter which ensues, the Boy comes in, hangs up his coat, puts on his office coat, then goes to the pay telephone.

5-23-40 (Continued)

B-5 (Cont'd)

HARRY
Hello, Jimmy.

THE BOY
Harya.

TOM
No, but the best one is you say this is the Edison Company, would you mind stepping outside and see if the street light is burning in front of your house, and when the mug comes back and says, "Yes, it is," then you say, "Well, blow it out, will you?"

During the laughter we hear the Boy at the telephone.

THE BOY
Is this the Parker House Company? Could you tell me if the jury has reached a verdict on the contest yet?...They haven't, huhh. Well. then I guess there's still hope for everybody, heh-heh-heh... Well, thanks just the same.

He hangs up, snaps his fingers nervously and starts past Tom, Dick and Harry.

HARRY
You in the contest, big boy?

THE BOY
You gotta keep trying.

He goes past the three.

HARRY
(Looking after the Boy)
Poor sucker! I wonder what one of these guys would do if they ever did win anything.

TOM
It's very easy to find out.

HARRY
Hunh?

TOM
All you need is a telegraph blank, some scissors and some glue. You cut it in strips and glue it on the blank.

5-23-40 (Continued)

B-5 (Cont'd)

DICK
Holy mackerel!

B-6 A VERY LARGE ROOM FULL OF DESKS

One half is occupied by girl stenographers, the other half by accountants, each one with a calculating machine at his elbow. In the FOREGROUND we see the Girl. As the Boy goes past her desk he pauses and whispers something. She crosses the fingers of both hands and holds them up for luck. He thanks her and moves away jerkily. All this to the song of the many typewriters. As the Boy reaches his desk --

B-7 CLOSE SHOT - THE BOY - SITTING AT HIS DESK

He seems very nervous. He drums on the desk with his fingers, smiles idiotically, catches himself doing it, then tries to get to work. After a moment he rests his chin on his hand and stares off into space.

B-8 CLOSE SHOT - TOM - AT HIS DESK

Harry stands next to him. Tom looks over toward the Boy, then continues cutting a message into strips. Suddenly Harry clears his throat warningly. Tom puts his implements away quickly as a manager comes through a glass door and starts a leisurely inspection. As Harry starts back for his own desk --

B-9 THE BOY - AT HIS DESK

He is still day-dreaming. The manager comes slowly into the SHOT behind him. After watching the Boy for a long moment he comes around and looks at him from the side. Suddenly the Boy becomes aware of the scrutiny. With a guilty jerk he goes to work on his calculating machine and succeeds in jamming it immediately.

THE BOY
(With a sheepish smile)
It's been doing that quite a lot recently.

He tries to clear the machine.

THE MANAGER
The wonder is that it works at all.

5-23-40 (Continued)

B-9 (Cont'd)

THE BOY
Yes, sir.

THE MANAGER
(After a pause)
Come into my office a moment, Mr. MacDonald.

THE BOY
Yes, sir.

He rises and precedes the manager.

B-10 THE GIRL - AT HER DESK

She watches in horror as the Boy goes into the manager's office.

B-11 INT. THE MANAGER'S OFFICE - SHOOTING OUT TOWARD THE BIG ROOM

The Boy enters followed by the manager. They both sit and there is an awkward pause.

THE MANAGER
I've been watching you for some time, Mr. MacDonald.

THE BOY
Yes, sir.

THE MANAGER (Pointing)
You see, your desk being just where it is, I have an unobstructed view of it.

THE BOY
Yes sir. I've noticed that...it used to make me kind of nervous, heh-heh-heh.

He drums miserably with his fingers.

THE MANAGER
You're not nervous any more...

THE BOY
Wh-who, me? No, sir.

THE MANAGER
Are you a drinking man, then?

THE BOY
(Stupefied)
Sir?

In reply, the manager lifts a sheet from his desk and examines it.

5-23-40 (Continued)

B-11 (Cont'd)

THE MANAGER
This is part of your yesterday's work...
I believe your number is a hundred and
twelve.

THE BOY
Yes, sir.

THE MANAGER
The Multometer computing machine is almost fool proof, Mr. MacDonald, and yet
you manage to miss your total by a little
matter of eleven thousand dollars just on
this one sheet. To what do you attribute that?

THE BOY
(Miserably)
I...I don't know, Mr. Waterbury. I...

THE MANAGER
You are familiar with simple arithmetic,
aren't you, Mr. MacDonald? I mean, you
know the difference between subtraction
and addition..possibly even multiplication.

THE BOY
Yes, sir... I'm pretty good at it.

THE MANAGER
Have you troubles at home then? Are you
henpecked? Are you suffering from a
broken heart. Have you had your teeth
examined? Do you play the races? or are
you purely and simply incapable of doing
your work?

THE BOY
I guess it's the contest, Mr. Waterbury...
The Parker House Contest...I didn't realize
that it was hurting my work.

THE MANAGER
Oh.

THE BOY
I'm very sorry, sir.

THE MANAGER
How much is the prize?

THE BOY
The first prize is twenty-five
thousand dollars.

THE MANAGER
(Gently)
Ah, yes, I used to think about
twenty-five thousand dollars too
and what I'd do with it and that I'd

5-23-40

(Continued)

B-11 (Cont'd) THE MANAGER (Cont'd)

be a failure if I didn't get ahold of it...and then one day I realized I was never going to have twenty-five thousand dollars, Mr. MacDonald: and then another day a little bit later, considerably later, I realized something else, something I am imparting to you now, Mr. McDonald: I'm not a failure. I'm a success. You see, ambition is all right if it works, but no system could be right where only half of one per cent were successes and all the rest were failures. That wouldn't be right. I'm not a failure, I'm a success, and so are you, if you earn your living and pay your bills and look the world in the eye. I hope you win your twenty-five thousand, but if you shouldn't happen to...don't worry about it.

(He pauses before concluding)

Now get the heck back to your desk and try to improve your arithmetic.

THE BOY

(Gratefully)

Yes, sir, Mr. Waterbury...thanks.

The Boy goes out.

B-12 THE GIRL - AT HER DESK

She looks toward the Boy with a worried expression.

B-13 THE BOY - COMING OUT OF THE MANAGER'S OFFICE

He smiles reassuringly toward the Girl and the CAMERA PANS him to his desk. As he is about to sit down he pauses at something he sees on his desk.

B-14 INSERT: A TELEGRAM ADDRESSED TO MR. JAMES MACDONALD E. BAXTER & SONS, THE BAXTER BLDG., NEW YORK CITY

B-15 THE BOY - AT HIS DESK

He picks the telegram up slowly, examines it again, looks at the back of it, then looks around the room with some nervousness.

5-23-40

B-16 PANNING SHOT - OVER THE DESKS OF TOM, DICK AND HARRY

They look PAST US with elaborately straight faces.

B-17 THE GIRL - AT HER DESK

She looks PAST US with a slight frown.

B-18 THE BOY - AT HIS DESK

He opens the telegram slowly, then reads it.

B-19 INSERT: THE TELEGRAM

After the hour, the date and the address, it says:

"WE TAKE GREAT PLEASURE IN INFORMING YOU THAT YOUR SLOGAN HAS WON TWENTY-FIVE THOUSAND DOLLAR FIRST PRIZE IN NEW SLOGAN CONTEST. KINDLY CALL AND PICK UP YOUR CHECK. CONGRATULATIONS.

THE PARKER HOUSE CO."

B-20 CLOSE SHOT - THE BOY - READING THE TELEGRAM

He tries to swallow but his tonsils bump against each other. He licks his lips nervously, then tries to whistle nonchalantly.

B-21 CLOSE SHOT - TOM

He has difficulty in controlling his laughter. The CAMERA PANS onto Dick, who watches the Boy with the cold scrutiny of a scientist. The CAMERA PANS onto Harry, who waits blinkingly to see what will happen next.

B-22 THE GIRL - AT HER DESK

She gets slowly to her feet and starts forward.

B-23 THE BOY - NEAR HIS DESK

Suddenly he lets out a war whoop.

5-23-40 (Continued)

B-23 (Cont'd)

THE BOY
Yippee !

He leaps onto his desk, waves the telegram and says:

THE BOY
Ladies and gentlemen....WOW ! Yippee !
Oska-ba-ba !

He starts to laugh hysterically.

B-24 HIGH CAMERA SHOT - DOWN ON THE ROOM

The girls and the young men hurry toward us.

B-25 TOM - AT HIS DESK

He is having hysterics. Dick moves INTO THE SHOT behind him and watches, straight-faced. Harry comes in laughing.

B-26 THE BOY - ON HIS DESK

He waves the telegram and tries to talk.

THE BOY
Boys and girls...and you, honey ...

B-27 CLOSE SHOT - THE GIRL

She looks around in embarrassment.

THE BOY'S VOICE
There are times in everybody's life
when....

B-28 THE MANAGER COMING THROUGH FROM HIS OFFICE

THE BOY'S VOICE
...you have to climb up on the desk
and let 'er go. Yippee !

B-29 CLOSE SHOT - THE BOY - ON HIS DESK

THE BOY
In other words, boys and girls, and
'specially you, honey, I've just won
the twenty-five thousand dollar first
prize in the....

5-23-40 (Continued)

B-29 (Cont'd)

THE BOY (Cont'd)
(He clears his throat)
....Parker House Contest!

There is a wild yell from all present. The Girl is helped up onto the desk where she throws her arms around the Boy's neck. The yelling doubles at this.

B-30 A DOOR MARKED - "J. B. BAXTER, PRES."

It opens, and a small middle-aged gentleman comes out frowning slightly. He frowns more heavily as his ears are smitten by another roar.

B-31 THE BOY AND THE GIRL - IN THE MIDDLE OF THE CROWD

THE BOY
Now give me a phone...this is going to be good.

He receives a phone and dials a number.

THE BOY
Hello ... is that Mrs. Schwartz? Mrs. Schwartz, this is Jimmy MacDonald... across the hall... I hate to bother you, but could you let me talk to my mother a minute? It's very important...thanks a lot, Mrs. Schwartz. I'll let you use my phone all you like -- when I get one.
(Then to the clerks around him)
Give me a cigarette, somebody, will you?

He receives a cigarette and flips a match with his thumbnail. After a second he speaks.

THE BOY
Hello, Mom? This is Jimmy. Mom ... I've got something to tell you, but don't get frightened, see?...No, of course I'm not hurt...I tell you I'm not. Would I call you up from under a street car? Listen, Mom, are you a rich woman or a poor woman? No, I'm not crazy with the heat. I'm asking you a simple question. Are you a rich woman or a poor woman?...

5-23-40 (Continued)

B-31 (Cont'd)

THE BOY (Cont'd)
You're all wet...Heh-heh-heh. I said you're all wet, Mom. You can buy yourself anything you want... automobiles, dresses, new furniture...

THE GIRL
...the electric washer....

THE BOY
Listen, you know that electric washer you saw - the green one? It's yours, Mom.

THE GIRL
The davenport.

THE BOY
And, Mom, that davenport that turns into a double bed at night - it's yours, Mom. And anything else you want. All you got to do is tell me, and it's all yours...

B-32 TOM, DICK AND HARRY - IN THE CROWD

They look quite miserable and avoid each other's eyes.

THE BOY'S VOICE
I'll tell the world I've got a raise, ha-ha....

B-33 THE BOY AND THE GIRL - IN THE MIDDLE OF THE CROWD

THE GIRL
And how he got a raise!

There is a roar of laughter from the crowd.

B-34 J. B. BAXTER - ARRIVING AT THE EDGE OF THE CROWD

MR. BAXTER
What's going on around here?

As nobody answers him, he starts forward.

B-35 THE BOY AND THE GIRL - IN THE MIDDLE OF THE CROWD

THE BOY
Mom, I can't even believe it myself yet, but I won the first prize, Mom,

5-23-40 (Continued)

B-35 (Cont'd) THE BOY (Cont'd)
in the Parker House competition ...
twenty-five thousand dollars ...
What? WHAT? What are you crying
for? But now listen, Mom ... Mom ...

B-36 TOM, DICK AND HARRY

HARRY
(To Tom)
That's going to cost you just one
davenport that turns into a double
bed at night.

TOM
(Sourly)
You and me both.
(Now he turns to Dick)
And you, too, babyface ... Come on,
let's put him out of his misery.

Suddenly Harry sees the approaching J. B. BAXTER.
He puts a warning hand on Tom's arm.

B-37 HIGH CAMERA SHOT - DOWN ON THE APPROACHING MR. BAXTER

As he works his way through the crowd he spots the
center of ~~the~~ rumpus.

MR. BAXTER
(Furiously)
What's going on around here? What is
this - a football game?

EMPLOYEES SURROUNDING HIM
(Simultaneously and
unintelligibly)
Just won the ... isn't that wonderful
...you'd never think it to look ...
and they say they give them ... twenty-
five thousand in ... and they never
said a word about.....

MR. BAXTER
(Roaring)
QUIET! I said quiet - or there will
be severe consequences for all of you!
What are you doing up on that desk,
young man?...NEVER MIND WHAT YOU'RE
DOING, YOU'RE FIRED AS OF NOW...THIS
MINUTE! What is your name ... and
yours, too, young lady?

5-23-40

B-38 THE BOY AND THE GIRL - LOOKING DOWN AT MR. BAXTER

THE BOY
(Cheerfully)
James MacDonald, sir -- and this is
my fiancee, Miss Jones.

B-39 CLOSE SHOT - MR. BAXTER

MR. BAXTER
(Somewhat at a loss)
Well, let that be a lesson to you.
A business office...

He is drowned out by a wild yell of laughter.

B-40 VARIOUS GROUPS

Laughing at the funniness of discharging a man with twenty-five thousand dollars.

B-41 TOM, DICK AND HARRY

They really look stricken. Harry steps forward, then hesitates.

B-42 CLOSE SHOT - MR. BAXTER

MR. BAXTER
What's so funny about that?

He looks around in astonishment - then sees the Manager and calls to him.

MR. BAXTER
What is the meaning of this demonstra-
tion, Mr. Waterbury? I demand an im-
mediate explanation - and it had better
be very good!

B-43 THE MANAGER - PAST BAXTER

THE MANAGER
(Chuckling)
It is very good, sir. It appears that
this young lad...

5-23-40

(Continued)

B-43 (Cont'd) THE EMPLOYEES AROUND THEM
(Simultaneously)
Just won the ... isn't that wonderful ... you'd never think it to look ... and they say they give them ... twenty-five thousand in ... and they never said a word about it....

B-44 BAXTER - PAST THE OTHERS

MR. BAXTER
(Deafened by the yelling)
What? What? What? Quiet!

As partial quiet is restored, Tom, Dick and Harry approach through the crowd.

TOM
(Coming ahead)
Mr. Baxter.....

MR. BAXTER
(Angrily)
What do you want?

TOM
If anybody ... ought to be fired around here ... it's me.

MR. BAXTER
(Angrily)
Yes, well never mind the noble gestures. I'll decide what's what around here ... You can save the Rover Boy stuff for your spare time!
(He turns to the Manager)
See that this young man is paid off, Mr. Waterbury, and don't let this type of nonsense re-occur.
(He turns away)

THE MANAGER
(Conciliatingly)
But Mr. Baxter...there's a very good reason....

MR. BAXTER
Has it anything to do with the affairs of this company?

THE MANAGER
Well, no, but...

MR. BAXTER
Then I don't care to hear any more about it.

5-23-40 (Continued)

B-44 (Cont'd)

He glowers at the employees - then turns and starts away.

B-45 THE MANAGER, THE BOY AND THE GIRL

THE MANAGER
(Suddenly courageous)
But you do care to hear more about it!

The Manager almost staggers at this effrontery, then steadies by putting a hand on the desk.

B-46 MR. BAXTER - WALKING AWAY FROM US

He stops, turns slowly and considers the Manager before replying.

MR. BAXTER
How was that?

B-47 THE MANAGER, THE BOY AND THE GIRL

THE MANAGER
(Swallowing)
I said, "You do care to hear more about it." You couldn't have understood what was said or you wouldn't have walked away...These children, are part of your family, Mr. Baxter, and anything that happens to them is happening to you. So I say, if you don't care to hear any more about it, you must have misunderstood.

B-48 CLOSE SHOT - MR. BAXTER

He ponders a moment, then comes forward and faces the Manager.

MR. BAXTER
What is all this, Waterbury?

B-49 THE MANAGER, THE BOY AND THE GIRL - PAST BAXTER

THE MANAGER
(Indicating the Boy)
This young man, this minor employee of yours, has just won the twenty-five thousand dollar Parker House new slogan contest, Mr. Baxter, He, and he alone, was chosen the winner over millions of contestants; and I say, that that is reason enough for rejoicing.

5-23-40

B-50 MR. BAXTER - PAST THE OTHERS

MR. BAXTER
(Considering the Boy)
Well, I should say it is.
(He smiles and steps forward)

There is a happy yell from all. Mr. Baxter shakes the Boy's hand, then, as the noise subsides:

MR. BAXTER
Congratulations uh ...

THE GIRL
Jimmy.

MR. BAXTER
... Jimmy, and more power to you...
Now I suppose I'll have to hire you back at a fat increase.

There is laughter from the onlookers.

B-51 TOM, DICK AND HARRY

They look more and more stricken.

B-52 THE BOY AND THE GIRL - PAST BAXTER

THE BOY
I don't think that'll be necessary, Mr. Baxter... I've always liked it here and.. and... of course a little raise would come in mighty handy.

There is more laughter from the onlookers.

B-53 MR. BAXTER - PAST THE OTHERS

MR. BAXTER
You really won the Parker House contest, hunh?

THE BOY
(Laughing)
That's what the telegram says.

MR. BAXTER
(Frowning)
You say they wanted a new slogan or something?

5-23-40 (Continued)

B-53 (Cont'd)

THE BOY
Yes, sir.

MR. BAXTER
Well, it's about time they changed the old one.

There is laughter.

MR. BAXTER
What was your slogan.

B-54 THE BOY - PAST THE OTHERS

THE BOY
"If you don't sleep at night"... "IT ISN'T THE COFFEE"... "IT'S THE BUNK," Do you get it? It's a play on words... it means...

MR. BAXTER
But coffee keeps you awake.

THE BOY
No, sir. You see, this scientist ---

B-55 MR. BAXTER - PAST THE OTHERS

MR. BAXTER
(Interrupting)
It's a very clever idea just the same. "It isn't the coffee, it's the bunk." ... That ought to be good for the whole industry.

Laughter.

MR. BAXTER
(Continuing)
You didn't ever happen to get any ideas for Baxter & Sons, did you, while you were inventing slogans for our competitors? ... We make coffee too, you know.

B-56 THE BOY - PAST MR. BAXTER

THE BOY
(Earnestly)
I certainly did, Mr. Baxter. I've been trying to tell 'em to the

B-56 (Cont'd)

THE BOY (Cont'd)
advertising department ever since I've been here. I guess I've been down there about a thousand times till I guess they got kinda sick of me... You see, we don't advertise enough! What do we do? A half a page in the Grocers' Gazette, free paper bags and a cutout that was designed in 1902.

MR. BAXTER
(Mildly)
No, no, 1910.

THE BOY
All right, 1910. And while we're giving out a 1910 lithograph what are our competitors doing? I pause for a reply...

Mr. Baxter looks around to right and left.

THE BOY
The Blue Rose Cavaliers drench the nation with chamber music on Tuesdays and carpet cutting on Fridays! Hunt & Dearborn have got Dummy McGurk, the ventriloquist of the radio. ANYBODY can be a ventriloquist on the radio! Parker House has contests, throw-aways, free Neon signs, beautiful outdoor advertising in every nook and dell, and ROSCOE BROTHERS HAVE GOT A LIVE CAMEL IN EVERY CITY OVER A HUNDRED THOUSAND INHABITANTS WITH "YUM-YUM" SHAVED IN ITS FUR...ON BOTH SIDES!

B-57 BAXTER - PAST THE OTHERS

MR. BAXTER
They do, hunh. That's very interesting, Jimmy. Make a note of that Mr. Waterbury.

THE MANAGER
Yes, sir.

MR. BAXTER
How would you like to come into my office and tell me a few of these ideas?

5-23-40

B-58 THE BOY - PAST THE OTHERS

THE BOY
I should say I would, Mr. Baxter,
but ...
(He waves the telegram)
... I wonder if I hadn't better
get over to Parker House and pick
up this check... while it's hot....
I wouldn't want them to change
their minds.

There is mild laughter.

B-59 MR. BAXTER - PAST THE OTHERS

MR. BAXTER
A big corporation doesn't change
it's mind that easily, Jimmy...
and we might have something for
you here... even more interesting
than Parker House... in the long
run, of course.
(He adds cautiously)

B-60 THE BOY AND THE GIRL - PAST BAXTER

THE BOY
(Slightly stunned)
Yes, sir.

THE GIRL
(Squeezing his arm)
Oh, Jimmy!

They start forward and the CAMERA PANS with them.

MR. BAXTER
(Gently)
You can come too, my dear... Oh,
Waterbury, ask Jenkins to join us
and then come along also.

THE MANAGER
Yes, sir.

As the four move OUT OF THE SHOT the CAMERA PANS onto Tom, Dick and Harry. The three of them reach for their handkerchiefs simultaneously and start to mop their brows.

SLOW DISSOLVE TO:

5-23-40

B-61 MR. BAXTER'S PRIVATE OFFICE

We are SHOOTING PAST the Boy who faces Baxter, the Girl, the Manager and Mr. Jenkins.

THE BOY
(Quietly)
And then I'd put out a secondary brand, maybe: "Waterbury's... it's the berries," to catch the inbetween trade, because if Baxter's is the best you've got to charge a little more for it and we've got to have a good slogan for it. Word of mouth is all right, but only if you've got the right words.

MR. BAXTER
(To the Girl)
Make a note of that, dear.

THE MANAGER
(Crossly)
What do you mean, "Waterbury's -- it's the berries?" Who do you think...

MR. BAXTER
Now, now, now. Let him go on.

THE BOY
So I'd try to find a slogan that implied that Baxter's was in a class by itself... something like, not the aristocrat of coffees, that's been done, but ... but...
(Suddenly he pauses and his eyes bulge)
"THE BLUE BLOOD COFFEE... It's bred in the bean!" See? As if every bean in our coffee had a pedigree.
(Now he places the lettering on an imaginary sign)
"Baxter's Best... The Blueblood Coffee..."

THE GIRL
"It's bred in the bean."

MR. BAXTER
It's bred in the bean. Wonderful!

5-23-40 (Continued)

B-61 (Cont'd)

MR. BAXTER (Cont'd)
(He turns to his Sales Manager)
How about that one, Jenkins?

MR. JENKINS
The only trouble with it is I didn't think of it myself.
(He repeats)
"It's bred in the bean." I can see it all over the nation.

MR. BAXTER
In every nook and dell.

He gets up and puts his hand on the Boy's shoulder.

MR. BAXTER
Jimmy, I'm proud of you, now that you're a capitalist I don't know how you feel about working for a living, but if you'd like to have a little office here...

THE BOY
You mean to myself?

THE GIRL
With his name on the door?

MR. BAXTER
Well, naturally with his name on the door, and this young lady as your secretary and a uh... reasonable stipend to be determined upon later. I see no reason...

THE BOY
A reasonable what?

MR. BAXTER
A salary... a good salary... I see no reason why we shouldn't shake hands on it.

THE GIRL
Go ahead, Jimmy -

THE BOY
Well, gee whiz, Mr. Baxter, I ... Well, I should say I would... and how I would!

He shakes the Girl by the hand.

5-23-40 (Continued)

B-61 (Cont'd)

MR. BAXTER
What was your Parker House slogan again?

THE GIRL
It isn't the bunk, it's the coffee!

THE BOY
No, "It isn't the coffee, it's the bunk."

MR. BAXTER
(To Mr. Jenkins)
Oh! Isn't that marvelous? If you don't sleep at night, it isn't the uh --- it's the uh ...

MR. JENKINS
(Wisely)
Yes... but: "It's bred in the bean" ... That's the one for my money.

MR. BAXTER
I suppose you'd like the afternoon off, Jimmy, while we get your office ready?

THE BOY
I'd certainly appreciate it, Mr. Baxter. Can she come too?

MR. BAXTER
(Benignly)
Well, of course she can. And a little bird tells me what kind of a store you'll be visiting first, heh-heh-heh. A little jewelry store I'll wager.

THE BOY
I guess you're not so far wrong, only first of all we'll just stop off at Parker House ... and pick up that little check.

MR. BAXTER
Ah, yes, we'd almost forgotten that, hadn't we?

THE BOY
Almost, but not quite.

He shakes hands.

5-23-40

(Continued)

B-61 (Cont'd)

THE BOY
Thank you, Mr. Baxter, I don't know what to say... thank you, Mr. Jenkins, it'll certainly be a pleasure working with you, and thank you, Mr. Waterbury, and, ... uh...

THE GIRL
And how!

They exit.

MR. BAXTER
(Shaking his head after a moment)
A big future.

JENKINS
Immense.

MR. BAXTER
I've had my eye on him for some time.

The manager gives him a look.

B-62 THE BIG ROOM

The Boy and the Girl hurry in and go to their respective desks. The Girl takes out her handbag and joins the Boy who's putting his things away neatly.

THE BOY
Say, am I snoring?

THE GIRL
What? No, who, what do you mean? Of course you're not.

THE BOY
Then I guess I'm awake.

She squeezes his hand.

B-63 TOM, DICK AND HARRY - AT THEIR DESKS

Tom looks at the other two, then gets to his feet. The CAMERA PANS him over to the Boy's desk

TOM
(Embarrassed)
Say, look, kid.

THE BOY
What?

5-23-40 (Continued)

B-63 (Cont'd)

TOM
Can I talk to you for a moment...
it's kind of important.

THE BOY
(Impatiently)
Look, tell me when I come back,
will you? I've got to go over
to Parker House and pick up the
check or they might think I wasn't
grateful or something and...

TOM
That's what I wanted to talk to
you about... You see Harry and
Dick and I... Well...

THE BOY
Well, what?

TOM
Well, it's like this... You see
we...

MR. BAXTER'S VOICE
Oh, MacDonald.

THE BOY
(Turning)
Yes, sir?

B-64 LONG SHOT - BAXTER - PAST THE BOY

MR. BAXTER
(Coming forward)
Was that: "It's bred in the bean,"
or just plain "Bred in the bean?"

B-65 THE BOY, THE GIRL AND TOM - PAST THE WALKING BAXTER

THE BOY
"It's." You see just plain "Bred
in the bean" might sound like bread,
you know, like bread and butter.

B-66 CLOSE SHOT - TOM

He watches the others and we hear their voices.

5-23-40 (Continued)

B-66 (Cont'd)

MR. BAXTER'S VOICE
(Retreating)
Of course it does. I don't know why I didn't realize it. Well, have a nice time, and don't spend all your money in one place, heh-heh-heh.

THE BOY'S VOICE
(Retreating)
No, sir, we'll be careful. Goodbye.

B-67 MEDIUM LONG SHOT - THE BOY AND THE GIRL GOING OUT THE DOOR - PAST TOM'S SHOULDER

Mr. Baxter comes back smiling. Suddenly he realizes that Tom is standing there.

MR. BAXTER
Did you want to speak to me, D'Arcy?

B-68 TOM - PAST BAXTER

TOM
(Startled)
Who, me? No, sir, I uh...I was just watching them go out.

MR. BAXTER
(Chuckling)
This has been quite an exciting day, hasn't it, heh-heh-heh?

He moves away.

TOM
(With a phoney smile)
Yeah, and it ain't even over yet, heh-heh-heh.

The smile falls off his face as Baxter walks away. He passes his hand over his brow and starts toward his accomplices.

FADE OUT:

END OF SEQUENCE "B"

5-23-40

SEQUENCE "C"

FADE IN:

C-1 DR. PARKER AND THE RADIO ANNOUNCER - IN THE FORMER'S SUPERB OFFICE

DR. PARKER
(Marching up and down)
... and I said: "you can stay here till Hoboken freezes over!" I should have fired the whole bunch of them.
(He shakes an angry finger)
The biggest moment in commercial annals muffed by a gang of horse whistles who wouldn't know a slogan from a.... slap in the belly with a wet fish!

THE ANNOUNCER
I thought I would die of embarrassment.

DR. PARKER
I wish they had died of lockjaw.

A buzzer begins to ring.

DR. PARKER
What good are these contests anyway? They disrupt your entire organization, they make you millions of enemies and all they prove is you're making too much money in the first place since you can afford to toss a large chunk of it to some sap who probably never had a cup of your coffee in his life but lives on goat's milk!

THE ANNOUNCER
Have they reached a verdict yet?

DR. PARKER
I don't know and I don't care!

THE ANNOUNCER
Maybe if they could hold off until our next broadcast....

DR. PARKER
(Sarcastically)
No, no... that would be an intelligent thing....that would be useful to the

5-23-40 (Continued)

C-1 (Cont'd)

DR. PARKER (Cont'd)
company that feeds and clothes them and sends their children to college so they can grow up to be dumbbells like their parents...
(He answers the dictaphone)
What do you want?

A GIRL'S WHINY VOICE
(On the dictaphone)
The contest winner is here, Dr. Parker.

DR. PARKER
The contest winner!
(He turns to the Announcer)
Well, how do you like that one! First they bottle up the biggest scoop of the year and then when they get good and ready they... ALL RIGHT, SEND HIM IN!
(Then to the Announcer)
But just wait until I get through with that Bildocker!

C-2 THE BOY AND THE GIRL - IN PARKER'S OUTER OFFICE

They sit nervously side by side, the boy clutching his telegram. An elderly lady secretary sits in the foreground. Through a partition in the background we see some more secretaries.

THE SECRETARY
(Turning from the dictaphone)
You can go in now.

THE BOY
Thanks.

He gets up and the Girl gets up too.

THE GIRL
I'll wait out here.

THE BOY
Come on in... well, no... maybe you'd better wait out here.
(He smiles sheepishly at the Secretary)
I guess we're kind of excited.

5-23-40 (Continued)

C-2 (Cont'd)

THE SECRETARY
I should think you would be. Congratulations.

THE GIRL
Thanks... I mean for him.

THE BOY
For us both.

The CAMERA PANS him to the door marked "Private." He knocks.

C-3 DR. PARKER AND THE ANNOUNCER

DR. PARKER
Come in.

C-4 THE BOY - PAST DR. PARKER AND THE ANNOUNCER

He comes in a little awkwardly.

THE BOY
How do you do, sir. I suppose I have the honor of addressing Dr. Parker, I presume.

C-5 DR. PARKER AND THE ANNOUNCER - PAST THE BOY

DR. PARKER
(Sharply)
That's right, and this is Don Hartman, my announcer.

C-6 THE BOY - PAST THE OTHERS

THE BOY
(With enthusiasm)
It's certainly a pleasure to meet you, Mr. Hartman... I've certainly enjoyed your personality on the air.

THE ANNOUNCER
Congratulations to you.

THE BOY
Thank you.
(He holds the telegram forward)

5-23-40 (Continued)

C-6 (Cont'd)

THE BOY (Cont'd)
Here's the telegram, Mr. Parker...
Dr. Parker.

He hands it to Dr. Parker who takes it.

C-7 DR. PARKER AND THE ANNOUNCER - PAST THE BOY

DR. PARKER
(Reading the telegram)
Yes, yes. "Kindly call and pick up
your check." Bildocker has a great
sense of the dramatic.

The Announcer clutches his head.

DR. PARKER
Are you by any chance a coffee
drinker, Mr. MacDonald?

THE BOY
Yes, sir, I certainly am.

DR. PARKER
That's surprising... you don't by
any chance drink... Parker House,
do you?

THE BOY
Well... no, sir, I've been drinking
Baxter's Best.

DR. PARKER
Ah, yes... that sounds more natural.

THE BOY
But I could easily change.

DR. PARKER
(Dryly)
That won't be necessary, Mr. MacDonald..
I wouldn't want anybody to think I had
any base commercial motives in all this..
I just give money away because I can't
sleep at night... I have a guilty con-
science.

THE BOY
(Happily)
That's my slogan! The one I won with.
Well, I guess you know about that.

5-23-40 (Continued)

C-7 (Cont'd)

DR. PARKER
A guilty conscience, hunh? I can see that my money is well spent. That's a great slogan.
(He talks into the dictaphone)
Bring me the contest check.

THE BOY
No, no. If you can't sleep at night.. it isn't the coffee, it's the bunk... do you get it?

DR. PARKER
Hunh?

THE BOY
It's a pun.

DR. PARKER
(After a slight pause)
It certainly is... It's great.

THE BOY
Thank you.

C-8 THE BOY - PAST DR. PARKER AND THE ANNOUNCER

THE BOY
I don't know whether you've ever had anything like this happen to you, Dr. Parker, but to be poor and...unknown one minute, and be sitting on top of the world the next minute, that's a feeling nobody can ever take away from me... to know I won this contest because I thought up a better slogan than anyone else means more to me than anything else on earth... and I'll tell you why: You see, I used to _think_ maybe I had good ideas and was going to get somewhere in the world...but _now_ I _know_ it... and that's what I want to thank you for, Dr. Parker... even more than the money.

A door opens behind him and a cashier comes in with a check.

THE CASHIER
(Reaching the desk)
Was this the one you wanted, Dr. Parker? The twenty-five thousand dollar one?

5-23-40 (Continued)

C-8 (Cont'd)

DR. PARKER
(Reaching for it)
That's right.
(He starts to write)

THE CASHIER
I didn't know they'd agreed on a winner yet.

The Boy mops his head.

C-9 DR. PARKER - PAST THE BOY AND THE CASHIER

DR. PARKER
Oh, yes... they don't bother to inform us about these things, of course... James MacDonald... is that "Mac" or "Mc?"

THE BOY
"Mac," sir.

DR. PARKER
(Writing)
Ah, yes... my grandmother was Scottish ....here we are.

He reaches the check across the desk.

DR. PARKER
Here you are, young man... it is customary under these circumstances to have a few photographers present.. a couple of reporters and even news reels and broadcasting machinery, but since we do everything around here on a very high non-commercial plane, I merely take pleasure in handing you this small check, Mr. Mac...
(He consults the check)
...Donald... AND THAT'S ALL THERE IS TO IT!

THE BOY
(Emotionally)
Thank you, Dr. Parker, I don't know what words I can use to...

DR. PARKER
(Interrupting)
Yes, well never mind them. Just.... goodbye...good luck to you.

The Boy turns, examines his check.

5-23-40 (Continued)

C-9 (Cont'd)

THE BOY
Oh, boy!

He starts to spring out of the room, knocks over a chair, picks it up, back away shyly and falls into the arms of another chair, gets up, laughs like a half-wit and hurries out.

DR. PARKER
(Into the dictaphone)
Now send for Bildocker!

C-10 THE BOY AND THE GIRL - IN THE OUTER OFFICE

The Girl is examining the check. Suddenly she throws her arms around the Boy's neck.

THE BOY
She's a little bit excited.

THE GIRL
He's as cool as ice.

They hurry out and the Secretary laughs.

C-11 DR. PARKER AND THE ANNOUNCER

DR. PARKER
Out of the millions of answers these birds had to pick from...
(Into dictaphone)
Well, why isn't he in his office? Where is he, down in the lobby playing the marble games? You find him and tell him... Never mind, I'll tell him myself.
(He hangs up and mumbles)
It isn't the coffee, it's the bunk.

C-12 THE CONFERENCE ROOM OF THE PARKER HOUSE COFFEE COMPANY

The jurors are sitting around in attitudes of extreme dejection. One of them is looking out the window, two of them are matching quarters lackadaisically. One gentleman is asleep, two gentlemen are playing tick-tack-toe and the other five surround Bildocker who glowers at the head of the table.

A LARGE ROUGH GENTLEMAN
Why don't you get wise to yourself? Who do you think you are? If it's

5-23-40 (Continued)

C-12 (Cont'd)

A LARGE ROUGH GENTLEMAN (Cont'd)
good enough for the eleven of us, who are you to say...

BILDOCKER
It stinks.

A LARGE ROUGH GENTLEMAN
(Indignantly)
It stinks!

THE THIN SOUR GENTLEMAN
He stinks!

BILDOCKER
One more crack out of you, Armbrewster, and I'll....

THE THIN SOUR GENTLEMAN
All right, let's see you do it.

BILDOCKER
All right, I will, you snake-eyed --

They are kept apart.

A LARGE ROUGH GENTLEMAN
Sit down before you burst a blood vessel!

THE LARGE GENTLEMAN
Let's talk this over in a nice friendly way. We think:
(He reads from a paper)
"Parker's Peps the Palate" is just what the doctor ordered. It's smooth, it's brief, it's pungent, it..."

BILDOCKER
It's putrid.

THE LARGE GENTLEMAN
(As to a child)
Why is it putrid?

BILDOCKER
Because it stinks!

THE MILD GENTLEMAN
(Clutching his forehead)
Oh, death, where is thy sting?

All resume attitudes of dejection. Mr. Bildocker glares around the room.

FADE OUT:

END OF SEQUENCE "C"

SEQUENCE "D"

FADE IN:

D-1 A CLOSEUP OF A DIAMOND SOLITAIRE

THE GIRL'S VOICE
Isn't it beautiful, Jimmy?

THE BOY'S VOICE
Holy smoke, I should say it is.

D-2 THE BOY, THE GIRL AND A VERY SUPERIOR SALESMAN - AT THE JEWELRY COUNTER OF A GREAT DEPARTMENT STORE

THE SALESMAN
(Condescendingly)
Of course this is a little on the large side...now here is a stone of more practical dimensions.

He picks up a ring and twiddles it.

THE SALESMAN
Fiery little devil, isn't it?

D-3 CLOSEUP OF THE LITTLE RING

D-4 CLOSE SHOT - THE BOY AND THE GIRL

The Girl's face has fallen considerably.

THE BOY
(Sourly)
Looks more like a glass cutter.

D-5 THE SALESMAN - PAST THE BOY AND THE GIRL

THE SALESMAN
(Resentfully)
Of course it's entirely up to you... I'm only trying to be helpful, you know. It's immaterial to me how bit a ring you ... look at heh-heh-heh.

He laughs nastily, then snatches up a superb emerald cut.

D-5 (Cont'd)

THE SALESMAN
(After examining the Boy's suit)
What do you think of this, for instance?

THE BOY
(Resenting his manner)
How much is it?

THE SALESMAN
(Examining the tag)
Twelve thousand dollars.

THE BOY
(Quietly)
I wouldn't care to spend that much.

THE SALESMAN
(With some sarcasm)
Oh, you wouldn't.

THE BOY
No, but I could.

THE SALESMAN
(Faintly worried)
Oh.
(He clears his throat)
Well, that puts everything on an entirely different basis. Now... uh, let me see....

THE GIRL
(Pointing to the first diamond)
I'm in love with that one.

THE SALESMAN
(Disappointed)
Oh. Do you think it's uh...showy enough.

THE GIRL
I wouldn't want it to be showy.

THE SALESMAN
(Sadly)
Ah, yes. Of course there's no denying it's a very handsome little piece.

5-23-40

(Continued)

D-5 (Cont'd)

THE BOY
Then I guess we'll take it.

THE SALESMAN
(Solemnly)
Yes, sir.

THE GIRL
Oh, Jimmy!

THE BOY
Of course I haven't got any cash with me....

THE SALESMAN
(His suspicions confirmed)
Ah!

THE BOY
(Pulling out the check)
But I got a check here.

THE SALESMAN
(Coldly)
Aha. May I see it, please?

THE BOY
Sure.

The Salesman takes it and does a triple-take.

THE SALESMAN
Oh. Well, well.
(Now he calls to someone in the distance)
Mr. Schmidt, could you step this way immediately, if you please?
(He turns back to the boy)
Well, well, well.

THE BOY
(Quietly)
I won the Parker House contest.

THE GIRL
Isn't it wonderful?

5-23-40 (Continued)

D-5 (Cont'd)

THE SALESMAN
Well...dog my cats, I should say it is! A thousand congratulations.. I mean twenty-five thousand congratulations... for heaven sakes!
(Calling peremptorily)
Mr. Schmidt!

D-6 CLOSE SHOT - MR. SCHMIDT OKAYING AN ORDER

MR. SCHMIDT
(Displeased)
Yes, yes, Mr. Hillbeiner, I'll be there presently.

D-7 THE SALESMAN, THE BOY AND THE GIRL

THE SALESMAN
(Forcefully)
Well, kindly cut a groove, will you?

D-8 MR. SCHMIDT

MR. SCHMIDT
(Aghast)
Sir?

He hands the order book pompously back to a girl and says in a low voice:

MR. SCHMIDT
Hillbeiner's been drinking again.

He walks forward coldly.

DISSOLVE TO:

D-9 DICTAPHONE - IN DR. PARKER'S OFFICE

A TINNY VOICE
Schindel Brothers want to know if that twenty-five thousand dollar check of yours is good, Dr. Parker.

5-23-40

D-10 DR. PARKER SIGNING LETTERS - AT HIS DESK

DR. PARKER
(Furiously)
What do they mean, is it good? Tell 'em I'll match mine against theirs any day and give them six to four!

D-11 THE DICTAPHONE

THE TINNY VOICE
Yes, sir.

There is a click.

DISSOLVE TO:

D-12 THE BOY, THE GIRL, MR. HILLBEINER, MR. SCHMIDT AND A FURNITURE SALESMAN - IN THE FURNITURE DEPARTMENT OF SCHINDEL BROS.

They are standing around a striped davenport.

THE FURNITURE SALESMAN
The Davenola - Now watch closely. I merely remove the two cushions and place my finger on the button marked "Night", which is next to the button marked "Day", and vice versa and with one easy push of the finger we have:

The divan changes into a double bed.

THE FURNITURE SALESMAN
...a double bed, a radio, an ash tray for those who smoke in bed, a reading lamp for the most voracious reader. Pausing merely to slip a pillowslip over the day cushion, we complete the metamorphosis.

THE GIRL
Isn't that wonderful?

THE BOY
Mom will go nuts.

MR. SCHMIDT
(Solemnly)
There is no limit to man's ingenuity.

5-23-40 (Continued)

D-12 (Cont'd)

THE FURNITURE SALESMAN
Comes the morrow... a flick of the wrist....
(He empties the pillow-slip and folds them up)
...a thorough airing....
(He flaps the sheet up and down once and picks up the cushions)
... a gentle pressure on the button marked "Day", et voila, as the French say.

The bed turns into a divan and he drops the cushions on it.

THE FURNITURE SALESMAN
Ready for the invigorating breakfast, the browsing book, or the gentle game of bridge. The price: One ninety-eight fifty plus tax.

THE BOY
We'll take it.

MR. SCHINDEL
(Approaching with the Boy's check in his hand)
And what a bargain you're getting. I'm Mr. Schindel, Mr. MacDonald. Congratulations and here's your check... what a check!

THE BOY
(Pointing to the davenport)
Say, how soon could you send it? My mother's wanted it for so long...

MR. SCHINDEL
(Raising a hand)
It's there! We'll make it a special. Take note, Hillbeiner.

HILLBEINER
Yes, sir.

THE BOY
(Suddenly to the Girl)
Say, do you think your mother would like one?

5-23-40 (Continued)

D-12 (Cont'd)

THE GIRL
Oh no, thank you, Jimmy, we haven't got room.

THE BOY
Well, we've got to get her something... we've got to get everybody something.

THE GIRL
(Diffidently)
Well, mamma's been wanting a new iron for a long time.

MR. SCHINDEL
She's got it!

THE BOY
(To Schindel)
Have you got irons?

MR. SCHINDEL
Have we got irons! They do everything but sing!

THE BOY
(Suddenly to the Girl)
And say: -- We've got to get something for Mrs. Schwartz...and a doll for Sophie...and old Mr. Zimmerman...and the Casey kids....

THE GIRL
Aren't you afraid of spending too much?

THE BOY
Nonsense...and the Finnegan kids...

THE GIRL
And Patrolman Murphy....

THE BOY
And Tony Mazeppo....

THE GIRL
And Mr. Rosenblatt....

THE BOY
Look: We'd better just work down one side of the street and then up the other...that way we won't forget anybody.

5-23-40 (Continued)

D-12 (Cont'd)

THE GIRL
(Happily)
Oh, Jimmy!

HILLBEINER
(Soaping his hands)
Well, well, well... What a day!

DISSOLVE TO:

D-13 THE MAIN ENTRANCE TO SCHINDEL BROS. - PAST A TAXICAB

Porters are coming out with quantities of packages. As they move down the line we PAN with them and see that they are filling several cabs.

D-14 THE BOY, THE GIRL, MR. HILLBEINER, MR. SCHMIDT AND MR. SCHINDEL - JUST INSIDE SCHINDEL BROS.

Some young employees are looking on in the background.

THE BOY
(With the check in his hand)
I don't like to take all this without paying for it, Mr. Schindel.

MR. SCHINDEL
Nonsense, Mr. MacDonald, I guess we know an honest man when we see him, don't we, boys?

Mr. Schmidt and Mr. Hillbeiner laugh horsily.

THE BOY
(Proffering the check)
If you'll just take the check and give me the change.

MR. SCHINDEL
(Laughing)
We should have change for such a check!

He exchanges a glance with his employees and they laugh again. Suddenly he leans forward to the Girl.

MR. SCHINDEL
Excuse me.

5-23-40 (Continued)

D-14 (Cont'd)

He takes a pair of blunt-noses scissors out of his pocket and cuts the price tag off a beautiful fox fur piece she is wearing.

THE GIRL
Oh, thank you.

She examines her solitaire.

MR. SCHINDEL
What a stone!

THE BOY
Well then...Mr. Schindel, I'll give you a check as soon as I put this in the bank...

MR. SCHINDEL
Who's in a hurry? Drop in any time... drop in tomorrow...Have a cigar.

THE BOY
Well, thanks, I....
(He fumbles the cigar and drops it)

Schmidt and Hillbeiner start to pick it up.

MR. SCHINDEL
(Stopping them)
Have another...
(He puts it in the Boy's breast pocket)
Goodbye....Don't forget to come back.

THE BOY
I won't. Goodbye, Mr. Schindel.

THE GIRL
Goodbye, Mr. Schindel.

THE BOY
Goodbye, Mr. Schmidt.

MR. SCHMIDT
Goodbye, Mr.. MacDonald.

THE GIRL
Goodbye, Mr. Schmidt.

MR. SCHMIDT
Goodbye, Mrs. uh...

5-23-40 (Continued)

D-14 (Cont'd)

MR. SCHINDEL
(Quickly, pointing to the engagement ring)
Miss.

MR. SCHMIDT
Miss.

THE BOY
Goodbye, Mr. Billheimer.

HILLBEINER
(Gently)
Hillbeiner.

THE GIRL
Goodbye, Mr. Heilbimmer.

As Mr. Hillbeiner opens his mouth to correct her, Mr. Schindel lays a heavy hand on his shoulder.

MR. SCHINDEL
That's close enough. Goodbye, goodbye.

THE BOY AND
THE GIRL
Goodbye.

They go OUT OF THE SHOT.

MR. SCHINDEL
(Coyly)
Don't forget.
(He shakes his head)

Mr. Hillbeiner and Mr. Schmidt shake their heads too.

MR. HILLBEINER
What a boy.

MR. SCHINDEL
(Picking up his cigar)
What a business!

He puts the cigar back in his pocket.

DISSOLVE TO:

5-23-40

D-15 THE BOY AND THE GIRL - IN THE TAXICAB

They are holding hands. They ride in silence for a moment, then she releases her hand and takes a look at the sparkler.

THE GIRL
I'm so happy.

THE BOY
I feel pretty good myself. Can you see the faces on everybody when we get out there?

THE GIRL
Yes...Like Christmas...in July.

THE BOY
Maybe I should have bought a beard!

She laughs at him.

THE BOY
Well...Happy New Year!

He kisses her on the cheek.

THE GIRL
It will be a happy New Year too... from now on. Everything new and clean and different, and just think, Jimmy, no more worry.

THE BOY
That's right.

THE GIRL
That's the only terrible thing about being poor. What kind of a house are we going to have?

THE BOY
Any kind you like.

THE GIRL
How about a penthouse?

THE BOY
They come kinda high, don't they?

5-23-40 (Continued)

D-15 (Cont'd)

GIRL
(Only getting it in the middle)
Oh, I don't think...Oh, you fool!

They both laugh and he hugs her tight to him.

THE BOY
How soon do we take the dive?

THE GIRL
(Blankly)
Hunh?

THE BOY
When do we get hitched?

THE GIRL
(Understanding)
Oh, you mean get married...Why don't we do it tonight after dinner.

THE BOY
You can't do that...You have to wait three days now.

THE GIRL
(Blankly)
What for?

THE BOY
The test.

THE GIRL
(Innocently)
What test?

THE BOY
(Frowning slightly)
Well, the test, that's all.

THE GIRL
What kind of a test?

THE BOY
Well, it's a kind of a test to see if you ought to get married or not.

THE GIRL
You mean like a literacy test?

THE BOY
Well, something like that.

D-15 (Cont'd)

THE GIRL
I'll never pass it.

THE BOY
(Turning slowly)
Hunh?

THE GIRL
I never passed a test in my life. I get so nervous I just can't do it. It was the same in history and geography and arithmetic...and ho-ho, you should have caught me in geometry.

THE BOY
Well, you're going to give yourself a big surprise this time.

THE GIRL
I hope so.
(She snuggles close to him)
Will you love me for always?

THE BOY
Of course I will.

THE GIRL
For always and always?

THE BOY
I don't know why not.

THE GIRL
(Smiling)
That might be a long time.

THE BOY
The longer the sweeter.

FADE OUT:

END OF SEQUENCE "D"

5-23-40

SEQUENCE "E"

FADE IN:

E-1 MRS. MacDONALD'S FRONT ROOM

She is talking to Mrs. Schwartz, Mrs. Casey and Mr. Zimmerman.

MRS. MacDONALD
(Worried)
And then he said: "You're all wet, Mom..."

Mrs. Schwartz clucks disapprovingly.

MRS. MacDONALD
"... you can buy anything you want: Automobiles, dresses, new furniture... the davenport ... anything!"

MRS. SCHWARTZ
(Sympathetically)
I know, my Irving drinks too, a little bit...once in a while.

MRS. MacDONALD
(Fervently)
I know, but Jimmy doesn't. I can't think of his taking a drink unless something terrible happened.

MR. ZIMMERMAN
Maybe he lost his job.

MRS. CASEY
But he said he got a raise.

MRS. SCHWARTZ
Who's giving raises these days?

MRS. MacDONALD
(Wringing her hands)
Well...
(She sniffles)
... I don't know what to think...

At this moment we hear a symphony of four taxi horns in the street below and some excited babble.

MR. ZIMMERMAN
(Dolefully)
They're bringing him home.

5-24-40 (Continued)

E-1 (Cont'd)

Mrs. Casey crosses hurriedly to the window.

MRS. SCHWARTZ
(Crossly to
Mr. Zimmerman)
What do you have to talk?
(Then to Mrs. MacDonald)
It's probably just a little accident
... a leg... maybe a finger...

MRS. CASEY
(Piercingly from the
window)
Come here!

She sticks her head back out the window.

E-2 EXT. - LOW CAMERA SHOT - UP AT MRS. CASEY FROM OUTSIDE THE WINDOW

She calls back into the room.

MRS. CASEY
Come here quick!

Now appear the heads of Mr. Zimmerman, Mrs. Schwartz, and finally Mrs. MacDonald.

MR. ZIMMERMAN
A funeral.

E-3 HIGH CAMERA SHOT DOWN ON THE LITTLE STREET

Four yellow cabs are coming to a stop. A crowd of children has gathered around them, across the street Sophie, the little crippled girl, watches from her wheelchair, there are heads in all the windows and people are emerging from doorways and basement stores. Patrolman Murphy is approaching from the corner.

E-4 CLOSE HIGH SHOT - DOWN ON THE FIRST CAB

The door flies open and the Boy jumps out.

THE BOY
(Hollering up)
Hey, Mom, come on down... and
you too, Mrs. Schwartz!

5-24-40 (Continued)

E-4 (Cont'd)

THE GIRL
(Joining him)
And you too, Mamma.

THE BOY
We've got presents for everybody.

E-5 LOW CAMERA SHOT - UP AT THE WINDOW

MR. ZIMMERMAN
He's drunk.

MRS. MacDONALD
(Emotionally)
Jimmy!

E-6 CLOSE SHOT - THE BOY AND THE GIRL - IN FRONT OF THE TAXI

They are looking up OVER THE CAMERA.

THE BOY
I'm all right, Mom, come on down.

THE GIRL
(Holding up the diamond ring and twinkling it)
Look!

The crowd grows and presses closer.

THE BOY
Come on, now, and give me some room.

He reaches in the cab, takes out a big box, then pauses before disappearing in the crowd.

THE BOY
(To the Girl)
You start with the others.

E-7 CLOSE SHOT - SOPHIE - IN HER WHEELCHAIR

Her mother stands behind her, wiping her hands on her apron.

5-24-40 (Continued)

E-7 (Cont'd)

SOPHIE'S MOTHER
(Looking across the street)
What happened? Was somebody hurt?

SOPHIE
Jimmy MacDonald came home in a taxicab.

E-8 REVERSE SHOT ACROSS THE STREET - PAST SOPHIE AND HER MOTHER

The Boy pushes his way through the crowd. He comes toward us carrying the big box.

THE BOY
(As he gets near)
I brought you a present, Sophie.

He puts the big box in her arms.

E-9 SOPHIE AND HER MOTHER - PAST THE BOY

SOPHIE
(Holding the box tight)
What for?

THE BOY
Go on, open it.

SOPHIE'S MOTHER
Open it up, honey.

Sophie looks around at her mother, then slips the string off, opens the box and starts separating the tissue paper with trembling hands.

E-10 LOW PANNING CAMERA SHOT - UP AT THE BOY AND THE CHILDREN AND GROWNUPS NEAR HIM

Jimmy smiles a little, but the others crane their necks. Suddenly there is an "Oh!" of wonderment as the beauty of the doll is seen.

5-24-40

E-11 CLOSE SHOT - SOPHIE AND HER PRESENT

Her head is bent over the doll as she lifts it tenderly and clasps it to her bosom. After a moment she looks up. The tears are streaming down her face.

E-12 THE DOORWAY OF THE HOUSE THE BOY LIVES IN

Mr. Zimmerman comes hurrying out followed a moment later by Mrs. Schwartz. Now come Mrs. Casey and Mrs. MacDonald.

MRS. CASEY
Betty!

MRS. MacDONALD
Jimmy!

E-13 THE FIRST TAXICAB - PAST MRS. MacDONALD, ET AL

The Girl is handing out packages, the Boy just appearing through the crowd.

THE BOY
Come on, now, take it easy...
one at a time. There's something
for almost everybody, I guess.
(Now he sees his
mother)
Hello, Mom.

THE GIRL
Hello, Mama.

He comes forward and takes her in his arms. Mrs. Casey rushes down the steps and puts her arms around the Girl.

E-14 THE BOY AND HIS MOTHER

We see the Girl and her mother in the background.

MRS. MacDONALD
I thought you was hurt. What
happened to you? What's all
this, Jimmy?

THE BOY
I wasn't lyin' to you, Mom. The

5-24-40 (Continued)

E-14 (Cont'd)

THE BOY (Cont'd)
davenport is comin' by special delivery and wait till you see it, oh, boy!

MRS. MacDONALD
Then you did get a raise.

THE BOY
Look, I got this.

He pulls the check out of his pocket. As his Mother looks at it stupefied --

E-15 THE GIRL IN HER MOTHER'S ARMS

MRS. CASEY
But what is it?

She looks around at the commotion. Mrs. Schwartz and Mr. Zimmerman come INTO THE SHOT.

MRS. SCHWARTZ
What happened?

MR. ZIMMERMAN
He won the swipsticks.

THE GIRL
No, he won the Parker House contest.

MRS. SCHWARTZ
What kind of a house is that?

MR. ZIMMERMAN
Is a hotel.

THE GIRL
(Holding up the solitaire)
Look, Mamma.

MRS. CASEY
(Taking her in her arms)
Oh, darling.

MR. ZIMMERMAN
(Suddenly seeing the diamond)
Aye-yi-yi-yi-yi-yi!

5-24-40 (Continued)

E-15 (Cont'd)

MRS. SCHWARTZ
(Trying to grab the Girl)
Oh, darlink, I'm so happy for you.

She bursts into tears.

E-16 THE GIRL AND HER MOTHER

THE GIRL
Well, what are you crying about? You ought to be laughing.

MRS. CASEY
(Between laughter and tears)
I know.

E-17 THE LITTLE CRIPPLE GIRL AND HER DOLL

She is surrounded by other little girls. Suddenly a look of consternation comes over the little cripple girl's face. She feels under the doll, then looks at the other little girls with a look of astonishment.

DISSOLVE TO:

E-18 DR. PARKER - AT THE DICTAPHONE

DR. PARKER
What do you mean, he isn't back? Why isn't he back? Where is he, in the barbershop...never mind him. Tell him to go soak his head in a barrel.
(He switches to another key)
Is Mr. Armbrewster there? Well, why isn't he there? Where is everybody, playing pool?
(He switches to the next key)
Is Mr. Groble there? He isn't! What's he having, an operation? What kind of a firm is this, anyway? What do you mean, he's in the contest room. The

5-24-40 (Continued)

E-18 (Cont'd)

DR. PARKER (Cont'd)
contest is all over... Well, what are they doing down there, playing poker... NEVER MIND...I'LL FIND OUT MYSELF!
(He rises to his feet. To no one in particular)
Horse feathers!

He starts out of the room.

E-19 THE CONFERENCE ROOM OF THE PARKER HOUSE COFFEE COMPANY

The gentlemen are as before.

BILDOCKER
All right: I say it stinks!

M. G.
Don't be vulgar, Bildocker.

BILDOCKER
(Vulgarly)
Who are you?

The door brusts open and Dr. Parker stamps into the room.

DR. PARKER
What are you arguing about now? Haven't you made enough trouble? Now that it's over would you be kind enough to get back to your offices and try to sell a little coffee for a change... or am I being too commercial? And while I'm on that subject, I just want to tell you that of all the congregations of fatheads I've ever had the pleasure of gazing upon... you take the lard pail! So kiss each other goodbye and all get back to your offices... all except Bildocker! You come with me.

BILDOCKER
Then what about the contest?

DR. PARKER
What about it? Now that you've killed it do you have to hold a post mortem on it?

5-24-40 (Continued)

E-19 (Cont'd)

BILDOCKER
Don't you want us to choose a winner?

DR. PARKER
You chose a winner!

BILDOCKER
(Scowling)
Who chose a winner? We certainly did not choose a winner...

DR. PARKER
Well, you certainly did choose a winner... WHAT DO YOU MEAN, YOU DIDN'T CHOOSE A WINNER?

BILDOCKER
I mean we haven't reached a verdict yet.

DR. PARKER
(Horrified)
You haven't reached a verdict yet!

BILDOCKER
No, sir.

DR. PARKER
Well you certainly have reached a verdict yet.... WHAT DO YOU MEAN YOU HAVEN'T REACHED A VERDICT YET? Are you trying to stand there and tell me that... that...you haven't reached a verdict yet!

BILDOCKER
We have not!

DR. PARKER
(Pointing helplessly)
Then why did you send him a telegram telling him he won?

BILDOCKER
(Stupefied)
Send who a telegram?

DR. PARKER
(Looking around the room wildly)
McTavish.

BILDOCKER
We didn't send any telegram. Who's McTavish?

5-24-40 (Continued)

E-19 (Cont'd)

DR. PARKER
You didn't send any telegram! Well, you certainly did send a telegram.

BILDOCKER
Well we certainly did not send a telegram.

DR. PARKER
You didn't? Then who...who... Holy smoke!

He sprints out of the room.

BILDOCKER
Now where were we?

THE LARGE GENTLEMAN
I was saying that "Parker's peps the palate..."

BILDOCKER
And I say it stinks!

E-20 DR. PARKER'S OUTER OFFICE

The door bursts open and flies in.

DR. PARKER
(Excitedly)
Get my lawyers!

THE SECRETARY
Which ones, Dr. Parker?

DR. PARKER
Schlummel, Schlimmel, Abercrombie and Schlitz! Get the police!

Another secretary screams.

DR. PARKER
Quiet! Get me Schindel Brothers.

SECRETARY
Yes, sir.

DR. PARKER
The important thing at a moment like this is to keep cool and collected... COLLECTED! Holy Moses! Don't get excited... bank the call!

THE SECRETARY
(Puzzled)
Bank the call?

5-24-40 (Continued)

E-20 (Cont'd)

DR. PARKER
CALL THE BANK! What's the matter with you? Holy mackerel!

He mops his head, runs into a room marked "Ladies," comes out and says:

DR. PARKER
Excuse me.

He hurries into his office.

DISSOLVE TO:

E-21 MR. SCHINDEL - AT A TELEPHONE IN THE GENT'S HAT DEPARTMENT

Mr. Schmidt is balancing on the balls of his feet in the background. A customer is trying on a hat in front of a mirror.

MR. SCHINDEL
(At the top of his lungs)
WHAT?
(He slams the phone down on the counter)
Give me a hat.
(He turns and yells at Schmidt)
Get me Minsk, Pinsk, Minsk and Pinsk!

SCHMIDT
Yes, sir.

THE HAT SALESMAN
What kind of a hat, Mr. Schindel?

MR. SCHINDEL
(Bellowing)
A hat!

THE SALESMAN
(Trembling)
Yes, sir.

He hands him a decorated ski hat with a badger in the back. Mr. Schindel puts it on his head, then throws it in his face.

MR. SCHINDEL
Schlemiel!

5-24-40 (Continued)

E-21 (Cont'd)

He grabs a derby off a stand, slaps it on his head where it slips down to his ears. He gallops OUT OF THE SHOT.

E-22 LOW CAMERA SHOT - UP AT AN ESCALATOR

The side nearest us is going up and this is the side Mr. Schindel chooses for his descent. His legs move very rapidly until he trips and falls OUT OF THE SHOT. A moment later he is carried slowly back INTO THE PICTURE. Now he gets to his feet and starts again. Slowly he makes headway.

E-23 THE DELIVERY PLATFORM OF SCHINDEL BROTHERS

Four men are loading the Boy's davenport onto a truck. On the side of the truck, glass panels which can be illuminated read:

SCHINDEL BROS.
"Everything from A to Zither"

Mr. Schindel appears followed by Messrs. Hillbeiner and Schmidt.

MR. SCHINDEL
Stop!... No! Go! We'll go with you! Step on it!

Mr. Schindel, Mr. Hillbeiner and Mr. Schmidt sit on the davenport. The truckmen hop on and the truck hurries away.

DISSOLVE TO:

E-24 THE DEAD END STREET

It looks like an Elks' picnic. The following props are in evidence: Dolls, boxing gloves, kiddiecars, tricycles, automobiles, badminton sets, baseball outfits, football outfits, one Indian outfit with bow and arrow, one traffic cop's outfit complete with whistle, one fireman's outfit with small ladder, several cowboys' outfits with lassoes and six-shooters, some large striped rubber balls, one diavolo outfit, half a dozen pogo sticks, an assortment of horns and siren whistles, an assortment of false faces, water pistols, noise makers, and a pair of stilts. A baseball game is in progress in the middle of the street, children are whizzing up and down on

5-24-40 (Continued)

E-24 (Cont'd)

kiddiecars, tricycles, and toy automobiles, a hurdy-gurdy is playing some invigorating music, Mrs. MacDonald and Mrs. Casey are distributing ice cream cones from an ice cream wagon, and the Boy and the Girl are giving out presents from the last taxi. The din is terrific. There are traffic accidents between toy automobiles, disasters to dolls accompanied by loud wails and a few fist fights. Over all this presides patrolman Murphy, a cigar in one hand and an ice cream cone in the other. Next to him stands a little boy in a cop uniform. He is directing traffic shrilly. Across the street are a fish wagon, a merry-go-round and a fruit and vegetable wagon.

E-25 CLOSE SHOT - THE BOY AND THE GIRL AT THE TAXI

They are happy and hot. He scoops some sweat off his brow and they grin at each other. Suddenly the Girl's face falls.

THE GIRL
Jimmy.

THE BOY
(Scowling over the din)
What?

THE GIRL
You forgot to get a present for yourself.

THE BOY
What?

THE GIRL
I said you forgot to get a present for yourself.

THE BOY
What do I want a present for? I've got you.

She smiles sweetly, kisses him on the cheek and they resume the distribution of presents.

E-26 THE END OF THE STREET

The Schindel Bros.' truck arrives and screeches to a stop.

E-27 A SMALL BOY - AT BAT

He takes a terrific crack at a baseball.

5-24-40

E-28 THE SIDE OF THE SCHINDEL BROS.' TRUCK

We see the ornate glass sign for one second before the baseball ruins it. As the glass tinkles to the street the heads of Mr. Hillbeiner, Mr. Schindel and Mr. Schmidt pop over the top of the truck. A toy airplane hits Mr. Schindel in the face. As he grabs it --

E-29 MR. SCHINDEL - FROM INSIDE THE TRUCK

He feels of his nose, then breaks the airplane over his knee. As he is giving it one last crunch he scowls at a label he sees on the plane.

E-30 INSERT: THE LABEL

It reads: SCHINDEL BROS. TOYLAND - SPECIAL $1.98.

E-31 MR. SCHINDEL - IN THE TRUCK

He throws down the remains of the airplane and starts forward, then stops in dismay.

E-32 A VERY SMALL BOY WITH A TIN MACHINE GUN

He aims his weapon at Mr. Schindel and it goes rat-tat-tat. Now the owner of the airplane appears.

BOY OWNER OF AIRPLANE
Hey, what's the idea in busting my plane?

He climbs up on the truck.

E-33 MESSRS. SCHINDEL, SCHMIDT AND HILLBEINER - PAST THE OWNER OF THE PLANE

MR. SCHINDEL
It happens to be my plane.
(Then to Schmidt and Hillbeiner)
Get down and grab something, what are you standing there?

The two go PAST THE CAMERA.

E-34 THE OWNER OF THE PLANE - PAST SCHINDEL

BOY OWNER OF AIRPLANE
What do you mean, it's your plane? Jimmy MacDonald give it to me.

5-24-40

E-35 MR. SCHINDEL - PAST THE OWNER OF THE PLANE

MR. SCHINDEL
Yes, and when I get through with Jimmy MacDonald ...

We hear a little girl's angry scream. Mr. Schindel looks over the side of the truck.

E-36 HIGH CAMERA SHOT - DOWN ON MR. SCHMIDT

He is trying to take a toy baby carriage away from a little girl.

MR. SCHMIDT
(To the descending truckmen)
Well, why don't you come and help?

E-37 CLOSE SHOT - THE TRUCKMEN

They look at each other uneasily and do not move. We hear the child squeal angrily again.

E-38 THE REAR OF THE TRUCK

Mr. Schindel hops off and looks around searchingly.

E-39 MEDIUM LONG SHOT - PATROLMAN MURPHY

E-40 MR. SCHINDEL

He starts forward and the CAMERA PANS him to Murphy.

E-41 CLOSE SHOT - SCHINDEL AND MURPHY

MR. SCHINDEL
(Arriving in front of Murphy)
I want all these people arrested.

MURPHY
(After a pause)
Who do you think you are, Hitler?

MR. SCHINDEL
(Angrily)
Listen to me.

5-24-40 (Continued)

E-41 (Cont'd)

MURPHY
Yeah? Well you listen to me, baby.

We hear an angry yell. Murphy scowls into the distance.

MURPHY
What's going on around here? ...

He starts to go, then turns and seizes Schindel in a grip of iron.

MURPHY
You come with me.

E-42 HILLBEINER FACING A SMALL BOY IN A TOY AUTOMOBILE AND THE LATTER'S FATHER

THE FATHER
What do you mean, it ain't his?

HILLBEINER
It belongs to Schindel & Company.
It was stolen this afternoon.

E-43 MURPHY AND SCHINDEL

MURPHY
(Shaking Schindel)
Does this guy answer the description?

SCHINDEL
(Furiously)
I am Mr. Schindel.

E-44 A SMALL BOY IN AN INDIAN SUIT

He lets an arrow go.

E-45 SCHINDEL AND MURPHY - PAST HILLBEINER AND THE FATHER

We hear a clop, Schindel reacts violently, then reaches behind him and removes an arrow with a vacuum cup end. Suddenly he points to the arrow.

SCHINDEL
You see? Schindel Bros... Toyland!

5-24-40

E-46 THE BOY AND THE GIRL - NEAR MRS. MacDONALD AND MRS. CASEY

The Boy hands out the last present and mops his brow and starts turning toward his Mother when something catches his eye.

E-47 LONG SHOT - THE END OF THE STREET

We see the Schindel Bros. truck. A crowd is gathering around it.

E-48 THE BOY AND THE GIRL - NEAR MRS. MacDONALD AND MRS. CASEY

THE BOY
Here comes your davenport, Mom.
Come on...wait till you see it!

He puts one arm around his mother, the other around the Girl and, followed by Mrs. Casey, they start forward. The CAMERA PANS them past Mrs. Schwartz and Mr. Zimmerman. Mr. Zimmerman wears a flowered Hawaiian shirt hanging outside his pants. Mrs. Schwartz wears a white feather boa.

THE BOY
Come and see the davenport.

MR. ZIMMERMAN
A what?

MRS. SCHWARTZ
A divan.

The CAMERA PANS them through the playing children. Suddenly the Boy stops and frowns.

E-49 MR. SCHINDEL, MR. SCHMIDT, MR. HILLBEINER AND PATROLMAN MURPHY PARTLY SURROUNDED BY A CROWD WHICH HOLDS THEM BACK AGAINST THE TRUCK

MR. SCHINDEL
(In a loud voice)
I tell you everything is stolen, down to the last pogo stick...everything! He came to my store with a phoney check and when I asked him...

5-24-40

E-50 THE BOY, THE GIRL, MRS. MacDONALD AND MRS. CASEY

THE BOY
(Menacingly)
Who came to your store with a phoney check?

E-51 MR. SCHINDEL AND PATROLMAN MURPHY

MR. SCHINDEL
(Pointing triumphantly)
There he is! He ain't even got the decency to run away, you low-life!
(He turns importantly to Patrolman Murphy)
Officer, arrest that man.

MURPHY
You wouldn't kid me, would you?

MR. SCHINDEL
What are you talking about?

MURPHY
(Getting hard)
What are you talking about? I've known that kid since he was knee high to a cockroach. What's he supposed to have done?

MR. SCHINDEL
(Sarcastically)
Supposed to have done?
(He looks at Schmidt and Hillbeiner)
Listen to him!
(He turns back to Murphy)
He's supposed to have come into my store and flashed a bum check in my face and then he's supposed to have walked out with a diamond ring I suppose I see on that girl's finger, and a fox fur piece I don't suppose I see around her neck yet and half the toys in my store and then waves the bum check in my face and takes a powder.

5-24-40

E-52 THE BOY AND THE OTHERS - PAST MR. SCHINDEL

THE BOY
(Pulling the check out of his pocket and coming forward)
Who says it's a bum check? Are you nuts?

E-53 MR. SCHINDEL AND THE OTHERS - PAST THE BOY

MR. SCHINDEL
Dr. Parker of Parker House said so...maybe he's nuts.

MURPHY
(Conciliatingly)
Maybe we're all nuts...look what they're doing in Europe.

E-54 THE BOY AND THE OTHERS - PAST MR. SCHINDEL

THE BOY
How can Dr. Parker say anything against this check when he gave it to me himself?

Mrs. Schwartz steps forward and raises a hand. Mr. Zimmerman hovers near.

MRS. SCHWARTZ
Mr. Schwindel...

MR. SCHINDEL
Schindel, kindly.

MRS. SCHWARTZ
I known dis boy since his papa and his mamma wasn't even married yet...he THINKS Mr. Parker House give him a check....

MR. ZIMMERMAN
(Interrupting helpfully)
The whole family is a little bit crazy.

5-24-40 (Continued)

E-54 (Cont'd)

MRS. SCHWARTZ
Twenty-five thousand dollars, can you imagine?

MR. ZIMMERMAN
Ah dreamer.

THE BOY
(Desperately)
But Mrs. Schwartz...Mr. Zimmerman...

MRS. SCHWARTZ
Sh!

MR. ZIMMERMAN
Let me handle it.

THE BOY
(Desperately)
I tell you he gave me the check.

MRS. MacDONALD
If he tells you they gave him the check...

MRS. CASEY
...they gave him the check.

E-55 A GROUP OF WOMEN - ON THE SIDEWALK

They are eating ice cream cones. A large strapping one turns quickly, recognizing her child's voice through the din. Now she frowns and steps quickly into the street.

E-56 MR. SCHMIDT STRUGGLING WITH THE CHILD

THE YOUNG WOMAN
(Coming INTO THE SHOT)
And what do you think you're doing?

MR. SCHMIDT
Just who are you to meddle ...

5-24-40 (Continued)

E-56 (Cont'd)

THE YOUNG WOMAN
I'll show you.

She squashes her ice cream cone on Mr. Schmidt's kisser and gives him a powerful shove backwards at the same time.

E-57 MR. SCHINDEL AND PATROLMAN MURPHY

MURPHY
Why don't you just go home and think it all over?

SCHINDEL
(Furiously)
Listen, you, I'll break you in so many pieces...
(He includes Hill-beiner and Schmidt in a gesture)
You're witnesses he refused to...

MURPHY
(Laying an iron mitt on his shoulder)
Are you trying to intimate an officer in the pursuit of his duty?

E-58 A LITTLE BOY

The little boy making a snowball of ice cream.

E-59 MR. SCHINDEL AND PATROLMAN MURPHY

MR. SCHINDEL
(At the top of his lungs)
When I get through with you you'll be pounding a beat in Sheepshead Bay!

MURPHY
(Beginning to get a little hard)
Yeah? Well when I get through with you, baby, you won't be...

5-24-40

E-60 THE LITTLE BOY

The little boy lets the ice cream go.

E-61 MURPHY, SCHINDEL AND THE BOY

Although partly blinded, Murphy grabs Schindel in an iron grip.

THE BOY
(Trying to separate them)
Cut it out, Murph, this guy's on the level, it's just...

He receives an ice cream ball in the face. Schindel sees this and laughs happily. He receives a tomato in the face.

E-62 THE FRUIT WAGON

A couple of boys are pitching fruit as fast as they can.

E-63 HILLBEINER STRUGGLING WITH A CHILD IN FRONT OF THE FISH WAGON

The fishman receives a tomato in the back of the neck, turns furiously on Hillbeiner and fells him with a fish. As he looks down at him triumphantly he receives an ice cream ball in the face.

E-64 SCHINDEL, MURPHY AND THE BOY

MURPHY
(Loudly)
All right, now, cut it out!
It's been all right up to now, but the next one who throws anything....

He receives a tomato in the face and brings his club down on Schindel, almost braining him. As some more projectiles are hurled we hear the scream of motor-cycle sirens.

5-24-40

E-65 THE KIDS AT THE ICE CREAM WAGON

One of them yells: "Cheese it, the cops!" They run away.

E-66 A BIG SHINY AUTOMOBILE FLANKED BY TWO MOTOR COPS

Dr. Parker leaps out and spots the boy. He is followed by two plain clothes men.

E-67 TWO KIDS PEEKING OUT OF A DOORWAY

E-68 DR. PARKER IN FRONT OF HIS AUTOMOBILE

DR. PARKER
(To a motorcycle cop)
Officer, arrest that man!

He receives an ice cream ball in the necktie. He feels of it, then looks up in indignation. As he opens his mouth to speak, he receives a tomato in the kisser.

E-69 THE BOY, SCHINDEL AND MURPHY

MURPHY
(Glaring around)
And this time I ain't kiddin'

E-70 A BOY IN A DOORWAY

He looks speculatively at a tomato in his hand, then takes a bite of it.

E-71 THE BOY, SCHINDEL AND MURPHY

SCHINDEL
(To Murphy)
Now I'll give you one more chance.

THE BOY
(Seeing Parker)
Wait a minute, there's the man who can explain the whole thing.
(He calls)
Dr. Parker!

5-24-40

E-72 PARKER AND THE MOTOR COPS - PAST THE BOY, SCHINDEL AND MURPHY

DR. PARKER
You have the effrontery to speak to me...
(He indicates the Boy to a motor cop)
Officer, arrest that man.

E-73 THE BOY AND THE OTHERS - PAST DR. PARKER

MR. SCHINDEL
That's been tried before.

THE BOY
(Holding out the check)
Dr. Parker, there's some kind of a mix-up here... would you tell these gentlemen that you gave me this check?

E-74 DR. PARKER - PAST THE BOY

DR. PARKER
Well, you'll have to let me see it first.

E-75 THE BOY - PAST DR. PARKER

THE BOY
(Handing Dr. Parker the check)
It's the same one.

E-76 DR. PARKER - PAST THE BOY

DR. PARKER
It certainly is.

Suddenly he tears the check in pieces.

DR. PARKER
Oh, baby! Do I feel better!

E-77 THE BOY AND THE OTHERS - PAST DR. PARKER

They are rooted to the ground in horror.

5-24-40 (Continued)

E-77 (Cont'd)

THE BOY
Wait a minute...

SCHINDEL
(Stepping forward)
What are you destroying the evidence, you crook!

E-78 DR. PARKER - PAST THE OTHERS

DR. PARKER
(Indignantly)
Who's a crook, you burglar!
(Then to a cop)
Officer, you'd better round up this whole gang... they're all confidence men.

E-79 THE BOY AND THE OTHERS - PAST THE OTHER OTHERS

MR. SCHINDEL
Including you!

DR. PARKER
Listen, you footpad!

THE BOY
Wait a minute, Dr. Parker, what did you give me the check for? Why did you send me the telegram if you didn't...

E-80 DR. PARKER - PAST THE BOY

DR. PARKER
You know perfectly well I never sent you a telegram. You never heard from me in your life and I never heard of you! So why should I...

E-81 THE BOY - PAST DR. PARKER

THE BOY
But you _did_ send me a telegram! You saw _it_... I showed it to you! It said: "You have just won the Parkerhouse contest... kindly call and pick up your check."

5-24-40

E-82 DR. PARKER - PAST THE BOY

DR. PARKER
How could you have won anything
when my jury is still dead-locked?
Answer me that! How could you win
when those fat-heads aren't any
nearer a verdict than they were
last Tuesday? The numbskulls!
You thought you were pretty foxy,
young man, but just let me tell
you: I was suspicious of you
from the moment I clamped my
eyes on you!

E-83 THE BOY - PAST DR. PARKER AND THE OTHERS

THE BOY
(Stunned)
You mean I didn't win?

He looks around hopelessly.

DR. PARKER
... you know perfectly well you
didn't win.

THE BOY
But... but...
(He makes an almost
idiotic gesture)

MR. SCHINDEL
(Suddenly inspired)
WAIT A MINUTE!
(he points an accusing
finger at Dr. Parker)
He is entirely responsible! I
see it all! I know how a big
firm works, God forbid.

He puts a hand on the Boy's shoulder.

MR. SCHINDEL
This is an honest boy, ladies and
gentlemen... I know it the minute
I looked at him.
(Now he turns accusingly
on Dr. Parker)
You gave him the check, you schnook,
so where do you get off to have any-
body arrested or I should take back
the merchandise I sold in good faith.

5-24-40 (Continued)

E-83 (Cont'd)

MR. SCHINDEL (Cont'd)
(He makes a gesture to his truck drivers)
Take down that davenport and carry it upstairs for the lady.
(He nods to Mrs. MacDonald)
Enjoy it in good health... a present from Dr. Parker.
(Then to the Girl)
And don't lose that ring or the fur piece... a present from Dr. P.
(Now he hands a five dollar bill to the policeman)
And buy the little children some more ice cream, they should enjoy my toys better... with love from Dr. Parker... who's paying for everything.

DR. PARKER
I'll see you in Hoboken before I'll pay for anything.

MR. SCHINDEL
I'll see you in court!... and I guarantee you'll pay for everything... with costs!

DR. PARKER
In a pig's nose!

MR. SCHINDEL
Pigs or no pigs.

E-84 CLOSE SHOT - THE BOY AND THE GIRL

THE GIRL
(Holding back her tears)
It doesn't matter, honey... you can't lose anything you never had...
(She looks at the ring)
I don't want his old...
(She sobs)
... ring... or his old skunk.
(She fondles the beautiful fur)

THE BOY
(Dully)
What I can't figure... is who sent that telegram.

5-24-40

E-85 TOM, DICK AND HARRY - PAST THE BOY

They are carrying a slightly worn davenport at a funereal pace. As they reach the Boy and the Girl they put the heavy piece down on the sidewalk and the crank falls off with a clank.

TOM
(In a dead voice)
Hello.. Jimmy... is this the kind of davenport your Ma wanted?

E-86 THE BOY AND THE GIRL - PAST THE OTHERS

Tears are streaming down the Girl's face. The Boy looks blankly at his co-workers.

E-87 TOM, DICK AND HARRY - PAST THE BOY

DICK
(Picking up the crank)
The crank fits on here, and when you turn it, it... it...

HARRY
(Avoiding the Boy's eye)
... it makes into a full size double bed at night. The guy says it works swell.

E-88 THE BOY AND THE GIRL - PAST THE OTHERS

THE BOY
(Hesitantly)
I don't know what you had to go and get that for.

E-89 TOM, DICK AND HARRY - PAST THE BOY

TOM
We... we kinda hoped... it would make up for the... the phoney telegram.

DICK
It was supposed to be a joke.

5-24-40 (Continued)

E-89 (Cont'd)

HARRY
It wasn't a very funny joke.

E-90 THE BOY AND THE GIRL

THE BOY
(After a long pause)
Oh... I get it.

THE GIRL
Oh, Jimmy!

FADE OUT:

END OF SEQUENCE "E"

5-24-40

SEQUENCE "F"

FADE IN:

F-1 CLOSEUP - THE HANDS OF A PAINTER

He is finishing the last "e" of "James MacDonald - Private" on the frosted glass of a door.

F-2 AN OLD PAINTER FINISHING THE SIGN

Beyond him we see that the great offices are deserted and most of the lights are out. The painter is working with a sort of floodlight attached to a tripod. He leans back, cocks his head to one side and smiles with satisfaction at his work. Now he gives the letter one more lick, then starts putting his implements away.

F-3 A COLORED PORTER

He is wielding a floor brush in front of the door that comes in from the elevator hall. A black cat is trying to rub against his legs.

THE PORTER
(Stuttering slightly)
G-git away, dere, Martin.

A flash of light appears on the glass door followed by a clang. The Boy and the Girl come in quietly.

THE BOY
The boss gone yet, Sam?

THE PORTER
Nawsuh, he's still in dere connivin' at sompin or other.

THE GIRL
Why don't you tell him in the morning?

THE PORTER
Sure glad to hear about your good luck, Mista Jimmy. You wouldn't be needin' a vallay, would you?

THE BOY
No thanks, Sam.

THE PORTER
Well, I guess you're right...

F-3 (Cont'd)

THE PORTER (Cont'd)
Pride rideth before a fall...but it sure ain't everybody hit de jack-pot while dey's young and all.

THE BOY
You said it.

At this point the black cat either does or does not rub against the Boy's legs or cross his path or something. If it muffs the whole thing we'll make an insert.

THE GIRL
(Pointing to the black cat)
Look.

THE BOY
Hello, pussy.

THE GIRL
Is it bad luck or good luck when they rub against you?

THE PORTER
'at all depends on what happen afterward.

THE BOY
You said it.
(Then to the Girl)
Come on.

They walk OUT OF THE SHOT.

THE PORTER
(Looking after them)
Yas-suh ... sure don't happen to everybody.

In reply the cat meows.

F-4 THE SIGN PAINTER

He is attaching a "Fresh Paint" sign to the door. The Boy and the Girl walk INTO THE SHOT behind him.

THE GIRL
(Almost in tears)
Oh, look.

5-24-40 (Continued)

F-4 (Cont'd)

The Boy starts to say something, then closes his mouth in swallows.

THE SIGN PAINTER
(Seeing him)
Pretty nifty, hunh? Say, who is this MacDonald who won the watcha-call-it contest?

THE BOY
It's me.

THE SIGN PAINTER
(Admiringly)
No foolin'! A young punk like you, hunh? Well, that sure is unusual, ain't it?

THE BOY
Yeah, I guess it is.

THE SIGN PAINTER
Private office...secretary to yourself...hot dog!

THE BOY
With mustard.

The painter looks at him blankly and the Girl opens the door to the private office.

F-5 REVERSE SHOT - FROM THE PRIVATE OFFICE

The Girl comes in followed by the Boy. He switches on a light and gives the door a push. It does not quite close, leaving just enough room for a cat to come in. The two kids look around the room sadly. Now the boy crosses, sits down and tries out his desk. The Girl sits down at her desk and tries it out.

THE BOY
It was going to be nice, wasn't it?

The Girl buries her head in her arms and starts to sob.

THE BOY
Quit it, willya?

He comes around his desk and pats her on the back.

THE BOY
Come on, cut it out, willya...
stop it.

5-24-40 (Continued)

F-5 (Cont'd)

He lifts her to her feet. She throws her arms around his neck. He pats her on the back and she stops sobbing.

F-6 THE HALL THAT GOES PAST JIMMY'S OFFICE

A door opens some distance down the hall and Mr. Baxter appears in hat, stick and gloves. He puts on the gloves as he walks toward us. The CAMERA PANS with him until we see the lighted door of the Boy's office, with the silhouette of the Boy and the Girl in each other's arms. Mr. Baxter looks at this in surprise, then chuckles. After a moment he crosses to the door and knocks.

F-7 THE BOY AND THE GIRL - IN THE NEW OFFICE

They spring apart and she wipes her eyes.

THE BOY
(After a pause)
Come in.

He starts to open the door. Before he gets to it, Mr. Baxter enters.

MR. BAXTER
(Slyly)
I hope I'm not intruding, heh-heh-heh.

THE BOY
Oh, no, sir. I was just coming down to see you...We just stopped in on the way to take a look at the office.

MR. BAXTER
So I noticed. I hope you like it.

THE GIRL
(Her lips trembling)
It's beautiful.

MR. BAXTER
It isn't every young man who gets his own office and a private secretary at your age. With many I would be afraid it might go to their heads, but I think you have your feet pretty solidly on the ground.

THE BOY
(Ill at ease)
Thank you, Mr. Baxter.

F-7 (Cont'd)

MR. BAXTER
I mean it sincerely, and if this all works out as well as we both hope it will, I know that neither of us will be disappointed.

THE BOY
(Miserably)
Yes, sir, thank you, Mr. Baxter. The only thing is...you see...

MR. BAXTER
(Who ignores interruptions)
And I have every reason to believe that it will work out. Mr. Jenkins and I discussed our little meeting at some length after you left and I want you to know that we were genuinely impressed, Jimmy ... genuinely so.

THE BOY
I'm certainly glad to hear that, Mr. Baxter...I... I...

MR. BAXTER
The more we talked about your ideas the more aware we became of their...
(He feels for the word)
....their pungency...their brevity... their uh...uh...crispness.

THE BOY
(Beginning to take hope)
Well, thank you, Mr. Baxter, that's certainly....

MR. BAXTER
You have a genuine talent for slogans, it must be something like having an ear for music, now you take me I sing flat, but you on the other hand are a born sloganeer.

THE BOY
Well, that's certainly wonderful to hear, Mr. Baxter. I...I...I uh... I've kinda got something on my mind but you certainly make me feel a lot better...
(He looks at the Girl)
I mean, they're still the same ideas, aren't they? I mean, if they were good this afternoon they're still good...they have to be...they're the same.

5-24-40

(Continued)

F-7 (Cont'd)

THE GIRL
(Encouragingly)
Of course they are!

THE BOY
Of course they are.
(He turns to Mr. Baxter with nascent hope)

MR. BAXTER
(Puzzled)
I'm not quite sure I have your thought.

THE BOY
I mean, if you thought the ideas were good this afternoon, you think they're good now, don't you?

MR. BAXTER
(Faintly suspicious)
Of course I do, why?

THE BOY
(His hopes returning fast)
I mean...since the ideas were good... and they're still good...then it wouldn't make so much difference... or any difference...if I hadn't won the contest...the Parker House contest.

MR. BAXTER
(Quietly)
Of course it would make a difference.

THE BOY
(His hopes falling again)
Oh...it would?

THE GIRL
(Defiantly)
Why?

MR. BAXTER
(Frowning slightly)
Well certainly it would. I'm no genius. I didn't hang onto my father's money by backing my own judgement, you know. I make mistakes every day. Sometimes several times a day. I have a whole warehouse full of mistakes... I should say it would make a difference! You see, I think your ideas are good because they sound good to me.
(He smiles)
I know they are good because you won this contest...over millions of aspirants.

5-24-40 (Continued)

F-7 (Cont'd)

THE BOY
(Dismally)
Yes, but you see...

MR. BAXTER
(Wound up)
It's what you might call commercial insurance...as when a horse wins the Derby...you back him for the Preakness...
(He smiles with pleasure)

THE BOY
Well, I didn't win it.

MR. BAXTER
(Mystified)
The Preakness!

THE BOY
The contest...I didn't win anything...it was a joke.

MR. BAXTER
(In horror)
A joke!

THE BOY
That's what they meant it for anyway.

MR. BAXTER
(Scowling)
Who did?

THE BOY
Some of the fellas. They didn't mean any harm...they wanted to see how I looked when I got the news.

MR. BAXTER
(Furiously)
Yes, well you tell me their names and I'll see how they look when I give them some news.

THE BOY
I wouldn't care to do that, Mr. Baxter, it doesn't matter.

MR. BAXTER
(Furiously)
What do you mean, "it doesn't matter?" After I spend a whole afternoon listening to a lot of ... your proposals...all predicated on the winning of this contest... and giving you this office and... and...

5-24-40

(Continued)

F-7 (Cont'd)

THE BOY
But if the ideas are good?

MR. BAXTER
(With irritation)
Well, we'll find out if they are...there's plenty of time for that...but I can't be made a fool of, you understand... I can't go around giving people private offices and private secretaries on the strength of some prank that personally I consider far from funny!

THE BOY
(Barely audible)
Yes, sir.

MR. BAXTER
(Concurring)
Yes, sir.

THE BOY
(Looking away)
It'll be kinda hard to face the gang again tomorrow morning... from back at the desk.

MR. BAXTER
(Still crossly)
Well, it would be just as hard to face them from in here if you didn't belong in here. Uneasy lies the head that....

THE GIRL
(Quickly)
He does belong in here, Mr. Baxter.

MR. BAXTER
(Scowling)
What's the joke this time?

THE GIRL
He belongs in here because he thinks he belongs in here, because he thinks...

MR. BAXTER
(Testily)
Yes, well that's all very deep-dish and highfallutin',

5-24-40 (Continued)

F-7 (Cont'd)

MR. BASTER (Cont'd)
but from a practical...

the girl
(Desperately)
It is practical, Mr. Baxter, it's the most practical idea you ever had. He belongs in here because he thinks he has ideas. He belongs in here until he proves himself or fails, and then somebody else belongs in here until he proves himself or fails and then somebody else after him and then somebody else after that, and then so on and so on for always. I don't know how to put it in words like Jimmy could, but all he wants...all any of them want...is a chance to show...to find out...what they've got while they're still young...and...and... burning...like a short-cut...or a ...or a...stepping stone.
(Now she changes her tone entirely)
Oh, I know they're not going to succeed...at least most of them aren't...they'll all be like Mr. MacKenzie soon enough...most of them, anyway...but they won't mind it...they'll find something else, and they'll be happy because they had their chance...because it's one thing to muff a chance when you get it...but it's another thing never to have had a chance.

The Boy looks away in embarrassment. Mr. Baxter scowls at him, then glares at the Girl. For once he seems at a loss for words. She blinks her eyes and two big tears roll down her cheeks.

THE GIRL
(Hardly above a whisper)
His name's already on the door.

MR. BAXTER
(After a pause)
Well....if anything decided me... that would be it.

The Boy turns quickly.

5-24-40 (Continued)

F-7 (Cont'd)

THE GIRL
Oh, Mr. Baxter!

MR. BAXTER
(Crossly)
Now you've talked enough... the desks have already been moved and the name is already painted on as you pointed out so skillfully...so we'll try it for a very short time, you understand...at no advance in salary you understand...and uh... for a very short time...this is a business institution...not a cultural project.

THE GIRL
(Excitedly)
You'll never be sorry, Mr. Baxter.

MR. BAXTER
(Crossly)
Yes, well, I'm a little bit sorry already, so just...let it go at that. Good night and...try and be on time in the morning.

Suddenly the Girl steps forward and kisses him on both cheeks.

MR. BAXTER
(Embarrassed)
Good...for heaven sa.....Oh, pshaw!

He turns and hurries out. The Girl turns gaily to the Boy.

THE GIRL
Isn't it wonderful?

THE BOY
(Without enthusiasm)
You were wonderful...you'll always be wonderful...but I'm a little bit leery about me.

THE GIRL
Don't talk like a fathead, will you? This is the chance of a lifetime. You know you've got

5-24-40 (Continued)

F-7 (Cont'd)

THE GIRL (Cont'd)
what it takes... you know
that...

THE BOY
But I don't know. I never did
know until I got that telegram
this morning. And now I don't
know any more. I'm like Mr.
Baxter, that's why I understood
him so well and I didn't say
anything, see?

THE GIRL
Well...even if it shouldn't work,
it brought us together...that's
something, and I've got the ring
to prove it...and you couldn't
back out on me now or I'd...I'd
sue you. Oh, you poor kid!

She throws her arms around his neck.

THE GIRL
So you see we have plenty to be
thankful for.

THE BOY
How'd that cat get in here?

He leads her to the door, puts out the light and they go out.

F-8 THE LONG CORRIDOR

They walk slowly toward us. As they get near we hear the cat meow.

THE GIRL
There it is again.

THE BOY
Yeah.

He opens the door for her.

F-9 THE ELEVATOR HALL

The Boy and the Girl cross to the elevator. Behind them there is a big window. The Boy pushes the

5-24-40 (Continued)

F-9 (Cont'd)

elevator button and far below we hear the clang of the night bell.

THE GIRL
(Suddenly pointing out of the window)
Look!

We see the Parker House tower in the distance and the head gulping its never-ending last gulp.

THE BOY
Yeah.

THE GIRL
(Chuckling)
He sure looked funny this afternoon.

THE BOY
Yeah, the old b...

F-10 S.E.D. ZOOM SHOT - TO PARKER HOUSE TOWER AND THROUGH WINDOW TO DR. PARKER - AT HIS DESK

The ZOOM is accompanied by the wail of a high siren. Dr. Parker is at the telephone.

DR. PARKER
All right, well, you meet with his lawyers and settle the best way you can. I can't stand the publicity.
(He hangs up)

The door behind him bursts open and Mr. Bildocker bursts in.

BILDOCKER
Dr. Parker...

DR. PARKER
(Glaring at him)
What do you want?

BILDOCKER
(Pleased with himself)
I got some good news for you. It took a little doing but I won those fatheads over in the end and...

5-24-40 (Continued)

F-10 (Cont'd)

DR. PARKER
(Interrupting)
The way I feel about it, Bildocker, it just doesn't matter any more.
(Now in crescendo)
This has been the stupidest, the most asinine, the most infuriating, the ga...

BILDOCKER
(Holding up a hand amiably)
But wait till you hear the slogan, oh, boy!

DR. PARKER
I don't wish to hear the slogan. I don't wish to hear any more about the whole mess. Pick your winner, send him a check and tell him to go and...

BILDOCKER
(Confidently)
Listen to this, willya?
(He reads from a paper)
If you don't sleep at night, it isn't the coffee, it's the bunk! Is that a slogan?

DR. PARKER
(Electrified)
WHAT!

He seizes his head.

BILDOCKER
It's what you call a pun...and believe me it's some pun! We just sent the winner a telegram of congratulations...a guy by the name of....

He pulls a paper out of his pocket as Dr. Parker picks up a lamp.

BILDOCKER
Here we are: James MacDon...
HEY!

5-24-40 (Continued)

F-10 (Cont'd)

He ducks and the lamp crashes against the wall behind him.

ZOOM DISSOLVE BACK TO:

F-11 THE BOY AND THE GIRL - IN FRONT OF THE WINDOW

THE GIRL
Aw, cheer up, will you?

THE BOY
I'm cheerful.

THE GIRL
Then smile, willya?

THE BOY
I'm smiling.

THE GIRL
(Holding back her tears)
Who wants a penthouse anyway?
Way up high where it catches all
the soot...and makes you dizzy...
when you look down.

THE BOY
I guess so.

THE GIRL
Then smile, gloomy Gus.

THE BOY
I'm smiling.

THE GIRL
(Looking down)
There's that cat again.

F-12 CLOSE SHOT - THE CAT PURRING AND RUBBING UP AND DOWN THE BOY'S LEGS

F-13 THE BOY AND THE GIRL

THE GIRL
What do you suppose he's
doing that for?

THE BOY
Probably got fleas.

5-24-40 (Continued)

F-13 (Cont'd)

THE GIRL
Probably...ah, cheer up, willya?

She kisses him and the light from the rising elevator appears on their faces. The night man opens the elevator door and they get in. The gate closes and the elevator moves out of sight. THE CAMERA, HAVING FOLLOWED IT DOWN, NOW ENDS UP ON A CLOSE SHOT ON THE CAT.

THE CAT
Meow!

FADE OUT:

THE END

5-24-40

The Lady Eve

Our account of Sturges's work on *The Lady Eve* (1941) begins with work by other writers—a story by Monckton Hoffe called "The Two Bad Hats" and a "synopsis" of this story, really an adaptation of it, by Jeanne Bartlett.[1] The presence of another writer in the genealogy of a Sturges film, let alone two, makes *The Lady Eve* unique among the scripts included in this volume and, indeed, among the eight films he wrote and directed for Paramount.[2]

Hoffe's nineteen-page story is undated. It must have been written before Bartlett's synopsis of February 12, 1938, but how long before, whether it was written for Paramount or bought by them, and whether it had been published are not clear. The story begins with Kitty Ardelaire—"the one bad hat" in General Ardelaire's reputable, very English family—who has run away to America with Ned Drusila, a horse dealer. They marry, and Ned gives his wife twin girls and himself delirium tremens; in fact, up to the time of his early death he remains a little unsure as to whether he has twin daughters—whom Kitty names Salome and Sheba—or double vision. Turning to alcohol herself, Kitty struggles along without him but eventually receives checks from the Ardelaires for the support of the two girls; later, when Sheba dies, Kitty does not tell the family so that she can continue to receive both checks.

Salome grows, in due course, into "that most pleasant thing of all pleasant things—a pretty girl," who sees life at the same angle as her mother, "not a very nice angle, but still an angle." Returning to England, Kitty and Salome rent a house in London where they conduct a discreet card game. They make money for a while but are eventually raided by the police, taken to court, and photographed by the press. The Ardelaires are horrified and cut off the checks.

Desperate at this point, Kitty and Salome decide to resurrect Sheba, who has of course been untouched by their scandal. After some coaching by her mother, Salome visits the Ardelaires as "a sweet, engaging Sheba" and successfully takes them in. Soon they have quashed the police proceedings and resumed the checks, and they want Sheba to become a permanent member of the family. Salome, however, hates the Ardelaires and hates being Sheba even more.

At this point enters Geoffrey Pallas, a wealthy, well-connected young man, who comes to the Ardelaires for a cricket weekend; he falls in love with "Sheba," and Salome falls in love with him. Although marrying him will lock her into the identity of Sheba, she consents. Kitty watches the wedding from the edge of the crowd.

The couple is happy for some time, but then Pallas takes up with a notorious woman named "Tommy" Ledgeworth and soon declines into drunkenness and disgrace. After a breakdown, Salome visits her mother and, in effect, becomes Salome again. "The young bad hat has joined the old bad hat: the spirit of the wild is in the air." They go to a dance club. Hoffe comments: "Never mind which dance-club it is. It is a dance-club. One we all know, who have to stick in London. The crowd is good: evil and decent, and damned well dressed. So-and-so is there, and so is so-and-so. What a crew! Still an alluring crew. Taken on the whole they're rather alluring."

Pallas visits the club that night and sees Salome, whom he takes to be Sheba's sister, and falls in love with her. Soon, after several weeks of teas and walks in the park, "Tommy" Ledgeworth is a thing of the past. Salome and Pallas go away together for "a wild and wicked and wonderful three days in the uttermost depths of the country." Salome is tempted to tell him the truth but Kitty advises against it. The story ends with the three on a ship to America. "For such disgraceful people there was only one thing to be done. The New World calls across the water for a second time." The author speculates that Kitty will probably never extinguish Sheba; she will keep her alive somewhere in Timbuktu, in case of accidents. Kitty packs herself in a deck chair and the young people find a place looking out over the ocean: "The wickedest man in the world squeezes his lady's fingers and has to confess to himself that he feels disgracefully happy and Salome knows that she's got her husband back for good and all this time and thats that, in itself, is a very nice sensation [*sic*]."[3]

Bartlett's sixteen-page "synopsis," called "Two Bad Hats" (without the article), cuts most of the background to Hoffe's story, getting to the romance almost immediately: she introduces Pallas on page 2, whereas Hoffe first presents him on page 9. Bartlett also takes literally Ned's double vision—he and Kitty have only one daughter, whom he sees through the eyes of delirium tremens as two and, "being at the religious stage in his drinking," names them Salome and Sheba, whereupon he dies. Receiving news of twins, the Ardelaires send Kitty two monthly checks, a swindle that allows her to devote herself to the bottle and to her child. Salome grows up to be "an outrageously pretty girl," and, Bartlett observes: "An outrageously pretty girl is somehow always suspect"—a rather different epigram from Hoffe's.

In Bartlett's story, Kitty and Salome set up a gambling house in New York, and Salome has become famous as an *Esquire* model, "drawn by Petty." One day, while visiting the photographic studio of Lord Forbes, Kitty overhears his conversation with a friend, the Earl of Pallas, M. P., who berates Forbes for his Americanization and, above all, for his wanting to marry a vulgar woman (Salome). Salome, who likes Forbes but repels his advances, decides to teach

Pallas a lesson in vulgarity. She walks in and makes a pass at him and later tries to seduce him at dinner, at the same time telling him everything bad about herself—her mother, her mother's lover, the gambling casino, her father, her past, etc. Pallas in fact falls in love with her and she with him; but he fights his desire with his moral convictions. Bartlett comments:

> The entire difference between them is that Salome could act murderously without bothering to invent delusions of justification for herself. Her action is in itself complete. Her pride in herself is great enough to feel that anything she does is completely right. But to Pallas, an act is only the basis for a delusion of justification. He is a guy who looks at an ending, not a beginning. He is the dull rule—Salome the lovely exception.

As Salome and Pallas go around New York, they keep meeting Kitty's lover, identified by Bartlett as "Roland Young." An Oxford graduate and a gambler, Young takes surreptitious pictures of Salome and Pallas, including one of them "in bed" in a wax works. Salome takes Pallas to her apartment on his last night in New York, drinks some gin—which makes her sneeze—and has to lie down, whereupon she manages to seduce him. He is most upset afterward—one should want to make love only to the right sort of woman. Nevertheless, because he is in love with her, he cannot leave her. Later, when he returns to the gambling house, Salome greets him coldly because she knows they are being observed by the other guests. He tells her he should marry her but cannot. She graciously understands, and he finds it even harder to leave. She agrees to accompany him on the boat trip back to England, after which she will return to America.

Meanwhile, the Ardelaire solicitor visits the gambling house, and Roland Young shows Pallas the photos he has taken, offering to part with them for a contribution to Kitty's champagne fund, which is very low. Pallas becomes convinced that Salome is part of a scheme to blackmail him and leaves. At this point there is a police raid, and all are arrested, including the Ardelaire solicitor, who learns about Kitty and Salome's scandalous life and has the family cut off their checks.

The only resort for Kitty and Salome is to have Salome impersonate the fictional Sheba, who of course has remained untouched by their scandal. Coached by Kitty, Salome succeeds so well that Kitty is soon receiving checks again, which allow her to live in a comfortable apartment with Roland Young, whom she now considers marrying although he is evasive. The Ardelaires, whose lifestyle Salome abhors, want her to become a permanent member of the family. She excels, through an unspecified "comedy routine," even at fox hunting. When Pallas unexpectedly arrives for the hunt, Salome exposes him to her family as the seducer of her unfortunate sister. He stays on, however, feeling that "marriage with the pure and perfect Sheba, who is at the same time the image of Salome, is the correct panacea for his feeling about Salome." In a scene reminiscent of Austen's *Pride and Prejudice*, he proposes to her with great condescension and insists that she break all ties with her family. To Pallas's surprise "Sheba" rejects him, claiming that as the seducer of her sister, it is he who is the inferior person. He starts to tell her just who seduced whom, but his sense of honor forbids it. He promises to make good his offense to her sister, then return to claim her. Salome gives him the address of her sister in London; she is delighted with the way her plan is working out.

She goes to London and takes over her mother's apartment, "deciding to really show Pallas that she's a fallen woman, not only to further his abasement, but in this glamorous role, she feels she can excite him into making love to her . . . and realize that he couldn't have the fine lust with her that she knows he has, unless it is LOVE . . . To love her as Sheba is only loving himself, but to love her as Salome is honest love, because it's against his every conviction."

During their scene, Salome gives him "a little Sadie Thompson (but dressed by Molyneux)" and "a little Camille"; he is filled with remorse and even offers to marry her. She refuses him harshly in the same manner in which he talked to her in New York—she loves to make love to him, but he is not the sort of person she could marry. He is hurt and, although he desires her, feels it is wrong to make love to a woman who is not his wife and leaves. Back at the Ardelaire country house, Salome (now as Sheba) receives Pallas, fearful that he will persist in loving the Sheba she despises. In fact he is trying to tell her that he loves Salome, but Salome panics and invents a phone call in which she learns of his scene with her sister the day before. She returns to the room in tears, upbraids Pallas for having seduced her unfortunate sister once more, and tells him she wishes never to see him again. As Salome again, she waits for him outside the Ardelaire country house in her "two-block long car." Reluctantly he gets into the car to avoid a scene but soon turns on her for her lying telephone call to her sister. She replies sweetly that she wanted to see him again, and getting him thrown out was the only way to do so. He thinks perhaps that she loves him and wants to marry him, but she says that she only wanted to kiss him. This is too much for him—sex is all she thinks about. They argue further, then he gets out, assisted by "a short uppercut" from Salome.

At the Ardelaire house, "Sheba" has disappeared—"returned to the convent," her mother says. "Her heart breaking," Salome decides to go to Pallas as Sheba—to marry him as Sheba is better than not marrying him at all. When she arrives, he is making preparations to go to Africa. She tells him that there is no need for him to run away; she forgives his conduct with her sister, whom she "rips up and down as a horrid girl." Pallas stops her diatribe to make a long speech about how wonderful Salome is. Pallas gives her a drink, which turns out to be gin, and she starts sneezing, whereupon "a horrible suspicion seizes Pallas." He laughs, picks her up, and says that he knew all the time, but Salome doesn't believe him. Pallas replies that he will be sure in a few minutes, "happily carrying her through the adjoining door."

A comparison between the Hoffe and Bartlett stories is of interest for the traces that each leaves upon *The Lady Eve*. The two stories reveal, among other things, a marked difference in gender perspective. Geoffrey Pallas is the pivotal figure of Hoffe's story, around whom the Sheba–Salome identity struggle revolves. Although marrying Pallas locks her into the hated identity

Henry Fonda, Sturges, and William Demarest prepare for a shipboard scene in THE LADY EVE*–Muggsy tells Charles, who is trying to shave, that Jean and her father are "a gang of sharpies."*

of Sheba, Salome gives up her true identity to do so. This creates no abiding conflicts within Salome—she is fulfilled and whole so long as she has her man. It is only when she loses her husband—to a notorious woman—that Salome is discontented with her false identity. Her problem, presented by Hoffe as a law of nature, is that a virtuous Sheba cannot hold a man. She becomes Salome again in order to get her husband back. When this succeeds, she settles happily into the Salome identity—again without telling her husband, let alone integrating her disparate selves. The core problem is one of male sexuality—no one woman can satisfy Pallas; only a mythical integration of the virtuous woman and the sexual woman can yield fulfillment.

In Hoffe's story, Pallas has all the power and all the sexual freedom; in Bartlett's story, Salome has all the sexual freedom and, in relational though not worldly terms, all the power. Salome is required to pose as Sheba for the same reason in Bartlett's story as in Hoffe's—to convince the Ardelaires to start up her mother's checks again. She refuses, however, to accept love or marriage on the basis of this false identity. She manipulates Pallas, shuttling him back and forth between the two sisters, until he works through his repressions and admits his feelings for Salome. Salome thus insists on love in her own person and identity and will give up love, at least until the very end, rather than lose her sense of self.

Bartlett reverses a number of plot elements also. Pallas meets the worldly and sensual Salome first, not, as in Hoffe, the repressed Sheba. This exposes his sexual puritanism, his rigidity of morals and personality, and of course, his snobbery. Salome is open, nondemanding, able to love without giving up her freedom; Pallas is drawn to her and repelled at the same time. Bartlett invents a number of subplots—the gambling house, the photographs, "Roland Young"—that are designed to bring Pallas to what is for him an inevitable conclusion: that Salome is no good and therefore he must leave her. Bartlett's needlessly complex plot reminds us of many thirties films, although its sexual sophistication is assuredly ahead of its time.

All of Sturges's script versions (1938 and 1940) follow Bartlett by eliminating Hoffe's background material and beginning with the romance, but they follow Hoffe by adhering to a simple structure without subplots. From Bartlett the scripts take the notion of Pallas (Charles Pike, an ale magnate's son in Sturges's version) as sexually repressed and morally rigid; his meeting the "bad" girl (Jean) first and then the "good" girl (Eve), who is a creation of the "bad" girl; and his eventual disillusionment with the "good" girl and his realization that he loves the "bad" girl. Besides these parallels, *The Lady Eve* also has its own version of Salome's revenge on Pallas by deliberately confusing him and its "therapeutic" result of ridding him of a puritanism that blocks his emotional and sexual desires.

Bartlett has Pallas explicitly realizing that "marriage with the pure and perfect Sheba, who is at the same time the image of Salome, is the correct panacea for his feelings about Salome." Sturges suggests a comparable, unconscious motivation in Charles. Eve physically resembles Jean, the woman he loved, but without her bad character—"You see, Eve, you're so beautiful, and so fine, and you're so . . . I don't deserve you" (pages 134–135). Sturges, however, resolves the conflict far more deftly and economically than Bartlett: her shuttling of Pallas back and forth between Salome and Sheba is tediously overplotted—so much so that the underlying feelings become obscured. Eve's "lesson" for Charles is severe and definitive: he will not equate social position with virtue again.

It is true that these undoubted parallels are situated at a rather general level. From the moment he began to work on *Two Bad Hats,* Sturges left behind the Hoffe-Bartlett plot, characters, and setting, preferring as usual to begin all over again. There is, however, a quite concrete reminder of the Hoffe and Bartlett stories not in Sturges's own *Two Bad Hats* but in his scripts for *The Lady Eve,* written nearly two years later, and in the film itself. When Charles reappears at the Pike party for Eve, now the Lady Eve, he mentions to Sir Alfred McGlennan Keith, alias Pearlie (Eric Blore), that a girl on the boat looked exactly like his niece. Horrified that his own fraudulent position might be discovered, Sir Alfred tells him, as he later describes it to Jean, "the plot of 'Cecilia, or the Coachman's Daughter' . . . a gaslight melodrama." The story he tells Charles—and his manner of telling it—is Sturges's derisive version of the Hoffe–Bartlett "Two Bad Hats":

> I'm afraid you have stumbled on the sorrow of Sidwich . . . the secret of the century. . . . You see, the Earl was considerably older than her mama who must NEVER be mentioned again. . . . A May–November romance . . . even a March–December . . . if you follow me. . . . [I]nto the gulf that separated this unfortunate couple . . . there was a coachman on the estate . . . a gay dog, a great hand with the horses . . . and the ladies . . . need I say more? They called him "Handsome Harry" . . . the father of the OTHER child . . . after the divorce, of course. . . . We must close our minds to [the fact that Jean and Eve look exactly alike] . . . as it brings up the DREADFUL and thoroughly unfounded suspicion that we must carry to our tombs . . . as it is absolutely untenable that the coachman, in both instances . . . need I say more? (pages 124-126)

Charles replies, "He did! I mean, he was! . . . I mean," swallowing the story "like a wolf," as Sir Alfred/Pearlie later tells Jean. Charles, of course, wants to believe that Eve is not Jean; but he also seems pleased at the blood relationship that, as it were, ensures the copy: Eve is Jean with the proper upbringing and character.

Sturges had finished the first draft of *If I Were King* (1938) by February 1, 1938, and the revised script by mid-April. He was then loaned out to MGM for work on *Broadway Melody of 1939*. Some time later, Sturges began work on a new screenplay for Paramount producer Albert Lewin; it was called *Two Bad Hats* after the Hoffe story on which it was supposedly based. Sturges's drafts and notes, referred to as "discards" in the register to the Sturges papers, are dated from September 14 to early December 1938. The pages of the completed screenplay itself are dated from September 20 to November 29, 1938. Sturges's characteristic note at the bottom of the last page says: "Script completed: 6:48 A.M., Nov. 30, 1938."

As had often been his practice as a screenwriter in the thirties whenever he "rewrote" the work of others, Sturges in effect threw out the Hoffe and Bartlett stories and began again from scratch. His first draft of the film's opening, written September 14–15, 1938, has the Pike yacht *Bittersweet* stop the SS *Serenia* at sea. Lady Pike is dispatching her son, the Right Honorable Percival Pike, and his valet Treekell (treacle?) for a stockholders' meeting in New York. But first, while the ship is waiting impatiently ("There is an angry blast from the *Serenia*," followed by "three angry toots"), they have a toast of "Pike's, the beer that won at Waterloo," and throw their glasses in the water. Lady Pike warns her son against Indians and buffalos and also against American "gels," who are all "gold baggers." Percival and Treekell's boarding is watched by "Mr. Brown, his daughter Eve and Murgatroyd the valet, known more affectionately as 'Muggsy.'"

On September 20, 1938, Sturges began again, this time with a snake.

After the Main Titles—

FADE IN:

A-1 THE LONG UPPER CORRIDOR OF AN ENGLISH MANOR
Into the beam of sunlight from a partly opened door comes a long black snake. As it slithers down the hall PAST THE CAMERA—

A-2 REAR SHOT OF A BUXOM HOUSEMAID ON HER KNEES
She is scrubbing some stone work.

A-3 CLOSE SHOT—THE SNAKE
It pauses in its travels, lifts its head to enjoy the vista, then passes on.

A-4 LOW CAMERA SHOT UP SOME STAIRS
The snake peers over the edge of the top step, then comes down PAST US.

A-5 LONG SHOT—DRAWING ROOM—FROM THE MAIN HALLWAY
In the distance we see Sir Harry and Lady Pike breakfasting on the terrace. The snake crosses the hallway and enters the living room.

A scene between Sir Harry and Lady Pike follows. Their oldest son Tommy, who is in America, is involved with a much-married chorus girl; they plan to send their younger son Charles to break up the romance. Charles, however, is in the midst of breeding a hoop snake in captivity—"one of the most extraordinary experiments"—and does not want to go. (He comes downstairs in his long chemist's coat when his mother's scream tells him where his snake "Emma" has gotten to.) Charles is nevertheless prevailed upon to sail for America that morning with his valet—now "Treekill," which sounds even more like "treacle." This is the beginning that Sturges retains throughout his 1938 work on the project.

The fact that the ship's departure is held for Charles brings him to the attention of Lord Sidwich, alias English John, and his daughter Eve. Sidwich's "valet" Murgatroyd, who is called Muggsy, has been dispatched to find out about the new arrival. Much of the opening dialogue here is retained in the film—Eve hopes that Charles is rich and that he thinks he's a good card player, Sidwich says a mug is a mug in everything, and "let us be crooked, but never common," etc. Later, in the ship's dining room, Charles reads something titled *Are Snakes Necessary?* He ignores the passes being made at him by every young woman in sight and the fact that everyone is drinking "Pike's Pale"; however, there is no narration of the scene by Eve (Jean) as yet. Charles gets a cable from his father, which he reads "with ill-concealed fury." It says that Tommy was married yesterday to a "choral singer" who has been married only four times, not six, so all is well and Charles should return at once. Charles forgets his reading matter, then tears it up when the page boy brings it to him. As he is leaving the room, Eve trips him, breaking her shoe as she does so. He takes her down to her cabin for a new pair of shoes; he enjoys putting them on, but in the 1938 script there is little romance in the scene, none of Charles's dizziness or references to Eve's perfume or, of course, to his having been up the Amazon for a year. Indeed, only a fraction of the later script's dialogue is in place here. Their scene is broken up by Murgatroyd, who is marking decks of the ship's cards in the adjoining room. He knocks on Eve's door, sticks his head in, and asks if he can be of assistance.

Back on deck, Charles tells Eve and Lord Sidwich of his aborted mission to rescue his brother and shows them some card tricks. In the first version of the scene, written September 29, the three do not yet play cards. Charles and Eve dance, and then he asks her to his cabin to see Emma. When Eve sees the snake, she flees to her cabin where Muggsy and her father tend to her. Charles, outside their cabin, apologizes; Eve starts to tell him off, but her confederates muzzle her, and the scene ends with her agreeing to swim with him in the morning.

By October 3, Sturges had rewritten the scene from the point of Charles's card tricks and the drink and toasts that follow. Instead of asking Eve to dance, Charles suggests they play a rubber of bridge; Lord Sidwich recalls a three-handed game, and they play. Sidwich reveals after the game that they were playing for money—sixpence a point—and, of course, Charles is $600 ahead. After Eve's line that her father's card playing is "more uneven sometimes than others," the two dance. Charles then escorts Eve to her cabin but ends up at his own cabin instead, a "coincidence" that she does not believe. He invites her in to see Emma, which she says is a new one; he tells her Emma is a snake. Once inside, Charles offers Eve an apple, to which she responds: "Oh, teacher. What is this, the Garden of Eden?" Charles opens the snake box and discovers that Emma has got out. Eve "picks her skirts up to her garters" and runs to her cabin, which is empty. Charles follows her inside and looks under the bed to assure her there is no snake there. She lies on the chaise longue, Charles sits on the floor next to her, and a two-page dialogue ensues (the shooting script expands this to six pages), which includes Charles's susceptibility to her perfume and his responding to her line, "I think I can sleep peacefully now," with "I wish I could say the same." This ends Sequence A, which also includes a brief scene in which Treekill loses at cards to Muggsy.

Sequence B in the 1938 version begins the next morning, as it does in the final script, with Treekill making Muggsy sick by ordering Emma's breakfast—except, of course, that Muggsy becomes the name of Charles's "valet" and bodyguard and Gerald the name of the valet-confederate of Colonel Harrington (formerly Sidwich). The 1938 script follows this, however, with a scene between Charles and the purser, who warns him about professional gamblers who let one win the first night; he refuses to name names, but he evidently has Lord Sidwich and his daughter in mind. Charles dismisses him and greets Eve, for whom he has been waiting. Their breakfast scene is followed by one of the purser ordering a photograph by wireless from the New York Police Department.

Next comes a seven-page scene in which Charles takes Eve all over the boat—from port to starboard, then to the engine room, the boiler room, the stuffing-box room, etc.—to find a place where he can tell her that he loves her; when he does say it, she cannot hear him due to the noise of the engines. (This scene is similar to the scene in *The Power and the Glory* where Tom Garner takes Sally ever higher up a mountain until he has the courage to ask her to marry him.)[4] When Eve returns to her cabin, Lord Sidwich and Muggsy are preparing to take Charles at cards that evening. She reports that Charles has asked her to marry him and says that of course they cannot cheat him now. When they object to this, Eve seizes two decks of marked cards and promises to oppose their plan. A good deal of what became the final dialogue for the scene is in place here, although some of it is unpolished, and several excellent later lines are missing.[5]

An inset scene in the wireless room shows a photo being received of John Chumway, Eve ("probably his daughter"), and Muggsy, along with a description of their aliases and crimes. The card game scene that follows plays very closely to that of the final version, except that here, after Lord Sidwich pretends to tear up Charles's check, Charles is called out, supposedly to answer the phone. It is in fact a summons from the purser, who shows Charles the photograph that he has just received.

Charles then meets Eve on deck; she tells him that the best women aren't as good as men think they are and the bad ones are not as bad. She also admits that she is an "adventuress." Charles proposes dancing, and Eve suggests that they do so on her private deck. Once there, they dance, then sit down while Eve smokes a cigarette.

CHARLES
(Suddenly)
Oh, God, how I love you.

He moves closer to her. She closes her eyes but does not move away. Now he crushes her in his arms. She sinks back against the chaise longue.

B-74 THE RAIL OF THE PRIVATE DECK AND THE MOONLIGHT WATER BEYOND

A lighted cigarette arcs over the rail and down into the water.

FADE OUT

Eve comes in the next day—Sequence C—and finds Charles looking at the incriminating picture. She says he had to know sooner or later and that at least they had two very beautiful days. Charles says, avoiding her eyes, "I'm still quite willing to marry you, Eve." She says forgivingly that she would have made him a very nice wife. "We're really very nice people except that we play cards too well . . . just think how useful that would be if anyone ever tried to cheat you . . . I don't think you have any idea what a miserable card player you are, darling." Eve says also that she is glad that the picture came this morning rather than last night. Charles responds harshly that it did come last night. Eve is hurt.

EVE

Then you knew who we were . . . before you told me you loved me.

CHARLES

(Miserably)

I tried to tell you . . . I swear it, but every time I looked into your eyes . . .

(His voice trails off)

Eve says that he should be very proud of himself and leaves, blowing him a kiss. Treekill comes in breathlessly ("puff, puff, puff") with the news that Emma has just laid her first egg; Charles tells him: "Oh, go to h . . ." The last word is drowned out by the powerful blast of the ship's whistle, accompanied by a close-up of same.

The next morning the *Serenia* docks in New York; Tommy and his bride shout greetings to Charles from the shore. Eve and Lord Sidwich have a conversation that is quite similar to the one that appears in the final script, including the revelation that Sidwich had not torn up Charles's check after all. This leads to Eve's final comment: "I feel better myself," which closes Sequence C.

Sequence D consists of a single scene between Charles and Eve in Charles's New York bank. Eve tries to cash the check her father palmed; she has difficulty because of its large amount. Just then Charles happens to be cashing a check of his own and directs the teller to pay Eve's check. Charles is cold and formal although his expression is "quite miserable" as he leaves; Eve says nothing. This scene survives in the final script (pages 77–79) but was cut from the film itself.

Sequence E takes place back at Pike Manor. This is, in essence, the second half of the script, and it begins, as did the first, with Emma.

Into the beam of sunlight from a partly opened door comes our old friend Emma. As she starts down the hall the door is thrown open violently and Charles appears fully dressed in country style. Possibly knickerbockers. He looks for Emma, spots her, then hurries PAST THE CAMERA after her.

CHARLES' VOICE

I've had about enough out of you! Now get back where you belong and look sharp about it. Go on, now!

Emma slithers back INTO THE PICTURE and disappears inside the room.

CHARLES

(Reappearing)

A little of you goes a long way.

He steps into the room and slams the door hard.

A seven-page conversation on the terrace between Sir Harry and Lady Pike, later joined by Charles, makes clear that they wish him to marry. Charles has been, his father says, "as gloomy as Shrove Tuesday." When Charles appears, Sir Harry says bluntly: "Why don't you get married? . . . What do you think you're on earth for? Why do you think we brought you into this world and have supported you in luxury and in whimsies till the mind revolteth? Do you think we like living in a house full of snakes?" An astonished Charles asks: "Who to?" Sir Harry suggests Sheba Ramsey, who lives on the next estate; Charles says she looks like a bullfrog and also pleads his ophiological duties—attending a meeting, seeing a new boa at the zoo, hearing a lecture on Saturday "that I dare not miss . . . Sunday, of course, is feeding day for me here . . ." When his father presses him, Charles says finally that it does not matter since he will never be in love again anyway.

Sir Harry notices in the newspaper that the entire family of the Earl of Northwood, their neighbors, has disappeared. A cut to Monte Carlo shows Eve, Lord Sidwich, and Muggsy at breakfast on the terrace of a villa. While Eve throws crumbs to pigeons and Sidwich reads the *London Times,* Muggsy peruses "a small sporting journal," which provides the occasion for the dialogue about horse racing that occurs in the track scene of the final script (page 81). Sidwich says that the *Serenia* will be sailing soon, their vacation is over; Eve says she hates the *Serenia*. Sidwich replies that it treated them pretty well.

EVE

And we're right back where we were.

SIDWICH

We've lived.

EVE

So have the slugs in the backyard.

Sidwich then notices in the newspaper the story about Northwood and reads it excitedly to Eve and Muggsy.

> "Entire family disappears! The Earl of Northwood and party of sixteen vanish into crevasse. One of the most shocking disasters in the history of mountain climbing occurred this morning above Zinf, Switzerland. The elderly Earl of Northwood and his entire lineage totalling sixteen members, tied together by a single rope, were hurled to instant oblivion in the unplumbed depths of the celebrated Kunzi Crevasse, the glacier of the Altfrau. The Earl of Northwood had refused a guide, the latter having demanded seventeen fees which his grace considered excessive. It is believed this catastrophe has extinguished the succession and that the Earldom of Northwood, created in 1192, is now no more."

Lord Sidwich states that the earl was his father's brother. The rest of Sequence E has to do with the arrival of Sidwich, Eve, and Muggsy at Northwood Manor to claim the title and with their settling into their new circumstances. Sidwich becomes the forty-first Earl of Northwood with an estate of £4 million; Eve becomes Lady Lucinda; Muggsy is introduced to the servants as "Dr. Leavenworth." The sequence ends with Eve's realization that the Pikes are their next-door neighbors.

Sequence F begins with Sir Harry and Charles arguing again about the issue of marriage. Charles says he has to buy a ring—"You can't propose without flashing the sparkler, anybody knows that." Sir Harry, however, has already bought a ring to fit Sheba Ramsey's finger and gives it to his son. Furious, Charles "picks up a snake, forces it into his father's hands, exits, and slams the door." Driving away from Pike Manor in anger, presumably to ask Sheba Ramsey for her hand in marriage, Charles sees Eve in a pony cart and drives off the road. He confronts her about the *Serenia*; she denies any knowledge—her name is Lady Lucinda, daughter of the Earl of Northwood. Charles goes over later to apologize to the earl for his rudeness to his daughter; he is admitted to their drawing room—"these are democratic days," says the earl to Muggsy. The earl accepts his apology, and Eve comes in. She and Charles talk about the lady on the boat who looked like her and "exit laughing." Charles comes home singing "Good-night, sweetheart . . ." and explains to his parents' questions that he could not ask her to marry him since he has only just met her. They are stupefied.

In Sequence G, Eve tells her father how much she hates Charles, then mystifies him by planning a campaign to seduce him into loving her. She pictures how it will be in three weeks, and there is a dissolve to the two of them on horseback, as in the final script. A wedding scene follows, after which Northwood and Muggsy wonder what Eve is planning to do to Charles. Sequence G continues with the long scene on a train in which Eve tells Charles of her sexual past; this scene survives almost intact in the final script and film. The sequence ends with Charles's fall in the mud as he exits the train; Eve grins, then bursts into tears.

At a party at Northwood Manor, Eve lies to various people that Charles is hunting in Africa and South America. Sir Harry tells Northwood and Eve that he has received a letter from his son asking him to arrange a divorce. Eve learns that Charles is in Monte Carlo and heads there herself. She finds him at the gambling tables; when he sees her, he is delighted. They have dinner that night. Charles says he has been in love with her since they met but that he has married someone who looked like her. She starts to tell him of how she has consoled herself in the meantime: first Herbert, then. . . . After a dissolve, she explains to a distraught Charles that she has not been able to look at another man because of her love for him. Charles faints, but she manages to get him to her villa, where his limp body pulls her on top of him; she gets to her knees and unties his tie. Then there is a dissolve to "The Bedroom of All Bedrooms"—Sturges comments: "It is small but oh my." Charles rests in bed with Eve next to him. When he revives, he asks who she is and she replies that she is Eve who loves him. He asks what he is doing there and says he is married. She says that she's married too but tells him to lie back and rest "because bye and bye . . . you're going to get the shock of your life." "She smiles at him like a mother looking at a baby. FADE OUT: THE END."

Sturges did not return to *Two Bad Hats* until August 1940 when he rewrote it for himself as director and called it, of course, *The Lady Eve.* Why the project was shelved in the meantime is not entirely clear. We do know that Albert Lewin had major reservations about Sturges's screenplay; it was for this reason, presumably, that the film was not scheduled for production and that Sturges did not proceed directly to revise the script, as was his normal procedure, but instead went on to another project. Lewin apparently voiced some of his criticisms to Sturges in person; he pursued them at length in a three-page, single-spaced letter to Sturges, dated January 17, 1939.

Lewin wrote the letter from New York City before sailing to England—he tells Sturges that he can be reached, if necessary, at Dorchester House, London. It is evident that relations between the two men were quite cordial, both before and after their disagreement over *Two Bad Hats*.[6] Lewin says he will speak with "unalloyed brutality," which he hopes Sturges will forgive since it hurts him more than it does Sturges. "Sit down, get yourself a highball and put your lovely Louise on one knee where she can kiss away your tears." He continues: "I am afraid that the first two-thirds of the script, in spite of the high quality of your jokes, will require an almost one hundred percent rewrite. The last third of the script, however, will need only minor revisions." This is not as bad as it sounds, he says, since "the last third of a story is four-fifths of it so to speak."

Lewin complains that the hero is an ophiologist for inadequate reasons, essentially to provide gags. It tells us what the hero's occupation is but nothing about his character. Since snakes do not appear in the climax of the film, the point builds to nothing. Lewin observes also that the business about saving his brother from a misalliance is "merely an amateurish detour in order to get Charles on the boat"; nothing is made of the brother and his wife later. He complains also that once Charles gets on the boat, the romance between him and Eve is "all too easy, mainly because there is absolutely no character problem between them." Her being a crook is a matter of very slight consequence, like his ophiology. "They should be kept apart because he is the kind of a guy he is and she is the kind of a gal she is."

Lewin continues: "Now when Eve is prepared to marry Charles without letting him know that she is a crook and when Charles, in his turn, embraces Eve without revealing to her that he knows she is a crook, I lose all respect for both of them. . . ." Lewin remarks that he has already spoken to Sturges about the "too fortuitous inheritance" of Lord Sidwich and Eve. He opposes "the convenience of this together with the extremely silly and haw-haw British nature of the middle episodes that follow from this point up to the point of the marriage. . . ."

Turning to "constructive" suggestions, Lewin refers to discussions they had held before the script was written: "I should like to revert in particular to certain elements in the original outline that I presented to you which I still feel are sound and, in fact, the only solution to the story." "Let me briefly rehearse the essentials the way we had them," Lewin continues, whereupon he summarizes what is essentially the Bartlett version of the story without her subplots:

Charles was a very supercilious Englishman, good-looking, rich, noble, cultured, but too well aware that he was all these things. When he found that his friend, who had been to dear old Balliol with him, was actually contemplating matrimony with so inferior an object as Eve he was shocked and scandalized at this sad falling off in his standards. This provided a challenge to Eve who, in contrast to Charles, is a helluva regular scout. In fact, I see her very much as Carole Lombard is in life. She laughs much too loud and too often. When she laughs she slaps herself. She also slaps you. She can bend an elbow with the best of them. She is in two words a hearty wench. And with all, completely adorable. Charles is fascinated with her and horrified at the same time. His remarks about her constitute a challenge. If he thinks she is vulgar she is determined to show him that he doesn't know the half of it. She intends to scandalize him right out of his noble skin with the unexpected result that he is completely captivated by her. But when she gets into an awful jam, what with her father and all, he runs like a scared rabbit leaving her annoyed, contemptuous and miserably in love with someone who, according to all of her lights, is a heel. Now the twin-business of the old story makes their meeting again and his acceptance of her as her own twin sister, completely believable. For this reason I think it is worth almost any amount of trouble to work the twin gag into the script. He finds himself falling in love with, as he thinks, a perfectly proper counterpart of the adorable, improper original whom he has never been able to forget. His proposal, however, is a model of condescension, so phrased as to enrage Eve. From there on she proceeds to punish him exactly as you have written it, only the scene on the train is much better because he is being punished not for something he has done but for something he is.

Lewin states what is apparent—that Sturges's script abandons the story that Lewin had given him—and makes clear his view that it was a mistake to do so. Lewin wishes Sturges to return to the original story, but his work has not been totally in vain: the last third of the script is a valuable contribution. Lewin writes: "I admit without equivocation that the outline I originally presented to you never had a last third at all. What you have done with the last third makes the story possible. For this I am prepared to pin the Congressional Medal on you and make any obeisance you require, but you must go back and do the early part over."

Despite this concession, it is evident that producer and writer disagree fundamentally about the project they have embarked upon and that unless the writer capitulates and agrees to start over again, they have reached an impasse. Sturges's response to Lewin's criticism was amiable and amusing (see note 6), but there is no evidence that he ever considered redoing *Two Bad Hats* to bring it closer to the original stories.[7]

By the time he received Lewin's letter, in any case, he was already at work on an original screenplay, also for Lewin, called *The Amazing Marriage.* (This was directed by Mitchell Leisen in 1939 and released in 1940 as *Remember the Night.*) Sturges finished a revised draft of this script by March 24, 1939, and was occupied with rewrites at least through July. Lewin left Paramount for another studio during the rewrite process, which put Sturges at the mercy of Leisen, who now became his own producer. According to James Curtis, Leisen preferred to cut passages he did not like in a script rather than to work with the writer to change them.[8] This so rankled Sturges, whose *Easy Living* script Leisen had also directed, that he threatened to leave Paramount. This apparently helped persuade Paramount head of production William LeBaron to let Sturges direct *The Great McGinty.* The rewriting, filming, and editing of *The Great McGinty* and *Christmas in July* occupied him through July 1940.

In August 1940, Sturges returned to his 1938 project in triumph. His two films as writer-director had been great critical and solid commercial successes. He was able to demand a larger budget, including star leads Barbara Stanwyck and Henry Fonda, who had to be borrowed from Twentieth Century–Fox. Sturges was also now free, it seems safe to say, to do whatever he wanted with the screenplay of *Two Bad Hats,* within the bounds of censorship. What he chose to do, of course, was to rewrite it extensively.

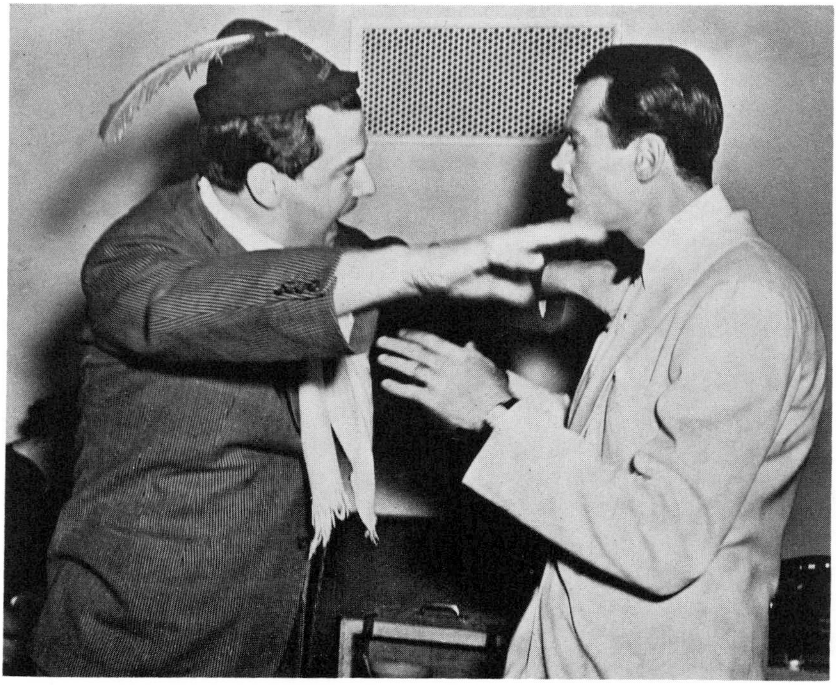

Sturges "motivates" Henry Fonda in THE LADY EVE.

Sturges seems to have decided upon certain general features of the revision right away. (Their exact working out, of course, took a long time to accomplish—not to mention their harmonization with other aspects of the script, some of which were themselves in process of revision.) Lewin, for instance, had criticized the "amateurish detour" of Charles's boarding the boat to save his brother from a bad marriage and also Charles's ophiology, which he said tells us nothing about his character and builds to nothing in the film. Sturges rightly dropped the rescue mission, but he increased the importance of snakes by starting the revised script with Charles's emergence from the Amazon and by making *that* the pretext of his boarding the ship. Sturges grasped in this respect what Lewin missed—that the very irrelevance of the snake business lends the film its delightful absurdity. (It is a "screwball" element and, as such, one of the things that pushes *The Lady Eve* toward screwball comedy. Lewin evidently had in mind a more traditional comedy of manners.) Charles's love of snakes also, of course, tells us about his character and functions as part of the film's Garden of Eden motif.

Lewin had also criticized the "too fortuitous inheritance" of Lord Sidwich and Eve. Sturges did indeed drop the inheritance plot in his 1940 rewrites, but this element was not so easily excised, or replaced, as had been the reason for Charles's getting on the boat. It was tied up with, among other things, the script's English characters and setting. Englishness had been essential to the project from the beginning. It plays an important, if distinct, role in the Hoffe story, in the Bartlett story, in Sturges's 1938 script, and in Lewin's fond and precise ideas about how the script and film should go. In Hoffe, all the characters are English, and, it seems, society, wherever it exists, is English. The New World provides an escape for the disreputable and an outlet for those who wish to fulfill their deepest, "most wicked" desires. In Bartlett, Salome is English, but she is born in America and somehow becomes American by association. Pallas had criticized the photographer Lord Forbes's Americanization, which means principally his willingness to ignore social barriers in matters of love and marriage. Pallas's very English propriety is equated by Bartlett with near-total instinctual repression—a very American view. (Hoffe's Pallas is not at all repressed.) That Bartlett names one of her characters after actor Roland Young is, in this respect, more than suggested casting. Beginning with *Ruggles of Red Gap* (1935), Young specialized in portrayals of the pleasure-loving, woman-chasing Englishman who found America very much to his taste. In American cinema, at least in comedies, Englishmen are Americanized to the extent that they are socially democratic, especially in their choice of marriage partners, and vice versa.

Sturges's *Two Bad Hats* treats the question differently. First, Sturges seems to put no particular emotional or sexual valence on Englishness as such; he treats it as simply a background like any other and, hence, as a source of gags. Sturges's American Charles in *The Lady Eve* is in fact more repressed than his English Charles in *Two Bad Hats*. After Eve trips the English Charles, they take the lift to her cabin—she topples against him and is stabbed with a fork still stuck in his shirt from his earlier fall. "They both roar with laughter," Sturges specifies, and Charles wants to keep the fork as a memento. When they get to Eve's cabin, Charles says, "Now isn't this jolly?"; as he puts on slipper after slipper, he wishes it could go on all night. Indeed, Sturges may have been obliged to put Murgatroyd in the next cabin to keep Charles from trying to seduce Eve then and there. *The Lady Eve*'s Charles would never say or do any of these things, needless to say, nor could he later seize Eve "expertly" and dance away with her "with perfect grace and rhythm," as does Sturges's English Charles. (John Ford's *Young Mr. Lincoln* [1939] established once and for all that the Fonda persona is by nature a stiff, inelegant dancer. Ford's *My Darling Clementine* [1946] is merely one of many later films that quote this axiom; Fonda's pratfalls in *The Lady Eve* extend it into the realm and idiom of overt comedy.)

Second, there is confusion about money in Sturges's *Two Bad Hats* (it is reckoned sometimes in pounds, sometimes in dollars) and about some linguistic expressions. When Lord Sidwich figures up what Charles has "won" the first night, his computations are even more complicated than in the finished film. "Purely nominal . . . at six-pence a point, let me see now . . . by six . . . divided by twelve and divided by twenty gives us one hundred and four pounds, seven shillings and sixpence ha'penny . . . would you accept five hundred dollars, my money has already been changed?" He then goes through an abbreviated form of the same to determine what Eve owes Charles—"roughly a hundred dollars." In the second card game, they bet in increments of twenty-five, fifty, and, finally, a hundred pounds, but the "cheque" which Charles pays after his round of "double or quits" with Lord Sidwich is for $32,000 ("and no pence"), as in *The Lady Eve.* Such double-entry terminology, amusing at first, quickly becomes tiresome, which comedy cannot afford.

Eve herself, in all versions of *Two Bad Hats,* is a changeling child in nationality, as in other respects. In Hoffe, she is born in "British Columbia or Alaska, or somewhere of that sort," and returns to England with her mother. In Bartlett, she is born in America, where she also has a career and works at her mother's gambling house. Sturges's *Two Bad Hats* eliminates the "gaslight melodrama" of the earlier versions; Eve is therefore uncomplicatedly English in genealogy, even if her character and speech are inconsistently so. Charles, indeed, plausibly asks her: "I say, you ARE funny, are you English?" "Half," she says, adding: "My mother was a French maid." Charles does not seem to know how to take this—is it a joke?—and neither does the reader.

Lewin had criticized the British gags of the second part of the script as silly, but this criticism undercut his call for a more English theme. When he had eliminated the British gags, Sturges had no further use for English characters and an English setting, and he dropped them. Sturges's choice to Americanize *The Lady Eve* was one of the most important of the revision process, affecting directly or indirectly many other aspects of the script and film.

Having begun on August 26, 1940, Sturges finished a revised screenplay, now called *The Lady Eve,* by October 7, 1940. Notes and discard pages in the Sturges archive indicate the exact process by which he achieved, bit by bit and with many detours and canceled initiatives, what we know as the final form of *The Lady Eve.* There isn't space here to trace in detail this painstaking process, as important as any other in the complex genesis of the film; perhaps a few examples will suffice.

The bulk of Sturges's rewriting concerned the second part of the script, but there were many important changes in the first part also. On September 4, for example, Sturges first uses Eve's voice-over to describe the women in the dining room vying for Charles's attention (pages 9–11). On September 25, the lines "Snakes are my life!" and "What a life!" (page 33) first appear, and "Eve," as far as I can tell, is first referred to by another name—"Jane." On October 5, Charles and "Jane's" dialogue on their ideal mates (pages 34–36) first appears, and on October 7, "Jane" is changed to "Jean," which remains the name of the character in all subsequent drafts and versions. "Jane" might have suggested the presence of an "Eve" behind every (plain) Jane; "Jean," the name that Sturges chose, might suggest "Jean d'Arc," the savior who triumphs over "Eve." (It takes Charles the entire film to understand and accept this.) The change of names is important also because it makes Jean herself the author of the name "Eve," which she adopts in the second half of the film.

In the second part of the film, the lines for Mr. Pike while he is on the telephone (page 85) first appear on September 20, Eve's dialogue about the subway (page 104) on the day after. On September 22, Charles's rough bodyguard-valet, now called Muggsy, first says: "That's the same dame" (page 111). By September 30, Sturges had revised the train scene to fit its new context; as late as this date, however, it is Eve who tells Charles the story about the coachman's daughter that Sir Alfred tells him in the revised script and film (pages 123–126), all but explicitly identifying "the girl on the boat" as her sister or half-sister (Sir Alfred only hints at this in the film).

The October 7 script of *The Lady Eve* embodied these and numerous other changes. It did not, however, end the revision process. Further changes resulted in the October 18 script, printed below, which is, of course, the shooting script. But the filming process itself entailed, as always with Sturges, considerable further refinements of the dialogue and, in this case, of important aspects of structure also.

Lewin had criticized the coming together of Eve and Charles as "all too easy," but this is part of the appealing fantasy of screwball comedy.[9] It is also true that the viewer of such a film may be sustained through later separations and complications only if the initial coming together has seemed irresistible. Sturges, in any case, never altered the coming together of the lovers—except to improve the dialogue—from the 1938 script to the finished film. What took him much longer to resolve were the reasons for their breaking up and the right way to present it.

The romance of Jean and Charles takes place over three days, although, like many a shipboard romance, it seems much longer. The first day includes Jean's tripping Charles, their going for a new pair of shoes, his card tricks, the first card game, the "Emma" scene in Charles's cabin, and the long dialogue on the chaise longue in Jean's cabin. This sequence of events remains constant from the 1938 script to the 1941 film. What changes from version to version and is finally resolved only by the film itself are the events of the second and third days. On the second day, the romance peaks, with Charles and Jean making plans for the future, and on the third day they part. What happens on the second day, the exact order and nature of its events, determines the nature of the third day's parting, and that, in turn, determines the nature of the second half of the film—Jean's revenge—and hence the relationship between the two parts of the film.

In the 1938 script, the second day begins with the scene in which Treekill (later Muggsy) orders Emma's breakfast and makes Muggsy (later Gerald) sick, followed by a scene in which the purser warns Charles against professional gamblers. Charles dismisses him and greets Eve, with whom he has breakfast. This scene is followed by one in which the purser orders a photograph from the New York Police Department. Following this is the long scene in which Charles takes Eve all over the ship to tell her he loves her, which is followed by the scene in which Eve tells her father not to cheat Charles that evening. The card game itself plays largely as in the film except that after Eve's father pretends to tear up his check, Charles is called out and the purser shows him the photo of Eve and her father. Charles and Eve spend a romantic evening, and when Eve joins Charles the next morning, he is looking at the photograph. Charles tells her "harshly" that the photo arrived the night before, and Eve says "in a cold small voice," "Then you knew who we were . . . before you told me you loved me," then leaves soon after.

The October 7 script begins the second day with Muggsy's making Gerald sick and follows this with a short scene in which Jean tells her father that Charles is "the real McPike," that is, the right sucker. This is followed by a scene in which Muggsy brings Emma her breakfast and voices to Charles his suspicions about Jean and her father, and then by the breakfast scene between Jean and Charles. Next comes the scene between Muggsy and the purser, who says he has confidential photos of some professional card players but does not admit that there are any on board. This is followed by a scene between Jean and Charles on the bow of the ship "against a magnificent sunset," in which he gives his long "I've always loved you" speech. (This speech, which substitutes for the journey-through-the-ship gag of the 1938 script, is an important stage in the gradually increasing seriousness of the Jean–Charles romance.) Next comes the scene in which Jean tells her father not to cheat Charles that evening, then the card game itself. After Jean's father tears up his check, Charles is called out, and the purser shows him the photo of Jean and her father. Charles and Jean talk, then go to her cabin. When Jean joins him the next morning, he is looking at the photograph. Charles confesses that he received the photo the night before. Jean asks why he did not tell her then, and Charles asks why she did not tell him (that she was a crook) when he said he loved her and asked her to marry him. Jean says she was going to tell him before they married—he must believe that. Charles says he does not know what to think. Jean says: "Then you were acting out of revenge . . . you wanted to hurt me . . . and make me feel cheap . . . when you knew you didn't want to marry me any more . . . that's why you came like a thief in the night." Charles says he will marry Jean if she wants; she replies that he must feel very proud of himself and leaves.

In the October 18 script, as in that of October 7, the scene of Muggsy and

Gerald at breakfast is followed by the scene of Jean and her father, and then the scene between Muggsy and Charles, the scene of Jean and Charles at breakfast, and the scene between Muggsy and the purser. Sturges inserted here a brief new scene (C-9, page 47) in which Jean and Charles say "good-bye for a little while," which is followed by the scene in which Jean tells her father not to cheat Charles, and the card game itself. This time Charles is not called away from the table, and he does not see the photo of Jean and her father. Instead, he meets Jean on deck, goes with her to the bow of the boat, and makes his "I've always loved you" speech, which is now the peak of their romantic evening.

The next morning begins with a scene in which Jean and her father reconcile; she tells him that she plans to marry Charles, and he asks that she not tell Charles "who we are" until he and Gerald get off the boat. Jean agrees "after a slight pause" and goes off to meet Charles. (This is a new scene in the October 18 script, obviously designed to show that Jean intends to tell Charles the truth about herself and to provide one of the reasons why she has not done so already.) While Charles is waiting for Jean on deck, Muggsy brings the purser, and Charles sees the photograph. In the scene between Charles and Jean that follows, he tells her that he knew who she was the night before. In the October 18 script, for the first time, this is a lie; Charles is trying to hurt Jean, and, although she says she does not believe him, she is hurt at the possibility and at his intentional cruelty. This provides a motivation for her revenge in the second part of the film that is far subtler than those of the earlier versions. It also implies, and helps create, a more intimate and intense love relation between Jean and Charles than before, wherein the pretense to betrayal is as wounding as betrayal itself.

Lewin had touched a sore point in the 1938 script when he criticized Eve's not telling Charles that she is a crook and Charles's "embracing" Eve knowing that she is one. It seems true that Charles cannot "embrace" Jean with this knowledge and still retain our sympathy; the romance, the film, and the genre itself (romantic or screwball comedy) would be violated if this occurred. It is fascinating that Sturges did not change either of these crucial elements in the nearly two years from the 1938 script to the October 7 script but changed them both in the eleven days that followed. In the October 18 script, for the first time, Charles does not know about Eve when he "embraces" her, and, thanks to the new scene between Jean and her father, we know that Jean wants to tell Charles the truth about herself but cannot yet do so.

The film itself makes several further changes in the order of events. The second day's breakfast scene with Muggsy and Gerald is followed by the scene between Muggsy and Charles. This makes a smoother transition: Muggsy brings Emma's breakfast directly from the scene in which he orders it; Charles's "Did you get it?" is the first line of the next scene. Jean's brief morning scene with her father follows ("He's the real McPike"), ending with her line, "Tell me my fortune." This is followed by a scene of Charles on deck waiting to have breakfast with Jean, perhaps while she has her fortune told. In the film he has to wait some time (none of the scripts indicates this), and to distract Charles and the viewer, Sturges invents a Tati-like character in a striped jersey who walks up and down the deck with a fishing rod.

The next change in order occurs directly after this scene. Instead of proceeding from Jean and Charles at breakfast to Muggsy's going to see the purser, Sturges postpones the purser scene and proceeds right to Jean's confrontation with her father (page 47). Her breakfast with Charles, and whatever may have followed it, has changed her mind—they are in love and Charles must not be cheated. This change of order also allows Sturges to cut the awkward good-bye scene (C-9, page 47), which formerly came between Muggsy's visit to the purser and Jean's confrontation with her father. (C-9 thus functioned in part as a "remotivation" scene for Jean's break with her father.) The card game itself follows, with Charles's speech on deck after that. Sequence D, the next day, begins with Muggsy's going to see the purser, and the rest of the sequence, some dialogue changes aside, plays as written.

Between "Jean" and "Eve" –Barbara Stanwyck in the bank sequence that was cut from the release print of THE LADY EVE.

The film's most conspicuous change concerns Sequence E (pages 77–79), the scene in which Charles and Jean meet at his New York bank as she tries to cash the palmed check, which it simply cuts. The film thus fades out from Jean's line as her party waits to disembark—"I feel better already" (about the palmed check)—and fades in on the racetrack scene in which she meets Pearlie ("Sir Alfred at the moment") and conceives her plan of revenge.

In the 1938 and October 7 scripts, the bank scene follows Charles's confession that he knew Jean was a crook during their romantic evening together. In the October 18 script, the bank scene follows Charles's false confession that he knew. In the film, Charles's confession is false, and the bank scene that was to follow it is cut. (The bank scene was, however, definitely shot—see accompanying illustration.)[10]

In itself, the bank scene is ambiguous. In the 1938 and October 7 scripts, the fact that Charles knows about Jean before their romantic evening and says nothing sufficiently motivates her revenge in the second half of the film. In both versions, however, the bank scene develops sympathy for Charles by showing him to be miserable. It also keeps alive for the second half of the film a sense of the couple's passion for each other, however suppressed—it shows that their parting was not as definitive as it seemed. But in the October 18 script, when Charles acts in good faith on their romantic evening—even though he lies about it the next day—Jean's revenge seems somewhat excessive. The bank scene in this case might serve to reinforce Jean's revenge drive by presenting Charles as condescending, stuffy, and unable to express his feelings. It does after all reiterate the social distance between the former lovers and hence reminds the viewer that Jean feels hurt and cheapened. On the other hand, the scene as written seems to emphasize the pathos of the lovers' estranged condition:

> He flips the check through the window, then turns to Jean. His expression becomes quite miserable.
>
> Jean looks down and whispers:
>
> JEAN
>
> Good-bye.
>
> Charles walks away fast. (page 79)

Unless the scene were played to underscore Charles's condescension, the sadness of the scene might undermine Jean's revenge drive. Indeed, what all of this suggests is that the way in which the bank scene was directed would have determined its meaning and its impact on the film as a whole. Since the scene as written seems to cut in several directions at once, some of them opposing, it is difficult to assess the effect of the scene's final omission.

The film's preservation of Charles's good faith from the October 18 script—combined with its deleting the bank scene, present in all previous versions—poses a new context for Jean's revenge. It also thereby displaces the problem of direction backward. Without the bank scene, our last view of the lovers in the first half of the film is the disembarkation scene, in which Sturges cuts back and forth between Jean and Charles. Charles never once looks over at Jean's group; Muggsy looks over once. The coldness of recently fiery emotions is realized with great restraint by what each of the lovers does not do—which is to acknowledge the existence of the other. Stanwyck in her traveling outfit is

Getting into the act–Sturges directing Barbara Stanwyck inside the train as she watches Henry Fonda fall in the mud outside. (Sturges is dressed for shooting the muddy exterior.)

already an elegant hunter, her hatred hidden beneath an icy exterior. In the absence of the bank scene, this scene becomes the hinge between the two parts of the film, and it is played with complete seriousness. It does not supply or replace, but stands in for, the rationalized "motivations" of all of the previous story and script versions. It thereby locates the spring of Jean's later actions in a somewhat obscure but powerful realm of interior feeling. The scene thus presents the nonlaughing other side of screwball comedy's battle of the sexes. Perhaps this accounts in part for the enduring power of the film.

The mesmerist–Sturges directs Barbara Stanwyck and Henry Fonda in the final embrace for THE LADY EVE.

Notes

1. Monckton Hoffe, author and playwright, was born in Connemara, Ireland, December 26, 1880. His plays *Hate Ship, Flame of Love,* and *Many Waters* were filmed in 1931, *The Faithful Heart* (directed by Victor Saville) in 1932, and *The Little Damazel* in 1933, all by British film companies. For several of these he made his own adaptations. From 1933 he worked as a screenwriter in Hollywood, writing "additional dialogue" for *Bitter Sweet* (1933), *The Mystery of Madame X* (1934), and *What Every Woman Knows* (1934). He collaborated on the screenplays of *The Runaway Queen* (1935), *Pagliacci* (1937), *The Last of Mrs. Cheyney* (1937), *The Emperor's Candlesticks* (1937), and *The Haunted Honeymoon* (1940). He died in London on November 4, 1951. My source for Hoffe's credits is the *International Motion Picture Almanac,* 1938–39 (page 367) and 1942–43 (page 278) (New York: Quigley Publishing Company, 1938 and 1942). Hoffe's credits were published without change from the *Almanac* for 1942–43 through 1948–49; ironically, the last credit in each of those entries was "In 1941: Screenplay, 'Lady Eve.'" I could find no information about Jeanne Bartlett.

2. Sturges's biographical film for Paramount, *The Great Moment* (1944), draws its facts from the book *Triumph Over Pain* by René Fulop-Miller, but all versions of the story and screenplay were written by Sturges alone. Among the four films directed by Sturges after his Paramount period, *Mad Wednesday* (1946) and *Unfaithfully Yours* (1948) were entirely written by Sturges. *The Beautiful Blonde from Bashful Bend* (1948) was based upon a story by Earl Felton, and *The French, They Are a Funny Race* (1955) was based upon the book *The Notebooks of Major Thompson* by Pierre Daninos.

3. This is the last sentence of Hoffe's otherwise perfectly typed story. Is it a typographical error or a mistake in the writing itself? The sentence has one "that" too many, or one too few. It might read, ". . . and that, in itself, is a very nice sensation," or "and that's that, and that, in itself, is a very nice sensation." It is tempting to see the error as emblematic of the story's sexism and as symptomatic of the psychic mechanisms that underlie sexism in society generally. The male only is granted subjectivity, desire, and will; the female is merely the object of male desire and, indeed, can transform herself, as needed, to satisfy that desire. The "repressed" of this thesis, which inevitably "returns" in some form, is the affirmation of women's subjectivity and desire, what older traditions of thought called simply their humanity. The last sentence of the story closes its narrative and its discourse; it thereby postpones definitively the resolution, or even the acknowledgment, of this contradiction. The stresses of this forced avoidance result in the condensation (one "that" too few) and/or the hyperbole (one "that" too many) of the last sentence. Hardly an accident, the clause in which the error occurs is one that attempts to describe female desire (or simply feeling), something the story has not done up to this point. Hence the proliferation of "that"s and the confusion of reference which a pile-up of "that"s nearly always involves. The "that" in question is that which cannot be named or described. The discourse can neither close without further attention to the question—"and that's that"—nor allow itself to admit its inability to treat the subject by too overtly confusing its reference and by running on too long: "and that's that, and that, in itself, is a very nice sensation." In another sense, it is the final "that" which is the site of the condensation; its nominal referent—"she's got her husband back"—has slipped overdeterminedly into an imagining of the female position in sex, the subject of male preoccupation and avoidance. "That, in itself, is a very nice sensation" is what the text cannot say directly.

4. In *The Power and the Glory,* the scene has a punch line lacking in Sturges's *Two Bad Hats.* After she says yes, Sally says: "Tom, couldn't you have asked me at the foot of the mountain?" In *Two Bad Hats,* Jean does not hear Charles's proposal in the engine room but nevertheless announces it to her father and Muggsy in the next scene. There is another, rather uncanny connection between the two scenes. Henry, the narrator of *The Power and the Glory* and, indeed, of the proposal scene itself (he even narrates the dialogue that we see the characters Tom and Sally mouthing to each other!) says of Tom's attempt to propose: ". . . then he opened his mouth a couple of times like a goldfish." Sturges notes of Charles's initial attempt to propose to Eve: "Charles opens and closes his mouth like a goldfish a few times. . . ."

5. One line that is not missing is Lord Sidwich's to Muggsy (later Gerald) after Eve seizes the cards: "Children don't respect their parents any more." This line, which concludes (or "caps") a rather serious scene, always gets a big laugh. What is interesting is that Sturges altered the line in his 1940 scripts (both the October 7 script and the October 18 script which is printed below). The colonel says: "Children don't respect their parents any more. If I'd spoken that way to MY father. . . ." The film itself drops the second line, that is, returns to the 1938 rendering.

6. Sturges began a letter to Lewin, who was still in England, on February 3, 1939, and continued it on February 6:

I waited a couple of days before mentioning the stories. As to TLE: I agree with much that you say. The beginning must be made to fit the end and many of the seeds I scattered in the early part to see what they would grow into can now be weeded. On the other hand I am frightened to death by the word "ruthless". O ruth, what crimes have been committed in thy name! What destructions of Carthage! What massacres of St. Bartholomew! What throttling of beautiful poker scenes! How well I know the fanatical look in the eye, the light foam on the lips, the orgastic tension of the face muscles, and the sadistic smile on the face of the one who says: "I am going to be ruthless." It is such a beautifully positive thing to be, so decisive and virile, fraught with such a feeling of well-being, that it is almost irresistible. There is nothing puny and Coolidge-like about it. It is Rooseveltian (I am writing all this hogwash on my own time.) In conclusion, I think we will get a very nice picture with a reasonable amount of rewriting. I mean I think that you will agree. After all, you liked the first two-thirds pretty much when you first read them. The audience should too. I showed your letter to Bill [LeBaron]. He agreed with both of us. As to that other turkey [*The Amazing Marriage,* which became *Remember the Night*]: like the "supplice du pal qui commence si bien et qui finit si mal . . ." it has been quite a pain in the arse. I almost committed hari-kari several times, but thinking of the pain it would cause you I postponed it for some later assignment. (I wonder why I never get any of those easy ones like *True Confession* or *Spawn of the North* or *Zaza* or *Knights of the Round Table?*) Anyway, when the District Attorney took the girl up to the mountains to reform her the picture died of pernicious anaemia. When he took her up because his conscience bothered him it perished from lack of oxygen. When he was moved through charitable impulse and Yuletide spirit it expired from galloping eunuchry. So I thought of a novelty. As it was not at all what we had discussed I sprang it first on your lieutenant producers Manny and Bill. They liked it and it gives me something to go on with besides conversation. The novelty is that the District Attorney takes her up to the mountains for the purpose of committing the Man Act [*sic*]. This has always been a good second act and there is no reason to suspect that it will fail us here. It is an act enjoyed by all, one that we rarely tire of and not above the heads of the audience. In *Rain* he starts to reform her and ends up by laying her like a carpet. In *Resurrection* he gets the errection first and hits the trail much much later. In ours Love will reform her and corrupt him. Which leaves us with the finely balanced moral that one man's meat is another man's poison or caveat emptor. I hope this letter doesn't bore you as much as it would me.

As a matter of fact I think the picture is going to have quite a lot of schmalz, a good dose of schmerz and just enough schmut to make it good box office.

With the assurance of my high regard and my most distinguished salutations, I have the honor to sign myself, dear Boss, Your most humble serf, [Preston].

On February 20, 1939, Lewin, still in London, wrote Sturges: "My boy: Your long letter dated February 3rd just reached me, and has given me the best laugh I have had since I last saw you. I surrender unconditionally. Follow your witty nose, my boy; it will lead you and me and Paramount to the Elysian pastures of popular entertainment . . . As ever, Al Lewin."

On March 19, 1941, Lewin, who was then at Universal Studios, about to embark on his own career as writer-director, sent Sturges a congratulatory note on *The Lady Eve:* "Dear Preston: I can't tell you how delighted I am with your brilliant success. Bob Gillham showed me 'Lady Eve' in the projection room in New York. I laughed till I cried. You have made a marvellous entertainment of it. . . . Regards, Al."

7. With a salary of $2750 a week (James Curtis, *Between Flops: A Biography of Preston Sturges* [New York: Harcourt Brace Jovanovich, 1982], page 116), Sturges's time presumably could not be wasted on projects for which he felt no affinity. (Mr. LeBrand says to Sullivan in *Sullivan's Travels:* ". . . at what you're getting I can't afford to argue with you.") Those who had worked with Sturges must have known his temperamental aversion to collaborating, let alone to writing by prescription. Lewin could veto Sturges's script, but he could hardly force him to rewrite it to his specifications—as Lewin no doubt knew.

8. Curtis, op. cit., p. 125.

9. Charles and Eve's coming together was "all too easy," according to Lewin, "mainly because there is absolutely no character problem between them. . . . They should be kept apart because he is the kind of a guy he is and she is the kind of a gal she is." Lewin's "character problem" formula is not the universal law that he suggests it is. From Greek New Comedy to present-day forms, lovers have also been kept apart by family opposition, by wealth or its absence, by prior commitments, by class differences, and/or by other circumstances. In Sturges's films, indeed, it is not usually character problems that keep lovers apart but external conditions of various kinds. In *Christmas in July* and *The Palm Beach Story,* it is a lack of money that keeps the lovers apart; in *The Miracle of Morgan's Creek,* it is Norvall's incarceration and flight from the police; and in *Hail the Conquering Hero,* it is the hero's pretense to be a hero, without which the lovers would not have been rejoined in the first place. What keeps the lovers apart in *The Lady Eve* is partly subjective (character differences) and partly objective (class differences, social prejudice). Jean, later Eve, says to her father about the inevitable disclosure of their profession to Charles: "He wouldn't be much of a man if he couldn't forgive." Charles sulks that he has been cheated and, with his card tricks, made to look ridiculous. He cannot get beyond his wounded pride to recognize that he loves Jean anyway. At the same time, he fears, despite the evidence of his own senses and emotions, that Eve's love is also a ruse designed to cheat him of his money. His social upbringing, finally, does not allow him to consider marriage to a professional crook. Jean's impersonation of Eve is a revenge on Charles for his rejection of her, but it is also a kind of therapy, allowing him to change his personality, or at least his behavior, and allowing Jean to get beyond her hurt.

10. Positive evidence in the Sturges papers shows that Sturges had in fact shot the bank scene and indeed had included it in an early version of the assembled film. He evidently removed it at a later stage of editing since, as noted, it does not appear in the release print of the film. One of my sources is the dialogue continuity of the film, a verbatim description of the finished film's dialogue. This presumably routine document of the studio era was evidently compiled for publicity and censorship purposes—for the Hays Office as well as for state and city boards. For *The Lady Eve* specifically, and as far as I could find, uniquely, there is also in the Sturges papers a production script, evidently compiled for or by the costume department since it contains costume lists for all the characters of the film and for all the scenes in which they appear. This script also has a single 35mm film frame for, apparently, every shot of the film. For the bank scene there are twenty-two stills, although some of these may have been taken from a single shot. As far as one can judge from stills, the bank scene seems to have been shot very much as indicated by the script.

P.1283

THE LADY EVE

October 18, 1940

THE LADY EVE

CAST OF CHARACTERS

JEAN..................................Barbara Stanwyck

CHARLES PIKE..........................Henry Fonda

COLONEL HARRINGTON....................Charles Coburn

GERALD................................

MUGGSY................................William Demarest

MR. PIKE..............................Eugene Pallette

MRS. PIKE.............................Janet Beecher

SIR ALFRED McGLENNAN-KEITH............Eric Blore

PIKE'S CHEF...........................Luis Alberni

PIKE'S BUTLER.........................Robert Grieg

THE PURSER............................

* * *

Prof. Jones, 1st-Class Steward, Bartender, 2nd-Class Steward, Bank Manager, Martha, the maid, Gertrude, middle-aged maid, Man with potted palm, Piano tuner, Footman, Lawyer at telephone, Second Lawyer, Third Lawyer.

* * *

SEQUENCE "A"

After the Main Titles, which will be an airbrush rendition of the Garden of Eden complete with snake --

FADE IN:

A-1 CLOSE SHOT - EMMA - IN HER BOX

She is a remarkably (Westmore) marked garter snake, coiled amiably in her box.

PROF. JONES' VOICE
... once a day is plenty. Just a couple of flies, a sip of milk and maybe a pigeon's egg on Sundays.

A-2 CHARLES PIKE, PROF. JONES, MUGGSY, TWO YOUNG SCIENTISTS, SEVEN INDIANS AND THE BRAZILIAN PILOT OF THE MOTOR LAUNCH - IN THE SELVA AT THE EDGE OF THE JUTAHY

In other words, the bank of a tropical river. Everybody is dressed for the tropics. Charles is receiving Emma's box from Prof. Jones and the others are gathered around in farewell. The launch, with the luggage piled on its deck, is chugging IN THE BACKGROUND.

CHARLES
I certainly will, Professor.

PROF. JONES
Keep her warm as you get further north and sometimes let her out of her box... to play a little.

CHARLES
I certainly will, Professor.

PROF. JONES
Tell Dr. Marzditz I have named her in his honor: Colubrina Marzditzia, and that this is only the beginning of what I am bringing out...when I come out.

CHARLES
I'll do that, Professor, and I want to tell you... all of you... how much I've enjoyed being on this expedition with you. If I had my way, believe me, this is the way I'd like to spend all my time... in the company of men like yourselves... in the pursuit of knowledge.

10-18-40

(Continued)

A-2 (Cont'd)

PROF. JONES
Good-bye, Charlie.
(Putting a hand on his shoulder)
If you get a chance to come back ... this is where we'll be... give my affectionate salutations to your father and thank him again for making the Pike expedition possible... and I hope... a success.

CHARLES
I will, Professor.

PROF. JONES
Good-bye, my boy... good-bye, Muggsy, my good friend.

MUGGSY
So long, Prof... don't take no wooden money.

CHARLES
(To one of the young scientists)
Good-bye, Sparky. Good-bye, Mac - good-bye, boys.

THE LEADER OF THE INDIANS
So long, Sarlie.

MUGGSY
So long, gang.

Now an Indian lady comes from behind a tree. She puts a wreath of flowers around Muggsy's neck.

MUGGSY
(A little self-consciously)
So long, Lulu... I'll send you a post card.

He climbs on the launch and helps Charles aboard. The pilot casts it loose.

PROF. JONES
Be careful of the traffic...you haven't dodged any in a long time.

MAC
And be careful of the dames. -- You haven't dodged any of them in a long time either.

CHARLES
(Laughing)
You know me, Mac... nothing but reptiles.

10-18-40 (Continued)

A-2 (Cont'd)

They all wave good-bye and the little whistle on the launch shrills sharply. As it lets off a cloud of steam --

DISSOLVE TO:

A-3 LOW CAMERA SHOT - UP AT A VERY PRETTY GIRL - AT THE RAIL OF THE S.S. "SOUTHERN QUEEN"

She's a sweetie in a sweater and looks particularly well, leaning on the rail of the ship.

THE YOUNG GIRL
There he is!

A-4 HIGH CAMERA SHOT - ON A LAUNCH SOME DISTANCE AWAY

A-5 AN OFFICER - ON THE BRIDGE

He throws the engine room telegraph to "Stop" then does whatever one does to make the whistle blow. As the whistle starts to blast --

A-6 LOW CAMERA - UP AT A STEAMSHIP WHISTLE

It is vibrating deafeningly.

A-7 CLOSE SHOT - THE LAUNCH WHISTLE

It peep-peeps its answer over the distant sound of the steamship whistle.

A-8 LOW CAMERA SHOT - UP AT THE PASSENGERS - AT THE RAIL OF THE S.S. "SOUTHERN QUEEN"

We start with the young lady we saw before but we don't hear the first few of them speak because of the boat whistle. Thus we see: The young girl, her mother, her father, a Spanish family, and a steward in uniform. Now the whistle stops blowing and we hear what the people say.

A MOTHER (A)
You mean the Charlie Pike?

ANOTHER MOTHER (B)
(To her daughter)
Go change your dress.

A MAN WITH GLASSES (C)
--- way up in the jungle looking for something or other. I read about it in the National Geographic.

10-18-40

(Continued)

A-8 (Cont'd)

A MIDDLE-AGED WOMAN (D)
No, I tell you Charles Pike.

ANOTHER WOMAN (E)
You mean the Bridgefield Pikes? ...
the brewers?

HER HUSBAND (F)
Why not?

A WOMAN (G)
You'd think he'd have a bigger yacht
than that if he's so rich.

HER HUSBAND (H)
That isn't a yacht; that's a tender.

THE WOMAN (G)
What's a tender?

ANOTHER GIRL (J)
(To her father)
I thought you said Schlitz.

HER FATHER (K)
I said Pabst.

THE MAN NEXT TO HIM (L)
It was Pike.

THE GIRL (J)
You mean the Pike... Charlie Pike?

THE YOUNG MAN WITH HER (M)
So what?

A MOTHER (N)
(To her daughter)
Go put on your shorts.

A DAUGHTER (O)
(To her mother)
But, I can't drink it, mamma, it
makes me sick.

HER MOTHER (P)
You can try, can't you?

THE GIRL (O)
(Confidentially)
It makes me puke.

HER FATHER (Q)
(Astonished)
Puke!

10-18-40 (Continued)

A-8 (Cont'd)

THE MAN NEXT TO HIM (R)
No, Pike.

HIS WIFE NEXT TO HIM (S)
You mean the Pike?
(Then to her daughter)
Go put on your peek-a-boo.

For the last six people the CAMERA HAS PICKED UP Gerald who is walking behind them. We reach the end of the people and follow Gerald a few steps more until he reaches Colonel Harrington leaning on the rail Colonel Harrington wears a black and white checked ca[

GERALD
Pike.

COL. HARRINGTON
Ah.

He turns and speaks to someone OUT OF THE PICTURE.

COL. HARRINGTON
Pike.

The CAMERA MOVES ON to Jean, whose real name is Eugenia. She is a smart looking girl engaged at the moment in nibbling an apple.

JEAN
Oh.

She looks down speculatively.

A-9 HIGH CAMERA SHOT - DOWN ON THE LAUNCH COMING ALONGSID

We see Charles and Muggsy.

A-10 JEAN, COL. HARRINGTON AND GERALD

JEAN
Is he rich?

Col. Harrington looks inquiringly at Gerald.

COL. HARRINGTON
Is he rich?

GERALD
I'll find out, but he'd almost have to be ... to stop a boat. He's been up a river somewhere ....

He moves OUT OF THE PICTURE and the CAMERA COMES INT(A TIGHT TWO.

JEAN
(Poising the apple)
Haven't we all....I wonder if I could clunk him on the head with this?

10-18-40 (Continued)

A-10 (Cont'd)

COL. HARRINGTON
Don't be childish, my child.

JEAN
(Fervently)
I hope he's rich; I hope he thinks he's a wizard at cards....

COL. HARRINGTON
From your mouth to the ear of the Almighty.

JEAN
....and I hope he's got a big, fat wife so I don't have to dance in the moonlight with him. I don't know why it is, but a sucker always steps on your feet.

COL. HARRINGTON
(Looking over the rail)
A mug is a mug in everything.

JEAN
I don't see why I have to do all the dirty work... there must be plenty of rich old dames just waiting for you to push them around...

COL. HARRINGTON
You find them and I'll push them.

JEAN
(Grinning)
Boy, would I like to see you giving some old harpy the three-in-one.

COL. HARRINGTON
Don't be vulgar, Jean... Let us be crooked but never common.

A-11 GERALD - APPROACHING WITH A PASSENGER LIST IN HIS HAN

The CAMERA PANS HIM INTO A THREE SHOT.

GERALD
He is.

COL. HARRINGTON
Hunh?

GERALD
As the steward so picturesquely put it: He is dripping with dough.

JEAN
Pike?

10-18-40 (Continued)

A-11 (Cont'd)

GERALD
You said it.

JEAN
What does he own, Pike's Peak?

GERALD
No, no.... Pike's Pale....

A-12 INSERT

He turns the passenger list over for their inspection. The back page is taken up by a beefy football player squatting, bracing himself with two fingers of each hand. Above and below this we see:

"PIKE'S PALE
The Ale That Won For Yale"

GERALD'S VOICE
(Reading)
Pike's Pale, the ale that won for Yale.

A-13 JEAN, COL. HARRINGTON AND GERALD

Jean holds the apple out over the side of the ship and squints down as if aiming.

COL. HARRINGTON
(Suddenly noticing what she's doing)
Don't do that!

He is, however, too late. The apple falls and the three of them lean way out to watch its descent. They hold this for quite a moment.

A-14 CHARLES - JUST STARTING UP THE JACOB'S LADDER FROM THE LAUNCH

Muggsy is steadying the ladder for him. The apple socks Charles on the head and splatters on to Muggsy. Charles' head gives a little and one foot slips off the lower rung of the Jacob's ladder and dunks in the sea. Muggsy steadies him, then looks straight up.

MUGGSY
(Wiping some apple out of his eye)
Hey!

FADE OUT

END OF SEQUENCE "A"

SEQUENCE "B"

FADE IN:

B-1 A SERVICE BAR AT ONE END OF THE MAIN DINING ROOM OF THE S.S. "SOUTHERN QUEEN"

A STEWARD
(Coming up to the bar)
Six more Pike's Pale, and snappy, my lad.

BARTENDER
What are you trying to do, embarrass me? We're all out of Pike's. Work something else off on them.

B-2 THE STEWARD AND THE DINING ROOM BEHIND HIM - PAST THE BARTENDER

THE STEWARD
They don't want nothing else... They want the ale that won for Yale...rah-rah-rah!

BARTENDER
Well, tell 'em to go to Harvard.

B-3 CLOSE SHOT - A BOOK - IN CHARLES' HAND

The title of it is: "ARE SNAKES NECESSARY?

by
Hugo Marzditz"

The CAMERA DRAWS BACK SLOWLY and we see Charles reading. The coffee and after-dinner mints on the table indicate that the meal is over. He turns a page, looks up vaguely, then recoils.

B-4 A FATHER AND A MOTHER AND TWO DAUGHTERS

The women are looking at us hungrily. Four bottles of Pike's Pale adorn the table.

B-5 CLOSE SHOT - CHARLES

He frowns a little, then looks the other way. Again he recoils.

10-18-40

B-6 TWO YOUNG WOMEN - AT A TABLE

They are looking this way sulphurously.

B-7 CLOSE SHOT - CHARLES

He looks back in the other direction, recoils once more, then returns to his book.

B-8 COLONEL HARRINGTON AND JEAN

They are at a table at the side of the main passage, i.e., I must be able to SHOOT PAST Jean AT Charles while she is looking at him, and Jean must be able to trip him up as he passes.

JEAN
(Looking into her mirror)
Not good enough.

COL. HARRINGTON
What did you say?

JEAN
I said they're not good enough for him. Every Jane in the room is giving him the thermometer and he feels they're just a waste of time.

B-9 JEAN'S HAND AND THE MIRROR - S.E. SHOT OF CHARLES IN MIRROR

JEAN
He's returning to his book...he's deeply immersed in it...He sees no one except watch his head turn when that kid goes by...it won't do you any good, dear, he's a book-worm, but swing them anyway...yes, they're straight...you don't have to worry, but she's a little flat in the front...now here comes one that's a little flat behind...that's right, dear, just a quick one then back to the book.

10-18-40

B-10 JEAN PAST COLONEL HARRINGTON

JEAN
The dropped kerchief! That hasn't been used since Lily Langtry... you'll have to pick it up yourself, madam... it's a shame, but he doesn't care for the flesh; he'll never see it.

B-11 JEAN'S HAND AND THE MIRROR - S.E. SHOT OF CHARLES IN MIRROR

NOTE: Only enough of this dialogue will be used to match the action.

JEAN
That's right...pick it up... it was worth trying anyway, wasn't it?...Look at the girl over to his left...look over to your left, bookworm...there's a girl pining for you... a little further... just a little further. THERE! Now wasn't that worth looking for? See those nice store teeth, all beaming at you. Why, she recognizes you! She's up...she's down, she can't make up her mind, she's up again! She recognizes you! She's coming over to speak to you. The suspense is killing me. "Why, for heaven's sake, aren't you Fuzzy Oathammer I went to manual training school with in Louisville? Oh, you're not? Well, you certainly look exactly like him... it's certainly a remarkable resemblance, but if you're not going to ask me to sit down I suppose you're not going to ask me to sit down... I'm very sorry. I certainly hope I haven't caused you any embarrassment, you so-and-so," so here goes back to the table. Imagine thinking she could get away with anything like that with me.... I wonder if my tie's on straight...I certainly upset them, don't I?

10-18-40 (Continued)

B-11 (Cont'd)

JEAN (Cont'd)
Now who else is after me? Ah! the lady champion wrestler, wouldn't she make an armful... Oh, you don't like her either... Well, what are you going to do about it... Oh, you just can't stand it any more... you're leaving... these women just don't give you a moment's peace, do they... Well, go ahead! Go sulk in your cabin! Go soak your head and see if I care.

B-12 CLOSE SHOT - CHARLES

He rises, places a finger in his book and starts for the door of the main dining room. The CAMERA PANS WITH him. As he gets a little distance away from Jean and her father --

B-13 POINT-OF-VIEW SHOT

Jean and her father watch us rigidly. Suddenly Jean gets lower in her seat as she stretches out under the table. Charles goes hurtling PAST THE CAMERA and we hear a frightful crash.

JEAN
(Half-rising)
Why don't you look where you're going?

B-14 CHARLES - BEING HELPED TO HIS FEET

CHARLES
Why don't I look?

He walks back toward Jean.

JEAN
Look what you did to my shoe... you knocked the heel off.

CHARLES
I did? Well I'm....certainly very sorry...

10-18-40

(Continued)

B-14 (Cont'd)

JEAN
You did, and you can just take me right to my cabin for another pair of slippers.

CHARLES
(Slightly rattled)
Oh...well...certainly...I guess it's the least I can do... by the way, my name is Pike.

JEAN
Everybody knows about that... nobody's talking about anything else... This is my father, Colonel Harrington...my name is Jean, it's really Eugenia.
(She takes his arm)
Come on.

With only one heel she starts out like Lady Gimp. As they move OUT OF THE SHOT, the CAMERA PANS ONTO Colonel Harrington and the Steward.

THE STEWARD
(Full of admiration)
Gorgeous... like Grant took Richmond.

Colonel Harrington gives the Steward a disapproving scowl.

B-15 JEAN AND CHARLES - LEAVING THE DINING ROOM

JEAN
Funny, our meeting like this, isn't it.

CHARLES
Yes, isn't it?

JEAN
(Looking up into his face)
Maybe fate.

DISSOLVE TO:

B-16 GERALD - IN COLONEL HARRINGTON'S CABIN

We see him from the rear. He is in his shirt sleeves, apparently writing a letter.

10-18-40

B-17 CLOSE SHOT - GERALD

Before him are perhaps fifty packs of the S.S. "Southern Queen's" private cards. One pack has been opened without breaking the stamp and Gerald is busy marking the cards. He finishes the pack, which had three cards to go, and puts them carefully back in the box. As he glues the stamp back in place we hear a peal of Jean's laughter. With one movement Gerald slips the cards into a drawer and leaps into his coat. The CAMERA PANS him to the door of Jean's room. He opens it a crack and peers through.

B-18 JEAN'S CABIN - FULL SHOT

It is SOMETHING...modern, handsome and romantic. It has its private deck. Jean limps in, followed by Charles who closes the door after him.

CHARLES
(Looking around)
Holy Moses!

JEAN
What's the matter?

CHARLES
(Inhaling deeply)
That perfume.

JEAN
What's the matter with it?

CHARLES
It's just that... I've been up the Amazon for a year... they don't use perfume.

JEAN
Oh...
(She points to a closet)
The shoes are in there...because you were so polite you can pick them out....and then put them on... if you like.

Charles looks at her strangely, then opens the closet door, revealing a compartmented shoe bag with fifty pairs of shoes.

10-18-40 (Continued)

B-18 (Cont'd)

CHARLES
Holy Moses!

He touches several pairs of shoes shyly, then lifts out a pair. Jean laughs behind his back, then sits down.

JEAN
Those the ones you want?

CHARLES
(Turning slowly)
Doesn't seem p ossible for anybody to wear anything... that size.

JEAN
That's pretty.

Charles gets on one knee clumsily. Jean extends the foot with the broken heel.

CHARLES
(Huskily as he takes hold of her foot)
I hope...I didn't hurt you.

JEAN
Of course you didn't.
(Looking at him)
Don't you feel well?

CHARLES
I'm all right.

He takes off her broken slipper and slips on the new one.

JEAN
What were you doing up the Amazon?

CHARLES
Looking for snakes...I'm an Ophiologist.

JEAN
I thought you were in the beer business.

10-18-40 (Continued)

B-18 (Cont'd)

CHARLES
Beer! Ale.

He takes off the other slipper and puts the new one on.

JEAN
What's the difference?

CHARLES
Between beer and ale?

JEAN
Yes.

CHARLES
My father would burst a blood vessel. There's a big difference... ale is sort of fermented on the top or something and beer is fermented on the bottom...or maybe it's vice versa.. There's no similarity at all. The uh...you see, the trouble with being descended from a brewer, no matter how long ago he brooded, or whatever you call it, is that you're supposed to know all about something you don't give a hoot about. It's funny to be kneeling here at your feet and talking about beer, isn't it? You see, I don't like beer, bock beer, lager beer, or steam beer.

JEAN
Don't you?

CHARLES
(With some fire)
I do not! And I don't like pale ale, brown ale, nut brown ale, porter or stout which makes me ulp just to think about it. Ulp! But that hasn't stopped everybody from calling me Hopsie ever since I was six years old. Hopsie Pike!

JEAN
Hello, Hopsie.

CHARLES
Make it Charlie, will you?

10-18-40 (Continued)

B-18 (Cont'd)

JEAN
All right, but there's something kinda cute about Hopsie and when you got older I could call you Popsie...Hopsie Popsie!

CHARLES
(Smiling)
That's all I need.
(He looks down at her feet)
Now, here's a business I wouldn't mind being in...I never realized before how lovely it could be.

JEAN
Thank you.

She reaches out and touches his hair. Charles seizes her hand, then slowly lets it go.

JEAN
We'd better get back now.

CHARLES
I guess so. You see, where I've been, I mean up the Amazon, you kind of forget how...how...I mean when you haven't seen a girl in a long time...I mean there's something about that perfume that... that...

JEAN
Don't you like my perfume?

CHARLES
Like it! I'm cockeyed on it!

JEAN
(Getting to her feet)
Why, Hopsie...you ought to be kept in a cage.

DISSOLVE TO:

B-19 COLONEL HARRINGTON - IN THE SMOKING ROOM - TOYING WITH A PACK OF CARDS

Some couples are dancing and new people are arriving.

10-18-40

B-20 THE DOORWAY - FROM THE ELEVATORS

Jean comes in on Charles' arm and the CAMERA PANS THEM OVER to the Colonel.

COL. HARRINGTON
Well, you certainly took long enough to come back in the same outfit.

JEAN
I'm lucky to have this on. Mr. Pike has been up the river for a year.

CHARLES
(Embarrassed)
Now look, I...

COL. HARRINGTON
Pay no attention to my daughter's ribaldry.....it always comes out in the women in our family. With the exception of myself, the men are all missionaries.

JEAN
And what an exception...Won't you have a drink with us?

CHARLES
Just a brandy, but you have it with me.

He picks up the pack of cards.

COL. HARRINGTON
Three brandies.

CHARLES
Have you seen this one?

He changes an ace of diamonds into a queen of spades.

JEAN
(Delighted;
to her father)
Oh, he does card tricks.

CHARLES
(Modestly)
Just in a small way, of course.

10-18-40 (Continued)

B-20 (Cont'd)

COL. HARRINGTON
Well, bless my soul. Do that again, will you?

Charles obliges.

COL. HARRINGTON
Extraordinary. How do you do it?

CHARLES
(Demonstrating)
You see, you palm it in this hand. That means you grip it with the palm of this hand... of course it takes quite a lot of practice.

COL. HARRINGTON
I can see how it might...amazing. It's a good thing I know who you are or I wouldn't play cards with you.

CHARLES
(Surprised)
Sir?

Jean points to a sign over Charles' head and he turns around and looks at it. The CAMERA ANGLES UP and we see the standard warning:

"BEWARE OF PROFESSIONAL GAMBLERS!
The Company is not
responsible, etc.,etc."

The CAMERA ANGLES DOWN again.

CHARLES
(Embarrassed)
Oh, say, you really didn't think that uh...

JEAN
Of course not, silly...you look as honest as we do.

The steward arrives with the drinks.

10-18-40 (Continued)

B-20 (Cont'd)

COL. HARRINGTON
(Raising his glass)
Washington and Valley Forge!

CHARLES
(Raising his glass)
Dewey and Manila!

JEAN
(After a fraction of a second's hesitation)
Napoleon and Josephine!

They drink. After a moment Charles gets a bright idea.

CHARLES
Say, how about a rubber of bridge?

JEAN
You're probably too good for us.

CHARLES
Well, I don't have to play my best, and besides, playing with you, no matter how you played, would always be a pleasure.

JEAN
Well, aren't you sweet.

CHARLES
(Looking around)
Who shall we get for a fourth?

COL. HARRINGTON
(Vaguely)
Isn't there a three handed game? I seem to remember vaguely having...,

CHARLES
(Remembering)
Of course there is, and it will be much cozier...
(He hands Col. Harrington the cards)
Will you shuffle?

10-18-40 (Continued)

B-20 (Cont'd)

COL. HARRINGTON
(Taking the cards clumsily)
I'll try.

He drops the cards on the table.

JEAN
Every man for himself.

Now she notices Charles staring at her.

CHARLES
(Coming to)
I, uh...What? Oh! Well...
(He chuckles)
...you go up the Amazon for a year and then you come out and meet you and...
(To the Steward)
Bring some more Brandy.

He beams at Jean.

B-21 COLONEL HARRINGTON - WATCHING THEM

He becomes so interested that he forgets what he is doing. He makes two expert passes with the cards, pulls them out once like an accordion and brings them together neatly before he catches himself and starts shuffling clumsily again.

DISSOLVE TO:

B-22 A DOOR WHICH IS MARKED: "SECOND CLASS SMOKING ROOM"

MUGGSY'S VOICE
(With irritation)
Here, let me see them conies.

GERALD'S VOICE
The pleasure is all yours.

B-23 CLOSE SHOT - GERALD AND MUGGSY - IN THE SECOND CLASS SMOKING ROOM

They are apparently playing rummy. Muggsy leans back after examining Gerald's cards.

10-18-40 (Continued)

B-23 (Cont'd)

MUGGSY
Well, I'll be a cock-eyed cookie-pusher.
(He throws down his cards)

GERALD
What's the matter now?

MUGGSY
Deal those shingles.

GERALD
(Smoothly)
You don't happen to have some beautiful damsel pining away for you, do you...That often explains it.

MUGGSY
Come on...let's go.

DISSOLVE TO:

B-24 GERALD AND MUGGSY - PLAYING CARDS

All the money is now in front of Gerald. Muggsy is in his shirt sleeves and looks very sour.

GERALD
(Raking in the last of the money)
There's no question about it; she's panting for you.

MUGGSY
(Furiously)
She must be croaking.

He rises and seizes his coat.

DISSOLVE TO:

B-25 JEAN, CHARLES AND COLONEL HARRINGTON - AT THE TABLE IN THE SMOKING ROOM

Charles seems in the act of making a grand slam.

CHARLES
I really feel very guilty about this...
(He laughs ruefully)

JEAN
Don't let it worry you.

10-18-40 (Continued

B-25 (Cont'd)

CHARLES
(Working on the score sheet)
It's a good thing we weren't playing for money or I'd have you in bankruptcy. This last hand alone...

COL. HARRINGTON
(Interrupting)
Weren't we playing for money?

CHARLES
(Aghast)
Of course not! I never play for...

JEAN
(Interrupting)
But, we always play for money, darling...otherwise it's like swimming in an empty swimming pool.

CHARLES
(Pointing to the empty score sheet)
Yes, but if you count that last re-double...

COL. HARRINGTON
(Taking up the score sheet)
Nonsense, my boy! What does it amount to at ten cents a point...

CHARLES
(Startled)
Ten cents a point!
(He points to the score sheet)
Why, at ten cents a point...

COL. HARRINGTON
Purely nominal...now, let me see... plus six and four is ten and eight is eighteen and seven is twenty-five and five is thirty, I carry three plus nine is twelve and eight is twenty plus four is twenty-four, I carry two, plus eight and yes and yes and yes plus two, I carry six, is four thousand, nine hundred and eighty-six, at ten cents a point...roughly five hundred dollars.

He opens his wallet and whips out five hundred.

CHARLES
Oh, but now, really...wait a minute!

10-18-40 (Continued)

B-25 (Cont'd)

JEAN
Father's in the oil business, dear, it just keeps bubbling up out of the ground.

CHARLES
Oh, I thought maybe with the title of Colonel...

COL. HARRINGTON
Purely honorary.

JEAN
(Scowling faintly)
How much do I owe the sucker?

COL. HARRINGTON
(Looking at the score sheet)
Let me see...plus five and seven are twelve and nine is twenty-one and...

Jean looks up at somebody and frowns.

B-26 MUGGSY PEERING AROUND SOME CONVENIENT BARRIER

He looks deeply suspicious.

B-27 JEAN, CHARLES AND COLONEL HARRINGTON - AT THE TABLE IN THE SMOKING ROOM

COL. HARRINGTON
Six, seven I carry two, and one is three and five is eight and nine is...

JEAN
(Tapping Charles on the arm)
Who's the funny looking gink watching us?

Charles turns, the Colonel looks up and the three look at Muggsy.

B-28 CLOSE SHOT - MUGGSY

MUGGSY
(Suspiciously)
Everything on the up and up?

10-18-40

B-29 JEAN, CHARLES AND COLONEL HARRINGTON - AT THE TABLE IN THE SMOKING ROOM

CHARLES
(Laughing)
Everything's okay. Go to bed... I'm way ahead.

B-30 CLOSE SHOT - MUGGSY

MUGGSY
(Reluctantly)
All right.

He disappears around the barrier.

B-31 JEAN, CHARLES AND COLONEL HARRINGTON - AT THE TABLE

Colonel Harrington exchanges a look with his daughter, then continues his calculation.

JEAN
(To Charles)
Who's that, your nurse?

CHARLES
(Chuckling)
That's Muggsy. My father took him off a truck to watch over me when I was a kid...you know, kidnappers and stuff like that, and he's been sort of bodyguard, governess and a very bad valet ever since...he saved my life one time in a brawl, so the family's crazy about him.

JEAN
I should think you would be, too.

CHARLES
He's my buddy.

COL. HARRINGTON
(Finishing his calculation)
...and five is twelve, put down two and...roughly, a hundred dollars.

JEAN
(Taking a hundred dollar bill from her bag)
That's rough enough.

CHARLES
Now look here, since I had no underst--

10-18 40 (Continued)

B-31 (Cont'd)

JEAN
(Threateningly)
Don't you worry, I'll get it back...

CHARLES
Well.....if that's a promise.....

He picks the money up very reluctantly..

JEAN
You can depend upon it.

CHARLES
(Looking at the money miserably)
Then I'll certainly feel better.

JEAN
You certainly will.

COL. HARRINGTON
(Rising)
I think, if you don't mind, I'll toddle off and leave you young people to continue this interesting conversation.

CHARLES
(Rising)
Good night, sir.
(He indicates the money)
I'm really awfully sorry about this.

COL. HARRINGTON
(Raising a hand)
Beeswax, my boy, Beeswax.
(He pinches Jean's ear)
Good night, Jeanie.

JEAN
(Sticking her face up to be kissed)
Good night, darling.

Colonel Harrington winks at Charles and departs.

CHARLES
(Looking after him)
He's a nice fellow, your father.

JEAN
He's a good card player, too.

10-18-40 (Continued)

B-31 (Cont'd)

CHARLES
(Surprised)
Do you think so? I don't want to be rude, but I thought he was kind of uneven.

JEAN
He's more uneven sometimes than others.

CHARLES
(Logically)
That's what makes him uneven, of course, but now you, on the other hand, with a little coaching, you could be terrific.

JEAN
(Charmed)
Do you really think so?

CHARLES
Yes, you have a definite nose.

JEAN
Well, that's very nice of you...do you like any of the rest of me?

CHARLES
(Hastily)
Oh, but what I meant was in the card-playing sense, like you say...

JEAN
I know what you meant, I was just flirting with you.

CHARLES
(Paralyzed)
Oh...

He taps her hand nervously a couple of times, then lets his hand rest on hers.

JEAN
(After observing him for a moment)
You're not going to faint, are you?

CHARLES
Who, me? It's that perfume.

JEAN
Oh.

CHARLES
Do you think they're dancing anywhere on-board?

10-18-40 (Continued)

B-31 (Cont'd)

JEAN
(After a moment)
Don't you think we ought to go to bed?

Charles looks ahead rigidly for a moment, then turns and looks at Jean who looks back at him innocently.

CHARLES
(With a silly grin)
You certainly are a funny girl for anybody to meet who's just been up the Amazon for a year.

JEAN
(Getting to her feet)
It's a good thing you weren't up there two years.

Rising, Charles trips on the foot of the table. Jean steadies him. As they start out of the smoking room --

DISSOLVE TO:

B-32 A LONG CORRIDOR WITH STATEROOMS ON BOTH SIDES

We still hear the strains of music as Jean and Charles appear in the distance. As they get near us, they look at the numbers on the staterooms.

CHARLES
(Suddenly)
Say, I'm afraid we're on the wrong deck.

JEAN
(Round-eyed)
Well, isn't that a coincidence.

Charles looks at the other side of the corridor and recoils in surprise.

CHARLES
Well, for heaven's sake, here's my cabin.

JEAN
(Too astounded)
Fantastic!

CHARLES
(He clears his throat)
Would you care to come in ...
(He clears his throat)
... and see Emma?

JEAN
That's a new one, isn't it?

10-18-40 (Continued)

B-32 (Cont'd)

CHARLES
(Putting his finger to his lips)
Sh!

Charles takes Jean's hand and enters the cabin. Jean looks up and down the corridor, then follows him.

B-33 INT. CHARLES' CABIN

On a banquette we see Emma's box. The lighting is shadowy and romantic. Charles leads Jean in and closes the door after her.

CHARLES
I don't want to wake her up.

JEAN
(Looking around)
Wake who up?

CHARLES
Emma.

JEAN
Who's Emma? I thought that was the fly paper.

CHARLES
Well, technically, she's a Colubrina Marzditzia, which seems to be a rare type of Brazilian glass snake that I'm taking back to ... Hello, she got out again.

This last as he opens the cover of the box.

JEAN
(Ready to yammer)
A s-snake!

CHARLES
She's around here somewhere...

Jean starts to pick her skirts up to her garters.

CHARLES
(Looking around)
Be careful where you step.

JEAN
(Yammering)
L-let m-me w-wout of h-here!

B-33 (Cont'd)

CHARLES
(Smiling and putting a
hand on her shoulder)
Don't be frightened. She's as gentle
as a kitten. People just don't
realize what affectionate, loyal,
playful little pets snakes can ...

Suddenly Jean points past his shoulder. Her eyes widen and her mouth stretches open.

B-34 CLOSE SHOT - EMMA - COILED ON CHARLES' PAJAMAS ON THE BED

We hear a devastating scream.

B-35 JEAN AND CHARLES - IN CHARLES' CABIN

CHARLES
(Urgently)
Sh! Don't be frightened, it's really...

Jean screams like a steam whistle.

CHARLES
Don't do that; how's that going to
sound to...

Jean opens her mouth wide and looks toward the door.

B-36 THE CORRIDOR OUTSIDE CHARLES' CABIN

Heads pop out as Jean comes catapulting out of the cabin with her skirts held higher than before. She flashes PAST US in nothing flat. Charles comes skidding after her, pauses to close his cabin door, then starts after Jean again. As he notices the people looking on, he changes from a run to a fast walk, then breaks into a run again.

B-37 THE CURVED STAIRCASE OF THE SHIP

Jean hurries PAST US and a second later Charles does likewise.

B-38 THE CORRIDOR OUTSIDE JEAN'S CABIN

Jean arrives panting and Charles overtakes her as she puts her hand on the knob.

10-18-40 (Continued)

B-38 (Cont'd)

CHARLES
(Desperately)
I'm terribly sorry ... I wouldn't have frightened you for the world. She just won't stay in her box. She's apt to show up at...

Jean looks down and around and ready to scream again.

CHARLES
(Holding her tightly)
Now, now, now.

JEAN
Why didn't you tell me you had a slimy...

CHARLES
(Interrupting)
But I thought you understood that Emma was a snake.

JEAN
How could I understand anything of the kind? Why should I suspect an apparently civilized man of ...

CHARLES
Please.

He opens the door and supports her into the cabin.

B-39 INT. JEAN'S CABIN

Charles brings Jean in and closes the door after her.

JEAN
(Pointing)
Look under the bed.

CHARLES
(As to a child)
How could she possibly get down here and ...

JEAN
(Almost in tears)
Please!

CHARLES
All right, all right.

10-18-40 (Continued)

B-39 (Cont'd)

He gets on his hands and knees and looks under the bed. Suddenly reaches way under for something. As he drags out something long and black --

B-40 FULL FIGURE SHOT - JEAN

She opens her mouth to scream but her vocal chords are paralyzed. She reaches for her skirts and climbs onto the chaise longue.

B-41 HIGH CAMERA SHOT - CHARLES - ON THE FLOOR

CHARLES
(Looking up at us)
It's only a stocking.

B-42 LOW CAMERA SHOT - JEAN - ON THE CHAISE LONGUE

JEAN
Well, if you see any more, leave them there. Now, look in the bed.

B-43 HIGH CAMERA - CHARLES

CHARLES
(Getting to his feet)
In the bed? How could she possibly...

B-44 LOW CAMERA SHOT - JEAN

JEAN
Go on, now.

B-45 CHARLES - AT THE BED

CHARLES
(Reaching inside the bed)
You know how fast we came down, so you can imagine...

Suddenly he pauses and yanks his hand out.

10-18-40

B-46 LOW CAMERA SHOT - JEAN

She steps onto the arms of the chaise longue to get up a little higher. Her mouth is ready for a scream.

B-47 HIGH CAMERA SHOT - CHARLES

He looks inside the bed and chuckles and reaches in.

CHARLES
It's nothing, but it might have given you a shock at that...There's nothing like a cold hot water bottle.

He pulls it out and chucks it on the bed.

B-48 LOW CAMERA SHOT - JEAN - PAST CHARLES, APPROACHING

JEAN
They would have had to bury me at sea... Help me down.

Charles takes her in his arms and seats her on the chaise longue.

JEAN
(Hanging on to him)
Don't let me go yet... sit down beside me...You don't know what you've done to me.

CHARLES
(Sitting on the floor)
I'm terribly sorry.

JEAN
That's all right.

She puts her arms around his neck.

CHARLES
I wouldn't have frightened you for anything in the world...I mean if there's one person in the world that I wouldn't have wanted to...

He smells of her hair and closes his eyes.

CHARLES
... it's you.

JEAN
(Putting her cheek against his)
You're very sweet... don't let me go.

10-18-40 (Continued)

B-48 (Cont'd)

Charles licks his lips nervously, steals a look at her gams and again seems on the verge of swooning. He looks away and pulls her skirt down a little.

JEAN
(Quietly)
Thank you.
(Then after a pause)
How was everything up the Amazon?

CHARLES
All right, thank you.

JEAN
(After another pause)
What are you thinking about?

Charles opens his mouth to speak, closes it again, then speaks almost with violence.

CHARLES
Nothing.

Jean looks at him innocently, then pursues.

JEAN
Are you always going to be interested in snakes?

She fools with his ear.

CHARLES
(Almost crossly)
In a way...snakes are my life.

JEAN
(After a very long pause)
What a life!

CHARLES
(After a pause)
I suppose it sounds kind of silly... I mean I suppose I should have married...and gone into the brewing business which I suspect my father's always wanted me to do... as a matter of fact he's told me so fairly plainly...but I just don't care for the brewing business.

JEAN
You say that's why you never married?

10-18-40 (Continued)

B-48 (Cont'd)

CHARLES
(Chuckling)
Oh, no... it's just that I've never met her, that's all...I guess she's somewhere in the world.

JEAN
It would be too bad if you never bunked into each other.

CHARLES
(Shrugging)
Well...

JEAN
I suppose you know exactly what she looks like and everything.

CHARLES
I... I think I do.

JEAN
I'll bet she looks like...Marguerite in "Faust."

CHARLES
No...she hasn't...she isn't...
(He helps out with a gesture)
...hefty enough for an opera singer.

JEAN
Oh. How are her teeth?

CHARLES
(Startled)
Hunh?

JEAN
You should always pick one with good teeth...it saves expense later.

CHARLES
Oh...you're kidding me...maybe you should.

JEAN
Not badly. You have a right to have an ideal. I guess we all have an ideal.

CHARLES
What does yours look like?

JEAN
He's a little short guy with lots of money.

10-18-40 (Continued)

B-48 (Cont'd)

CHARLES
Why short?

JEAN
What does it matter if he's rich enough...it's so he'll look up to me...so I'll be his ideal.

CHARLES
That's a funny way of reasoning.

JEAN
Well look who's reasoning. And when he takes me out to dinner he won't ever add up the check or smoke greasy cigars...and he won't use grease on his hair either...and he won't do card tricks...

CHARLES
Oh.

JEAN
(Sweetly)
Oh, I don't mind your doing card tricks, Hopsie, I just mean you naturally wouldn't want your ideal to do card tricks.

CHARLES
I shouldn't think that kind of an ideal would be very hard to find.

JEAN
Oh, he isn't...that's why he's my ideal...what's the use of having an ideal you can't ever find any place? Mine is a practical ideal you can always find two or three of in every barber shop... getting the works.

CHARLES
Then why don't you marry one of them?

JEAN
(Almost indignantly)
Why should I marry anybody who looked like that? When I marry it's going to be somebody I've never seen before...I mean I don't know what he looks like or where he'll come from...

10-18-40

(Continued)

B-48 (Cont'd)

JEAN (Continuing)
(She holds him a little tighter)
...or what he'll be...I want him to sort of take me by surprise.

CHARLES
Like a burglar.

JEAN
That's right...the night will be heavy with perfume.

Charles inhales deeply.

JEAN
...and all of a sudden I'll hear a step behind me and somebody breathing heavily...and then...

She settles herself langorously as if for sleep. Her cheek brushes against his and she gives him a butterfly kiss. Charles looks ahead stonily and puts his fingertips to his forehead, then examines them for traces of sweat. Jean sighs softly and Charles looks around uneasily. Jean opens her eyes and discovers Charles still in the room.

JEAN
You'd better go to bed, Hopsie...I think I can sleep peacefully now.

CHARLES
(Almost angrily)
Yes, well I wish I could say the same.

He gets to his feet and hurries to the door.

CHARLES
Good night.

He looks at her indignantly, then goes out and slams the door after him.

JEAN
Why, Hopsie!

She giggles.

FADE OUT:

END OF SEQUENCE "B"

10-18-40

FADE IN:

C-1 GERALD BREAKFASTING IN THE SECOND CABIN DINING ROOM

He finishes a boiled egg, then removes a cover from a dish, takes a good whiff of the fish revealed, and starts to dissect it. Muggsy comes in behind him.

GERALD
(Seeing Muggsy)
Ah, good morning, Mr. Murgatroyd, I trust I see you full of zip and sparkle.

MUGGSY
(Looking around for the steward)
Morning.

GERALD
A dish of tea?

MUGGSY
I had my breakfast...where I come from we get up in the morning.

GERALD
(Waspishly)
Ah yes, and where did it get you, may I ask...or is that a personal question?

MUGGSY
(Resentfully)
Where did it get me! I'll tell you where it got me...

The Second Class Steward hurries INTO THE SHOT.

SECOND CLASS STEWARD
(Heartily)
Goodmorning, sir. Fruit, cereal, bacon and, roe, kipper, or how about a nice bloater?

MUGGSY
(To the horror of Gerald and the Steward)
Gimme a spoonful of milk, a raw pigeon's egg and four house flies. If you can't catch any I'll settle for a cockroach. I'll be on deck.

He moves OUT OF THE SHOT.

10-18-40 (Continued)

C-1 (Cont'd)

Gerald and the Steward watch him in stupefaction, then look at each other blankly. Now Gerald returns to the dissection of his fish. After a second he slams down the knife and fork, bangs the cover down on the dish and hands it to the Steward, his appetite destroyed.

DISSOLVE TO:

C-2 JEAN IN BED

Through the louvres, the bars of sunlight move slowly back and forth across the counterpane as the ship rolls a little. Suddenly she sits up and screams. She looks around wildly, then holds her heart.

C-3 THE DOOR TO COL. HARRINGTON'S CABIN

It bursts open and the Colonel appears in a dressing gown, a pack of cards in his hand. Gerald appears behind him.

COL. HARRINGTON
What's the matter?

C-4 JEAN IN BED

JEAN
I'm sorry....that slimy snake...I've been dreaming about him all night.

COL. HARRINGTON
(Coming INTO THE SHOT)
You mean Pike?

JEAN
(Smiling wryly)
No, his reptile. He travels with a snake act. He's an ophi...an ophalol... he likes snakes.

COL. HARRINGTON
(Horrified)
You mean he isn't in the beer business?

JEAN
He's in the ale business...It seems there's a very big difference....

10-18-40 (Continued)

C-4 (Cont'd)

COL. HARRINGTON
(Chuckling)
You had me worried...I thought
we'd sweetened the wrong kitty.

He stretches his fingers, then starts dealing hands on the bed.

JEAN
No, he's the real McPike...the
poor sap...that card trick!

COL. HARRINGTON
Tragic.

JEAN
What are you dealing?

COL. HARRINGTON
Fifths.

JEAN
Like heck you're dealing fifths!

COL. HARRINGTON
You want to bet.

He shows her four aces on top of the pack, puts them back on the pack, then starts dealing five hands.

JEAN
I don't believe it.

In reply, Col. Harrington peels the four aces off the deck and shows them to her.

COL. HARRINGTON
(Modestly)
You never really need it....it's
just virtuosity....

JEAN
Harry.

COL. HARRINGTON
Yes, darling.

JEAN
(Smiling like a little girl)
Tell me my fortune.

Colonel Harrington chuckles as he gathers his cards together.

10-18-40

C-5 CHARLES SHAVING - IN HIS CABIN WITH A SAFETY RAZOR

He is singing "Love in Bloom" in a voice that leaves something to be desired. Muggsy comes in behind him bearing a plate covered with another plate.

CHARLES
(Without turning around)
Did you get it?

MUGGSY
Close enough.

He sticks the plate in the snake box.

MUGGSY (Cont'd)
There, dunk your whiskers in that.
(He turns)
How much you say you win last night?

CHARLES
(Shaving)
About six hundred dollars...but I'm going to try to lose it back to them.

MUGGSY
I don't get it...I lose forty bucks to their valay and I figure the guy is a cutie.

CHARLES
Because he took you?...Who do you think you are...Houdini?

MUGGSY
You don't have to be a whodunit to tell a cold deck when you get your mits on one. All you have to know is the difference between hot and cold. That guy rung in a cold deck in on me.

CHARLES
Balderdash! You're always suspicious of everybody. Remember that clergyman you said was a pickpocket and he turned out to be a bishop?

MUGGSY
Well, I still ain't so sure.

10-18-40 (Continued)

C-5 (Cont'd)

CHARLES
(Laughing)
And the guy you poked for trying to slip you a mickey only he was taking aspirin.

MUGGSY
I ain't so sure about him neither.

CHARLES
I suppose you think this gentleman and his daughter lost six hundred dollars to me just so they can fleece me later. First of all he happens to be Colonel Harrington, a very important oil man, and in the second place I'm an expert card player...I've been fooling with cards all my life...I do tricks with cards.

MUGGSY
They might know a couple you ain't seen yet.

CHARLES
Yeah. Go get some flowers some place and take them to Miss Harrington with my compliments and ask her if she'll have breakfast with me.

MUGGSY
Okay, it's your funeral.

CHARLES
Don't forget the flowers.

SLOW DISSOLVE TO:

C-6 CHARLES - AT A BREAKFAST TABLE - ON THE SIDEWALK CAFE OF THE S.S. "SOUTHERN QUEEN"

BEYOND and BELOW we see the swimming pool in use. Charles is watching anxiously for Jean. Suddenly he rises happily and his chair falls over. As he starts to pick it up --

C-7 JEAN - PAST CHARLES

She comes toward him in a pair of very elegant slacks. She carries one rose in her hand.

C-7 (Cont'd)

JEAN
Good morning. Thank you for the roses.
(She sits down)

CHARLES
I hope you slept well.

JEAN
I'm still a little jumpy...how is the uh...Emma?

CHARLES
She's just having her breakfast.

JEAN
(Without any pause in the middle)
What does she eat don't tell me.

CHARLES
I won't. I hope you didn't mind my asking you to breakfast.

JEAN
Well, it wouldn't be very polite if I said I did, would it?

CHARLES
(Vaguely hurt)
No, I don't suppose it would.

JEAN
(Leaning forward)
And it wouldn't be true, either.

CHARLES
(Happy again)
You've got the darndest way of bumping a fellow down and then bouncing him up again.

Jean laughs.

JEAN
And then bumping him down again.

CHARLES
Oh. I was just going to say that I could imagine a life with you being a series of ups and downs...

10-18-40 (Continued)

C-7 (Cont'd)

CHARLES (Cont'd)
lights and shadows...sometimes irritation...but very much happiness.

JEAN
Why Hopsie! Are you proposing to me....so soon?

CHARLES
No, of course I'm not, I'm just...

He stares at her hypnotized.

JEAN
Then you ought to be more careful... people have been sued for much less.

CHARLES
(Warmly)
Not by girls like you.

JEAN
(After a slight pause)
Don't you know it's dangerous to trust people you don't know very well?

CHARLES
But I know you very well.

JEAN
I mean people you haven't known very long.

CHARLES
I've known you a long time....in a way.

A DECK STEWARD
(ENTERING THE SHOT, briskly)
Breakfast, sir?

CHARLES
(Bemused, turning slowly)
What did you say?

THE DECK STEWARD
(Surprised)
I said, breakfast, sir.

10-18-40 (Continued)

C-7 (Cont'd)

CHARLES
Two Scotch and sodas with plain water....you take it plain, don't you?

JEAN
(With a faint smile)
Don't you take cream and sugar in it?

CHARLES
No, I always drink it black.
(Suddenly he shakes his head)
Say, what am I talking about?

JEAN
That's what I was wondering.

THE DECK STEWARD
(Confidentially)
How about a nice bicarbonate of soda, sir, with an egg in it.... it does wonders.

CHARLES
(To Jean, pointing to the Deck Steward)
He doesn't understand.

DISSOLVE TO:

C-8 THE PURSER'S DESK IN THE LOBBY OF THE S.S. SOUTHERN QUEEN

The Purser and some of his assistants are visible. Muggsy COMES INTO THE SHOT and points a finger at the man with the most braid.

MUGGSY
You the purser?

THE PURSER
Yes, what is it, please?

MUGGSY
Wanta ask you a hypodermical question.

10-18-40 (Continued)

C-8 (Cont'd)

THE PURSER
(Keeping a straight face)
Maybe that would be better to ask the doctor.

MUGGSY
Never mind the wise cracks. What I want the dope on is this: if they happened to be a gang of card sharks on this tub...

THE PURSER
(Looking around uneasily)
Not so loud, please. In the first place there isn't, and in the second place...

MUGGSY
(Interrupting)
What I want to know is could you prove it if they was?

THE PURSER
(Severely)
A passenger is a passenger, my friend. If he pays for his ticket and doesn't steal the ship's towels, who are we to go slandering him? Furthermore, what do you mean by card shark? One man's card sharp is another man's bridge expert.

MUGGSY
I mean a guy who cheats.

THE PURSER
What do you mean by "cheating"? It's a very hard thing to prove. The companies have been trying for years...

MUGGSY
You don't happen to be a mouthpiece, do you? You talk like a law school.

10-18-40 (Continued)

C-8 (Cont'd)

THE PURSER
I was admitted to the bar, if that's what you're talking about.

MUGGSY
Well, the drinks are on you, baby. I watch out for the kid, see? ... the Pike Kid. I watch out for him and you're gonna watch out for him or you'll be right on the beach sellin' popcorn, you get me? His old man knows your president, a wire from me is all it takes, and when old man Pike goes into action you'll be in the side pocket, see? All I gotta do is...

THE PURSER
(Angrily)
You needn't try to intimidate me, Mr. uh...er...

MUGGSY
Murgatroyd to you.

THE PURSER
If I should discover that Mr. Pike was in any danger of being swindled, not that I admit there is any such possibility, you understand, I would consider it my duty to warn him.

MUGGSY
He's already been warned. What I need is some proof. You got any?

THE PURSER
In the event that I should consider it necessary, I might have some photographs, confidential, of course, of some of the better known... ALLEGED professional card players... NOT THAT I ADMIT THERE ARE ANY ON THIS SHIP, YOU UNDERSTAND

MUGGSY
Naw, they're swimmin' alongside in the water. You keep your eyes peeled, baby, 'cause I got mine right in the middle of your back.

10-18-40 (Continued)

C-8 (Cont'd)

He turns and walks away. The Purser looks after him with extreme irritation, then turns to his assistants.

THE PURSER
(Crossly)
Well, get on with your work; what's stopping you?

DISSOLVE TO:

C-9 THE HALLWAY OUTSIDE JEAN'S CABIN - CHARLES AND JEAN

Jean takes Charles' hand, then opens the door.

JEAN
Goodbye for a little while.

CHARLES
It's been a wonderful day...will you meet me in the bar before dinner?

JEAN
I will.

CHARLES
Thank you.

Suddenly he kisses her hand and hurries away. Jean watches him go, then slowly enters her cabin and closes the door.

C-10 COL. HARRINGTON'S CABIN - HARRINGTON AND GERALD

Col. Harrington is in his shirtsleeves buttoning his waistcoat which has extra pockets in the small of the back.

GERALD
(Approaching with several packs of cards)
Do you want the strippers on the right or on the left?

COL. HARRINGTON
(Massaging his fingers)
I hardly need them, Gerald.

10-18-40 (Continued)

C-10 (Cont'd)

He picks up a pack of cards and shuffles them with lightning rapidity.

COL. HARRINGTON
I could take this boy with a deck of visiting cards.

GERALD
(Sticking two packs in the back of the Colonel's vest)
It's always better to be on the safe side...high card cuts are on the outside...cold hands in the middle.

COL. HARRINGTON
(Singing tonelessly)
Cold hands I love da-daddle-daddle da da...

GERALD
(Putting two more packs in the back of the Colonel's waistcoat)
Blue readers on the outside...red nearest the heart.

COL. HARRINGTON
(Chuckling)
I could play the whole ship with this.

Jean comes in from her cabin.

JEAN
(Quietly)
Hello, Harry.

COL. HARRINGTON
(Happily)
Greetings, my little minx. I hope I see you well and that your little pal hasn't fallen overboard...with our six hundred dollars.

JEAN
He's all right. He's just gone to dress for dinner.

10-18-40 (Continued)

C-10 (Cont'd)

COL. HARRINGTON
Then you'd better do the same, my pearl of price, because we're going to play a little cards tonight... and I don't mean bumble-puppy.

JEAN
(After a pause)
I think Charles is in love with me.

COL. HARRINGTON
Well of course he's in love with you...who is he not to be in love with you...who have beautified the north Atlantic...better men than he...

JEAN
(Quietly)
I mean on the level, Harry.

COL. HARRINGTON
(With mock severity)
Are you suggesting that the others were on the bias? Name me but their names, my little Lorelei, and I will see to it...

JEAN
Stop kidding, will you?

COL. HARRINGTON
I'm not kidding. I've never been more delighted, you have as usual taken...

JEAN
(Interrupting)
You don't get the point. I like him too.

COL. HARRINGTON
Why shouldn't you like him? That's as fine a specimen of the sucker sapiens as I have ever encountered. There's a man who does card tricks! There is a sap who...

JEAN
I think he's going to ask me to marry him, Harry.

10-18-40 (Continued)

C-10 (Cont'd)

COL. HARRINGTON
No.

GERALD
No.

JEAN
Yes.

GERALD
(Coming forward and
taking her hand)
But that's wonderful, Jean.

COL. HARRINGTON
(Taking her other hand)
No wonder you're blushing! Standing breathlessly on the threshold of life...and it seems only yesterday you were a little howler fastened together with safety pins.

Jean lowers her eyes, puts her hands on her father's chest and sniffles.

COL. HARRINGTON
And that fortunate young man.

GERALD
Fortunate indeed.

COL. HARRINGTON
Can't you hear his pulses pounding... his ears must be ringing like telephone bells.

GERALD
His hands clammy with excitement.

COL. HARRINGTON
He won't know an ace from a deuce.

JEAN
(Looking up slowly)
You weren't thinking of taking him, Harry?

10-18-40 (Continued)

C-10 (Cont'd)

COL. HARRINGTON
(Astonished)
Well, what were you thinking of?

JEAN
You can't rob your own son-in-law.

COL. HARRINGTON
Well, in the first place he isn't my son-in-law yet, and in the second place, if you can't rob your own son-in-law...

GERALD
Then who can you rob?

JEAN
(Levelly)
I don't think you understand, either of you...this is on the up and up... I think I'm in love with the poor fish...snakes and all...he's kind of touched something in my heart and I'd...I'd give a lot to be, I mean I'm going to be...exactly the way he thinks I am...the way he'd like me to be.

COL. HARRINGTON
(Exchanging a glance with Gerald)
I'm sure that's very noble, Jean, and I certainly wish you all the happiness in the world...all the little boys and all the little girls you want, and...

JEAN
(Quickly putting a hand on his arm)
And you'll go straight, too, won't you, Harry?

COL. HARRINGTON
(Blankly)
Straight to where?

10-18-40 (Continued)

C-10 (Cont'd)

JEAN
You know what I mean. You can come and live with us...part of the time anyway...we probably have a very beautiful place... and think how peaceful you can be...

COL. HARRINGTON
You mean playing cribbage with the gardener. I can just see myself wandering around your estate with a weed sticker and fifty cents a week...and some new slippers for Christmas. The trouble with people who reform is they always want to rain on everybody else's parade too. You tend to your knitting and I'll play the cards.

JEAN
Not with him.

COL. HARRINGTON
(Crossly)
Do you happen to remember that that sucker has six hundred dollars of ours in his kick?

JEAN
I suppose you could take that back...

COL. HARRINGTON
You said it...and a little gravy along with it.

JEAN
Oh, no.

COL. HARRINGTON
Oh, yes.

JEAN
Oh, no.

COL. HARRINGTON
Oh, yes.

10-18-40 (Continued)

C-10 (Cont'd)

JEAN
You'll find out I can play a
little cards myself.

COL. HARRINGTON
You think so.

JEAN
(Harshly)
I know so. I'm not your daughter
for free, you know.

She snatches a pack of cards from Gerald's hand.

JEAN
Give me a pack of those.
(As she starts to leave)
You'll find out.

She slams the door.

COL. HARRINGTON
(To Gerald)
Children don't respect their
parents any more. If I'd
spoken that way to my father...

Gerald looks toward heaven.

DISSOLVE TO:

C-11 JEAN, CHARLES AND COL. HARRINGTON - PLAYING THREE-HANDED POKER - IN THE SMOKING ROOM

CHARLES
(Examining a small
stack of chips)
Well, I haven't been quite as
lucky as usual, have I?

JEAN
You don't know how lucky you've
been...the Colonel has been
drawing wonderful cards.

10-18-40 (Continued)

C-11 (Cont'd)

She looks at her father who is shuffling the cards.

JEAN
(Coldly)
I believe it's my deal.

COL. HARRINGTON
(Chuckling apologetically)
I'm sorry.

He hands over the cards.

I'm so overcome by the news you brought me, I can't keep my mind on the game.

JEAN
I noticed that.
(She turns to Charles)
How much are you behind.

CHARLES
(Lightly)
Oh... about three thousand dollars.

Jean gives her father a look, shuffles expertly and starts dealing. As she finishes dealing, Charles picks up his cards and starts with pleasure. Now he changes his smile into a scowl, looks around suspiciously, then glances once more at his cards.

C-12 CLOSE SHOT - CHARLES' HAND

It contains four queens and a nine.

C-13 THE THREE PLAYING CARDS

Col. Harrington is looking intently at the back of Charles' cards. Now he gives Jean a look, then examines his own. He appears to be pleasantly surprised.

COL. HARRINGTON
Well, well, you've given me a good hand at last.

C-14 COL. HARRINGTON'S HAND

It contains a two, a five, a nine, a jack and a four of assorted suits.

10-18-40

C-14 THE THREE PLAYING CARDS

JEAN
I'm glad you like it.

CHARLES
I warn you, sir, you'll have to be pretty good to beat me.

COL. HARRINGTON
(Shoving in some chips)
Nevertheless, my lad, I shall have to bet you a hundred dollars on this.

CHARLES
(Shoving in some chips)
I'm afraid I'll have to raise you a hundred.

JEAN
(Throwing down her cards)
Too high for me.

COL. HARRINGTON
(Looking at the cards)
Well, well, you must have something good...still...

He smiles at his hand, starts to cough and with the hand that holds the cards reaches for his handkerchief. He coughs into this for a second, says:

COL. HARRINGTON
Excuse me.

and examines his hand once more.

COL. HARRINGTON
Still...

C-15 CLOSE SHOT - HIS HAND

which contains four kings and a two.

C-16 CLOSE SHOT - JEAN

Her lips are compressed and she looks at her father through narrowed eyes.

C-17 THE THREE AT THE CARD TABLE

COL. HARRINGTON
(Putting his cards face down on the table)
Still I must raise you a hundred.

C-17 (Cont'd)

He pushes some chips into the middle of the table.

CHARLES
I'm sorry to see you lose your money, but I can't let that challenge go unanswered.

He shoves some chips into the middle of the table.

CHARLES
And a hundred.

COL. HARRINGTON
You're making me very nervous.

He picks up his cards, looks at them speculatively, then puts them down again.

COL. HARRINGTON
But I'll raise you two hundred.

CHARLES
(Chuckling)
A Pike doesn't know the meaning of the word fear. And a hundred.

He shoves some chips in.

COL. HARRINGTON
A Harrington does not know the word "defeat". And two hundred. This is getting exciting, isn't it?

As he shoves the chips in Jean reaches out suddenly.

COL. HARRINGTON
(Abruptly)
What are you doing?

JEAN
I'm so sorry, dear, I thought I'd given you six cards.

COL. HARRINGTON
Far from it, my little minx -
(He examines his cards and adds in a dead voice)
...far from it.

C-18 COL. HARRINGTON'S HAND

It contains two sixes, a four, an eight and a ten, of assorted suits.

10-18-40

C-19 THE THREE PLAYING CARDS

Col. Harrington gives his daughter a gentle pained look. She glares back at him.

CHARLES
(Pushing his chips out)
And a hundred.

COL. HARRINGTON
My gracious. I hope I have enough money with me.

He takes out his wallet, places it on the table over his cards, looks inside, then says:

COL. HARRINGTON
Oh, yes, plenty.

He puts the wallet back in his pocket without showing us the bottom of it.

COL. HARRINGTON
I'll raise you a thousand.

Jean glares at the cards in front of her father.

CHARLES
(Frowning)
Oh, I don't want to win so much from you.
(He pushes his chips in)
I'll cover and show you how hopeless it is.

JEAN
Cards?

COL. HARRINGTON
(Amiably)
I see no necessity for it.

JEAN
And you, Charles?

CHARLES
(Laughing)
Not unless you have another queen, which I doubt.

JEAN
(Laughing nervously)
I'll see what I can do.

She flips the top card face up on the table.

10-18-40

C-20 CLOSE SHOT - THE ACE OF SPADES

C-21 THE THREE PLAYING

JEAN
(Chuckling)
Well, what do you know about that...
I thought at least one of you had
four aces.

She turns and giggles at her father who gives her a very dirty look, then examines his cards sadly.

C-22 CLOSE SHOT - COL. HARRINGTON'S CARDS

They consist of four aces and a deuce.

C-23 THE THREE PLAYING

Charles turns up his cards.

CHARLES
Four queens, sir. What have you?

COL. HARRINGTON
(Folding his cards without
showing them)
I regret to say that I was bluffing.
Spare me the shame of showing you on
what.

He gathers in the cards and starts shuffling them.

CHARLES
(Before Col. Harrington
can reply)
Say, I feel kind of embarrassed about
this. Maybe I should have laid my
cards down and...

JEAN
(Laughing)
You don't think he minds, do you?
Father loves to lose. How do you
stand now?

CHARLES
Let me see, I started with uh...I'm
just a thousand dollars behind.

JEAN
(Firmly)
You're going to stop right there.

10-18-40 (Continued

C-23 (Cont'd)

CHARLES
Just one more round.

JEAN
You can play all night if you'd rather do that than be with me.

CHARLES
(Apologetically to Col. Harrington)
I'm afraid she's going to be firm.

COL. HARRINGTON
I'm afraid you don't know how firm.

JEAN
(Rising)
I'll meet you on "A" deck in five minutes, dear.

Colonel Harrington riffles the cards.

JEAN
(Pausing close to Charles)
But I want your word of honor that you won't play even one more hand.

CHARLES
You have it.

JEAN
(Smiling sweetly at her father)
You know any more games, Harry?
(She exits)

CHARLES
(Seating himself)
Wonderful girl.

COL. HARRINGTON
(Dryly)
Yes, isn't she?

CHARLES
I uh...I don't know whether you've noticed it or not but uh...well, if you have no objections, it was my intention to uh...ask Miss Harrington, I mean your daughter, to uh...
(He clears his throat)
...be mine.

10-18-40 (Continued)

C-23 (Cont'd)

COL. HARRINGTON
(Astonished)
Why my dear boy! You see me astonished! That was the last thing that entered my mind. Why bless my soul, we must have a drink on that. Steward! I'm all emotional.
(He seizes Charles' hand)

THE PASSING STEWARD
Yes sir.

CHARLES
Thank you, sir.

COL. HARRINGTON
To say that I am thunderstruck is an understatement. She'll probably turn you down, but anyway...

CHARLES
I intend to make her as happy as...I can.

COL. HARRINGTON
(Riffling the cards)
She asks very little.

CHARLES
I suppose you know I'm very rich.

COL. HARRINGTON
(Sadly)
Aren't we all.

CHARLES
(Sadly)
I'm sorry in a way. It would be so pleasant to buy lovely nonsensities for somebody ...who hadn't ever had them.

COL. HARRINGTON
Yes, wouldn't it...that's the tragedy of the rich: they don't need anything.

The steward brings the drinks.

COL. HARRINGTON
You know, as a matter of fact, Charles, I don't even like winning a thousand dollars from you.

CHARLES
(Embarrassed)
But my dear sir, it isn't a drop in the ocean. Every time the clock ticks fourteen people swig a bottle of Pike's, and there you are.

10-18-40 (Continued)

C-23 (Cont'd)

COL. HARRINGTON
(Raising a finger)
It is the principle of the thing that bothers me: a father who wins from his son-in-law...how does that look? Here...
(He plunks the deck of cards on the table)
...double or nothing...let's get rid of it.

CHARLES
But I promised Jean I wouldn't play any more.

COL. HARRINGTON
(Frowning)
This isn't playing...this is undoing an absurdity...a thousand dollars, the high card takes it...go ahead.

CHARLES
Well...
(He cuts a queen)

COL. HARRINGTON
(Cutting a king)
Darn it all, now we'll have to try again.

CHARLES
That's two thousand I owe you.

He cuts a deuce.

COL. HARRINGTON
(Cutting a trey)
Tt-tt...four thousand...keep on, keep on, you're bound to win.

CHARLES
(Cutting an ace)
There!... and I thank you for your courtesy.

COL. HARRINGTON
Don't mention it, my boy. Believe me, I feel better about the whole thing.

CHARLES
Are you conceding the cut?

10-18-40 (Continued)

C-23 (Cont'd)

COL. HARRINGTON
Oh, well, just for the fun of it....
(He also cuts an ace)

CHARLES
We're tied.

COL. HARRINGTON
(Sadly)
Continue, continue, it's only a matter of time.

CHARLES
What is it, four thousand?

COL. HARRINGTON
(Apologetically)
For the moment...

Charles cuts a ten and with some embarrassment Col. Harrington cuts a jack.

CHARLES
(With a trace of a frown)
What's that, eight thousand?

COL. HARRINGTON
(Frowning with displeasure)
It looks like it.

Charles cuts a four. As Col. Harrington reaches for the cards --

DISSOLVE TO:

C-24 JEAN - ON "A" DECK

She is walking up and down in a beautiful outfit convenient for walking or sitting in the moonlight. She looks a little impatient. Now a terrible thought crosses her face. She pauses, then hurries toward the door which leads to the stairs.

C-25 CHARLES AND COL. HARRINGTON - AT THE TABLE

Charles is writing a check.

10-18-40 (Continued)

C-25 (Cont'd)

COL. HARRINGTON
(Distressed)
I wish you wouldn't do that... I'm sure if you tried once more...

CHARLES
(Writing)
No... I'd rather pay thirty-two thousand than lose a really large amount.

COL. HARRINGTON
This is very embarrassing...just make it out to "cash".

CHARLES
(Wisely)
It could be even more embarrassing...

C-26 CHARLES' HAND WRITING THE CHECK

The date, the name of a New York bank and the word "bearer" have already been written in.

CHARLES' VOICE
(As he writes)
Thirty-two thousand dollars and no cents.

He signs: "Charles Poncefort Pike".

C-27 THE PURSER AND MUGGSY LOOKING ON

Now they exit.

C-28 CHARLES AND COL. HARRINGTON - AT THE TABLE

CHARLES
(Handing over the check)
Don't mention the middle name, I wouldn't want Jean to know it... as a matter of fact, I'd prefer that you didn't tell Jean anything about...the whole transaction.

COL. HARRINGTON
You may depend upon it, my boy.

JEAN'S VOICE
You certainly may.

As they turn guiltily --

10-18-40

C-29 JEAN - PAST CHARLES AND COL. HARRINGTON

JEAN
(Accusingly to Charles)
You promised me you wouldn't play any more.

CHARLES
(Worried)
I didn't play any more, dear. We were just wiping out my loss.

JEAN
You need a keeper.
(Jean turns to her father)
And now that you've taught Charles not to play double or quits, what are you going to do with that check?

COL. HARRINGTON
Just this...my pretty child...

He takes the check in both hands, rolls it into a ball, then tears it in little pieces which he deposits in the ash tray.

CHARLES
(Stupefied)
You mean it was a joke?

COL. HARRINGTON
(Roaring)
Of course it was. You don't actually think I'd bleed my own... daughter's friend, do you?

JEAN
Perish the thought...Come on. She drags Charles out.

THE STEWARD
That'll be two dollars and eighty cents, sir. The Colonel gives him a look.

DISSOLVE:

C-30 THE DECK OUTSIDE THE SMOKING ROOM

Charles and Jean enter.

CHARLES
That was a terrible lesson the Colonel almost taught me.

10-18-40 (Continued)

C-30 (Cont'd)

JEAN
He's a great joker.

CHARLES
He certainly had me fooled...gee you look lovely.

JEAN
Thank you.

CHARLES
I spoke to your father about something.

JEAN
Did you?

CHARLES
Yes. Do you want to go up in the bow of the boat and stand in the wind?

C-31 THE BOW OF THE BOAT

In the BACKGROUND we see a moonlit sky. Jean and Charles come INTO THE SHOT.

JEAN
The air is good, isn't it?...It makes you feel all clean inside and nice.

CHARLES
(Suddenly)
Don't move.

JEAN
What?

CHARLES
I've just understood something...you see, every time I've lookd at you here on the boat it wasn't only here I saw you: you seemed to go way back...I know that isn't clear but I saw you here and at the same time further away, and then still further away, and then very small...like converging perspective lines... no, that isn't it, more like figures following each other in a forest glade. Only way back there you were a little girl in short dresses with your hair falling on your shoulders, in the middle distance your hair is up but you're still gawky like a colt...then when you get nearer you look more like you do now, except not so pretty...but I've only told

10-18-40 (Continued)

C-31 (Cont'd) CHARLES (Continued)

you half of it, because way back there a little boy is standing with you, holding your hand, and in the middle distance I'm still with you, not holding your hand any more because it isn't manly, but wanting to. And then still nearer we look terrible: you with your legs like a colt and mine like a calf... what I'm trying to say, only I'm not a poet, I'm an ophiologist, is that I've always loved you...I mean I've never loved anyone but you...I suppose that sounds as dull as a drug store novel, and what I see inside I'll never be able to cast into words...but that's what I mean.

Jean looks at him lovingly.

CHARLES

I wish we were married and on our honeymoon now.

JEAN

So do I.

He crushes her to him.

JEAN

But it isn't as simple as all that, Hopsie...I'm terribly in love.... and you seem to be too, so one of us has to think and try to keep things clear,..and maybe I can do that better than you can...they say a moonlit deck is a woman's business office.

Charles kisses her passionately.

JEAN

(Freeing herself)

What kind of a business is that?

FADE OUT:

END OF SEQUENCE "C"

10-18-40

SEQUENCE "D"

FADE IN:

D-1 COL. HARRINGTON - IN HIS CABIN - DAY

He is brushing his hair in front of a mirror. He wears a dressing gown. The remains of some breakfast are in evidence. He seems quite cheerful. Finishing with his hair he goes to the door of the adjoining cabin and knocks.

D-2 JEAN - IN FRONT OF HER DRESSING TABLE

She is nearly dressed and is finishing her makeup.

JEAN
Come in.

The adjoining door opens and the Colonel enters and pauses in the doorway.

COL. HARRINGTON
Good morning.

JEAN
(Faintly contrite)
Good morning, Harry.

COL. HARRINGTON
Think you're pretty smart, don't you?

JEAN
(Apologetically)
You know I had to.

She gets up and crosses to him.

JEAN
You're such an old scoundrel you'd skin me if you got the chance.

She kisses him on the cheek and he pats her on the back.

JEAN
Aren't you ashamed of yourself?

COL. HARRINGTON
Are you really in love with this mug?

JEAN
Unhunh.

10-18-40 (Continued)

D-2 (Cont'd)

COL. HARRINGTON
Don't you think it's a little bit dangerous...I don't mean for us, I mean for your heart. They're apt to be slightly narrow-minded... these righteous people.

JEAN
A man who couldn't forgive wouldn't be much of a man.

COL. HARRINGTON
How about his family?

JEAN
Well...

COL. HARRINGTON
You're going to tell him who we are, of course, before you...marry him... I presume he offered you marriage.

JEAN
(Laughing)
Of course he did.

COL. HARRINGTON
And you're going to tell him.

JEAN
Of course.

COL. HARRINGTON
But not until we get off the boat...you'd have to be fair...to Gerald and me.

JEAN
(After a slight pause)
Naturally.

COL. HARRINGTON
I hope you'll never be unhappy.

JEAN
I hope I'll never be more unhappy than I am right now.

COL. HARRINGTON
He's waiting for you?

JEAN
Unhunh.

COL. HARRINGTON
And you're in a hurry to join him?

JEAN
(Smiling)
Unhunh.

10-18-40 (Continued)

D-2 (Cont'd)

COL. HARRINGTON
Then hurry up.

He kisses her on the forehead and she returns to her preparations.

DISSOLVE TO:

D-3 THE SIDEWALK CAFE

Charles is pacing up and down near a prettily set table.

D-4 MUGGSY AND THE PURSER - IN THE DOORWAY OF THE SMOKING ROOM

The purser carries an eight by ten envelope in his hand. They watch Charles for a moment.

MUGGSY
(To the purser)
Come on.

D-5 CHARLES LOOKING OUT OVER THE RAIL

Muggsy and the Purser come up behind him and Muggsy taps him on the shoulder. Charles swings happily, then his face falls.

CHARLES
Oh....what do you want?

MUGGSY
How much you lose last night?

CHARLES
Nothing, why?

THE PURSER
(Triumphantly to Muggsy)
You see.

MUGGSY
There's something screwy somewhere, this is a gang of sharpies.

CHARLES
(To the Purser, pointing to Muggsy)
Sherlock Holmes.
(Then to Muggsy)
How much did you lose?

MUGGSY
The guy lets me win a few fish for a change.

10-18-40 (Continued)

D-5 (Cont'd)

CHARLES
So that makes you twice as suspicious.

MUGGSY
That's right.

CHARLES
You ought to have some handles fastened onto your skull and you could grow geraniums in it.

Muggsy snatches the envelope from the Purser's hand and hands it to Charles.

MUGGSY
Yeah? Well get a load a this and see what you can grow in it.

He starts out. As he passes the Purser he says:

MUGGSY
Gratitude ! ... 'at's what you get for savin' a guy's life.

He walks OUT OF THE SHOT

THE PURSER
(Indicating the envelope)
If you didn't happen to lose any money last night, Mr. Pike, I would prefer you didn't look in there.

CHARLES
I didn't lose any money.

THE PURSER
Then there's only one other possibility... they might be aiming at higher game.

CHARLES
(Irritably)
What are you talking about?

THE PURSER
(Suddenly inspired)
You haven't fallen in love?

CHARLES
(Crossly)
What's that got to do with you?

THE PURSER
(Decisively)
Look at the photograph. I will take the consequences. Good morning.

He walks out.

10-18-40 (Continued)

D-5 (Cont'd)

Charles stands watching him go, then slowly turns his attention to the envelope. Now he takes out the picture. As he looks at it miserably --

D-6 INSERT: PHOTOGRAPH

It is a candid camera shot of Jean, her father, and Gerald descending the gangplank of their vessel. Below it the description reads:

"Patrick Henry Harrington, alias 'Handsome Harry,' and Jean, probably his daughter. Harrington also known as Dr. Hersher, Major Charles D. D. Brown, the Reverend Doctor Upswitch, Captain Julius Joyce, retired, C. K. J. Malvern, etc., etc., poses also as dentists, physicians, and explorers. Specialty: cards, occasionally bunko, oil wells, mines and war charities. Third character, valet type, accomplice known as Gerald."

D-7 CHARLES - LOOKING AT THE PHOTOGRAPH

He sticks it carefully back in the envelope, looks around vaguely, then goes into the bar.

D-8 THE MAIN STAIRWAY

Jean comes up happily and the CAMERA PANS her to the entrance of the smoking room.

D-9 JEAN - IN THE ENTRANCE OF THE SMOKING ROOM - PAST CHARLES

She looks astonished to see him at the bar.

JEAN
Why Hopsie, what are you doing at the bar at this hour?

CHARLES
Good morning.

JEAN
(Very gently)
Good morning, darling.

She kisses him behind the ear.

JEAN
You look like the last grave over near the willow. Are you worried about something?

10-18-40 (Continued)

D-9 (Cont'd)

CHARLES
Should I be?

JEAN
Of course you should...falling in love with a girl in the middle of an ocean... you see, you don't know very much about girls, Hopsie: the best ones aren't as good as you probably think they are... and the bad ones aren't as bad...not nearly as bad.

Charles looks at her miserably.

JEAN
So I suppose you're right to worry... falling in love with an adventuress on the high seas.

CHARLES
Are you an adventuress?

JEAN
(After a pause)
Of course I am...all women are. They have to be. If you waited for a man to propose to you from natural causes you'd die of old maidenhood. That's why I let you try my slippers on... and then I put my cheek against yours... and then I made you put your arms around me and hold me tight...and then I fell in love with you...which wasn't in the cards.

CHARLES
(Looking away)
Jean.

JEAN
(Tenderly)
Yes, darling.

In reply he hands her the photograph.

JEAN
What's that?

CHARLES
You'd better look.

Slowly Jean takes the picture out of the envelope. She doesn't bat an eyelash as she looks at it.

JEAN
(In a small voice, after a moment)
Rotten likeness, isn't it? I never cared for that picture.

10-18-40 (Continued)

D-9 (Cont'd)

The smoking room Steward hurries INTO THE SHOT.

THE STEWARD
Good morning, Miss Harrington...breakfast? Melon, grapefruit, orange juice, sliced peaches...

JEAN
Just some coffee, please.

THE STEWARD
Yes indeed.

Jean reaches out and pats Charles' arm.

JEAN
Please don't look so upset, darling... I was going to tell you when we got to New York...I would have told you last night only it wouldn't be fair to Harry and Gerald, I mean you never know how someone's going to take something like that...and maybe I wanted you to love me a little more...too.
(She looks at him)
Well you believe me, don't you? You don't think I was going to... marry you without telling you... you don't think that badly of me...or do you?

CHARLES
(Bitterly)
Why didn't you let your father rob me last night?

JEAN
If you don't believe what I just told you you wouldn't believe that either... you wouldn't understand...anyway, I'm glad you got the picture this morning instead of last night, if that means anything to you...it should.

CHARLES
You thought you were having a lot of fun with me, didn't you?

JEAN
I was having a lot of fun with you, Hopsie...more fun than I've ever had with anybody.
(She laughs ruefully)
You were certainly very funny showing Harry how to palm a card.

10-18-40 (Continued)

D-9 (Cont'd)

CHARLES
(Stung)
You were pretty funny yourself.

JEAN
When?

CHARLES
Trying to play me for a sucker when they told me who you were... the morning after I met you.

JEAN
(Unbelievingly)
Who told you?

CHARLES
Never mind who told me..

JEAN
(After a pause)
You mean you were playing me for a sucker...I don't believe it, but if you were, if you just wanted to make me feel cheap...and hurt me and... and...you succeeded handsomely.

She closes her eyes for a moment, then gets off the bar stool.

JEAN
You ought to be very proud of yourself, Mr. Pike...
(Her lips tremble and she bites them before repeating:)
...very proud of yourself.

She starts out. The Steward hurries INTO THE SHOT with the cup of coffee.

THE STEWARD
Your coffee, Miss.

Jean shakes her head and stumbles out of the smoking room.

DISSOLVE TO:

D-10 JEAN'S CABIN

She hurries in, gulps once, then throws herself on her face across the bed. She is racked with sobs.

10-18-40

D-11 THE DOOR OF THE ADJOINING CABIN

Col. Harrington appears with a deck of cards in his hands. He quickly puts the cards in his pocket and crosses to Jean's bed.

COL. HARRINGTON
(Sitting beside his daughter and patting her)
There, there, there, my gracious... you know you shouldn't draw to a middle straight.

JEAN
(Through her tears)
I hate him. Oh, how I hate that m-mug.

COL. HARRINGTON
There, there, there.

VERY SLOW DISSOLVE TO:

D-12 CLOSE SHOT - SHIP'S WHISTLE

Steam and noise emit from it.

D-13 LONG SHOT - THE S.S. "SOUTHERN QUEEN" BEING WARPED INTO HER DOCK IN NEW YORK

The whistle is still blowing.

D-14 JEAN, COL. HARRINGTON AND GERALD

They stand next to a pile of luggage. Jean looks ver beautiful and very sore in a smart traveling outfit. She is looking in Charles' direction. Now she turns to her father.

JEAN
When I think we let that sucker get off Scott free, it makes my blood boil.

COL. HARRINGTON
(Airily)
I told you not to mix business and pleasure.

JEAN
(Bitterly)
I won't again you can believe me.

10-18-40 (Continued)

D-14 (Cont'd) COL. HARRINGTON
However, "Scott free" is perhaps an exaggeration, dear.

JEAN
Hunh?

In reply Col. Harrington takes the crumpled check out of his waistcoat pocket and hands it to her. Jean unfolds the check.

D-15 JEAN'S HANDS AND CHARLES' CHECK FOR $32,000

D-16 JEAN, COL. HARRINGTON AND GERALD

JEAN
(Quietly)
How did you do it?

COL. HARRINGTON
(Amused)
Don't you remember, he showed me how to palm things.

GERALD
(Taking a good look at the check)
It should come out like new with a hot iron.

JEAN
(Smiling faintly in Charles' direction)
I feel better myself.

FADE OUT:

END OF SEQUENCE "D"

10-18-40

SEQUENCE "E"

FADE IN:

E-1 THE SIDEWALK OUTSIDE A N.Y. BANK

A cab pulls up and Charles steps out of it.

CHARLES
Wait, please.

DRIVER
I can't wait here, buddy.

CHARLES
(Sternly)
You can wait where you like.

He marches into the bank.

E-2 INT. BANK - LONG SHOT - JEAN WAITING

Charles moves into the foreground and stops at a desk with his back to her. He writes a check. Suddenly Jean sees him.

E-3 CLOSE SHOT - JEAN

Her eyes become wide with fright. She looks around for a way out. At this moment the wicket opens beside her and we see the teller accompanied by a middle-aged manager.

MANAGER
Miss Harrington?

JEAN
(Turning her back
on Charles)
Yes.

MANAGER
(With a wolfish smile)
This check is for such a large amount that uh...heh heh heh...

JEAN
(Smiling also)
Of course, heh heh heh... just what do you want to know?

10-18-40

E-4 REAR VIEW OF CHARLES

He blots his check, faces us and looks slowly from right to left.

E-5 THE BANK ROOM - PAST CHARLES

All the windows have waiting queues except the one at which Jean stands with her back to us. Charles crosses toward her.

E-6 JEAN - AT THE WINDOW

JEAN
I don't know why not. The check is made to "Cash," and it seems to me..

MANAGER
(Interrupting)
You are quite correct, Miss Harrington, but after all, thirty-two thousand dollars is a rather large amount to uh...

The CAMERA DRAWS BACK AND BRINGS Charles INTO THE SHOT. He stands directly behind Jean.

MANAGER
...to pay over...to a complete stranger. If you would deposit this check in some other bank... or even in this one...

JEAN
(In a low voice)
But I tell you I'm going away.

CHARLES
Perhaps I can be of some assistance...

Jean swings and faces him but says nothing. Charles steps to the window.

CHARLES
I am Mr. Pike.

MANAGER
Why yes, Mr. Pike...

10-18-40 (Continued)

E-6 (Cont'd)

CHARLES
(Holding out his hand)
May I see the check you were discussing?

The manager gives it to him.

CHARLES
(Examining the check)
Ah, yes.
(He looks up at Jean)
You'd never know it had been crumpled, would you?... a good trick.
(Now he turns back to the Manager)
I believe we have ample funds to cover this.

MANAGER
(Embarrassed)
Of course we have, Mr. Pike, it wasn't at all a question of that...

CHARLES
Then pay it, please.

He flips the check through the window, then turns to Jean. His expression becomes quite miserable. Jean looks down and whispers:

JEAN
Good-bye.

Charles walks away fast.

FADE OUT:

END OF SEQUENCE "E"

10-18-40

SEQUENCE "F"

FADE IN:

F-1 FOUR HORSES - AT THE GATE AT AN EASTERN TRACK

They break and we hear the distant roar: "They're off!"

F-2 FULL SHOT - A GRANDSTAND

The crowd gets more and more excited.

F-3 THE HORSE RUNNING

F-4 JEAN, COLONEL HARRINGTON AND GERALD

Jean is lackadaisical. Her father twists his program nervously.

GERALD
(Excitedly)
Come on baby....Oh, you sweet pappy!...roll dem hoofs.

JEAN
He took it too wide.

GERALD
He'll be all right. He only faltered for a second there.

JEAN
In a pig's nose he'll be all right.

GERALD
Come on baby!...Papa needs dem pennies!

COL. HARRINGTON
Keep it down to a riot, will you?

Colonel Harrington and Jean exchange glances.

GERALD
(Suddenly)
Oh, baby, don't do that!

F-5 THE FOUR HORSES - POUNDING DOWN THE STRETCH

One of them is losing ground. Now the racing and the yelling gets very intense. There's a roar from the crowd and the race is over.

F-6 THE BOX CONTAINING OUR FRIENDS

Somewhat disheveled, Gerald gets down off his chair and starts tearing up his tickets. Colonel Harrington does likewise.

GERALD
What I don't understand is how he could have finished fourth.

JEAN
There were only four horses in the race...What do you expect when you bet on a goat called "After You?"

COL. HARRINGTON
Don't pick on him.

JEAN
I'm not picking on him; compared to you he's ahead.

Now a gay little man in a checked suit sticks his head INTO THE SHOT.

SIR ALFRED McGLENNAN-KEITH
I beg your pardon, is this seat...
(Now he recognizes Colonel Harrington)
Why, Harry, bless my soul!

COL. HARRINGTON
(Quickly)
William, at the moment.

SIR ALFRED
(Instantly)
William, of course, I'm enchanted to see you, my dear William, and you, Gerald, and the little lady still as pretty as a pack of aces.

JEAN
(Taking his hand)
Hello, Pearlie.

ALFRED
(Clearing his throat)
Sir Alfred, at the moment, my pretty child...Sir Alfred McGlennan-Keith at your service. Well, you're certainly a sight for lame peepers. I've seen no one, positively not anybody, I mean of our set, of

10-18-40 (Continued)

F-6 (Cont'd)

SIR ALFRED (Cont'd)
course, since the boats stopped running...but, tell me about yourself...How is the...market?

COL. HARRINGTON
We went south and back a few times...but there're so few boats.

SIR ALFRED
Ah, yes, and one so quickly wears out one's welcome, doesn't one?
(He chuckles)

Now he puts a confidential hand on Colonel Harrington.

SIR ALFRED
Ah, but my dear boy, there's nothing like the land...had I know how thick they come and how voluptuously they play, believe me, I would have given up the sea long ago.

GERALD
Where's your pitch, Pearlie?

SIR ALFRED
Sir Alfred. I have a little nest on the edge of a town called Bridgefield, Connecticut...a town that's full of mugs --
(He corrects himself quickly)
-- millionaires.

Jean pricks up her ears.

SIR ALFRED
(Continuing)
In the heart of the contract bridge belt, a wonderful game. I have my horses, I have my dogs, I have my little house, I have my antiques. We play a little game here and a little game there, and then we play somewhere else. Sometimes my luck is good and sometimes my luck is better, and what with one thing and another, my dear boy...What a dream.

COL. HARRINGTON
How did you meet them?

10-18-40 (Continued)

F-6 (Cont'd)

SIR ALFRED
The chumps? My dear boy, when your name is Sir Alfred McGlennan-Keith, R.F.D., you don't have to meet them; you fight them off with sticks...and just think...there's no hurry...you have them by the year...like a lease.

COL. HARRINGTON
(Laughing)
Ah, Pearlie.

JEAN
Do you know the Pikes?

COL. HARRINGTON
(Gently)
What do you care if he does?

SIR ALFRED
Do I know them? I practically swill in their ale...good old Horace. What a card player!

JEAN
Do you know...Charles?

Colonel Harrington tries to stop her.

SIR ALFRED
Is that the backward boy who's always toying with toads and things? I think I've seen him slinking about.

JEAN
He isn't backward; he's a scientist.

SIR ALFRED
Oh, is that what it is. I knew he was peculiar. Ah, well, it's delightful to see you again. Now, what have we in the fifth?

Jean leans close to him and speaks in a low voice.

JEAN
Pearlie.

SIR ALFRED
(Also in a whisper)
Yes?

F-6 (Cont'd)

JEAN
Could I visit you sometime?

SIR ALFRED
Could you visit me sometime?

JEAN
As your niece.

SIR ALFRED
As my niece?

COL. HARRINGTON
Why don't you stop talking nonsense?

JEAN
(Coldly)
Because I want to see that guy.
(Now she grits her teeth)
I've got some unfinished business with him...I need him like Dempsey needed Firpo.

SIR ALFRED
The only thing, darling...you'd have to be English, you see.

JEAN
I've been English before, dear. I shall be as English as necessary.

A bell rings.

JEAN
Go make your bets.

The men look at her peculiarly and depart.

FADE OUT:

END OF SEQUENCE "F"

10-18-40

SEQUENCE "G"

FADE IN:

G-1 THE MAIN HALL OF THE PIKE RESIDENCE SHOWING THE STAIRS

We hear a bass voice singing: "Roll Out the Barrel" and Mr. Pike trots down the stairs and INTO VIEW. He pauses at a console for his mail, starts for the terrace, then is stopped by the ringing of one of the telephones on the console.

MR. PIKE
(After picking up the wrong phone)
Yes... yes... that's right... black tie or white tie?... You can wear a green tie for all I care... What party is that? Who's giving it?... Oh, we are... You'd think they'd tell me something about it...
(He chuckles)
This is Mr. Pike, speaking... Mr. who?... I don't get it... I'll probably meet you at the party tonight. By the way what time is it... thanks.
(He hangs up)
Nuthouse!

He picks up his mail and starts for the terrace. His good humor returning, he reprises: "Roll Out the Barrel."

G-2 THE BREAKFAST TABLE - ON THE TERRACE

It is beautifully laid and well covered with silver covers and a silver coffee set. We hear the singing of "Roll Out the Barrel." A second later Mr. Pike appears, sits down at the table, takes a sip of water, tucks a napkin under his chin, licks his lips and peeks under a cover. His face falls as he lifts the cover higher and discovers positively that there is nothing there. With less hope he tries the second cover. With no hope at all he tries the third. He looks around the table indignantly, then tries unsuccessfully to pour himself a cup of coffee. He bangs the empty pot down on the table.

MR. PIKE
Hey! Where is everybody? Where's my breakfast?

10-18-40

G-3 FULL SHOT - THE KITCHEN

In the FOREGROUND an elaborate cake, next to it the Chef and Mr. Burrows. Mr. Burrows is a large English butler, the Chef a small Latin. Great activity is going on behind them. Chefs, maids, kitchen boys are slamming pots and pans around, boning chickens, peeling potatoes and performing the general mess necessary for a big dinner. Squirt gun in hand, the Chef is trying to put on the cake the design read aloud by Mr. Burrows.

MR. BURROWS
(Reading from Burke's Peerage)
Arms: Quarterly: First and fourth argent three fusils, conjoined in fesse, gules, within a border sable for Mordant.

THE CHEF
Hunh?

G-4 INSERT - A PAGE IN BURKE'S PEERAGE

We see the coat-of-arms and above it the word "Sidwich".

MR. BURROWS' VOICE
Second and third, or, a fesse, dancettee, between three crosses crosslet, fitchee, azure, for Sidwich. Supporters: two wyverns, argent, beaked and membered, vert.

G-5 BURROWS AND THE CHEF

MR. BURROWS
Crest: A lion couchant gardant, or, holding between the paws an escocheon sable, charged with a cock proper. Motto: Hyphen "sic erat in fatis."

THE CHEF
(Offering him the squirt gun)
Here, you do it.

MR. BURROWS
Nonsense, Emile, it's very simple: Second and third, a fesse dancettee, between three crosses crosslet...

10-18-40 (Continued)

G-5 (Cont'd)

THE CHEF
Crosses crosslet!

MR. BURROWS
That's right.

THE CHEF
(Insultingly)
Horses horselet!

MR. BURROWS
(Sternly)
Emile!

THE CHEF
Nutzes nutslet!

MR. BURROWS
Remember who you are.

THE CHEF
(Shaking the squirt gun at him)
Wit gules!

He slams it down and as it arcs it squirts some cream into Mr. Burrows' face.

G-6 MR. PIKE - AT THE BREAKFAST TABLE

He is ringing a bell violently. A pretty Maid rushes out from the house.

THE MAID
Yes, sir?

MR. PIKE
(Crossly)
When do I eat?

THE MAID
They must have overlooked you in the rush for the party, Mr. Pike. I'll get you something right away.

MR. PIKE
'Sabout time. Who's the party for, anyway?

THE MAID
Sir Alfred McGlennan-Keith's niece, the Lady Eve Sidwich.

MR. PIKE
I didn't know he had a niece.

10-18-40

G-7 MR. BURROWS AND THE CHEF - IN THE KITCHEN

MR. BURROWS
(Wiping his face)
You'll regret this day, my lad.

THE CHEF
Fusils!

MR. BURROWS
That's all very well....

THE CHEF
Fitchee!

MUGGSY
(Coming in with a tail
coat over his arm)
Where's the snake food?

MR. BURROWS
(Furiously)
Get it yourself, Ambrose.

MUGGSY
(Looking at him)
Lay off the Ambrose, willya?
(Now he watches him
continuing to wipe
the cream off his face)
Why don't you shave in your room?

MR. BURROWS
I'll thank you to keep your remarks
to yourself, Mr. Murgatroyd.

He walks toward a sink.

MUGGSY
(To the Chef)
What's the matter with him?

THE CHEF
(Tapping his forehead)
Fitchee!

MUGGSY
Oh... Where's the snake food?

THE CHEF
In the ice box.... where do you
think it is, in the gules?

MUGGSY
(Walking toward the
ice box)
'Smatter with everybody?

10-18-40 (Continued)

G-7 (Cont'd)

The pretty Maid runs in.

THE MAID
The master's breakfast, please,
Mr. Burrows.

MR. BURROWS
Yes, well you can take it up with
somebody else.

THE MAID
(To the Chef)
Give me some breakfast for the
boss, will you Chef?

THE CHEF
All my time is taken up wit
crosses crosslet.

MUGGSY
(Coming from the ice box
with a plate)
Here, take him this.

THE MAID
Oh, you.

A VOICE
The madam wants you, Martha.

The Maid runs out of the kitchen and Muggsy follows her.

G-8 MR. PIKE - AT THE BREAKFAST TABLE

He is drumming angrily on the surface of the table. Now a stupid looking gook walks INTO THE SHOT carrying a potted palm.

MR. PIKE
Hey, you, while you're inside there...

THE MAN WITH THE PALM
No speak.

He vanishes inside the house. Mr. Pike seizes the bell and rings it violently.

G-9 MRS. PIKE AND GERTRUDE, A MIDDLE-AGED MAID - AT THE FLOWER SINK UNDER THE STAIRS

We hear Mr. Pike's bell ringing.

10-18-40 (Continued)

G-9 (Cont'd)

MRS. PIKE
If that's the knife sharpener, take him around to the back.

GERTRUDE
Yes, madam.

She starts out. The phone rings.

MRS. PIKE
(Into the telephone)
Oh, hello, Janet... no, dear, it's for his niece... the Lady Eve.

The Man with the potted palm comes INTO THE SHOT.

MRS. PIKE
Take it upstairs to the solarium.

THE MAN WITH THE POTTED PALM
Hunh?

Martha enters.

MARTHA
You wanted me, madam?

MRS. PIKE
Take this man upstairs and show him where the solarium is.

MARTHA
I was going to get breakfast for...

MRS. PIKE
Do as you're told, dear.

MARTHA
Yes, m'am.

THE MAN WITH THE POTTED PALM
No speak.

MARTHA
Come on.

She draws him OUT OF THE SHOT.

MRS. PIKE
(Into the telephone)
I'm sorry I kept you waiting, dear...
No, Sidwich... I think her mother

10-18-40 (Continued)

G-9 (Cont'd)

MRS. PIKE (Cont'd)
was a McGlennan-Keith...Although she may not have been....you know these English families.
(She chuckles)

A social secretary comes in with a table plan, a pile of cards, a pencil in her hand a fountain pen between her teeth.

G-10 MR. PIKE - AT THE BREAKFAST TABLE

He is shaking the bell.

MR. PIKE
Hey, somebody!

GERTRUDE
(Hurrying INTO THE SHOT)
Why, Mr. Pike, you haven't had your breakfast yet, you poor dear. Why didn't you ask somebody? Now, you just sit there quietly and I'll be back before you can say....

A foreign looking man with a satchel comes INTO THE SHOT.

THE PIANO TUNER
Piano?

MR. PIKE
What do you want?

THE PIANO TUNER
I said, vere iss de piano, kindly?

MR. PIKE
(Irascibly)
Well, where do you think it is, out on the lawn?

GERTRUDE
(Quickly)
I'll show you.

She drags him away.

MR. PIKE
But don't forget to come back.

He drums on the table..

10-18-40

G-11 MRS. PIKE AND HER SECRETARY

MRS. PIKE
(To the passing Gertrude)
Oh, Gertrude!

GERTRUDE
(Stopping suddenly)
Yes, m'am.

The Piano Tuner almost bumps into her.

MRS. PIKE
Run upstairs to the string closet and get me some gold-edged place cards.... they're in the third drawer on the left.

GERTRUDE
Yes, m'am.

She hurries away and the Piano Tuner trots after her. We hear a terrible clatter from outside.

MRS. PIKE
What is that dreadful noise?

G-12 MR. PIKE - AT THE BREAKFAST TABLE

He is hitting the silver covers with the handle of a knife.

G-13 A STAIRCASE

Gertrude hurries up, followed dutifully by the Piano Tuner.

G-14 THE UPPER LANDING OF THE STAIRS

Gertrude hurries INTO THE SHOT, followed by the Piano Tuner. As they disappear down the hall, we find ourselves POINTING toward an open door. WE GO IN.

G-15 CHARLES' LABORATORY

A camera is set up for the purpose of photographing something on the workbench. Charles, wearing a laboratory coat, has his head under the focusing cloth. Muggsy is putting down the snake food and talking at the same time.

10-18-40 (Continued)

G-15 (Cont'd)

CHARLES
(Under the cloth)
What?

MUGGSY
Your old lady wants me to see
if it fits.

CHARLES
(Under the cloth)
If what fits?

MUGGSY
Your tail coat.

CHARLES
(Coming out from under
the cloth)
Who's going to wear a tail coat when?

MUGGSY
You are... tonight.

CHARLES
That's what you think. I'm going
to a lecture at Yale...

He goes back under the focusing cloth.

MUGGSY
That's what you think.

THE PIANO TUNER
(Coming in)
Vere do I tune de piano?

MUGGSY
Get outta here, this is the
snake house.

The Piano Tuner hurries out.

MUGGSY
Look, if your old lady wants you
to show up at the party, the least
you can do...

CHARLES
(Under the cloth)
I've got to go to a lecture.

MUGGSY
Look: Suppose when you die 'stead
of hearing ten thousand lectures you
only heard nine thousand, nine hundred

G-15 (Cont'd)

MUGGSY (Cont'd)
and ninety-nine... You gotta realize these things mean more to a dame than to guys like us... If it makes the old lady happy...

During this speech Charles has come out from under the cloth and is looking around the room. Now he interrupts.

CHARLES
Where did she go? I was photographing a little black crotalis colobrinus with pink spots and...

THE PIANO TUNER'S VOICE
Help!

CHARLES
There she is.

He starts out of the room, followed by Muggsy.

G-16 THE MAIN STAIRS

The Piano Tuner comes tearing down PAST US.

G-17 A LITTLE SNAKE - SLITHERING DOWN THE SIDE OF THE STAIRS

G-18 CHARLES AND MUGGSY - IN THE UPPER HALL

CHARLES
She's around here someplace; somebody hollered.

G-19 MR. BURROWS - ENTERING THE MAIN HALL

The CAMERA PANS WITH him to the middle of the hall. He stops at Charles' voice.

CHARLES' VOICE
Say, Burrows.

G-20 BURROWS - CUT OFF AT THE KNEES

MR. BURROWS
(Coming to a stop and looking up)
Yes, sir; good morning, sir.

10-18-40

G-21 LOW CAMERA SHOT - UP AT CHARLES AND MUGGSY - ON THE STAIRS

CHARLES
You haven't seen a little black crotalis colobrinus, have you?

MUGGSY
With pink spots.

G-22 BURROWS - CUT OFF AT THE KNEES

MR. BURROWS
I rejoice to say that I have not, sir...that's all I'd be needing this morning.

G-23 LOW CAMERA SHOT - UP AT CHARLES AND MUGGSY

CHARLES
She slipped out on us.

G-24 BURROWS - CUT OFF AT THE KNEES

MR. BURROWS
Yes, sir... thank you, sir.

He starts away. The CAMERA TRUCKS WITH him and ANGLES DOWN to his feet. We see the little snake securely wrapped around his right ankle.

G-25 MR. PIKE - AT THE BREAKFAST TABLE

He is banging two covers together like cymbals. He pauses momentarily to watch the Piano Tuner rush past him and across the lawn, mutters: "Nuthouse," and resumes the banging of his covers.

FADE OUT

END OF SEQUENCE "G"

10-18-40

SEQUENCE "H"

FADE IN:

H-1 CLOSE SHOT - THE CAKE

The Sidwich emblem has been beautifully worked upon it. A fine-pointed pastry gun puts one last blob on it for the eye of the lion.

H-2 THE CHEF - SURROUNDED BY HIS KITCHEN STAFF - IN THE PIKE KITCHEN

THE STAFF
(Variously)
Ah!..
Superbe!...
Wunderbar!...
Magnifico!...
Unmoeglich!...
A work of art!...

The Chef chucks his pastry gun onto Burke's Peerage, shakes his head and says:

THE CHEF
(Sadly)
Yes...but where is it tomorrow?

As he turns away --

H-3 EXT. THE PIKE MANSION - (NIGHT)

A line of cars is discharging its fashionable occupants. Muggsy is acting as doorman. Muggsy closes the door of a car, then speaks to the chauffeur.

MUGGSY
Okay, and try and keep off the grass.
(He hollers to the next car)
Next!

A very elegant but slightly old-fashioned Rolls-Royce with right-hand drive pulls up.

MUGGSY
(To the chauffeur)
Where'd you get that thing?

H-3 (Cont'd)

He opens the door and Sir Alfred McGlennan-Keith steps out in full regalia.

SIR ALFRED
Good evening, my man.

MUGGSY
(Instantly)
How are you?
(He looks inside the car)
Come on, lady, we're holding up the traffic.

Sir Alfred has a slight take-it at this, then stretches a hand inside the car.

SIR ALFRED
Come, my dear.

H-4 THE LADY EVE - INSIDE OF THE CAR - (DARK)

Sir Alfred's hand is in the foreground. She wears a veil over her head through which we see the glittering of a small tiara. The collar of a great fur coat comes up to her ears. She looks slightly scared. She closes her eyes, takes a long breath, then --

THE LADY EVE
Right you are, Glenny; coming.

She seizes the hand.

H-5 SHOT ALONGSIDE THE CAR - FROM THE REAR

Sir Alfred stands three-quarters back to us, Muggsy full face looking into the car. As the Lady Eve steps out --

MUGGSY
Evening.

He slams the car door and it pulls away. Now he calls:

MUGGSY
Next!

10-18-40 (Continued)

H-5 (Cont'd)

Suddenly he turns and looks after Sir Alfred and the Lady Eve. As he stands rooted to the ground, another car pulls up and the door opens, catching Muggsy in the rear with the handle. He arcs forward violently, looks resentfully over his shoulder, then starts slowly toward the door of the house. The CAMERA PANS WITH HIM.

H-6 INT. OF THE GREAT HALL - SHOOTING FROM THE DOORWAY

Sir Alfred and the Lady Eve stand with their backs to us. Gertrude and Martha are receiving the ladies' coats and a man servant, the men's coats.

H-7 MUGGSY - PEERING IN AT THE DOOR

He moves to one side as some guests approach. Now the CAMERA STARTS FORWARD as if it were the Lady Eve. We discover Burrows standing in the doorway at the edge of the step down into the living room. He bows.

MR. BURROWS
Your Ladyship...Sir Alfred.
(He steps forward
and announces)
The Right Honorable, the Lady
Eve, Countess of Sidwich...
Sir Alfred McGlennan-Keith.

The CAMERA CONTINUES TO MOVE, THEN STOPS in the doorway. We see the FULL SHOT of the living room with the alcove bar in the corner. Near us stand Mr. and Mrs. Pike. For the rest there are twenty-seven people in the room, not including the servants. All heads turn and stare.

H-8 REVERSE SHOT - THE LADY EVE AND SIR ALFRED - IN THE DOORWAY

Behind them stands Burrows. Sir Alfred wears a tail coat with decorations, the Lady Eve a silver lame dress which I am baffled to describe. Around her throat she wears a pearl dog collar, below this two pearl necklaces. The little tiara gleams

H-8 (Cont'd)

in her hair. On her right wrist she wears some bracelets, in her left hand she carries a scintillating vanity-cigarette case. She looks gorgeous and she knows it. The conversation dribbles into silence.

THE LADY EVE
(With a faint smile)
Good evening.

SIR ALFRED
(Galvanized)
Hello, hello, hello.

The CAMERA PULLS BACK as Mr. and Mrs. Pike move forward.

MRS. PIKE
(Taking Eve's hand)
Welcome, my dear.

MR. PIKE
(Pumping Sir Alfred's hand)
How are you, Glenny; glad to see you, you old rascal.

SIR ALFRED
Horace, my lad! My niece, Lady Sidwich.

MR. PIKE
(Somewhat at a loss)
Well, for heaven's sake...
What a surprise...How do you do...How do I...I mean, what do I...call you?

MRS. PIKE
(Faintly embarrassed)
Well, Horace, I should think that you'd...

THE LADY EVE
(Quickly)
Please just call me Eve.

10-18-40 (Continued)

H-8 (Cont'd)

MR. PIKE
(Enthusiastically)
Well, for heaven's sake...
You're just the kind of a girl
I've been looking for...the
name is Horace.

H-9 CLOSE SHOT - MR. PIKE AND THE LADY EVE

Mr. Pike leans close.

MR. PIKE
(Confidentially)
We'll get this over quick!
Then you and I will have a
drink.

THE LADY EVE
Ripping.

MR. PIKE
(Hardly taken aback
at all)
Uh...the very word for it.
Come on.

As they move forward --

H-10 MRS. PIKE AND SIR ALFRED

MRS. PIKE
(Faintly worried)
I hope Horace doesn't frighten
her to death. How long has
she been in America?

SIR ALFRED
Three days.

MRS. PIKE
And to meet Horace right
away...
(Now she gets
a thought)
How did she come over... I
didn't know the boats were
running.

10-18-40 (Continued)

H-10 (Cont'd)

Sir Alfred clears his throat twice, looks all around, then very confidentially says:

SIR ALFRED
Battleship.

MRS. PIKE
(Round-eyed)
They sent a...
(She mouths the word "battleship")

SIR ALFRED
Oh, yes...Actually a...cruiser.

MRS. PIKE
(Raising her hand by stages)
But then she must be...very... very...

SIR ALFRED
Very.

Mrs. Pike smiles pleasantly.

H-11 MUGGSY - PEERING IN THE DOORWAY

Now he walks to the first big window of the living room and the CAMERA PANS WITH HIM. As he looks in the window --

H-12 SHOT - PAST MUGGSY

Through the window we see Mr Pike, the Lady Eve, Sir Alfred and Mrs. Pike coming slowly forward, meeting the guests. Some of the ladies try curtsies, but most of them do not. Some of the gentlemen indulge in jack-knife bows. One or two try the hand kiss. As the Lady Eve passes the window --

H-13 CLOSE SHOT - MUGGSY

His face is a poem of perplexity. Now he moves along the house, off the terrace and tries to get into a flower bed. The little wire hoops around it trip him and he takes a nice fall.

10-18-40

H-14 THE BIG LIVING ROOM WINDOW - FROM THE INTERIOR

We hear the buzz of conversation, the shaking of drinks, and some introductions of the Lady Eve. Muggsy raises up from the bottom of the window and looks into the room. He brushes himself off.

H-15 WHAT MUGGSY SEES FROM THE OUTSIDE

The introductions are almost complete now. The CAMERA DRAWS BACK, revealing Muggsy looking in. After a moment he turns and scratches his head. Now he starts out of the flower bed. We hear a grunt as he disappears PAST THE CAMERA.

H-16 LONGER SHOT OF MUGGSY - STRETCHED FLAT ON THE GROUND

He picks himself up, looks up toward the second floor and yells:

MUGGSY
Hey!

The CAMERA PANS UP and we see a window with a light in it.

MUGGSY'S VOICE
Hey, boss!

A stone bangs on the window.

H-17 CHARLES - IN HIS ROOM

He wears evening dress, minus the coat. He is looking into a microscope. A handful of pebbles rattles against the window. He looks toward the window, then gets up and crosses to it.

H-18 EXT. OF THE SECOND FLOOR

Charles appears and opens the window.

CHARLES
(Sticking his head out)
Has it started yet?

10-18-40

H-19 HIGH CAMERA SHOT - DOWN ON MUGGSY

MUGGSY
You said it.

H-20 CHARLES - IN HIS ROOM

He leans out the window in the matching position.

CHARLES
I'll be right down.

He pulls his head in, closes the window and crosses to put on his coat. The CAMERA PANS WITH HIM. He checks his tie in front of a mirror, brushes his hair a little, starts out, remembers a handkerchief, goes back and gets one, then hurries out.

H-21 THE LADY EVE MR. PIKE AND FOUR ADMIRING GENTLEMEN - AT THE BAR

In the background we see the living room and the door from the hall. Sir Alfred is holding forth to some ladies in the middle distance. The bartender is finishing six champagne cocktails.

THE LADY EVE
(In the middle of a story)
Naturally, I was frightfully anxious to see Uncle Alfred and I didn't know just where Connect-i-cut was, so I took the tube...

MR. PIKE
(To the others)
The subway.

THE LADY EVE
...and to the official I said: "Be so good as to let me off at Connect-i-cut."

The gentlemen laugh happily.

10-18-40 (Continued)

H-21 (Cont'd)

THE LADY EVE
You see, I thought we'd have the boxes sent up on a dray later that afternoon.

MR. PIKE
(After an instant's hesitation)
Trunks... on a truck.

Charles enters the room and starts wending his way toward us, shaking hands as he goes.

THE LADY EVE
So the official said: "Where did you want to get off?" and I said: "Just anywhere in Connect-i-cut."

There is laughter from the gentlemen.

THE LADY EVE
So he said: "Lady, I don't know where Connect-i-cut is but this train goes to Harlem."

There is a wild guffaw from the gentlemen.

THE LADY EVE
I don't know how he knew I was a lady.

The gentlemen slap each other on the back.

THE LADY EVE
So I said: "Isn't Connect-i-cut on your shed-ule?" And he said: "No, m'am, not if that means what I think it means."

The gentlemen holler.

THE LADY EVE
So I said: "Do you think I could do better with a tram?" and he said: "Well, you couldn't do worse," so I thanked him and returned to the street...I must say, I felt an awful fool.

10-18-40 (Continued)

H-21 (Cont'd)

A GENTLEMAN
Then, how did you get here?

THE LADY EVE
I took a taxi.

ANOTHER GENTLEMAN
From New York?

THE LADY EVE
Oh, yes.

There is a roar of laughter and Charles joins the group.

MR. PIKE
(Seeing his son)
Charlie, I want you to meet the Lady Eve Sidwich.

THE LADY EVE
(Very pleasantly)
How do you do.

MR. PIKE
(To Eve)
Go on.

THE LADY EVE
The chauffeur said it wasn't far and I said: "Veddy well..."

H-22 CLOSE SHOT - CHARLES' FACE

His jaw hangs open.

THE LADY EVE'S VOICE
"... but don't you try any hanky-panky such as going in a round-about way because I've been there many times before," and he said: "I can see that."

There is a holler from the gentlemen.

H-23 THE GROUP - INCLUDING CHARLES

THE LADY EVE
...so here I am... but I must say the city seemed enormous.

10-18-40 (Continued)

H-23 (Cont'd)

GENTLEMAN
(Pounding the bar)
At twenty cents a mile!

THE LADY EVE
(Laughing)
I must say it was an awfully good joke on Uncle Alfred...he had to be given smelling salts when he saw the meter.

She roars with laughter, and looks from one to another for approval. As her eyes come to rest on Charles, her expression changes to slight puzzlement. Now she turns to Mr. Pike.

THE LADY EVE
Isn't your son feeling well?

MR. PIKE
(Turning to Charles)
What's the matter with you?

CHARLES
(Idiotically)
Well, I uh... I mean uh.. uh...
(He stops and swallows and points vaguely toward Eve)
Did you uh... uh...

THE LADY EVE
(Courteously)
I beg your pardon?

CHARLES
What I mean to say is uh.. uh.. haven't we met?

THE LADY EVE
(Charmingly as to a child)
Of course we have... your father just introduced us.

MR. PIKE
(To his son)
Don't you feel well?

10-18-40 (Continued)

H-23 (Cont'd)

CHARLES
(Trying to laugh
it off)
Why, uh...heh-heh-heh... sure.

He looks, however, far from well.

THE LADY EVE
(Charmingly, to
cover his embarrass-
ment)
Oh, you meant had you met me before someplace?

CHARLES
Yes.

THE LADY EVE
Very probably... Now, where could it have been? Deauville?

CHARLES
No.

THE LADY EVE
Biarritz?

CHARLES
No.

THE LADY EVE
I know: Le Touquet! ... You had a mustache at the time... you tried to meet me at a dance in the casino.

CHARLES
No.

THE LADY EVE
Then, I give up.

MR. PIKE
Well, let's have a drink.

CHARLES
It couldn't have been on the S.S. "Southern Queen" between here and South America, could it?

H-23 (Cont'd)

THE LADY EVE
(Almost regretfully)
I'm afraid it wasn't... I've never been in South America.

CHARLES
(Dumbly)
You've never been in South America?

MR. PIKE
She's never been in South America.

THE LADY EVE
As a matter of fact, I've never been in North America until three days ago.

CHARLES
Oh, you haven't... then you weren't on the S.S. "Southern Queen".

MR. PIKE
What's the matter with you?

CHARLES
I, uh...
(He makes a helpless gesture)
I'm sorry.

THE LADY EVE
Were you in love with her?

This is regarded as hilariously funny by the gentlemen at the bar. They slap each other on the back.

MR. PIKE
He was in love with her but he don't remember what she looks like.

More hilarity.

THE LADY EVE
(To Charles)
Don't let them tease you... You can tell me all about her.

CHARLES
Ha.

10-18-40 (Continued)

H-23 (Cont'd)

Unfortunately, as he says this he looks like an idiot.

MR. PIKE
My son is brighter on some days than he is on others.

Charles laughs sheepishly.

MR. PIKE
(Raising his glass)
Well... I don't know what the other girl looked like, but if she was anything like you, here's to her.

H-24 THE DOORWAY - FROM THE HALL

Mr. Burrows enters.

MR. BURROWS
Dinner is served, madam.

H-25 MRS. PIKE AND SIR ALFRED IN THE MIDST OF SOME GUESTS

MRS. PIKE
(Pitching her voice over some people's heads)
Dinner, Horace.

H-26 THE GROUP - AT THE BAR

MR. PIKE
(Finishing his drink)
Come on, let's put on the feed bag.
(He extends his arm to Eve)
You take my arm and we'll fight our way through.

Eve laughs and they all start for the dining room. The CAMERA STAYS ON Charles as he slowly follows the others. In a moment we see the window through

10-18-40

(Continued)

H-26 (Cont'd)

which Muggsy is peering. Charles sees him and makes a helpless gesture. Muggsy points toward the Lady Eve. Charles replies with another helpless gesture and as he isn't watching where he's going he dives right over the end of a low sofa and with his extended hands upsets a coffee table heavily laden with cocktail glasses, appetizers, cigarette boxes and a crystal bowl of flowers. The CAMERA PANS ONTO the exiting guests as they turn in astonishment. The Lady Eve, Mr. Pike and the others hurry back and the CAMERA PANS them back to Charles.

THE LADY EVE
(Helping him to his feet)
Did you hurt yourself?

CHARLES
No, I'm fine; I uh...

MR. PIKE
(Suspiciously)
You haven't been hitting the bottle lately, have you?

THE LADY EVE
(Protectingly)
Of course, he hasn't...

She peels a caviar sandwich off his shirt front.

THE LADY EVE
Anybody's apt to trip.

MR. PIKE
Not over a sofa... that sofa's been there fifteen years and nobody ever fell over it before.

THE LADY EVE
(Cheerfully)
Well, now the ice is broken... You just go upstairs and take a bath... and I'll like you just as much as ever... au revoir.

She and the men start for the dining room and Charles starts for the door to the hall. The CAMERA TRUCKS AHEAD of him and just before he leaves the room we see them both in line. She turns and waves and enters the dining room. Charles waves, stands a moment.

10-18-40

H-27 MUGGSY - COMING INTO THE DOORWAY OF THE LIVING ROOM

MUGGSY
Why don't you watch where
you're....

H-28 CHARLES - PAST MUGGSY

CHARLES
I'm wa...

He steps forward, forgetting the step, and gets a death hold on the portieres. There is a cracking sound and, accompanied by dust and falling plaster, the whole structure comes down.

H-29 THE LADY EVE, MR. PIKE AND THE OTHERS

They turn in astonishment.

H-30 AN ANIMATED PORTIERE - ON THE FLOOR

A wild struggle is going on under it. Now an opening is found and the heads of Charles and Muggsy appear, their hair on end.

H-31 CLOSE SHOT - THE LADY EVE

She claps a handkerchief to her mouth and laughs very hard.

DISSOLVE TO:

H-32 CHARLES AND MUGGSY - IN CHARLES' ROOM

Charles has put on a clean shirt which still hangs outside his trousers. He is trying to tie a black tie and at the same time look at the police photograph Muggsy is holding.

MUGGSY
That's the same dame... she
looks the same, she walks the
same and she's tossing you just
like she did the last time.

(Continued)

10-18-40

H-32 (Cont'd)

CHARLES
She doesn't talk the same.

MUGGSY
Anybody can put on an act.
(He says a sentence in low comedy Swedish and finishes with:)
Guess who I am?

CHARLES
Weren't her eyes a little closer together?

MUGGSY
They were not... they were right where they are... on each side of her nose.

Charles takes the picture, looks at it, then hands it back silently. He puts one tail of his shirt in.

CHARLES
Why should she do it?

MUGGSY
I don't know... Maybe she wants you to fall for her again.

CHARLES
Do I look that dumb?

He sticks the other tail of his shirt in.

MUGGSY
You wouldn't be the first one. I knew a guy married the same dame three times, then turned around and married her aunt.

CHARLES
(After a pause)
No.

MUGGSY
Hunh?

CHARLES
They look too much alike....

10-18-40 (Continued)

H-32 (Cont'd)

MUGGSY
You said it. They couldn't be two Janes as.....

CHARLES
You don't understand me: They look too much alike to be the same.

MUGGSY
That's what I been telling you, they....hunh?

CHARLES
You see, if she came here with her hair dyed yellow and her eye-brows different and...

MUGGSY
(Interrupting)
What's hair to a skirt? I used to go with a little Eskimo dame and one night....

CHARLES
Yes, but she didn't dye her hair and she didn't pretend she'd never seen me before which is the first thing anybody would do. She says I look familiar..

MUGGSY
Why shouldn't you?

CHARLES
Because if I did she wouldn't admit it.... If she didn't look so exactly like the other girl I might be suspicious, but.... you see you don't understand psychology. If you wanted to pretend you were somebody else you'd glue a muff on your chin and the dog wouldn't even bark at you.

MUGGSY
(Indignantly)
You tryin' to tell me this ain't

1-18-40 (Continued)

H-32 (Cont'd)

MUGGSY (Cont'd)
the same rib was on the boat? She even wears the same perfume.

CHARLES
(Vascillating)
I don't know.

He picks up a dinner jacket and Muggsy helps him on with it. Charles walks out.

H-33 CHARLES - COMING DOWN THE STAIRS

A few steps behind, comes Muggsy. As they reach the ground floor --

MUGGSY
The same.

Charles walks away and the CAMERA PANS him to the dining room entrance.

H-34 THE DINING ROOM - PAST CHARLES

We see the sumptuously set table lit by candles. With his back to us sits Mr. Pike. The Lady Eve is on his right. At the far end of the table Mrs. Pike has Sir Alfred on her right. Mr. Burrows stands behind Mrs. Pike. Two maids and a footman are passing dishes.

THE LADY EVE
(Seeing Charles)
There he is.

Everybody turns and stares.

H-35 CHARLES - PAST THE LADY EVE AND MR. PIKE

CHARLES
(Feeling where his coat tails were before)
Had to change my coat.
(He grins and starts down the table looking for his place)

10-18-40 (Continued)

H-35 (Cont'd)

MR. PIKE
Don't knock the table over.

Charles laughs faintly and the CAMERA MOVES WITH him as he looks for his place. As he reaches the end of the table --

SIR ALFRED
(Twisting his neck around)
All right now?

CHARLES
Fine, thanks.

SIR ALFRED
It happens to the best of us, you know.
(He turns to Mrs. Pike)
I remember a night in Bombay....
Have you ever been in Bombay?
(To the lady on his right)
Have you ever been in Bombay, madam?

MRS. PIKE
(Pointing but trying not to point... to her son)
You're just there, dear.

She points four seats up on the CAMERA SIDE of the table.

THE LADY ON SIR ALFRED'S RIGHT
No, but I've been to Egypt.

CHARLES
(To his mother)
Thanks.

SIR ALFRED
Well, for that matter, I can remember a night in Egypt... I was on a Dahabia with a small party of friends....

The CAMERA MOVES WITH Charles to his place. As he sits --

10-18-40

H-36 REVERSE SHOT - CLOSE - CHARLES SITTING

He nods to the ladies on either side of him, then unfolds his napkin.

THE LADY ON HIS RIGHT
(Leaning INTO THE SHOT)
You missed some very nice soup.

CHARLES
That's too bad.

THE LADY ON HIS LEFT
(Leaning INTO THE SHOT)
The fish was a poem.

CHARLES
That's fine.

THE LADY ON HIS RIGHT
Did you hear how the Lady Eve got to this country?

CHARLES
(With vague interest)
How?

THE LADY ON HIS RIGHT
You promise not to tell a soul?

CHARLES
I won't.

THE LADY ON HIS LEFT
On a battleship!

CHARLES
Is that so?
(He leans way forward and looks down toward Eve)

The CAMERA TRAVELS DOWN the guests and comes to rest on Eve. As we reach her she leans forward, looks toward Charles, then turns to Mr. Pike.

10-18-40 (Continued)

H-36 (Cont'd)

THE LADY EVE
Do you know that I find your son very handsome?

MR. PIKE
(Astonished)
No.

THE LADY EVE
Quite.

She looks back toward Charles, smiles and waves.

H-37 CHARLES

Charles smiles, waves vaguely, then pulls his neck back. The ladies on each side of him exchange a glance.

H-38 CLOSE SHOT - A PANTRY DOOR

It opens an inch and we see an eye. It opens a little more and we see half of Muggsy's face.

H-39 MUGGSY - IN THE PANTRY - PEEKING INTO THE DINING ROOM

Suddenly he grunts and grabs his nose, then is thrown backwards as a footman comes through from the dining room with a plate.

MUGGSY
(Rubbing his nose)
Why don't you look where you're goin'?

THE FOOTMAN
Why don't you keep your nose out of other people's business?

MUGGSY
Listen, Fish-eye, for two cents...

THE FOOTMAN
Oh, pish!

He hurries OUT OF THE SHOT. Muggsy opens the door and peeks out.

10-18-40

H-40 LONG SHOT - THE DINING ROOM - CENTERING ON EVE

H-41 THE PANTRY DOOR - FROM THE DINING ROOM SIDE

We see Muggsy's eye in the crack. Suddenly the door flies open and Muggsy is reluctantly propelled into the room by the Footman bearing a platter of roast beef with gravy. Under the platter there is a cloth to prevent the man from burning his hand.

MUGGSY
Here!.... gimme that.

He snatches the cloth from under the platter, whips it over his forearm in good restaurant style and grabs the platter with both hands.

THE FOOTMAN
(Indignantly)
What are you....

MUGGSY
Come on.

He wrenches it away from him and starts for Eve's end of the table. The CAMERA PANS WITH him until it comes to rest on Mr. Burrows who sees with horror what is going on. Muggsy goes PAST THE CAMERA. Mr. Burrows looks about, then starts after Muggsy.

H-42 MR. PIKE'S END OF THE TABLE

THE LADY EVE
(Telling an anecdote)
... so the deaf man said: "What did you say?" and the other passenger said: "I hear you buried your wife."

MUGGSY
(Coming INTO THE SHOT... To Mr. Pike)
Roast beef?

He stares intently at the Lady Eve.

THE LADY EVE
(After returning his glance)
So the deaf gentleman said: "I didn't quite hear you."

10-18-40 (Continued)

H-42 (Cont'd)

MUGGSY
Roast beef?

MR. PIKE
Hunh?
(Then to Eve)
Go on.

He takes a large slice of roast beef and holds it about six inches above where his plate ought to be.

THE LADY EVE
So the other passenger said:
"I hear you buried your wife."

Having abandoned Mr. Pike, Muggsy appears on Eve's left. By now Mr. Pike has noticed the lack of the plate and is looking around to his left for Muggsy. Eve reaches for the serving knife and fork but there is none.

MUGGSY
Oh.

He gives her another look, then goes back to Mr. Pike's left, the latter, in the meanwhile, having turned to the right.

MUGGSY
Over here.

MR. PIKE
(Furiously)
What the... What do you think you're doing in the dining room?

MUGGSY
What does it look like I'm doing?

Mr. Pike puts the meat and the serving implements back on the platter.

MR. BURROWS
(Hurrying INTO THE SHOT)
There you are, sir.

10-18-40 (Continued)

H-42 (Cont'd)

He slips a plate in front of Mr. Pike.

MR. PIKE
All right.

He turns to take the meat but Muggsy has gone.

H-43 CLOSE SHOT - THE LADY EVE

THE LADY EVE
So the deaf gentleman said: "What did you say... "

She yields slightly as Muggsy forces his platter down on her right.

MUGGSY
I said, do you want some roast beef.

She turns in surprise to her right and almost rubs noses with Muggsy who gets a good look at her.

H-44 EVE, MUGGSY AND THE GENTLEMAN NEXT TO HER

THE LADY EVE
Thank you.

She reaches for the fork and spoon at the same time as the gentleman on her right who has just discovered the platter to his left. The gentleman reaches the implements first.

MUGGSY
Ladies first.

THE GENTLEMAN
(Astonished)
I'm so sorry, I thought he was passing it to me.

MUGGSY
(To Eve)
Go ahead.

With some difficulty, she helps herself. As she finishes, the gentleman reaches for the implements but does not succeed because Muggsy steps back with the platter. As the gentleman looks around helplessly --

H-45 MR. PIKE - TALKING IN BURROWS' EAR

MR. PIKE
Will you get that roughneck out of here... or do I have to?

MR. BURROWS
With enthusiasm, sir.

H-46 CHARLES - BETWEEN THE TWO LADIES

They are looking toward Eve's end of the table. Muggsy comes INTO THE SHOT and passes Charles the roast beef.

MUGGSY
(In a stage whisper)
It's the same dame. I can tell by the way...

MR. BURROWS
(Hurrying INTO THE SHOT)
I'll take over from here, Mr. Murgatroyd.

MUGGSY
You and who else?

CHARLES
(Warningly)
Cut it out, Muggsy.

MR. BURROWS
(Seizing the salver)
I said, I'll take over from here, Ambrose.

MUGGSY
Ambrose!

CHARLES
(Turning to stop this)
Cut it out, will you?

MR. BURROWS
(Threateningly)
I said...

Muggsy starts to twist the salver away from Burrows. All the gravy on it rolls slowly onto Charles' shirt front and down his sleeves. As he rises, dripping --

10-18-40

H-47 EVE AND MR. PIKE - AT THE HEAD OF THE TABLE

MR. PIKE
(Seeing Charles)
Well, I'll be.

Eve turns and they twist their heads as the unhappy Charles goes by.

THE LADY EVE
Oh, deah, again?

MR. PIKE
Put on a bathing suit.

THE LADY EVE
(Laying a restraining hand on Mr. Pike's arm)
The poor lamb.

DISSOLVE TO:

H-48 THE GUESTS - COMING INTO THE LIVING ROOM FROM THE DINING ROOM

Eve and Mr. Pike lead the way, surrounded by gentlemen of the party.

THE LADY EVE
(Concluding a story)
And then the countryman said: "But dash it all, mester, if I muss the moss I'll miss the mass ... and I've never been behind before besides."

She hollers with laughter.

THE LADY EVE
(Continuing)
It was absolutely priceless!

MR. PIKE
(Happily)
Ripping.

A GENTLEMAN
You mean, top hole.

They go PAST THE CAMERA which PANS ONTO Charles looking in from the hallway. He now wears a white dinner jacket. As he comes forward sheepishly, the CAMERA PANS IN WITH him. We see Sir Alfred coming in last from the dining room.

10-18-40 (Continued)

H-48 (Cont'd)

SIR ALFRED
(Perceiving Charles)
Ah, there you are, laddy, and very nice too.
(He admires the dinner jacket)
Did you purchase it locally?

CHARLES
It's the last one... anything happens to this I'll have to wear a bath towel.

SIR ALFRED
Don't let it depress you, laddy ... worse things happen in the best families. I remember an incident...

CHARLES
(Interrupting)
I hope your niece doesn't think I'm a half-wit.

SIR ALFRED
Oh, bumble-puppy! She's quite used to young men... falling for her!
(He laughs delightedly)
You know, I think that's quite neat... for a nobleman.

CHARLES
(Frowning)
No, it's just that this girl on the boat...

SIR ALFRED
There was a girl om a boat?

CHARLES
She looked so exactly like your niece that...

SIR ALFRED
(Violently)
SH!

He looks all around, then lays a hand on Charles' arm.

SIR ALFRED
Had she the McGlennan eyes... the cornflower blue?

CHARLES
I...I think so.

10-18-40 (Continued)

H-48 (Cont'd)

SIR ALFRED
You must never mention a word of this to a soul.

CHARLES
(Surprised)
What do you mean?

SIR ALFRED
Sh!
(He looks around again before continuing)
You are r-rattling the skeletons in our family closet.
(He looks all around before continuing)
I'm afraid you have stumbled on the sorrow of Sidwich... the secret of the century.

CHARLES
I don't quite follow...

SIR ALFRED
Sh!
(He looks all around, then indicates a window)
Meet me in yonder window embrasure... look as if you knew nothing.

Charles looks exactly like this and walks away. Sir Alfred looks around like a conspirator, then clasps his hands behind his back and follows deviously. The CAMERA TRUCKS AFTER him. He peeks into the bar where the Lady Eve is holding court over the coffee, then joins Charles in the window embrasure.

H-49 REVERSE SHOT - CHARLES AND SIR ALFRED - IN THE WINDOW EMBRASURE

We see part of the bar room and the living room beyond.

SIR ALFRED
Sh!

He looks all around, then jerks his thumb toward Eve.

SIR ALFRED
You see, the Earl was considerably older than her mamma who must never be mentioned again.

10-18-40 (Continued)

H-49 (Cont'd)

CHARLES
Oh.

SIR ALFRED
A May-November romance...even March-December...if you follow me.

CHARLES
You mean...

SIR ALFRED
Sh! She'd die of shame if she knew I told you this...except that she doesn't know it herself... hasn't a suspicion of it, in fact...
(He looks all around before continuing)
You see, into the gulf that separated this unfortunate couple... there was a coachman on the estate... a gay dog, a great hand with the horses...and the ladies...need I say more?

CHARLES
A coachman!

SIR ALFRED
A man who drives horses.

CHARLES
(Irritably)
I know what a coachman is, I just don't..

SIR ALFRED
(Raising a hand for silence)
Sh! They called him "Handsome Harry."

CHARLES
(Electrified)
Handsome Harry!

SIR ALFRED
Sh!

CHARLES
(Making an effort to keep quiet)
But, that's the father of the girl on the...

10-18-40 (Continued)

H-49 (Cont'd)

SIR ALFRED
(Waving him quiet)
Of course it is...the father of the other child...after the divorce, of course.

CHARLES
They look exactly alike.

SIR ALFRED
We must close our minds to that fact...as it brings up the dreadful and thoroughly unfounded suspicion that we must carry to our tombs, you understand...as it is absolutely untenable... that the coachman, in both instances...need I say more?
(He mops his head)

CHARLES
He did! I mean, it was! ... I mean...

SIR ALFRED
(Seizing him for silence and looking up)
Do you want to bring the walls down about our heads? Silence! To the grave!...and even beyond!
(He mops his head again)

In the background, the Lady Eve appears in the doorway from the bar.

H-50 CLOSE SHOT - EVE - IN THE DOORWAY FROM THE BAR

She steps down.

THE LADY EVE
(Pleasantly)
There you are in your nice white coat. Would you like to come and talk to me?

10-18-40

H-51 SIR ALFRED AND CHARLES

Charles comes forward and the CAMERA PANS HIM into a TWO SHOT WITH EVE.

CHARLES
(Happily)
I certainly would...and I want to apologize for seeming so clumsy tonight. I...

THE LADY EVE
(Charmingly)
Well, that's quite all right. As a matter of fact, I rather enjoyed it.

CHARLES
I'm not that way all the time.

THE LADY EVE
(Consolingly)
Of course you're not.
(She takes his arm)
Now, where shall we go?

CHARLES
(Happily)
Well, there's a conservatory...

THE LADY EVE
Jolly.

She steps forward and stops instantly.

THE LADY EVE
Oh.

CHARLES
What's the matter?

THE LADY EVE
I'm caught.

She looks around sheepishly.

H-52 INSERT - THE END OF EVE'S TRAIN UNDER A CHAIR LEG

10-18-40

H-53 EVE AND CHARLES

CHARLES
(Happily)
Well, I'm glad it isn't my fault
this time.

He moves around her and we see Burrows approaching with a large tray containing a coffee service and quantities of cups. The CAMERA PANS DOWN AND TRUCKS IN with Charles as he squats to release her train. Burrows' feet come into the shot as he waits for the young man to complete his task.

CHARLES
(Happily)
There you are...all clear.

He straightens up quickly to a resounding crash as the contents of the tray are tipped over and down on him.

H-54 EVE - TURNING SUDDENLY

She claps her hand over her mouth to stop from having hysterics.

H-55 THE MISERABLE CHARLES - NEXT TO BURROWS

He is drenched with black coffee, including his hair which hangs in wisps.

H-56 MR. PIKE - RISING FROM HIS CHAIR

MR. PIKE
(Stupefied)
Well, I'll be.

FADE OUT

END OF SEQUENCE "H"

FADE IN:

J-1 SIR ALFRED - AT THE HEAD OF HIS CHARMING BREAKFAST TABLE

SIR ALFRED
Entirely disgraceful. I've never seen such a farce in a respectable house.

J-2 EVE - LOUNGING IN A WINDOW SEAT

A cup of coffee next to her, a cigarette in her hand.

THE LADY EVE
If I didn't hate him so I would have felt sorry for him. He certainly took some nice falls... he's going to take some more too.... Do you know why he didn't recognize me?

SIR ALFRED
Yes.

THE LADY EVE
No you don't. I hardly recognized him; he seemed shorter and bonier...it's because we don't love each other any more...You see on the boat, we had an awful yen for each other, so I saw him as very tall and very handsome and he probably thought I had big melting eyes and a rosebud mouth and a figure like Miss Long Beach, the Dream of the Fleet.

SIR ALFRED
You have, for that matter, but I took the further precaution of telling him the plot of "Cecilia, or the Coachman's Daughter"...a gaslight melodrama.

THE LADY EVE
(Awe-struck)
No!

SIR ALFRED
Yes, I have to protect myself, too, you know. I have a shouting interest

10-18-40 (Continued)

J-2 (Cont'd)

SIR ALFRED (Cont'd)
around here. I fed him full of handsome coachmen, elderly Earls, young wives, and the two little girls who looked exactly alike.

LADY EVE
You mean he swallowed that?

SIR ALFRED
Like a wolf...so now that you have him, what are you going to do with him?

THE LADY EVE
(Solemnly)
I'm going to finish what I started. I'm going to dine with him, dance with him, swim with him, laugh at his jokes, canoodle with him and then one day, about six weeks from now...

A Manservant enters with an enormous box.

MANSERVANT
Some red roses for Your Ladyship.

THE LADY EVE
Who could they be from?

MANSERVANT
(Examining the card)
From Mr. Charles Pike, Your Ladyship.

THE LADY EVE
Ah, yes, the brewer's son. Just stick them in the umbrella stand, will you?

MANSERVANT
Very good, Milady.
(He exits)

THE LADY EVE
It won't take six weeks. One day, two weeks from now, we'll be riding in the hills...

10-18-40 (Continued)

J-2 (Cont'd)

SIR ALFRED
I don't think he rides.

THE LADY EVE
He'll have to learn...and the sunset will be so beautiful I'll be overcome and have to get off my horse to admire it...and as I stand there against the glory of Mother Nature the horse will steal up behind me and nuzzle my hair...AND SO WILL CHARLES, THE HEEL.

Sir Alfred looks astonished.

DISSOLVE TO:

J-3 A MAGNIFICENT SUNSET THROUGH SOME TREES

J-4 HIGH CAMERA SHOT - EVE AND CHARLES - ON HORSEBACK

They stop their horses to look. Eve gets to the ground gracefully and Charles slides down the saddle.

J-5 EVE AND HER HORSE'S HEAD - AGAINST THE SUNSET

THE LADY EVE
(Dreamily)
How too, too beautiful!

J-6 EVE - WITH CHARLES BEHIND HER

He moves between her and her horse.

THE LADY EVE
Stop that.

CHARLES
(Steamily)
Must I?

THE LADY EVE
I'm sorry...I thought it was the horse.

10-18-40 (Continued)

J-6 (Cont'd)

CHARLES
No, it was me. Eve...

THE LADY EVE
Yes, Charles?

CHARLES
I suppose you know what I'm thinking about.

THE LADY EVE
(Closing her eyes)
Possibly I have an idea.

CHARLES
The...union of two people for life...that is marriage.... shouldn't be taken lightly.

THE LADY EVE
How wise you are.

CHARLES
Men, that is lots of men, are more careful in choosing a tailor than they are in choosing a wife.

THE LADY EVE
That's probably why they look so funny.

CHARLES
(Gently)
No, dear, they're more careful in choosing a tailor than in choosing a wife.

THE LADY EVE
Oh....but not you, Charles.

CHARLES
That's right. I think if there's one time in your life to be careful...to weigh every pro and con ...it's at a time like this.

THE LADY EVE
You can't be too careful.

10-18-40 (Continued)

J-6 (Cont'd)

CHARLES
That's right. Now, you might think that having known you such a short time...

THE LADY EVE
I feel I've known you always.

CHARLES
That's the way I feel about you... I don't see you just here in front of the sunset...

Eve narrows her eyes slightly.

CHARLES
...you seem to go way back... I see you here but at the same time, further away and still further away, way, way back always...in a long place like a...like a....

THE LADY EVE
(Inspired)
Like a forest glade...

CHARLES
(Happily)
That's right...how did you guess?

THE LADY EVE
Because, that's where I see you... always...We held hands...way, way back.

CHARLES
That's remarkable. That's what you call telepathy.

THE LADY EVE
I can read many of your thoughts.

CHARLES
Then, I hardly have to tell you of the doubts I've had before I brought myself to speak like this...You see, darling, you're so beautiful, you're so fine,

10-18-40 (Continued)

J-6 (Cont'd)

CHARLES (Cont'd)
you're so...I don't deserve you.

THE LADY EVE
(Gently)
Oh, but you do, dear....if anybody ever deserved me...you do, dear...so richly.

CHARLES
(Passionately)
Eve!

THE LADY EVE
(Turning slowly)
Charles.

The horse licks his head.

DISSOLVE TO:

J-7 CLOSE SHOT - SIR ALFRED - BEHIND HIS DESK

His forehead is furrowed with worry. We hear the first momentous chord of the MUSICAL MONTAGE. As it holds a quivering note --

SIR ALFRED
(Over the music)
But you can't do that! You'll get us all in trouble! You'll jeopardize what has taken me years to build up. I'll most certainly telephone to your father...

The wild laughter of violins mocks him.

J-8 EVE - PAST SIR ALFRED

She is laughing gleefully. Now she waves her riding crop and runs out of the room.

J-9 SIR ALFRED - AT HIS DESK

He seizes a telephone.

10-18-40

J-10 CHARLES - IN HIS MOTHER'S ARMS - IN THE GREAT HALL OF THE PIKE MANSION

His father stands by, listening. Now his mother releases him and his father squeezes his hand in a grip of iron. Charles releases the hand, shakes it and sprints up the stairs. Mr. and Mrs. Pike fall into each others arms. The CAMERA PANS ONTO Muggsy who looks very sour.

J-11 SIR ALFRED - EXPOSTULATING ON THE TELEPHONE

J-12 COL. HARRINGTON - IN THE NEW YORK APARTMENT

He seems to say: "What?" Gerald listens with his mouth open.

J-13 SIR ALFRED - AT THE TELEPHONE

He hangs up and mops his brow.

DISSOLVE TO:

J-14 THE CHEF - IN THE KITCHEN OF THE PIKE MANSION

He is decorating the first great layer of the wedding cake, about the size of a millstone.

J-15 SOME OF THE PIKE'S SERVANTS - POLISHING SILVER

J-16 EVE - CONSERVATORY PIKE MANSION (PICKUP)

She is getting the first fitting on the wedding dress.

J-17 CHARLES - IN CORNER OF HIS ROOM (PICKUP)

He is being fitted into a cutaway. The CAMERA PANS ONTO Mr. Pike. He is being fitted into a cutaway. The CAMERA PANS ONTO Sir Alfred. He is being fitted into a cutaway and looks very nervous about it. The CAMERA PANS ONTO Burrows being fitted into a dress suit. The CAMERA PANS ONTO Muggsy. He is being fitted into a very stylish French chauffeur's uniform with a frogged tunic.

10-18-40 (Continued)

J-18 THE CHEF - IN THE KITCHEN OF THE PIKE MANSION (PICKUP)

He is decorating the second layer of the wedding cake. Mr. Burrows tries to give him some advice and the Chef threatens him with the pastry gun.

J-19 MRS. PIKE - IN THE CONSERVATORY (PICKUP)

She is being fitted to a lovely afternoon gown. The CAMERA PANS OVER ONTO Gertrude and Martha, the maids, being fitted to new uniforms.

J-20 THE CHEF - WORKING ON ANOTHER LEVEL OF THE WEDDING CAKE

J-21 CHARLES AND MR. PIKE - AND A JEWELER - IN PIKE HALL (PICKUP)

With his hands, Mr. Pike motions for something bigger.

J-22 EVE - IN CONSERVATORY (PICKUP)

She is trying on a traveling outfit.

J-23 THE CHEF - ON A STEPLADDER

He is putting the top on the wedding cake.

J-24 FULL SHOT - THE KITCHEN - SLOW CRANKED

The servants are flying in all directions, making last moment preparations.

J-25 THE MAIN HALL OF THE PIKE MANSION

Furniture and flowers are flying around in all directions. UNDERCRANKED.

J-26 SIR ALFRED

Dressed for the wedding. He stands in front of a cellaret. He drinks a powerful drink to fortify himself.

10-18-40

J-27 THE PIKE LIVING ROOM ARRANGED FOR THE WEDDING

The guests are ranged on both sides. Charles and his father stand near the CAMERA. The wedding march thunders out. All heads turn and Eve appears in the doorway on the arm of Sir Alfred. Eve comes straight toward us. Charles moves closer. As we get two big heads of them, Eve turns and gives Charles a peculiar smile. The music reaches a climax.

DISSOLVE TO:

J-28 EXT. OF THE PIKE MANSION - FROM BEYOND MUGGSY - AT THE WHEEL OF THE CAR

The guests are ranged inside and outside the house. Now there is excitement and they start throwing rice as Eve and Charles appear in traveling clothes. They jump into the car, slam the door and the car PULLS OUT OF THE SHOT to the tune of tin cans tied to the rear bumper.

DISSOLVE TO:

J-29 COL. HARRINGTON AND GERALD - IN THE NEW YORK APARTMENT

Col. Harrington is at the telephone.

COL. HARRINGTON
(Into the telephone)
Did she look pretty...she did, hunh? Well... thanks, Pearlie.

He hangs up. Now he gets up and addresses Gerald.

COL. HARRINGTON
Very depressing to have your daughter married and not be there.

GERALD
Especially under an assumed name. By the way, is that legal?

10-18-40 (Continued)

J-29 (Cont'd)

COL. HARRINGTON
Seems to be quite legal...women change their names so much anyway, it doesn't seem to matter... But, why did she do it?

GERALD
Maybe to teach him a lesson.

COL. HARRINGTON
How? All she said is: "You'll see," and "Wait till the time comes," and "It won't be long now," and now she's honeymooning on a train with a man she hates.

GERALD
Maybe she's going to shoot him.

COL. HARRINGTON
She's afraid of guns.

GERALD
Maybe she's going to push him out of the window.

Col. Harrington stops for a moment in thought, then relaxes.

COL. HARRINGTON
You can't open a window on a train.

DISSOLVE TO:

J-30 RAILS STRETCHING AWAY FROM US (NIGHT)

The CAMERA is just safely TO ONESIDE of where the train will pass. Clouds are running across the face of the moon and we see an occasional lightning flash. The streamlined train appears in the distance and thunders PAST US. The CAMERA TURNS UP to the windows.

DISSOLVE TO:

J-31 THE PASSING CARS

10-18-40

J-32 CHARLES - IN HIS STATEROOM

He whistles a little as he ties his dressing gown around him, then goes to the communicating door and knocks.

J-33 EVE - AT A DRESSING TABLE IN HER STATEROOM

This is the stateroom of all staterooms. It is necessarily small, but oh my! Terrific is an understatement. The rails are singing beneath us and we can almost smell, in fact we can smell, the perfume that Eve is squirting on herself. Our senses reel as we see her bridal negligee. She turns toward the door in answer to the knock, gives it one long level look, then smiles like a leopardess and almost purrs.

THE LADY EVE
Come in, dear.

The CAMERA PANS OVER TO the door. Charles enters, somewhat shyly, closes the door after him, then crosses to Eve who rises to meet him. She takes his hands.

CHARLES
(Looking around)
I must say Father picked out a swell compartment. You've got to admit that for a brewer he does things nicely.

THE LADY EVE
It's very beautiful.

She shakes her head, then starts to laugh.

CHARLES
What are you laughing about?

THE LADY EVE
Oh, it's nothing... It's just that it's so different it reminds me of that other time.

10-18-40 (Continued)

J-33 (Cont'd)

CHARLES
(Amiably)
What time was that?

He laughs slightly, wishing to join in the fun. Eve starts laughing so hard that she braces herself against the partition, then sits on the bed.

THE LADY EVE
I must be a little bit hysterical. We didn't have any money so we went third class... and there was a farmer on the opposite bench with a cheese on his lap... Haven't you ever noticed I never eat cheese?... It was very unromantic.

She laughs so hard she bends over.

CHARLES
(Amiably)
But, where were you going?

THE LADY EVE
We eloped.

CHARLES
(With a trifle less smile)
Who?

THE LADY EVE
Me.

Upon seeing his face she becomes serious at once.

THE LADY EVE
It was really nothing, darling...I was only sixteen at the time. You know how romantic young girls are... It wasn't of the slightest importance, I assure you. I'm

10-18-40 (Continued)

J-33 (Cont'd)

THE LADY EVE (Cont'd)
sorry I mentioned it; now, let's pretend I didn't; kiss me, and that's the end of it.

Charles smiles a faint smile and they peck each other on the lips.

THE LADY EVE
Now it's all finished, isn't it?

CHARLES
But, who did you elope with?

THE LADY EVE
(Distressed)
Oh, now I've planted a seed in your mind...Are you sure you want to know? Why don't we just forget the whole thing?

CHARLES
(A little more firmly)
Who was it.

THE LADY EVE
(After a little pause)
Angus.

CHARLES
Angus?

THE LADY EVE
(Reluctantly)
I assure you he was no one of the slightest importance, darling. What a way to spend a wedding night! He was just a groom on Father's estate.

CHARLES
(As if he had swallowed vitriol)
A groom!

THE LADY EVE
Not really the groom, of course. He just put on the groom's uniform on his day off and then he'd be the groom that day...the rest of the time he was the stable boy.

CHARLES
The stable boy!

THE LADY EVE
The boy who cleans up the stable.... Oh, you mean you don't think much

10-18-40 (Continued)

J-33 (Cont'd)

THE LADY EVE
of my choice...but he didn't look so bad in the groom's uniform, with the little tight pants and the boots with the yellow tops and the little fat silk hat. Don't you think they're cute?

CHARLES
(Emphatically)
I do not!

THE LADY EVE
(Ruefully)
Now you're upset. I never know when to keep my mouth closed. I was always taught to be frank and honest... It was really nothing, dear..nothing at all... We ran away but they caught us and brought us back, and that's all there was to it...except they discharged him.

CHARLES
(With conviction)
Good!

Eve shrugs as if she thinks the punishment was rather severe.

CHARLES
And when they brought you back it was before nightfall, I trust.

THE LADY EVE
(Round-eyed)
Oh, no...

CHARLES
You were out all night?

THE LADY EVE
(Almost on the verge of tears)
It took them weeks to find us, darling. You see, we'd make up different names at the different inns we stayed at.

She starts to giggle.

THE LADY EVE
You'd die at some of the names we thought of. I remember....

10-18-40 (Continued)

J-33 (Cont'd)

CHARLES
(Interrupting)
Yes, I'm sure I would.

THE LADY EVE
(As sweet as molasses)
Now you're all upset.

She clasps her hands and holds them between her knees. She steals a glance at him then looks away.

J-34 THE NIGHT SKY

Lightning flashes and we hear the rumble of thunder.

J-35 THE EXTERIOR OF THE COMPARTMENT

Raindrops appear on the window.

J-36 EVE AND CHARLES - IN THE COMPARTMENT

Eve is looking up toward the thunder but Charles sits stationary, like Rodin's Thinker. She steals a look at him, then looks away again. We hear the clickety-clack of the rail joints for a while.

CHARLES
(Suddenly and in a stern croak)
Eve!

THE LADY EVE
(Startled)
Yes, darling.

CHARLES
(Nobly, in a voice which gets gentler and gentler)
If there is one thing that distinguishes a man from a beast, it is the ability to understand.... and understanding, forgive.
(He pauses and Eve steals a look at him)
Surely the qualities of mercy, understanding and sweet forgiveness....

His voice trails off so that Eve doesn't hear the last words.

THE LADY EVE
(Leaning forward)
Sweet what?

10-18-40 (Continued)

J-36 (Cont'd)

CHARLES
(Yelling at her savagely)
SWEET FORGIVENESS!

THE LADY EVE
Oh.
(She looks down
at her knees)

Charles glares at her for a moment while recapturing his qualities of deep understanding and sweet mercy.

CHARLES
(As noble as possible)
I won't conceal from you that I wish this hadn't happened but it has... and so it has. A girl of sixteen is practically an idiot anyway, so I can't very well blame you now for something that was practically done by somebody else.
(He clears his throat)
I want to thank you for being so frank with me... The name of Angus will never cross my lips again and I hope that you will do likewise. Now, let's smile and be as we were.

With a superhuman effort he turns to her and smiles like a gargoyle. Eve takes his hand and pets it.

THE LADY EVE
I knew you'd be that way... I knew it the first moment I saw you standing beside me. I knew you'd be both husband and father to me. I knew I could trust you and confide in you... I suppose that's why I fell in love with you.

CHARLES
Thank you.

THE LADY EVE
(In a small voice,
looking away)
I wonder if now would be the time to tell you about Herman?

CHARLES
(Electrified)
Herman! Who was Herman?

Eve gives him a frightened look before getting ready to begin.

10-18-40

J-37 THE ENTRANCE TO A RAILWAY TUNNEL - (NIGHT)

On the side of the entrance an antique sign reads:

"PULL IN YOUR HEAD -
WE'RE COMING TO A TUNNEL"

With a loud shriek the train roars into the tunnel, It is raining.

DISSOLVE TO:

J-38 THE EXIT OF THE TUNNEL - HIGH CAMERA SHOT

The train roars out PAST US.

J-39 INT. OF THE SWAYING COMPARTMENT

CHARLES
(Outraged)
Vernon! I thought you said Herman!

THE LADY EVE
(Looking away)
Vernon was Herman's friend.

CHARLES
(To no one in particular)
What a friend!

J-40 THE NIGHT SKY

We see some violent flashes of lightning.

J-41 A RAILWAY BRIDGE

The train roars TOWARD US.

J-42 EXT. OF THE CAR

Eve rolls up the curtain to see what the noise is. Charles stands behind her, apparently yelling questions.

J-43 INT. OF THE CAR

THE LADY EVE
(Turning from the window)
What did you say, dear?

CHARLES
I said, now do you mean Hubert or Herbert?

10-18-40

(Continued)

J-43 (Cont'd)

THE LADY EVE
They were John's twin cousins.

CHARLES
John's! Who was John?

Eve clutches her head.

J-44 EXT. OF THE TRAIN

It is flashing by us. As it moves away the CAMERA PANS WITH it. It disappears into the distance.

J-45 A VERY SMALL COUNTRY STATION - (NIGHT)

This can also be a watertower. It is raining cats and dogs. The train is squeaking to a stop.

J-46 LONG SHOT - AT A CAR

The door flies open and a suitcase is pitched out into the mud. It is followed by a second one, and a third one which bursts open, scattering its contents in all directions. We hear the locomotive whistle, and the train starts to move.

J-47 CLOSE SHOT - THE DOOR OF THE CAR

Charles appears in dressing gown and pajamas, a hat on his head and his pants hanging over his arm. His dressing gown catches on something which delays him for a moment. Now he leaps clear, slips and sits down in the mud.

J-48 MEDIUM CLOSE SHOT - EVE - IN THE COMPARTMENT

She watches out of the window for a while, then lowers the shade. She is neither laughing nor triumphant. Rather forlornly she sits by the window.

FADE OUT.

END OF SEQUENCE "J"

10-18-40

SEQUENCE "K"

FADE IN:

K-1 MR. PIKE'S OFFICE - IN THE BRIDGEFIELD BREWING COMPANY - (NIGHT)

This is somewhat oaky and Germanic and suggests the lair of a beer baron. Through a window we see part of the brewery. Mr. Pike is at his desk, watching a lawyer at the telephone. This lawyer is watched by two other lawyers. Two more lawyers hold a conference in the background. Charles stands unhappily near the desk.

LAWYER AT TELEPHONE
Well, you can give her a message, can't you?

MR. PIKE
Raise it fifty.

One of the two lawyers holding the conference in the background leaps forward.

THE LAWYER
Don't be too hasty.

MR. PIKE
(Roughly)
Lay off.
(Then to the lawyer at the telephone)
You tell her...

LAWYER AT TELEPHONE
Our client has authorized us....

He is apparently shut off by a stream of conversation.

LAWYER AT TELEPHONE
(Indignantly)
But, that's unheard of... that's what lawyers are for...

He reacts unpleasantly to something, then holds his hand over the phone.

LAWYER AT TELEPHONE
He says...

MR. PIKE
Who says?

LAWYER AT TELEPHONE
I don't know. I naturally presumed it was her lawyer, but he says she says she won't have anything to do with lawyers.

10-18-40

(Continued)

K-1 (Cont'd)

A LAWYER
But, that's entirely irregular.

MR. PIKE
Well...it's a thought.

K-2 EVE, HER FATHER AND GERALD - IN THE NEW YORK APARTMENT

In the BACKGROUND we see Sir Alfred at the telephone.

THE LADY EVE
I tell you I won't see any lawyer.

COL. HARRINGTON
But these things are always handled by lawyers.

THE LADY EVE
Well, this is one time it isn't going to be. This is entirely between....my husband and myself.

COL. HARRINGTON
What's the matter with you? They want to make a settlement. They'll give you half when you leave for Reno and the balance at the end of six weeks...name your own price. For once that we have a chance to make some honest money...

THE LADY EVE
Tell them to go peel an eel.

Her father and Gerald exchange a look.

COL. HARRINGTON
I don't think you understand the beauty of your situation... You have a royal flush.

GERALD
You have him right by the ears.

COL. HARRINGTON
You know, I had nothing to do with this arrangement, but now that you're in it you might as well...

Eve gets up, crosses to the telephone held by Sir Alfred and says:

K-2 (Cont'd)

THE LADY EVE
(Into the telephone)
Will you let me speak with Mr. Pike, please?

K-3 MR. PIKE'S OFFICE IN BRIDGEFIELD

LAWYER AT TELEPHONE
(Holding his hand over the tlephone; excitedly)
She's on the phone...she wants to talk to Mr. Pike.

A LAWYER IN THE BACKGROUND
We can't allow that...that's entirely irregular.

MR. PIKE
(Roughly)
Shut up!

Now he turns to his son.

MR. PIKE
Will ,ou talk to her?

CHARLES
(Violently)
I'll rot before I'll talk to her.

Mr. Pike reaches for the phone.

THE LAWYER IN THE BACKGROUND
Mr. Pike, I advise you against...

MR. PIKE
(Ignoring him - into telephone)
Hello, Eve... this is Horace talking.

K-4 EVE - AT THE TELEPHONE

THE LADY EVE
Hello, darling... I'm awfully sorry about the trouble I've made you all... I thought I had a reason, but now...
(Her lips tremble as she pauses before continuing)

K-4 (Cont'd)

THE LADY EVE (Cont'd)
I just wanted to tell you: I won't see any lawyers because there's nothing to see them about... I don't want any money... I don't want any anything... He can have back his jewelry... and anything else there is... and I'll go to Reno at my own expense... I think that's only fair... There's only one thing I want: I want to see him first and I want him to ask me... to be free. That's all... no money, no nothing, only he has to come here to ask me... because I have something to tell him... before we part.

She lowers her eyes and a big tear rolls down her cheek.

K-5 MR. PIKE - AT THE TELEPHONE

MR. PIKE
Just a minute.
(He puts his hand over the receiver; to his son)
All she wants is for you to go to New York and ask her.

THE LAWYER
It's a trick.

MR. PIKE
Will you shut up!
(Then to his son)
That's all she wants. Now, what time can you...

CHARLES
Oh, it is, is it? Well, you tell her that if she waits till I ask her anything she'll wait till Havana freezes over. And I'll tell you something else that you can tell her.

A LAWYER
Quite right.

MR. PIKE
(Into the telephone)
I'll have to call you back, Eve... He stepped out of the office for a minute; I'll call you back.

10-18-40 (Continued)

K-5 (Cont'd)

MR. PIKE (Cont'd)
(Now he turns to his son)
Now, listen, you numbskull....

CHARLES
Go ahead and talk... I'm listening.

DISSOLVE TO:

K-6 EVE - STANDING IN FRONT OF A WINDOW - IN THE NEW YORK APARTMENT

Behind her we see the Manhattan night skyline. In different seats in the room sit her father, Sir Alfred and Gerald looking very glum. Suddenly the phone rings. Eve turns and runs to it. The CAMERA PANS WITH her.

THE LADY EVE
(Hopefully)
Hello...Yes, Horace.

K-7 MR. PIKE - AT THE TELEPHONE

His lawyers stand in the BACKGROUND but there is no sign of Charles.

MR. PIKE
I'm sorry, Eve, he won't do it... I thought it was a pretty fair offer... As a matter of fact, I think you're a sucker to make it.

One of his lawyers clutches his head in horror.

MR. PIKE (Continuing)
But he won't do it... He seemed very bitter... I'm sorry...

K-8 EVE - AT THE TELEPHONE

THE LADY EVE
(Distressed)
Let me talk to him, please, Horace.

K-9 MR. PIKE - AT THE TELEPHONE

MR. PIKE
I don't think he'd talk to you, Eve, and anyway he's gone to say good-bye to his mother.

10-18-40

K-10 EVE - AT THE TELEPHONE

THE LADY EVE
Oh.
(Suddenly sitting up)
Where's he going?...............
WHAT?

She turns around and looks at the clock, then hurries to her feet. She finishes in a very small voice.

THE LADY EVE
Thank you, Horace.

She hangs up, then holds her hand over her mouth for a moment.

DISSOLVE TO:

K-11 LONG SHOT - THE S. S. SOUTHERN QUEEN LEAVING MANHATTAN - (NIGHT)

DISSOLVE TO:

K-12 A LONG CORRIDOR OF THE SHIP

Charles appears in a lounge suit, slams his cabin door after him, walks to the corner NEAR US and starts up the steps. The CAMERA PANS WITH him.

K-13 THE ENTRANCE TO THE SMOKING ROOM

The CAMERA PANS Charles into the room. As he gets squarely in front of us he trips and the CAMERA FLIES a few feet with him as he regains his balance and turns indignantly.

K-14 JEAN AND COL. HARRINGTON - ON A BANQUETTE

JEAN
(Examining her shoe)
Why don't you look where you're...

Now a look of astonishment comes across her face.

JEAN
Hello, Hopsie.

COL. HARRINGTON
(Sourly)
Good evening.

10-18-40

K-15 CHARLES

CHARLES
(Stupefied)
Hopsie!

He comes forward a few feet.

CHARLES
(Continuing)
Hopsie!

The CAMERA PANS him INTO THE SHOT with them.

CHARLES
Jean!

JEAN
(Her eyes wet with tears)
Hello, Hopsie.

He crushes her mouth to his. As she relaxes in his arms Colonel Harrington looks around uneasily.

K-16 A GROUP IN THE ROOM - LOOKING ON

K-17 ANOTHER GROUP IN THE ROOM - LOOKING ON

K-18 A THIRD GROUP IN THE ROOM - LOOKING ON

They begin to pound on the table with their glasses.

K-19 JEAN, CHARLES AND COLONEL HARRINGTON

CHARLES
(Separating from Jean)
I'm sorry... but if you knew... what it means to me... to find you. Can we go to your cabin or some place?

COL. HARRINGTON
(Severely)
Now, just a minute.

CHARLES
(Seizing his hand and pumping it up and down)
I'm delighted to see you, Colonel... We must play cards this trip... lots of cards.

10-18-40

(Continued)

K-19 (Cont'd)

CHARLES (Cont'd)
(He waves to a steward)
Some champagne for the Colonel.
(Then to Jean)
Come on.

They hurry out of the smoking room.

K-20 ONE OF THE GROUPS

THE LADY
(Shocked)
That is probably one of the most scandalous meetings I've ever seen anywhere.

HER HUSBAND
(To a Steward)
What kind of a boat is this?

K-21 THE STAIRS LEADING DOWN TO JEAN'S DECK

Jean pauses on the last step.

JEAN
You really haven't the right to drag me off like this, Hopsie.

He kisses her again. An old lady and an old gentleman come around from a corridor and stop in amazement.

THE OLD LADY
Are you sure we're on the right boat, Sylvester?

Charles and Jean spring to life. He puts his arm around her and they hurry down the hall.

K-22 INT. OF JEAN'S CABIN

It is dark. The door opens and Charles and Jean step inside. Once more they kiss passionately.

JEAN
(Fighting for breath)
Why didn't you take me in your arms that day in the bank... Why did you let me go? Why did we have to go through all this nonsense? Don't you know you're the only man I ever loved, you big fathead? Don't you

K-22 (Cont'd)

JEAN (Cont'd)
know I couldn't look at another man if I wanted to? Don't you know I waited all my life for you... and then talked too much... you big mug.

CHARLES
Will you forgive me?

JEAN
For what? Oh, you mean...on the boat...the question is, will you forgive me.

CHARLES
What for?

JEAN
Oh, you still don't understand.

CHARLES
I don't want to understand...I don't want to know...Whatever it is, keep it to yourself. All I know is that I adore you, that I'll never leave you again, we'll work it out somehow...and that...I have no right to be in your cabin.

JEAN
Why?

CHARLES
Because I'm married.

JEAN
(Softly)
But so am I, darling, so am I.

She pushes the door closed. After four seconds it opens stealthily and Muggsy flattens out through it. He closes the door very softly. He looks straight INTO THE CAMERA.

MUGGSY
Positively, the same dame.

FADE OUT:

THE END

10-18-40

Sullivan's Travels

Sturges finished shooting *The Lady Eve* in late November 1940. According to James Curtis, Sturges was apprehensive about the film's reception, feeling perhaps, after the unqualified raves for *The Great McGinty* and *Christmas in July*, that critics would not allow him a third success in a row, particularly for a film like *The Lady Eve*, which was "simply an amusing story."[1] *Eve* eventually earned Sturges the best reviews of his career, but he may have considered what to do next amid worries about its likely reception.

Paramount owed Sturges to Darryl Zanuck of Twentieth Century–Fox for one film; this, plus a small sum of money, had been the trade for lending Fox star Henry Fonda for *The Lady Eve*. After finishing *Eve*, Sturges sent Zanuck his script for *Song of Joy*, the Hollywood satire that he had conceived and written around the time that he worked on *Diamond Jim* (1935) and a number of lesser projects at Universal. At that time Universal had needed a film about a foreign opera singer, which was to star Marta Eggerth, a Hungarian singer who had made several films in Europe. Sturges proposed a film about this situation to Eddie Sutherland, the director of *Diamond Jim*.

The only record of *Song of Joy* in the Sturges archive is an undated, double-spaced, nineteen-page prose treatment of the film and three pieces of correspondence concerning it. The treatment begins backstage at the Paris Opera House at the end of a production of *Faust*. The star, Lilli Pogany, hurries off-stage and races with her entourage to catch a plane that will take them to Hollywood. The script then cuts to Adolph Apex, head of the Apex Film Company, who is told that a famous opera star, Miss Lilli Pogany, has arrived at the studio. Hoping to get rid of her, he orders a tour, lunch, and some flowers, then discovers that she is there to make a film under a contract that pays her $19,000 a week, starting immediately. Because she is singing in four weeks at La Scala, the film has to be made in one month. Apex rails at his subordinates for allowing such a situation, but it is soon disclosed that Apex himself hired Pogany and that, further, he has no script. These scenes launch the film's lampoon of yes-men and incompetent directors, writers, and producers bumbling to make a film from scratch in four weeks.

Next there is a cut from Apex's office to a Pennsylvania Dutch village, whose quaint lifestyle is lovingly rendered until the entrance of a Hollywood crew makes clear that this is a movie within a movie. "What comes next?" asks Apex. "This is as far as I've gone," says the writer. Later it is decided that Lilli is to sing "Ave Maria"; which one, she asks—there are thirty-two versions. "We want the latest one," says Apex.

Alternating with the filmmaking scenes are scenes between Lilli and a young man. She is reading an English conversation book in her dressing room and asks for the help of a personable young studio employee she sees outside her window. She refers several times to a "gwat," which turns out to be "goat." He asks her what Pogany is like.

An Apex conference decides that Lilli will sing "Blue Danube" even though, it is objected, it is not from an opera. Apex becomes very interested in Lilli's education as an opera singer, wanting to know details. Meanwhile, Lilli and the young man go out for dinner—she hides her Mercedes. They go to a cafeteria and he takes both checks. She insists on paying her own check and gives the cashier a fifty-dollar bill; the cashier gives her a dirty look "and a bale of change like a cabbage." She takes the young man to a record store, where she records a song and gives it to him. A record agent happens to be there and wants to take the record and sign her; she says she is just an "extra girl" and deliberately drops the record. At the agent's insistence, she makes another record, this one very bad, and thereby gets rid of him. She and the young man go to a movie, where they see *One Night of Love, One Heavenly Night,* and *It Happened One Night.* (Next week's show will be *The Night Was Made for Love, Night After Night,* and *What a Night.*) The young man insists on taking her home; she tries to get away from him so he will not find out who she is; she finally goes into a house to escape him and waves from the second floor—a sign outside reveals that the house is a mortuary.

On the set, the director tells Lilli she will sing "Blue Danube," someone else suggests she sing "Dixie," someone else that she not sing at all, but dance. The director prevails and says that "she sits in something with somebody" as she sings "Blue Danube"; Lilli sings it then and there, without any scene-setting. In the next scene, Lilli makes Hungarian goulash for the young man, who, however, angers her by putting down actresses in general and opera singers in particular. They fight, he goes, and Lilli ends up eating haute cuisine with her entourage.

The young man is a songwriter and has written "Song of Joy," which, of course, Lilli eventually sings. Apex fires the young man, however, not for writing songs to an extra girl on his time, but for writing a noncommercial song to an extra girl on his time. Later Lilli goes looking for the young man and finds that he is not in the office he shares with several other young composers. Later still, the young man looks for Lilli as the extra girls leave for the day. Just then Lilli drives by in her Mercedes looking the other way; they do not see each other. (This recalls the ending of Chaplin's *A Woman of Paris* [1923].)

Eddie Sutherland reacted to Sturges's script in tones of dread worthy of the Hollywood Chamber of Commerce. In a November 7, 1935, letter written to Universal's Carl Laemmle, Sr., Fred S. Meyer, Paul Kohner, and Sturges, he said:

When Mr. Sturgis [*sic*] told me the story it sounded entirely different than it does in black and white. I feel without question that we are on the wrong track, and although naturally being under contract, I do not refuse to go ahead with it, I am dreadfully afraid of making a five or six hundred thousand dollar failure for Universal. I am sure that making fun of producers, writers, etc. is not entertainment. I also think, after seeing it on paper, that the situation where the girl, a big star, is not recognized by the boy does not hold water. . . .

In conclusion . . . THIS seems to me a DANGEROUS, EXPENSIVE experiment and one that will unquestionably reflect on our taste, due to such things as stressing the throwing away of money by producers, the over-paying of stars by companies—in fact, it attempts to point out specifically that we are all inefficient in our jobs. Such is not the case, and not only do I feel we would fail to entertain an audience with this, but am sure we would make enemies of all the other motion picture companies and producers.

Sturges responded in a November 8 letter to Laemmle in which he offers his "unsolicited opinion about the matter":

"Song of Joy," if given any sort of chance, should be one of the outstanding musical pictures of the year. It is fresh in concept, contains two of the most beautiful musical production numbers ever put into a picture, and cannot fail, with the assistance of the charming Miss Eggereth, to furnish thorough satisfaction and pleasure to those who see it. [Sturges later comments: "that she is of the same opinion, I mention in passing."]

. . . in "Song of Joy" the humor is based upon the predicament in which find themselves some perfectly normal business men. It is my belief that the Motion Picture Industry is sufficiently well established and sufficiently dignified to be able to withstand some "spoofing." Without fear of permanent, or even temporary damage, professors tell jokes on professors, doctors are most fond of doctor's stories, hardware men laugh about other hardware men. This is healthy.

Needless to say, Sturges lost the battle in 1935, and he lost it again in 1941, which was, as far as *Song of Joy* was concerned, loss of the war itself.[2] On January 20, 1941, Zanuck wrote to Sturges's agent, Frank Orsatti, who had evidently sent him a script called *Santa Ana* as well as Sturges's *Song of Joy:*

I finally had a chance to read *Santa Ana* and *Song of Joy. Santa Ana* is, of course, impossible to do at this time. The Government would not permit us to do it. Right now everyone is breaking their backs to appease Mexico, Central and South America. We are crossing out anything that might even remotely offend the people of these nations, and you would be surprised how easily they can be offended even by a musical picture. The story of *Santa Ana* would raise bloody hell and the State Department would throw the Alamo monument at us if we even attempted it.

The other story—*Song of Joy*—is, I am sure, something out of Preston's trunk. It is not bad and probably with some work on it, it could be whipped into shape; but with a man who is as clever as he is, it seems a shame not to settle down on something completely original and new. He has made a success by tackling unique subjects and handling them in a smart, modern vein. I believe that the handicaps on this story, *Song of Joy,* are too heavy.

I told you that in the near future I will submit to him two or three stories that I think he can knock the hell out of.

Zanuck did not know that Sturges's three films to date had all been "trunk items" or that Sturges had in each case so thoroughly overhauled the earlier project as to transform it. What Sturges would have done with *Song of Joy* is a tantalizing possibility. The material with Lilli and the young man is, as it stands, simply terrible. Its only (dubious) merit is that it anticipates all those films of the forties that used real musical figures like Lauritz Melchior and Jose Iturbi, who was in real life a friend of Sturges. (*Anchors Aweigh* [1945], the best of these films, is the exception which proves the rule.) But Sturges never let even good material go unimproved, so we do not know what he would have done with the romance in *Song of Joy.*

The backlot Hollywood scenes, however, are something else. Scenes that begin as though "real" only to be interrupted and revealed as movie scenes; scenes that abort because the writer has got no further than what we have seen, but then continue as arguments about how to continue—these are fraught with "metafilmic" and "self-reflexive" possibilities beyond anything achieved in *Sullivan's Travels. Song of Joy*'s view of Hollywood is also, it seems safe to say, far more savage than the finally rather benevolent view of the later film. These are somewhat idle speculations, however, since it is impossible to know how Sturges would have transformed his six-year-old material under the conditions of imminent production, which always seemed to galvanize him and bring out his best.

What is beyond all doubt is that Zanuck closed the lid on Sturges's trunk once and for all. Whatever Sturges did from now on, *The Great Moment* (1944) aside, was indeed "something completely original and new"—there were no more bankable materials from the past for Sturges to adapt. We can see in retrospect what was not apparent at the time—that this imposed mandate implied nothing less than a revolution in Sturges's work methods and led, even less realized at the time, to a new kind of comic screenplay and film.

Perhaps determined to make a satire on Hollywood, Sturges began writing the script of *Sullivan's Travels* on February 3, 1941. The commercial and critical success of *The Lady Eve,* released later that month, put Sturges in a stronger position than he had ever enjoyed before, able—within the limits of censorship and commerce—to make whatever he wanted to make. This situation was not immediately affected by the change in the Paramount hierarchy that was to prove momentous for Sturges in the long run; William LeBaron left Paramount for Fox in February 1941 and was quickly replaced by B. G. "Buddy" DeSylva. In March 1941, as a favor to DeSylva, Sturges wrote and directed a new ending for *New York Town* (1941), a Paramount film that was in trouble.

There are only two versions of *Sullivan's Travels* in the Sturges archive, but there are three scripts with different cover pages on them: one dated February 3, 1941; another dated April 22, 1941; and the May 3, 1941, script, which is printed below. Work on the composition of the February 3 script in fact extended from February 3 to April 21, 1941. Sturges apparently made up the February 3 cover page on the day that he began *Sullivan's Travels* and left it in place when he had finished it. The last page of the February 3 script contains this characteristic Sturges note:

Finished:
April 21, 1941
12:25 A.M.
Preston Sturges—spoke
Edwin Gilette—wrote
Ernst Laemmle—assisted

The April 22 script was obviously typed the next day, probably at the studio, from the work completed the night before. It differs from the February 3 script only in its cover page, the dating and numbering of its pages, and its omission of the final note. The individual pages of the February 3 script are not dated; the first page of each sequence, or part of a sequence, is dated by its starting date, and sequences revised later bear the date of revision as well as the original date of writing. The April 22 script, unlike that of February 3, is an "official" studio script, like those printed in this volume. The April 22, 1941, date appears uniformly at the bottom of every page, but the script also retains from the February 3 script the beginning date of work on each sequence. The May 3 script, the last before shooting, embodies minor additional changes.

The internal markings of the February 3 script corroborate what we know from external evidence: that Sturges did not work continuously on *Sullivan's Travels* from February 3 to April 21 but was subject to a variety of interruptions, particularly in late February and March. Louise was five months pregnant in February 1941, and Sturges made elaborate plans for the baby's birth, converting an upstairs room into a nursery and taking great care of Louise. At the same time Sturges's restaurant, The Players, which had lost money in its first year, was in the process of being remodeled. February also marked the turnover of Paramount production from LeBaron to DeSylva, and much of Sturges's March was devoted to the attempted salvage of *New York Town*.

Every version of the *Sullivan's Travels* script has eleven sequences, A through K. This is an unusually high number for a Sturges film, reflecting, of course, the story's picaresque subject and variety of scenes. In principle, like Cervantes's *Don Quixote*, Ibsen's *Peer Gynt*, or Feuillade's serials, Sullivan's adventures on the road could go on forever. In fact the film is ninety minutes long, shorter than *The Lady Eve, The Miracle of Morgan's Creek*, and *Hail the Conquering Hero.*

Sturges wrote Sequence A on February 3, 1941, Sequence B and most of Sequence C on February 10. Then he stopped work and did not resume, presumably for the reasons mentioned above, until March 24, when he finished Sequence C and wrote Sequence D. On March 26 he wrote twenty-five pages of Sequence E, following which there is another hiatus until April 7, when Sturges wrote three more pages of Sequence E and began Sequence F. Sequence F, which is the longest sequence of the film, extends from Sullivan's initial setting out with the Girl to the death of the tramp in the railroad yard; Sturges continued writing on April 10 and 14 and finished it on April 18, on which date he also wrote the bulk of Sequence G. The end of Sequence G was written on April 21, as were all of Sequences H, J, and K.

Sturges also rewrote some of the pages of earlier sections as he went along, thirteen of them to be exact, including a new half-page occasioned by his expansion of the butler's warning speech in Sequence B. Ten of these revised pages were written on the prodigious day and night of April 21. The April 22 script consolidated all of these changes but—as mentioned earlier—rather unusually preserved on the first page of each sequence the date on which it was begun. (The dates of the pages revised later and of the parts of sequences completed on a later date than they were begun are omitted.)

As the reader can see, the May 3 script—the shooting script—also dates its sequences and, indeed, even parts of sequences:

A-1 to A-8	May 2, 1941
A-9 to A-11	May 3, 1941
B-1 to B-9	May 2, 1941
C-1 to C-6	May 2, 1941
C-7 to C-11	May 3, 1941
D-1 to D-13	May 2, 1941
D-14 to D-15	May 3, 1941
E-1 to E-2	May 2, 1941
E-3 to E-15	May 3, 1941
E-16 to E-27	May 5, 1941
F-1 to F-37	May 5, 1941
G-1 to G-7	May 5, 1941
H-1 to H-7	May 5, 1941
J-1 to J-6	May 5, 1941
K-1 to K-5	May 5, 1941
K-6 to K-12	May 8, 1941

The most important revisions of *Sullivan's Travels* took place not between the script versions but between the May 3 script and the finished film itself. The compositional table above shows that in fact Sturges finished the May 3 script on May 8, the day after shooting began; whatever revisions were made after this date were necessarily done during filming. These are for the most part small, subtle changes, but they are frequently suggestive of underlying tensions or problems in the script.

The most interesting thing perhaps is that, despite the meticulous dating of all versions of the *Sullivan's Travels* script, the revision process as a whole changed it very little. There are no major substantive changes from version to version and surprisingly few, rather unimportant changes of dialogue and other details. The February 3 script, finished in fact on April 21, is very close to the May 3 shooting script. The February 3 script, as noted, itself embodies revisions made as Sturges wrote it, but even it, with a few exceptions and despite important interruptions, was written sequentially from A to K. *Sullivan's Travels* as a whole was written in slightly more than two months. This is astonishing given the complex revision process, spanning literally years, that we have traced for *The Great McGinty, Christmas in July,* and *The Lady Eve.*

Sullivan's Travels was also Sturges's first script written from first to last in full knowledge that he would direct it. As we have indicated, Sturges revised the scripts of his first three films in preparation for directing them, and *The Vagrant* (1933), at least, was written originally in the hope that Sturges himself would direct it. But with *Sullivan's Travels* for the first time Sturges, as a working director, conceived and wrote a script which he knew he would direct, which he was indeed under contract to write and direct, with even the likely casting and approximate production schedule already in mind. *Sullivan's Travels* thus marks, arguably, Sturges's full attainment of the status of writer-director; from now on, at Paramount anyway, he was to write only new, original scripts and those only for his own direction. The relation of this new work situation to Sturges's methods of work, including his mode of revision, poses interesting questions. Since

Sturges directs Veronica Lake in S*ULLIVAN'S* T*RAVELS.*

the scripts printed in this volume do not include *The Palm Beach Story, The Great Moment, The Miracle of Morgan's Creek,* and the films made after *Hail the Conquering Hero,* it is not possible to generalize confidently. There seem to be fewer drafts of the later scripts than of *The Great McGinty, Christmas in July,* and *The Lady Eve,* but *Hail the Conquering Hero,* as we shall see, went through a complex and protracted revision process before reaching its final form. Finally, if writing *Sullivan's Travels* in two months was an undoubted feat, filming the script, which is far more vigorous in action and diverse in locale than anything Sturges had done before, was certainly another.

The May 3, 1941, script of *Sullivan's Travels* begins with the phrase "After the Main Titles." In the film itself, released in January 1942, those main titles begin with the Paramount logo; then the camera pulls back and reveals that it is in fact a seal on a large package. A woman's arms enter the frame, an expensive-looking bracelet on one hand, a ring with a precious stone on the other, lacquered nails on both. She gently pulls away the seal and removes the paper wrapping; inside is an oversized, gilt-edged book—a "DeLuxe Edition." Across the top of the cover of the book, in bold letters, is the title *Sullivan's Travels*; on the right side of the cover "by Preston Sturges." Thus, in effect, Sturges identifies himself as the author of the novel or at least of the original story on which the film is based—in any case, as the film's author in a sense beyond the "written and directed by Preston Sturges" credit that appears, as usual, at the end of the credit sequence. Perhaps Sturges was still smarting over the fact that Monckton Hoffe was given credit for *The Lady Eve*'s original story—as we have seen, Sturges really supplied his own original story—and wished to set the record straight at the outset here.

The cover of the "DeLuxe Edition" is also illustrated—on it we see a huge Joel McCrea and a proportionately huge Veronica Lake, both in tramp's costume, towering over and standing at the head of long columns of people that wind around behind them. McCrea and Lake are looking down on scenes apparently of human suffering (it is hard to tell because the woman's right hand quickly covers the lower right-hand corner), in the lower foreground. Perhaps the idea is that McCrea and Lake stand witness to the scenes of misery for the masses of people that stand behind them. The graphic design of the cover is reminiscent of rather old-fashioned book illustration, and the iconography suggests *Gulliver's Travels,* particularly Gulliver's adventures among the Lilliputians. The woman's hand opens the cover, and as she turns successive pages, we see, of course, the credits of the film, the last page being the film's dedication.

In *Sullivan's Travels,* as in *The Great McGinty,* Sturges experimented with several epigraphs, dedications, and postscripts—and several combinations of them—in its successive versions. The February 3 script has no epigraph or foreword. What became the film's foreword appears in that script at the end of the dialogue in the last scene on the airplane that is flying Sullivan, the Girl, and the producers back to Hollywood.

SULLIVAN
I'd like to make a comedy . . . if I still can.

MR. LeBRAND
A comedy!

MR. HADRIAN
Now he wants to make a comedy!

SULLIVAN
There's a lot to be said for making people laugh. Quite a lot. I've already got the prologue for it. It says: "To the memory of those who made us laugh . . . the motley mountebanks, the clowns, the buffoons in all times and in all nations . . . whose efforts lightened our burden a little . . . in this cockeyed caravan . . . this picture is affectionately dedicated."

In the April 22 version, a foreword has been added between the title page and the "Cast of Characters" page:

This is the story
of a man who wanted
to wash an elephant.
The elephant darn
near ruined him.

The postscript and its setting in the dialogue remain the same.

The May 3 script, the shooting script, retains the foreword from the April 22 version but completely eliminates the lines quoted above from the final airplane scene. That dialogue now reads:

SULLIVAN
(Gently)
And I'll tell you something else: there's a lot to be said for making people laugh . . . did you know that's all some people have? It isn't much . . . but it's better than nothing in this cockeyed caravan . . .
(He shakes his head reminiscently)
Boy!

The film retains this dialogue, eliminates the "washing an elephant" foreword, and puts in its place the "dedication," which was dropped from the April 22 script's dialogue. Thus, the dedication to Sullivan's proposed comedy has become the dedication to *Sullivan's Travels* itself:

To the memory of those who made us laugh: the motley mountebanks, the clowns, the buffoons, in all times and in all nations, whose efforts have lightened our burden a little, this picture is affectionately dedicated.

If the credit sequence creates literally a bookish atmosphere—it ends with that most literary item, a high-flown dedication—that atmosphere is promptly shattered by cinema: the rip-roaring, train-top fight-to-the-death, which turns out to be the conclusion of the film that Sullivan and the two producers are watching in the film's first scene.[3]

Whose film, by the way, are Sullivan and the producers screening? It cannot be Sullivan's since it becomes clear that he has never made a serious film, and this one, one of the producers informs the other, is already a financial success at Radio City Music Hall. If it were a Sullivan film, his producers would have seen it before it opened, and both would know its box-office record to date without having to be told. Sullivan seems to be using this film's success and artistic excellence as an argument for making *Oh Brother, Where Art Thou?*, a social problem film in a similar vein. The producers disparage what they have seen in part from genuine distaste, in part to dissuade Sullivan from undertaking a similar project.

But many Sturges commentators, including Manny Farber and James Ursini, have concluded that this is a film by Sullivan himself, and certainly the script and film of *Sullivan's Travels* create this ambiguity.[4] Sullivan speaks in the projection room as though what they have been watching is his film—at least his words can be construed that way: "You see the symbolism of it? Capital and labor destroy each other. It teaches a lesson, a moral lesson . . . it has social significance." (This remark perhaps suggests Sullivan's naïveté—a railroad "shack" [hobo slang for a railroad detective] and a vagrant, as the script identifies the fighting figures on the train, seem dubious symbols of capital and labor.) The ensuing exchange establishes that the two producers do not like the film, even if it was held over a fifth week at Radio City Music Hall. Mr. Hadrian says: "Who goes to the Music Hall? Communists!" Sullivan replies "explosively":

> Communists! This is an ANSWER to Communists . . . it shows we're awake and not dunking our heads in the sands like a bunch of ostriches! I want this picture to be a commentary on modern conditions . . . stark realism . . . the problems that confront the average man.
>
> MR. LeBRAND
>
> But with a little sex in it.
>
> MR. SULLIVAN
>
> A little, but I don't want to stress it. I want this picture to be a . . . true canvas of the suffering of humanity.

Here it becomes clear that the three are talking about a proposed film that Sullivan wishes to make, even though in his "Communists!" speech Sullivan refers to "this picture" in a way that seems to indicate the film we have just seen. Why else would the scene as a whole—and the film itself—proceed as if Sullivan were a comedy director attempting for the first time to make a social film? At the end of the film, of course, he decides not to make a social film, which would make no sense if he has already made one. In Sturges's defense, it might be said that the producers and Sullivan know that this is not his film and hence do not need to keep their "this" references meticulously clear.

The two producers of Sequence A are not the producers of *Song of Joy*, alas! They are entirely reasonable men and, indeed, for producers anyway, nice guys. Perhaps Sturges modeled them on those producers who had helped him over the years: Charles Abramson in New York, Henry Henigson, Albert Lewin, William LeBaron, and Paul Jones in Hollywood. Perhaps he did not wish to offend Paramount's new production chief right off the bat with an unflattering portrait of Hollywood producers, although such a prudent Sturges could hardly have made the films that bear his name. Sturges gets in his jibes, it is true; the producers clearly care only about profits and hypocritically claim to have risen from the gutter. Best of all, Sturges makes Hadrian and LeBrand seem completely interchangeable, a nice feat with character actors as different as Porter Hall and Robert Warwick. It is critical heresy to question *Sullivan's Travels*, but *Song of Joy*, transformed by the alchemy of Sturges's revising, might have made a better film; on the other hand, despite Sturges's best efforts, it was apparently unfilmable in the Hollywood of his day.

Sequence B remains essentially unchanged in all versions of the script and in the film. Each version, but not the film, begins with Mrs. Sullivan's telephone call; the April 22 version begins with the butler answering Sullivan's phone, the May 3 one with a shot of Mrs. Sullivan on the phone. (The dialogue continuity for *Sullivan's Travels*, dated July 22, 1941, makes clear that the opening indicated by the May 3 script was in fact shot, hence that Sturges later removed the first two shots—B-1 and B-2 below.) The released film improves on all previous versions by beginning Sequence B with a shot of Sullivan in his tramp costume, carrying stick and bandanna, trying out his hobo walk before a three-way mirror, asking his valet "How's this?" to which he replies: "Isn't that overdoing it a bit, Sir? Why break their hearts?" After another exchange, the telephone rings, and the scene plays pretty much as written. The way that Sequence B opens in the film has the advantage of direct continuity with Sequence A; we learn, before any dialogue, that Sullivan is going ahead with his journey as announced. This established humorously, the film then introduces Sullivan's alimony-demanding ex-wife, a necessary complement to any successful director—necessary also to create a barrier later between the film's lovers. Sturges also no doubt loved the idea of having a director wear tramp's clothes while speaking to his ex-wife about alimony.

We might pause at this image of Mr. Sullivan, fabulously successful director. If Farber is right that Sturges films all deal in one way or another with American success and failure, then *The Lady Eve* and *Sullivan's Travels* seem to be exceptions. *The Lady Eve* is true to the screwball ethos that love is all that matters—Jean as Eve has a chance to make a bundle from her divorce, but, by this time in the film, she is not interested in money. Nevertheless, Jean herself is not rich at the outset of the film, and she will become so by marrying Charles Pike. Sullivan, however, begins very rich and successful and ends the same way. True, he loses his "privilege" and his identity for a while, suffers a loss of memory, and is even threatened by death; but he is never afflicted by failure—it's all waiting for him when he gets out—which makes him an exception among Sturges heroes.

Nevertheless, even here, in the sanctuary of a fantasy figure of success, there is a return of the Sturgean repressed. Sullivan is no Sturges ideal of talent or brilliance—he and his films are ridiculed by their very titles—but of unfailing success, of the unworried enjoyment of the smile of the gods. No matter how unlikely Joel McCrea may be as a director of comedy, the stolidity and smugness he brings to the role effectively project that freedom from anxiety and fear of failure that Sturges sees in Sullivan.

But there is a ghost haunting all success in Sturges's films—the ghost of failure and poverty. As Farber says, Sturges's characters

> work feverishly as every moment brings them the fear that their lives are going to pieces, that they are going to be fired, murdered, emasculated, trapped in such ridiculous situations that headlines will scream about them to a hooting nation for the rest of their lives. They seem to be haunted by the specters of such nationally famous boneheads as Wrong-Way Corrigan, Roy Riegels, who ran backward in a Rose Bowl game, or Fred Merkle, who forgot to touch second base in a crucial play-off game, living incarnations of the great American nightmare that some monstrous error can drive individuals clean out of society into a forlorn no man's land, to be the lonely objects of an eternity of scorn, derision, and self-humiliation. This nightmare is of course the reverse side of the uncontrolled American success impulse, which would set individuals apart in an apparently different but really similar and equally frightening manner.[5]

Sturges's Sullivan is a smug, thick-skinned success, haunted by no fear of failure, protected as it were by his very mediocrity. But the iconography of the film supplies the anxiety that Sullivan himself lacks, by posing again and again images of fabulous wealth and privilege against images of poverty, failure, and devastation. As usual in Sturges, there is no middle ground, no comfortable middle state, nothing but absolute failure and absolute success. There are, above all, the shots of Sullivan stalking through his mansion in a tramp's outfit, as though preparing himself for the inevitable collapse to come, trying it on for size. When the Girl finds out who the tramp she pitied really is, she says: "So you're the washed-up director." Sullivan replies: "I'm afraid I exaggerated that part a little bit." Unfortunately, McCrea's flat reading robs the line of its wonderful ambivalence.

Sequence B ends when producers Hadrian and LeBrand burst into Sullivan's mansion suddenly full of passion for his bum's expedition. Accompanied by public relations specialists Casalsis (Franklin Pangborn) and Jones (William Demarest), they propose that a team of publicity people follow Sullivan in a "land yacht" equipped with every convenience in order to flash news of his journey far and wide and thereby promote his film. Sullivan, of course, wants no part of the scheme, but the producers slap him with a court order restraining his expedition.

The presence of publicity people, a doctor, a secretary, a chauffeur, a cook, and a radioman in the land yacht that follows Sullivan at the outset of Sequence C indicates that the producers have won. These "eight stooges," as one of their number calls them, include some of Sturges's most distinctive supporting players—William Demarest, Frank Moran, Torben Meyer, Charles Moore, and Vic Potel—and some players new to Sturges: Margaret Hayes as the secretary, Byron Foulger as a publicity writer, and Richard Webb as the radioman. They are introduced all at once, however—a squabbling gaggle—and are never much differentiated at any later point either. (The beginning of an introduction to them is cut short by the arrival of the whippet tank driver and the chase that follows. We have been introduced to the characters—and to the cook's galley—only to see them tumbling and sprawling a moment later and the inside of the yacht a shambles.) The impression they give, in fact, is that of a *Mad Magazine* cluster of press agents, chauffeurs, photographers, doctors, radiomen, and secretaries. Even the way the secretary's underwear shows in her ungainly sprawls in the tank–yacht chase has a *Mad Magazine* aspect. This is only one respect in which *Sullivan's Travels* is ahead of its time, opening the way not only to the free-wheeling style of Sturges's own later comedies, but to much of the best postwar comedy as well, notably that of Frank Tashlin and Jerry Lewis.

Even more conspicuously ahead of its time is the boy whippet tank commander himself (Robert Winkler), the infernal child of the day's technology, not only abreast of it but coequal with it, therefore a monster. He walks from *Sullivan's Travels* (1941), by way of *Mad Magazine* and the *National Lampoon*, into *The Loved One* (1965), by which time the speed-demon driver has become a homemade-rocket engineer. He is played there, of course, by Paul Williams, who had a corner on the type for a certain period (for example, *The Phantom of the Paradise*). As the boy drives off, Sullivan says appropriately: "What a future!"

The chase of the land yacht after the whippet tank is a rather long comic set piece. It has often been said—Agee was the first—that Sturges knowingly mixed the verbal sparring of the sound era with the best slapstick techniques of silent comedy. *Sullivan's Travels* is often cited as typical of this mixture, indeed as possibly its best example, but to me it is neither typical nor the best. Its slapstick passages at their worst are heavily applied and seem somewhat arbitrarily inserted for overtly "rhythmic" considerations—periodically to liven up a conceit that might be considered as too intellectual or satirical. The slapstick elements in *Christmas in July*, *The Lady Eve*, *The Miracle of Morgan's Creek*, *Hail the Conquering Hero*, and, for that matter, *Mad Wednesday* are expertly built up to and descended from. They are dramatically prepared and placed so as to release tensions at exactly those points where they have crystallized. Perhaps because *Sullivan's Travels* has a picaresque subject, because it is episodic rather than dramatic, the slapstick passages cannot grow out of the dramatic process; they can only alternate as autonomous passages with the verbal passages. In the second half of the film, melodramatic passages take the place of the slapstick ones, but one might argue that the principle of simple alternation rather than full dramatic integration remains the same.

After the chase, Sullivan convinces the studio gang to let him go on alone and promises to meet them in Las Vegas in a few weeks. Sturges cuts here from the top of page 31 in the script printed below to the bottom of page 36, the scene in which Sullivan is chopping wood with his shirt off as Miz Zeffie leans out of her window to ogle him. This eliminates a page and a half of needless further dialogue with the studio crew, but it also eliminates an interesting scene between Sullivan and "Mr. Carson" on pages 33–36. The dialogue continuity establishes that this scene was shot; indeed most cast lists identify Harry Hayden as Mr. Carson. Neither character nor actor, of course, appears in the finished film. In the missing scene Mr. Carson has picked up hitchhiker Sullivan and offers to take him to Miz Zeffie, who needs yard work done. Sullivan demurs until Carson turns out to be a sheriff who will arrest him for vagrancy if he does not take the job. Carson's function in the plot is to deliver Sullivan to Miz Zeffie and thus to set up the scene that follows. As such it is expendable, particularly since Sullivan has told the studio gang at the end of the previous sequence that he will be "just up ahead mooching a lunch off a farmer's wife," a description that more or less fits the Miz Zeffie scene.

But the dialogue between Sullivan and Mr. Carson raises a number of issues that seem important to the film's theme and the times in which it is set—issues that are treated nowhere else in the film. Sullivan's exchange with Carson suggests that in early 1941 there is already some recovery from the depression—the "airplane factories and all." The character of Carson also serves to introduce some right-wing thinking on poverty and hobos—bums are bums and they deserve their lot. This might have better prepared us for the brutality of the railroad shack and the prison "Mister" later, indicating that theirs is not simply the behavior of aberrant individuals. The exchange also serves to raise, if it does not resolve, the issue of work in the film: are most tramps in 1941 tramps by choice, or are they workers who cannot find work? The film as it stands takes hobos as a given; it never asks why they are there. (The film seems to share the Christian notion that "the poor we have always with us"; in its ultimate shrug at the problem of poverty, *Sullivan's Travels* is arguably Sturges's most conservative film.) Sullivan's evasions of Carson's questions also perhaps reveal his own attitudes toward physical work, an important issue that the film otherwise does not address. He does not want to work, it seems, or to try different kinds of work. At the outset of the film he wants to be a hobo to find out what being poor is like; on the airplane at the end of the film he says that he hasn't suffered enough to make *O Brother, Where Art Thou?*, which indicates that suffering has been his goal and that hobohood, rather than work, is his idea of suffering. There is perhaps a lack of the sharpest focus here, something rarely lacking in a Sturges script or film; or perhaps there is a sea-change that occurs in the course of Sullivan's quest. At the start he wants to "know" what poverty is like, suggesting a project of research; at the end, on the airplane, he reveals that "suffering enough" in order to make a serious work has been his object and that he has failed.

In any case, the nature of bums and hobos is important to determining both the nature of Sullivan's quest and the theme of the film itself. One of the two bums (Harry Rosenthal) in the railroad car that Sullivan and the Girl jump disapproves of their technique with the word "amateurs" (which does not appear in the script). If this is ambiguous—one may take pride in mounting a train well whatever one's reasons for doing so—the next exchange is not. Sullivan asks the two "Weary-Willies," as the script calls them (page 79), "How do you feel about the labor situation?" whereupon they "gather their bindles sourly" and exit for another car. The other bum is played by Georges Renavent, who had much earlier introduced Sturges to Brock Pemberton; Renavent figures later in the plot as the thief of Sullivan's shoes and still later as the bum who assaults Sullivan and subsequently dies in the railroad yard. (The script specifies simply "Two Weary-Willies" in this scene, not the later bum.)

The rest of Sequence D deals with Miz Zeffie's romantic interest in Sullivan, his avoidance of her advances, and his final escape from his second-floor room via knotted sheets, during which he snags his trousers on a nail and lands in a barrel of water. The sequence might have been turned to give Sullivan a pointed lesson in reverse sexual exploitation, but it settles instead for more familiar comedy about lecherous country widows.

Sequence E, twenty-seven pages long, presents the meeting of Sullivan and the Girl (this is her only identification in the script) and their subsequent interactions up to their departure via freight car in Sequence F. True to Hollywood convention, she meets the great director in his tramp disguise so that he and we can be assured of her kindness of heart. Almost broke herself, she buys this hobo ham and eggs. Her remarks on this and other matters are pointed and amusing: "You know the nice thing about buying food for a man is you don't have to laugh at his jokes." But does she not later sink to the status of ironic groupie to the famous director, who even follows him on the road? At first, it is true, she is angry at him for fooling her and taking advantage of her good nature. In this state she throws him into his swimming pool, but he drags her in with him. Then the butler comes in with food for them, and there is a dissolve to the two of them in bathrobes finishing breakfast on the terrace.

Are there hints that they have made love in the meantime? Yes, but there are denials at the same time—standard ambivalence in Hollywood films of the classical period. The Girl's first line after the dissolve to the terrace is: "You might have shaved," which may even refer simply to their having breakfast together. She says he needed the dunking in the water, that is, a bath, but also that she had had a yen for him as a hobo that she does not have for him as director. In proposing to go along with him on his "Noble Experiment," she says that she can just keep going when he reaches the farthest point of his journey. "It'll make a nice ending . . . and we'll finish what we started this morning." He responds that it is out of the question, that she would take his mind off his work.

When he still refuses, even after the butler chimes in on her behalf, the script notes:

THE GIRL
(Bouncing up and down
on Sullivan's lap)

I will, I will, I will! I'm going with you.

At such moments in the script and film it is difficult to take this relationship seriously. Their conversation after their second journey, which is their actual exploration of the lower depths (pages 102–107), is another example. Here Sullivan rather imperially reverses his decision to send her on her way and orders two tickets to take them both back to Hollywood. The script duly notes, "She smiles through her tears" (page 107), which is how the scene is played in the film.

The consequence of transforming the Girl from wisecracking independent to rather dependent groupie is to drain their relationship of much of its potential interest—there seems little at stake in it. Sullivan's decision to take her back to Hollywood with him may seem plausible, but his later decision to marry her, even after his solo ordeal in prison, is simply not believable.

One aspect of the problem is that Sullivan does not seem to need this Girl or, indeed, any particular one. As a famous director, he presumably can get anyone he wants. (Unlike Charles Pike in *The Lady Eve,* Sullivan has definitely not been up the Amazon for a year.) The film hints at this in a variety of ways without coming right out and saying it. For instance, when Mr. Jones (William Demarest) lists the creature comforts of the land yacht, his last item is "a hot shower and a secretary." Indeed, when Sullivan and the studio crew talk it over after the whippet tank chase, the secretary (Margaret Hayes) rubs her backside and tilts herself toward Sullivan as though to say: "Give it up, Boss, and come with me." (Cut from the film is her line as she watches him continue up the road: "You know, I have a feeling he's really on the level." This cut avoids an explicit acknowledgment that she is coming on to Sullivan but preserves a hint of her disappointment that he has turned her down.)

Sturges had to proceed most carefully here. The Hays Office report on the April 22 script had warned:

> In shooting this picture, we strongly urge that you give serious thought to avoiding anything that could in any way reflect in a derogatory manner on Hollywood or the motion picture industry, or that might cause us to be accused of deliberately befouling our own nest. Some of the lines we ask eliminated below as sex suggestive, are also doubly questionable, from the standpoint that they might be considered as reflecting unfavorably, and possibly unfairly on the habits of the motion picture industry. We strongly urge that you give unusual care and attention to this phase of the picture.

When Sullivan tells the Girl "you can't get a divorce without collusion" and that his wife "won't collude," there is an additional exchange that is cut from the film:

THE GIRL
How about you? [colluding]

SULLIVAN
She said she'd overlook it.

Indeed, presumably for reasons of censorship, Sturges banishes sexual desire even from Sullivan's past—it is made clear that he married his wife only for a tax break. Nevertheless, as mentioned, Sullivan's extreme calm in the face of the Girl's advances tells its own story.

Sturges wanted Veronica Lake for the part of the Girl and finally got her despite the opposition of Buddy DeSylva, who thought she was wrong for the part; the studio suggested instead Ida Lupino, Lucille Ball, Claire Trevor, Frances Farmer, Betty Field, or Ruby Keeler.[6] One is tempted to say that for once the studio was right and Sturges was wrong. Any of these actresses, Keeler excepted, might have transformed the film, making the Girl more a figure to be reckoned with throughout and shattering Sullivan's smugness and insularity. It is easy, however, to suggest this or that change in a script or film but very difficult to calculate the impact of a change on all of the other elements, something Sturges was particularly expert at gauging. For instance, if Trevor or Farmer or Lupino had said to Sullivan, "I know fifty times as much about trouble as you ever will," we might believe her—as we do not believe Lake. On the other hand, this might create the expectation that the Girl will vindicate her remark later by street-smart behavior on the road—getting food, lodging, etc.—which would make *Sullivan's Travels* a different film from the one that Sturges had in mind.

The meeting of Sullivan and the Girl in the "owl wagon," so called presumably because it is open all night, raises another point, akin to the film's unintegrated slapstick but distinct from it. Sturges cuts again and again to reaction shots of the counterman (Roscoe Ates) exaggeratedly guffawing at the Girl's outrageous remarks. Also, in the black church scene later, Sturges has his convicts laugh much too uproariously at the Mickey Mouse cartoon. As Farber writes:

> Sturges' faults are legion and have been pretty well gone over during his most successful period. Masterful with noisy crowds, he is liable to let a quiet spot in the script provoke him to burden the screen with "slapstick the size of a whale bone." A good businessman believes that any article can be sold if presented with eardrum-smashing loudness and brain-numbing certitude. From a similar approach, Sturges will represent hilarity by activating a crew of convicts as though he were trying to get Siberia to witness their gleeful shrieks. To communicate the bawdy wit of a fast blonde, he will show the tough owner of a lunch wagon doubled up like a suburban teenager hearing his first dirty joke.[7]

One might add to Farber's hyperbolic inventory the three reaction shots to Sullivan's butler (Robert Grieg) that Sturges cuts into the poolside breakfast scene between Sullivan and the Girl. Each of the shots of Grieg's uncharacteristically smiling face reacts to one of the Girl's lines to Sullivan—"I liked you better as a tramp"; "I'll throw you in the water"; and "I'll follow you and tell everybody who you are . . . like a kid sister" (pages 70–72). It is true that these shots prepare Grieg's entry into the conversation, but this might have been done with a single nonreaction shot that established the butler's presence, as indeed the script specifies (top of page 73). Perhaps Sturges felt that Lake's line readings needed this sort of bolstering. In any case, no Sturges film before or after *Sullivan's Travels* resorted to audience nudging of this kind, so familiar in mainstream comedy of all eras.

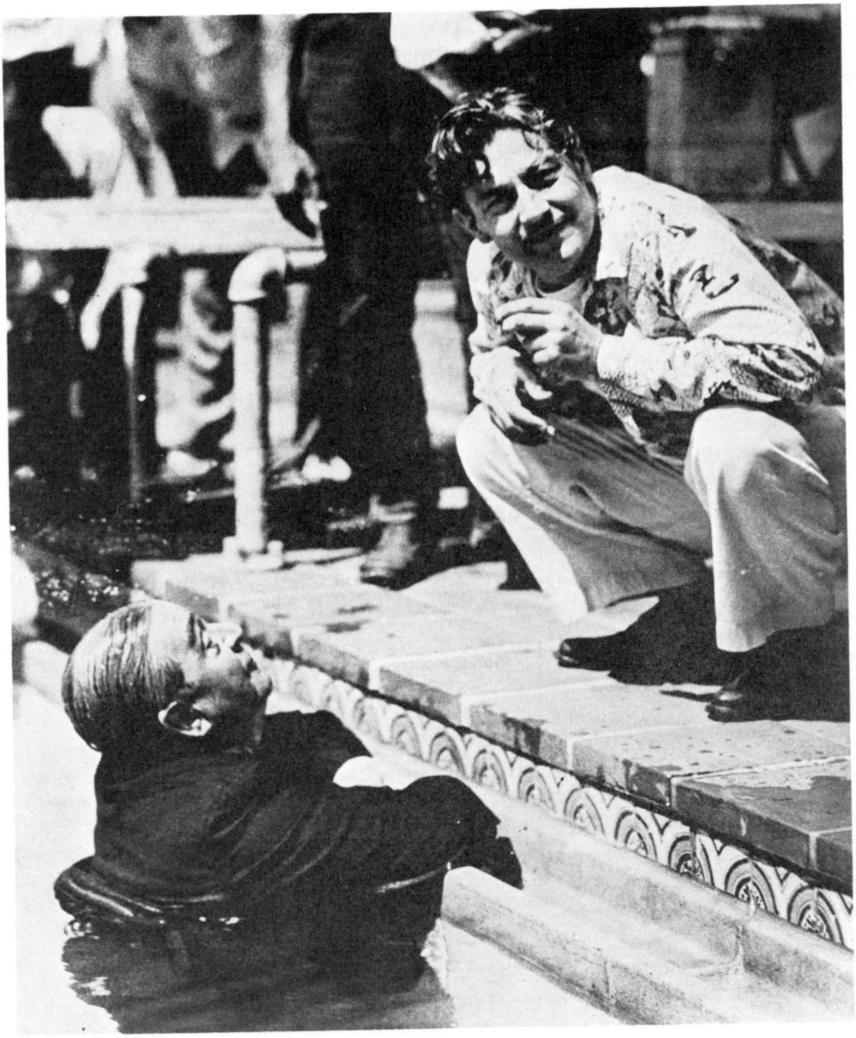

Sturges directs Robert Grieg as Sullivan's butler Burroughs in the pool scene in SULLIVAN'S TRAVELS.

The central if late-blooming plot of *Sullivan's Travels* is elaborated in the thirty-seven-page Sequence F, which comprises the two journeys Sullivan takes with the Girl and his solo trip to distribute five-dollar bills to the tramps who helped him learn about poverty (his fourth journey altogether), which ends disastrously with Sullivan being attacked by an old bum and the bum's death in a railroad yard. Sequences G, H, J, and K develop the consequences of these last events. Sequence G shows the Girl waiting for Sullivan with the studio crowd, then hearing of his "death" when his shoe with a studio identification card hidden in the sole is found among the dead tramp's otherwise unrecognizable remains. The sequence then picks up Sullivan's story as he "comes to" in a boxcar that is just arriving in a railroad yard. He is caught and knocked down by a railroad shack, whom he in turn hits with a rock. Sequence H presents Sullivan's trial for trespass and atrocious assault, rendered through frosted glass to suggest his temporary amnesia and confusion. He is sentenced to six years in the state penitentiary and, when he is first brought there, is struck on the head by the "Mister" and chained to his bunk when he demands to see a lawyer. In Sequence J, Sullivan takes a newspaper from the pocket of a prison trusty and reads the report of his own strange death. The "Mister" puts him in the sweatbox for reading without permission. He spends a whole day there but is allowed to go to the picture show at a black church that Sunday. At the church, everyone, including the convicts, laughs at the comedy that's being shown, and Sullivan finds himself laughing along with them. Sequence K begins with Sullivan's wife and his business manager visiting his supposed grave and conversing cynically. The script calls for the camera to discover the Girl sitting at a bench near the graveside (page 134), but this is cut from the film. Back at the prison, we see Sullivan talking to the trusty about how to get his picture in the paper; then Sullivan suddenly "confesses" to the murder of John L. Sullivan. His scheme works: the Girl, whom we see in costume on the set of a movie, sees Sullivan's picture and runs to LeBrand's office with the news. The film's last scene is on an airplane back to Hollywood, as Sullivan and the Girl plan to marry. (His wife, believing him dead, has married his business manager, so she will have to give Sullivan his divorce.) Sullivan also informs his distraught bosses that, despite the great publicity his experience has created for *O Brother, Where Art Thou?*, he is no longer interested in the project and wishes to make a comedy.

The film's treatment of several of these script passages deserves a close look. The middle part of the script's Sequence F (pages 95–101) describes a "Montage with Music" in the slums of a big city at night. This is what the film gives us, but the passage as shot and edited differs from the passage described in the script. The cop, Sullivan's picking up a cigarette butt, the Girl's following him at a discreet distance, then catching up and offering him a fresh cigarette, and Sullivan's ordering her away again—all are dropped. Instead, we see Sullivan and the Girl walking hand in hand through a shanty town and, as in the script, standing in line in a soup kitchen where the studio photographer snaps their picture. The script then has them eating out of a can of beans by a fire and afterward lying in a piano box, each in turn scratching for fleas while the other laughs and the photographer takes their picture. The film eliminates the fire scene and stages the scratching scene on the second floor of a mission, where the photographer more plausibly catches up with them, as the two try to sleep sitting up.

The shots of the couple in the "his" and "hers" fumigation rooms of a mission correspond to the script's description as does the "meek-looking orator addressing the bums in a mission" that follows. The film makes a good deal more of this, however, by cutting to several shots of desolate-looking people listening to him, then to a long tracking shot down row after row of listeners, coming finally to Sullivan and the Girl. At the mission's long table in the scene following, they do reluctantly eat the food before them—rather than pass it along to someone else as the script describes—and they eat from plates, not from a can. Sturges also adds a shot of a toothless man chewing vigorously and returning Sullivan's stare.

The script's description of Sullivan and the Girl looking for a place to sleep on the crowded mission floor is realized in the film without alteration, but the film's treatment in this scene of the snoring bum who later steals Sullivan's shoes has one important difference. The script specifies a shot that begins with "a horrendous pair of feet," then "moves up the torn clothes, the shredded shirt, to the horrible face of the big man. Here all the mechanism of a snore is exposed" (page 98). The script then calls for an extreme close-up of the snoring drunk's face, which in fact ends the scene. In the film, there is a close-up of the bum's dilapidated shoes but only a dark medium shot of his face with his eyes closed—by no means enough to identify him later as the same man who steals Sullivan's money and dies in the railroad yard.

This detail is important because the rest of the plot depends upon the discovery of Sullivan's identification cards that his valet (Eric Blore) has taken "the extreme liberty" of having sewed in the sole of each of Sullivan's boots in Sequence B. As noted, the bum that Sullivan and the Girl see on the train early in Sequence F is the same person who turns up at the hobo shelter and steals Sullivan's boots (pages 98–99) and who later attacks Sullivan at the railyard and gets killed by the train (pages 108–111). The tramp's body is mangled, but his shoes identify him as Sullivan. Hence, the real Sullivan is stuck in prison for hitting back at a railroad shack, his wife remarries, etc. All this is clear in the script passages just mentioned, but in the film it is not so clear because the bum sleeping next to Sullivan in the shelter is not at all recognizable as the man whom we have seen earlier on the train and will see later attacking Sullivan and being run over by a train. Since these events are not clear visually, we tend not to believe the far-fetched coincidence the plot depends upon.

The shots that follow those of the bum in the shelter are for the most part as the script specifies them: Sullivan's discovering the loss of his shoes and the pitiful substitutes left for them, the gag of Sullivan and the Girl carrying opposing signs, and their walk down an alley looking for food in garbage cans. In the film this occasions a revulsion that leads to the cancellation of their trip, which is much preferable to the script's treatment (pages 100–101): Sullivan and the Girl go out to dinner in formal dress and then revert to bumhood again—they sit around a fire under a bridge with a one-legged bum—only to return suddenly to the studio crowd at a Kansas City hotel declaring the entire expedition to be over. As though to make up partially for the omitted "dinner out" scene, the film retains a shot of Sullivan and the Girl (both still in tramp's costume) walking along a beautiful river in the country; though they are tired and beaten down, he is moved to put his arm around her and she to put her arm around him.

Sequence F concludes with another montage with music (and railyard sounds)—pages 108–111—in which Sullivan hands out five-dollar bills to the tramps whose company he has just left "in gratitude for what they done for him," as Mr. Jones tells Mr. LeBrand (page 102). This passage follows the script rather closely from beginning to end, although there are some small differences. The film's Sullivan passes out bills to a middle-aged woman, a young girl, an old man, and three men standing together—a somewhat different group of recipients from what the script indicates—before giving one to "the old bum who stole Sullivan's shoes" (page 108). Also, instead of dropping an additional bill that the old bum picks up, as the script has it, the film's Sullivan holds his wad of bills in his hands for anyone to see, which leads the bum to follow him. In the script Sullivan sees the apparently sleeping bum—who has taken a shortcut to put himself in Sullivan's path—tucks a bill in his hand and then is hit by him. In the film the bum hides, Sullivan walks past him, and the bum hits him from behind. The film also adds a long-held shot of the train that takes the unconscious Sullivan away—this is the last we see of him until he wakes up in the freight car in Sequence G. Following this shot is the scene where we see the bum attempting to escape across the tracks with his stolen bills but being hit by a train.

Sequence F ends with a dark shot of the bum's shoe, possibly with his severed foot in it, surrounded by some falling bills. Sequence G begins with a scene of the Girl and some of the studio crew waiting for reports on Sullivan by other crew members who are combing the city. The chauffeur reports from the morgue that "they got a guy in a basket you can't tell who he is." The Girl mentions the studio card between the soles of Sullivan's shoe; the chauffeur recovers the card and reads Sullivan's name on it with some difficulty—"It's all splattered," he says, a line added by the film. Here is another plausibility problem—the Girl knows very well that Sullivan's shoes were stolen by a bum when they were in the mission and that the shoes he was wearing when he disappeared were those that the thief had left in their place.

The chauffeur's identification scene is followed by a newspaper headline of Sullivan's strange death. The script then cuts back to Sullivan in the freight car and carries the action through Sullivan's hitting the railroad shack with a rock (page 117); it then cuts to a telephone scene between LeBrand and Mrs. Sullivan (she threatens to sue the studio), which is followed by LeBrand's bawling out the studio crew but deciding not to fire them and his and Hadrian's promising the distraught Girl that they will take care of her. This is followed by Sequence H, which begins with Sullivan's trial. The film, on the other hand, proceeds from the newspaper headline about Sullivan to the scenes with the studio people and the Girl and then cuts back to Sullivan as he wakes up in the freight car. This order has the advantage of proceeding directly from Sullivan's assault on the railroad shack to his trial scene and the prison scenes that follow it, thereby increasing the dramatic continuity of Sullivan's frightening adventures.

Sequence H, which comprises Sullivan's trial and his arrival at the penitentiary, is shot very much as the script indicates, as is most of Sequence J, which includes the sweatbox scenes and the scenes at a black church. The singing of a hymn as the chained convicts walk into the church is moving despite its evident intention to move. The song the congregation sings is not specified by the script—it just says "a spiritual"; in the film it is "Go Down, Moses."[8]

What the church-goers, Sullivan, and the other convicts see on the church's movie screen was changed by Sturges at least twice. All of the script versions specify "a silent comedy, possibly Chaplin in 'The Gold Rush,' possibly a Laurel and Hardy two-reeler" (page 133). We know from the film's dialogue continuity, dated July 22, 1941, that before resorting to the Mickey Mouse and Pluto Walt Disney cartoon that we see in the released film, Sturges had used another comedy passage. All that remains of this passage is the following elliptical exchange from the dialogue continuity:

SISTER:	How, do.
COLORED MAN:	Swing it, boy . . . Harder . . . Still harder.
FAT ONE:	Suppose you try wrestling with it for awhile.
FIRST ONE:	Come on, swing it . . . Ah, that did it. That did it.

It seems impossible to guess from this record of its dialogue what the passage was like—which is frustrating indeed since Sturges presumably shot the passage himself! In any case, this whatever-it-was must have failed to motivate the degree of collective mirth that the scene required; alas, we will probably never know.

The early part of Sequence K—Sullivan's conversation with the trusty, his confession to his own murder, and the newspaper stories that follow—was filmed very much as the script indicates. But the film makes the studio pandemonium at the news about Sullivan entirely silent—or, rather, yet one more montage with music. Thus LeBrand's and Hadrian's dialogue on page 138 is cut, as is the studio crew dialogue on page 139. The dialogue between Sullivan and the Girl on pages 139–140 is retained and, due to Sturges's cutting all of the studio dialogue on pages 141 and 142, is in effect carried over unbroken to the airplane scene, ending with Sullivan's "And then I'll be free . . . but not for long, I hope." This is followed, due to some further dialogue cuts on pages 142–143, by LeBrand's extolling *O Brother, Where Art Thou?*, with the results discussed above.

It is only in the airplane scene that we see at last the book itself, *Oh Brother, Where Art Thou?* by Sinclair Beckstein, whose name is an obvious play on those of Sinclair Lewis and John Steinbeck. The cover illustration, held very briefly, shows stylized human sufferers menaced by at least one death figure, and the scene as a whole is arranged as a crucifixion. The cover adds dimension to Sullivan's observation on the book, omitted by the film, on the last page of the script:

> Besides, it's already been done . . . they made it a couple of thousand years ago and I don't believe in re-makes. There's nothing like original material.

Despite the ironic context of this speech, its last line reminds us of Sturges's own apparent aesthetic credo. In deciding not to adapt a book but instead to write or at least to direct an original comedy, Sullivan draws closer to Sturges after all. It is worth noting also that *Sullivan's Travels* ends in an airplane in mid-air, which is where *Unfaithfully Yours* (1948), Sturges's next ironic "portrait of the artist," begins.

NOTES

1. James Curtis, *Between Flops: A Biography of Preston Sturges* (New York: Harcourt Brace Jovanovich, 1982), page 149.

2. There is some evidence in the Sturges papers that Paramount at some point considered making *Song of Joy* but decided against it.

3. There is an opposition between cinema and the book that runs intermittently through *Sullivan's Travels*. After Mr. LeBrand has ordered a second copy of *O Brother, Where Art Thou?* for his colleague Mr. Hadrian, he says to Hadrian: "Why should I suffer alone?" (page 11). Producers are not the only movie people who find reading painful—Sullivan himself is also an object of the film's Hollywood satire. After Sullivan's butler Burroughs (Robert Grieg) had delivered his elegantly expressed reservations on his employer's proposed venturing into the realm of the poor, a mystified Sullivan says to his valet (Eric Blore): "He gets a little gruesome every once in a while." The valet comments, "Always reading books, sir," to which Sullivan responds, a bit resentfully: "Oh" (page 16). The doctor (Torben Meyer) in the land yacht following Sullivan asks Mr. Jones (William Demarest): "Why doesn't he [Sullivan] read a book if he wants to learn something?" "Maybe he don't know how to read," Jones answers, referring to the cook rather than Sullivan. Still the doctor has a point—Sullivan might read about poverty and hobos in addition to going out among them.

4. Manny Farber, *Negative Space* (New York: Praeger, 1971), page 95; James Ursini, *The Fabulous Life and Times of Preston Sturges* (New York: Curtis Books, 1973), page 89.

5. Farber, op. cit., page 98.

6. Curtis, op. cit., page 153.

7. Farber, op. cit., page 99.

8. William Faulkner had published his story "Go Down, Moses" in *Collier's* for January 25, 1941, and it was later reprinted in the novel of the same name in March 1942. Sturges, who shot *Sullivan's Travels* between May and July 1941, might have seen the *Collier's* story, or he might have chosen the hymn without such prompting. Sturges and Faulkner first met in late 1942 when the latter visited Sturges's Players restaurant. According to Joseph Blotner, the following initial dialogue took place: "'I hear you've made some fine pictures,' Faulkner remarked after the introductions. 'I hear you've written some fine novels,' Sturges replied" (Joseph Blotner, *Faulkner: A Biography,* vol. 2 [New York: Random House, 1974], pages 1134–1135).

P.1304

SULLIVAN'S TRAVELS

May 3, 1941

SULLIVAN'S TRAVELS

This is the story
of a man who wanted
to wash an elephant.
The elephant darn
near ruined him.

SULLIVAN'S TRAVELS

CAST OF CHARACTERS

JOHN L. SULLIVAN.....................Joel McCrea

THE GIRL...........................Veronica Lake

MR. LeBRAND (Head of studio)........Raymond Walburn

MR. JONES..........................William Demarest

MR. CASALSIS.......................Franklin Pangborn

MR. HADRIAN........................Porter Hall

MR. VALDELLE.......................Byron Foulger

PRETTY SECRETARY...................Margaret Hayes

THE DOCTOR.........................Torben Meyer

SULLIVAN'S BUTLER..................Robert Grieg

SULLIVAN'S VALET...................Eric Blore

MR. CARSON, (the sheriff)..........Al Bridge

MIZ ZEFFIE.........................Esther Howard

URSULA.............................Almira Sessions

TOUGH CHAUFFEUR....................Frank Moran

OLD BUM............................George Renevant

* * *

B I T S

Candid cameraman, young man with ear-phones, colored cook, Bud, truck driver, counter man, motor cops, police sergeant, information clerk, 2nd counter man, big R.R. shack, yardman, small-town judge, sheriff, etc.

Form F-62—G-39

PARAMOUNT PICTURES INC.

West Coast Studios

INTER-OFFICE COMMUNICATION

Date May 8, 1941

SULLIVAN'S TRAVELS - Prod. 1304

NOTE:

In the script of SULLIVAN'S TRAVELS, wherever the title "FOR WHOM THE NIGHT FALLS" appears, please change it to "OH BROTHER, WHERE ART THOU?"

SEQUENCE "A"

After the Main Titles -

FADE IN:

A-1 LONG SHOT - A FREIGHT TRAIN ROARING TOWARD US THROUGH THE NIGHT

There is snow in the foreground. As the train starts past us -

A-2 THE SWAYING TOP OF A BOXCAR

It is shiny with sleet. A brutal battle is in progress between a railroad shack and a young vagrant. They clinch, fall and roll to the end of the car.

A-3 HIGH CAMERA CLOSE DOWN - ON THE STRUGGLING MEN

We see the couplings and the shining rails below. The young vagrant almost falls, catches himself, and kicks out desperately. The shack falls back onto the roof of the car OUT OF THE SHOT.

A-4 THE SHACK - FALLING ON THE TOP OF THE BOXCAR

He pulls a revolver and holds it close to his side.

A-5 THE VAGRANT

He crouches and comes forward.

A-6 LONG SHOT - OF A BRIDGE

The locomotive roars onto it.

A-7 THE SHACK

He raises his gun and fires.

A-8 THE VAGRANT - PAST THE SHACK

He clutches his belly, falters, then staggers forward. The shack fires again as the vagrant closes with him. The boxcar comes onto the bridge. The vagrant seizes the shack's collar in a death grip as he starts to

5-2-41 (Continued)

A-8 (Cont'd)

fall sideways. The shack fires once more, than screams as he is dragged over the side of the car. As they disappear -

A-9 HIGH CAMERA SHOT - THE FALLING BODIES

The train whistles wildly. As the bodies strike the water -

A-10 CLOSE SHOT - THE BLACK AGITATED WATERS

The current is strong. The men rise to the surface, the vagrant rigid, the shack struggling and kicking. He fires twice more point-black then sinks below the waters with the man he has killed. The waters rush by for a moment, then slowly the words: "THE END" DISSOLVE IN under the water. The finale music swells.

A-11 MESSRS. LE BRAND, HADRIAN AND SULLIVAN - IN A DARK PROJECTION ROOM

Behind them we see the apertures opening into the projection room. The beam of light from the projector goes PAST US. The music ends in a shocking silence and the lights come on. Mr. LeBrand blows out his cheeks with relief.

MR. HADRIAN
(Wiping his forehead)
Phooey!

MR. SULLIVAN
(Getting to his feet enthusiastically)
You see? You see the symbolism of it? Capital and labor destroy each other. It teaches a moral lesson...it has social significance. It...

MR. HADRIAN
Who wants to see that kind of stuff? It gives me the creeps.

MR. SULLIVAN
(To Mr. LeBrand)
Tell him how long it played the Music Hall.

5-2-41 (Continued)

A-11 (Cont'd)

MR. LeBRAND
(Reluctantly)
It was held over a fifth week.

He opens the door to his private office and the other two follow him.

A-12 MR. LeBRAND'S PRIVATE OFFICE

MR. HADRIAN
(Still in the projection room)
Who goes to the Music Hall? Communists!

He and Sullivan enter the private office and close the door.

MR. SULLIVAN
(Explosively)
Communists! This is an answer to Communists...it shows we're awake and not dunking our heads in the sands like a bunch of ostriches! I want this picture to be a commentary on modern conditions...stark realism... the problems that confront the average man.

MR. LeBRAND
But with a little sex in it.

MR. SULLIVAN
A little, but I don't want to stress it. I want this picture to be a.....document. I want to hold a mirror up to life. I want this to be a picture of dignity... a true canvas of the suffering of humanity.

MR. LeBRAND
But with a little sex in it.

MR. SULLIVAN
(Reluctantly)
With a little sex in it.

MR. HADRIAN
How about a nice musical?

5-2-41 (Continued)

A-12 (Cont'd)

MR. SULLIVAN
How can you talk about musicals at a time like this? With the world committing suicide...corpses piling up in the street, grim death gargling at you around every corner...people slaughtered like sheep....

MR. HADRIAN
Maybe they'd like to forget that.

MR. SULLIVAN
(Jerking his thumb)
Then why do they hold this one over for a fifth week at the Music Hall... for the ushers?

MR. HADRIAN
It died in Pittsburgh.

MR. LeBRAND
Like a dog.

MR. SULLIVAN
(Contemptuously)
What do they know in Pittsburgh?

MR. LeBRAND
(Mildly)
They know what they like.

MR. SULLIVAN
(Sneeringly)
If they knew what they liked they wouldn't live in Pittsburgh! That's no argument. If you pandered to the public you'd still be in the horse age...

MR. HADRIAN
You think we're not? Look at Hopalong Cassidy, look at...

MR. SULLIVAN
<u>You</u> look at him. We'd still be making Keystone chases, bathing beauties, custard pie operas...

MR. LeBRAND
And a fortune.

5-2-41 (Continued)

A-12 (Cont'd)

MR. SULLIVAN
(Taking a new tack)
Of course I'm just a minor employee here, Mr. LeBrand....

MR. LeBRAND
(To Mr. Hadrian)
He's starting that one again.

MR. SULLIVAN
I wanted to make you something outstanding, something you could be proud of, something that would realize the potentialities of film as the sociological and artistic medium that it is, with a little sex in it. Something like...

MR. HADRIAN
Something like Capra. I know.

MR. SULLIVAN
What's the matter with Capra?

MR. LeBRAND
Look: You want to make "For Whom the Night Falls."

MR. SULLIVAN
Yes.

MR. HADRIAN
Now wait a minute.

MR. LeBRAND
Then go ahead and make it, at what you're getting I can't afford to argue with you.

MR. SULLIVAN
That's a fine way to start a man out on a million dollar production.

MR. LeBRAND
(Crossly)
You want it? You've got it! I can take it on the chin! I've taken it before.

MR. SULLIVAN
Not from me, you haven't.

5-2-41 (Continued)

A-12 (Cont'd)

MR. LeBRAND
Not from you, Sully, that's true. Not with pictures like "So Long, Sarong," "Hey, Hey in the Hayloft", or "Ants in Your Plants of 1939"... but they weren't about tramps, and lockouts, and sweatshops, and people eating garbage in alleys and living in piano boxes and ashcans and... and...

MR. HADRIAN
And phooey!

MR. LeBRAND
They were about nice clean young people who fell in love, with laughter and music and...legs you take that scene in "Hey-hey in the Hayloft"....

MR. SULLIVAN
Yes, but you don't seem to understand conditions have changed. There isn't any work...there isn't any food...these are troublous times...

MR. HADRIAN
What do you know about troubles?

MR. SULLIVAN
(Indignantly)
What do I know about trouble?

MR. HADRIAN
(Pressing the point)
Yes. What do you know about trouble?

MR. SULLIVAN
What do you mean, what do I know about trouble?

MR. HADRIAN
Just what I'm saying. You want to make a picture about garbage cans... what do you know about garbage cans...when did you eat your last meal out of one?

MR. SULLIVAN
(To Mr. LeBrand)
What's that got to do with it?

5-2-41 (Continued)

A-12 (Cont'd)

MR. LeBRAND
He's asking you.

MR. HADRIAN
You want to make an epic about misery. You want to show hungry people sleeping in doorways....

MR. LeBRAND
With newspapers around them.

MR. HADRIAN
You want to grind ten thousand feet of hard luck and all I'm asking you is what do you know about hard luck?

MR. LeBRAND
Yes.

MR. SULLIVAN
What do you mean, what do I know about hard luck? Don't you think I've....

MR. HADRIAN
No.

MR. SULLIVAN
What?

MR. HADRIAN
You have not. I sold newspapers till I was twenty, then I worked in a shoe store and put myself through law school at night. Where were you at twenty?

MR. SULLIVAN
I was in college, but...

MR. LeBRAND
When I was thirteen I was supporting three sisters and two brothers and a widowed mother. Where were you at thirteen?

MR. SULLIVAN
I was in boarding school. I'm sorry.

5-2-41 (Continued)

A-12 (Cont'd)

MR. LeBRAND
You don't have to be ashamed of it, Sully. That's why your pictures have been so light, so cheerful, so inspiring....

MR. HADRIAN
They don't stink with messages.

MR. LeBRAND
That's why I paid you five hundred a week when you were twenty-four.

MR. HADRIAN
Seven-fifty when you were twenty-five.

MR. LeBRAND
A thousand when you were twenty-six.

MR. HADRIAN
When I was twenty-six I was getting eighteen.

MR. LeBRAND
Two thousand when you were twenty-seven.

MR. HADRIAN
I was getting twenty-five then.

MR. LeBRAND
I was just opening my first shooting gallery. Three thousand after "Thanks for Yesterday."

MR. HADRIAN
Four thousand after "Ants in Your Plants."

MR. SULLIVAN
I suppose you're trying to tell me I don't know what trouble is.

MR. HADRIAN
Yes.

MR. LeBRAND
In a nice way, Sully.

5-2-41 (Continued)

A-12 (Cont'd)

MR. SULLIVAN
(Ruefully, after a pause)
You're perfectly right...I haven't the slightest idea what it is. It's funny I never thought about it from that angle.

MR. HADRIAN
People always like what they don't know anything about.

MR. SULLIVAN
(Pensively)
I really had a lot of nerve wanting to make a picture about human suffering.

MR. LeBRAND
You're a gentleman to admit it, Sully...but then you are anyway.

MR. HADRIAN
How about making "Ants in your Plants of 1941?" You can have Bob Hope, Mary Martin...

MR. LeBRAND
Maybe Bing Crosby....

MR. HADRIAN
The Abbey Dancers...

MR. LeBRAND
Maybe Jack Benny and Rochester....

MR. HADRIAN
A big-name band and...

MR. SULLIVAN
(Coming out of a trance)
What? Oh, no...I want to make "For Whom the Night Falls," but I'll tell you what I'm going to do first: I'm going to get some old clothes and some old shoes from wardrobe and start out with ten cents in my pocket...I don't know where...and I'm not coming back till I know what trouble is.

5-3-41 (Continued)

A-12 (Cont'd)

MR. LeBRAND
What!

MR. SULLIVAN
You don't have to worry. You can take me off salary.

MR. LeBRAND
Who's talking about taking you off salary?

MR. SULLIVAN
(Shaking Mr. LeBrand's hand)
So long...and thanks for the idea.

MR. LeBRAND
Now wait a minute...don't be so impulsive. How long will you be gone?

MR. SULLIVAN
I don't know...maybe a week... maybe a month...I'll come back when I've had enough. Don't worry about me. So long -

He squeezes Mr. Hadrian's hand.

MR. SULLIVAN
So long, Dracula, you gave me a great idea.

He hurries out and slams the door.

MR. LeBRAND
(After a moment's silence)
Now look what you've done.

MR. HADRIAN
What _I've_ done!

MR. LeBRAND
With your lies about selling newspapers.

MR. HADRIAN
I sold as many newspapers as you supported a family at thirteen.

5-3-41 (Continued)

A-12 (Cont'd)

MR. LeBRAND
Well, I opened a shooting gallery, didn't I?

MR. HADRIAN
With money you borrowed from your uncle.
(Then after a pause)
We'd better insure him for a million.

MR. LeBRAND
He's worth more.

MR. HADRIAN
(Looking toward the door)
Bone-head!

MR. LeBRAND
But what a genius.

He crosses to his dictaphone.

MR. LeBRAND
(Into the dictaphone)
Get me a copy of that "For Whom the Night Falls"...I guess I'll have to read it.

He lets go the lever, looks at Mr. Hadrian, then pushes the lever down again. Giving Mr. Hadrian a dirty look he says:

MR. LeBRAND
(Into the dictaphone)
Make that two copies. Why should I suffer alone?

FADE OUT:

END OF SEQUENCE "A"

5-3-41

SEQUENCE "B"

FADE IN:

B-1 MRS. SULLIVAN - IN BED IN HER RESIDENCE (DAY)

MRS. SULLIVAN
(Unpleasantly into telephone)
I want to talk to Mr. Sullivan,
please...this is Mrs. Sullivan.

B-2 THE BUTLER - IN SULLIVAN'S PANTRY

Next to him there is a silver breakfast set and some tomato juice in a bowl of ice.

THE BUTLER
(Into the telephone, his
face falling)
Ah, yes, Mrs. Sullivan.

He looks up at a calendar which says September 14th, 1941. He peels off a leaf and crumples it up.

THE BUTLER
I'll see if he's at home, madam.

MRS. SULLIVAN'S VOICE
(Through the phone)
He'd better be at home.

The Butler scowls at the telephone, then directs his finger toward a button.

B-3 SULLIVAN AND HIS VALET - IN THE BEDROOM

Mr. Sullivan stands in front of a three-piece tailor's mirror dressed in a fearful tramp outfit.

THE VALET
I think that's overdoing it a
bit, sir. There's no use breaking
their hearts.

The phone rings and the valet answers it.

THE VALET
(After a moment)
Your wife is on one, sir.

SULLIVAN
What does she want?

B-3 (Cont'd)

THE VALET
I was speaking to Jeffry, sir, but I suspect it has something to do with today's being the fifteenth.

SULLIVAN
(Grunting)
Oh, yes...payday. Put her on.

THE VALET
(Into the telephone)
You may connect Mrs. Sullivan.

Sullivan takes the phone.

B-4 MRS. SULLIVAN - AT THE TELEPHONE

MRS. SULLIVAN
(With false sweetness)
You don't happen to remember what day this is do you, dear?

B-5 SULLIVAN AND HIS VALET - IN THE BEDROOM

SULLIVAN
(Into the phone)
Yes..., I happen to remember what day it is.....No, I haven't forgotten anything, have you.... Well, maybe I could be a little more polite, but somehow, Mrs. Sullivan, when I talk to you I just don't feel polite; I regret it but that's the way it is...... Maybe you'd better take it up with the postal authorities.....I don't know whether I signed it or not...When I sign your checks I always close my eyes; maybe I signed the blotter.....

He hangs up roughly, then dials "one, one."

SULLIVAN
(Into telephone)
You make out the Panther Woman's check yet?.....Well, you better get it down to her before she shows up with the sheriff....She has a very peculiar sense of humor.

5-2-41 (Continued)

B-5 (Cont'd)

THE VALET
(Holding up a coat)
I think this one is sufficiently seedy, sir. Why overplay it?

THE BUTLER
(Entering with the breakfast tray)
Good morning...
(Now he stops in astonishment, then recovers his equanimity)
...Sir.

SULLIVAN
Good morning, Burrows; how do you like it?

THE BUTLER
I don't like it at all, sir. Fancy dress, I take it.

He gives Sullivan the tomato juice.

SULLIVAN
(Taking the tomato juice)
What's the matter with it?
(He starts drinking the juice)

THE BUTLER
I have never been sympathetic to the caricaturing of the poor and needy, sir.

SULLIVAN
(Indignantly)
Who's caricaturing...

THE VALET
Burrows doesn't know about the expedition, sir.

SULLIVAN
I'm going out on the road to find out what it's *like* to be poor and needy....and then I'm going to make a picture about it.

5-2-41 (Continued)

B-5 (Cont'd)

THE BUTLER
If you'll permit me to say so, sir: The subject is not an interesting one. The poor know all about poverty and only the morbid rich would find the topic glamorous.

SULLIVAN
(Exasperated)
But I'm doing it for the poor.

THE BUTLER
I doubt that they would appreciate it, sir. They rather resent the invasion of their privacy...I believe quite properly, sir. Also, such excursions can be extremely dangerous, sir. I worked for a gentleman once who likewise, with two friends, accoutred himself as you have, sir, and then went out for a lark.....They have not been heard from since.

SULLIVAN
That was some time ago?

THE BUTLER
1912, sir.
(Then after a pause)
You see, sir, rich people and theorists, who are usually rich people, think of poverty in the negative...as the lack of riches ...as disease might be called the lack of health...but it isn't, sir. Poverty is not the lack of anything, but a positive plague, virulent in itself, contagious as cholera, with filth, criminality, vice and despair as only a few of its symptoms. It is to be stayed away from, even for purposes of study....It is to be shunned.

Sullivan exchanges a look with his valet, then looks back at the butler.

SULLIVAN
Well, you seem to have made quite a study of it.

5-2-41 (Continued)

B-5 (Cont'd)

THE BUTLER
(Dryly)
Quite unwillingly, sir. Will that be all, sir?

SULLIVAN
Thanks.

He watches him exit, then turns to the valet.

SULLIVAN
He gets a little gruesome every once in a while.

THE VALET
Always reading books, sir.

SULLIVAN
Oh.

THE VALET
As a matter of fact, sir, I don't like the idea of a gentleman of your inexperience leaving with only ten cents in his pocket, so I...took the extreme liberty, sir, of having a studio identification card sewed in the sole of each of your boots...

Sullivan looks indignantly at his feet.

SULLIVAN
(Indignantly)
You must think I'm a child or something. The whole purpose of this expedition...

THE BUTLER
(Re-entering)
Mr. LeBrand, Mr. Hadrian, Mr. Casalsis and a Mr. Jones to see you, sir. I asked them to wait in the Blue Room but...

The four gentlemen brush past him in the order in which they were announced.

MR. LeBRAND
Good morning, Sully.

SULLIVAN
Hello.

5-2-41 (Continued)

B-5 (Cont'd)

MR. LeBRAND
I brought Casalsis and Mr. uh...
(He looks at Jones)

JONES
Jones.

MR. LeBRAND
....along to tell you....

SULLIVAN
All right, but before you all
get started I just want to tell you
one thing: my mind is made up.

MR. LeBRAND
Nobody's here to argue with you,
Sully. You know that your slightest
wish...

MR. HADRIAN
We talked it all over and there's
quite a lot to the idea at that.

MR. LeBRAND
There's a great deal to it.

Mr. Casalsis opens his mouth to speak.

MR. JONES
(Beating him to it)
It's a pip.

MR. CASALSIS
(After directing a frown at
Jones)
Stupendous.

He opens his mouth to speak again.

MR. LeBRAND
(Pointing to Mr. Casalsis)
Cassy has it all worked out:
it's as safe as a church, as
big as a cathedral and...

MR. CASALSIS
Bigger. This is the story of
the year, Sully. It'll break
the front page of every newspaper
in the country...THE WORLD!
It'll put the war back....

B-5 (Cont'd)

MR. JONES
...with the want ads...right next to the lost dogs.

MR. CASALSIS
I'm sending five of my boys with you...

MR. JONES
With me in charge.

MR. CASALSIS
An advance man in front, a follow-upper behind...

MR. JONES
A cook and a still man.

MR. CASALSIS
I want lots of eight by tens.

SULLIVAN
Now listen.

MR. CASALSIS
I guarantee that no one will be able to open a newspaper...

MR. JONES
...without staring right into your kisser...

MR. CASALSIS
...and reading about "For Whom The Night Falls." It's the topic of the nation. Furthermore...

SULLIVAN
(Desperately)
Will you wait a minute?

MR. JONES
(Impatiently)
We're coming to that part of it. We got everything figured out.

MR. CASALSIS
We're revamping that lovely land-yacht DeMille used in "Northwest Mounted," and it follows you at a discreet distance with...

5-2-41 (Continued)

B-5 (Cont'd)

MR. JONES
...hot coffee, sandwiches and a little bar in the back.

MR. CASALSIS
It's connected directly to the studio by short-wave and it carries also...

MR. JONES
...a hot shower and a secretary.

MR. CASALSIS
....a physician...

MR. JONES
...and two strong-arm guys....

MR. CASALSIS
(Triumphantly)
...all dressed like tramps!. What a novelty! You see, we have thought of everything..

SULLIVAN
Look: I'm looking for trouble and I'm not going to find it with six acts of vaudeville on my tail....at least not the kind I'm looking for.

MR. LeBRAND
(Gently)
Be reasonable, Sully.

MR. CASALSIS
I'm re-upholstering it from stem to stern.

MR. JONES
Wait'll you see...

SULLIVAN
I've already told you my mind is made up.

MR. LeBRAND
Definitely?

SULLIVAN
Definitely.

Mr. LeBrand turns and looks at Mr. Hadrian.

5-2-41 (Continued)

B-5 (Cont'd)

MR. HADRIAN
In that case there's nothing else to do...

SULLIVAN
You said it...

MR. HADRIAN
(Pulling it out of his pocket)
...but serve you with this summons to appear and show cause why you should not be restrained from jeopardizing your unique and extraordinary services by willfully, recklessly and unnecessarily...

SULLIVAN
(Backing away from the summons)
Now wait a minute.

MR. LeBRAND
(Gently)
We have all day, Sully...but you must realize that we also have minds...also made up.

MR. CASALSIS
If you saw that upholstery...

FADE OUT:

END OF SEQUENCE "B"

5-2-41

SEQUENCE "C"

FADE IN:

C-1 THE BROW OF A HILL, U.S. HIGHWAY 99

The extraordinarily long shadows from left to right indicate very early morning looking south. In the distance we see a beautiful valley. Sullivan comes over the hill wearing his tramp outfit and carrying a little bundle over his shoulder.

C-2 CLOSE TRUCKING SHOT - SULLIVAN

He walks along side of us long enough for us to see that he is unshaven and that his shoes are not entirely comfortable. After a moment Sullivan scowls back over his shoulder and the CAMERA PANS BACK ONTO a land yacht coming over the crest of the hill. As it moves TOWARD US -

C-3 TRUCKING SHOT - THE LAND YACHT COMPLETE

It is a magnificent looking outfit, its occupants visible through the windows.

C-4 THE DRIVER'S SEAT OF THE LAND YACHT

A very tough looking chauffeur is at the wheel. Next to him sits a strong-arm man, next to him sits a candid camera man with his camera slung around his neck, next to him sits Mr. Valdelle, binoculars in hand dictating to a pretty girl secretary who sits next to him.

MR. VALDELLE
(Dictating)
Thus begins this remarkable expedition into the valley of the shadow of adversity.

THE GIRL SECRETARY
The shadow of the what?

THE CHAUFFEUR
The valley of the shadow of adversity.... It's a paraphrase.

MR. VALDELLE
Alone and unattended,....

5-2-41 (Continued)

C-4 (Cont'd)

THE GIRL SECRETARY
With nine stooges!

MR. VALDELLE
... prey to passing prowlers, poverty and policemen, with only ten cents in his pocket, John L. Sullivan, the Calef of Comedy, departed Hollywood at four o'clock this morning...

THE GIRL SECRETARY
You said it!

C-5 INT. OF THE LAND YACHT

At the breakfast table we see the Doctor, Mr. Jones, and the young man with the earphones fooling with short-wave set. A colored cook is leaning over the table.

COLORED COOK
Can I get you another stack, Doctor?

JONES
Get me some bicarbonate of soda and don't call me "doctor".

THE DOCTOR
He was talking to me, I think.
(Then to the cook)
No, thank you.

COLORED COOK
You say you don't want any bicarbonate of soda, Doctor?

JONES
Don't call me "Doctor".

THE DOCTOR
(To the cook)
No, I don't want any bicarbonate of soda.

THE COOK
I thought you said you did.

He walks out.

THE DOCTOR
This pace is very depressing.

JONES
So was the breakfast.

5-2-41 (Continued)

C-5 (Cont'd)

THE DOCTOR
Why doesn't he read a book if he wants to learn something?

JONES
Who, the cook? He could learn plenty.

THE DOCTOR
No, Sullivan.

JONES
Maybe he don't know how to read.

THE DOCTOR
The cook?

JONES
No, the... say, this is going to be a great trip.

THE YOUNG MAN WITH THE EAR PHONES
I'm sorry, I must have the wrong number.
(He takes off his ear phones)
That was the lighthouse on San Clemente Island.

JONES
(To the doctor)
How about a little gin rummy?

THE DOCTOR
I don't drink, thank you. Never touch it.

C-6 TRUCKING SHOT - AHEAD OF SULLIVAN

Behind him we see the land yacht. We hear the toot of a horn and a low-cut Ford roadster comes around the land yacht and speeds toward Sullivan. He turns his head, then jerks his thumb. The Ford screams to a stop.

C-7 CLOSE SHOT - THE FORD - PAST SULLIVAN

It looks clumsily like a tank. At the wheel sits a rural youngster wearing a football helmet.

5-2-41 (Continued)

C-7 (Cont'd)

SULLIVAN
How about a lift, Bud?

BUD
If you don't mind goin' fast...
I'm studyin' to be a whippet
tanker.

Sullivan looks over his shoulder toward the land yacht, then steps into the car.

SULLIVAN
Go to it, lieutenant.

BUD
You're there, general.

He lets in his clutch and howls OUT OF THE SHOT.

C-8 THE DRIVER'S SEAT OF THE LAND YACHT

THE CANDID CAMERAMAN
(Pointing up ahead)
Hey!

MR. VALDELLE
(Raising his binoculars)
Step on it!

THE CHAUFFEUR
Hang on!

There's a roar of the big motor. As the car leaps forward -

C-9 INT. OF THE LAND YACHT

Jones, the doctor and the young man with the ear-phones pile onto the floor.

C-10 THE GALLEY OF THE LAND YACHT

The colored cook is sitting on the floor, removing a bowl of flapjack dough from his head.

C-11 AUTOMOBILE SHOT - AHEAD OF RACING FORD

Sullivan gets a better grip on the car.

5-2-41

C-12 DRIVER'S SEAT OF THE RACING LAND YACHT

The chauffeur grits his teeth with determination and the other four occupants hang onto each other, each around the other's neck.

C-13 LOW CAMERA SHOT - A SHARP CURVE IN THE ROAD

The Ford whizzes by us on two wheels, the land yacht does almost the same.

C-14 A MOTOR COP - READING A NEWSPAPER

He is in a little side road at its juncture with the main highway. Some mud and water from the side road has leaked onto the highway. He lowers his newspaper and turns his head in astonishment as the Ford races past and splatters him with mud. He throws his newspaper to the ground and his leg over the saddle. As he throws his weight up to start the motorcycle, the land yacht roars by and really gives him some mud.

C-15 CLOSE SHOT - THE MOTOR COP - SCOOPING THE MUD OUT OF HIS EYES

C-16 CLOSE SHOT BEHIND THE HEADS OF SULLIVAN AND BUD

SULLIVAN
Can a whippet tank make a sharp turn?

BUD
What?

SULLIVAN
(Hollering)
Can a whippet tank go up a side road?

BUD
A whippet tank can go anywhere. Hang on!

There is a terrible screeching, the car lurches and the background swings ninety degrees. Now the car bumps down a country lane.

C-17 THE DRIVER'S SEAT OF THE LAND YACHT

THE CHAUFFEUR
Hang on!

5-2-41 (Continued)

C-17 (Cont'd)

He takes a mighty grip and spins the wheel. As the four other occupants slide toward him -

C-18 INT. OF THE LAND YACHT

Jones, the doctor, and the young man with the ear-phones flop over to the side of the body then bounce back.

C-19 THE COOK - IN THE GALLEY

He is upside down on the floor. Another pile of dishes fall on him.

C-20 THE DRIVER'S SEAT OF THE LAND YACHT

It is listing badly as it completes the turn. The girl screams.

C-21 THE MOTOR COP - ROARING TOWARD US

He is scooping mud out of his eyes.

C-22 THE MOTOR COP - ROARING AWAY FROM US

As he disappears down the road the CAMERA PANS and LOOKS UP THE LANE. The land yacht is moving AWAY FROM US in a series of leaps.

C-23 THE FRONT SEAT OF THE LAND YACHT

The occupants bounce high, return to the seat and bounce up again.

C-24 INT. OF THE LAND YACHT

The doctor, Jones and the young man with the ear-phones are being turned over like potatoes in a skillet.

C-25 THE CHEF - IN THE GALLEY

He is catapulted toward the roof; we hear a crash but to our astonishment, instead of coming down he stays there.

5-2-41

C-26 CLOSE SHOT - THE CHEF'S HEAD - FROM OUTSIDE

His head protrudes through the splintered roof of the land yacht. He is hanging by his chin and looking very much surprised.

C-27 CLOSE SHOT - LOOKING BACK AT SULLIVAN AND BUD

Suddenly Sullivan points ahead in horror.

C-28 THE ROAD - AHEAD OF SULLIVAN AND BUD

A hay wagon is just pulling across the road. As we get within five feet of it we sheer off to the right.

C-29 THE FORD - BOUNDING AWAY FROM US IN AN OPEN FIELD

It leaps like a hop toad.

C-30 THE FRONT SEAT OF THE LAND YACHT

With a screaming of brakes it comes to a stop.

C-31 THE OPEN FIELD

The Ford makes one bound INTO THE SHOT and stops. Sullivan gets out hurriedly and stands half bent.

SULLIVAN
Thank you, major. This is where I get out.

BUD
(Enthusiastically)
She's some tank, ain't she?

SULLIVAN
(Feeling his rear end)
In a class by itself, major. I never felt anything like it.

BUD
Well, I guess I'd better be gettin' to school now, anyway.

SULLIVAN
I guess maybe you better had... drive carefully.

5-3-41 (Continued)

C-31 (Cont'd)

BUD
(Happily)
You know me.

SULLIVAN
By the way, how old are you?

BUD
(Racing his motor)
Thirteen. So long.

His car bounds OUT OF THE SHOT.

SULLIVAN
(Feeling of himself again)
What a future!

He limps a little toward the road.

C-32 THE LAND YACHT

The hay wagon has just worked its way by, by going into the field across the road and then coming back. The occupants of the front seat are helping each other to the ground, all except the chauffeur who leans dismally on his wheel. He looks back toward the hay wagon before speaking.

THE CHAUFFEUR
Wasn't for that thing he never would a got away.

THE GIRL
Well, thank heaven something showed up.

She starts to sit on the running board, then gets up again quickly. Now Mr. Jones, the doctor and the young man minus the earphones appear. A moment later the colored chef comes out on his hands and knees.

MR. VALDELLE
He got away.

MR. JONES
(Holding his kidneys)
What were you chasing, a jack rabbit?

THE COLORED CHEF
Felt more like a kangaroo.

5-3-41 (Continued)

C-32 (Cont'd)

THE DOCTOR
Any broken bones... I mean seriously broken?

THE GIRL
(Looking up suddenly)
There he is.

C-33 SULLIVAN - LEANING AGAINST A TREE

SULLIVAN
(Laughing)
How'd you like it?

C-34 THE GROUP - PAST SULLIVAN

MR. VALDELLE
That was a dirty trick, Boss.

THE CHAUFFEUR
(Scowling)
I nearly lost my rear end -

C-35 SULLIVAN APPROACHING - PAST THE GROUP

SULLIVAN
I lost mine. Look: That was just to give you a rough idea ... unless you play ball with me. You know I can't do what I started out to do with you guys chasing me around... so I'll make you a fair proposition. You go on to some place you like; take it easy for a couple of weeks and I'll join you then or sooner. If the boss wants to talk to me, I'm just up ahead there bumming a lunch off a farmer's wife... you can see me but you can't get me on the phone. Is that a square proposition or isn't it?

C-36 THE GROUP - PAST SULLIVAN

THE CANDID CAMERAMAN
How about the pictures? I've got a job to think of, you know. I've got a wife, four children, a sister-in-law, my aunt...

5-3-41

C-37 SULLIVAN

SULLIVAN
We'll take all the pictures you like on the way back. I'll pose in every dump from here to Hollywood. This is on the level, kids... I want you to help me.

C-38 THE GROUP

THE GIRL
Well...I always wanted to see Boulder Dam.

SULLIVAN
You're there!

MR. JONES
(Indignantly)
Yeah, well if you think I'm going to look at Boulder Dam for two weeks...

THE DOCTOR
(Mildly)
How about Yellowstone National Park?

MR. JONES
(To the doctor)
And that goes for Yellowstone National Park.

MR. VALDELLE
Now, if you said Las Vegas....

MR. JONES
Then you'd be saying something.

THE GIRL
Well, that's only thirty miles from Boulder Dam.

THE CHAUFFEUR
You could take side trips.

THE DOCTOR
What do they do in Las Vegas?

THE CHAUFFEUR
Everything, doctor... It's an education.

5-3-41 (Continued)

C-38 (Cont'd)

SULLIVAN
(Cutting all this short)
All right... I'll see you in Las Vegas on or about the first... and thanks, kids...thanks sincerely.

He turns and starts up the road.

THE GIRL SECRETARY
You know, I have a feeling he's really on the level.

THE CANDID CAMERAMAN
And I have a feeling this is all going to turn out very badly.

He clicks a shot of Sullivan. The others frown at him.

THE CANDID CAMERAMAN
Just a personal observation.

A TINNY VOICE
Calling Mobile Station W - six - X - O - X ... Calling Mobile Station W - six - X - O - X. Come in, Station W - six - X - O - X.

The young man leaps into the land yacht and the others follow.

C-39 THE YOUNG MAN - AT THE PANEL

THE YOUNG MAN
(Into the microphone)
Yes, sir, Mr. LeBrand, how are you. He's right here....

He hands the earphones to Mr. Jones.

THE YOUNG MAN
It's Mr. LeBrand.

MR. JONES
Hello, boss....Yes...everything is lovely... I can just see him down the road there, asking a farmer's wife for a handout... Yes, it's very interesting... No, I don't think I'll be able to call him to the phone for some little while... You know

5-3-41 (Continued)

C-39 (Cont'd)

MR. JONES
(Continued)
how it is... You bet we've got our eye on him... Yes, sir!... wonderful stories! You'll be surprised at some of the things that are going to happen to him in the next few days. Yes, sir, Mr. LeBrand, don't you worry your head any... you let me do the worrying... Yes, sir.
(Wiping his head)
Yes, sir.

THE CANDID CAMERAMAN
Yes, I have a feeling this is going to be very depressing for all concerned.

They all look out of the land yacht down the road.

C-40 LONG SHOT - SULLIVAN, VERY SMALL, FRAMED IN THE ARCHING TREES

FADE OUT:

END OF SEQUENCE "C"

5-3-41

SEQUENCE "D"

FADE IN:

D-1 A COUNTRY ROAD - (DAY)

a 1935 Ford coupe bounces gaily toward us. As it comes abreast of us ---

D-2 INT. OF THE COUPE - SULLIVAN AND MR. CARSON

MR. CARSON
(Sympathetically)
Is that a fact, tt-tt-tt. Thought Roosevelt had that all fixed up... with them airplane factories and all... I thought work was the one thing there wasn't nothin' else but.

SULLIVAN
That isn't the way I found it.

MR. CARSON
That just goes to show you can't believe nothin' you read in the papers... I read even where some people even went off relief...to accept jobs.
(He cackles happily)

Sullivan gives him a pitying look.

MR. CARSON
You sure you looked in the right places...while you were lookin' for all this work you couldn't find?

SULLIVAN
I sure did.

MR. CARSON
Where did you look?

SULLIVAN
(Slightly unprepared)
Why, uh....high and low.... I walked up one side of the country and down the other...but you just can't find anything...no work, no food, no ... anything.

MR. CARSON
You sure you wasn't too choosy ... I mean about what you'd do?

D-2 (Cont'd)

SULLIVAN
A guy can't be choosy with only ten cents in his pocket.

MR. CARSON
Ain't it the truth.
(Then innocently)
Ain't it against the law to have only ten cents in your pocket?

SULLIVAN
I wouldn't know about that. All I know is I'm tryin' to get east ... there might be some work around the Great Lakes... Very kind of you to give me a lift.

MR. CARSON
Sure, sure. By the way, what do you do when you do work?

SULLIVAN
Who, me?

MR. CARSON
Yes, your hands look kinda soft for a worker, so I was just kinda figurin'... you wouldn't be a professional bum, would you?

SULLIVAN
(Chuckling)
No, no... it's just that I haven't worked in so long... conditions are so terrible.

MR. CARSON
Sure.

SULLIVAN
(After a pause)
What do you do?

MR. CARSON
Who, me?

SULLIVAN
Yes.

MR. CARSON
I'm the sheriff of this county.

SULLIVAN
(Startled)
Oh.

5-2-41 (Continued)

D-2 (Cont'd)

MR. CARSON
(Amiable)
That's right... that's how I come to know about the law agin havin' only ten cents in your pocket...that's what you call vagrancy...that calls for sixty days.

SULLIVAN
Oh!

MR. CARSON
But in hard times like you talk about we try to be as lenient as possible, and when we find a man is on the level about looking for work... we don't lock him up...

SULLIVAN
I see.

MR. CARSON
It's the next lane to the right.

SULLIVAN
What is?

MR. CARSON
This job I'm takin' you to.

SULLIVAN
(Startled, reaching for the door)
But, I'm not lookin' for a...

MR. CARSON
(Coldly)
You're not lookin' for a what?

SULLIVAN
I think I forgot to tell you that the one kind of work I'm absolutely unfamiliar with is any kind of agricultural work. I wouldn't know which end of the whiffle-tree you... whiffle with. I wouldn't know...

MR. CARSON
(Coldly)
Willing to learn, ain't you?

SULLIVAN
(With false indignation)
Certainly I'm willing to learn, but do you think at my age that I'm apt

5-2-41 (Continued)

D-2 (Cont'd)

SULLIVAN (Cont'd)
to? Don't you think it's an imposition on these poor people to wish such an incompetent clunk...such an untalented oaf as...

MR. CARSON
You're quite a talker, ain't you?

SULLIVAN
Well, I mean, let's be fair about it. Let's not think of ourselves, let's think of them...

MR. CARSON
I ain't goin' to force you, brother, this is a free country. If you'd rather spend the next few weeks in the hoosegow...

SULLIVAN
Who's talking about hoosegows? All I say is... I am, by trade, a chauffeur...What possible good is a chauffeur going to be to these people?

MR. CARSON
But that's what they're looking for, Miz Zeffie and her sister, a chauffeur and handy man.

SULLIVAN
(Dying)
Oh.

MR. CARSON
She's a widow lady...They just can't seem to keep a man on the place.

DISSOLVE TO:

D-3 A SECOND-STORY WINDOW OF A PRETTY WHITE HOUSE

Miz Zeffie peers around the curtains coyly, then sticks her head out.

MIZ ZEFFIE
You-hoo!

D-4 HIGH CAMERA SHOT - DOWN ON SULLIVAN

He is in the middle of a big pile of wood, pausing in his chopping. He is nude to the waist and sweating freely.

5-2-41 (Continued)

D-4 (Cont'd)

SULLIVAN
(Looking up)
Yes, M'am.

He swats a horsefly on the back of his neck.

D-5 CLOSE SHOT - MIZ ZEFFIE - IN THE WINDOW

MIZ ZEFFIE
Don't you try to run away, now, you naughty boy, or I'll tell the sheriff on you.

D-6 HIGH CAMERA SHOT - DOWN ON SULLIVAN

SULLIVAN
Yes, M'am.

He goes back to his chopping.

D-7 MIZ ZEFFIE AND HER THIN SISTER - IN THE SECOND FLOOR BEDROOM

It is a prettily decorated room more suited to a woman than a man and certainly exceptional for a farmhand. Miz Zeffie is hollering out the window while her sister, dust cloth around her hair, is cleaning the room unenthusiastically.

MIZ ZEFFIE
(Out the window)
And don't get too tired.
(She turns in to her sister and adds)
First day's work.

Now she feels of the softness of the bed and adds:

MIZ ZEFFIE (Cont'd)
I do hope he'll like everything here...
It's so hard to keep a man...
(She feels of her back hair)
D'you know what I need?

URSULA
Yes.

MIZ ZEFFIE
I need a permanent.

5-2-41 (Continued)

D-7 (Cont'd)

URSULA
A permanent what?

MIZ ZEFFIE
(Occupied with her thoughts)
You don't suppose we're overworking him, do you... Oh, I doubt it...he seems very strong.
(She takes a peek out the window)
Did you notice his torso?

URSULA
I notice that you noticed it.

MIZ ZEFFIE
Don't be vulgar, dear... Some people are just naturally more sensitive to some things in life than some people are... Some are blind to beauty, while others... are not... even as a little girl you were more of the acid type, dear, whereas I, if you will remember...

URSULA
I remember better than you do.

MIZ ZEFFIE
Well, forget it... and furthermore, I have never done anything that I was ashamed of, Ursula.

URSULA
Neither have I.

MIZ ZEFFIE
(Charmingly)
Yes, but nobody ever asked you to, dear.

URSULA
(Burning)
Why Zeffie Kornhauser...

MIZ ZEFFIE
(All sweetness and light)
And now that you have had your attack for the day, let us endeavor to recapture our good humor...and remember our breeding. I was thinking of celebrating this day by taking in a picture show...and that brings up the problem of clothes for the young man.

5-2-41 (Continued)

D-7 (Cont'd)

URSULA
It certainly does.

MIZ ZEFFIE
(Looking at a picture
on the wall)
Do you think dear Joseph would mind
if we gave this poor young man some
of the clothes he has so little need
for now?

URSULA
Well...
(She looks at the pic-
ture on the wall)

D-8 INSERT - AN ENLARGED HAND-COLORED PICTURE OF JOSEPH

A piece of crepe is draped across the top of the frame. Joseph looks rather displeased at the whole situation. He seems to have been a man who went in for stripes.

URSULA'S VOICE
...he's never minded before.

D-9 MIZ ZEFFIE AND URSULA

MIZ ZEFFIE
(With a hand at her throat)
Do you suppose dear Joseph's clothes
would fit him?

URSULA
I hope they fit him better than they
fitted Joseph.

D-10 HIGH CAMERA SHOT - DOWN ON SULLIVAN

Sweating healthily, he is looking suspiciously up at the window.

DISSOLVE TO:

D-11 LOW CAMERA SHOT UP AT - A RURAL THEATRE MARQUEE

On it we read: "Three Features Tonight - BEYOND THESE TEARS - THE VALLEY OF THE SHADOW - THE BUZZARD OF BERLIN - Also Bingo."

DISSOLVE TO:

5-2-41

D-12 INT. OF THE THEATRE - SULLIVAN - BETWEEN MIZ ZEFFIE AND URSULA

We see a few spectators around them. All look bored to tears.

D-13 THE SCREEN

A Bund parade is marching toward us in the rain. An old professor type rushes out and tries to wrench the Nazi flag away from the flag bearer. He is killed in the ensuing melee. As they cart him away --

D-14 SULLIVAN - BETWEEN MIZ ZEFFIE AND URSULA

As they watch the scene dejectedly their attention is attracted by a snore. The three of them look to their right and the CAMERA PANS OVER TO the local drunk sleeping with his mouth open. The CAMERA PANS BACK ONTO Sullivan and the two ladies. Sullivan looks down at his hand nearest Miz Zeffie and scowls.

D-15 INSERT - THE TIPS OF MIZ ZEFFIE'S FINGERS ARE TICKLING HIS WRIST

D-16 CLOSE SHOT - SULLIVAN

He folds his arms, steals a look at Miz Zeffie, then glares at the screen.

DISSOLVE TO:

D-17 JOSEPH - GLARING OUT OF HIS FRAME

A patch of light across his kisser makes him look unusually unpleasant. We hear three pairs of feet coming up the stairs.

URSULA'S VOICE
Good night, John.

MIZ ZEFFIE'S VOICE
And sleep tight.

SULLIVAN'S VOICE
Yes, M'am.

The CAMERA PANS OVER to Sullivan closing the door. He is nattily dressed in Joseph's clothes, including the hat.

5-2-41 (Continued)

D-17 (Cont'd)

MIZ ZEFFIE
(Leaning in the door)
And don't let the skeeters bite.

SULLIVAN
Yes, M'am.

MIZ ZEFFIE
You sure you have everything you want?

SULLIVAN
Yes, M'am.

MIZ ZEFFIE
Absolutely sure?

SULLIVAN
Positive.

MIZ ZEFFIE
(Suddenly)
Oh, your bed isn't opened.

SULLIVAN
Oh, that's all right. I'll take care of it.

MIZ ZEFFIE
(Forcing her way into the room)
Nonsense. That is woman's work...
(She starts to sing)
Men must work and women must weep, or however it goes.

The CAMERA PANS her to the bed.

MIZ ZEFFIE
(Opening and patting the bed)
There. Would you like a hot water bottle?

SULLIVAN
No, M'am.

MIZ ZEFFIE
And you haven't any pyjies!

SULLIVAN
Never use 'em.

5-2-41 (Continued)

D-17 (Cont'd)

MIZ ZEFFIE
Oh!
(Then after a moment)
Joseph wore a nightgown.

SULLIVAN
Is that a fact?

MIZ ZEFFIE
(Looking around)
Well...I guess there's nothing
else.

SULLIVAN
I guess not.

MIS ZEFFIE
(Pointing)
I'll let you know as soon as
the bathroom is free...it's uh
...community.

SULLIVAN
Ah.

MIZ ZEFFIE
(Musically)
Well, then...Good night.

SULLIVAN
Good night.

He closes the door and gives it a dirty look, then slips a bolt. Now he tears off Joseph's coat.

D-18 MIZ ZEFFIE AND URSULA - OUTSIDE SULLIVAN'S DOOR

URSULA
(In a whisper)
Do you think he'll stay?

MIZ ZEFFIE
I do, do hope so.

She turns the key in Sullivan's door, pulls it out and takes it with her.

DISSOLVE TO:

D-19 A CLOCK - ON THE MANTELPIECE

It strikes "One."

5-2-41

D-20 SULLIVAN - IN BED

He sits up, puts on the bed light and we see that he is in his underwear. Now he hurries out of bed, crosses the room and from a waste basket retrieves his tramp clothes. He hurries into them, then gets his bindle and his old shoes from the bottom of the bureau drawer. Holding his bindle and his shoes in one hand he starts for the door. He pauses to salute Joseph's enlargement, reaches the door and returns to put out the bed light. Now his shadow crosses to the door. We hear a couple of low bangs and the lights go on, revealing Sullivan with his hand on the switch, giving the door a very dirty look. He makes sure that the bolt is pulled back, tries the door again, then directs a foul look toward the bathroom. Now he crosses to this and opens the door cautiously. Very cautiously he opens the door on the far side of the bathroom and peeks through.

D-21 MIZ ZEFFIE - IN THE ROMANTIC LIGHT OF A NIGHT LIGHT

Her eyes are closed but she smiles sweetly.

MIZ ZEFFIE
(Languorously)
Who is it?

D-22 CLOSE SHOT - SULLIVAN

He closes the door hastily and the CAMERA TRUCKS AHEAD of him as he comes into his room, closes the door to the bathroom and stops, looking very irritated. After a moment he gives the window a long look, then crosses to it cautiously. He opens the window, looks back once over his shoulder, then looks out.

D-23 LOW CAMERA SHOT - UP AT SULLIVAN

This is from the ground and gives an idea of the height of the second-story window. It is a black night.

D-24 CLOSE SHOT - SULLIVAN - FROM OUTSIDE

We see him squinting around, trying to see something, then he goes back in the room and crosses

D-24 (Cont'd)

to the bed. The CAMERA MOVES TO THE OTHER WINDOW as he crosses and we see him take the two sheets from the bed, knot them together, tie one sheet to the foot of the bed, then come back to the first window. We MOVE WITH HIM. He lets the sheet down PAST US, picks up his bindle, grips it in his teeth, throws a leg over the window sill and starts down cautiously and somewhat clumsily. We GO DOWN WITH HIM. At one point, although he keeps descending, his pants remain stationary. With great difficulty he hangs on with one hand and reaches around to his rear with the other.

D-25 CLOSE SHOT - SULLIVAN'S PANTS CAUGHT ON A NAIL

His hand comes INTO THE SHOT and tries to free the pants, but for this he would have to hoist his weight up with one arm.

D-26 SULLIVAN - ON THE SHEET

He tries to hoist himself up with both hands now, but he is not as strong as he was, so he lets himself down and there is a slow dramatic ripping sound. As he moves OUT OF THE SHOT -

D-27 THE GRANNY KNOT HOLDING THE TWO SHEETS

It slips a little.

D-28 SULLIVAN - COMING DOWN THE STREET - DESCENDING CAMERA SHOT

After a moment he reaches the end of the sheet and damn near falls off. With a Herculean effort, he gets one hand back over the other and starts looking around to see what there is below him. The bindle in his teeth impedes his vision quite a lot. Now his feet start feeling around for something and the CAMERA MOVES DOWN to watch their futile efforts. After a moment he reaches one foot way down below the other, trying to reach ground. The CAMERA SLIDES DOWN A LITTLE and reveals the top of a rain barrel full of water. Sullivan's feet are doing a rather delicate ballet within a quarter of an inch of the water. Now the CAMERA MOVES UP again to Sullivan's upper half. He lets one arm go, takes

D-28 (Cont'd)

another look around and prepares to drop. He drops. There is a loud splash and a "Wow!" from Sullivan.

D-29 MIZ ZEFFIE'S ROOM

Ursula, in hair-curlers, comes in with a shotgun. The CAMERA PANS her to Miz Zeffie's bed.

URSULA
Did you hear something?

MIZ ZEFFIE
(Sitting up)
Yes, we'd better wake up...
John.

URSULA
This is no time for men...get
your gun.

We hear a crash outside as Ursula hurries out.

D-30 DARK SHOT - SULLIVAN - CRAWLING OUT OF THE TIPPED-OVER RAIN BARREL

A light goes on in a window behind him and he hurries, wetly, OUT OF THE SHOT. The CAMERA PANS ONTO a door which opens, revealing Ursula with a shotgun followed by Miz Zeffie with another shotgun.

URSULA
(Indicating)
You take that side; I'll take
this side.

D-31 SULLIVAN - IN THE DOORWAY OF A SHED

He hurries inside and we hear the wild cackling of hens.

D-32 URSULA - GOING AWAY FROM US

She swings and hurries back toward the cackling.

D-33 THE CANVAS WINDOW - IN THE BACK OF THE CHICKEN HOUSE

This tears in twain and the shadow of Sullivan comes through it. He jumps to the ground and dives into a low shed. Immediately we hear the oinking of pigs.

5-2-41

D-34 MIZ ZEFFIE - IN FRONT OF THE CHICKEN HOUSE

She hears a step and backs around the corner.

D-35 THE OTHER SIDE OF THE CHICKEN HOUSE

Here Ursula hears something and backs stealthily around the chicken house.

D-36 THE FAR SIDE OF THE PIG SHED

Sullivan comes through on hands and knees, falls over some fencing and disappears in the darkness. We hear the wild cackle of guinea hens.

D-37 THE REAR OF THE CHICKEN HOUSE

Ursula comes around backwards on the qui vive, waving her gun from right to left. Around the other side of the chicken shed Miz Zeffie appears backwards, waving her gun from left to right. As the sisters approach each other we hear the mooing of a startled cow. The sisters bump, scream piercingly, fire their shotguns into the air and sit down simultaneously.

DISSOLVE TO:

D-38 A HIGHWAY

We hear a motor truck approaching. As its headlights begin to light up the road Sullivan comes out of the bushes, still dripping wet. He jerks his thumb for a ride. We hear a squealing of brakes, Sullivan is lit brilliantly by the headlights and the truck comes to a stop, blocking him from view.

D-39 SULLIVAN - TALKING TO THE DRIVER OF THE TRUCK

SULLIVAN
(His teeth chattering)
Say....clink, clink, clink....
could you give me a lift...click,
click, click....I'm freezing to
death.

THE TRUCK DRIVER
What did you fall into?

5-3-41 (Continued)

D-39 (Cont'd)

SULLIVAN
Everything there was.

THE TRUCK DRIVER
Okay. Hop in the back...here.

He pulls an old blanket from a compartment behind his head.

THE TRUCK DRIVER
Drape that around you.

SULLIVAN
(Throwing the blanket around himself)
Thanks a m-m-million, b-buddy.

THE TRUCK DRIVER
Okay.
(Then after a moment)
Y'all right?

SULLIVAN'S VOICE
F-fine.

THE TRUCK DRIVER
Okay.

He grinds his gears and the truck pulls away. The CAMERA PANS WITH IT.

FADE OUT:

END OF SEQUENCE "D"

5-3-41

SEQUENCE "E"

FADE IN:

E-1 THE TRUCK DRIVER AND SULLIVAN - INSIDE THE TRUCK - (NIGHT)

The truck driver is shaking Sullivan to wake him up.

THE TRUCK DRIVER
Come on, buddy, wake up...this is as far as I go..

SULLIVAN
(Sitting up sleepily)
Hunh? What?... Who are you? Oh.

THE TRUCK DRIVER
Come on, wake up... I don't want the boss to see you. We ain't supposed to give no lifts.

SULLIVAN
Oh... sure... thanks a lot.

As he moves toward the rear of the truck he sees the houses for the first time.

SULLIVAN
What city is this?

He hops onto the ground.

THE TRUCK DRIVER
(Following him)
Hollywood.

SULLIVAN
(Surprised)
Hollywood! What state?

THE TRUCK DRIVER
Hollywood, California... How many is there?... You'll get a chanst to meet the moom-pitcher stars... so long.

He hurries to the front of the truck. Sullivan is too stupified to answer as the truck grinds away. Now he rubs the sleep out of his eyes and looks around angrily. If swearing were permitted he would do so

E-1 (Cont'd)

at this point. He shivers, notices an owl wagon, feels in his pocket for his ten cents, then crosses to the owl wagon. As he slides the door open -

E-2 INT. THE OWL WAGON

Sullivan comes in and rubs his hands.

SULLIVAN
Give me a cup of coffee and a...
doughnut, if that's enough for it.
(He puts his dime
on the counter)

THE COUNTER MAN
You want it plain or with powdered
sugar.

SULLIVAN
With a little cream.

THE COUNTER MAN
The sinker.

SULLIVAN
Oh, just any kind... or some rolls,
I don't care.

He shivers, rubs his hands again and climbs on the stool. The CAMERA PANS WITH him and brings the Girl into view. She is getting some cigarettes from a slot machine. She is young, dressed in evening dress with a coat over it. Now she turns, starts taking the cellophane off her cigarettes and looks at Sullivan pitifully.

THE GIRL
Give him some ham and eggs.

She takes thirty-five cents from her bag, walks next to Sullivan and puts the money on the counter.

SULLIVAN
(Embarrassed)
That's very kind of you, sister,
but I'm not hungry... a cup of coffee
and a... sinker will fix me fine.

THE GIRL
Don't be a sucker... give him some
ham and eggs.

5-2-41 (Continued)

E-2 (Cont'd)

THE GIRL (Cont'd)
(Then to Sullivan)
The way I'm fixed, thirty-five cents isn't going to make any difference...here.

She offers him a cigarette.

SULLIVAN
Thanks.

He lights her cigarette and then his own.

SULLIVAN (Cont'd)
Thanks....things a little tough, huh?

THE GIRL
I'm not sitting in an owl wagon for local color...they locked me out of my room.

SULLIVAN
Oh, that's too bad....Things are tough every place...The war in Europe...the strikes over here... There's no work...there's no food...

THE GIRL
Drink your coffee while it's hot.

SULLIVAN
Thanks.
(Then after a sip)
What did they lock you out of your room for?

THE GIRL
Did I ask _you_ any questions?

SULLIVAN
I'm sorry.

THE GIRL
(Relenting)
That's all right.

SULLIVAN
You been in Hollywood long?

THE GIRL
Long enough.

5-3-41 (Continued)

E-2 (Cont'd)

SULLIVAN
Trying to crash the movies or something?

THE GIRL
Something like that.

SULLIVAN
I guess that must be pretty hard to do, hunh?

THE GIRL
I guess so...I never got close enough to find out.

SULLIVAN
I'm sorry.

THE GIRL
Say, who's being sorry for who? Are you buying <u>me</u> the eggs or am I buying them for <u>you</u>?

SULLIVAN
I'd like to repay you for them.

THE GIRL
All right, give me a letter of introduction to Lubitsch.

SULLIVAN
I might be able to do that too... ...Who is Lubitsch?

THE GIRL
Eat your eggs.

SULLIVAN
(His mouth full)
Can you act?

THE GIRL
What did you say?

SULLIVAN
(Swallowing)
I said, can you act?

THE GIRL
Sure I can act...Would you like me to give you a recitation?

SULLIVAN
Go ahead.

5-3-41 (Continued)

E-2 (Cont'd)

THE GIRL
(Not expecting to be
taken seriously)
Skip it. My next act will be an
impersonation of a young lady going
home....on the thumb.

SULLIVAN
In that outfit?

THE GIRL
How about your own outfit?

SULLIVAN
(After a moment)
Haven't you got a car?

THE GIRL
No, have you?

SULLIVAN
Well...no...but...

THE GIRL
Then don't get Ritzie. And I'll
tell you some other things I haven't
got: I haven't got a yacht, or a
pearl necklace, or a fur coat, or a
country seat or even a winter seat...
and I could use a new girdle too.
(Protection: stockings)

SULLIVAN
I wish I could give you...a few of
the things you need.

THE GIRL
You're not trying to lead me astray,
are you? You big bad wolf!

Sullivan laughs sheepishly.

THE GIRL
You know the nice thing about buying
food for a man is you don't have to
laugh at his jokes...Just think, if
you were some big shot like a casting
director or something, I'd be staring
into your bridgework...
(She rests her chin
on her hand)
...saying: "Yes, Mr. Smearkase...
not really, Mr. Smearkase....Now
there's a funny one, Mr. Smearkase,

E-2 (Cont'd)

THE GIRL (Cont'd)
ha, ha, ha! How you carry on, Mr. Smearkase. Stop it, that's my knee!
(She laughs archly, then speaks to the counter man)
Give Mr. Smearkase another cup of coffee...make that two.
(Then to Sullivan)
You want a piece of pie?

SULLIVAN
No, thanks, kid.

THE GIRL
Why, Mr. Smearkase, aren't you getting a little familiar on such short acquaintance?

SULLIVAN
(Seriously)
Look: If you wanted to stay in Hollywood a little longer...

THE GIRL
(Bitterly)
Well, I don't want to stay in Hollywood a little longer! I've used up all my money and all my going home money and my date got fresh...and they locked me out of my room and...

SULLIVAN
(Interrupting)
I was going to say I've got a friend who's out of town and you could use his place for a couple of weeks and maybe by then things would break a little better or he might even be able to help you a little.

THE GIRL
No thanks.

SULLIVAN
(Quietly)
They're no strings to this, kid. You don't know who I am but I used to know...a few people around here and this guy is really out of town...

5-3-41 (Continued)

E-2 (Cont'd)

THE GIRL
... and you know the way in through a window or something. No thanks. The guy always comes back unexpectedly... or his wife drops in...or they take away the furniture or something.

SULLIVAN
I'm pretty sure that in this case...

THE GIRL
I'm going home, big boy. I'll get a ride out of here in the morning.

SULLIVAN
(After a pause)
I don't like to think of your asking a bunch of thugs for lifts along the highway.

THE GIRL
Then, don't think about it.

SULLIVAN
You just get in any car that comes along?

THE GIRL
Anything but a Stanley Steamer...my uncle blew up in one.

SULLIVAN
But, that's terrible. You can't tell what kind of a heel is apt to be...behind the wheel.

THE GIRL
All heels are pretty much the same.

SULLIVAN
Say, look:

THE GIRL
(Archly)
Yes, Mr. Smearkase.

SULLIVAN
This friend of mine... this guy who's out of town... I don't think he'd mind if I borrowed his car.

THE GIRL
What is it, a street car?
(Cover with a Saxon)

5-3-41 (Continued)

E-2 (Cont'd)

SULLIVAN
(Rising)
It's a car. You wait here.

THE GIRL
(Anxiously)
You're just going to get yourself in trouble.

SULLIVAN
I'm not going to get myself in trouble and I want to repay you for that ham and eggs.

THE GIRL
(Touched)
That isn't necessary, big boy... Some day, when your ship comes in, buy somebody who's hungry some ham and eggs... and we'll be all square.

SULLIVAN
(Putting his hand on her shoulder)
You wait here... I'll be back here before you can say... what's that big director's name?

THE GIRL
Lubitsch.

SULLIVAN
(Raising a finger)
Lubitsch.

DISSOLVE TO:

E-3 INT. OF A HANDSOME COUPE - (DAY)

SULLIVAN
Now where would you like to go?

THE GIRL
Oh, well, uh...if you could just drop me off at uh... or maybe that would be too far for you.

SULLIVAN
That depends entirely on where it is.

THE GIRL
Well...would Chicago be too far?

5-3-41 (Continued)

E-3 (Cont'd)

SULLIVAN
Chicago!...You mean Chicago, Illinois?

THE GIRL
Yes.

SULLIVAN
Well, I wasn't actually thinking of driving as far as Chicago.

THE GIRL
That's all right. Just drop me anywhere...I just happened to say Chicago because it's a little better than halfway and I could hitch a ride out of there easily.

SULLIVAN
Where do you live, in Bermuda?

THE GIRL
(Vexed)
You don't have to get funny...You can drop me anywhere...I didn't ask you for a ride.

SULLIVAN
Well, you don't have to get on your high horse either...If I wasn't solicitous about your welfare I wouldn't have gone into this in the first place.

THE GIRL
(Indignantly)
You wouldn't have gone into it!...I suppose you bought me eggs.

SULLIVAN
Look: I'm not denying the eggs and I'm very anxious to repay you. I just haven't time to go rubber-necking all over the United States. I'm a busy man and...

THE GIRL
You are?

SULLIVAN
I mean, I'm not. Now..wait a minute... How's this: Suppose you drop me somewhere, drive home and I'll pick up the car later. Now, that's what you call an idea.

5-3-41 (Continued)

E-3 (Cont'd)

THE GIRL
(Looking at him slowly)
You don't happen to operate out of a boobyhatch, do you? You'd better drop me in the next town and then take this bus back where you stole it from.

SULLIVAN
Look: If there's one thing in the world you don't have to worry about it's this...
(He chuckles)
it would certainly be funny if they arrested me for taking it, though.

THE GIRL
A panic.

Sullivan laughs joyously.

THE GIRL
You have a very peculiar sense of humor. I can't think of anything funnier than a year in the cooler to remember you by.

SULLIVAN
Don't talk nonsense...I left a note saying I was taking the car...or did I?

THE GIRL
Time will tell.

SULLIVAN
(After a moment's thought)
I certainly meant to leave a note... I must have left a note...but did I?

THE GIRL
That is the question. Who does it belong to?

SULLIVAN
Did I ask you any questions?
(Then after a moment of triumph)
It belongs to a picture director... a fellow called Sullivan.
(He gives her a quick look)

E-3 (Cont'd)

THE GIRL
Oh.

SULLIVAN
You never heard of him.

THE GIRL
No.

SULLIVAN
(Airily)
He's made a few pictures: "Ants In Your Plants Of 1939."

THE GIRL
(Mildly interested)
Oh, did he do that?

SULLIVAN
You saw it?

THE GIRL
Yes.

SULLIVAN
Well, well...did you like it?

THE GIRL
Not much.

SULLIVAN
Ah. Some people thought it was pretty good.

THE GIRL
I don't care for musicals...they hurt my ears.

SULLIVAN
I see.
(Then after a pause)
Did you like uh..."Hey, Hey, in the Hayloft"?

THE GIRL
(Brightly)
Oh, I was crazy about that.

SULLIVAN
Yes, I thought that would just...about fit.

5-3-41 (Continued)

E-3 (Cont'd)

THE GIRL
Do you remember that scene where the two are up in the hayloft...

SULLIVAN
Perfectly.

THE GIRL
...and she made him close his eyes and count three before kissing her...
(She starts to laugh violently)
...and the pig came out and he kissed the pig instead...
(She goes into a gale of laughter)

SULLIVAN
Yes, that was on a very high plane.

THE GIRL
(Through her laughter)
...and then he fell through the hole and sneezed at the horse?

SULLIVAN
(Dismally)
And the horse sneezed back at him.

THE GIRL
(Happily)
That was a wonderful scene, of course it was stupid, but it was wonderful. Who directed that picture?

Sullivan looks at her sternly for a moment before speaking.

SULLIVAN
Don't you think with the world in its present condition...with death snarling at you from every street corner...people are a little tired of comedies?

THE GIRL
No.

SULLIVAN
(Taking a deep breath)
Perhaps I didn't make myself clear...

5-3-41 (Continued)

E-3 (Cont'd)

THE GIRL
(Suddenly suspiciously)
Say! How come you know a picture director well enough to borrow his car?

SULLIVAN
What about it?

THE GIRL
And you never even heard of Lubitsch?

SULLIVAN
(Uneasily)
Oh...I thought you said Von Sternberg.

THE GIRL
(With narrowed eyes)
Say, what <u>is</u> this?

SULLIVAN
(Uneasily)
Well, as a matter of fact, I used to know...most of those boys. Naturally, you don't like to mention it in a suit like this.

He gives her a look and she gives it right back to him.

SULLIVAN (Cont'd)
As a matter of fact, I used to <u>be</u> a uh..picture director.

THE GIRL
(Almost with tears)
Oh, you poor kid.

SULLIVAN
Don't get emotional...I'll be all right.

THE GIRL
What kind of pictures did you make?

SULLIVAN
More along...educational lines.

THE GIRL
No wonder. There's nothing like a deep-dish movie to drive you out in the open.

5-3-41 (Continued)

E-3 (Cont'd)

SULLIVAN
What are you talking about? Film is the greatest educational medium the world has ever known. You take "Hold Back Tomorrow"...

THE GIRL
You hold it.

Sullivan bares his teeth and looks away disgustedly.

THE GIRL
Did you ever meet Lubitsch?

SULLIVAN
Yes.

THE GIRL
I bet he wouldn't even speak to you now, hunh?

SULLIVAN
He spoke to me the day before yesterday.

THE GIRL
Gee, isn't that swell. Is Capra nice, or don't you know him?

SULLIVAN
Very nice.

THE GIRL
Is Hitchcock as fat as they say he is?

SULLIVAN
Fatter.

THE GIRL
Do you think Orson Welles is crazy?

SULLIVAN
In a very practical way.

THE GIRL
(After a moment)
Funny, isn't it...to meet your first picture director on the day you're leaving Hollywood...all washed up... even a washed up picture director.

SULLIVAN
Don't get sympathetic...I might make a comeback, you know.

E-3 (Cont'd)

THE GIRL
They all say that...the man had the room ahead of me in the hotel was always going to make a come-back...he was a picture director... then one day he shot himself instead.

Sullivan winces.

THE GIRL
They had to re-paper the room.

Sullivan winces again.

THE GIRL
(Putting her hand on his arm, very sympathetically)
You wouldn't ever do anything like that, would you, big boy?

SULLIVAN
(Firmly)
Not on your wall paper.

We hear the sirens of two motorcops.

THE GIRL
(After a look over her shoulder)
What do you suppose that is?

SULLIVAN
Well, it isn't a banshee...but whatever it is, there's absolutely nothing they can do...remember that!

DISSOLVE TO:

E-4 EXT. OF THE BEVERLY HILLS POLICE STATION - (DAY)

DISSOLVE TO:

E-5 SULLIVAN AND THE GIRL - IN ADJOINING CELLS

THE GIRL
What did you say?

SULLIVAN
I said there's absolutely nothing they can do.

5-3-41 (Continued)

E-5 (Cont'd)

The Cop appears and unlocks Sullivan's cell.

THE COP
All right, you.

SULLIVAN
(Passing the girl)
Don't give it a thought.

E-6 A DESK SERGEANT - BEHIND HIS DESK

Next to the desk stands Sullivan's butler and his valet. They are looking toward the door to the cells.

E-7 THE DOOR

Sullivan is brought in by the cop.

SULLIVAN
(Spying his servants)
Well...
(He starts forward)

E-8 THE SERGEANT, THE VALET AND THE BUTLER

THE VALET
Oh, good morning, sir, I'm so sorry.

THE BUTLER
(Sternly)
Good morning, sir.

THE SERGEANT
You ever seen this man before?

THE BUTLER
That is Mr. Sullivan, sir, the owner of the alleged hot car.

THE SERGEANT
Then what's all the hullabaloo?

E-9 SULLIVAN - WALKING INTO THE SHOT

SULLIVAN
(Coming into the shot)
That's what I'd like to know.

5-5-41 (Continued)

E-9 (Cont'd)

THE SERGEANT
You John L. Sullivan?

SULLIVAN
Yes.

THE SERGEANT
What is your occupation?

SULLIVAN
Motion picture director.

THE SERGEANT
(To the valet)
Is that right?

THE VALET
Yes, sir.

THE SERGEANT
(To Sullivan)
Let me see your driver's license.

SULLIVAN
I haven't got it.
(To the valet)
Did you bring it?

THE VALET
No, sir.

THE SERGEANT
Driving without your license, hunh?

SULLIVAN
Yes, isn't that terrible. That must call for a dollar fine and ten minutes in jail.

THE SERGEANT
(To the butler)
You sure this is Sullivan?

THE BUTLER
Oh, quite, sir.

THE SERGEANT
(Suddenly to Sullivan)
Then, what are you doing in those clothes?

SULLIVAN
I just paid my income tax.

5-5-41 (Continued)

E-9 (Cont'd)

THE SERGEANT
(After looking around)
All right... case dismissed... but you don't drive that car without a license.

SULLIVAN
Okay, and let the girl out too, will you? She's getting bored in there.

THE SERGEANT
(Scowling)
How does the girl fit into this picture?

SULLIVAN
There's always a girl in the picture... haven't you ever been to the movies?

DISSOLVE TO:

E-10 SULLIVAN AND THE GIRL - IN THE BACK OF A LIMOUSINE

THE GIRL
(Nervously)
Where's he taking us now? Whose car is this?

SULLIVAN
The same guy. Sullivan.

THE GIRL
Where's he taking us?

SULLIVAN
Down to the depot to buy you a ticket and send you home and stop fooling around.

THE GIRL
Who's buying me a ticket?

SULLIVAN
Sullivan.

THE GIRL
What did I ever do for him?

SULLIVAN
You bought him some eggs.

5-5-41 (Continued)

E-10 (Cont'd)

THE GIRL
(After turning slowly
and looking at him)
Oh.
(Then after a pause)
So you're the washed-up director.

SULLIVAN
I exaggerated that part a little
bit.

THE GIRL
What are you doing in those
clothes?

SULLIVAN
I just pulled that one in the
police station.

THE GIRL
Hunh?

SULLIVAN
I made up a joke.
(Then crossly)
Look: I'm not sore at you, I'm
sore at those cops dragging me all
the way back here. It doesn't
matter where I go, I end up right
in Hollywood. You're a very nice
girl; as a matter of fact, I en-
joyed meeting you and if ever
there's anything I can do for you,
at any time, I'll do it. Honestly.

THE GIRL
You mean that?

SULLIVAN
Sincerely.

THE GIRL
Then buy me some ham and eggs...
before I bite you.

Sullivan picks up the telephone, hesitates, looks at his clothes, then says:

SULLIVAN
Home.

DISSOLVE TO:

5-5-41

E-11 CLOSE SHOT - SOME HAM AND EGGS - COOKING IN A SKILLET

DISSOLVE TO:

E-12 SULLIVAN'S LIVING ROOM - LOOKING INTO THE HALL

We see some handsome stairs in the background. The girl comes in, followed by Sullivan. She looks rather sadly at the rich trappings of the room Sullivan looks slightly sheepish. As they walk toward us she touches a piece of satin here, a polished wood surface there.

THE GIRL
(As they get close to us)
Where is the swimming pool?... You must have a swimming pool.

SULLIVAN
(Pointing)
Out there.

As they LEAVE THE SHOT -

E-13 A BEAUTIFUL TERRACE - NEXT TO THE POOL

The girl comes out and Sullivan follows sheepishly. The CAMERA PANS them to the edge of the pool.

SULLIVAN
(Nearer the pool)
Pretty, isn't it?

The girl looks at it sourly.

SULLIVAN
(Pointing vaguely)
The barbecue is over there and the tennis court on this side.

Now he notices the ferocity of her expression.

SULLIVAN
What are you looking at me that way for?

With a squeal of anger the girl pushes Sullivan into the pool.

5-5-41 (Continued)

E-13 (Cont'd)

THE GIRL
(Leaning over the pool)
There, you fat-head, that's for your swimming pools and your tennis courts and your limousines and your barbecues...

E-14 HIGH CAMERA SHOT - SULLIVAN - IN THE POOL

He sputters to the surface and hangs onto the gutter.

SULLIVAN
(Furiously)
What's the big idea?

E-15 LOW CAMERA SHOT - UP AT THE GIRL - PAST SULLIVAN

THE GIRL
That's for making fun of a poor girl who only tried to help you, you faker!

SULLIVAN
Who made fun of you?

THE GIRL
You did, you big clunk!... with your stories of being a washed-up director...

SULLIVAN
Oh, I did, did I!

He half leaps out of the pool, grabs her ankle and pulls back with all his might. With a scream, the girl falls forward and there is a hell of a splash.

E-16 THE BUTLER - COMING OUT OF THE HOUSE WITH AN ENORMOUS SILVER TRAY

He stops in amazement.

E-17 SULLIVAN AND THE GIRL -IN THE SHALLOW END OF THE POOL

The water comes to a little above her waist.

THE GIRL
You b...uzzard!

She hauls off and nails him with a terrific slap.

5-5-41 (Continued)

E-17 (Cont'd)

SULLIVAN
Oh, you will, will you!

He puts both hands on her shoulders and dunks her under water.

E-18 THE BUTLER

THE BUTLER
(Clearing his throat)
Breakfast is served, sir.

DISSOLVE TO:

E-19 THE GIRL AND SULLIVAN - AT A GLEAMING BREAKFAST TABLE NEXT TO THE POOL

They each wear voluminous white terry-cloth bathrobes. They have already eaten the eggs. Sullivan pours the girl some more coffee. She crosses her legs which are sensational and picks up a cigarette. Sullivan lights it for her.

THE GIRL
You might have shaved.

SULLIVAN
I need these whiskers... for my experiment.

THE GIRL
Oh, yes... the noble experiment.

SULLIVAN
You don't have to make any cracks.
I don't starve and suffer because
I like it, you know.

THE GIRL
Neither does anybody else.
(Contrite)
... I'm sorry.

SULLIVAN
S'all right.

THE GIRL
I'm sorry I pushed you in the water, too.

SULLIVAN
I probably needed it.

5-5-41 (Continued)

E-19 (Cont'd)

THE GIRL
You certainly did.

SULLIVAN
(Worried)
Did I?

THE GIRL
I didn't mind you... as a matter of fact, I had kind of a yen for you...

SULLIVAN
(Surprised)
You have?

THE GIRL
(Pointing to his kimono)
Not in that thing... I liked you better as a bo.

SULLIVAN
Well, I can't help what kind of people you like.

THE GIRL
Maybe I'm vicious... it's funny... I suppose I ought to be very happy for you, as if you'd just struck oil or something... instead of that, I'm sore.

SULLIVAN
Don't frown, it'll make lines in your face.

THE GIRL
You've taken all the joy out of life... I was all through with this kind of stuff...
(She indicates around)
I mean I knew I'd never have it... there was no envy in my heart... I'd found a friend who'd swiped a car to take me home... and now I'm right back where I started.

SULLIVAN
(Crossly)
So am I.

THE GIRL
Just an extra girl having breakfast with a director... only I didn't use to have breakfast with them... maybe that was my trouble.

5-5-41 (Continued)

E-19 (Cont'd)

SULLIVAN
Did they ever ask you to?

THE GIRL
No.

SULLIVAN
Then don't pat yourself on the back.

The butler comes INTO THE SHOT and takes the coffee pot to a side table to refill it.

THE GIRL
Take me with you.

SULLIVAN
(Indignantly)
What?...

THE GIRL
I don't want to be sent home on the rattler.

SULLIVAN
(After a pause)
Don't be childish. I'll tell you what I'll do. You can stay here for a couple of weeks like I told you in the owl wagon... and when I come back I'll see what I can do for you... or I'll write you a couple of notes before I go.

THE GIRL
I don't want you to write me any notes... I don't want to start all that stuff again... take me with you and when you get as far as you're going we'll say goodbye and I'll go the rest of the way alone... it'll make a nice ending... and we'll finish what we started this morning.

SULLIVAN
That is absolutely out of the question.

The girl crosses and sits on the arm of his chair.

THE GIRL
Please. You don't know anything about... anything. You don't know how to get a meal; you don't know how to keep a secret... you can't even stay out of town.

5-5-41 (Continued)

E-19 (Cont'd)

SULLIVAN
Thanks.

THE GIRL
I know fifty times as much about trouble as you ever will ... and besides, you owe it to me, you sort of belong to me... when you're a bum... I found you.

SULLIVAN
Piffle!

THE GIRL
(Leaning closer)
Please.

SULLIVAN
I tell you it's absolutely out of the...

THE GIRL
(Leaning still closer)
I'll throw you in the water.

SULLIVAN
You'd take my mind off my work.

THE GIRL
(Mockingly)
Ho, ho, the big director... who has all the girls panting for him...

SULLIVAN
(Wearily)
I tell you...

THE GIRL
(Inspired)
I'll follow you and tell everybody who you are... like a kid sister.

SULLIVAN
(Tauntingly)
You'll follow me!

THE GIRL
Yes I'll follow you, and I'll holler: this guy is a phoney, ladies and gentlemen... this is Sullivan, the big director from Hollywood, a phonus balonus, a faker, a heel who's just trying to...

5-5-41 (Continued)

E-19 (Cont'd)

THE BUTLER
(Coming into THE SHOT
with a pot of fresh
coffee)
If I may join in the controversy,
sir, I believe the young lady's
suggestion is an excellent one for
the reason ...

SULLIVAN
(Severely, looking
around the girl)
Yes, well you may not join in the
controversy, Mr. Burrows.

THE GIRL
(Bouncing up and down
on Sullivan's lap)
I will, I will, I will! I'm going
with you.

SULLIVAN
Well, you're not going to do any-
thing of the kind. Burrows, you
go down to the station and....

The Girl puts her hand over his mouth and Sullivan starts to yammer.

THE GIRL
Will you get me some tramp clothes,
Mr. Burrows?

THE BUTLER
Certainly, Miss.

SULLIVAN
(Getting up with the
struggling girl in
his arms)
You go down to the station and get
me a ticket to...
(Then to the girl)
Where do you live?

THE GIRL
I won't tell you. I won't be sent
home, I'll...

She grabs Sullivan's ears and starts to kick her feet up and down.

5-5-41 (Continued)

E-19 (Cont'd)

SULLIVAN
Stop that! ... grab her feet, Burrows!

THE BUTLER
Yes, sir... now, Miss...

THE GIRL
I won't be sent home. You leave me alone. Let go my feet.

THE BUTLER
Now, Miss.

THE GIRL
Oh, you will, will you!

She straightens out her legs and the Butler starts teetering backwards.

SULLIVAN
Stop that!

The girl gets a death-grip around Sullivan's neck and the Butler gets a death-grip on the girl's legs. The result is inevitable and the three of them swan-dive into the pool. At the splash --

E-20 THE DOOR OF THE HOUSE

The Valet comes hurrying out and stops in dismay.

THE VALET
(Under his breath)
Good God!

He hurries to the edge of the pool where Sullivan and the girl are occupied in dunking each other.

THE VALET
(Seizing Burrows's hand)
My dear Burrows... here now, one, two, three, PULL HARD!

With a tremendous effort on Burrows part the Valet flies into the pool.

FADE OUT:

END OF SEQUENCE "E"

5-5-41

SEQUENCE "F"

FADE IN:

F-1 THE BUTLER AND THE VALET - AT THE TELEPHONE IN THE PANTRY - (DAY)

They are both in rather loud dressing gowns and the valet is still wiping his back hair with a bathtowel.

THE BUTLER
(Into the telephone)
Union Depot? Information, please. Hello, information? Have you any freight trains going east this afternoon or early this evening...five forty-eight? Thank you very much indeed, sir...oh, and could you tell me: does that train carry tramps and if so where do they get on? Tramps!

F-2 THE INFORMATION MAN - IN THE UNION DEPOT

THE INFORMATION MAN
(Bitterly into the telephone)
How would you like to take a flying...
(He hangs up the receiver and to his colleague says)
Wise guy.
(Now he moves forward wearily)
Yes, madam.

DISSOLVE TO:

F-3 AN OLD CLERK IN THE FREIGHT DEPARTMENT OF THE RAILWAY TERMINAL

THE OLD CLERK
Yes, this is the freight department...
What was that again?

F-4 THE BUTLER AND THE VALET - IN THE PANTRY

This time the Valet is at the telephone.

THE VALET
(Into the telephone)
I said, I wonder if you'd be kind enough to settle a bet for us...just a few of us here in the club...if a tramp were going to board your five-forty-eight this afternoon from where would he board it.

5-5-41 (Continued)

F-4 (Cont'd)

THE VALET (Cont'd)
(He holds up his finger for silence)
I see, I see...but not within the yard limits...I think that gives me the complete picture. Thank you very much for your trouble and, by the way, I win, ha, ha. Good day.
(He hangs up)

Now he looks at the Butler.

THE VALET
Different approach to the same problem.

DISSOLVE TO:

F-5 A BIG FREIGHT LOCOMOTIVE - JUST PAST A SIGN READING: "YARD LIMIT"

Behind it stretches a long row of cars ending with a caboose. The engineer stands next to the engine oiling the link mechanism. He looks toward the waiting people, back to his mechanism, then to the waiting people again.

F-6 LOW CAMERA SHOT OF THE RIGHT-OF-WAY

Here, on a slight embankment, we see about thirty men. They are of all nationalities including Chinese, Filipino and Negro.

F-7 HIGH CAMERA SHOT - SOME FREIGHT CARS - AT THE YARD LIMIT

Sullivan's limousine comes around a freight car and turns to the left across the tracks. Now it stops, backs up and passes UNDER US. We see the butler and the valet on the front seat.

F-8 A BROKEN-IN SHACK - NEAR THE WAITING PEOPLE

Sullivan's car comes out from behind it and stops.

F-9 CLOSE SHOT - THE VALET AT THE WHEEL AND THE BUTLER BEHIND HIM

THE BUTLER
(Over his shoulder)
I think this is it, sir.

5-5-41 (Continued)

F-9 (Con*'d)

The CAMERA PANS to the rear of the car. Peeking out of the window we see Sullivan and the girl. Sullivan looks as he did before. The girl's hair is tucked up inside a boy's cap and her face is dirty.

SULLIVAN
Back up behind this shack.

As the car MOVES OUT OF THE SHOT -

F-10 LONGER SHOT - OF THE CAR BACKING TO A PLACE BEHIND THE SHACK

Sullivan, the girl and the butler get to the ground. The girl wears a turtle-neck sweater, a cap slightly sideways, a torn coat, turned-up pants and sneakers.

SULLIVAN
Why don't you go back with the car...
You look about as much like a boy as
Mae West.

THE GIRL
All right, they'll think I'm your
frail.

THE BUTLER
I believe it's called a beazle, Miss...
if memory serves.

SULLIVAN
(Shaking hands)
So long, Burrows, I'll see you in a
little while.

THE BUTLER
Goodbye, sir. Goodbye, Miss.

THE VALET
(Joining them)
Goodbye, sir. Goodbye, Miss.

SULLIVAN
Goodbye....goodbye.

THE BUTLER
May I close, sir, by reiterating the
fervent wish that you might abandon
the entire expedition which I en-
vision with deep apprehension and
gloomy foreboding.

5-5-41 (Continued)

F-10 (Cont'd)

SULLIVAN
Thanks.

We hear a whistle.

SULLIVAN
(To the girl)
Come on.

He takes her hand and runs OUT OF THE SHOT. The butler removes his derby tragically and holds it over his left forearm as for the passing of a funeral.

F-11 THE FREIGHT CONDUCTOR - NEAR THE CABOOSE

He snaps his watch, puts it back in his pocket, then gives the high-ball.

F-12 LOW CAMERA - THE LOCOMOTIVE

It snorts, jerks forward and we hear the distant bangings of the stretched couplings. The engine blasts again and moves PAST US.

F-13 SHOT LOOKING FORWARD - FROM THE ROOF OF THE FIRST BOXCAR

PAST the engine and the tender we see the waiting transients.

F-14 CLOSE TRUCKING SHOT - PAST THE EMBANKMENT

Sullivan and the girl tear INTO THE SHOT and PAST US.

F-15 HIGH CAMERA SHOT - SHOOTING FORWARD ALONG THE TRAIN

We see the vagrants swarming on the train.

F-16 SHOT FROM INTERIOR OF A CATTLE CAR

There is some straw on the floor. A typical old Weary-Willie flips on board expertly and is joined a moment later by another one. Now Sullivan and the girl appear. She gets aboard with considerable

5-5-41 (Continued)

F-16 (Cont'd)

difficulty and boosts from Sullivan. Eventually he lands flat on his stomach on the floor of the car with his legs hanging out. She grabs him by the seat of the pants and yanks him on board.

F-17 THE TWO OLD WEARY-WILLIES - IN THE CORNER OF THE CAR

They watch this exhibition with disgust but no comment.

F-18 SULLIVAN AND THE GIRL - BRUSHING EACH OTHER OFF

SULLIVAN
(Seeing the Weary-Willies)
How do you do.

One of the Weary-Willies grunts in reply.

SULLIVAN
(After a moment)
Beautiful weather.

THE GIRL
If it doesn't rain.

To this the Weary-Willies do not reply.

SULLIVAN
How do you feel about the labor situation?

The Weary-Willies gather their bindles sourly and go to the door of the car. The first one reaches expertly for the ladder and disappears. As the second one starts out:

SULLIVAN
(In surprise)
Where are you going? I hope we didn't disturb you.

In reply, the Weary-Willie spits richly onto the right-of-way and disappears.

THE GIRL
Very interesting couple.

5-5-41 (Continued)

F-18 (Cont'd)

She sits down and Sullivan sits beside her. After a moment he inhales deeply, then speaks.

SULLIVAN
Do you smell anything?

THE GIRL
I certainly do.

SULLIVAN
What does it smell like to you?

THE GIRL
Hogs.

SULLIVAN
That's what I was afraid of.

THE GIRL
I'm getting hungry.

SULLIVAN
How can you be hungry...when you just ate?

THE GIRL
I'm not a scientist. All I know is I'm hungry.

Sullivan sneezes.

THE GIRL
You'd better tell the porter to close the window.

SULLIVAN
(Gently)
I didn't want to bring you in the first place...so now that you're here....
(He sneezes)
......don't start baking wise cracks.

THE GIRL
Do, sir.

SULLIVAN
Blasted draft id here ad thad.

5-5-41 (Continued)

F-18 (Cont'd)

THE GIRL
Where does this train go?

SULLIVAN
I don't know.

THE GIRL
Well, how long is it going to take to get there?

SULLIVAN
I didn't ask you to come along.

THE GIRL
I think that's a perfectly reasonable question.

SULLIVAN
Look: Haven't you got enough imagination to pretend that we're broke, hungry, homeless....drifting in despair.

THE GIRL
That doesn't take much imagination as far as I'm concerned....especially about the hungry part.... but I'd still like to know where the train was going. Suppose it was going to Mexico.

SULLIVAN
Well, suppose it was....now let's sit here and try to feel like a couple of tramps.

THE GIRL
(After a moment)
Where do you suppose they took those hogs?

SULLIVAN
Probably Kansas City, I wish you'd stop talking about them. Do you want to try to climb to another car?

5-5-41 (Continued)

F-18 (Cont'd)

THE GIRL
(Looking out)
No thanks. Do you know what they make out of hogs?

SULLIVAN
Tooth brushes.

THE GIRL
They make hams...Boy, what I could do to a ham....with some rye bread and dill pickles. Do you suppose we're going to Kansas City?

SULLIVAN
Maybe, I don't know.

THE GIRL
How long does it take to get there?

SULLIVAN
I don't know.

THE GIRL
You don't suppose they all died in here on the way, do you?

SULLIVAN
Who?

THE GIRL
The hogs.

Sullivan sneezes.

THE GIRL
This is a nice airy car you picked.

Sullivan gets up and slides the slatted door closed.

THE GIRL
That ought to make a big difference.

FADE OUT:

5-5-41

FADE IN:

F-19 VERY LONG SHOT - THE MOON - IN THE SKY

The clouds are silver-edged around it. We hear a train whistle and the freight train in silhouette creeps across the BOTTOM OF THE SHOT, very small.

DISSOLVE TO:

F-20 THE CATTLE CAR IN THE MOONLIGHT

Sullivan has the girl in his arms to keep her warm.

SULLIVAN
Are you cold?

THE GIRL
I'll be all right.

SULLIVAN
It's the desert.

THE GIRL
I'll be all right.

SULLIVAN
As soon as this blasted thing
comes to a town some place I'll
send for a car and have you
takid hobe. This is a lot of
hoky-baloky. This is a terrible
way to travel...with a girl.

THE GIRL
It's better with a girl than
without one...you would have
frozen to death. If I go back
will you go back with me?

SULLIVAN
Dod sense.

THE GIRL
Then, I won't go back either.
You're so simple, you're apt
to get into a lot of trouble.

5-5-41 (Continued)

F-20 (Cont'd)

SULLIVAN
Whud you thig I'bout here for?

THE GIRL
I like that in you. You're like those knights who used to ride around looking for trouble. Who was it that rode on the pure white horse?

SULLIVAN
Lady Godiba.

THE GIRL
(Chuckling)
She must have been a nut. I bet her husband was sore... are you jealous?

SULLIVAN
Why don't you shut ub and try to get some sleeb?

THE GIRL
Will you sleep with me?

SULLIVAN
I'll try.

THE GIRL
Try counting the hogs jumping over a hedge.

He sneezes and narrowly misses her.

FADE OUT:

FADE IN:

F-21 LONG SHOT - THE FREIGHT TRAID - (EARLY BORDIG)

In the distance we see a towd. The locomotive whistles.

F-22 CLOSE SHOT - THE ENGINEER - IN HIS CAB

He whistles again.

QUICK DISSOLVE TO:

5-5-41

F-23 SULLIVAN AND THE GIRL - ASLEEP IN THE HAY

We hear the whistle a third time. Sullivan sits up, blinks, looks around in some surprise, takes a good look at the girl, remembers and opens his mouth to sneeze. Slowly he closes it again. He opens it again, lingers longer on the brink, then relaxes and starts to close his mouth. Just as he is about to close it he opens it rapidly and sneezes like a cannon shot. The girl sits up frightened.

THE GIRL
What was that?

SULLIVAN
Dothing...just be.

THE GIRL
What?

SULLIVAN
I sdeezed.

THE GIRL
You what?

SULLIVAN
I....
(His mouth begins to work)

His mouth works more and he explodes like a bomb.

SULLIVAN
....sdeezed.

THE GIRL
Oh, you poor darling. Have you got hay fever?

SULLIVAN
I thing ids hog fever.

He taps his chest, opens his mouth and wheezes at her gruesomely.

THE GIRL
Oh, you poor lamb.

SULLIVAN
I'll be all right as sood as the sud cubs ub ad id geds a liddle warber.

5-5-41 (Continued)

F-23 (Cont'd)

THE GIRL
Are you huggry?
(She laughs)
You've god be doig id. Have we
got any eating money?

SULLIVAN
Ted seds.

THE GIRL
Can we spend it for breakfast or
are you saving it for something?

SULLIVAN
(Sourly)
Loog, I've already told you: I'll
sed for a car ad...

THE GIRL
I can't help it if I'm good-natured...
I like to be with you and it puts me
in a good humor. You take lots of
girls and you made them sleep in a
hog sty all night and then didn't
tell them where their breakfast was
coming from in the morning...they
wouldn't take it lying down.

SULLIVAN
We'll fide sub breakfast subwhere.

THE GIRL
In some swill pail, I suppose.

SULLIVAN
(On the defensive)
Well, whad do the other bubs do?

THE GIRL
(Forcefully)
They steal chickigs...chickens,
and roast them over campfires with
baked potatoes and green corn-on-
the cob roasted in the ashes with
melted butter and...

SULLIVAN
Shud ub!
(Then after a pause)
Where do they ged the budder?

THE GIRL
They steal it.

5-5-41 (Continued)

F-23 (Cont'd)

SULLIVAN
Well...they doadt. It isnit as easy as all that...there is a lot of suffering id this world that ordidary people don'd know anythig aboud.

The girl sniffles.

SULLIVAN
What's the badder?

THE GIRL
I'm hungry.

Two tears roll down her cheeks.

SULLIVAN
Well, there's a towd up ahead... We'll ged off ad...see whad happeds.

THE GIRL
What town is it?

SULLIVAN
I don't know. I suppose it's Hollywood.

THE GIRL
Lock, there's a lunch stand.

SULLIVAN
All right, come on.

He jumps off and runs alongside the car. The girl hesitates.

SULLIVAN
Well, come on. I can't keep ruddig along here all day.

She takes a wild jump into his arms. Sullivan staggers, falters for about three steps, then the two of them go down in a heap.

F-24 CLOSE SHOT - SULLIVAN AND THE GIRL - ON THE GROUND

They untangle from each other like a pair of wrestlers.

THE GIRL
Did I hurt you?

5-5-41 (Continued)

F-24 (Cont'd)

SULLIVAN
Well, you didit do be any good.

He chuckles and opens his mouth preparatory to a sneeze. She opens her mouth sympathetically and closes it slowly as he does.

SULLIVAN
Cub od.

At this point he sneezes like a depth bomb. She clutches her heart.

DISSOLVE TO:

F-25 THE COUNTERMAN OF A ROADSIDE LUNCH STAND

He looks up with his best smile which freezes on his face.

F-26 SULLIVAN AND THE GIRL COMING IN

They look pretty dilapidated.

SULLIVAN
Coffee and sinkers for one.

The girl looks at him quickly.

SULLIVAN
I dever eat before dood; it gives be idigestion.

THE GIRL
(To the counterman)
Just make that two coffees.

F-27 THE COUNTERMAN - PAST SULLIVAN AND THE GIRL

THE COUNTERMAN
That'll be ten cents.

SULLIVAN
That's all right.

He starts looking in his pockets and the girl climbs on a stool. The counterman picks up two cups and pauses as he sees Sullivan feeling in another pocket. Now the girl looks uneasily at Sullivan.

5-5-41 (Continued)

F-27 (Cont'd)

SULLIVAN
It's right here sub place.

He keeps looking, then lets his hands fall at his side.

SULLIVAN
Holy Boses! I bust have spent it id that owl wagon.

F-28 CLOSE SHOT - THE GIRL

She turns slowly away from Sullivan and gives a slight double-take to something below her.

F-29 INSERT - A GLASS BELL COVERING A MOUNTAIN OR DOUGH-NUTS AND CRULLERS

Some are plain, some smeared with jam and some snowy with powdered sugar.

F-30 CLOSE SHOT - THE GIRL

Two big teas roll down her cheeks. The CAMERA PANS ONTO Sullivan. He looks at her in great embarrass-ment.

F-31 THE COUNTERMAN

He looks at them sourly with the empty coffee cups in his hand. Now with a furious look, he fills the cof-fee cups and bangs them down in front of Sullivan and the girl. Looking still more angry he slaps a plate down in front of each, lifts the bell from the sinkers and gives them each a doughnut.

THE COUNTERMAN
I'll never get rich.

F-32 THE GIRL AND SULLIVAN - PAST THE COUNTERMAN

THE GIRL
Oh, gee.

SULLIVAN
Well, you're a little richer than you were. Hudreds of biles frub everythig...cut off frub the world ...I taste of hubab kideness. I'll dever forget this as long as I live.
5-5-41 What towd is this? (Continued)

F-32 (Cont'd)

THE COUNTERMAN
Las Vegas, Nevada.

SULLIVAN
(Repeating)
Las Vegas, Devada. And this is the Busy Bee.
(Then with a sharp rise in inflection)
LAS VEGAS! You mean Las Vegas?

THE COUNTERMAN
What about it?

SULLIVAN
(Scowling)
Is there a lad yacht waitig here?

THE COUNTERMAN
A land yacht?
(He points out back)
You mean that thing?

DISSOLVE TO:

F-33 THE LAND YACHT - IN A TRAILER CAMP

The CAMERA PUSHES IN TO A CLOSE SHOT of a window. Through it we see Sullivan and the girl at the breakfast table, surrounded by the gang. The colored cook forces his way in to place another stack of wheat cakes on the table.

F-34 INT. OF THE LAND YACHT

SULLIVAN
Just dowd there by the tracks. Give hib a hundred dollars. Dever bide who frub.

THE GIRL
That's swell.

MR. JONES
A great human interest story.

THE GIRL SECRETARY
It'll probably ruin him....He'll give turkey dinners to every bum who comes in and never hit the jackpot again.

5-5-41 (Continued)

F-34 (Cont'd)

SULLIVAN
All right, all right. Buy a few clothes for the kid here, and beet be in Kansas City, sub place near the station...I'm going the hard way.
(He gets to his feet)
So long, gang.

THE DOCTOR
(Rising)
Just a minute.

SULLIVAN
Hunh?

THE DOCTOR
(After feeling of Sullivan's forehead)
Sit down a second.

SULLIVAN
Hunh?

He sits down. The doctor sticks the thermometer in Sullivan's mouth, puts a finger on his pulse and takes out his watch. As Sullivan looks at him sourly,

DISSOLVE TO:

F-35 THE COUNTERMAN - AT THE LUNCH STAND - PAST THE CHAUFFEUR OF THE LAND YACHT

THE CHAUFFEUR
Just sign there.

THE COUNTERMAN
What is it?

THE CHAUFFEUR
(Handing him a flat envelope)
It's Christmas. So long.

He hurries out and slams the door. The counterman tears open the envelope and takes out an assorted wad of bills. We hear the heavy door of the land yacht slam and the grinding of its gears as it crunches away on the gravel. The counterman hurries around the counter and looks out the door.

F-36 LONG SHOT - THE LAND YACHT PULLING AWAY FROM US

DISSOLVE TO:

5-5-41

F-37 THE BATHROOM OF THE LAND YACHT

The shower is steaming. The girl secretary comes in with a kimono over her arm.

THE GIRL SECRETARY
(Hollering)
Here's a wrapper for you and some slippers.

THE GIRL
(Sticking her head out of the shower)
What? Oh, thanks. Boy, this water's good.

THE GIRL SECRETARY
There's some makeup in the medicine cabinet.

THE GIRL
Thanks, I can use it.

THE GIRL SECRETARY
You sure can.

F-38 SULLIVAN - IN A BERTH IN A STATEROOM - PAST THE DOCTOR

SULLIVAN
But lissid, Doc....

THE DOCTOR
(Picking up a hypodermic needle)
You listen: It's three days in bed, minimum....This is just a cold shot. You won't even feel it.
(He bends over Sullivan and we do not see injection)

SULLIVAN
(Hollering)
Ouch!
(Then rubbing his arm)
I havud got tibe to sped three days id bed.

THE DOCTOR
(Picking up an atomizer)
You'll take the time. You'll get to Kansas City just as soon, and you can imagine that you went there

5-5-41 (Continued)

F-38 (Cont'd)

THE DOCTOR (Cont'd)
on the cow-catcher or whatever you use. What have you got an imagination for?

SULLIVAN
(Opening his mouth wide)
But....

The doctor pops the atomizer in his mouth and gives him a thorough squirting.

SULLIVAN
Hey!

The doctor gives him a quick shot up each nostril. Sullivan sneezes.

DISSOLVE TO:

F-39 MR. JONES - AT THE SHORT-WAVE SET

MR. JONES
Yes, sir, Mr. LeBrand...he's right here in the next stateroom, taking a little snooze....He looks great... this whole thing is doing him a power of good. Getting the feel of humanity, the stink of sweat...the sound of the symphony of suffering... but in a nice way, you understand. He'll come out of this a bigger man...immensely bigger. And what human interest stories we're getting: Let me tell you about a little incident this morning at the Busy Bee lunch room...it'll tear your heart out, What a story!

DISSOLVE TO:

F-40 THE GIRL - IN THE BATHROOM

She finishes her makeup in front of the mirror, ties the kimono more tightly around her and exits.

F-41 SULLIVAN - IN HIS BERTH

There is a knock on the door.

5-5-41 (Continued)

F-41 (Cont'd)

SULLIVAN
(Sourly)
Cub id.

He looks toward the door.

F-42 THE GIRL - COMING IN

She looks very lovely in the kimono.

THE GIRL
(Closing the door after her)
Hello.

The CAMERA TRUCKS BACK WITH HER as she comes forward.

THE GIRL
Do you feel better now?

SULLIVAN
Do, I'b sore. There's dothig the batter with be except a little fever... and even if I did get sick I could have gone to some free hospital or somethig...wherever they take you... It would have been very interestig.

THE GIRL
They give you a nice free burial too...in potter's field.

SULLIVAN
A free burial! Why does everybody exaggerate everythig so much. I've got a little cold in the head...You take a dose of salts and there you are.

THE GIRL
Because you're a very valuable person.

SULLIVAN
Bushwa.

THE GIRL
You make lovely, funny pictures that...

SULLIVAN
Phooey!

THE GIRL
Well, you do, and...

5-5-41 (Continued)

F-42 (Cont'd)

SULLIVAN
It's a funny thing the way everythig keeps...shovig be back...to Holly-wood...or Beverly Hills..or this monstrosity we're ridig in...albost like.. like...gravity..as if some force way sayig: "Get back where you belong..don't you try stickig your nose out here, you don't belong to real life, you phoney."

THE GIRL
(Putting her hand on his forehead)
You're a little feverish.

SULLIVAN
Baybe there's a universal law that says: "Stay put..as you are, so shall you remain." Baybe that's why tramps are always in trouble. They don't pay taxes...they don't vote... they violate the law of nature...you look very pretty in that outfit... that's why they don't want trailer colonies...or ab I gettig a little bit profound?

THE GIRL
(Putting her hand on his forehead)
You're getting a little bit hot.

SULLIVAN
Your hand is very cool...but dothig is going to stop be: I'b going to find out how it feels to be alone... in trouble..without friends...with-out credit...without check book and without name.

THE GIRL
And I'll go with you.

SULLIVAN
How can I be alone if you're with be?

DISSOLVE TO:

F-43 MONTAGE WITH MUSIC - THE SLUMS OF A BIG CITY (NIGHT)

1. TRUCKING SHOT OF SULLIVAN AS HE WALKS DOWN THE STREET COLDLY

5-5-41 As he passes a cop. (Continued)

F-43 (Cont'd)

2. THE COP

He watches Sullivan pass, then turns his head toward somebody following Sullivan. As the cop watches he frowns slightly.

3. TRUCKING SHOT - ALONGSIDE THE GIRL

As she goes by the cop.

4. TRUCKING SHOT - AHEAD OF SULLIVAN SHAMBLING ALONG

We see the girl following him. Suddenly he stops and picks up a cigarette butt. He examines it for a moment before putting it in his mouth, then feels for a match. The girl catches up to him, takes the cigarette out of his mouth, tells him not to be disgusting, throws the cigarette in the gutter, and offers him a fresh cigarette and a match. He orders her away as the brother does the kid sister. She hangs her head but does not move. He starts to get more eloquent but the approach of a cop stops this and they move down the street. Now the cameraman steps out and takes their picture with a flash bulb. Sullivan walks on disgustedly, followed by the girl. The cop walks inquiringly up to the cameraman who takes his picture.

DISSOLVE TO:

5. A LOT OF BUMS - IN FRONT OF A SOUP KITCHEN

Near them is a Salvation Army Band. As Sullivan and the girl come INTO THE SHOT there is a flash.

6. THE CAMERAMAN - GETTING DOWN OFF A BOX

DISSOLVE TO:

7. SULLIVAN AND THE GIRL - IN A HOBO JUNGLE

They are eating out of a can of beans in the light of a fire. Sullivan stops eating to scratch himself.

DISSOLVE TO:

5-5-41 (Continued)

F-43 (Cont'd)

8. SULLIVAN AND THE GIRL - LYING IN A PIANO BOX IN THE HOBO JUNGLE

We see them in the light of the fire. Sullivan sits up suddenly and starts scratching the small of his back. The girl watches him with big eyes. Now he tries to scratch himself between the shoulders. The girl starts to laugh, then yanks her shirt tail out of her pants and starts scratching herself. It is Sullivan's turn to laugh. At this point a fearful looking vaudeville tramp sticks his head into the piano box. His beard doesn't quite fit. He removes a handkerchief from the package he bears and flashes their picture.

DISSOLVE TO:

9. SULLIVAN - IN THE FUMIGATION ROOM OF A MISSION

He is lathering himself with soap.

10. THE GIRL - IN THE WOMEN'S FUMIGATION DEPARTMENT

Action to be devised later.

DISSOLVE TO:

11. A MEEK LOOKING ORATOR - ADDRESSING THE BUMS IN A MISSION

12. SULLIVAN AND THE GIRL - SNOOZING DURING THE LECTURE

The bums around them rise and start out. Sullivan and the girl wake up.

DISSOLVE TO:

13. SULLIVAN AND THE GIRL - AT A LONG TABLE - EATING SOME SLOPS OUT OF A CAN

All around them wolf it greedily. Sullivan passes his to the man next to him and the girl does likewise.

DISSOLVE TO:

14. SULLIVAN AND THE GIRL - LOOKING FOR A PLACE TO SLEEP ON THE PACKED FLOOR OF THE MISSION

The CAMERA TRUCKS WITH THEM. They step on a few people's hands and finally arrive at a

5-5-41

(Continued)

F-43 (Cont'd)

14. (Cont'd)

damp place near the swinging doors of the toilet. They arrange themselves and Sullivan gallantly gives the girl his arm as a pillow. As they try to compose themselves to slumber, a drunk comes roaring out of the toilet singing merrily. He steps on Sullivan's face, apologizes profusely, steps on somebody else's stomach while doing so, then stretches out next to Sullivan and immediately goes to sleep.

15. CLOSE SHOT - THE HEADS OF SULLIVAN AND THE GIRL

They exchange a look, then Sullivan turns distastefully and takes in the bum from his feet to his head.

16. CLOSE TRUCKING SHOT - ALONGSIDE THE SNORING DRUNK

We begin with a horrendous pair of feet; the toes stick out through the gaping shoes which have brass eyelets and hooks (so that we will remember them.) Now the CAMERA MOVES UP the torn clothes, the shredded shirt, to the horrible face of the big man. Here all the mechanism of a snore is exposed. We are reminded of a CLOSE SHOT of hippopotamus at feeding time.

17. SULLIVAN AND THE GIRL

Sullivan jerks his head back from an overpowering snore, pulls his coat up over his head, pulls the girl close to him and covers her also. A second later his rump moves. He grabs for the small of his back, scratches himself again, then pokes his head up from under the coat and looks around in despair.

18. CHOKER SHOT - OF THIS SNORING DRUNK

Through his snores he smiles happily.

SLOW DISSOLVE TO:

19. A FROWSY SLEEPY-LOOKING MISSION COOK - BEATING A FRYING PAN WITH A BIG SPOON

20. FULL SHOT - THE MISSION FLOOR - (IN THE GRAY LIGHT OF DAWN)

The cook goes PAST US, beating his frying pan and the rabble wakes up slowly. As they start sitting up here and there -

5-5-41 (Continued)

F-43 (Cont'd)

21. CLOSE SHOT - SULLIVAN AND THE GIRL - CUTTING THEM OFF AT THE KNEES

Sullivan sits up stiffly and rubs his eyes. Suddenly he looks down OUTSIDE THE SHOT and scowls. The CAMERA TRUCKS BACK and we see that he is barefooted. He looks around in alarm, then again fixes his gaze on something OUTSIDE THE SHOT. The CAMERA PANS OVER to the space occupied by the big snoring drunk. It is empty, but in the middle of it we see the revolting shoes with the brass eyelets and hooks. Sullivan looks at his bare feet, then back at the shoes, once more at his bare feet, then reaches daintily for the shoes.

DISSOLVE TO:

22. TRUCKING SHOT - ALONGSIDE AND SLIGHTLY AHEAD OF SULLIVAN'S FEET IN THE SHOES WITH THE BRASS EYELETS AND HOOKS

They are walking on a sunny sidewalk. Now the CAMERA PULLS SLIGHTLY AHEAD AND ANGLES UP. We see that Sullivan is encased between a pair of sandwich boards, the front one of which reads:

"WHY LOOK LIKE A TRAMP?

MOE'S SLIGHTLY DAMAGED

MISFITS ON YOUR OWN TERMS"

The CAMERA PANS ONTO the girl who is following Sullivan closely. She carries a sign which reads:

"MOE UNFAIR TO

UNITED PANTS MAKERS"

DISSOLVE TO:

23. SULLIVAN AND THE GIRL - IN AN ALLEY - (NIGHT)

It is raining. They are looking at a garbage can. Now the girl looks at Sullivan to see if he is really going to make her eat it. Suddenly he takes her arm and they hurry out of the alley.

DISSOLVE TO:

5-5-41 (Continued)

F-43 (Cont'd)

24. A SHINING SILVER COFFEE SET - ON A SNOWY TABLE CLOTH

Here we see also some flowers and a candle stand. The CAMERA TILTS UP and we see Sullivan in a dinner jacket and the girl in a lovely dinner dress. They smile at each other. Sullivan stops smiling and sniffs pleasantly toward her. He says: "You smell very nice," and smells of her shoulder. She points to behind her ear and says that it's here. She toys with a swizzle stick. He takes a whiff at this spot and seems to be smelling the spices of Araby. Now he sighs with content, puts a bill on his plate and looks at his watch. The girl frowns at him, then says: "Just one more dance." Sullivan looks at her, then back at his watch and says: "All right." They rise and start toward the dance floor.

DISSOLVE TO:

25. CLOSE HIGH CAMERA - ON THE GIRL AND SULLIVAN DANCING

She seems to enjoy this enormously. She almost seems to be in love with him.

DISSOLVE TO:

26. SULLIVAN AND THE GIRL - IN BUMS' OUTFITS AGAIN - WALKING ALONG THE RIVER'S EDGE - RAINING - (NIGHT)

DISSOLVE TO:

27. A SMALL FIRE - UNDER A BRIDGE

A one-legged bum is tending the fire. Sullivan and the girl come INTO THE SHOT, nod to the bum and sit near the fire. They stretch their hands toward its warmth. Their shadows dance behind them. Now Sullivan takes a sniff at the girl. He scowls at her. She toys with a swizzle stick and points behind her ear. After a moment's hesitation he takes a whiff of it, then reacts to the look of the one-legged bum.

5-5-41 (Continued)

F-43 (Cont'd)

28. THE ONE-LEGGED BUM

He inhales of the perfume and looks blearily toward his guests.

29. SULLIVAN AND THE GIRL - PAST THE OLD BUM

She takes off her cap, shakes her hair, puts the cap back on, arranges her head on Sullivan's shoulder and prepares to sleep.

FADE OUT:

END OF MONTAGE

FADE IN:

F-44 A BANK TELLER - COUNTING OUT TWO HUNDRED NEW FIVE-DOLLAR BILLS TO MR. VALDELLE

DISSOLVE TO:

F-45 MR. JONES - AT THE TELEPHONE - IN A KANSAS CITY HOTEL SUITE - (DAY)

MR. JONES
Yes, sir, Mr. LeBrand, it's all finished...The greatest expedition of modern times...almost the greatest sacrifice ever made by human man...He's suffered everything from adenoids to eczema...He's had lice, fleas, bedbugs, colds, chills, fever, chilblains, corns, boils, hookworm, pellagra, the colic, tonsillitis and the epizootic, but in a nice way, you understand... He's the past-master of poverty ... he knows everything....yes, sir, Mr. LeBrand, I agree with you. He's all washed up except tonight he's just going through for a quick tour...and do you know what for?...it'll tear your heart out. He calls it the payoff...he's taking a thousand dollars in five-dollar bills and

5-5-41 (Continued)

F-45 (Cont'd)

MR. JONES (Cont'd)
he's going to hand them out to these bums...in gratitude for what they did for him...Now is that a story...does that give you a lump in your throat or does that give you a lump in your throat?

DISSOLVE TO:

F-46 A WASTE PAPER BASKET CONTAINING THE GIRL'S TRAMP CLOTHES

The girl secretary is writing on a typewriter. The CAMERA ANGLES UP and we see the girl fixing her make-up. She turns, crosses and knocks on the door to the adjoining room.

F-47 SULLIVAN - SNORING ON TOP OF A BED

He wears a dressing gown, under it shorts and an under shirt. The knock is repeated, then the door opens and the girl comes in.

SULLIVAN
(Waking up a little late)
Oh, hello.

THE GIRL
Hello.

She crosses and sits on the edge of the bed.

THE GIRL
Tired?

SULLIVAN
No, no...I was just thinking.

THE GIRL
(Laughing)
You were thinking out loud.

SULLIVAN
Well, here we are at the end of the adventure...and the funny part is I don't know any more about trouble than when I started...

5-5-41 (Continued)

F-47 (Cont'd)

SULLIVAN (Cont'd)
I mean about how to cure it...
and what's wrong with the world
and all that stuff. It's like
Shaw said: The trouble with
the poor seems to be poverty...
and what we're going to do about
it I don't know.

THE GIRL
Well, you tried....they can't
say we didn't wallow in it.
(She scratches her hip)

SULLIVAN
I'll go down and give them a little
money tonight and that winds it
up.
(He pats her hand)
You were a big help too.......
several times there I wouldn't
have got in any trouble at all
if it hadn't been for you.

THE GIRL
Are you sorry you took me?

SULLIVAN
Far from it.
(He smiles at her)
Now what do you want to do, go
home...or take another crack at
Hollywood...with a letter to
Lubitsch.

THE GIRL
(Looking away)
I want to go where you go.

Sullivan gives her a long look.

THE GIRL
(Avoiding his glance)
I mean...I hoped maybe you'd...

5-5-41 (Continued)

F-47 (Cont'd)

THE GIRL (Cont'd)
I mean we got along so well,
I hoped maybe you'd, well...
I mean...I hoped maybe you'd
want us to keep on together...
a little longer...
(She looks up at him)
...now that we're kinda used
to each other.

SULLIVAN
(Taking her hand)
Of course I would...

THE GIRL
Oh, gee.

SULLIVAN
..if I wasn't married.

THE GIRL
(Startled)
Who's married?

SULLIVAN
Didn't you know that? I thought
everybody had heard of my mis-
fortune.

THE GIRL
(Indignantly)
Of course I didn't.

SULLIVAN
(Resenting the tone)
What do you mean: "Of course
I didn't"? As if I'd swan-
dangled you away from your
loving grand-mother or something.

THE GIRL
Are you in love with her?

SULLIVAN
That vulture?

THE GIRL
Then, why did you marry her?

SULLIVAN
(Sourly)
Income tax.

THE GIRL
Income tax!

5-5-41 (Continued)

F-47 (Cont'd)

SULLIVAN
It was to save twenty-four thousand dollars a year. It's what you call a joint return...it's a California law. Each one pays half and the total is less than the aggregate surtax or the surtax is less than the something-or-other...it was an idea of my business manager's.

THE GIRL
I think it's disgusting.

SULLIVAN
It was practical. I wasn't in love and she agreed to give me a divorce if ever I fell, and in the meantime she got twelve thousand a year which was better than the eighteen bucks a week she was getting from the business manager.

THE GIRL
I still think it's revolting.

SULLIVAN
(Irritated)
It was not supposed to be romantic! It was supposed to save me twelve thousand dollars a year.

THE GIRL
Hunh!

SULLIVAN
But it didn't...it turned out that she couldn't live on twelve thousand a year.

THE GIRL
Good!

SULLIVAN
Lovely! She needed twenty-four thousand a year to live.

THE GIRL
That took care of the profit.

SULLIVAN
I'm not finished. Then I got a raise and she heard about it, and she demanded half of that.

THE GIRL
Good!

5-5-41 (Continued)

F-47 (Cont'd)

SULLIVAN
Don't keep saying "good" all the time or I'll poke you in the nose. So I cut her off without a cent and she moved into my house...and wouldn't get out until I settled with her.

THE GIRL
Good!

SULLIVAN
(Threateningly)
Now, listen...so I demanded the divorce she'd promised me...

THE GIRL
And she told you to go fry an egg.

SULLIVAN
She said it would break her mother's heart.

THE GIRL
Your business manager certainly gave you some fine advice.

SULLIVAN
I found out why...He was getting half of it.

THE GIRL
(Unbelievingly)
And you really can't get a divorce ...<u>ever</u>?

SULLIVAN
Never...you can't get a divorce without collusion...she won't collude.

THE GIRL
How about you?

SULLIVAN
She said she'd overlook it.

THE GIRL
I suppose I ought to go home now.

SULLIVAN
You could still have the letter to Lubitsch.

THE GIRL
Could I come and push you in the pool sometimes?

SULLIVAN
5-5-41 Of course you could. (Continued)

F-47 (Cont'd)

THE GIRL
Well...it's better than nothing.

She starts to cry and puts her arms around his neck.

SULLIVAN
There, there, there...my gracious.

He pats her on the back. There is a knock on the door and the girl sits up.

SULLIVAN
Come in.

F-48 THE DOOR OPENING

MR. VALDELLE
(Entering)
Here are the five-dollar bills, Mr. Sullivan.

He goes OUT OF THE SHOT.

F-49 SULLIVAN AND THE GIRL

SULLIVAN
Thanks....

Valdelle comes INTO THE SHOT.

SULLIVAN (Continued)
...and get me two tickets on the midnight plane.

MR. VALDELLE
Yes, sir.

SULLIVAN
(Examining the money;
to the girl)
Pretty, aren't they? You want one?

THE GIRL
(Impulsively)
Yes!

SULLIVAN
Here, you can have two of them.

She smiles through her tears.

DISSOLVE TO:

5-5-41

F-50 AN OLD WOMAN - IN A DOORWAY - (NIGHT)

She is examining a new five-dollar bill. Now she looks in the direction just taken by Sullivan.

F-51 FULL SHOT - SULLIVAN - WALKING AWAY FROM US

He turns toward another doorway.

DISSOLVE TO:

F-52 A YOUNG MAN AND A LITTLE GIRL

He is looking after Sullivan in astonishment.

F-53 SULLIVAN - COMING TOWARD US

He comes INTO THE SHOT FROM RIGHT TO LEFT, goes to a dark hallway where we see only a pair of feet, then goes OUT OF THE SHOT, CAMERA LEFT. The CAMERA TRUCKS IN TO A CLOSE SHOT ON THE FEET, THEN PANS UP onto the revolting head of the old bum who stole Sullivan's shoes. He looks at the five-dollar bill, then glares after Sullivan like a maniac. Now he rises and follows.

F-54 TRUCKING SHOT - ALONGSIDE SULLIVAN'S FEET

He overtakes some shuffling feet walking ahead of him and there is a pause. A five-dollar bill drops to the sidewalk. The man scoops it up hurriedly and Sullivan's feet go OUT OF THE SHOT. We STAY ON the man's feet. Now the old bum's feet COME INTO THE SHOT and the CAMERA PANS WITH THEM as they go after Sullivan. Presently we see the old bum following Sullivan down the street.

DISSOLVE TO:

F-55 A DARK ALLEY

Sullivan comes INTO THE SHOT and enters this. The old bum appears, looks after Sullivan, then breaks into a run and goes past the alley.

F-56 ANOTHER ALLEY

The old bum comes tearing around a corner and lopes past us. He is feeling his hip pocket for something.

5-5-41

F-57 THE LOADING PLATFORM SIDE OF A WAREHOUSE

A couple of empty freight cars stand on the spur track. The old bum hurries INTO THE SHOT, looks over his shoulder, then pulls his hat over his eyes and seats himself in an attitude of sleep against a couple of barrels.

F-58 CLOSE SHOT - HIS RIGHT HAND

It holds a blackjack which he hides in a fold of his coat. The CAMERA ANGLES UP ONTO the old bum's face. In the shadow of the brim of his hat his eyes narrow.

F-59 SULLIVAN - FROM NEAR THE OLD BUM'S POINT OF VIEW

He comes out of the alley and starts past the loading platform, then looks almost straight toward us.

F-60 LONG SHOT - THE OLD BUM APPARENTLY ASLEEP NEAR THE FREIGHT CARS

F-61 CLOSE SHOT - SULLIVAN

A look of compassion passes over his face and he starts forward. The CAMERA TRUCKS BACK as he climbs onto the loading platform and PANS WITH HIM AS HE takes out a five-dollar bill and FOLLOWS HIM as he approaches the old bum.

F-62 CLOSE SHOT - THE OLD BUM - LOOKING UP THROUGH NARROWED EYES

F-63 LOW CAMERA SHOT - UP AT SULLIVAN APPROACHING

F-64 SULLIVAN - BENDING OVER THE OLD BUM

He crumples up a five-dollar bill and tucks it in the limp left hand. Suddenly he is seized by the lapel and pulled forward. Holding him struggling, the bum hits him a terrible blow on the back of the head. Sullivan falls limp. After a pause, the bum hits him once more for good measure, then scrambles to his feet, looks all around and drags the limp form of Sullivan into the open boxcar. He disappears in the shadows.

5-5-41

F-65 SWITCH ENGINE APPROACHING WITH BELL CLANGING LAZILY

A brakeman stands on the front platform, a lantern in his hand. As it bangs onto the nearest boxcar -

F-66 THE DOORWAY OF THE BOXCAR CONTAINING SULLIVAN AND THE OLD BUM

Clutching a handful of five-dollar bills the old bum appears and looks toward the engine in horrible anxiety. We hear the banging of the safety chain.

A MAN'S VOICE

Okay!

There is a low toot on the whistle and the cars start to move. The old bum slides the door to within fifteen inches of closing and peers out. The train squeaks away and grinds around a corner.

DISSOLVE TO:

F-67 PANNING SHOT - THE END OF THE FREIGHT CAR WHICH CONTAINS SULLIVAN

A brakeman hangs onto this, signalling with a lantern. The car bangs into another car, the brakeman drops to the ground, hooks the safety chain, then goes back toward the engine. The CAMERA FOLLOWS HIM as FAR AS the partly opened door of the freight car. One eye of the old bum appears as he watches the brakeman hurry away. Now we see all of him. Clutching the money in both hands, he jumps to the ground and the CAMERA PANS WITH HIM as he ducks under a freight car on another track.

F-68 LONG SHOT - BETWEEN TWO LINES OF STATIONARY CARS

The old bum comes dancing towards us, casting long shadows from the arc lights. As he passes us --

F-69 A FENCE - BETWEEN THE FREIGHT YARDS AND THE MAIN LINES

The shadow of the old bum precedes him INTO THE SHOT. He gets over the fence, drops a bill, picks it up, then starts hurrying across the main lines. The CAMERA PANS WITH HIM. Suddenly he stumbles and falls. The money flies in the air.

5-5-41

F-70 CLOSE SHOT - THE OLD BUM

He is almost in silhouette as the arc source is from behind him. He sits up, rubs his knee in pain, then makes a dive for one of his bills. Almost hysterically he starts pecking at the money. We hear a wild whistle. The old bum looks up vaguely, then dives back for more bills. The headlights begin to flicker across him. He looks up blearily, moves between the tracks, then in the improving light makes a dive for some bills between the next set of rails. The light gets stronger and the old bum looks up. Now he squints toward the headlight.

F-71 AN APPROACHING STREAMLINER - ON ONE OF THE MANY CURVED TRACKS

F-72 CLOSE SHOT - THE OLD BUM

He looks down to see if he's on the tracks or between them. Blinded and in a panic now, he jumps onto the next set of tracks and peers toward the locomotive. He can't tell what track the light is coming from. Now, like a rabbit between the moving headlights of a car, he jumps from side to side and starts to run away.

F-73 CLOSE SHOT - THE OLD BUM - LOOKING OVER HIS SHOULDER

ONE-FOOT DISSOLVE THROUGH THIS TO:

F-74 BROKEN-MIRROR SHOT - OF AN APPROACHING STREAMLINER

There is a wild whistle as the mirror breaks.

F-75 THE NEXT TRACKS

A shoe falls heavily into the THE FIELD OF THE CAMERA and is followed by some drifting five-dollar bills as the window-squares flash by. Now we hear the whining of the brakes.

FADE OUT:

END OF SEQUENCE "F"

5-5-41

SEQUENCE "G"

FADE IN:

G-1 THE CLOCK - ON THE MANTELPIECE OF THE KANSAS CITY HOTEL SITTING ROOM - (DAWN)

It reads a few minutes past "five." The CAMERA PANS FROM THE CLOCK DOWN ONTO THE GIRL who looks white and worried. Next to her is an ash tray full of cigarette snipes.

THE GIRL
Did you cancel the plane tickets?

The CAMERA PANS ONTO Jones who sits next to a telephone. Beyond him we see the short-wave operator at another telephone and next to him the girl secretary, asleep.

MR. JONES
They canceled themselves. I'm going to give him just fifteen minutes more.

G-2 THE GIRL

THE GIRL
(Falteringly)
I'm sure he's all right...He probably got interested in a revival meeting or something and...

A phone rings. She presses her hand to her heart and hurries to Jones' side. The CAMERA PANS WITH HER.

MR. JONES
Yes, Doc...not in the hospitals, hunh?...Sure...I guess that's all you can do.
(He hangs up)
Anyway, he didn't have an accident.

The other phone rings.

THE SHORT-WAVE OPERATOR
Yeah?...He isn't hunh?
(Now he speaks to Jones)
Val has covered the police stations.

5-5-41

(Continued)

G-2 (Cont'd)

MR. JONES
Okay.

THE SHORT-WAVE
OPERATOR
(Into the telephone)
I guess you can come back now.
So long.
(He hangs up)

THE GIRL
I should have gone with him...
I knew he'd get in trouble without me. I told him...

MR. JONES
I'm going to give him just twelve minutes more, and then I'm going to lay it in LeBrand's lap and let him figure it out.

THE GIRL
Sully'll be awful sore if you raise a big holler and then he walks in for br....

MR. JONES
Well, let him be sore. I got a job too, you know. If LeBrand ever found out...

THE GIRL
He came back the other time.

MR. JONES
He didn't have reservations on a plane, or people waiting for him...You don't know him like I know him.

THE GIRL
That's what you think. I guess I know him better than...

The phone rings and the girl clutches her heart again.

MR. JONES
(Into phone)
Yeah?

5-5-41

G-3 THE LAND YACHT CHAUFFEUR - AT A WALL TELEPHONE

THE CHAUFFEUR
Say, I'm down here to the morgue ...they got a guy in a basket you can't tell who he is...did the boss have any...any identification..you know, like a cut or something?

G-4 THE GIRL AND JONES

MR. JONES
Did he have any identification that you know of?

THE GIRL
Well, he had...I think he said he had...
(Suddenly she points accusingly to the telephone)
Who's that? Have they found him?

MR. JONES
Take it easy, willya...We got to check everywhere...What identification did he have?

THE GIRL
In his shoes...I think there was a... card...between the soles of his shoes.

She puts the back of her hand to her mouth.

MR. JONES
(Into the telephone)
Look in the soles of his shoes ...between the leather.

G-5 THE CHAUFFEUR - AT THE WALL TELEPHONE

THE CHAUFFEUR
(Into the telephone)
If I can find them...hold the wire.

He lets the ear-piece dangle and goes OUT OF THE SHOT.

5-5-41

G-6 THE GIRL AND JONES

She watches him rigidly for approximately twenty seconds.

MR. JONES
He's coming now... I can hear his footsteps.

G-7 THE WALL TELEPHONE - IN THE MORGUE

The receiver is swinging just a little bit now. We hear the footsteps of the chauffeur ringing on the marble. He comes INTO THE SHOT, looking at a card in his hand.

THE CHAUFFEUR
(Into the telephone)
There's a card here that says...
(He squints at it)
... It's kinda hard to read...

G-8 NEWSPAPER HEADLINE:

"STRANGE DEATH OF HOLLYWOOD DIRECTOR"

Below this in small letters:

"Under circumstances cloaked in mystery, the remains of John L. Sullivan, Hollywood ace comedy director, were found today on the right-of-way...

DISSOLVE TO:

G-9 SULLIVAN - ON THE FLOOR OF A MOVING FREIGHT CAR - (DAY)

A patch of sunlight comes through the nearly closed door. He lies immobile on his face. We hear the click of the rails and the panting of the locomotive. The locomotive whistles for the yards and there is a slight jolt and bang as the train slows down. At this, Sullivan moves, rolls over part way and looks around through half-opened eyes. Now, with an effort, he sits up, closes his eyes in pain and feels of the back of his head. He winces and licks his lips several times thirstily. Now he staggers to his feet

5-5-41 (Continued)

G-9 (Cont'd)

and immediately loses his balance and falls down again. He gets on his hands and knees and crawls to the door and pulls it open about two feet. About this time the train is entering the yards. It slows down and we flash past a few railroad employees.

G-10 THE TRAIN - IN THE YARDS - EXT.

It comes to a jolting stop.

G-11 CLOSE SHOT - SULLIVAN

With great difficulty he starts to let himself down. As he hits the ground and braces himself --

G-12 A BIG MEAN-LOOKING RAILROAD SHACK WATCHING SULLIVAN

Now he walks slowly toward him and the CAMERA PANS WITH HIM until Sullivan is also IN THE SHOT.

THE SHACK
What's the idea of riding into the yards, bo?

SULLIVAN
(Stupidly)
Hunh?

THE SHACK
I said, what's the idea of riding into the freight yard, you drunken scum?

SULLIVAN
Lay off, willya?

THE SHACK
I got a good mind to run you in for trespass.

SULLIVAN
Go soak your head, you dumb cluck; can't you see I'm sick?

He turns and staggers away.

G-13 A COUPLE OF YARD MEN - LOOKING ON.

They laugh.

5-5-41

G-14 THE SHACK

THE YARDMAN'S VOICE
That's tellin' him, bo.

THE SHACK
(Furiously)
Get out of this yard, you dirty rat!

He hurries behind Sullivan and gives him a terrible mule kick. Sullivan flies OUT OF THE SHOT.

G-15 SULLIVAN - LANDING NEAR THE BOGIE OF A FREIGHT CAR

Sick unto death, he feels the back of his head, then looks back toward his aggressor.

THE SHACK'S VOICE
Come on, get out of here, you bum!

Sullivan's hand fumbles for a rock.

THE SHACK'S VOICE
Come on.

His foot kicks Sullivan. Rigid with fury, Sullivan straightens to his feet and we see him PAST the railroad shack.

THE SHACK
(Slapping him on the back of the head)
Come on!

Sullivan brings up his right fist which contains the rock and hits the shack full in the face. As the shack staggers, Sullivan hits him again. The shack falls OUT OF THE SHOT and Sullivan looks down at his fist which is dripping with blood. Now he clutches the back of his head with his left hand and pitches forward on his face.

DISSOLVE TO:

5-5-41

G-16 MRS. SULLIVAN - AT A TELEPHONE

Near her stands the business manager.

MRS. SULLIVAN
(Furiously)
What do you mean, he's dead?

G-17 MR. LeBRAND - AT THE TELEPHONE IN KANSAS CITY

MR. LeBRAND
(Resenting the tone)
Well, what do you think it means?
Do you think I like it any better
than you do?

G-18 MRS. SULLIVAN - AT THE TELEPHONE

MRS. SULLIVAN
Well, what do you send him on
jobs like that for....I've got
a good mind to sue you...in
fact I will sue you....I'll
teach you to....Operator!
(She clicks the
phone up and down)
Operator!....I was talking to
Kansas City.

G-19 MR. LeBRAND - HANGING UP THE TELEPHONE

He walks over to Hadrian and in the background we see Jones, Valdelle, the doctor, the girl secretary, the chauffeur, the short-wave operator and the cook.

MR. LeBRAND
(To Hadrian)
She's going to sue me.
(He shrugs his
shoulders and
looks at the group)
I suppose I ought to fire the whole
bunch of you...but somehow I don't
feel like firing anybody. Well...
There's no use hanging around here.
Get your things together and leave
this afternoon...I'll fly back.

Nobody answers except the cook.

THE COOK
Yassuh.

5-5-41

G-20 THE GIRL - IN HER ROOM

She seems far away. Mr. LeBrand comes in, followed by Mr. Hadrian.

MR. LeBRAND
(Very gently)
And I'd like you to come with us, my dear....Jones has explained to me...you were his last discovery ...his last gift to the world. We'll take care of you always.

HADRIAN
(After a pause)
She didn't hear you.

After a second, the girl sobs.

DISSOLVE TO:

G-21 PERPENDICULAR SHOT OF A BIG PLANE OVERHEAD

As it flies away WE ANGLE DOWN WITH IT, DOWN A TREE AND ONTO the rear of the land yacht which grinds AWAY FROM US.

FADE OUT:

END OF SEQUENCE "G"

5-5-41

SEQUENCE "H"

FADE IN:

H-1 A LITTLE COURTHOUSE - SOMEWHERE IN THE SOUTH - (DAY)

DISSOLVE TO:

H-2 SULLIVAN - CLOSE SHOT - LISTENING TO THE VOICES AROUND HIM

Occasionally he rubs the back of his head and looks around woozily.

H-3 THE COURTROOM - FROM SULLIVAN'S POINT-OF-VIEW

Everything is blurred and swimming: The Judge at the bench, the Clerk of the Court, the Yard Bull in bandages, the Public Defender, the Sheriff and Deputies, the few spectators.

VOICES

Trespass, resisting arrest, atrocious assault and battery with intent to kill...

We object, your honor, my client had been injured and denies all knowledge...

Objection over-ruled, proceed.... Trespass, resisting arrest...

Object, your honor, the man was a railroad employee and not an officer of the law...

Sustained...trespass and atrocious assault...

Objection, your honor...

Objection over-ruled, get down to business...prisoner at the bar! PRISONER AT THE BAR!

H-4 SULLIVAN

A Deputy nudges him.

5-5-41 (Continued)

H-4 (Cont'd)

THE DEPUTY
Answer when you're spoken to.

SULLIVAN
(Vaguely)
Hunh?

He tries to focus on the Judge.

THE JUDGE'S VOICE
Do you plead guilty or not guilty?

SULLIVAN
Hunh?

THE JUDGE'S VOICE
Guilty or not_guilty to trespass and atrocious assault with a rock upon the person of the employee of the railroad.

SULLIVAN
(Vaguely)
I guess I must have hit him all right...
(He looks at his hand)
... the way my hand feels.
(He looks around for the bandaged Yard Bull)
I'm very sorry... I'll be glad to make it up to you...

H-5 SWIMMING SHOT OF THE BANDAGED YARD BULL

SULLIVAN'S VOICE
... give you any damages you like...

H-6 SULLIVAN

SULLIVAN
(Looking toward the Yard Bull)
Very sorry.

THE JUDGE'S VOICE
So you still refuse to give your name?

SULLIVAN
'Ll come to me in a minute... I've got such a headache... all mixed up.

5-5-41

H-7 SWIMMING SHOT OF THE PUBLIC DEFENDER

PUBLIC DEFENDER
We plead guilty, Your Honor, with extenuating circumstances due to temporary insanity and throw ourselves upon the mercy of the Court.

H-8 SULLIVAN

SULLIVAN
(To the Deputy)
What'd he say?
(He sits down)

THE JUDGE'S VOICE
Stand up!

Sullivan is jerked to his feet by the Deputy.

THE JUDGE'S VOICE
Prisoner at the bar...

H-9 SWIMMING SHOT OF THE JUDGE

THE JUDGE
These are parlous times and we have no desire to be severe. Vagrancy is rampant in the country and the railroads and municipalities have been more than indulgent and sympathetic with our present conditions.

H-10 SULLIVAN - TRYING TO FOCUS ON THE JUDGE

THE JUDGE'S VOICE
On the other hand, the line must be drawn somewhere... property must be protected...

SULLIVAN
Just a minute.

There is a rap of the gavel.

THE JUDGE'S VOICE
Silence!

5-5-41

H-11 SWIMMING SHOT OF THE JUDGE

During this shot the focus becomes sharp at the moment of sentence.

THE JUDGE
When confronted with violence and hoodlumism this Court has no alternative... since you still refuse to remember your name but have pleaded guilty to trespass and atrocious assault...having heard the arguments of your counsel and weighed his plea of self-defense and temporary insanity... mindful also of the fact that you have waived trial by jury and thrown yourself on the mercy of this court, thus saving the tax-payers the expense of long litigation, I will be as lenient as my conscience permits and will not impose upon you the maximum penalty that your crimes ordinarily permit... Richard Roe: I sentence you to six years at hard labor as prescribed by the laws of our sovereign state.
(He bangs the gavel)

H-12 SULLIVAN

SULLIVAN
(To the Deputy)
What's he talking about?

THE DEPUTY
You got off easy.

SULLIVAN
(With mounting panic)
But wait a minute... get me a telephone... I want to send a

THE DEPUTY
(Dragging him away)
Come on.

SULLIVAN
But wait a minute... wait a minute... I'm all mixed up here!

DISSOLVE TO:

5-5-41

H-13 THE HANDS OF A BLACKSMITH - FORGING THE ANKLET ON SULLIVAN'S ANKLE

(Check research for correct way of doing this.)

DISSOLVE TO:

H-14 EXT. A CONVICT BARRACKS - AT NIGHT

Sullivan is dragged out of a car and toward the barracks, by the Sheriff and his Deputy. Waiting to receive are the Chief Guard and a Trusty.

SULLIVAN
Wait a minute, boys; I wanta...
I wanta....

The receiving guard slaps him hard across the face.

THE "MR."
You speak when you're spoken to...
and not before, see? You raise
your arm and wait.

SULLIVAN
Listen, you....

The guard socks him again and hard.

THE "MR."
You say "Mister."

Sullivan tries to pull loose of his handcuffs.

H-15 CLOSEUP - HIS HANDS

They strain until a drop of blood runs out from under a handcuff.

H-16 THE GROUP

THE "MR."
(To his assistant)
Take him to the can, then find him
a bunk.

THE TRUSTY
Come on.

SULLIVAN
But...

5-5-41 (Continued)

H-16 (Cont'd)

The Trusty shakes his head violently in the negative.

THE SHERIFF
Wait a minute... those cost me sixteen-fifty.

He chuckles and takes the handcuffs off Sullivan. As they enter the barracks, the "Mr." turns to the Sheriff and his Deputy before following Sullivan.

THE "MR."
How's everything up to the house, Charlie?

THE SHERIFF
Fine, Jake.

THE "MR."
Give my regards to the Mrs.

THE SHERIFF
I'll do that little thing...so long.

He walks into the barracks.

H-17 INT. THE CONVICT BARRACKS - SULLIVAN - BEING LED ALONG BETWEEN THE BUNKS, BY THE TRUSTY

SULLIVAN
I got to get outta here.

THE TRUSTY
Take it easy, boy.

SULLIVAN
(Raising his voice a little)
Listen: I'm John L. Sullivan, a Hollywood director. Somebody slugged me... I've got to get out of here.

THE TRUSTY
(Lowering his voice)
Take it easy, will you... you're going to lose your privilege... no letters, no writin', no smokes... you don't want that.

SULLIVAN
(Excitedly)
I want a lawyer... I want a telephone.. you can't do things like this to people!

5-5-41 (Continued)

H-17 (Cont'd)

THE TRUSTY
Will you pipe down before he hears you.

SULLIVAN
(Loudly)
I want a lawyer... I demand my right to have a lawyer... you take me to a telephone.

As he started talking, the "Mr." came in and stood behind him. He reached for something in his hip pocket, Now he speaks.

THE "MR."
You startin' in again? You're goin' to be here a long time, see, so you gotta learn and learn quick.

The CAMERA TRUCKS UP ON HIM as he speaks.

SULLIVAN'S VOICE
I want a lawyer and I want him quick. I want to get to a telephone....

The "Mr." steps PAST THE CAMERA, raising his arm. We hear a crack, a cry of pain and two more cracks. Then the dragging of a body.

H-18 THE "MR." AND THE TRUSTY - CHUCKING SULLIVAN ON A BUNK

As he is released Sullivan clutches his head and rolls on his face.

THE "MR."
All right, chain him in.

While the Trusty is fastening Sullivan's leg chain to the end of the bunk (check this with research), the "Mr." speaks.

THE "MR."
No privilege... fresh guy.

FADE OUT:

END OF SEQUENCE "H"

5-5-41

SEQUENCE "J"

FADE IN:

J-1 SULLIVAN AND THREE OTHER CONVICTS - NEAR THE BANK OF A RIVER

This has been piled with sandbags and they are occupied in filling more. Sullivan fills the sandbags which are suspended to a chute or rack to hold the mouth of the bag open. An old convict fits a new bag to the chute and ties up the filled bag. The other two convicts drag the bags to the water's edge and pile them up. More convicts are doing the same work IN THE BACKGROUND. It is very hot where Sullivan is working. The men are stripped to the waist. The "Mr." is sitting under a tree reading a newspaper. The Trusty circulates among the men with a pail of water and a dipper. He speaks to the "Mr." in the background. The "Mr." finishes the paper and gives it to the Trusty. Now he strides away. The Trusty sticks the newspaper in his hip pocket, gives drinks to men on the way and eventually reaches Sullivan who takes a dipper of water.

THE TRUSTY
(In a low, excited voice)
Goin' to a pitcher show Sunday. They asked us over again.

SULLIVAN
(Sourly)
When can I write a letter?

THE TRUSTY
When you get your privilege back.

SULLIVAN
How long is that going to take?

THE TRUSTY
That all depends on the "Mr." He's all right if you take it nice and quiet.

SULLIVAN
(Raucously)
Well how long does it take him to make up his mind?

THE TRUSTY
Take it easy, will you, or you'll never get it.

Sullivan resumes his work. The Guard gives a dipper of water to one of the men behind him, which brings the newspaper in his hip pocket into view. We see part of the headline concerning Sullivan's strange death. The CAMERA MOVES CLOSE on the newspaper.

-5-5-41

J-2 CLOSE SHOT - SULLIVAN

He takes the paper out of the Trusty's pocket and opens it.

J-3 INSERT: THE NEWSPAPER HEADLINE

Through this, DISSOLVE Sullivan looking at the paper in astonishment.

THE TRUSTY'S VOICE
Look out!

J-4 THE "MR." - WATCHING SULLIVAN

THE "MR."
Who give you leave to read the paper... you won't learn, hunh?
(He starts forward)

J-5 SULLIVAN AND THE TRUSTY - PAST THE "MR."

SULLIVAN
(Desperately)
It's about me... I just happened to see it and...

THE "MR."
(Interrupting)
Shut up and turn around.

Sullivan turns.

THE "MR."
Put your hands behind your back.

Sullivan does so. The "Mr." puts handcuffs on him.

THE "MR."
Put him in the sweatbox.

THE TRUSTY
For how long, "Mr."

THE "MR."
Till I tell you to take him out...
You goin' to start now?

THE TRUSTY
No, sir... I mean yes, sir; I mean no, sir.

THE "MR."
Well get movin'.

DISSOLVE TO:

-5-5-41

J-6 SWEATBOX IN THE WOODS

It is a little structure not quite high enough to stand up in, not quite wide enough to sit down in. There is a small door within the door to give the man water.

J-7 THE TRUSTY - APPROACHING WITH A LONG-SPOUTED OIL CAN AND A PAIL OF WATER

He fills the oil can from the pail, looks over his shoulder, then opens the little door and sticks the spout of his oil can in it.

J-8 CLOSEUP - SULLIVAN

His eyes are wild and the sweat is streaming down his face. The spout of the oil can squirts water in his mouth and he licks it greedily.

J-9 THE TRUSTY - SQUIRTING THE WATER IN TO HIM

THE TRUSTY
Tastes good, don't it? I'll try to get him to let you off early.

He fills his oil can again, looks over his shoulder guiltily, then squirts Sullivan's face with the cold water.

THE TRUSTY
There.

He closes the little door and hurries away.

DISSOLVE TO:

J-10 THE SWEATBOX IN THE WOODS - (NIGHT)

We hear running shuffling footsteps and the Trusty comes INTO THE SHOT with a lantern. He fumbles at the door, has some difficulty, then yanks it open. For a moment we see Sullivan, knees bent, head lolling on his shoulders. He tries to speak but just mutters gibberish. Now he falls forward into the Trusty's arms. The Trusty seats him gently to the ground.

5-5-41 (Continued)

J-10 (Cont'd)

THE TRUSTY
(Almost tenderly)
You'll be all right... you got to learn, that's all... it ain't so easy at first ... but after while you don't mind... We ain't so bad off... He ain't bad... accordin' to his lights...has to deal with pretty tough hombres...got us chicken last Thanksgivin'...and some turkey wunst...for Christmas...and there ain't another Mister takes his gang to the pitcher show... Maybe.. Maybe if I ask him...he'll let you go to the pitcher show on Sunday... hunh?

Sullivan pants hoarsely.

DISSOLVE TO:

J-11 A NEGRO CHURCH - (NIGHT)

We see its reflection in the bayou and we hear somewhat off-key harmonium music. We hear the shuffling of feet and the clanking of chains. Now BETWEEN US and the church march the silhouettes of the convicts.

DISSOLVE TO:

J-12 CLOSE SHOT - THE COLORED PREACHER - BEFORE A RUDE ALTAR

THE OLD PREACHER
(To somebody out of sight)
Now let it down easy, Charlie.

A sheet tacked to a piece of wood descends INTO THE SHOT.

J-13 THE CONGREGATION

It is all negro, and for the most part very poor. There are some very old and some very young. They smile in anticipation of what's coming. The first two rows are roped off. Two members of the flock are carrying an antique motion picture projector to a table in the middle of the aisle.

J-14 THE PREACHER

The sheet finishes descending about two feet from the floor and the harmonium piece comes to an end.

-5-5-41 (Continued)

J-14 (Cont'd)

THE OLD PREACHER
Once again, brethren and sisters, we're goin' to have a little entertainment.... I don't have to tell you what 'tis.

There is a laugh from the congregation.

THE OLD PREACHER
The sheet kinda gives it away.

There is a little more laughter.

THE OLD PREACHER
(Solemnly)
And once again, brethren and sisters, we are goin' to share our pleasure with some neighbors less fortunate than ourselves... and when they gets here I'm goin' to ask you once more, neither by word, nor by action, nor by look to make our guests feel unwelcome... nor to draw away from them or get high-tone.
(Now he thunders)
For we is all equal in the sight of God and He said: "Let him who is without sin cast the first stone... and their chains shall be struck from them... and the lame shall leap... and the blind shall see... AND GLORY IN THE COMING OF THE LORD.

There is a chorus of "Amens" and "Hallelujahs" from the congregation.

THE OLD PREACHER
Now let's rise and give them a little welcome.

He turns toward the harmonium player and mentions the name of a spiritual. He lifts his hands and starts the singing.

J-15 THE CONGREGATION SINGING

After fifteen seconds of music, the door at the back of the church opens and the convicts shuffle in, followed by the Trusty and the "Mr.", a revolver strapped to his side. As they reach the first pew and start moving in --

5-5-41

J-16 TWO COLORED BOYS OUTSIDE THE CHURCH STARTING A PORTABLE GENERATOR PLANT ON WHEELS

As it sputters off --

J-17 SULLIVAN - TAKING HIS SEAT

The "Mr." sits alone in the row behind him. The old Preacher is walking up the aisle toward the projection machine. In passing he nods gravely to the "Mr."

J-18 SULLIVAN - LOOKING FROM RIGHT TO LEFT

J-19 THE PREACHER AND THE MOVIE OPERATOR

The song comes to an end.

THE OLD PREACHER
Will those of you nearest the lights kindly turn them low.

J-20 A SISTER TURNING A LIGHT LOW

J-21 THE PREACHER AND CHARLIE

THE OLD PREACHER
Let her go, Charlie.

He smiles in anticipation toward the screen.

J-22 THE HARMONIUM PLAYER

She looks toward the screen and lifts her hands to start. Now she bangs out the beginning of some very gay music, the type that was played long ago with silent one-reelers.

J-23 SULLIVAN AND THOSE AROUND HIM

The wriggling beam of light shoots PAST US from the projector. Suddenly there is a yell of laughter from everybody except Sullivan. He looks to his left, up at the screen, then to his right and glumly up at the screen.

5-5-41

J-24 THE SCREEN - PAST SOME SILHOUETTES

On it we see a silent comedy, possibly Chaplin in "The Gold Rush," possibly a Laurel and Hardy two-reeler. As each funny thing happens we hear a roar from the audience. After a while --

J-25 SULLIVAN - AMIDST THE LAUGHING AUDIENCE

Alone he is glum.

J-26 CLOSE SHOT - SULLIVAN

Imperceptibly, as he watches the screen, his expression softens and he smiles very faintly.

J-27 A VERY FUNNY BIT ON THE SCREEN

J-28 CLOSE SHOT - SULLIVAN

As if it pained him, he snorts a couple of times.

J-29 ANOTHER FUNNY PIECE ON THE SCREEN

J-30 SULLIVAN

He laughs outright. Now there is a roar from the audience; Sullivan throws back his head and laughs with them.

J-31 A GOOD PIECE OF THE FUNNY BUSINESS ON THE SCREEN

J-32 A FULL SHOT OF THE AUDIENCE LAUGHING

DISSOLVE THROUGH:

J-33 SUPERIMPOSED CLOSE SHOT - BIG HEAD OF SULLIVAN LAUGHING SEEN THROUGH THE ENTIRE AUDIENCE

DISSOLVE TO:

J-34 THE LITTLE NEGRO CHURCH REFLECTED IN THE LAGOON

We hear the music and the distant laughter.

FADE OUT:

-5-5-41 END OF SEQUENCE "J"

SEQUENCE "K"

FADE IN:

K-1 A GRAVESTONE MARKED: "JOHN LLOYD SULLIVAN 1909 - 1941"

In light intaglio behind these words we see the silhouette of the Academy Oscar resting on his sword. A hand comes INTO THE SHOT and jabs some flowers into a tin flower container. The CAMERA PANS UP and we see the heavily weeded Mrs. Sullivan and Sullivan's ex-business manager.

MRS. SULLIVAN
(Narrowing her eyes)
You don't suppose this is a trick, do you?

THE BUSINESS MANAGER
He'd have to be a Houdini.

MRS. SULLIVAN
Well.....I wouldn't put it past him.

They walk OUT OF THE SHOT and the CAMERA PANS SLOWLY to a little bench in an alley. The Girl sits here quietly.

DISSOLVE TO:

K-2 SULLIVAN AND THE TRUSTY - UNDER A TREE

It is the lunch hour. Sullivan is smoking a cigarette, and the Trusty is finishing a sandwich.

SULLIVAN
Don't you understand, they think I'm dead but I'm not dead.

TRUSTY
Well, that's fine, just think what a nice surprise they'll have when you get out.

SULLIVAN
You don't seem to understand: I haven't got the time to spend six years here.

THE TRUSTY
But you were sentenced.

5-5-41 (Continued)

K-2 (Cont'd)

SULLIVAN
(Patiently)
I know that but I still haven't got the time.

THE TRUSTY
You'll have to find the time.

SULLIVAN
Don't you understand: They don't sentence people like me.... to places like this for a little...., disagreement with a Yard Bull.

THE TRUSTY
Don't they?

SULLIVAN
They do not.

THE TRUSTY
(Tactfully)
Then maybe you ain't a pitcher director ....maybe that idea just come to you when you got hit on the head.

Sullivan feels of his head and gives the trusty a searching look.

THE TRUSTY
(Apologetically)
Maybe.
(Then after a pause)
We used to have a fellow here thought he was Lindbergh...used to fly away every night...but he was always back in the morning.

SULLIVAN
(Scowling)
Don't I look like a picture director?

THE TRUSTY
'Course I never seen one...to me you look more like a soda jerk...or maybe a plasterer.

SULLIVAN
(After a pause)
If ever a plot needed a twist, this one does.

THE TRUSTY
Hunh?

K-2 (Cont'd)

SULLIVAN
I've got to get my picture in the paper.

THE TRUSTY
(Amiably)
That would be swell...you could paste it over your bunk.

SULLIVAN
What kind of people get their pictures in the papers?

THE TRUSTY
Ball players?

Sullivan shakes his head in the negative.

THE TRUSTY
(Sadly)
Girls? They take 'em with their legs crossed. I cut one out; she was sittin'...

Sullivan shakes his head.

THE TRUSTY
When you die...if you was important enough....

SULLIVAN
I've had that.

THE TRUSTY
Murderers.

Sullivan starts to shrug his shoulders, then becomes rigid.

THE TRUSTY
There was a swell pitcher of a friend of mine...he was a lodge brother... they called him "The Blowtorch Killer."

SULLIVAN
(Forcefully)
That's it! You tell the "Mr." I'm ready to make a full confession.

THE TRUSTY
(Drawing away nervously)
Hunh?

SULLIVAN
There isn't a minute to lose... my conscience has got me...I'm ready to confess...I want to confess about killing somebody!

DISSOLVE TO:

K-3 NEWSPAPER HEADLINES:

"SULLIVAN'S MURDERER CONFESSES!"

"ASSASSIN ADMITS CRIME!"

"RAIL YARD MYSTERY CLEARED!"

"SULLIVAN'S SLAYING SOLVED!"

K-4 THE GIRL - STARING AT A NEWSPAPER

She is in costume on a picture set.

K-5 THE HEADLINE:

"I KILLED SULLIVAN" --
CONFESSES CONVICT

Now she turns to the bottom of the paper where we see a large photograph of Sullivan in a Kansas City jail. The caption reads:

"CONFESSED SLAYER OF PICTURE ACE"

K-6 THE GIRL

She screams jubilantly and runs PAST THE CAMERA.

DISSOLVE TO:

K-7 A LONG HALL - IN THE PICTURE STUDIO

The Girl gallops down this in nothing flat. People flatten against the walls as she flies by.

K-8 MR. LeBRAND'S OUTER OFFICE

The girl knocks three people down as she tears through this and into the door marked "PRIVATE".

K-9 MR. LeBRAND'S PRIVATE OFFICE

He is talking to Hadrian as the girl rushes in, shoves the picture under his nose, then throws her arms around his neck and starts dancing with him. Mr. Hadrian picks up the newspaper, yells and grabs a phone. Mr. LeBrand grabs another phone. The girl grabs a third phone.

5-5-41

K-10 MR. CASALSIS - AT A TELEPHONE

He lets out a yell and walks right up on the top of his desk from where he starts issuing instructions.

K-11 THE STUDIO SWITCHBOARD

We see an UNDERCRANKED SHOT of pandemonium.

K-12 MR. LeBRAND - AT THE TELEPHONE

He hollers:

MR. LeBRAND
Get me the governor of California...
GET ME THE PRESIDENT OF THE UNITED
STATES!

K-13 MR. HADRIAN - AT A TELEPHONE

MR. HADRIAN
Get me Cohen, Cohen, Kirshbottom
and Cohen!

K-14 THE GIRL - AT A TELEPHONE

THE GIRL
Get me Crestview eight - one, four,
nine, two!

K-15 MRS. SULLIVAN - IN A TWIN BED

Her breakfast tray is on her lap. As she listens to the phone her eyes widen. She issues a piercing scream, the breakfast tray flies in all directions. The Business Manager sits up from the depths of the other bed. She breaks a lamp over his head.

K-16 UNDERCRANKED SHOT - MR. LeBRAND, THE GIRL, MR. HADRIAN, MR. CASALSIS, MR. VALDELLE, MR. JONES, SULLIVAN'S BUTLER, HIS VALET, THE GIRL SECRETARY, THE DOCTOR AND THE CHAUFFEUR OF THE LAND YACHT - PILING INTO A LARGE PLANE

DISSOLVE TO:

K-17 THE HOTEL SUITE IN KANSAS CITY

We hear an eight-cylinder Hubub approaching. The double doors burst open as a crowd of photographers and reporters comes in backwards. In the middle of the group of all our friends we see Sullivan with his arm around the girl. Light bulbs flash and the conversation becomes deafening.

-5-5-41

(Continued)

K-17 (Cont'd)

MR. CASALSIS
(Shouting to a camera-
man)
Get a picture of him with Sullivan
and the book.

THE CAMERAMAN
(Hollering)
What?

MR. CASALSIS
A picture with Sullivan and the
book!

He produces a copy of "Oh Brother, Where Art Thou?", places it in the hands of a dignified official, then looks around.

MR. CASALSIS
Where's Sullivan?

K-18 CLOSE SHOT - SULLIVAN AND THE GIRL - IN THE MIDDLE OF THE CROWD

THE GIRL
I'm so happy.

SULLIVAN
What did you say?

THE GIRL
I said: "I'm so happy."

SULLIVAN
Thanks, so am I.

THE GIRL
I said: "I'm so happy."

SULLIVAN
What?

THE GIRL
Your wife got married last week.

SULLIVAN
Who got buried last week?

(Continued)

K-18 (Cont'd)

THE GIRL
She got <u>married</u> last week.

SULLIVAN
Who got married last week?

THE GIRL
Your wife.

SULLIVAN
My wife!
(Now he adds hopefully)
You say they buried her?

THE GIRL
(Screaming)
SHE GOT MARRIED!
(She points to her
wedding finger)
She married your business manager.

SULLIVAN
(Not daring to believe
his ears)
She married <u>him</u>?

THE GIRL
(Screaming)
Yes!

SULLIVAN
He married <u>her</u>?

THE GIRL
Yes!

SULLIVAN
(Still not daring to
believe his ears)
But how?

THE GIRL
BECAUSE YOU WERE DEAD.

SULLIVAN
Dead?

THE GIRL
Dead.

Sullivan looks to heaven with gratitude, throws his arms high, then stoops and picks up the girl and does a wild Indian dance with her in his arms.

DISSOLVE TO:

K-19 INT. A COMMERCIAL PLANE (DAY)

Sullivan and the Girl are jammed next to the window. Next to them sit Mr. Hadrian and Mr. Casalsis. Opposite them, Mr. LeBrand and Mr. Jones. IN THE BACKGROUND are placed Mr. Valdelle, Sullivan's Butler, his Valet, the Girl Secretary, the Chauffeur of the Land Yacht and the Doctor. On the table are several copies of "Oh Brother, Where Art Thou?" Glasses, whiskey, cigarettes and ashtrays are also in evidence. Everybody seems to be talking at once.

MR. CASALSIS
...tell you it's going to be the most dynamic tragedy in the history of film. I further predict...

JONES
(Simultaneously)
...in the history of the industry. We got more free publicity...
(He picks up a book)
...more coverage, more picture breaks than Hitler's funeral.

MR. LeBRAND
(Simultaneously)
No man in history has gone to such lengths...
(He picks up a volume)
...overcome such obstacles...
(He waves the book at Sullivan)
run such risks, made such sacrifices.
(He puts the book back on the table and pats it fondly)

SULLIVAN
Thanks very much.
(He turns back to the Girl)

K-20 TWO BIG HEADS - SULLIVAN AND THE GIRL

Sullivan turns back to the Girl in this also.

SULLIVAN
Don't you understand, she'll have to! Otherwise it's bigamy, unfaithfulness, alienation of affections and corpus delicti.

The girl smiles up at him.

K-21 THE PREVIOUS SHOT

MR. JONES
If he'd a done it on purpose
he couldn't a done it as good.

MR. HADRIAN
(Simultaneously)
It will be sensational.

MR. CASALSIS
It will be monumental.

MR. JONES
(Simultaneously)
The greatest drama since the
Johnstown flood.

K-22 TWO BIG HEADS - SULLIVAN AND THE GIRL

THE GIRL
(Looking up at Sullivan)
And then you'll be free.

SULLIVAN
(With eyes only for her)
And then I'll be free...but not
for very long...I hope.

THE GIRL
(Looking up)
You don't hope it any sooner than
I do.

SULLIVAN
And you know where we'll spend
our honeymoon?

THE GIRL
In a hog car, I suppose.

He laughs at her.

K-23 THE PREVIOUS SHOT

MR. CASALSIS
Furthermore, with a hookup of
the syndicates, a forty-nine
cent edition of a million copies,
and...

(Continued)

K-23 (Cont'd)

JONES
(Simultaneously)
Hookup with every brotherhood, every lodge, every benevolent association, a club in every city over ten thousand...

MR. LeBRAND
(Rapping for silence)
Just a moment, gentlemen.

He gets silence, picks up a copy of the book and turns to Sullivan.

MR. LeBRAND
Sully, I just want to tell you that "Oh Brother, Where Art Thou?" is going to be the greatest tragedy ever made! The world will weep! Humanity will sob when you...

JONES
It'll put Shakespeare back with the shipping news.

MR. LeBRAND
Quiet!
(Then again to Sullivan)
Your personal courage...your sacrifice...the lengths to which you went to sample the bitter dregs of vicissitude will make "Oh Brother, Where Art Thou?" positively and beyond dispute the greatest...

SULLIVAN
I'm sorry to disappoint you.

MR. LeBRAND
(Politely)
You're sorry to disappoint me...

SULLIVAN
Yes...and I say this with some embarrassment...but I don't want to make "Oh Brother, Where Art Thou?".

MR. LeBRAND
(Dully)
You don't want to make "Oh Brother, Where Art Thou?"

(Continued)

K-23 (Cont'd)

SULLIVAN
And I say it with some embarrassment. I want to make a comedy.

MR. LeBRAND
(Monotonously)
And you say it with some embarrassment?
(Now he turns to Mr. Hadrian)
He doesn't want to make "Oh Brother... Where Art Thou?", he wants to make a comedy.

JONES
He don't mean that, Boss, he's still a little stir-crazy.

SULLIVAN
Oh, yes I do... oh no, I'm not.

MR. LeBRAND
(Smiling a sickly smile)
You're joking, aren't you, Sully? It's in bad taste, but it's a joke.

SULLIVAN
(Firmly)
No.

MR. CASALSIS
But it's had more publicity than the Johnstown flood! What are we going to do with all that publicity?

MR. JONES
(Clutching his head)
Oh Brother!

MR. HADRIAN
(Gently)
Why don't you want to make "Oh Brother, Where Art Thou?", Sully?

SULLIVAN
Well, in the first place I'm too happy to make "Oh Brother, Where Art Thou?"
(He takes the Girl's hand in his)
In the second place, I haven't suffered enough to make "Oh Brother, Where Art Thou?"

MR. HADRIAN
You haven't suffered enough?

(Continued)

K-23 (Cont'd)

MR. LeBRAND
He hasn't suffered enough. What does he want?

SULLIVAN
In the third place, I never will have suffered enough to make "Oh Brother, Where Art Thou?" Besides, it's already been done... they made it a couple of thousand years ago and I don't believe in re-makes. There's nothing like original material.

His listeners look at each other goggle-eyed.

MR. LeBRAND
(Despairingly picking up the book)
But, Sully...

SULLIVAN
(Gently)
And I'll tell you something else: there's a lot to be said for making people laugh...did you know that's all some people have? It isn't much... but it's better than nothing in this cockeyed caravan...
(He shakes his head reminiscently)
Boy!

The Girl looks up at him and he chuckles as what he thinks about. We hear the echo of distant laughter, and ON THE SCREEN, SUPERIMPOSED ON THE IMAGES OF SULLIVAN AND THE GIRL we see THE LAUGHING CONVICTS, what they are laughing at, and THE LAUGHING NEGROES. IN AN AIR-RAID SHELTER we see the people laughing at a singing comic. BEHIND THE LINES we see soldiers laughing at a vaudeville act. We see a HOSPITAL WARD with the patients laughing at a Punch and Judy show. We see children in a BOMBED STREET laughing at an organ grinder's monkey. To this the PREVIOUS MONTAGE SHOTS ARE ADDED: SOLDIERS, REFUGEES, CONVICTS, WOUNDED CHILDREN AND NEGROES SHARE THE SCREEN. The sound builds into wild and deafening laughter. ON THE SCREEN appear the words:

"THE END"

Hail the Conquering Hero

The earliest note on *Hail the Conquering Hero* that I was able to find in the Sturges papers is a two-page story idea dated May 29, 1943.[1] Thirteen days later, on June 11, Sturges submitted to Paramount a thirteen-page, single-spaced "original story" entitled *Hail the Conquering Hero,* which was promptly approved for production. Sturges called the completed screenplay, which is printed below, *The Little Marine;* its cover page is dated June 21, but most of its pages bear a later date, some as late as July 12.

Shooting of the film began on July 14 and was completed by early September. The dialogue continuity for the film, which had in the meantime been retitled *Hail the Conquering Hero,* is dated September 20, 1943, which means that the film was edited, at least in a "rough cut" version, by this date. It was not previewed, however, until December, by which time its fate had become enmeshed in Sturges's deepening estrangement from Paramount, particularly from its chief of production, B. G. "Buddy" DeSylva. When two previews—the second on December 9—received mixed audience responses, DeSylva threatened cuts and retakes, as he had already done with the unreleased *Great Without Glory.* To complicate matters further, Sturges's contract expired on December 10, 1943. His demand for more control of his films was refused, so he left Paramount with three films unreleased.

The Miracle of Morgan's Creek opened in New York on January 19, 1944, and was an instant critical and popular success, indeed the biggest moneymaker of Sturges's career. Back at Paramount, DeSylva had already had *Hail the Conquering Hero* recut to eliminate the "talkier" passages, but a February preview of this version in New York proved disastrous. Sturges offered to return to Paramount without pay to adjust *Hail the Conquering Hero* and *Great Without Glory* "to everyone's satisfaction."[2] Sturges wrote a new ending for *Hail the Conquering Hero* in late March 1944 and shot four days of retakes in early April. (This new ending appears as the conclusion to the script below.) He devoted the rest of the month to integrating the new footage and restoring the film to his original vision. *Hail the Conquering Hero* was released in August 1944 to great critical acclaim and modest commercial success. DeSylva refused to let Sturges touch *Great Without Glory*, however, further souring the writer-director on Paramount and on big studios generally. The film was retitled *The Great Moment* and released late in 1944 to the bewilderment of critics and the indifference of audiences.

Like *Sullivan's Travels, The Little Marine* developed from earliest note to a shooting script in a very short time—two months for *Sullivan's Travels*, about six weeks for *The Little Marine*. Among the scripts included in this volume, moreover, *The Little Marine* alone exists in just one version, the one completed on July 12, 1943, and printed below; Sturges wrote two versions of *Sullivan's Travels* and more than two of *The Great McGinty, Christmas in July*, and *The Lady Eve*. It is in the next phase of its production, however—from shooting script to finished film—that *Hail the Conquering Hero* poses unique difficulties for analysis.

The dialogue continuity of September 20, 1943, tells us what sort of film Sturges originally shot. Aside from those small changes in the wording of lines that Sturges always made on the set, the shooting process as a whole stayed quite close to the July 12 script. It is from the point at which Sturges left Paramount that the fate of the film becomes mysterious. We simply do not know what Buddy DeSylva and his Paramount cutters did to the film that Sturges had shot and assembled; only that, praise the god of cinema (that is, the public), the film revolted audiences when it was previewed in February 1944 and that, as a result, Sturges got a second chance to put the film back together and, indeed, to improve it.

The new ending that Sturges wrote for the film is dated March 30, 1944, and is seven pages long—three pages shorter than the original ending. It is also marked by page and scene numbers to fit exactly into the original script. In capital letters at the top of this document are the words "ADDED SCENES AND RETAKES—HAIL THE CONQUERING HERO." In April 1944 Sturges shot this new ending, which itself entailed, strictly speaking, both new scenes and "retakes." Did Sturges at the same time retake any other shots or scenes besides those in the seven-page revised ending? It is difficult to answer with certainty since Sturges was also at this time undoing the damage that DeSylva and his cutters had done. By itself, this might or might not have entailed recutting the entire film or at least making changes in every part of it. Since we do not know what DeSylva and his cutters did to the film, we do not know what Sturges had to do to restore it.

Sturges did more, however, than simply restore the film that he had shot in July and August 1943. We know by comparing the September 20, 1943, dialogue continuity with the released film that Sturges made a number of important changes of his own in several other parts of the film besides the ending, notably in Sequence B's kaleidoscopic reception sequence. As the reader can see by comparing script and film, Sturges also eliminated a number of scenes, mainly small ones, and cut a number of speeches and a fair amount of incidental dialogue here and there throughout the film. Could it be that any of these changes were accomplished by DeSylva's cutters and carried over by Sturges in whole or part in his overall revision of the film? There is simply no way to tell, at least based upon the data that I was able to find.

What is beyond question is that Sturges's new ending and the other changes that he made in April 1944 improve the film enormously. Perfecting what was already a remarkable dramatic and cinematic structure, they make it what Sturges believed to be (and many of his critics concur) perhaps his most remarkable film.[3] The opposition of DeSylva was arguably disastrous for Sturges in both the short and long run if only because it soured him on the studio system and led him to two underproductive years in "partnership" with Howard Hughes. In regard to *Hail the Conquering Hero*, however, DeSylva's opposition and interference—while no less erroneous and mean-spirited—turned out to be a kind of Miltonic "fortunate fall," since it worked beyond anyone's intention to allow Sturges the opportunity, all but unprecedented in Hollywood or anywhere else, to revise substantially a studio film finished six months earlier.

The 1944 changes in *Hail the Conquering Hero*, while extensive, are of a particularly intimate or "internal" sort. They do not take the film in a new direction; they quicken its rhythms and sharpen its focus. It would be misleading therefore to treat these changes as though they were a distinct version of the script—they can best be understood as improvements of what was already there. Thus, although we will consider the story idea and the story in separate stages, we will treat the script, the 1944 changes, and the released film itself in a single run-through. That is, in comparing the July 12 screenplay with the June 11 story, we will also take note of the most important changes realized by Sturges in his March–April 1944 work on the film. We can do the last operation with assurance because, as mentioned, though we do not know the state in which Sturges received the film from the Paramount cutters, we do know from the release print itself what he did to it overall and how that compares with the film that he had assembled in September 1943, which, as the dialogue continuity shows, followed the July 12 screenplay quite closely.

In the two-page story idea of May 29, 1943, a little man departs heroically from his hometown for military service but suffers a minor injury in camp and is honorably discharged. He cannot bear to return home, so he takes a job in a neighboring town and returns home a year later. On the train he meets a returning war hero whose homecoming he envies. The hero offers to exchange clothes with him for a few days, saying: "What harm can it do?"

At this point Sturges shifts gears, writing "HOLD EVERYTHING! IS IT POSSIBLE I HAVE BEEN SMITTEN BY AN IDEA?? ??? ??? ???" He begins again, this time making the hero the center. "Our hero is really a hero," he says, "covered with medals." He is returning to his hometown and has lost all his money in a crap game. He offers to "shoot his medals," but the men he is playing with are lousy with medals themselves. Disconsolate, he returns to his seat and finds a young civilian, who is also going home. The civilian tells him his story. He was drafted, left home in a blaze of glory, then was honorably discharged for ulcers. Because of his send-off he has stayed away for a year. The hero sympathizes. The civilian says it was not so bad; he worked in an airplane factory and made plenty of money.

> "Did you save any of it" says our hero. "All of it" says the civilian. Our hero looks at him speculatively. "You know something?" he says. "What?" says the civilian. "I got an idea" says the hero.
> DISSOLVE TO:
> THE TRAIN ARRIVING AT THE STATION

The differences between these two story sketches do not seem great enough to merit Sturges's eureka. One begins with the civilian, the other with the hero; one involves a free offer, the other an exchange for cash; but the circumstances and the likely consequences of the two meetings seem quite similar. Sturges's first line after his exclamations, "Our hero is really a hero . . . covered with medals," is, given Sturges's penchant for exaggeration and extreme situations, suggestive. It may have been the vision of an excess of medals that ignited his imagination, summoning up hysterical responses—a whole town going berserk. In any case, it is only the second story, the one that begins with the medals, that brings him to the small-town station, portal to the script and film as we know them.

The June 11 story begins in fact with the civilian (Woodrow Lafayette Pershing Truesmith) and essentially tells his story, as do all the later versions of *Hail the Conquering Hero*—although, also like them, it divides its attention among civilian, marines, and townspeople, sharing the exclusive perspective of none. The story's first two paragraphs describe Woodrow's predicament at the outset of the film-to-be:

> The film begins many months later in a waterfront saloon. Six Marines from Guadalcanal, dripping with medals, are thirsty and broke. A little man in a blue serge suit puts his shipyard pay at their disposal. "Semper Fidelis" he says as they drink and in a few moments they know his story. At first sympathetic they end up by bawling him out for what he has done to his mother. They telephone his mother then and there and tell the boy he is going home. He resists but six Marines are hard to resist.

Above all, ot course, the June 11 story tells what happens at the train station and after and thereby develops the consequences of the story idea's premise:

> The seven Marines are on the train, parley voo? But as it rolls into Hickory Flat they realize something has gone wrong. It is one thing for a boy to kiss his mother, show her his two medals and then take off his uniform. It is another to face the entire populace with six bands and fourteen banners, photographers and the local press. The boy makes a dive for the Gents' room but the porter has just locked it.

The marines load Woodrow with medals and carry him from the train. Despite Woodrow's reluctance, the story has him say a few words at the reception, after which the opposing candidates for mayor try to get his endorsement.

When Woodrow tries to say a few words for one candidate, the opposition band drowns him out, and vice versa.

> After this the Chairman of the Reception Committee drags him away, reading off the list of things the hero must do the rest of the day: The wreath on the grave of General Zabriski, then the cornerstone of the Housing Project, a few words at the luncheon of the D. A. R., a flying trip to the Chamber of Commerce and little side trips to the Elks, the Lions, the Moose and the Rotary Club—just so there won't be any jealousies. He is just given time to kiss his mother and his girl, then yanked away.

In the script and film, Sturges has Woodrow say nothing at the reception, and he visits only the general's grave before returning home.

The story's scene now shifts from the railroad station reception to the kitchen of Mrs. Truesmith as she prepares for the return of her son and the six marines, with the aid of complimentary groceries and "points" from kindly Mr. Schultz. She shows the marines her living-room shrine to her husband, a hero killed in World War I. Woodrow changes into his blue suit and accuses the sergeant of getting him into trouble; the sergeant replies that everything will be all right. Downstairs Judge Dennis, Dr. Houser, and the sheriff are waiting for Woodrow. The marines pick up objects in preparation for a battle, and Woodrow is ready to give himself up, but it turns out that they want Woodrow to run for mayor. They drag him to a crowd waiting outside, where he stammers that there are "many, many men far, far more deserving" of the honor than he; "you could practically say that the medals were pinned on by mistake." The sergeant cuts in with a false war story about Woodrow's heroism; Woodrow staggers into the house and starts drinking cooking wine.

The scene shifts to the offices of the Noble Chair Company where Mr. Noble, who is also the incumbent mayor, is dictating his acceptance speech. A character identified by the script as a "political boss" comes in and tells him that Woodrow is running for mayor as a write-in candidate and will probably win. Back at Mrs. Truesmith's, Woodrow, his girlfriend Libby, her aunt, and the marines are finishing dinner. One of the marines is telling a heroic story about how Woodrow saved his life; Woodrow goes out on the porch, and Libby follows him. She asks what's wrong and wonders whether, now that he is famous, he still wants to go through with their marriage. Woodrow assures her that he wants nothing more, but he is worried about the effect on her—he's a phony; he's never been in Guadalcanal or received any medals. A photographer snaps their picture, and Woodrow demands the plate, attempting when words fail to take it by force. The marines come out of the house, and Woodrow tells them to catch the photographer; instead, they push Woodrow into the house, explaining to Libby that he is tired and overexcited. The sergeant takes him to task—he shouldn't tell people he wasn't in Guadalcanal. Woodrow says he wasn't, and the sergeant says: "Then how could you have saved my life?"

> After a dreadful moment Woodrow says, "I didn't REALLY save your life, did I? I mean, just here between the two of us." "I'm alive, ain't I?" says the

> Sergeant, "How could I be alive if you hadn't? There I was surrounded by four hundred Japs and my foot caught in a . . ."

Earlier the sergeant had said to Woodrow about the medals: "You're entitled to them . . . It ain't what you did, it's what you wanted to do." The script and film eliminate both Woodrow's doubting of reality and any suggestion that, when it comes to heroism, thinking makes it so. Whether prompted by the War Department Pictorial Board or by Sturges's own sense of propriety about such matters or by characterological considerations, Woodrow is at all times painfully aware of the reality of his nonheroism, and the sergeant never equates doing with wanting to do.[4]

The story continues with the marines guarding the door and window of Woodrow's room; then the scene shifts to the office of Mayor Noble, who complains to the political boss about the return of war heroes upsetting the political scene at home. The boss decides to wire the marine base in San Diego to find out if Woodrow is really a hero. We then see Woodrow having a nightmare about warfare and falling out of bed. Bugsy, the marine who is guarding Woodrow's door, comes in and says that Woodrow is lucky not to have nightmares all the time, then pulls the covers over Woodrow, laughs, and goes out. Bugsy is first mentioned on page 6 of the thirteen-page story, when the sergeant explains Woodrow's denial that he was in Guadalcanal to Libby before the marines push Woodrow into the house: "'Sure, we all get a little that way sometimes . . . You ought to hear Bugsy in a thunderstorm.' Bugsy laughs a little unnaturally, looks up suddenly to the skies, then laughs again."

These two passages are the genesis of the script's and film's Bugsy—we can almost see him developing in the course of the story—but he is by no means there yet. The story's Bugsy is not mentioned in the bar scene, he has no mother fixation, and he does not fight with Juke or with Woodrow or make his walk up the aisle during Woodrow's confession—all of which occur in the film. In the story he has nightmares all the time and whimpers, or whatever, in thunderstorms, but he is entirely good-natured—he laughs at the mention of both. The story does, however, give him its final line of dialogue: to Woodrow's parting "I knew the Marines could do almost anything but I never knew they could do anything like this," he replies: "You got no idea." The script's expansion of the role of Bugsy involves him intimately in the structure of the narrative and gives this line, which concludes both the script and the film, a fuller resonance.

The next morning, which is Sunday, all of the characters go to church; the minister, Reverend Upperman, burns Mrs. Truesmith's mortgage on behalf of the grateful citizens of the town. Woodrow, of course, is horrified by this and even more so by the news he hears outside church that a monument to him and his father is to be erected by the town.

In his office, meanwhile, the mayor's fulminations against war heroes continue; Western Union brings the news that Woodrow was discharged from the Marine Corps for medical unfitness. The mayor and the boss go to a political rally for Woodrow hoping to spring their exposé. Instead Woodrow makes his confession before the crowd, claiming that he bought medals for his impersonation and fooled the marines also, whom he brought home to make his act look good. He says that he will pack his things and go; he then leaves the stage. The five marines escort Libby and Mrs. Truesmith home; the sergeant stays to tell the audience the truth.

Libby joins Woodrow as he is packing and asks him to make room for her too. The marines are sitting on the porch and see the whole town coming toward the house. Woodrow suspects a lynching, but it turns out that they still want him to run for mayor. Mayor Noble hears the news in his office and faints. The next day:

> We see a Montage of the election. The Marines are stumping again and being simple men they slip in to their earlier stories of the heroism of Woodrow. "But he wasn't there," says a voice. "Well if he was there that's what he would have done," says a Marine. "You tryin' to make a liar out of the Marine Corps?" Now we see Mr. Noble making a hopeless speech. At the end of a sentence a voice says, "Hurray." "Who said that?" says a Marine stepping through a crowd. "I have nothing to say . . ." says Woodrow. "Hurray," says the crowd enthusiastically. "I don't know why you should want me, but if you do, I'll do my best." The crowd is delighted . . . and the election is a landslide for Woodrow.

The next day is the farewell scene: the whole town is gathered at the railroad station to say good-bye to the marines. Woodrow as mayor bids them farewell, saying that everyone wishes they were going along, but that they will do everything they can to do their part on the home front. He says he doesn't know much about being mayor but he guesses that Mr. Noble will help him. Mr. Noble says with irritation: "We're a minute late"; Woodrow corrects him: "You're a minute fast." This may have to do with the train, but it has also to do with the Noble Chair Company; Sturges specifies that at the beginning of the scene we see "its smokeless smokestack," but at its end:

> The Marines raise their hands as they pull away. The townspeople raise their hands and now a little smoke curls out of the chimney of the Noble Chair Company, "Seats of all Descriptions" . . . The Marines, now quite small, continue to hold the salute.

Sturges seems to stress by this conclusion the union of home-front manufacturing and war-front fighting. Hence also, perhaps, Mr. Noble is brought back into the fold of patriotic citizens—his contribution too is important.

The Little Marine, the script completed on July 12, 1943, keeps rather close to the June 11 story's outline of external events. It changes, however, among other things, the characters of Libby and Bugsy, and these changes in turn affect the other characters and the relations among them. The script differs most from the story, of course, in being a full shooting script with completely worked-out dialogue.

The script is divided into five sequences: A, B, C, D, and E. Sequence A presents the meeting of Woodrow and the six marines in a waterfront café. The story tells that they meet there; precisely how they meet and how that meeting is to be presented are left for the screenplay to determine.

The script and film begin with a shot of a tap dancer's feet; then the camera slowly moves around a café:

> Service men, girls, Merchant Sailors and shipyard workers, behind them a little band. The girl finishes her number to great applause, the lights dim and a spotlight picks out another girl who starts to sing . . . We now see SPOT SHOTS of different customers reacting to the song. The last shot is on the girl and the CAMERA STARTS pulling away from her. It leaves the dancing room, moves all the way down the bar and comes to rest on Woodrow.

Woodrow sits resolutely alone at the bar, bristling at the bartender's suggestion that he have a good time. Outside, the marines emerge from the fog like fairy-tale characters. They have lost all their money in a crap game, with five days of leave remaining; they quarrel but hang together, "partners in the soup." Inside the café they try to fool the manager with a phony souvenir. When beer and sandwiches arrive magically, they grab them and rush off to meet their benefactor. Then there is a cut to a shot with Woodrow in the foreground and the marines emerging, through a beaded curtain, from the background. Neither heroes nor civilian merely emerges into the ongoing story of the other; the stories of both are under way when they meet. A long dialogue scene ensues, A-5 to A-14, that takes up the rest of Sequence A.

Sturges directs Eddie Bracken and the marines in the opening saloon scene from Hail the Conquering Hero.

The song the girl sings, written by Sturges after completion of the screenplay, is "Home to the Arms of Mother," the pertinence of which to the plot and theme of the film is obvious. The cuts from the singer to a blubbering patron and others, the track from her to Woodrow, and the later cuts from him back to her, even the faint strains of the song that we hear as the marines walk up to the café, unify the diverse spaces of the film's opening and make the point perhaps that momism is everywhere in America. But this opening also raises the question: whom is this film about?—which is equated by the camera and the editing with the question: whom does this song affect? The reaction shots and the camera's slow turn around the room and track down the bar seem to search for the subject of the film. It discovers Woodrow only at the last, self-positioned as far from the action as possible.

This is what *Cahiers du cinéma* terms a "feigned indecisiveness,"[5] what might better be called here a "feigned indeterminacy." Although the rest of the film is a mad rush, what the political boss refers to as a "snowslide," Sequence A unfolds slowly, in order to make the chance meeting of heroes and civilian seem indeed like chance. The retarded discovery of Woodrow, the separate introductions of and extended time spent with the marines, even the rambling conversation between Woodrow and the marines that follows, serve to "naturalize" the meeting, and thereby the film's premise, deemphasizing its arbitrary, far-fetched nature. The meeting of Woodrow and the marines will close and determine the narrative but must itself appear open and undetermined. It is the mover of all the events of the narrative but must itself seem unmoved. Even the first time that we see the film, we may know that this indeterminacy is indeed feigned, but it works anyway. However often we see the film, moreover, the leisurely opening still serves to validate the chance meeting. (Perhaps only psychoanalysis, with its economies of double and contradictory knowledges, can explain this effect.) At the second preview of the film a viewer wrote: "Fix that grade C beginning—it crawls."[6] The answer to the objection is that in some cases a film must crawl before it can snowslide.

The ten-page conversation between Woodrow and the marines is one of Sturges's finest achievements in group dialogue. It is made possible in no small measure by the script's reinvention of Bugsy, who is now a near-psychotic marine obsessed with mothers because he never had one. One of Sturges's most original creations, Bugsy is startling in a film of 1944 and remarkable in a comedy at any time. It is now Bugsy, not all six marines, who bawls out Woodrow for staying away from home and for lying to his mother, and it is he who places the telephone call that launches the plot. Bugsy's extremity in the script—one thinks of Molière—allows the other marines to be more balanced here than in the story. They are sympathetic to Woodrow's problem but remain casual; it would all be just bar talk if Bugsy had not committed them by his phone call.

Bugsy has gone out on a limb; whether he was right or wrong to do so, the other marines rally in support. Sturges specifies actual war footage of Guadalcanal for the credits of *Hail the Conquering Hero;* whether or not the footage was gathered and, if so, whether it was used in the original version of the finished film,[7] Sturges wisely omits it from the release print. The other marines' support for Bugsy and many other incidents show marine solidarity and teamwork better than such footage would have done and, of course, integrally to the action of the film.

The script adds a connection between Woodrow's father, killed in World War I on the day that Woodrow was born, and Sergeant Heffelfinger, who served under the elder Truesmith and saw him fall. This makes the marine interest in Woodrow less idle than in the story, even noble, and removes the last trace of a mercenary interest, still hanging over the story from the May 29 note. Indeed, the script's line, "Why don't we go with him, seeins as how we ain't got any dough anyway" (page 17), does not appear in the film. As the sergeant says in the revised conclusion: "Anything for the son of an old pal." Nevertheless the marines are penniless, as we know from the bar scene, and they may expect to be fed, housed, and cared for in Oakridge—just one instance of the conjunction of satirical observation and sentiment that makes *Hail the Conquering Hero* so remarkable.

After Bugsy and Woodrow speak to Mrs. Truesmith—Woodrow denies Bugsy's story that he was wounded—the sergeant gets on the phone to straighten things out and in effect commits all six marines to delivering Woodrow to his mother the next day. Note that the film cuts all of the sergeant's lines except "Hello, Mrs. Truesmith? This is Sergeant Heffelfinger . . ." (page 14). This is perhaps to avoid spelling out the obvious or repeating what has gone before; but it also serves the snowslide principle, which in fact governs the script's revisions of the story, the film's revision of the script, and the revised conclusion of script and film. The remarkable headlong pace of *Hail the Conquering Hero,* its hurtling forward through spiraling misunderstandings until its conclusion, is the result of revisions and cuts, many quite small, at every stage of its making. In this case Sturges cuts, after a brief fade, from the sergeant's first few words on the telephone to the direct result of his call—the train that will take them all to Oakridge—while a marching version of "Mademoiselle from Armentières" follows his voice on the sound track.

Sequence B comprises the departure of Woodrow and the marines from San Francisco and their arrival in Oakridge to an unexpectedly large and tumultuous reception. The story specifies that the marines get on the train with Woodrow "to make sure that he gets there without changing his mind and also because they have no place to go." In the screenplay and film Woodrow refuses to get on the train at all, and the marines have to force him on; to keep him from getting off immediately, they end up going along with him. The script is very careful to avoid, as much as is possible, Woodrow's complicity in his impersonation of a hero, and the film increases this emphasis in a number of ways. Thus, the story has Woodrow say a few words at the reception; in script and film he says nothing. The story's list of appearances for Woodrow following the reception is reduced in the script and film to a mere mention of his laying a wreath at General Zabriski's grave; the script builds up this event beforehand in three pages of dialogue (pages 37–39) that the film cuts entirely. Indeed, the film's only reference to the wreath laying is Woodrow's anger after the event—toward the sergeant for the whole mess and toward Libby for complimenting his speech, for which he thanks her impatiently as he goes up to take off his uniform. All this "saves" Woodrow for his later confession and apotheosis, another reason why actual footage of Guadalcanal could not be shown in the credits—it would make Woodrow's impersonation unacceptable to the wartime audience, no matter how hard he resisted it.

The presentation of the reception differs greatly from the story to the script, and the film makes some important additional changes. The story describes the reception scene from the point of view of the arriving marines: Woodrow tries to hide; they load him up with medals and carry him off by force. The script has a page and a half of dialogue between Woodrow and the marines on the train (pages 18–20), then cuts to the train station for a kaleidoscopic series of scenes with the townspeople waiting for Woodrow. This ten-page passage (pages 20–30) is followed by a return to the train and Woodrow's saying: "What's that music?" The scenes of his resistance, of the marines' forcing him into more medals and off the train, and of the reception itself immediately follow.

The ten-page interlude allows Sturges to introduce the waiting townspeople before the pandemonium of the arrival. There are more characters to introduce than in the story and more complex relations among them: the entire network of relationships—romantic, familial, and political—that Woodrow will step into and affect. The snowslide principle precludes time for character exposition later; from the minute Woodrow steps off the train until film's end, he will bounce like a ball among the individuals and groups gathered at the station—and make them bounce against one another. Therefore, we must know who they are before this process begins. The passage also allows Sturges to show us a small town and small-town types delirious with war fever.

Ten major characters and several minor ones are differentiated by the sequence. The chairman of the Reception Committee (Franklin Pangborn) begins as a nervous wreck and deteriorates further throughout the sequence; his attempts to control the four bands, a soprano, the warring political factions, and a little girl with flowers and a speech to recite are seen in advance as impossible. A dialogue between Woodrow's mother and Libby's aunt, a new character in the script, makes it clear that Woodrow has broken off with Libby, formerly his fiancée (page 21); another between Libby and the mayor's son, Forrest Noble (another new character in the script), indicates that they are engaged but that there is already tension over Libby's role in Woodrow's homecoming (pages 21–22). Libby asks Mrs. Truesmith and her aunt to tell Woodrow of her engagement, but they refuse. Libby justifies her actions on the ground that Woodrow wrote that he did not love her any more. Forrest joins his father, the mayor, who is disputing with the chairman of the Reception Committee over who will speak first. Libby joins them to ask Mrs. Noble if she may postpone telling Woodrow of her engagement; she agrees, but Forrest and the mayor strenuously object. Judge Dennis and others of the Progressive party, including Doc Bissell, their candidate for mayor, discuss Bissell's speaking before or after the mayor and hint at a plan to draft Woodrow to run instead. The chairman of the Reception Committee, who has put the program together in one morning, continues to strive unsuccessfully for order.

The film makes some important changes in this scheme. For one thing, it cuts to the waiting townspeople earlier than the script indicates, specifically on Sergeant Heffelfinger's lines projectively describing Woodrow's homecoming and his reunion with his mother.

> You slip outta your uniform . . you salt it away in moth balls and there you are . . . home. SHE'S happy . . . you're happy . . . EVERYBODY's happy . . . and nobody's hep to nothin'. (page 19)

Sturges's cut from this line to the throngs of people and the loud band music in Oakridge makes the ironic point. Toward the end of the Oakridge passage, he cuts back to the train—just after Libby has given her engagement ring to her aunt to hold until after Woodrow's arrival (page 27). After the cut Woodrow says to the marines on the train: "It isn't only my mother . . . I gotta girl too . . . I mean I did have . . ." (page 19), and the scene then continues to the script's designated point of cutting to the waiting townspeople. This occurs on Woodrow's line "What can happen? . . . anything can happen" (page 20). At this point in the film Sturges cuts back to the train station for the chairman of the Reception Committee's final struggle with the various band leaders (pages 27–29). From now on, the sequence plays as written in the script, in which this final scene of chaos—and a subsequent scene of Woodrow's final desperation on the train as he grasps what is about to happen—prepares us for the reception itself.

Sturges's actual shooting and cutting of the waiting townspeople is also considerably more fragmentary than the script's version. He cuts from one group to another after just a few lines of dialogue, seeming never to finish a scene but achieving a vivid sense of the interrelationship of all of the characters present and of the kaleidoscopic simultaneity of the event as a whole.

One consequence of this treatment is a striking spatial dislocation of the viewer. It is impossible to determine in most cases where one group is standing in relation to the others, even when a character leaves one shot and enters the next. Sturges precedes his montage of the waiting townspeople with a very brief "establishing shot" of the crowd as a whole. This is the shot, itself a gag, that undermines the sergeant's description of a quiet return; but it is held too briefly to orient the viewer spatially, and, in any case, it is shot from too far away for the viewer to identify the characters.

An effect of this mode of shooting and editing is that we share the confusions of the characters awaiting Woodrow's arrival, with which their problems and aspirations are projectively mixed. Sturges's directorial treatment here, even more than in his script, dissolves the town—and with it the mythical

Sturges shooting Woodrow's welcome home in
HAIL THE CONQUERING HERO.

coziness and homogeneity of all small towns—into a number of conflict-ridden groups and individuals. The legendary serenity of small-town life is dissolved into a cacophony of four bands playing simultaneously.

Sturges's visual style in *Hail the Conquering Hero* marks a new turn in his cinema, even if it is, in some ways, an intensification of methods that he used earlier. Never particularly strong on physical atmosphere or set design, Sturges here makes that "defect" into the very principle of his filmmaking. His landscape becomes a human one—his characters are his landscape. In scene after scene, physical reality is all but eclipsed by wall-to-wall characters; faces and bodies literally fill the screen. With a greater number of characters active in more scenes than ever before in his films, Sturges does not move his camera back to take them all in; he boldly moves it forward, virtually eclipsing their setting and making the characters and only them the film's mise-en-scène.

Sturges's wonderful character actors, as well as his "leads"—themselves in this case character actors—withstand this intensified scrutiny and at the same time yield to it as never before. In *Hail the Conquering Hero,* the turn of a head has great visual and emotional leverage; so does the failure to turn it, as later when Sergeant Heffelfinger avoids Woodrow's accusing gaze. In many scenes it is Woodrow's excruciating expression and posture within an otherwise harmonious scene that creates overwhelming tension. Only he knows, and he reminds us, that the ceremony so moving to all is based upon a lie; even the marines get carried away by the general good feeling and forget the truth. The visual tension and emotional force of such scenes are greater perhaps than anything Sturges had done before or was to do subsequently.

The reception complex—one can hardly call it a scene or even a sequence—is such a tour de force that it threatens to stop the film, or at least the snowslide. But Sturges expertly keeps the momentum going in a number of ways. For one thing, he makes the reception ceremony itself quite brief, at least in relation to its lengthy, elaborate build-up. The only people who speak at the ceremony are little Mamie, who presents Woodrow with a "beautiful bunch of delphaminimums," which of course make him sneeze repeatedly; the chairman of the Reception Committee, who is barely able to introduce the mayor above the din and who blows his whistle and yells "Quiet!" as each band strikes up a song; and the mayor himself, whose speech is interrupted by three bands, each in response to what seems like a cue in his speech—"Home to the Arms of Mother," "Hail the Conquering Hero," and the Marine Hymn—and by a fourth band that starts up "There'll Be a Hot Time in the Old Town Tonight" with no cue at all. Perhaps the writer-director himself provides the fourth cue since its song predicts what only he knows is in store for Woodrow.[8]

The script's other incidental dialogue for the reception ceremony is either cut or drowned out by the crowd and band noise, for instance, the Libby–Woodrow exchange on page 33. A far more important cut is the entire script passage from pages 37 to 39. (The cut actually begins on the bottom of page 36 because Sturges eliminates from the film the action described there—Woodrow, his mother, and Libby moving through the crowd after the ceremony, exchanges of glances between Libby and Forrest, etc.) In this passage, the chairman of the Reception Committee coerces a reluctant Woodrow to get in the first of several cars that will escort the hero's party to General Zabriski's grave and suggests the sort of things that Woodrow might say there. There is also a brief exchange between the sergeant and Libby's aunt and a subscene in which Forrest reacts to Libby's having gone with Woodrow in the first car. The most important omission, however, is an exchange between Libby and Woodrow in the back of the car—she says twice to a distracted Woodrow that she has something to tell him and then, getting only a blank "What?" in response, says that she will tell him later.

This little scene puts Libby and Woodrow alone together in a car—why doesn't she just tell him then and there about her engagement to Forrest? There are, to be sure, reasons why she does not do so, but they would have to be spelled out at this early point in the film, either by Libby or by the writer-director of the film. Far better, as the released film has it, that she genuinely try again and again throughout the film to tell Woodrow the news, only to be foiled each time by the cascade of events engulfing him—each of which also adds to the difficulty of her telling him later and to the gradual process that will finally change her mind.

The film thus cuts directly from the chaos of the reception ceremony at its height to the calm scene in Mrs. Truesmith's kitchen (pages 40–42) that opens Sequence C. She and Libby's aunt are preparing a turkey for Woodrow and the marines and receive groceries from Mr. Schultz, as in the story. This cut not only serves the snowslide principle and avoids the discordant Libby-Woodrow scene; it also deemphasizes Woodrow's further complicity in his impersonation of a hero by laying a wreath at General Zabriski's grave. That scene itself is elided in the film as it is in the script, but now there is no discussion of it beforehand, just a few quick references after the event.

In the story, Mrs. Truesmith shows the arriving marines her shrine to her dead husband while Woodrow watches from the doorway. As he heads upstairs to change into civilian clothes, Libby asks him if he's going to kiss her, which he does hurriedly. The sergeant finds Woodrow undressing in his room and assures him that "Everything went perfect," which Woodrow miserably and accusingly denies; their conversation is interrupted by the arrival of Judge Dennis, Dr. Houser, and others, who want Woodrow to run for mayor. In the screenplay and film, Woodrow and the sergeant have an angry exchange as they come in the door. Libby says to Woodrow that she has something to tell him; he replies that she'll just have to wait and hurries upstairs to change, a scene we do not see, while Mrs. Truesmith shows the marines her shrine to her husband. This scene is interrupted by church bells, and all hurry off except for Libby's aunt, who stays to tend the turkey. Woodrow and the sergeant have another brief exchange on the way to church ("Everything went perfect." "Sure . . . except that I'm a haunted man for the rest of my life.")

The film's rendering of the church scene does not so much depart from the script's description of it as fill it out and make it more resonant. Sturges the director judiciously and subtly redistributes the emphases of Sturges the writer. Moreover, he does this without much change of dialogue since, of course, Reverend Upperman alone speaks during the service. (Upperman's sentence beginning "Mortgages . . ." on page 49 is cut from his speech.) Part of Sturges's direction of the scene is to eliminate the transition shots and scene-setting shots specified by the script. Indeed, this is something that he does throughout the film, serving what we have called the snowslide principle—hurtling the action constantly forward without interval or break. Also, however, by cutting directly to scenes (often already in progress) without separately introducing their exterior (or even interior) settings, Sturges assumes and thereby strongly suggests our familiarity with them in advance—railroad station, church, mayor's office, auditorium. This by itself increases our participation in Woodrow's and the town's dilemmas; indeed, from Woodrow's perspective it turns the film's action into a nightmarish phenomenology of horrible events streaming by without transitions, separations, or scene-settings. We are plunged with him into an infernal element and do not emerge until the end of the film.

Thus, on the way into church, Sturges cuts the shots of the church tower and the church steeple (C-10 and C-12) and Libby's crossing to the Noble party (C-11)—in the film she is sitting with the Nobles from the beginning of the first shot inside the church—and, on the way out of the church, the shots of the congregation congratulating the Truesmiths (C-27 and C-28). Instead, Mrs. Truesmith says to the minister inside the church: "Everyone has been so kind," and the sergeant says: "Very nice, Reverend"—there are no exteriors of the church at the beginning of the sequence, although there are two brief exterior scenes at the end.

In the left front pew of the church are Sergeant Heffelfinger, Woodrow, Mrs. Truesmith, and Bugsy; in the right, Mayor Noble, Mrs. Noble, Libby, and Forrest. The Noble party leans over and looks across disapprovingly as the marines rather raucously sing the opening hymn. During the sentimental scenes of the service they lean and look with different reactions—the mayor ceremonial and curious, Mrs. Noble carried away by it all, Libby moved, Forrest detached. On the Truesmith side, there are Mrs. Truesmith's tears and modest glorying in the events, Woodrow's mounting horror, the sergeant's genuine involvement with the ritual, and Bugsy's doting on Mrs. Truesmith. Woodrow never rises out of his seat, as the script indicates, and Sergeant Heffelfinger never pushes him back down or otherwise admonishes him—he is too caught up in the ceremony himself.

Outside the church the chairman of the Reception Committee tells Woodrow and the sergeant that the town is erecting a monument to Woodrow and his father. Woodrow protests, sees that it is in vain, and hurries out of the shot. A brief scene between Libby and Forrest outside the church has him irritated that she hasn't yet told Woodrow the news, and he asks that she hurry up and do so. (Except for this brief exchange, the film cuts everything from C-30 on the bottom of page 51 to the middle of page 53.) Outside the Truesmith house, Woodrow and the sergeant have an extended argument about the statue and other matters.

WOODROW

What do I do now?

SERGEANT

Well . . . you just let it blow over.

WOODROW

Did you ever see a statue blow over?

Libby comes up to the gate and asks to see Woodrow for a moment. He says "Certainly," but just then Mrs. Truesmith announces that dinner is on the table and invites Libby to join them.

There is a dissolve to "THE CARCASS OF THE TURKEY," and Libby asks Woodrow to come outside with her for a moment because she wants to tell him something. Woodrow agrees and starts to get up, but just then there is a heavy knock at the front door. Woodrow fears exposure and arrest, and his fears are intensified when it turns out that the judge, the sheriff, and others wish to see him in the parlor. The marines prepare for action by picking up household objects, and the tension is prolonged by the ambiguity of the judge's remarks (for example, "Woodrow, there is something rotten in this town.") It turns out of course that they wish to run Woodrow for mayor as the candidate of the Progressive party. Over his protests, they drag Woodrow out to the front porch, before which the whole town is gathered. Woodrow tells them they are making a big mistake, that there are "many, many men far, far more deserving" of the honor than he. He is cheered anyway, and he finally withdraws into the house, where the leaders of the party follow him. He refuses to speak again—he believes that he has turned down the nomination—but he slowly realizes that the sergeant is telling the crowd phony war stories about him; he starts to drink cooking wine. When his mother points this out, Woodrow says: "Well, I'M cooked."

There is a cut back to the sergeant continuing his story with exuberance, but the camera, moving back over the heads of the crowd, picks up and follows Libby, who is sobbing as she walks down the street away from the rally. There is a fade-out and a fade-in on the mayor's office as he prepares his acceptance speech—this is the beginning of Sequence D. Forrest, standing in for Libby as the mayor's secretary, tries to take it down. Libby comes in—Forrest asks if she has been crying—and takes over as secretary. She tries to tell the mayor about Woodrow's nomination, but he insists on going ahead with his speech. The political boss comes in and tells him the news, followed by Mrs. Noble bubbling with excitement—"You'll have a chance to use ALL of your oratory, dear." The mayor fulminates and Libby takes offense at his likening Woodrow to a loose character and a convict. The mayor refuses to apologize, demands to know which side Libby is on, and she leaves. Forrest follows her, and they have a long dialogue as he walks her through the town to her door (pages 75–78). He is even more irritated than before that she has not yet told Woodrow about their engagement; she says that she will go over in a little while and do so. Libby and Forrest have made peace by the time they part, but the breaches that have been opened in their relationship seem irreparable—their dialogue is one of Sturges's understated triumphs in intimate bickering. (The opening of *Christmas in July* is another.) The script and film stay with Libby for a brief scene as she goes into her bedroom, looks at a portrait of Woodrow, then puts it face down on her dresser, throws herself on her bed, and sobs. The film adds a visit and speech by Libby's aunt, which may have been written for Elizabeth Patterson, who played a similar role (the unmarried aunt) in *Remember the Night* (1940): "Well that's the war for you. It's always hard on women. Either it takes a man away and never sends him back home. Or it sends him back unexpectedly just to embarrass you. Just no consideration at all. There . . . there . . . there."

The story proceeds directly from Woodrow's line "Well, I'M cooked" to the scene in which Mayor Noble dictates his acceptance speech, after which it cuts back to the Truesmith household for the end of the dinner scene. One of the marines starts telling another war story, Woodrow leaves, Libby follows, and they have their long scene together. Except that they are—or will be—political rivals, the scenes at the mayor's office are unconnected with the story of Woodrow. The script's and film's following Libby from the political speech-making at the Truesmith house toward the mayor's office points up their reinvention of the character of Libby. She now links the two families (the Nobles and the Truesmiths), their two spaces, the two candidates for mayor, and the two young men. The extended drama of her choice between these groups and her physical movements between their respective spaces constitute a focus for the film second in importance only to Woodrow's own dilemma. The story's Libby has remained true blue so that there is nothing for her to do except to ask Woodrow why he has not kissed her and whether he is still in love with her, and to show her loyalty when he is exposed as a fraud. The Libby of the script and film is a far more complex conception and a dynamic link between the two stories.

Following the brief scene in Libby's bedroom, the script and film cut back to the Truesmith porch, where a marine corporal is telling war stories about Woodrow. The film preserves the corporal's first line, "And when I say surrounded I mean surrounded . . ." (page 79), but cuts the rest of his speech, indeed cuts everything from that point to D-15 on the top of page 82 except for a few lines between the chairman and a sign painter ("We Want Woodrow for Our Mayor") and an exchange between Judge Dennis and a citizen at a sandwich table at the rally—"A Woodrow special . . . means the best of everything." The scene in which Bugsy takes away Woodrow's cooking wine in the Truesmith kitchen (page 82 to the top of page 84) is the first hint of their later antagonism. Woodrow's exchange with the sergeant (page 84) amusingly continues their running dispute. The sergeant "hurries out" to the rally, and Libby, wearing "a very pretty summer dress" (page 85), enters through the back door.

Libby tells Woodrow of her engagement, and he is greatly relieved—"That's the best news I've heard all day." Libby is hurt by this, gives back Woodrow's fraternity pin, and runs out the back door. Woodrow starts after her, but he is stopped by the sudden entrance of Judge Dennis, Mr. Schultz, and the sergeant. They insist that he come out and address the crowd again, which will no longer accept substitute speakers. Woodrow insists adamantly that he is not running for mayor; they say just as adamantly that he has been drafted. "Can they do that?" he asks the sergeant, who replies: "They done it." "Listen to them," says Schultz, as the crowd outside lustily sings a catchy campaign song, "Win with Woodrow." Sturges here achieves a masterstroke. The judge, the sergeant, and Schultz are so transfixed by the singing that they do not notice that Woodrow has slipped away to pursue Libby. Caught up in the Woodrow they have created, they do not need the actual Woodrow. The town is uniting as never before around Woodrow, who is becoming more and more alienated from it. The ritual of unification carried on in his name does not need him; indeed, it specifically excludes him.

The scene between Libby and Woodrow (pages 88–93), played with the crowd's still singing "Win with Woodrow" off-screen, has been long delayed. Aside from a few lines spoken later as Woodrow is packing his bags (pages 130–131), this is their only scene together. Everything must therefore be packed into it—the present, the past, and the future of their relationship; and it also must fit precisely, and advance, the dramatic situation in which it occurs. The scene in fact realizes these requirements superbly. Oddly, the usual requirement of a romantic scene—that we feel the attraction and emotion between the characters—does not apply here or is transcended. Each character is caught up in his or her individual agony; their expressing this in relation to the other moves us more deeply than conventional "rapport." What the characters say, their recriminations and regrets in the present, assumes such closeness in the past. This, of course, is "classical construction" in more than a cinematic sense—possibly informed by Sturges's early exposure to the great plays and operas.

As in the story, the marines overtake Woodrow as he tries to convince Libby that he is no hero. They put him to bed and guard his room all night so that he does not escape. The film cuts to another scene at the mayor's office, as indeed had the story also; thanks, however, to Libby's earlier walk, this cut is now a link between two integrally related stories.

The script invents Woodrow's Sunday morning plan to get out of his predicament by pretending to be called back into the Marine Corps (pages 102–114, with page 103 to the top of page 105 elided). The breakfast scene in which this occurs also develops the Woodrow–Bugsy conflict and the disappointment of the Progressive party at Woodrow's announcing his leaving just before the big rally for Woodrow—this helps motivate their later decision to run Woodrow anyway after his confession. Aside from Bugsy's scowling at Woodrow along the parade route and later moving from the audience to the stage in honor of Woodrow's courage, the confession sequence in the script and film is substantially as it is in the story. The script also adds a brief scene in which Libby tells Mrs. Truesmith outside the rally that she will be over in a few minutes, and the triumphant scene in the mayor's office (pages 128–130), which Libby interrupts by dropping her engagement ring in Forrest's glass.

It is from this point that the new ending (pages 131–137), dated March 30, 1944, and filmed in April 1944, replaces the ending of the July 12, 1943, script. One of the principal things altered by the new ending is the script's chronology; since we have not yet discussed this, a word on the chronologies of story, script, and film is order.

In the story, the meeting of Woodrow and the marines takes place on a Friday night. On Saturday they take the train to Oakridge and are met by the town; Woodrow is nominated for mayor before dinner and talks with Libby afterward. Sunday begins with the church sequence in which the Truesmith mortgage is burned and Woodrow hears of the town's plan for a statue of himself; this is followed by the political rally at which Woodrow confesses, the scene with Libby as he is packing his bags, and the arrival of the townspeople asking him still to run for mayor. The story also specifies a "montage of the election," including campaign speeches, which presumably takes place the next day, and a farewell to the marines at the train station, which seems to occur on the day after the election since Woodrow is by that time already the mayor.

The script follows this chronology except that it moves the church sequence, and hence the mortgage burning and the statue announcement, from Sunday to Saturday—they immediately follow Woodrow's return from the train station.[9] The script's reordering of events significantly advances the snowslide principle: hero's reception, mortgage burning, monument, then nomination for mayor, and the ensuing uproar that keeps expanding until Woodrow makes his confession. In retrospect this seems the proper, even inevitable order. Each event marks a new degree in the town's hysteria and in Woodrow's misery, in his and our dread that the penalty to be paid is steadily increasing. By contrast, the story's placing the reception and the nomination on Saturday and the mortgage burning and the monument announcement on Sunday is anticlimactic; it also reduces Woodrow's nomination to an incident squeezed between the reception and the family dinner. In the script the nomination caps the snowslide of events preceding it—this is Woodrow's highest honor yet—then itself snowslides all the way to the confession scene near the end of the film. This onrush takes up in its path, without missing a beat, the two scenes with the mayor, the scene between Forrest and Libby, and, of course, the scene between Woodrow and Libby. The script's arrangement also allows Sturges to continue the political motif without break through Sunday's rally and beyond rather than interrupt it with the church and monument scenes. The script replaces the transposed church sequence with the Sunday morning breakfast scene, in which Woodrow pretends to be ordered back into the Marine Corps and also hits a defenseless Bugsy, who of course got Woodrow into the mess in the first place. These futile attempts to escape his fate lead far more plausibly than the story's sequence of events to Woodrow's confession at the rally.

The script's reorganization of the story's events also provides a firm scaffolding for Sturges's other revisions, notably the transformation of the character of Libby, and hence of the Woodrow–Libby relationship, and the substantial enhancement of the Woodrow–sergeant relationship.

As mentioned, the screenplay greatly expands the role of Libby by making her both the bridge and the object of contestation (along with the mayoralty) between the Woodrow camp and the mayor's camp, which involves putting her into many more scenes and giving her a great deal more dialogue than the story indicates. Also, by having Libby try again and again to tell Woodrow of her engagement to Forrest, Sturges creates a second crucial center of dramatic tension: how will Woodrow take Libby's news? in addition to: what will happen when Woodrow's impersonation of a hero is exposed (including Libby's reaction to it)? Libby's frustration itself creates dramatic tension and also enhances the impact of all those interruptions, which in fact constitute the film's plot, that prevent her from telling her news. At the level of character, these frustrations, Forrest's repeated insistences, and the time she is spending with Woodrow in the meantime all increase Libby's agitation and confusion; by the time she does tell Woodrow the news, she has serious doubts about Forrest and renewed feelings for Woodrow. Woodrow's unexpected joy at her revelation brings her to the breaking point. All this prepares her—and the viewer—for her declaration of loyalty to Woodrow after his confession, just as in the story. In the screenplay, of course, she has traveled a vastly greater distance to get to this point, and her arrival there has far more dramatic and emotional power and thematic interest than in the story.

As for the Woodrow–sergeant relationship, in the story Woodrow talks with the sergeant in the saloon, then argues with him on the train and in his room while he is changing out of his uniform and also at the end of the day when the marines put him to bed. In the screenplay, Sturges greatly expands the exchanges between Woodrow and the sergeant, multiplying the number of scenes between them and the amount of dialogue they speak in them. Sturges also spreads their encounters throughout the film so that they become, in effect, a single, long, interrupted dialogue. In scene after scene, indeed, Woodrow and the sergeant start talking to each other as though continuing a conversation rather than beginning one. (This is one of the secrets of Sturges's superb dialogue generally, although rarely, if ever, is it carried through an entire film as it is in *Hail the Conquering Hero.*) Their exchanges also, of course, comment on each stage of the snowsliding action, allowing us to gauge Woodrow's mounting despair and to marvel at the unflappable sergeant's increasingly outrageous assurances and rationalizations.

Thus, the script's chronology of events serves its dramatic and thematic purposes far better than did the story's sequence of events. In his March–April 1944 work, as noted, Sturges judiciously pared and trimmed *Hail the Conquering Hero* to make it considerably more streamlined and efficient than the script and the first version of the film had been. What his new ending supplied was a conclusion that sustained the intensity of the rest of the revised film, avoiding in particular the anticlimax of showing the actual campaign and election for mayor and the marine farewell after that. What Sturges did was simply to eliminate the campaign and election—they will take place after the end of the film, but it is made clear that Woodrow will win. Sturges has Woodrow and Libby not only pack but go to the train station with five of the marines. It is here that the town, led by Sergeant Heffelfinger (who has stayed behind at the rally to tell the whole story), confronts Woodrow and asks him to run for mayor. The train arrives, and the six marines board it and leave. The new ending thus allows Sturges to follow the emotional scene of the town's asking Woodrow to run, though he is not a hero, with the equally emotional farewell to the marines. It compresses the two climaxes into one final train station scene, thereby achieving symmetry with the reception sequence as well as considerable dramatic acceleration. Thus the confession scene, the scene of the town's asking Woodrow to run, and the farewell scene succeed one another without a break, and the snowslide principle is maintained to the very end of the film.

It could be argued that these changes amount to a revolution in Sturges's dramatic method that is comparable to and correlative with the changes in his visual style discussed above. Instead of writing and directing discrete comic scenes, each with its own build-up, high points, and climax, Sturges here tends to run his scenes together, with motifs like Woodrow's conflicts with the sergeant, Libby's attempts to tell Woodrow her news, and the town's spiraling hysteria continuing from scene to scene without a break. Perhaps this is something like Wagner's substitution of "endless melody" for the previous mode of opera based upon the unit of the discrete aria.

Notes

1. Sturges's widow, Sandy Sturges, reports that Sturges made this note on *Hail the Conquering Hero* in an "Idea Book" much earlier than the May 29, 1943, story idea: "July 1942: Story of a boy, turned down by every branch of service, who gets hold of a uniform—what happens to him."

2. James Curtis, *Between Flops: A Biography of Preston Sturges* (New York: Harcourt Brace Jovanovich, 1982), page 190.

3. Andrew Sarris reports from a 1957 interview with Sturges: "Of his own films, he felt that *Hail the Conquering Hero* had 'less wrong with it' than any of his other films" (Andrew Sarris, *Hollywood Voices: Interviews with Film Directors* [Indianapolis: Bobbs-Merrill, 1971], page 93).

4. The only censorship information on *Hail the Conquering Hero* that I found in the Sturges papers is this June 19, 1943, "interoffice communication" to Sturges from Luigi Luraschi, Paramount's in-house censorship expert and liaison man to the Hays Office, state and local censorship boards, and other interested agencies:

As I mentioned to you verbally the other day, we have sent this on to Washington for their reaction. I feel the only comments that they can possibly make are, naturally, that the Marines conduct themselves in a proper fashion and are not shown to be drunks, hoodlums, etc. etc. This, particularly, because of the first three or four lines of the third paragraph of the first page of your story line. The second observation will be about the medals. I feel that they will undoubtedly okay the business of lending their decorations to our boy, but I am sure we will be asked not to treat the matter of decorations lightly because this is one of the biggest moral [*sic*] builders that the Government has, and it doesn't want it undermined. I think we will also be told that the men in the services never wear their decorations except at the time they are presented and when they are in full dress. Otherwise they just wear the ribbons. We will be asked to do the same. They will probably make some comment as to the boy's wearing the uniform to go home. Although I think we should be able to treat this to their satisfaction.

As you know, I am merely guessing, but pass these thoughts on to you so that if we should receive a request along these lines, you will not be wholly unprepared. I can't see any criticism that they could make of the balance of the story. As a matter of fact they should be very pleased with the fraternizing of the civilians and the boys in uniform.

L. L.

cc: Mr. DeSylva.

The passage in Sturges's June 11, 1943, story that Luraschi refers to is this: "The film begins many months later in a water-front saloon. Six Marines from Guadalcanal, dripping with medals, are thirsty and broke. A little man in a blue serge suit puts his shipyard pay at their disposal. 'Semper Fidelis' he says as they drink and in a few moments they know his story."

5. The editors of *Cahiers du cinéma,* "John Ford's *Young Mr. Lincoln*," in Bill Nichols (ed.), *Movies and Methods* (Berkeley: University of California Press, 1976), pages 493, 503.

6. Curtis, op. cit., page 187.

7. The "dialogue continuities," at least those I found in the Sturges papers, were literally and solely that—transcripts of the assembled films' spoken dialogue. No other narrative information and nothing whatever about the visuals of the films are included. There is thus no way to know from this document whether the specified Guadalcanal footage was used in the titles section of the September 1943 version of the film.

8. After "There'll Be a Hot Time in the Old Town Tonight," there can be heard brief fragments from several of the other songs previously heard in this passage or earlier in the film—"Hail the Conquering Hero," "Mademoiselle from Armentières," and the Marine Hymn. The sound editing of this scene, particularly in relation to the complex visuals, seems to me remarkable.

9. The story does not indicate the day of the week that the meeting of Woodrow and the marines in San Francisco takes place, although a reference to Woodrow's shipyard pay perhaps suggests Friday night. We know from the exterior shot of the marines' arrival that it is night, hence that the daytime train and reception sequences take place the next day, as do Woodrow's nomination for mayor, the dinner with the Truesmiths, Libby, and the six marines, and the extended scene between Woodrow and Libby, which is interrupted by the marines who put Woodrow to bed. The story's next day begins with a church bell ringing in the village steeple and the church service itself, which begins with Reverend Upperman's saying: "Usually on Sundays I have to scold you because that is what I am paid for but this is a day of rejoicing." This remark clarifies the chronology as Friday night for the meeting, Saturday for the arrival and subsequent events in Oakridge, and Sunday for the church service in which Mrs. Truesmith's mortgage is burned. This is followed by the chairman of the Reception Committee's mention of the monument to Woodrow, then by the political rally at which Woodrow makes his confession, then by the scene of Woodrow's packing and Libby's asking to go with him. The town arrives at this point, and its leaders announce that they still want Woodrow; a scene at the office of the mayor shows him fainting at the news. The story specifies a "montage of the election," which must take place on the next day, and the farewell to the marines at the railroad station, which seems to occur on the day after that since Woodrow is already the mayor.

The script specifies the meeting of Woodrow and the marines as taking place on a Friday night. The train and reception scenes therefore take place on Saturday morning. (Both Bugsy and the sergeant say to Woodrow on Friday night that he can "go home tomorrow.") They are followed promptly by the church scene with the mortgage burning, which is followed in turn by announcement of the monument. The script thus moves the church scene from Sunday morning to Saturday morning or afternoon; this departure from custom is explainable by the extraordinary circumstances of a local hero's arrival. Just to confuse matters, however, Reverend Upperman says: "Usually on Sundays I have to scold you a little because that is what I am paid to do and I try to earn my keep . . . but today is a day of rejoicing." Possibly an oversight on Sturges's part, this is nevertheless a warp in the script's and film's chronology. This gap seems to require a baroque interpretation, such as that of a lost day between the Friday meeting and a train departure on Sunday morning or a lapse on the part of the minister who is used to services on Sunday morning, or, on the other hand, a simple recognition of textual contradiction.

SF 8604

"SAVE FILM! HELP WIN THE WAR!"

This Script is the personal property of PARAMOUNT PICTURES INC. provided for your use and convenience.

Please treat it as private and confidential and make sure it is not lost or stolen or left in any place where it may get into the wrong hands.

If you do not care to place it in your personal file when you have finished with it, please return to Stenographic Department, Second Floor Writers' Annex.

THE LITTLE MARINE

(HAIL THE CONQUERING HERO)

For Bert
from
Preston

Preston Sturges
June 21, 1943

THE LITTLE MARINE

CHARACTERS

WOODROW...

SERGEANT..

CORPORAL..

MRS. TRUESMITH..................................

MR. NOBLE.......................................

POLITICAL BOSS..................................

JONESY..

BUGSY...

BILL..

JUKE..

LIBBY...

JUDGE DENNIS....................................

REVEREND UPPERMAN...............................

DR. HOUSER......................................

BARTENDER.......................................

LIBBY'S AUNT....................................

CHAIRMAN COMMITTEE..............................

TRAIN PORTER....................................

WESTERN UNION MAN...............................

DOCTOR MEYER....................................

NEWSPAPER EDITOR................................

MR. SCHULTZ, the grocer.........................

* * *

SEQUENCE "A"

During the Main Titles we have seen some heroic stuff of fighting Marines, preferably jungle fighting, if available some official war footage. To a great screaming of sirens we see the Newsreel stuff of the debarkation of the Guadalcanal Marines. The last shot is a walking INSERT of the Blue Diamond bearing the big 1 with GUADALCANAL written down it, surrounded by the Constellation of the Southern Cross. After the Main Titles,

FADE IN:

A-1 INT. WATER FRONT CAFE - CLOSE SHOT - TAP DANCER'S FEET

As the girl dances away the CAMERA ANGLES UP and we see the interior of the establishment: Service men, girls, Merchant Sailors and shipyard workers, behind them a little band. The girl finishes her number to great applause, the lights dim and a spotlight picks out another girl who starts to sing "OH HOW I MISS YOU TONIGHT" or some other sentimental ditty, preferably owned by Paramount Pictures, Inc. We now see SPOT SHOTS of different customers reacting to the song. The last shot is on the girl and the CAMERA STARTS pulling away from her. It leaves the dancing room, moves all the way down the bar and comes to rest on Woodrow, a depressed young man, dressed like a shipyard worker on Friday night. Four singing waiters now join the girl singer and reenforce her with some close harmony.

BARTENDER: Fill her up?

WOODROW: Yeh.

BARTENDER: (Filling the beer)
Why don't you grab yourself off a skirt and have yourself a time?

WOODROW: Your beer is running over.

The bartender shrugs, knocks the collar off the beer and takes the money.

WOODROW: Why don't they sing something gay?

BARTENDER: Why don't you acquire a gay viewpoint? It's all mental...every bit of it... smile and the world smiles with you, frown and you frown alone.

WOODROW: Yes, well I'd just as soon be alone if it's just the same to you.

BARTENDER: Gratitude.

6-19-43 (Continued)

A-1 (Cont'd)

He goes about his business. Woodrow starts to drink his beer.

CUT TO:

A-2 THE GIRL SINGING AND THE SINGING WAITERS

They finish the number to much applause and the girl starts "JINGLE JANGLE JINGLE".

CUT TO:

A-3 THE FOGGY SIDEWALK - (NIGHT)

This is in front of the joint that we were just in. The six Marines are approaching. We HEAR them before we see them.

SERGEANT: If you could shoot craps like you can shoot your mouth off, you'd be the biggest breeze shooter this side of Hong Kong.

JONESY: He's the two biggest.

CORPORAL: (Defending himself)
I was fading the guy...how am I supposed to know the guy is going to pass eight times...

SERGEANT: You was fading the guy with our money.

By now they are pretty well in view.

CORPORAL: Well it was my money too, wasn't it? We're partners, ain't we?

SERGEANT: 'Specially now.

JONESY: Partners in the soup.

BILL: No dough.

JUKE: Nothin' to do.

SERGEANT: And five days to do it in.

They come to a stop in front of the joint and look longingly toward the music which drifts out.

JONESY: If you wasn't so big, I'd take one poke at that dumb kisser of yours.

CORPORAL: Why don't you try it, Joe?

SERGEANT: Save it for the Japs.

6-19-43 (Continued)

A-3 (Cont'd)

BUGSY: (Solemnly)
You shouldn't of faded so many times.

CORPORAL: You gonna start now?
(Then to the Sergeant)
give me one last ten spot...I'll go back and...

SERGEANT: (Sourly)
You had it, fancy fingers.
(Then mimicking him)
'Give me one last ten spot.' Who do you think you're talking to, Morganthau?

Bugsy starts for the door.

SERGEANT: Where you goin'?

BUGSY: I got fifteen cents.
(He laughs a little queerly)
I held out on you.

The other Marines look at each other, then follow the moneyed man into the establishment.

CUT TO:

A-4 INT. THE CAFE

The Marines enter and are given a ringside table by a waiter. He passes around about four large menus.

BUGSY: (Clutching his fifteen cents)
One beer.

WAITER: (In astonishment)
One beer!

SERGEANT: One beer and no cracks.

The waiter departs.

CORPORAL: You gonna share it or swill it all down yourself?

Bugsy laughs but says nothing.

SERGEANT: (To Jonesy)
Give me your Elk's tooth.

JONESY: Wait a minute my old man gimme that...

SERGEANT: Come on.

Jonesy gives it to him reluctantly. The Sergeant motions to the manager.

6-19-43 (Continued)

A-4 (Cont'd)

SERGEANT: You the manager?

MANAGER: Yes sir.

SERGEANT: We're just a little bit short of cash see, or I'd never make you this proposition. I was gonna save it for the museum, see, but when you're out on a limb you gotta make sacrifices that's all. I'm gonna let you in on the ground floor of something very rare.

MANAGER: Ahah.

SERGEANT: (With great secrecy) You remember when General Yamatoho committed Harry Carey?

MANAGER: Possibly.

SERGEANT: I happened to be very close by, see?

MANAGER: Unhunh.

The Sergeant now goes through the motions of removing a tooth from his mouth then pops the Elk tooth under the nose of the Manager who recoils visibly.

MANAGER: (Looking at the tooth) Big man, wasn't he?

SERGEANT: Immense. This is one of the rarest mementos...

MANAGER: (Taking it out of his coat pocket and displaying its whole 4x6) You wouldn't like to buy the flag they buried him in, would you? I could make it very reasonable. I have it in several sizes.
(He starts pulling more truck out of his pocket)
MacArthur's suspenders, the first bullet to land in Pearl Harbor...you can take your pick...a piece of a Japanese submarine; if you look at it this way it becomes a German submarine, and this way it's a piece of shell that just missed Montgomery...Here we have the seat of Rommel's pants and last but not least we have a button from Hitler's coat although that one I don't personally believe.

6-19-43 (Continued)

A-4 (Cont'd)

SERGEANT: Wise guy.

Now the waiter arrives with a heavy tray. On it there is a plate of sandwiches, pickles and six beers. The Marines exchange looks then Bugsy takes one beer off the tray and puts down his fifteen cents.

WAITER: (Waving back his money)
It's all paid for.

The Marines look at each other, then around questioningly at the Manager.

MANAGER: Not by me, it wasn't. You don't have to give me any credit.

WAITER: A guy at the end of the bar.

The Marines each grab a sandwich and a beer then start out of the room.

CUT TO:

A-5 SHOT DOWN THE LONG BAR

In the foreground we see Woodrow. The Marines come through in the beaded curtains in the background, look around, then spot Woodrow. He gives them a polite smile then looks away. The Marines comes closer.

SERGEANT: Was this from you?

WOODROW: That's all right, I just happened to hear the waiter say something about six Marines and one beer...and to serve it with six straws or something.

SERGEANT: Oh he did, did he?

CORPORAL: Where is he?

WOODROW: I already told him.

SERGEANT: Anyway that was a very nice gesture, Civilian.

WOODROW: Don't mention it.

SERGEANT: (Holding it up)
You want General Yamatoho's tooth?

WOODROW: No, thanks.

6-19-43 (Continued)

A-5 (Cont'd)

BUGSY: You could send it to your mother... if you got one.

WOODROW: No, thanks I already sent her some souvenirs.

The Sergeant lifts his glass and the others do likewise.

SERGEANT: Well, then...here's to you.

WOODROW: (Lifting his glass) Semper Fidelis.

THE MARINES: (Somewhat surprised but gravely) Semper Fidelis.

SERGEANT: (Not making much of it) You know our motto, hunh?

WOODROW: (Quietly) Yeh, I know the motto.

BUGSY: Was you in the Marine Corps, maybe?

WOODROW: Yeh, I was in the Marine Corps.

SERGEANT: That's too bad, Joe.

WOODROW: That's all right. Set 'em up again... Don't you want anything besides beer?

CORPORAL: Well, personally I never touch anything stronger than Rye Whiskey.

WOODROW: Seven Ryes...You can use the beer for chasers.

SERGEANT: Thanks...You sure you ain't spendin' too fast like fancy Feelix, the Crap King, here? (he indicates the Corporal)

CORPORAL: Listen.

WOODROW: I just got paid tonight, besides I can't think of any way I'd rather spend my money than for Marines...from Guadalcanal.

BUGSY: It's a great place to be from. (He laughs)

CORPORAL: (Lifting the Rye) Well, Sukiyaki.

They drink and Woodrow motions for another round.

SERGEANT: How long you out?

6-21-43 (Continued)

A-5 (Cont'd)

WOODROW: From the Marines?

SERGEANT: Yeh.

WOODROW: I was only in a month.

BUGSY: That's too bad.

CORPORAL: You hardly had time to get corns on your feet.

BILL: Were you wounded?

SERGEANT: How could he get wounded in Bootcamp?

JONESY: He could of fell off a roof.

SERGEANT: What would he be doing on a roof?

WOODROW: It was Hayfever...Chronic Hayfever.

JUKE: (Sympathetically)
That's the worst kind, too.

CORPORAL: It's terrible...I had a girl once had it. Every time you'd get close to her she'd sneeze right in your kisser.

SERGEANT: She wasn't so dumb.

CORPORAL: It was the excitement.

BILL: Well, better luck next time.

WOODROW: Thanks.

SERGEANT: Did you try any of the other branches of the Service?...like the Army or the Navy...they'll take anything.

WOODROW: They wouldn't take me. I went into a shipyard.

JUKE: My grandmother is a WAAC.

SERGEANT: What good is that gonna do him?

WOODROW: I don't know why Hayfever is so terrible...
(He snuffles)

CORPORAL: It's because you never know when it's gonna hit you...I remember one night...this dame.. had a bowl of noodle soup in front of her and all of a sudden...
(he wipes the noodles out of his eyes)

6-21-43 (Continued)

A-5 (Cont'd)

WOODROW: Anyway, I was kinda born to be a Marine... my father was killed in Belleau Wood the day I was born...almost the same hour...all I ever thought about was being a Marine... I did exercises...I never drank or smoked... I studied about them...I can tell you every battle the Marines were in from 1775 down to now: New Providence, Fort Nassau, the second Battle of Trenton, the Bonhomme Richard and the Serapis, 'I have not yet begun to fight'...

THE CAMERA STARTS TO PUSH IN to a BIG HEAD

Tripoli in 1805, Nukuhive in 1812, the Battle of Hatchee-Lustee River, 1837, Vera Cruz in '46...., Chapultepec...The Halls of Montezuma...Panama in '85, Quantanamo Bay in '98, then the Philippines, the Boxer Rebellion in China, Nicaragua, Coyotepe Hill, Fort Riviere in Haiti...then Chateau-Thierry... Belleau Wood...Soisson...Saint Mihiel...and now Wake Island...Guam...Bataan...Corregidor.. Guadalcanal...they bled and died...

Now the CAMERA STARTS TO PULL BACK

They gave me a big send-off when I left home...the band was playing and everybody hollering and all the dogs barking...my mother crying...everybody wondering if I'd come home a general or just a sergeant like my father...It's one thing to go home with things like that on your chest and another thing to go home with hayfever...and a medical discharge.

BUGSY: (Horrified)
You mean you ain't been home?

WOODROW: I wrote I was leaving for overseas.

BUGSY: You shouldn't do that to your mother.

WOODROW: I wrote a couple of letters to say I was all right, and asked a kid to mail them...from overseas.

BUGSY: Suppose he didn't get a chance to mail them!

WOODROW: Well....

BUGSY: (Indignantly)
That's a terrible thing to do to your mother...you ought to be ashamed of yourself.

6-21-43 (Continued)

A-5 (Cont'd)

WOODROW: (Quietly)
I am.

SERGEANT: (Faintly suspicious)
You say your father was a sergeant at Belleau Wood?

WOODROW: That's right...fill 'em up again...

SERGEANT: (After exchanging a wise look with the others)
What was his name? I was at Belleau Wood.

WOODROW: Truesmith.

SERGEANT: (Galvanized)
Truesmith! You mean Hinky Dinky Truesmith?

WOODROW: That's right.

SERGEANT: But he was my Sergeant...I saw him fall.

WOODROW: Well, right then I was being born...in Oakridge,California.

SERGEANT: Did you know your father got the Congressional Medal of Honor?

WOODROW: I grew up with it...they hung it on me.

BUGSY: (A man of single purpose)
Is that where she lives?...Oakridge?

WOODROW: Who?

BUGSY: Your mother.

WOODROW: Sure.

BUGSY: You ought to be ashamed of yourself.

He walks out of the SHOT.

SERGEANT: (With some embarrassment for Bugsy's rudeness)
It's an honor to meet you, kid.
(He takes him warmly by the hand)
What's your name?

WOODROW: (Bitterly)
Woodrow LaFayette Pershing Truesmith...
go ahead and laugh.

6-21-43 (Continued)

A-5 (Cont'd)

SERGEANT: That ain't anything to laugh at...to anybody who knows anything...Boys, I want you to shake hands with Hinky Dinky Truesmith's boy, Woodrow: Corporal Candida, Pfc's Jones, Gillette and Swenson. My name is Heffelfinger. Julius...and you can just call me Sarg...set 'em up...excuse me.

WOODROW: (To the Bartender)
Certainly.

SERGEANT: (Happily)
I guess you never got to know your father very well, hunh?

WOODROW: Well not exactly...as he...fell the day I was born.

SERGEANT: (After a second's puzzlement)
That's right. It's...hard to realize... he was a fine lookin' fellow...he didn't look anything like you at all.

WOODROW: I know. We got a picture of him.

SERGEANT: (Indicating Bugsy who comes back into the shot)
And this is Bugsy Walewski.

BUGSY: (Sourly)
Pleased to meet you.
(He does not shake hands but looks at the change on the bar)
Can I borrow fifty cents?

SERGEANT: (Indignantly)
Listen, after a guy's bought you...

WOODROW: (To Bugsy)
Go ahead.

SERGEANT: (To Bugsy)
You ought to be ashamed of yourself.

BUGSY: (Indicating Woodrow)
He ought to be ashamed of himself... Treatin' his mother that way.

He goes out of the SHOT.

SERGEANT: (Apologetically)
He never had any mother...He's from a Home.

CORPORAL: He's a little bit screwy too.

6-21-43

(Continued)

A-5 (Cont'd)

SERGEANT: He's all right...he got a little shot up that's all...nothing serious.

He brushes the subject aside:

So you're Hinky Dinky's boy...I travel one hundred thousand miles and run into Hinky Dinky's boy...He was a brave kid...not quite as old as you are...

WOODROW: I know.

SERGEANT: They was sixteen of us, see, in this wood... You couldn't see nothin'...They'd be a German right there and you'd be right here and you couldn't see him and he couldn't see you.

WOODROW: I know.

SERGEANT: All of a sudden, almost right under our feet we hear the rat, tat, tat, tat...

CUT TO:

A-6 BUGSY - <u>IN THE PHONE BOOTH</u>

He looks back, then puts two quarters in the telephone.

CUT TO:

A-7 <u>A RURAL TELEPHONE EXCHANGE</u> - (NIGHT)

THE OPERATOR: Oakridge........sure I know her number, but isn't it kind of late to be calling somebody up in the middle of the night...just a minute.. yes, Doctor...I don't think she's home yet, the third feature don't let out 'till twelve seventeen...You're welcome.
(She flips another toggle switch)
Are you sure it's important...He did! Well why didn't you say so in the first place... for Heaven's sake.
(She plugs a trunk in and starts ringing.)

DISSOLVE TO:

A-8 WOODROW AND THE MARINES - <u>AT THE BAR</u>

SERGEANT: (Excitedly)
Somebody had to get 'em, see, the Louie is lyin' there holding his belly, one of the kids is cryin' and somebody says 'let's draw lots' but Hinky says 'I'm the Sergeant, see...I already won...you'll hear 'em when I get there.. then come in' and he starts through the bushes.. so there we are...on your mark...get set...all of a sudden...

6-21-43 (Continued)

A-8 (Cont'd)

BUGSY: (Walking into the SHOT)
Your Mother's on the telephone...She wants to talk to you.

SERGEANT: (Irritated at the interruption)
Just a minute...WHAT?

WOODROW: (Stunned)
You mean my Mother?

BUGSY: That's right.

WOODROW: But how can I talk to her if I'm overseas?

SERGEANT: (To Bugsy)
You dumb clunk.

BUGSY: Because you ain't overseas...you just come home with us...from Guadalcanal...you're goin' home tomorrow...

WOODROW: Goin' home?

Thunderstruck, Woodrow looks toward the telephone, then starts for it.

CORPORAL: Are you nuts or something? This guy is tryin' to keep his mother from knowin' he ain't...

BUGSY: You want to make somethin' of it?

SERGEANT: Pipe down.

CUT TO:

A-9 TELEPHONE BOOTH

Woodrow comes into the SHOT and enters the booth, looks back at the Marines, then speaks.

WOODROW: Hello, is that you Mama......hello, Mama... Well sure I'm all right...Of course I am... never felt better in my life. How have you been, Mama?

CUT TO:

A-10 THE MARINES

They are walking toward the phone booth on tiptoe.

BUGSY: (Triumphantly)
See?

CUT TO:

6-21-43

A-11 WOODROW - IN THE BOOTH

WOODROW: Did you get my letters...You did, hunh? Well, that's fine...I was afraid you might have been worried...Well I don't know about that, Mama... It's very hard to get leave these days with the war and all...I just got up to Frisco for this evening, see...That I was wounded and honorably discharged from the service! Who told you I was wounded and discharged from the service?
(He turns and looks at Bugsy)

THE CAMERA PANS off him to the Marines who have come right up to the booth.

BUGSY: (To the Marines)
Then she won't have to worry no more.

CUT TO:

A-12 WOODROW - IN THE BOOTH

WOODROW: Now wait a minute, Mama...you'd hardly call it a wound...it was more like a scratch...it was more like a fever...just a little fever that's all.....well maybe it's called jungle fever, mama. I don't know...No I'm not being brave, but I just don't see how I'll be able to get home for quite some time, Mama, no I'm not seriously wounded, I wish I was...I said I wished I could come home but I just can't make it...You can't do that, Mama...They don't allow visitors where I am...Well then she must have known the Colonel or something...I'm in wrong with him...I can't tell you that, Mama... that's military information. No I'm not in jail what would I be in jail for? I don't know...why he said I was comin' home tomorrow, Mama...He was probably talking about somebody else...He had several calls to make, you know how it is...Well of course I want to come home, Mama...Why wouldn't I..I'm crazy to see you and Libby and, and everybody...but this is war, Mama.

SERGEANT: (Suddenly)
Wait a minute.

WOODROW: Hunh?
(He claps his hand over the phone)

SERGEANT: You can go home tomorrow, I figured it all out.

WOODROW: (Struggling)
What are you talking about? How can I go home when I...

SERGEANT: Like rolling off a log...Gimme that phone.

(Continued)

A-12 (Cont'd)

WOODROW: (Resisting)
Now wait a minute.

SERGEANT: (Snatching the phone away from him)
Hello, Mrs. Truesmith? This is Sergeant Hef-felfinger...I guess you never heard of me, hunh? But I was a friend of Hinky Dink's... I certainly was...Well I got some good news for you. I fixed it up with the Colonel and your boy's comin home tomorrow...Yes mam... that sounds pretty good, hunh? Your boy is comin' home.

FADE OUT:

END OF SEQUENCE "A"

SEQUENCE "B"

FADE IN:

B-1 A LOCOMOTIVE - IN THE SAN FRANCISCO STATION - (DAY)

It pants pleasingly. We hear the strains of "MADEMOISELLE FROM ARMENTIERRES."

DISSOLVE TO:

B-2 SEVEN PAIRS OF MARINES' FEET

We TRUCK with them as they march down the platform past pretty girls' legs, a couple of babies and a dog. The three leading pairs and the three trailing pairs of feet are in perfect step. The pair in the middle seems reluctant. It drops back, then hops forward again as if it had been pushed.

CUT TO:

B-3 A CONDUCTOR AND BRAKEMAN

They stand in front of a pullman car watching the approaching Marines.

CONDUCTOR: Guadalcanal.

BRAKEMAN: Gee!

CUT TO:

B-4 THE APPROACHING MARINES

There are seven of them. The CAMERA PANS them to the entrance of the Pullman car. Bugsy carries one of Woodrow's suitcases and Jonesy the other. Woodrow's right hand covers a medal on his chest.

WOODROW: Look, it's bad enough to wear the uniform without wearing this on it.

He uncovers an unusually small medal on his chest.

SERGEANT: What are you talking about? I don't even remember what I got it for.
(He points to a ribbon on the Corporal's chest)
You know what he got this for? Some Japs was roasting a pig across the stream and the breeze was blowing it all right over in his kisser...so he went over and got it.

CORPORAL: Boy that was some dish.

6-21-43 (Continued)

B-4 (Cont'd)

SERGEANT: Just a hog.

WOODROW: (Pointing to his chest)
I know but...

JUKE: You gotta wear something.

JONESY: You can't come back from the Solomons without nothing.

BILL: Not the son of Sergeant Truesmith.

WOODROW: I can't help it! I don't like the whole idea.

BUGSY: You gotta think of your Mother.

WOODROW: (Wearily)
The regulations are very clear: you can wear the uniform home but not longer than thirty days.

CORPORAL: Suppose you was paid off in South Africa?

SERGEANT: And you went home on foot?

CORPORAL: They can't tell you how to go home.

SERGEANT: You could go home on a pogo stick.

WOODROW: But the regulation distinctly says...

SERGEANT: That only applies to Marines...You ain't really a Marine any more...besides regulations is very elastic, I was even a Colonel once for a couple of days...once.

CORPORAL: And a brig hound for a couple of months.
(Suddenly under his breath)
'Shun.

The Marines come to attention.

CUT TO:

B-5 AN APPROACHING MARINE GENERAL

He is accompanied by his wife and a young daughter. The CAMERA PANS him into the SHOT with the Marines.

GENERAL: (Answering the Marines' salute)
How are you boys?

SERGEANT: (Very basso)
Fine, sir, thank you sir.

The Marines put their hands down but Woodrow keeps his up.

6-21-43 (Continued)

B-5 (Cont'd)

WOODROW: (His hand in salute and his knees in rubber)
Let's go back to my room and talk it over.

SERGEANT: Nonsense.
(He snatches Woodrow's hand down but it goes up again automatically)
Keep your lip buttoned...keep your hand down and nobody will be the wiser.

WOODROW: (Firmly)
No.

CONDUCTOR'S VOICE: All aboard.

SERGEANT: Come on, get on the train.

The train starts to move.

WOODROW: No.

SERGEANT: Come on will ya, chuck his gear on.

WOODROW: No, no.

SERGEANT: Will you get on that train?

WOODROW: No.

SERGEANT: Hoist him on...after we went to all this trouble.

The four Pfcs pull the struggling Woodrow on the train. They lose their balance a little. The Corporal and the Sergeant are now running alongside.

SERGEANT: All right now, get off there.

JONESY'S VOICE: He's sitting on me.

WOODROW'S VOICE: Let me off of here.

BUGSY'S VOICE: You gotta think of your Mother.

CORPORAL: Why don't we go with him, seeins as how we ain't got any dough anyway.

SERGEANT: (Beginning to puff)
Well get on or get off or anything except running along here.

6-21-43 (Continued)

B-5 (Cont'd)

CORPORAL: Come on.

He hoists the Sergeant aboard. The MUSIC reprises "MADEMOISELLE FROM ARMENTIERRES" as we:

CUT TO:

B-6 A RAILROAD SEMAPHORE AGAINST THE SKY - (DAY)

It swings up to the all clear position or words to that effect. The MUSIC continues under this.

CUT TO:

B-7 ANGLE DOWN SHOT

A train passes under us and the smoke fills the screen.

SLOW DISSOLVE TO:

B-8 WOODROW AND THE MARINES - IN THE SMOKING ROOM OF A PULLMAN CAR

The scenery is going by outside.

WOODROW: Look, I don't want to sound ungrateful.... I know you mean it for the best and I don't mind the seven tickets or anything I'ma, I'ma honored to have you go home with me....it's just the uniform...it makes me nervous.

BUGSY: Well you can't go home without it.

WOODROW: I shouldn't go home with it....and this....
(He points to the medal)

BUGSY: You shouldn't have lied to your Mother.

SERGEANT: I think it was for pulling a Frenchman out of a river or something.

JONESY: (Pointing to his)
He ought to have the Battle Blaze....that don' look right.

WOODROW: Well I'm not going to have the Battle Blaze.... It's bad enough like this.

SERGEANT: Who's gonna notice anything...you slip off the train...We'll kinda surround ya...We slip up a side street...Your mother is waiting on the front porch...You put your arms around her...

6-21-43 (Continued)

B-8 (Cont'd)

BUGSY: That's right.

SERGEANT: You get outta your uniform...you salt it away in moth balls and there you are... home. She's happy...you're happy...everybody's happy...and nobody's hep to nothin!

WOODROW: It isn't only my mother...I gotta girl too...I mean I did have...

SERGEANT: What'd you tell her...you was goin' in the Navy?

WOODROW: No...I told her I fell for somebody else... so she wouldn't wait for me.

SERGEANT: What are you gonna tell her now?

CORPORAL: Tell her you're married.

SERGEANT: What good does that do? Tell her you're divorced.

WOODROW: I'm no good at lying...maybe she doesn't care anymore anyway....

BUGSY: Is your ma a good cook?

WOODROW: Wonderful.

BUGSY: Gee you're lucky.

WOODROW: (Crossly)
Well I don't feel lucky...I tell you the whole thing is...suppose I see somebody I know at the station?

SERGEANT: We'll surround you...you got nothin' to worry about.

WOODROW: I hope not.

PORTER: (Sticking his head through the curtain)
Oakridge.

Woodrow immediately salutes him and keeps his hand glued to his forehead.

SERGEANT: Don't do that...keep cool will you...what can happen?

BUGSY: Does your ma put up preserves?

B-8 (Cont'd)

WOODROW: (Barking at Bugsy!
Yes!
(Then to the Sergeant)
What can happen?...anything can happen.

The Sergeant shrugs his shoulders at this childishness.

DISSOLVE TO:

B-9 FULL SHOT - STATION AT OAKRIDGE, CALIFORNIA

Across the tracks a big banner reads "WELCOME WOODROW - HAIL OUR HERO" and that is only the beginning. The entire town seems to be here with music. The Progressive's Party's band with placard: "WELCOME WOODROW...VOTE FOR DOC BISSELL, YOU CLEANED UP GUADALCANAL HELP HIM CLEAN UP OAKRIDGE." Then The Regular Party band with placard, "WELCOME WOODROW, OAKRIDGE IS PROUD OF YOU...REELECT EVERETT J. NOBLE, VICTORY THROUGH VIGI-LENCE." Next a Junior Sheriff's Auxiliary Band under a flag inscribed simply: "OUR HERO." Next is an American Legion band under a banner which says "WE DID IT BEFORE, WE'LL DO IT AGAIN ...WELCOME SON OF HINKY DINK" and a little old Western Union man with a sign which says "WELCOME FROM WESTERN UNION." Surrounding all of this are townspeople young and old, Mamie, a little girl in white with a bunch of flowers, loose children, squalling babies, barking dogs, an ice cream man with tricycle, a few soldiers and sailors, a colored delegation from the Odd-fellows, a Chinese with welcome sign in Chinese, the village photographer with a tripod camera and the cast: Woodrow's Mother, Libby and her Aunt, the Chairman of the Reception Committee, Mr. Noble, his wife, his son Forrest, the Political Boss, the Newspaper Editor, Judge Dennis, Doc Bissell, Schultz the grocer, and the Rev. Doctor Upperman...all wearing badges. A band starts to play.

CUT TO:

B-10 THE CHAIRMAN

CHAIRMAN: Not yet...not 'till I give the signal.

He blows on a whistle which STOPS the music.

CHAIRMAN: Not 'till I give the signal.

The Western Union man comes into the SHOT.

CHAIRMAN: Not here! Go stand some place else.

B-11 WOODROW'S MOTHER - WITH A BIG BUNCH OF FLOWERS IN HER ARMS

LIBBY'S AUNT: (Coming into the SHOT)
I'm very happy for you, Sally.

WOODROW'S MOTHER: Isn't it wonderful...when he was away for so long...and only hearing from him twice... and <u>then</u> being his father's son...you can imagine the chances he would take...the risks he would run.

(Continued)

B-11 (Cont'd)

LIBBY'S AUNT: Do you suppose he knows about Libby?

WOODROW'S MOTHER: I don't know, Martha...I certainly didn't tell him.

LIBBY'S AUNT: Do you suppose he'll be broken-hearted?

WOODROW'S MOTHER: I...hope not.

LIBBY'S AUNT: Well...he broke off with her...her skirts are certainly clean.

WOODROW'S MOTHER: I don't know anything about it, Martha.

LIBBY'S AUNT: She would have waited 'til, 'til Judgement day...

WOODROW'S MOTHER: I'm sure she would have, Martha.

LIBBY'S AUNT: (Looking away)
I wish she had.

WOODROW'S MOTHER: So do I dear but...
(Then forcing a smile)
anyway my boy is coming home.

She takes Martha in her arms.

CUT TO:

B-12 LIBBY AND FORREST NOBLE, THE LATTER A TALL HANDSOME YOUNG CIVILIAN

Libby is a pretty girl.

LIBBY: I don't know what to do.

FORREST: (Faintly annoyed)
Well it really isn't your problem, dear, you're engaged to me and that's all there is to it.

LIBBY: (Looking at her engagement ring)
I know...but it's his homecoming. And homecoming means to find everything the way you left it...at least for a little while. I mean after all we were...sweethearts when he left...whoever he may have fallen in love with afterwards.

FORREST: I don't see that that has anything to do with it...if he'd waited a year longer there might have been three of us to welcome him...if he'd waited two years there might have been...

LIBBY: Oh shut up.

(Continued)

B-12 (Cont'd)

FORREST: Well that's what marriage is for isn't it?

LIBBY: I suppose so if you look at it from a purely unromantic standpoint....like a breeding farm.
(She makes a hopeless gesture)
I mean if you don't see anything soul-stirring in the return of a, a...

FORREST: Hero.

LIBBY: All right, a hero. If you don't find anything heart-warming...

FORREST: My dear girl: I tried to get into the Army by every possible means. I even lied about my condition.

LIBBY: I know you did.

FORREST: It is not my fault that I have...

LIBBY: ...chronic hay fever. I know that Forrest.. I've heard it a thousand times...but since you bring it up I am forced to remind you that Woodrow also had hay fever.

Forrest opens his mouth helplessly.

LIBBY: (Looking out of the SHOT)
Your father wants you.

Forrest hesitates, then goes out of the SHOT. Now Libby crosses to Woodrow's mother. THE CAMERA PANS her over.

LIBBY: I'm very happy for you, Mrs. Truesmith.

WOODROW'S MOTHER: Of course you are, dear.

LIBBY: (In some hesitation)
Will you tell him I'm going to be married to Forrest, please?

WOODROW'S MOTHER: No I won't Libby, I think that's up to you.

LIBBY: Will you tell him, Aunt Martha?

LIBBY'S AUNT: Who me? Hah!

LIBBY: Well you know it wasn't my fault...I would have waited for him...forever.

She turns to Woodrow's mother.

LIBBY: He asked me not to.
(She turns to her aunt)
He told me to forget him.

(Continued)

B-12 (Cont'd)

LIBBY: (Cont'd)
(She turns to Woodrow's mother)
He wrote me he didn't love me anymore.

WOODROW'S MOTHER: Maybe you should have read between the lines a little.

LIBBY:
(On the verge of tears)
Oh I don't know what to do...I don't want to tell him I'm engaged to somebody else...I just want to take him in my arms and tell him I'm so glad he's safe and so proud of him...After all I grew up with him.

LIBBY'S AUNT: Then why don't you?

LIBBY:
(Tempted)
I don't know how Forrest would feel about it.

WOODROW'S MOTHER: I'm sure I don't know either, dear.

LIBBY'S AUNT: Why don't you ask him? If you can't handle a man the week before you marry him he'll have you carrying in the wood on the wedding night. (Would 'laying the fire' be better?).

Libby hesitates a second, then goes out of the SHOT. The two ladies exchange a significant look...

CUT TO:

B-13 MR. NOBLE, MRS. NOBLE, THE POLITICAL BOSS, THE CHAIRMAN AND FORREST

MR. NOBLE:
(Indignantly)
What do you mean I don't speak first? If anybody speaks first it's the mayor...I mean to say if you think I'm going to stand around like a door post and, and...

CHAIRMAN: Very well, Mr. Mayor, I'm only the chairman of the Reception Committee but as I visualize it...

MAYOR:
(To his son)
Did you bring the keys to the city?

FORREST: Yes, father, right here.

He pulls them half out of his pocket and looks back toward Libby.

MAYOR: Because I don't want to pull out my fountain pen like I did that time General what-che-ma-call-it...

B-13 (Cont'd)

MRS. NOBLE: Why don't you let Mr. Pash arrange things?

MAYOR: (Threateningly to his wife)
If it's all the same to you, my love...

BOSS: It's always better to talk last, Evvy.

As Mr. Noble turns to argue this:

CHAIRMAN: As I visualized it, the ceremony began with a little girl in white with a bunch of posies...

MAYOR: ...in her grimy little mitts. I know, I've listened to her before.

CHAIRMAN: Whatever you say, Mr. Mayor.

MAYOR: She forgets her lines till rigor mortis sets in.

CHAIRMAN: Very well, Mr. Mayor, you arrange the reception.

He folds his arms and looks in the distance.

THE BOSS: I tell you it's better to talk after Bissell... then you can give him the needle.

MAYOR: All right have it your own way...after all I'm only the Mayor.

CHAIRMAN: (Departing)
Thank you very much, Mr. Mayor.
(Now to the Western Union man who has just come)
Not in front of the Mayor...Out in the fringe somewhere.
(He leads him out)

MAYOR: You'd think this was a political campaign instead of a...did you bring the keys to the city?

FORREST: Yes, Father.

LIBBY: (Coming into the SHOT)
Mrs. Noble.

MRS. NOBLE: Oh call me mo....Myrtle, dear.

LIBBY: Do you think it would be all right if I didn't tell Woodrow I was engaged to Forrest right away?

THE MAYOR AND FORREST: (Together)
WHAT!

MAYOR: Well it most certainly would not be all right! Of all the confounded...what are you talking about?

(Continued)

B-13 (Cont'd)

LIBBY: I mean not to spoil his homecoming with with...by striking a single sour note.

FORREST: Thanks.

LIBBY: I don't mean that darling.

MRS. NOBLE: (Putting her arm around her)
Why of course it would be all right...I understand perfectly.

FORREST: (Coldly)
Well I'm not sure that I do, Mother.

MRS. NOBLE: That's because you're not a woman, dear.
(Then to Libby)
It's perfectly all right.
(Then to Forrest)
Why under similar circumstances I'd be perfectly willing to pretend I wasn't married to your father for several...weeks even.

MAYOR: You could make it several months as far as I'm concerned.

MRS. NOBLE: He talks that way in public...we understand perfectly...you go right down and take him in your arms and...kiss him all you like.

FORREST: Well I may have something to say about that...

MAYOR: Oh I suppose she could kiss him on the cheek.

MRS. NOBLE: Oh kiss him wherever you like, of all the nonsense: two men telling us how to welcome a hero.

LIBBY: (Kissing her)
Thank you...Myrtle.

Mrs. Noble winks at her.

LIBBY: (Starting out of the SHOT)
And thank you, Mr. Mayor...and you Forrest.

She pecks him on the cheek and goes happily out of the SHOT.

MRS. NOBLE: (To her son)
You're going to have her the rest of your life...let him have her for an hour.

MAYOR: (To his son)
This is war you know.

THE BOSS: (To Forrest)
And you know what Sherman said about it.

CUT TO:

B-14 JUDGE DENNIS, DOC BISSELL, MR. SCHULTZ, THE CHAIRMAN, THE LEADER OF THE PROGRESSIVE BAND AND SOME CHARACTERS

DOC BISSELL: Then he talks first? (Continued)

B-14 (Cont'd)

CHAIRMAN: No, no, no it's just as I visualized it: little Mamie Reynolds, then the Mayor, then you.

JUDGE DENNIS: You can take him apart a little.

CHAIRMAN: Precisely. Now if I can ever get the music straight...

PROGRESSIVE BAND LEADER: I've got it straight, I start with "There'll Be A Hot Time In The Old Town Tonight."

CHAIRMAN: You start with "Home To The Arms Of Mother" I've told you a thousand times.

PROGRESSIVE BAND LEADER: I thought Ed started with that.

CHAIRMAN: Well aren't you Ed?

PROGRESSIVE BAND LEADER: No, I'm Ned, Ed is playing for the Mayor.

CHAIRMAN: Then where is Ned?

PROGRESSIVE BAND LEADER: I am...we'd better get together on this while there's still time.

CHAIRMAN:
(Hollering to somebody out of the SHOT)
Oh Ned...
(Then to the Western Union Man who has just come into the SHOT)
Not here.
(He drags him out with him)
...just a minute.

The Band Leader exchanges a helpless look with Judge Dennis and says to the Chairman:

PROGRESSIVE BAND LEADER: I'm Ned.

He follows the Chairman out of the SHOT

JUDGE DENNIS: This boy Woodrow is going to be very popular in this town, Doc.

DOC BISSELL: He deserves to be.

JUDGE DENNIS: I wonder if the same thought has occurred to you that flashed through my mind?

DOC BISSELL: Probably.

CUT TO:

B-15 WOODROW'S MOTHER, LIBBY'S AUNT AND LIBBY

LIBBY: Well that's settled, I'm just going to hug him as if he'd never written to me at all.

WOODROW'S MOTHER: I think that is a very sweet thought, dear.

LIBBY'S AUNT: Do you want me to hold your engagement ring?

LIBBY: Oh.

(She looks around toward Forrest then gives her ring to her Aunt who puts it on her own finger)

CHAIRMAN: (Hurrying into the SHOT with two bandleaders)
If I could just move you over about six feet this way, Mrs. Truesmith, next to the band that plays "Home To The Arms Of Mother."

WOODROW'S MOTHER: Certainly.

THE REGULAR BAND LEADER: (Pointing in the opposite direction)
Well, I'm playing that over there.

CHAIRMAN: (Putting the back of his hand to his forehead)
Are you Ned or Ed?

REGULAR BAND LEADER: I'm Ed.

CHAIRMAN: Very well, Mrs. Truesmith, then would you mind moving about twelve feet over that way.

WOODROW'S MOTHER: Surely.

REGULAR BAND LEADER: I begin with "Mademoiselle From Armentierres" then go into "Hail The Conquering Hero Comes".

CHAIRMAN: (Stunned)
You begin with "Mademoiselle From Armentierres"

REGULAR BAND LEADER: That's right.

CHAIRMAN: (To the Progressive Band Leader)
Then what do you play?

PROGRESSIVE BAND LEADER: "There'll Be A Hot Time In The Old Town Tonight

CHAIRMAN: Then who plays "Home To The Arms Of Mother"?

B-15 (Cont'd)

LEADER OF THE AMERICAN LEGION BAND: (Coming into the SHOT)
I do.

CHAIRMAN: (Looking at his sheet)
What's your name?

LEADER OF THE AMERICAN LEGION BAND: Eddie.

LEADER OF THE JUNIOR SHERIFF'S AUXILIARY BAND: (Coming into the SHOT)
I thought I started with that.

CHAIRMAN: With what?

L. OF THE JUNIOR SHERIFF'S A. BAND: "Hail The Conquering Hero Comes".

CHAIRMAN: Who's talking about "Hail The Conquering Hero Comes"?

L. OF THE JUNIOR SHERIFF'S BAND: I am.

CHAIRMAN: (Expiring)
No, no, no, you play...
(He puts the back of his hand to his forehead)
Oh death where is thy sting?

L. OF THE JUNIOR SHERIFF'S A. BAND: We don't know that...all we know is "Hail The Conquering Hero" and half of "Marching Through Georgia". We were only formed last week.

PROGRESSIVE BAND LEADER: Now wait a minute, Teddy...
(The Chairman reacts to this)
I lead off with "A Hot Time In The Old Town Tonight", Ed follows with "Mademoiselle From Armentierres" and modulates into "Hail The Conquering Hero Comes", Eddie takes "Home To The Arms Of Mother" and you play anything you know.

LIBBY: Can anybody play "Let Me Call You Sweetheart"?

PROGRESSIVE BAND LEADER: Sure I can modulate into that from "There'll Be A Hot Time In The Old Town Tonight".

REGULAR BAND LEADER: Or I could take it after "Mademoiselle" and let Teddy take "Hail The Conquering Hero."

B-15 (Cont'd)

CHAIRMAN: Certainly if you want to upset all of my plans...after all I've only had one morning to whip this all together you know.

LIBBY: I'm sorry.

CHAIRMAN: Play it! Play anything you like.

Now a large lady in white comes into the SHOT, and grabs the Leader of the American Legion Band.

LADY IN WHITE: (With an accent)
Mr. Pash.

CHAIRMAN: What?

LADY IN WHITE: (Menacingly)
I am here to help...I do it for nothing... with joy...but I got to have cooperation: I sing the hymn in seven flats and he won't play it in seven flats.

LEADER OF THE LEGION BAND: (Desperately)
We don't know how to play in seven flats... we're not musicians.

LADY IN WHITE: You don't have to tell me.

CHAIRMAN: (Wearily)
Each work in your own key and do your best.

PROGRESSIVE BAND LEADER: (To the American Legion Band Leader)
Why don't we take it for her and you take "Mademoiselle From Armentierres"?

LADY IN WHITE: I refuse to sing it.

PROGRESSIVE BAND LEADER: You don't understand, Madam.

CHAIRMAN: (At the top of his lungs)
Will you stop bawling things up...everything was clear and simple and now
(Now he grabs a woman who is hurrying through the shot)
Where is Mamie? She's always disappearing.

MAMIE'S MOTHER: She'll be back in a minute...it's the excitement.

A STENTORIAN VOICE: Here comes the train.

Two bands start PLAYING immediately, all the leaders rush out of the SHOT.

B-15 (Cont'd)

CHAIRMAN: (Running in all directions at once)
Not yet! Not yet!

He blows his WHISTLE, starts off in one direction then stops and blows his WHISTLE in the other direction. The Western Union Man comes into the SHOT and settles himself for the Reception. After a moment he narrows his eyes and watches evilly as another little old man walks into the SHOT and stands beside him. The new arrival bears a placard which says simply: "POSTAL TELEGRAPH IS PROUD OF YOU."

CUT TO:

B-16 THE JUNIOR SHERIFF'S AUXILIARY BAND

The boys start playing "Marching Through Georgia."

CHAIRMAN: (Running into the SHOT)
No, no, no.

Now he clutches his head and rushes out of the SHOT.

CUT TO:

B-17 THE BIG LADY IN WHITE WITH AMERICAN LEGION BAND

The latter is playing something we can't make out and she is singing likewise. The Chairman blows his whistle in her face. She looks at him indignantly and with one powerful shove shoots him out of the SHOT.

CUT TO:

B-18 MAMIE AND HER BUNCH OF FLOWERS

The Chairman staggers into the SHOT and sits on her. Mamie starts to holler and the Chairman is immediately spoken to very roughly by Mamie's Mother.

CUT TO:

B-19 WOODROW AND THE MARINES - IN THE SMOKING ROOM

WOODROW: (Frightened)
What's that music?

PORTER: (Entering)
Brush you off, Gents?

He locks the toilet.

Fix you up for de reception?

(Continued)

B-19 (Cont'd)

WOODROW: (Freezing)
The reception!

PORTER: I reckon it's for you all...They's half a dozen bands and all de 'ficials...

WOODROW: (At bay)
Let me outta here.

SERGEANT: Now wait a minute...it's probably for somebody else...We'll wait here 'till they get it over with and then slip off quietly on the other side when the train starts up again.

In the meanwhile Bill, Juke, Bugsy and Jonesy have stepped into the corridor to look. Now they start bringing back reports.

JONESY: (Hollering above the MUSIC)
It ain't for anybody else...It says "WELCOME WOODROW"...

BILL: "You cleaned up Guadalcanal..."

JUKE: "...help us clean up Oakridge."

JONESY: "Vote for Doc Bissell."

BILL: "Welcome Woodrow...Oakridge is proud of you."

JUKE: "Reelect Everett J. Noble."

WOODROW: (Leaping to his feet)
Let me outta here.

He starts unbuttoning his coat.

SERGEANT: You're just gonna make things worse.

WOODROW: Where's my suitcase?

PORTER: They's up ahead in the vestibule.

SERGEANT: Keep cool, will ya.

WOODROW: (Pointing to the toilet)
Open that up...
(He sneezes)
I'll hide in there...you can all get off and tell 'em I couldn't...
(He sneezes)
...come. Make them...

(Continued)

B-19 (Cont'd)

WOODROW: (Cont'd)
(He sneezes)
My apologies.
(To the Porter)
Will you open that...
(He sneezes)

PORTER: Not while it's in the station, boss... You'll have to wait.

WOODROW: (Struggling out of his coat)
Then I'll get off in my underwear.

SERGEANT: Cut that out, we're just pullin' in the station.

JONESY: I told you he ought to have the Battle Blaze...with all those people.

CORPORAL: (Forcing Woodrow back into his coat)
Be a Marine, will you.

JUKE: They got four bands...That don't look good with only one medal.

The Sergeant is nonplussed only for one second.

SERGEANT: (Decisively)
Come on take that blouse off.

He pulls it off Woodrow and while doing so says to the Corporal.

Come on, gimme yours.

CORPORAL: (Holding back)
What?

SERGEANT: It's gotta have the Blaze on it...with four bands...come on, get outta that.

The Corporal sheds his blouse and helps force it on the struggling Woodrow.

WOODROW: Quit it, will you?

SERGEANT: Button him up.

They all go to work on Woodrow except the Corporal who struggles into Woodrow's blouse with considerable difficulty.

SERGEANT: It's a matter of honor...here.

(Continued)

B-19 (Cont'd)

He reaches into his breast pocket and starts pinning some additional medals on Woodrow. By now the MUSIC is deafening.

DISSOLVE TO:

B-20 MOVING SHOT - DOWN THE RAILS OF THE WAITING POPULACE

Everybody starts hooraying.

CUT TO:

B-21 PANNING SHOT - THE VESTIBULE OF THE PULLMAN CAR

The struggling Woodrow appears covered with medals, supported by the Marines. The train comes to a stop. The front Marines get off and Woodrow's knees start to sag.

SERGEANT: Hurrah! Pick him up.

The Marines hoist Woodrow to their shoulders. The crowd goes wild. As they carry Woodrow forward,

CUT TO:

B-22 TRUCKING.SHOT - THROUGH THE CROWD - (DAY)

We push through the populace, end up CLOSE SHOT OF WOODROW'S MOTHER, LIBBY AND HER AUNT.

WOODROW'S MOTHER: (Opening her arms wide)
Woodrow.

CUT TO:

B-23 WOODROW - PAST HIS MOTHER

The Marines take him down off their shoulders. As his feet hit the ground his knees give way and the Marines hoist him up again. He takes his Mother in his arms, gets an eyefull of his medals while he does so and tucks them behind his arms. Now he sees the Battle Blaze; he puts his right hand over it.

LIBBY: Hello, Woodrow.

WOODROW: Hello, Libby.

LIBBY: We're so proud of you.

WOODROW: What did you say?

LIBBY: (Hollering)
I said, we're so proud of you.

(Continued)

B-23 (Cont'd)

WOODROW: Thank you.

He kisses her.

CUT TO:

B-24 MAMIE - AT WOODROW'S FEET

She yanks on his blouse and starts talking in a voice like a bugle.

MAMIE: Welcome young warrior...your nattle city rejoices at your safe homecoming and takes great pleasure in presenting you with this beautiful bunch of chrys..chryszanthanamums.

There is a spatter of applause.

CHAIRMAN: (Coming into the SHOT)
And now, Woodrow, if you can spare a moment.

He drags Woodrow, his mother and Libby away and the Marines follow. THE CAMERA PANS them over.

CHAIRMAN: (Cont'd) Mr. Noble has prepared a little speech.

MR. NOBLE: (Seizing his hand)
Welcome home, Woodrow.

WOODROW: Thank you Mr. Noble.

Mr. Noble now puts a cough drop in his mouth and starts hollering in Woodrow's ear so that his speech will carry to the ends of the station.

MR. NOBLE: Friends, voters, returning hero and ex-employee of the Noble Chair Company, Seats of all Descriptions...home to the arms of your mother ...it is with a sense of deep humility...

CUT TO:

B-25 AMERICAN LEGION BAND

It starts playing "Home To The Arms of Mother" with much force (words and music will be supplied on request).

CUT TO:

B-26 WOODROW, HIS MOTHER, LIBBY AND THE MAYOR

Having nothing else to do the Mayor shakes Woodrow's hand again, smiles wolfishly at the crowd and glares at the band

(Continued)

B-26 (Cont'd)

which seems to be wound up. Now the photographer taps the Mayor on the shoulder and he looks at Woodrow again with a beautiful smile. A flash goes off, they all look back toward the band. The Chairman hurries out of the SHOT.

CUT TO:

B-27 AMERICAN LEGION BAND PLAYING "HOME TO THE ARMS OF MOTHER"

The Chairman hurries into the SHOT and gestures for silence.

CUT TO:

B-28 WOODROW, HIS MOTHER, LIBBY AND THE MAYOR

THE MAYOR: It is with a sense of deep humility that I hail this conquering hero! On what foreign shores has he not...
(Now he turns his head at the new interruption)

CUT TO:

B-29 THE REGULAR PARTY BAND

It is playing "Hail The Conquering Hero Comes"

CUT TO:

B-30 THE CHAIRMAN IN FRONT OF THE PROGRESSIVE PARTY BAND

He leaves hurriedly.

CUT TO:

B-31 MR. NOBLE, WOODROW'S MOTHER, LIBBY, AND WOODROW AND THE OTHERS

They are glaring at tha Regular Band. The photographer taps Mr. Noble on the shoulder and gets another smiling picture. The Chairman tears through the SHOT. We HEAR the band stop raggedly.

MR. NOBLE: I say it is with a sense of deep humility that I welcome this young Marine. Actions speak louder than words.
(He points to the medals)
Here are his words. From the Halls of Montezuma to the shores of Tripoli...

He turns and glares at the American Legion Band which picks up this cue in nothing flat. The Chairman hurries into the SHOT, mops his head with a handkerchief and hurries out the other side.

(Continued)

B-31 (Cont'd)

PHOTOGRAPHER: (Coming into the SHOT)
Just once more Mr. Mayor and a big smile this time.

CUT TO:

B-32 THE AMERICAN LEGION BAND PLAYING THE MARINE HYMN

The Chairman hurries into the SHOT and gesticulates but these are not men who take their eyes off their music. The Leader waves the Chairman away; as the latter stands there nonplussed the Lady In White comes into the SHOT, strikes an attitude and starts to sing. The Leader of the Junior Sheriffs' Band now comes into the SHOT and hollers something to the Chairman.

CHAIRMAN: (Throwing his arms to the sky)
Go ahead do anything you like.

CUT TO:

B-33 PROGRESSIVE PARTY BAND

The leader sees the Chairman's gesture and starts playing "Mademoiselle From Armentierres."

CUT TO:

B-34 CHAIRMAN - IN FRONT OF THE AMERICAN LEGION BAND

He turns wearily at the new music, then winces.

CUT TO:

B-35 REGULAR BAND

It is playing "There'll Be A Hot Time In The Old Town Tonight.

CUT TO:

B-36 THE CHAIRMAN

He registers great frustration, then scowls to his left as the Junior Sheriffs' Band marches through the SHOT playing "Marching Through Georgia." They are followed by the Western Union man who is followed in turn by the Postal Telegraph man.

CUT TO:

B-37 MR. NOBLE, WOODROW AND THE MARINES

Mr. Noble has his fingers in his ears. Now the Junior Sheriffs Band comes into the SHOT. Mr. Noble gives up. He gets the keys to the city from his son, presses them in Woodrow's hand and starts waving his hat goodbye. The chairman rushes

(Continued)

B-37 (Cont'd)

into the SHOT and apparently says: "But, Mr. Mayor." Mr. Noble threatens him with the back of his hand, Mrs. Noble smiles to show the Mayor doesn't mean it, Forrest looks at Libby who takes Woodrow's arm in reply. Now the Noble family departs. Woodrow, his mother and Libby move through the hooraying crowd, the Western Union Man and the Postal Telegraph Man fall in behind them, the Marines bring up the rear and are followed in turn by all the bands. There is a scramble and the Junior Sheriff's Band moves up ahead. Judge Dennis, Doc Bissell and Mr. Schultz shake Woodrow's hand. The Chairman goes mad trying to get up in front but is prevented from so doing by the crowd.

DISSOLVE TO:

B-38 THE SIDEWALK ON THE STREET SIDE OF THE STATION - (DAY)

Some open cars decorated with bunting are waiting here with drivers. The crowd comes through eventually squeezing out Woodrow, his mother and Libby, and the Marines. Now Libby's Aunt joins them.

WOODROW: (Hollering)
Goodbye, goodbye, thank you very much.

He shakes hands high in the air like a fighter and exchanges a look with the Marine Sergeant, who pantomimes that it is really nothing.

WOODROW: Goodbye, come on Mama.

He starts down the sidewalk.

CHAIRMAN: (Fighting his way through the crowd)
Where are you going?

WOODROW: (Crossly)
I'm going home...where do you suppose I'm going?

CHAIRMAN: Well you certainly are not going home like that...what do you think these cars are for anyway...you're going home with escort and besides you have to lay a wreath on General Zabriski's statue...now if you'll just get in here.

He tries to push Woodrow in the car.

WOODROW: (Holding back)
Come on Mama.

(Continued)

B-38 (Cont'd)

WOODROW'S MOTHER: You take Libby, dear...I've got to get some more food...I didn't know you were bringing quite so many friends...you ride with him, Libby.

LIBBY: (Looking around nervously for Forrest)
Oh...well I suppose it'll be all right.

WOODROW: What do I have to do at General Zabriski's statue?

CHAIRMAN: Oh just say a few words: Unprepared as I am, it is with a sense of both reverence and admiration that I place this wreath, and so forth, and so forth, at the feet of, and so forth and so forth.

CUT TO:

B-39 THE SERGEANT AND LIBBY'S AUNT

SERGEANT: What did he do?

LIBBY'S AUNT: Who?

SERGEANT: General Zablitski.

LIBBY'S AUNT: Oh...nobody can remember...but I think it was a battle or something.

SERGEANT: I get you.

LIBBY'S AUNT: You always start there.

SERGEANT: I get you.

CUT TO:

B-40 WOODROW, LIBBY, THE CHAIRMAN AND THE OTHERS

Libby is already in the car and Woodrow is getting in. The Chairman gets in on the far side and raises his whistle to his lips.

WOODROW: Wait a minute...how about the Marines?

CHAIRMAN: Oh...well we hadn't exactly counted on so many Marines.
(Then with a generous wave)
Oh put them in the third car...make it the second.
(Now he hollers to somebody out of the shot)
Put the other Marines in the second car.

(Continued)

B-40 (Cont'd)

He blows his whistle and a Band starts PLAYING "Praise the Lord and Pass the Ammunition". The car pulls out slowly. THE CAMERA FOLLOWS it and PANS onto the Noble family getting into its car.

FORREST: (Looking around)
Where's Libby?

Now he sees her and takes a step forward.

FORREST: Say wait a minute.

IN PANTOMIME his mother says "What does it matter?"

DISSOLVE TO:

B-41 WOODROW AND LIBBY - IN THE BACK SEAT OF THE CAR - (DAY)

The band music and the hooraying is quite loud. Woodrow is saluting to the both sides of the street.

LIBBY: I have something to tell you, Woodrow.

WOODROW: (Not hearing)
What?

LIBBY: I said I have something to tell you.

WOODROW: (Saluting off scene)
What?

LIBBY: I'll tell you later.

WOODROW: What did you say?

Libby gives up.

FADE OUT:

END OF SEQUENCE "B"

SEQUENCE "C"

FADE IN:

C-1 CLOSE SHOT - A TURKEY BEING BASTED BY WOODROW'S MOTHER - KITCHEN - (DAY)

The CAMERA PULLS BACK and we see Woodrow's Mother and Libby's Aunt preparing some big eats.

WOODROW'S MOTHER: I do wish he'd told me he was bringing six friends...if everybody hadn't been so kind I just don't what we'd have done.

The phone RINGS.

LIBBY'S AUNT: I'll get it.

She hurries toward the hall. There is a KNOCK on the door.

WOODROW'S MOTHER: Come in...oh dear.

CUT TO:

C-2 A SMALL BOY AND MR. SCHULTZ COMING IN THE DOOR

MR. SCHULTZ: Just in case you was short I brought over a few little knicknacks.

WOODROW'S MOTHER: That's terribly kind of you, Mr. Schultz, but I haven't a single point left.

MR. SCHULTZ: Who asked you? It's all complimentary, including the points with the compliments of Schultz' market.

TEDDY: Boy I wished I was a Marine.

MR. SCHULTZ: You will be.

TEDDY: Aw, it'll probably be over by the time I'm big enough.

MR. SCHULTZ: From your mouth to Heaven's ear.

WOODROW'S MOTHER: Just put it here Mr. Schultz...everybody has been so kind.

Mr. Schultz deposits his merchandise on a table that is practically collapsing with its load of home canned and home smoked delicacies.

TEDDY: How many Nips did Woodrow get, Mrs. Truesmith?

(Continued)

C-2 (Cont'd)

WOODROW'S MOTHER: I'm sure I don't know, Alfie...I hope he wasn't too bloodthirsty.

The little boy does the machine gun act.

MR. SCHULTZ: Quiet! And if there is anything else... the slightest thing...when we're open or when we're closed...Teddy will be happy to run over.

TEDDY: I'm bow-legged now.

Mr. Schultz points to the door.

MR. SCHULTZ: Raus. Goodbye Mrs. Truesmith and I'm very happy for you...one in the family is enough to lose.

He exits.

LIBBY'S AUNT: (Hurrying into the SHOT with a paper and pencil) Well that's done...you sleep the Sergeant and the one they call Bugsy...I'll take the tall blonde one that looks so much like my brother, Charles. Madame Lebovska spoke for the big Corporal...

WOODROW'S MOTHER: Do you suppose he'll be safe with her?... I don't mean that to be unkind.

LIBBY'S AUNT: Let him look out for himself...Myra Winstead will take the Southern boy so that's one left over and Madame Lebovska said she could really manage two in a pinch.

WOODROW'S MOTHER: It might be better at that.

LIBBY'S AUNT: (Seeing the new arrival of food) Good Gravy! When did that come?

WOODROW'S MOTHER: Just now, Mr. Schultz brought it.

LIBBY'S AUNT: What are we going to do with it?..even seven Marines can't wolf away <u>that</u> much.

WOODROW'S MOTHER: We can always send it to the poor.

LIBBY'S AUNT: Where are you going to find any? There just aren't any. Why down at the Assistance League we're getting desperate...everything piling up...we have to keep dusting it and brushing it...and...here they are.

(Continued)

C-2 (Cont'd)

WOODROW'S MOTHER: Oh dear, he'll just have time to wash for church...do I look all right, Martha?

LIBBY'S AUNT: Of course you look all right...I'll stay and get their dinner ready.

WOODROW'S MOTHER: Oh would you? That's so very kind of you.

She takes off her apron and starts fixing her hair.

CUT TO:

C-3 THE FRONT DOOR OF WOODROW'S HOUSE FROM INSIDE THE CORRIDOR

Woodrow and Libby are coming through the screen door followed by the Marines. Woodrow has the keys to the city and a papyrus scroll, Libby has a bunch of flowers, the Marines have cigars, flowers and candy. THE CAMERA PULLS them back into the kitchen.

WOODROW: (Starting to unbutton his uniform)
Well...that's that.
(Now he glares at the Sergeant)
That was a great idea you had.

SERGEANT: What are you talking about...everything was lovely.

LIBBY: I thought your speech at General Zabriski's monument was very moving.

WOODROW: Thanks. Now if you'll excuse me...

LIBBY: I have something to tell you, Woodrow.

WOODROW: Well you'll just have to wait 'till I get out of these clothes.

LIBBY: (Holding onto his arm)
Well the sooner I tell you, Woodrow...

WOODROW: Yes, well the sooner I slip into something else...the better, too.

LIBBY: Aren't you going to wear your uniform for a few days anyway? You look so splendid in...

WOODROW: (Fiercely)
I am not.

SERGEANT: You could wear it 'till tomorrow...the regulations is very elastic.

C-3 (Cont'd)

WOODROW: (Fiercely)
Well if it's all the same to you I'm not going to stretch them any further... if it's all the same to you.

WOODROW'S MOTHER: (Coming into the SHOT)
Where are you going, dear?

WOODROW: To put on my blue suit.

WOODROW'S MOTHER: (Holding on to him)
But we'll be late for church, dear.

WOODROW: THEN WE'LL BE LATE FOR CHURCH.

WOODROW'S MOTHER: But shy can't you wear your uniform for a little while?

WOODROW: I JUST FINISHED EXPLAINING. IT'S AGAINST REGULATIONS.

WOODROW'S MOTHER: Well I think that's perfectly ridiculous....

LIBBY: So do I.

WOODROW'S MOTHER: Your grandfather wore his Civil War uniform the rest of his life...he kept having new ones made.

WOODROW: (Departing)
Well his case was different.

WOODROW'S MOTHER: He said it helped to remind people that brother fought brother. HURRY UP WOODROW.

LIBBY: (Looking after Woodrow)
He seems a little upset.

WOODROW'S MOTHER: I suppose that's natural after what he's been through, dear...he has jungle fever, you know.

LIBBY'S AUNT: (horrified)
Jungle fever!

LIBBY: Oh the poor darling....I thought he looked a little bit yellow.

LIBBY'S AUNT: (Horrified)
They run through the woods without any clothes on with knives in their teeth.

(Continued)

C-3 (Cont'd)

SERGEANT: Oh no they don't at all, lady...you're thinkin' of Boksok...the Marines always dress very nice.

WOODROW'S MOTHER: Of course they do...you must be Sergeant Heffelfinger...who knew my Sergeant.

She takes his hand.

WOODROW'S MOTHER: I want you to see him...I want you all to see him.

She takes Bugsy's hand and the Sergeant's arm and leads the way toward the front room.

LIBBY'S AUNT: (after the others have left) You'd better get back to the Royal family.

LIBBY: I will...I'll meet them at church.

LIBBY'S AUNT: How did Woodrow take the news?

LIBBY: I haven't had a chance to tell him yet...there was so much noise.

LIBBY'S AUNT: You sure you tried your best?

LIBBY: (indignantly) Of course I did.

CUT TO:

C-4 THE SMALL FRONT ROOM

Woodrow's mother comes in followed by the six Marines. She pulls up a curtain to get more light, then indicates a framed enlargement under which are suspended, also framed, the Medal of Honor above a great many other medals.

WOODROW'S MOTHER: There he is.

SERGEANT: (very gruffly) 'Shun.

The six Marines come to attention and salute in unison.

WOODROW'S MOTHER: Thank you.

The Marines lower their hands.

(Continued)

C-4 (Cont'd)

WOODROW'S MOTHER: He looks so young...compared to me.
(Now she smiles)
Now I have two heroes.
(She puts her arm around the Sergeant and Bugsy then adds)
I have eight heroes.

BUGSY: You can sure put me on your flag...I sure ain't got anybody else.

WOODROW'S MOTHER: I'll be very proud to.

We hear a church bell.

WOODROW'S MOTHER: Oh dear we're going to be late....WOODROW.

She hurries the Marines out of the room.

CUT TO:

C-5 WOODROW - IN HIS BEDROOM - CHURCH BELL RINGING

He is half way into a blue serge suit, just putting on his tie. The room is decorated with baseball bats, pennants, pictures of American heroes, a beautiful framed "Semper Fidelis," an American flag and some movie stars.

WOODROW'S MOTHER'S VOICE: Hurry up, dear.

WOODROW: I'm doing the best I can, Mama...boy do I feel better.

CUT TO:

C-6 THE HEAD OF THE STAIRS - CHURCH BELL RINGING

The Corporal appears.

CORPORAL: Your ma says to hurry up...gimme back my blouse will ya?

WOODROW: And how. Here....
(He hands it to him)

CORPORAL: (Slipping into it)
Boy does that feel better.

WOODROW: Where's the Sergeant? I'd like to have a little talk with him.

He slips into his coat and THE CAMERA PANS them to the stairs.

(Continued)

C-6 (Cont'd)

CORPORAL: He's talkin' to you ma.
Everything went nice, didn't it?

WOODROW: (Sarcastically)
Marvelous.

CUT TO:

C-7 THE CHURCH STEEPLE AGAINST THE SKY - (DAY)

We hear the BOOMING of the bell.

CUT TO:

C-8 THE FRONT OF WOODROW'S HOUSE - (DAY)

The door opens and Woodrow's Mother and Libby come out followed by Woodrow, the Sergeant and the Marines.

CUT TO:

C-9 WOODROW AND THE SERGEANT

SERGEANT: You see...it's all over and everything went perfect.

WOODROW. (Bitterly)
Sure...except I'm a haunted man for the rest of my life. What do I do from now...

SERGEANT: Boy I wish that's all I ever had to worry about.

THE CAMERA PANS around after them and we see the little procession go up the street. One of the trailing Marines does a two step to get into step.

DISSOLVE TO:

C-10 THE CHURCH TOWER - (DAY)

The bell is still ringing. Now THE CAMERA PANS DOWN to people standing in front of the church. In the background people are entering the doors. In the foreground we see the Mayor, Mrs. Noble and Forrest. Suddenly Forrest sees the approaching Libby.

CUT TO:

C-11 WOODROW, HIS MOTHER, LIBBY AND THE MARINES

THE CAMERA PANS them into the group with the Nobles. Libby moves over next to Forrest and they all enter the church.

CUT TO:

C-12 THE CHURCH STEEPLE (DAY)

The bell stops ringing.

DISSOLVE TO:

C-13 DR. UPPERMAN BEATING TIME AS THE CONGREGATION FINISHES A HYMN

CUT TO:

C-14 WOODROW, HIS MOTHER, THE SERGEANT AND BUGSY

Behind them are the four other Marines. These latter finish the hymn in a fine barber shop chord with sliding half tones. The Sergeant turns and gives them an evil glance. Woodrow is too far gone to notice. Bugsy smiles at Woodrow's Mother. Now the congregation sits down.

CUT TO:

C-15 REV. DR. UPPERMAN

REV. UPPERMAN: And now, I have a very pleasant task to perform...

There is a rustle from the audience.

CUT TO:

C-16 PART OF THE CONGREGATION AND WOODROW'S GROUP

People turn and smile at Woodrow and his mother. Woodrow looks back in some alarm. This makes the congregation laugh.

CUT TO:

C-17 DR. UPPERMAN

DR. UPPERMAN: Usually on Sundays I have to scold you a little because that is what I am paid to do and I try to earn my keep...but today is a day of rejoicing.

There is a BUZZ of excitement and Dr. Upperman holds his hand aloft for silence:

Home from the hills cometh the hunter...
home from the wars...the hero.

CUT TO:

C-18 WOODROW'S GROUP

Woodrow sinks very low in the pew. His mother looks very happy. The Sergeant tries to look detached.

CUT TO:

C-19 DR. UPPERMAN

DR. UPPERMAN: Homecoming...what a beautiful word. Home to the arms of his mother, the widow of yet another hero...cut down in the bloom of young manhood.

CUT TO:

C-20 WOODROW'S MOTHER, BUGSY AND WOODROW

Woodrow's Mother's eyes are full of tears. Bugsy pats her hand.

CUT TO:

C-21 THE NOBLES AND LIBBY. FORREST TURNS AND LOOKS AT LIBBY.

CUT TO:

C-22 DR. UPPERMAN

DR. UPPERMAN: The arms of a mother who struggled through poverty and privation to raise her son rightly and courageously, that he might follow in the honorable footsteps of his father.

CUT TO:

C-23 CLOSE SHOT - WOODROW AND HIS MOTHER

His mother lowers her eyes and Woodrow sits up a little during this part of the speech.

DR. UPPERMAN'S VOICE: The years were hard, not always was there work...and the winds of reality blew coldly against this frail woman protecting her infant son.

THE CAMERA PANS OVER to include Bugsy who shakes his head sadly.

DR. UPPERMAN'S VOICE: She had one possession.... her home, the little white house at the end of Oak Street...the home of heroes.

THE CAMERA PANS OVER to include the Sergeant. Woodrow sinks a little lower.

(Continued)

C-23 (Cont'd)

DR.
UPPERMAN'S
VOICE: She clung to it tenaciously but one day she reached the end of her rope and a mortgage was her only solution.

The Sergeant sniffles.

CUT TO:

C-24 DR. UPPERMAN

DR. UPPERMAN: Mortgages have a way of growing... like beautiful trees...this one increased, then increased again and still again till the widow owned very little of the house she loved so well.
(He reaches calmly behind him and picks up a roll of paper tied with a ribbon)
I have here the document in question, purchased by the grateful citizens of our township.

CUT TO:

C-25 WOODROW AND HIS GROUP

His mother looks ecstatic. Woodrow looks horrified. He waggles no, no, no and starts to rise. The Sergeant pushes him down in his seat.

DR.
UPPERMAN'S
VOICE: ...purchased with deep respect by the grateful citizens of our township, who have asked me to perform the following ceremony.

Woodrow makes a sudden move and the Sergeant pulls him down again.

CUT TO:

C-26 DR. UPPERMAN

DR. UPPERMAN: (Happily)
You will notice that I have nothing up my sleeve...
(He laughs at his little joke then suddenly touches the rolled mortgage to the flame of a taper)

(Continued)

C-26 (Cont'd)

We hear a SINGLE ORGAN NOTE. Now Dr. Upperman holds the torch aloft and as the flames increase so does the roar of the music.

CUT TO:

C-27 WOODROW AND HIS GROUP

As they start out of the church they are congratulated from all sides. Woodrow's hand is pumped up and down continuously.

DISSOLVE TO:

C-28 EXT. OF THE CHURCH

The crowd is coming out. Woodrow's mother, her eyes full of tears is congratulated from all sides.

WOODROW'S MOTHER: Thank you...thank you so very much...I don't know what to say.

LIBBY: (Coming into the SHOT)
I'm so happy for you.

She kisses her.

CUT TO:

C-29 WOODROW HOLDING BACK FROM THE CROWD WAITING FOR THE SERGEANT

Now the Sergeant appears and avoids his eye.

WOODROW: Everything went perfect, hunh?

SERGEANT: It was a very beautiful ceremony.

WOODROW: Yes but how do I pay it back?

SERGEANT: They shoulda done it a long time ago on accounta your old man.

WOODROW: Wait 'till they find out.

SERGEANT: Who's gonna find out...

Now he pauses as the Chairman hurries into the SHOT.

CHAIRMAN: Oh Woodrow, we want your opinion.

WOODROW: (Suspiciously)
On what?

(Continued)

C-29 (Cont'd)

CHAIRMAN: On the location of the monument. Naturally General Zabriski has the choice spot...but then he's been there so long...

WOODROW: (Fearful already)
What monument is that?

CHAIRMAN: Oh didn't you know? But of course you didn't ...we're raising you a little monument by public subscription, I always say it's better to do these things while they're hot.

WOODROW: (Horrified)
Now wait a minute...
(He gives the Sergeant a fulminating look but the latter tries to avoid his eye)

CHAIRMAN: Oh just something modest, in granite probably ...bronze is simply impossible to get...it's just to our first hero of this present war.

WOODROW: Look, if anybody deserves a monument...it's my father, not me.

CHAIRMAN: (Happily)
Oh he's on it, too...you're both on it... shaking hands. It will be called: "Like Father, Like Son".

Woodrow feels of his head.

CHAIRMAN: Now I thought just in front of the station but there is much to be said for...

He stands with his mouth open as Woodrow hurries out of the SHOT.

CHAIRMAN: Did I say something wrong?

CUT TO:

C-30 MR. NOBLE, THE BOSS, MRS. NOBLE, FORREST AND LIBBY

MR. NOBLE: A statue!

He looks around from one to another;

MR. NOBLE: Wasn't General Zabriski enough of a pain... now I suppose every function starts with laying two wreaths...going and coming. I certainly hope this war ends in a hurry...holy moses.

MRS. NOBLE: Maybe you could be standing in the middle, dear...introducing them.

(Continued)

C-30 (Cont'd)

MR. NOBLE: Really, Myrtle, there are times...

MRS. NOBLE: Well I think he's cute...you're just hungry.

MR. NOBLE: Men let's eat.

He leads the way.

MRS. NOBLE: Come on, Libby.

LIBBY: Would you please excuse me for a few minutes ...I have one more errand to do.

MRS. NOBLE: Oh...oh of course darling.

She follows her husband out of the SHOT, leaving Forrest and Libby in the SHOT.

FORREST: What's the errand?

LIBBY: Oh nothing, I just have to tell Woodrow something.

FORREST: What about?

LIBBY: About...us.

FORREST: You mean you haven't told him yet?

LIBBY: I didn't get a chance to, dear. Every time I started to a band started playing or they burned the mortgage on his house or, or...

FORREST: ...raised him a statue.

LIBBY: Well I can't help it.

FORREST: I suppose you're very proud of him now?

LIBBY: Why shouldn't I be...I grew up with him.

FORREST: So did I, but I don't walk around starry-eyed..

LIBBY: Oh you're just jealous.

FORREST: Well make it snappy, will you?

LIBBY: Of course I will: I'll just say, Woodrow, I thought you'd like to know Forrest and I are going to be married next Sunday morning...I'm so glad you got back in time...to be there. That's all.

FORREST: Well you don't look glad.

(Continued)

C-30 (Cont'd)

LIBBY: Well I am glad...I'm terribly glad.

FORREST: Well you certainly conceal it beautifully.

LIBBY: Women have to conceal things beautifully, Forrest, that's their role in life.

She looks at him, then hurries out of the SHOT. Forrest looks after her a moment, then tightens his tie and goes after his father. The CAMERA PANS him a little way so that we see the Noble Chair Company, Seats of All Descriptions, in the distance. Forrest looks back toward us.

CUT TO:

C-31 WOODROW'S FRONT YARD FROM THE PORCH - (DAY)

Woodrow and his mother lead the little procession. Way in the distance Libby is following. Woodrow opens the gate for his mother who kisses him as she goes by.

WOODROW'S MOTHER: Now all wash your hands, dinner must be ready ...all this lovely sentimental nonsense...and seven hungry men to feed.

CORPORAL: Oh boy.

They all file past the Camera except Woodrow.

WOODROW: (Looking after the Sergeant)
Hey.

CUT TO:

C-32 THE SERGEANT - ABOUT TO ENTER THE HOUSE

SERGEANT: You talkin' to me?

CUT TO:

C-33 WOODROW - AT THE GATE

He comes in and closes the gate after him and walks up the steps until the Sergeant is included in the SHOT.

WOODROW: What do I do now?

SERGEANT: Well...you just let it blow over.

WOODROW: Did you ever see a statue blow over?

(Continued)

C-33 (Cont'd)

SERGEANT: Maybe you could be sort of hard to please... they want it standing up, you want it sitting down...they want it shaking hands, you want it with the hands behind the back...they want it in front of the station, you want it where General Zablizki is, 'till one day they say: do you want it or don't you? And you say: in that case no...and there you are.

WOODROW: And what do I do about the mortgage?

SERGEANT: Well, you a...well you could kinda...look, I didn't get you into this I just...

WOODROW: Oh yes you did...I was gonna hide in the Gents Room until...

SERGEANT: A Marine never hides in the Gents Room... that's what Semper Fidelis means. It means face the music.

WOODROW: Yes, well it doesn't happen to mean that at all...it means 'always faithful'.

SERGEANT: That's right...faithful to your mother...all right you're...

WOODROW: It doesn't mean faithful to your mother...it means...

SERGEANT: What's the matter with you? You're home... your mother is happy, did you see that look in her eyes?...your girl still loves you, and the town give you a nice little reception.

WOODROW: I'll say they did, but in the first place...

SERGEANT: Boy I wished I was in your shoes.

WOODROW: Boy I wish you were too. Look: I don't want to sound ungrateful...I know you meant it for the best and I thank you for your good intentions...

SERGEANT: I tell ya it'll all blow over. Everything is perfect...except for a couple of details.

WOODROW: They hang people for a couple of details.

SERGEANT: What are you talking about? I been a hero, you could call it that, for twenty-five years and does anybody ever ask me what I done? If they did I could hardly tell 'em, I've told it so different...so many times...it ain't as if you done it on purpose...by Tuesday it'll be forgotten.

(Continued)

C-33 (Cont'd)

WOODROW: I hope you're right.

SERGEANT: (Fortified as he sees Woodrow weakening)
I know I'm right. You take General Zabliski for instance...

WOODROW: Zabriski.

SERGEANT: All right, where did he tend bar?

WOODROW: That's a different case entirely...the town bought him from an iron works that was going out of business...he just happened to be a bargain.

SERGEANT: Well you're the only guy that knows it...all everybody else knows is he's a hero...he's got a statue in the park...and the birds sit on it...and except I ain't got no birds on me I'm in the same boat.

WOODROW: Look...

LIBBY'S VOICE: Woodrow.

WOODROW: (Turning)
Yes.

CUT TO:

LIBBY - AT THE GATE

LIBBY: Woodrow, could I see you for a moment please?

She comes through the gate and, with some diffidence, up to the house. When she is in the SHOT with the other two:

WOODROW: Yes, Libby.

SERGEANT: (Gallantly)
I'll leave youse two alone.

He winks at Libby.

LIBBY: Thank you, Sergeant.

SERGEANT: It's a pleasure.

He opens the door to go into the house and Woodrow's mother pops out of it.

(Continued)

C-33 (Cont'd)

WOODROW'S MOTHER: Hurry up, dear, dinner is on the table...you can come too, Libby...we're glad to have you... after all your Aunt practically cooked it... hurry up now while it's hot.

She shoos them inside.

DISSOLVE TO:

C-34 THE CARCASS OF THE TURKEY

THE CAMERA PULLS BACK and we see Woodrow, Libby and the six Marines at the table, Woodrow's mother and Libby's aunt hovering behind them.

WOODROW'S MOTHER: Now just a little pie to fill in chinks.

CORPORAL: Yes mam, I'll have to eat it in small pieces.

LIBBY: Aren't you hungry, Woodrow?

WOODROW: I guess the excitement kind of twisted my stomach a little

LIBBY'S AUNT: It's the fever.

WOODROW: No it isn't the fever...that never bothers me at all except...
(He sneezes)

LIBBY'S AUNT: You see.

WOODROW: Not at all...
(He sneezes again)

WOODROW'S MOTHER: Don't blow the house down, now that we own it.

Woodrow faintly shakes, no, no, no.

LIBBY'S AUNT: Wasn't that a lovely gesture?

WOODROW'S MOTHER: This is the happiest day of my life.

LIBBY: (A little sadly)
If you're all finished, Woodrow, would you come outside with me a moment...there's something I want to...

WOODROW: Sure.
(He starts to get up)

(Continued)

C-34 (Cont'd)

There is a heavy KNOCK on the screen door outside. Woodrow caught in a jumping position, slowly sits down again.

WOODROW: Here it comes.

SERGEANT: Here what comes?

WOODROW'S MOTHER: I'll see what it is.

She exits. Woodrow drinks a glass of water with a shaking hand.

LIBBY: What's the matter, Woodrow?

LIBBY'S AUNT: Does he feel hot? Feel his head.

She comes over to do so.

WOODROW: (Almost barking at her)
No I don't feel hot!...if I feel anything I feel...
(He sneezes, then looks up fearfully at his mother who is coming back in the room)

CUT TO:

C-35 WOODROW'S MOTHER

WOODROW'S MOTHER: Woodrow, Judge Dennis and the Sheriff and Doc Bissel and a lot of other men want to see you right away...they're in the parlor.

CUT TO:

C-36 WOODROW AND THE OTHERS - AT THE TABLE

WOODROW: (Having difficulty forming the words)
What about?

WOODROW'S MOTHER: (Coming into the SHOT)
They didn't tell me, dear, they just said they wanted to see you right away.

WOODROW: Well...
(He starts to get up and makes it on the second try)

SERGEANT: (Roughly)
They probably want to baptize a baby after ya.

WOODROW: I'll say.

(Continued)

C-36 (Cont'd)

He slips the knot of his tie so tight he nearly chokes himself.

WOODROW'S MOTHER: What's the matter, dear?

WOODROW: (Smiling only with the teeth)
Oh...nothing.

The smile drops off his face like a dry mud pack. The Sergeant wiggles his finger over his head and whistles the proper bugle call, it may be Assembly, the author does not remember. The Marines get to their feet instantly. As Woodrow starts out of the room, the Sergeant, in an unconcerned manner, picks a rolling pin off a side table. The Corporal picks up the whistling and seizes a potato masher. Woodrow and all the others start toward the front room.

CUT TO:

C-37 THE SITTING ROOM OF WOODROW'S HOUSE

Here we see Judge Dennis, Doc Bissell, the Sheriff, Mr. Schultz, the Rev. Dr. Upperman, the Chairman and about six other local business men. Judge Dennis is walking up and down gravely. Suddenly he turns.

JUDGE DENNIS: Ah there you are, Woodrow.

CUT TO:

C-38 WOODROW - IN THE DOORWAY

Behind him stand his Mother, Libby and the six Marines.

WOODROW: Good afternoon, Judge...Dennis.

CUT TO:

C-39 THE JUDGE AND THE OTHERS

JUDGE: (Severely)
Where are the medals?

CUT TO:

C-40 WOODROW AND HIS GROUP

WOODROW: Oh, the medals...
(He indicates them weakly)
Oh I justa wore those to get off the train...
I...suppose I shouldn't have but...

CUT TO:

C-41 THE JUDGE AND HIS GROUP

DOC BISSELL: What do you mean you shouldn't have? If all good men wore medals it wouldn't be so hard to tell the good from the bad.

JUDGE: That's a good line, Doc, make a note of it, Richard.

CHAIRMAN: (Writing it down)
I have it.

CUT TO:

C-42 WOODROW AND HIS GROUP

WOODROW: I guess that's right all right...well... I'm ready...Iya guess I deserve it all right.

NOTE: I am tired of cutting back and forth. The rest of this will be written as a master scene.

MR. SCHULTZ: You certainly do.

DR. UPPERMAN: Beyond question.

WOODROW: Goodbye, Mama.

WOODROW'S MOTHER: Where are you going?

JUDGE DENNIS: Who told you about it?

WOODROW: I can put two and two together.

SERGEANT: Now, wait a minute.

WOODROW: Come on, let's go.

JUDGE: What are you talking about?

WOODROW: Aren't you taking me somewhere?

JUDGE: Not at all, we're going to do it here.

CORPORAL: Oh yeh?

All the Marines move up.

JUDGE: Woodrow, there is something rotten in this town...

WOODROW: I know it.

(Continued)

C-42 (Cont'd)

MR. SCHULTZ: That's why we're here.

WOODROW: I know it, but I don't see why you have to do it in front of my mother.

WOODROW'S MOTHER: What are you talking about, dear?

SHERIFF: Then let's get down to business...the trouble with our party is that everybody talks too long all the time.

JUDGE: All right...Woodrow, there is something rotten in this town...

WOODROW: You don't have to keep rubbing it in...I'm ready.

JUDGE: Nothing you can put your finger on exactly but a kind of something you can feel. It's like the town was selfish...Everybody thinking about little profits and how not to pay the taxes and reasons for not buying bonds and not working too hard, and not working at night because it's nicer in the daytime... all things that are all right in peace time... things you used to call thrift and relaxation...that made many a fortune but things that are plain dishonest in war time. The motto of this town is 'Business as usual' but a lot of us feel war time ain't a usual time and that business as usual is dishonest. That's why we need an honest man for Mayor, an honest man who will wake us up and tell us the truth about something he knows all about.

SHERIFF: An honest man who will tell us the truth and who can win.

MR. SCHULTZ: We got an honest man who'll tell us the truth but he only pulls thirty-two votes outside of his brother and his wife.

DOC BISSELL: And I'm not even sure about her...I have everything but popularity.

JUDGE: In other words, Woodrow, we want you to take Doc Bissell's place.

DOC BISSELL: I will retire in your favor.

WOODROW: But I'm not a...veterinary...I hardly know one end of a horse from...

(Continued)

C-42 (Cont'd)

JUDGE: (Gently)
We want you to run for Mayor, Woodrow...in the coming election.

DOC BISSELL: The good of the party comes first.

DOC UPPERMAN: The right shall prevail.

WOODROW: (Looking around like a hunted animal)
You want me to run for m-m-mayor.
(He smiles idiotically and his knees give way)

The Marines grab him. He waggles no, no, no.

WOODROW'S MOTHER: (Grabbing him around the neck)
But that's wonderful, Woodrow, your father would be so proud of you.

Woodrow waggles a vehement no, no, no. Libby embraces him also and he is nearly strangled.

JUDGE: Three cheers for the new mayor.

DR. UPPERMAN: Hip, hip, hip.....

ALL: Hooray.

MR. SCHULTZ: Hip, hip, hip.....

ALL: Hooray.

CHAIRMAN: Hip, hip, hip.....

ALL: Hooray.

JUDGE:. (Leading the way)
Bring him out boys!

DR. UPPERMAN: (With magnificent gesture)
Forward...
(The Chairman blows his WHISTLE)
...march.

The band outside starts to PLAY. The Committee hurries out.

CUT TO:

C-43 THE STRUGGLING WOODROW

The Marines start pushing him ahead. THE CAMERA TRUCKS AHEAD of him and out through the door. On seeing the crowd, Woodrow grabs the side of the door and hangs on desperately like a bum resisting a bum's rush.

CUT TO:

C-44 THE FULL CROWD - TRAMPLING WOODROW'S LAWN

In the foreground we see the band and the committee.

THE CROWD: Hooray.

CUT TO:

C-45 WOODROW

He struggles to get back into the house and is lifted out bodily by the Marines.

CUT TO:

C-46 THE CHAIRMAN AND THE BAND

He blows his whistle for silence.

CUT TO:

C-47 THE JUDGE

JUDGE: Ladies and Gentlemen I give you...
OUR NEW MAYOR.

The band starts to PLAY and the crowd goes wild.

CUT TO:

C-48 WOODROW

He waggles no a thousand nevers as he is dragged to the railing by the Marines. The Chairman WHISTLES for silence, some voices holler "Speech."

JUDGE: First we'll have a few words from Doc Bissell.

CHAIRMAN: (With gestures)
A big hand please, a big hand.

DOC BISSELL: I'm gonna be even briefer than usual...you know what I stand for in this town...you know what I'm against. Our party is fortunate in having found a worthier standard bearer than I have ever been or ever could be...a man who fought for you overseas...a man who will fight for you here...AND WIN!

THE CROWD: Hooray.

DOC BISSELL: For the good of the party, for the good of the town and its war effort, for the good of the United States of America...I herewith retire in favor of, and ask you to vote for... Corporal Woodrow Lafayette Pershing Truesmith.

(Continued)

C-48 (Cont'd)

The crowd goes wild and the band plays "There'll Be A Hot Time In The Old Town Tonight." The Chairman stops the band after a moment.

JUDGE: Before introducing the principal speaker I wish to point out that he appears before you NOT as a hero, NOT with decorations he so heroically won and so richly deserves... but as a simple citizen...a home town boy... back home. I need say no more of the character of this young man than that HE REFUSED TO WEAR HIS MEDALS! Ladies and Gentlemen, Mr. Truesmith.

CUT TO:

C-49 THE CROWD

It hollers with pleasure and the band starts to PLAY. The Chairman stops it with difficulty.

CUT TO:

C-50 WOODROW

He loosens his collar, reaches in his pocket, grins not too brightly, looks back at the Marines, laughs at the crowd and stops laughing as suddenly as he had begun.

CUT TO:

C-51 THE CROWD

It is enchanted with Woodrow's modesty and laughs happily.

CUT TO:

C-52 WOODROW

WOODROW: Ladies and Gentlemen, Iya..wished I was dead.

The crowd laughs happily. Woodrow laughs and unlaughs suddenly.

WOODROW: You're making a big mistake.

The crowd hoorays and the band starts to PLAY. We hear the Chairman's WHISTLE and the band STOPS.

WOODROW: Iya...love my Mother very much.

The crowd hoorays and the band starts to PLAY. Woodrow's Mother kisses him.

(Continued)

C-52 (Cont'd)

WOODROW: But she shouldn't have told you I was coming home and made all that fuss down at the station.

There is a ROAR of laughter.

WOODROW: (Hollering)
I REALLY DON'T DESERVE IT.

All the Committee bursts out laughing and Woodrow now receives a kiss from Libby. The crowd hoorays and the band starts to play "Let Me Call You Sweetheart."

CUT TO:

C-53 A GROUP IN THE CROWD

AN OLD MAN: What a modest boy.

CUT TO:

C-54 A GROUP OF WOMEN

AN OLD LADY: Don't they make a handsome couple.
(She blinks away a tear)

CUT TO:

C-55 WOODROW - ON THE PORCH

WOODROW: There are many, many men...
(He points to the Sergeant and the Marines)
any one of these young men for instance... far, far more deserving than myself...

The Sergeant winks at the crowd which roars back at him.

WOODROW: The medals you saw on me you could practically say were...PINNED ON BY MISTAKE.

The Sergeant winks at the crowd again. The crowd roars. Woodrow looks around a little nonplussed.

WOODROW: I want you to believe me.

There is a wild hooray from the crowd.

CUT TO:

C-56 THE JUDGE AND DR. UPPERMAN

JUDGE: He has a natural flair for politics.

DR. UPPERMAN: A born speaker.

CUT TO:

C-57 WOODROW

WOODROW: I've known you all, all my life... I've mowed your lawns and delivered milk...for your babies.

There is a wild hooray. Woodrow tries to stop it.

CUT TO:

C-58 THE JUDGE AND DR. UPPERMAN

JUDGE: That milk and baby part is remarkable.

DR. UPPERMAN: After that he could be President.

CUT TO:

C-59 WOODROW

WOODROW: I even know the dogs and cats...
(Laughter)

He holds his hand up for silence.

WOODROW: Nothing would be dearer to my heart than to be worthy of the honor you offer me...I wish I could accept it. Iya... I'm no hero, Iya haven't Doctor Bissell's long experience with a...animals...

The laughter starts.

WOODROW: Iya...there is the man for you...I thank you.

He waves and hurries into the house to a tremendous burst of MUSIC and hooraying.

CUT TO:

C-60 THE KITCHEN OF WOODROW'S HOUSE

Libby's Aunt is basting the turkey. Woodrow staggers in.

(Continued)

C-60 (Cont'd)

LIBBY'S AUNT: Land sakes what's all the noise this time? It's a good thing somebody keeps cool.

WOODROW: You said it.

He goes to the sink and puts some cold water on his face.

WOODROW: That was a close one. Boy!

WOODROW'S MOTHER: (Hurrying in)
My boy.

She takes him in her arms and pats him on the back. Now the Judge, the Chairman, Mr. Schultz, Dr. Upperman and Doc Bissell come in.

JUDGE: Remarkable, Woodrow, remarkable.

MR. SCHULTZ: Wonderful.

DR. UPPERMAN: That's as good a political speech as I've heard since Bryan and the Crown of Thorns.

DOC BISSELL: You don't need any lessons from <u>me</u>.

JUDGE: If I might make <u>one</u> suggestion, Woodrow ...I wouldn't play down the hero part quite so much hereafter, modesty notwithstanding...they like it you know... anyway the Sergeant is taking care of that part of it.

WOODROW: (Astonished)
Hereafter? What are you talking about? What's the matter with him? What the... what's he doing?

He crosses to the hall where he can hear the Sergeant.

CUT TO:

C-61 THE SERGEANT AND THE MARINES - <u>ON THE FRONT PORCH</u> - PAST PART OF THE CROWD

SERGEANT: (With some embarrassment)
I been asked to tell you a couple of things about Woodrow...I don't know just how he's gonna take this.. in fact, he's so modest, I'm pretty sure he ain't gonna like it at all ...in fact I may get quite a sock on the jaw before I'm through
(Laughter)

(Continued)

C-61 (Cont'd)

SERGEANT: (Cont'd) anyway I'm gonna give ya just one sample...of his courage...and his resoursafullness...I'm gonna tell you how he saved my life.
(There is a wild hurray)
We're on the beach, see, at Tenaru Bay. All of a sudden we hear "HERE THEY COME"... take cover and out of the jungle come two, maybe three hundred Japs preceded by a hail of bullets. I turn, and my foot catches in a...I didn't see exactly what it was, I was kinda in a hurry but I'm stuck, I'm lost, see? Now a voice says "keep cool, pal" and beside me I see... Woodrow.

There is a wild hooray.

CUT TO:

C-62 WOODROW AND THE OTHERS - IN THE DOORWAY OF THE KITCHEN

WOODROW: (Gesturing no, no, no)
What's the matter with him? He can't do that.

He starts forward but the others hold him.

DR. UPPERMAN: Relax, Woodrow, relax...everything is all right.

JUDGE: That's doing you a lot of good.

WOODROW: (Struggling)
But I tell you I'm not running for mayor.

JUDGE: (Amused)
You're not running for mayor!

DOC BISSELL: Why you couldn't stop from being mayor if you, if you...

DR. UPPERMAN: A miracle couldn't stop you.

Woodrow staggers to the kitchen table and tosses off a glass of wine.

WOODROW'S MOTHER: Don't drink that dear...it's cooking wine.

WOODROW: Well I'm cooked.

CUT TO:

C-63 THE SERGEANT AND THE MARINES - PAST THE CROWD

SERGEANT:
(In full swing)
Zing, he got another one...zang another one hits the deck...zowie he clubs two of them with the butt end of his gun. We duck and run another little piece then drop, zing, zing, and two more brown brothers bite the dust. Now he picks up a machine gun...rat, tat, tat, tat, tat, tat...

The CAMERA WHICH STARTED MOVING BACK over the heads of the crowd at the beginning of this is now way down the street. Now it picks up Libby. Sobbing she walks down the street.

FADE OUT:

END OF SEQUENCE "C"

SEQUENCE "D"

FADE IN:

D-1 A BUNTING DRAPED BANNER WHICH SAYS: "VICTORY THROUGH VIGILENCE - Reelect Mayor Everett J. Noble, Your Humble Servant." THE CAMERA NOW ANGLES DOWN onto the bunting hung doorway of the Noble Chair Company, Seats of All Descriptions. Through this we see men walking in and out. Inside they stand around in groups. On the back wall there is an eight sheet of Mayor Noble.

CUT TO:

D-2 MAYOR NOBLE'S PRIVATE OFFICE

This is done in simple magnificence. The Mayor, toying with a twenty dollar gold piece, is strutting up and down and dictating to his son, who is taking it down in long hand.

MR. NOBLE: Once again fellow citizens you have chosen me to be your mayor and once again I accept the charge...make that responsibility... I accept the responsibility...make that deep responsibility...no just make that plain responsibility.

FORREST: I wish you'd make up your mind.

MR. NOBLE: (Indignantly)
What?

FORREST: And don't go so fast...I don't know how to do this.

MR. NOBLE: Then why isn't Libby here?

FORREST: She'll be back.

MR. NOBLE: She's still getting paid as my secretary you know, no matter who she marries.

FORREST: What do you mean "no matter who she marries?"

MR. NOBLE: I mean even if she is engaged to you. Now where was I?

FORREST: (Reading)
I accept the charge...make that responsibility. I accept the responsibility...make that deep responsibility...no just make that plain responsibility...

MR. NOBLE: (Not believing his ears)
Are you simple-minded or something?

(Continued)

D-2 (Cont'd)

MR. NOBLE: (Now he hollers:)
I accept the responsibility with a sense of both humility, satisfaction and gratitude.

FORREST: You dictated 'plain' responsibility.

MR. NOBLE: That's right, that means responsibility without adjectives. Now where was I...
DON'T TELL ME: I accept the responsibility with a sense of both humility, satisfaction and gratitude.

FORREST: You can't say both humility, satisfaction and gratitude. "Both" means two and you have humility, satisfaction and gratitude... that's three.

MR. NOBLE: (Furiously)
I can't say it?

FORREST: You can not.

MR. NOBLE: I've been saying it for years.

FORREST: It isn't correct grammar.

MR. NOBLE: I am not running on a platform of correct grammar...I even let my grammar slop over a little sometimes.

FORREST: You certainly do.

MR. NOBLE: Purposely.

FORREST: Unh-hunh

MR. NOBLE: It gives that homey quality...horny hands and honest hearts...Now where was I?

FORREST: With a sense of both humility, satisfaction and gratitude.

MR. NOBLE: (Generously)
All right, take out humility.

FORREST: (Shrugging)
Leave it in.

MR. NOBLE: (Hollering)
Take it out! Will you do what I tell you? Instead of sitting there like a stuffed nincompoop trying to annoy me.
(Now he adds meanly)
Just because your girl-friend is out with somebody else.

(Continued)

D-2 (Cont'd)

FORREST: (Menacingly)
What?

MR. NOBLE: Now where was I?

FORREST: With a sense of both satisfaction and gratitude.

MR. NOBLE: And humility.

His son looks at him unbelievingly.

MR. NOBLE: (Bushing off his vest)
What are you gaping at?

FORREST: Nothing.

MR. NOBLE: Well...cut it out...now...Well, it's about time...

CUT TO:

D-3 LIBBY - COMING IN THE DOOR

LIBBY: I'm sorry.
(Then seeing what Forrest is doing)
I'll take it, Forrest.

MR. NOBLE: I trust the conquering hero is home and that's that.

LIBBY: Yes sir.

FORREST: Have you been crying?

LIBBY: It's nothing.

MR. NOBLE: Now let's get this speech out of the way without further interruption. Dictating to my son is like dictating to a sponge.

LIBBY: Mr. Noble, before you go on with this there's one thing you might like to...

MR. NOBLE: (Severely)
I said without further interruption, if you please.

LIBBY: Yes sir.

MR. NOBLE: If it's all the same to you.

FORREST: (In a low voice)
What were you crying about?

(Continued)

D-3 (Cont'd)

MR. NOBLE: You can fight that out later. Now where was I?

LIBBY: With a sense of both humility, satisfaction and gratitude...You can't say that, both means two and you have humility, gratitude...

MR. NOBLE: (Slapping the desk)
Will you be so kind as to permit me to dictate my own speech, or do you just want to...

LIBBY: I'm sorry.

MR. NOBLE: As president and owner of the Noble Chair Company, Seats of All Descriptions, I am to most of you...make that many of you...make it some of you...your employer.. But as mayor of our fair city, I am to <u>all</u> of you...your servant. That's a nice twist. <u>Mine</u> not to reason why, mine but to...

FORREST: Do or die.

MR. NOBLE: When I want your assistance I'll ask for it... <u>mine</u> but to...don't keep looking at me... mine but to...What's all that hollering down the street?

LIBBY: It's for Woodrow. That's what I thought you'd like to...

MR. NOBLE: (Interrupting)
Statues! Well I suppose that's natural so long as they don't overdo it. Now:

LIBBY: Mine not to reason why, mine but to...

MR. NOBLE: (Pleased)
Harken and obey. Heaven knows I did not seek this distinction but since you force it upon me what alternative have I but to...

THE BOSS: (Coming in)
Save your voice, Evvy.

MR. NOBLE: Huh?

THE BOSS: Bissell's just retired in favor of Woodrow, the local hero...We got a fight on our hands.

MR. NOBLE: (Repeating like a parrot)
In favor of Woodrow, the local hero. THAT I WELCOMED AT THE STATION?

(Continued)

D-3 (Cont'd)

THE BOSS: That's right.

MRS. NOBLE: (Fluttering into the office)
Isn't it exciting, Evvy?...now you have some real opposition...that boy made the loveliest speech...wasn't it thrilling, Libby?

MR. NOBLE: (To his wife)
Will you kindly shut up for a minute?
(Then to the Boss)
You mean he's running for Mayor?

THE BOSS: That's right.

MRS. NOBLE: He was so shy and embarrassed...but at the same time so manly.

MR. NOBLE: (To his wife)
Will you kindly...
(Then to the Boss)
You mean running for Mayor against me?

LIBBY: That's what I was trying to tell you.

MR. NOBLE: Will you kindly...
(Then to the Boss)
But he can't do that...with the election only two days off.

THE BOSS: He can...he has.

MRS. NOBLE: You'll have a chance to use all your oratory, dear.

MR. NOBLE: (To his wife)
Will you...
(Then to the Boss with desk slaps)
He most certainly can not...that's entirely illegal...why if, if, if such was the case I mean to say why any Tom, Dick or Harry, any loose character whatsoever...fresh from the penitentiary could come along...

LIBBY: (Forcefully)
A loose character, Mr. Noble...Woodrow doesn't happen to be a loose character...and he's fresh from a battlefield not from a penitentiary.

MR. NOBLE: That was a figure of speech.

LIBBY: Well I don't care for it.

FORREST: Father didn't mean it the way it sounded.

(Continued)

D-3 (Cont'd)

MR. NOBLE: Well maybe father did...Which side are you on, anyway?

MRS. NOBLE: The romantic side, of course, dear.

MR. NOBLE: Because I don't want any spies around my office.

FORREST: Father, please.

MRS. NOBLE: Everett for heaven's sake...he doesn't mean that, Libby.

MR. NOBLE: Oh yes I do!

LIBBY: Well if you don't want me around your office, you certainly don't have to have me.

MRS. NOBLE: (Shaking her husband)
This is your daughter, you old idiot, this is your son's fiancee.

MR. NOBLE: Well she isn't my fiancee...when I lose confidence in people...

MRS. NOBLE: She's going to live in your house with you.

MR. NOBLE: She isn't going to live in my house with me... I'll move into the dog house first.

LIBBY: Then goodbye, Mr. Noble.

MR. NOBLE: Goodbye, Miss...whatever your name is.

FORREST: (Following Libby out)
Libby, for heaven's sake.

MR. NOBLE: That's right...abandon the shinking sip, sinking ship, whatever the...

MRS. NOBLE: Aren't you ashamed of yourself, Evvy. You're not sunk yet...you're very popular...in some quarters.

MR. NOBLE: Anyway the whole thing is entirely illegal...
(Then getting a thought)
Why his name isn't even on the ballot.

THE BOSS: It don't have to be. He's a write-in candidate...that's what that blank space is for down at the bottom.

(Continued)

D-3 (Cont'd)

MR. NOBLE: Well that most certainly is not what it's for. It's to, to count them wi...it's to put the date on. You call my lawyer.

THE BOSS: I already called him, Evvy. You could take my word for it...this is a free country... they can vote for anybody they like.

MR. NOBLE: But that's disgraceful.

THE BOSS: I know, but that's how it is, and the way it looks it don't look so good.

MR. NOBLE: You mean he actually has a chance?

THE BOSS: A chance! Did you ever see a snowslide?

Mr. Noble recoils and clutches his collar as if to protect himself from the cold.

DISSOLVE TO:

D-4 WALKING SHOT - LIBBY AND FORREST

FORREST: (Catching up with Libby)
I'm terribly sorry, Libby. Father is naturally a little upset...I guess we all are a little bit.

LIBBY: (Seething with indignation)
Talking that way about a boy who risked his life so the Noble Chair Company can make its twelve percent...Business as Usual!

FORREST: The Noble Chair Company makes twenty-four percent, just enough to cover its taxes, but he doesn't mean it, Libby...politicians always talk that way about each other... Woodrow is probably calling Father an old... windbag, right this minute.

LIBBY: Well if he is, he's right.

FORREST: (Frigidly)
Thank you.

LIBBY: I'm sorry...we all are a little upset, I guess.

FORREST: You weren't going to stay on as Father's secretary anyway...after our marriage so what does it matter?

LIBBY: What was I going to do, stay home and weave?

FORREST: You might stay home and take care of your children...with the servant problem as it is.

LIBBY: Thank you for warning me.

(Continued)

D-4 (Cont'd)

FORREST: Do you mean that?

LIBBY: Of course I don't mean it, I don't mean anything...but that ass of a father of yours...going around talking about people he doesn't know anything about.

FORREST: (Mildly)
You're still talking about your children's grandfather.

LIBBY: What are you trying to do, depress me? If I thought they'd look anything like him...

FORREST: Well I don't look anything like him.

LIBBY: I've noticed that...I pin my hopes on it.

FORREST: We're getting a little disagreeable again, aren't we?

LIBBY: We seem to be.

FORREST: Maybe now that the 'hero' is home, you feel a little differently about me.

LIBBY: No I don't. I feel just exactly the same about you as I've always felt...that you're upright...and honorable, and tall, and handsome, and, and wealthy and exactly what any girl in her right mind would hope for.

FORREST: (Gravely)
Thank you.

LIBBY: I just wish Woodrow hadn't come home exactly when he did that's all.

FORREST: Well what's he got to do with us?

LIBBY: It just spoils things a little, that's all.

FORREST: Why should it?...or do you think I ought to offer you to him like the keys to the city, on a silver platter?

LIBBY: Don't talk like an idiot.

FORREST: (Wound up)
And say: here oh noble hero, it happens to be my fiancee, but I'm only a civilian after all, so if you'd rather have her just help yourself...don't bother to stand on ceremony.

LIBBY: In the first place he doesn't want me...

(Continued)

D-4 (Cont'd)

FORREST: (Quickly)
Oh you asked him, did you?

LIBBY: I did not. And in the second place I'm engaged to you and that's all there is to it. I had plenty of time to think it over before I accepted you and that's all there is to it. A girl who kept changing her mind wouldn't be much good I don't think.

FORREST: She wouldn't be much good to me.

LIBBY: She wouldn't be much good to anybody.

FORREST: (Taking her arm)
Thank you.
(Suddenly he notices something)
Where's your ring?

LIBBY: My aunt has it...I was afraid of losing it in all that excitement.

FORREST: Oh..how did he take the news anyway?

LIBBY: (Uneasily)
What news?

FORREST: (Surprised)
Of our engagement.

LIBBY: (Stalling for time)
Who?

FORREST: Well how many people did you have to break it to?

LIBBY: Oh you mean Woodrow.

FORREST: Well naturally I mean Woodrow.

LIBBY: Well I didn't quite get the chance to tell him yet.

FORREST: (Indignantly)
You haven't told him yet!

LIBBY: I didn't get the chance.

FORREST: Then what have you been doing all day...basking in his glory?

LIBBY: I just didn't get an opening.

(Continued)

D-4 (Cont'd)

FORREST: Well do you want me to tell him?...
I'll create an opening.

LIBBY: No I don't.

FORREST: Holy mackerel!

They arrive in front of Libby's house.

LIBBY: Don't sound like your father.

FORREST: Well when are you going to tell him?

LIBBY: I'll go over in a little while.

FORREST: Be sure to put on something pretty.

LIBBY: I will.

FORREST: And try not to break his heart.

LIBBY: I won't.

FORREST: Holy mackerel...will I see you anymore tonight?

LIBBY: No.

FORREST: Well then...goodnight.

LIBBY: (Holding up her face to be kissed)
Goodnight, dear.

Forrest kisses her and she turns away. Forrest takes two steps, then looks back.

FORREST: Say...you haven't got any more boy-friends in the Army, the Navy or the Marine Corps, have you?

LIBBY: (Quietly)
No, dear...he was the only one.

FORREST: I was just wondering...holy moses.

He strides down the street. Libby looks after him a moment then sniffs twice, gulps and hurries into the house.

CUT TO:

D-5 INT. LIBBY'S HOUSE - HIGH CAMERA SHOT

Libby comes in downstairs slowly.

LIBBY: (At the newel post)
Aunt Martha.

(Continued)

D-5 (Cont'd)

As there is no answer she comes slowly up the stairs. As she goes into her room --

CUT TO:

D-6 LIBBY'S BEDROOM

Libby comes in slowly, closes the door behind her and leans against it. We HEAR the speech making in front of Woodrow's house and the band playing. Libby looks at a big picture of Forrest, then goes over and sits by the edge of her bed. Suddenly she gets up, throws a picture of Woodrow out the window, then throws herself face down and sobs broken-heartedly.

DISSOLVE TO:

D-7 THE CORPORAL - ADDRESSING THE CROWD - (NIGHT)

A pitcher of ice water has been placed on the porch.

CORPORAL: And when I say surrounded I mean surrounded, you get me...they was no hope, we was surrounded.

(He takes a sip of ice water, gargles it and continues)

Suddenly a figure comes through the trees, hopping from tree to tree. We can't see who it is, see...now there is a little opening, he's gotta cross it...we hold our breaths...he makes a dive for it...half way across we hear rat, tat, tat, tat, tat, tat, tat, tat, tat...He grabs his belly and falls...he got it, see. We say, so long Joe.

(He starts to take a sip of ice water. He puts it down suddenly and continues talking)

But wait a minute! He's on his feet, he's running toward us carrying the machine gun with him...He fooled them, see, their guns begin to chatter, but he's reached the trees...We're saved and as he comes staggerin' in to us we see for the first time who it is...do I have to tell you who it was?

There is a wild hooray. The Corporal takes a sip of water and pulls Jonesy into the SHOT.

CORPORAL: The next speaker will be Texas Jones, who is gonna tell you <u>his</u> experience with you know who.

(Continued)

D-7 (Cont'd)

He picks up a drumstick. The crowd hoorays.

NOTE: The following short scenes will be intercut with the above.

CUT TO:

D-8 THE CHAIRMAN, THE PROGRESSIVE BAND LEADER AND SIGN PAINTER - SURROUNDED BY PEOPLE - (NIGHT)

The Chairman is passing out buttons and at the same time supervising the painting of the stanzas of "We Want Woodrow" on the four sides of the box sign. The Progressive Band Leader holds the lyric in his hand.

CHAIRMAN: (Passing out buttons)
Be careful the ink is still a little fresh... and one for the little boy of course.

PROGRESSIVE BAND LEADER: (To the sign painter)
We Want Woodrow For Our Mayor.

SIGN PAINTER: M-a-r-e?

CHAIRMAN: M-a-y-o-r..what's the matter with you? What have horses to do with it.

A VOICE FROM THE CROWD: Give me a half dozen of them.

CHAIRMAN: (Handing them out)
A half dozen by all means...be careful the ink is still a little fresh...now don't stick yourself, Lurella...why certainly it's all right to wear it on the hat.

PROGRESSIVE BAND LEADER: (Hollering up to the sign painter)
Win with Woodrow, Win with Woodrow, Let's give Everett the air.

SIGN PAINTER: I wouldn't want to get in wrong with Mr. Noble.

CHAIRMAN: You paint it the way he tells you or you'll be in wrong with the new administration I can tell you.
(Then to the crowd)
Win with Woodrow...button, button who's got the button?...be careful the ink is still a little fresh.
(Now he hollers up to somebody out of the SHOT)
STRETCH IT OUT, IT'S ALL DROOPY.

CUT TO:

D-9 TWO MEN - ON TWO LADDERS - (NIGHT)

They are nailing up a sagging banner which reads, "Win With Woodrow". They look around.

CUT TO:

D-10 THE CHAIRMAN

CHAIRMAN: (Making a lifting movement)
Hoist it up...stretch it out flat.

He falls off his box and disappears.

CUT TO:

D-11 MR. SCHULTZ

MR. SCHULTZ: (Working the beer barrel)
Step right up...a glass of ice cold beer? Free lunch and pickles is to the left, step right up...not too much foam? We knock it off. Win with Woodrow.

CUT TO:

D-12 THE JUDGE AND THE SHERIFF - AT THE SANDWICH TABLE - (NIGHT)

JUDGE: A Woodrow special?
(Then to the Sheriff)
One Woodrow special...that means the best of everything...the ice cream? The ice cream is on the lawn...no, no, no everything is free, everything.

CUT TO:

D-13 WOODROW'S MOTHER AND LIBBY'S AUNT - (NIGHT)

WOODROW'S MOTHER: Ice cream for the children?

LIBBY'S AUNT: It's a good thing that food came in when it did.

WOODROW'S MOTHER: It's a good thing Woodrow came in when he did...Oh, I'm so happy.

CUT TO:

D-14 JONESY AT THE RAIL (NIGHT)

JONESY: He said don't give up kid...it may be hard, but we'll git back...I said how? He said we'll swim back...and I said look, Woody, there's only one trouble I don't know how to swim and he said just hang onto me, partner...and that's how we come back.

During the hooraying that follows this, we:

DISSOLVE TO:

D-15 WOODROW'S HANDS, A GLASS AND A BOTTLE OF COOKING WINE

This is in the kitchen. The hands clench and unclench nervously, then slap the table with futility. Now, shaking they pour the wine into the glass, the neck of the bottle rattling against the glass.

CUT TO:

D-16 BUGSY STANDING IN THE KITCHEN DOORWAY (NIGHT)

He is looking out toward the front of the house, listening to the speech-making with a happy smile. He looks back toward Woodrow and the smile vanishes. He crosses to the kitchen table which brings Woodrow into the shot.

BUGSY: (Severely)
Your ma said not to drink anymore of that stuff.

He takes the wine away from Woodrow and starts pouring it back into the bottle.

WOODROW: (Indignantly)
Say am I four years old or something...you gimme that.

BUGSY: You behave yourself and do like your ma tells you. You made her enough trouble.

WOODROW: I made her trouble!

BUGSY: (Severely)
That's right.

WOODROW: You made me trouble...you and your mother complex!

BUGSY: (Roughly)
Listen, knucklehead, you take one more crack at your mother and I'll...

(Continued)

D-16 (Cont'd)

WOODROW: (Belligerently)
Who's taking cracks at my mother? All I said was...

BUGSY: Well don't say it.

WOODROW: Are you nuts or something?

BUGSY: Maybe.

As the two men stand and look at each other, Woodrow's mother hurries into the kitchen.

WOODROW'S MOTHER: Isn't it wonderful, darling? I'm so proud of you.

She hugs him and kisses him in passing:

WOODROW'S MOTHER: We're running out of ice cream plates there's so many people out there.

She scoops up a stack of saucers and starts out, kissing him again on the way.

BUGSY: You see that look in her eyes?

WOODROW: Yes I saw it.

BUGSY: That's what we're working for, see?

WOODROW: (Desperately)
Can't you get it through your thick skull that...

SERGEANT: (Hurrying in)
All right you're on next.
(He grabs Bugsy's arm)
Just shoot 'em some bull about how you was in a hot spot with your foot caught in a gizmo and the ringtails is comin' from all sides and just when you ain't got a chancet who should come along but...
(He jerks his finger toward Woodrow)

WOODROW: (Grabbing him, desperately)
Will you quit telling lies and getting me in deeper and deeper so there'll never be a way out?

SERGEANT: They're eatin' it up...let 'em enjoy it.

BUGSY: (Turning to go)
Can I tell 'em about me and Smitty at Tulagi?

(Continued)

D-16 (Cont'd)

SERGEANT: Maskee, only you gotta be Smitty and he's gotta be you and you both gotta come out alive.

BUGSY: (Disappearing)
Ding how.

SERGEANT: (Reassuringly)
Everything's going great...you're gonna win in a walk and once you're in...you're in.

WOODROW: (Holding on to the Sergeant)
Don't you understand an election based on fraud....

SERGEANT: (Interrupting him)
Where's the fraud? You was in the Marines! Look: I didn't expect this anymore than you did...but now that it's happened...let it happen...they want heroes? We got six of 'em...all right we throw in a seventh for good luck...who's counting? We're doin' it for your ma, kid...they say opportunity's only got one hair on its head and you gotta grab it while it's goin' by and dog it down or you mightn't get another chancet.

WOODROW: (Desperately)
I don't want the chance...I don't want anything to do with it.

SERGEANT: Well you got it whether you want it or not.

WOODROW: Don't you understand this is all based on lies?

SERGEANT: (Indignantly)
What lies? You put on the wrong blouse when the train come into the station, that could happen to anybody...

WOODROW: (Pointing)
The lies they're telling out front!

SERGEANT: (Virtuously)
Who's telling lies out front? Every one of those boys is telling the truth...except they change the names a little so's not to give out military information. Lies!
(He turns and starts out of the room, now he pauses in the doorway)
Anyway those ain't lies...those is campaign promises...they expect those!

He hurries out, crossing Libby who is just coming in.

(Continued)

D-16 (Cont'd)

She wears a very pretty summer dress.

LIBBY: Hello, Woodrow.

CUT TO:

D-17 WOODROW - AT THE KITCHEN TABLE - (NIGHT)

WOODROW: (Dejectedly)
Hello, Libby.

He sinks into his chair and starts pouring himself a glass of cooking wine.

CUT TO:

D-18 LIBBY - IN THE DOORWAY - (NIGHT)

THE CAMERA PANS her over to Woodrow. She puts her hand on his shoulder.

LIBBY: (Gently)
You shouldn't drink too much of that stuff, dear...no matter how much you feel like celebrating.

WOODROW: (Looking up at her balefully)
Are you going to start now?

Libby steps back hurt.

LIBBY: Why Woodrow...I'm only thinking of your own good.

WOODROW: (Violently)
Yes, well there are too many people doing it.. they're thinking about my own good so much they're going to land me in the calaboose... if they haven't already.

LIBBY: (Pointing to the bottle)
Woodrow, you've been nipping.

WOODROW: (Getting to his feet)
I have not been nipping and I'll tell you something else...

LIBBY: I have something to tell you, Woodrow.

WOODROW: All right. But the less you hang around here and are seen with me, the better it's going to be you understand...I'm telling you that for your good.

(Continued)

D-18 (Cont'd)

LIBBY: (Indignantly)
Oh you needn't think I want to cash in on your glory! All I came here to tell you...

WOODROW: Who said anything about that?

Outside we hear the crowd start singing "We Want Woodrow."

LIBBY: All I came to tell you is that I'm going to marry Forrest Noble next Sunday morning at ten o'clock and the only reason I didn't tell you all day...

WOODROW: (Taking her arms)
But that's marvelous!

LIBBY: ...was because I didn't want to spoil your homecom...

WOODROW: But that's marvelous! That's the first good news I've had all day.

LIBBY: (Frigidly)
I'm glad you feel that way about it...

WOODROW: At least I don't have to worry about you!

LIBBY: ...because I think it's marvelous too and, and, and
(She starts to blubber)
I hope I never see you again as long as I live...here's your frat pin.

She presses it in his hand and turns and runs out the back door.

WOODROW: Will you wait a minute?

He starts after her but is stopped by the sudden entrance of Judge Dennis followed by Mr. Schultz and the Sergeant.

JUDGE DENNIS: (Grabbing Woodrow)
Woodrow, you've just got to come out and address the crowd again.

MR. SCHULTZ: They will no longer accept substitutes any longer.

WOODROW: Well I'm not going to address the crowd again, I've already told them how I feel and...

JUDGE DENNIS: But that's no way to run for Mayor.

MR. SCHULTZ: Or is it?

(Continued)

D-18 (Cont'd)

WOODROW: How many times do I have to tell you I'm not running for...

MR. SCHULTZ: But you are running for Mayor.

SERGEANT: Whether you like it or not.

JUDGE DENNIS: You have been drafted.

WOODROW: (To the Sergeant)
Can they do that?

SERGEANT: They done it.

MR. SCHULTZ: (Pointing outside)
Listen to them.

He, the Sergeant and Judge Dennis move forward a little which drops Woodrow out of the shot.

CUT TO:

D-19 WOODROW

WOODROW: You listen to them.

He turns and looks in the direction taken by Libby.

CUT TO:

D-20 JUDGE DENNIS, MR. SCHULTZ AND THE SERGEANT - (NIGHT)

MR. SCHULTZ: (Beating time to the song)
Beautiful.

CUT TO:

D-21 THE CHAIRMAN LEADING THE SONG - (NIGHT)

Behind him we see the Progressive Party Band, around him the people. He holds aloft the four-sided box, now completed, on each side of which is printed a verse of the song.

First side: We want Woodrow
We want Woodrow
We want Woodrow for our Mayor

Second side: Win with Woodrow
Win with Woodrow
Let's give Everett the air

Third side: Up with Woodrow
Down with Noble
Let's kick Evvy off the chair

(Continued)

D-21 (Cont'd)

Fourth side: Up our hero goes and down this zero goes 'cause we want Woodrow for our mayor.

CUT TO:

D-22 THE JUDGE, MR. SCHULTZ AND THE SERGEANT - IN THE KITCHEN - (NIGHT)

The song is approximately in its third verse.

JUDGE DENNIS: It's like Lincoln said 'You can fool all of the people part of the time and part of the people...' where did he go?

Now the Sergeant and Mr. Schultz turn.

MR. SCHULTZ: What happened to him?

They walk back into the deserted kitchen. The Sergeant sticks his head out of the window.

SERGEANT: (Pulling his head back in)
We'll find him...he won't get far.

DISSOLVE TO:

D-23 A BACK ALLEY - (NIGHT)

In the distance we hear the crowd singing "We Want Woodrow." Libby comes toward us. As she gets closer we hear her sobbing. Woodrow appears way in the background. He calls, 'hey'. She pauses near the Camera. Now he catches up to her.

LIBBY: What do you want?

WOODROW: Look: I'm in enough trouble without you turning against me.

LIBBY: When did I turn against you? I've been loyal to you all my life...I, I you know how I felt about you... you broke off with me... I would have waited for always...even so I asked my...my fiancee's permission to to welcome you the way I thought you'd like to be welcomed...although I may have been wrong... I defended you all afternoon and got fired for it by Mr. Noble and nearly broke off my engagement with Forrest...and now you say I'm t-t-turning against you.

WOODROW: I'm sorry.

(Continued)

D-23 (Cont'd)

LIBBY: (Starting away)
Well you can go to...

WOODROW: (Interrupting her)
Will you quit that.

He catches up with her and the CAMERA MOVES ALONG with them.

LIBBY: No I won't...you made me enough trouble with everybody saying I threw you over while you were fighting overseas to marry F-f-f-forest... as if I'd do such a thing...but I couldn't go around wearing your letter in my hat telling me you'd f-f-fallen in love with somebody else...which is your perfect right...and I'm deeply in love with Forrest...and then you have to come back a he-he-he...

WOODROW: (Finishing it for her)
A heel.

LIBBY: (Reproachfully)
A hero! So now they can say, you see? It served her right! She got just what she deser-deser-deserved.

She weeps copiously.

WOODROW: Cut it out, will ya? I've got enough troubles.

LIBBY: (Indignantly)
You have troubles...

WOODROW: And how I have.

LIBBY: I should say so...you can have any girl in town you want and then you get a mom-mo-monument and they b-b-burned your mother's mom-mo-mortgage and you're going to be m-m-m-mayor and I'm going to m-m-m-marry F-f-f-orrest.

WOODROW: But you said you loved him deeply.

LIBBY: Well of course I do but what's that got to do w-w-with it?

WOODROW: Libby.

LIBBY: What?

WOODROW: You don't know how well off you are.

(Continued)

D-23 (Cont'd)

LIBBY: Don't talk that way...you're just going to make me feel worse.

WOODROW: If you knew what a heel I was you'd be very happy.

LIBBY: I am very happy and I know exactly how much of a heel you are.

WOODROW: You do?

LIBBY: Anybody who could write a letter like you wrote six weeks after we parted, like we parted...you wouldn't have to tell me any more about.

WOODROW: Oh...then you don't know anything.

LIBBY: I don't want to know anything about her... whether she's tall or short or thin or fat or blond or...I just hope she's awful... no I don't, I hope she's beautiful and that you have ten children by her.

Then as Woodrow doesn't answer:

LIBBY: Is she?

WOODROW: If you only knew.

LIBBY: (Crossly)
Well I don't want to know.

They reach her garden gate.

LIBBY: Do you want to come in a minute? I suppose you shouldn't...but we'll have to start being grownup sometime and it might as well be now.

She opens the gate and he follows her in. They walk to the old apple tree. Around the trunk of which there is, as if on purpose, a bench. They sit.

CUT TO:

D-24 CLOSE SHOT - LIBBY AND WOODROW

LIBBY: (Archly, after a moment)
It's a beautiful night isn't it?

WOODROW: Great.

LIBBY: Are you worried about something?

(Continued)

D-24 (Cont'd)

WOODROW: (Also archly)
Who me? How could I be?...ha ha.

LIBBY: Don't you want to be mayor?

WOODROW: Naturally I want to be mayor...I'd like to have a million dollars, too.

LIBBY: Well then...of course I don't know what it's like to be famous...I suppose it even has its drawbacks but I should think you'd be so proud, Woodrow...so satisfied...I know I certainly am for you...no matter how I talked out there.

WOODROW: I'm going to be famous all right.

LIBBY: I was so proud even sitting beside you this afternoon...
(She makes a helpless gesture)
Do you remember when we used to come and sit here...in the cool of the evenings?

WOODROW: Naturally I do.

LIBBY: I thought maybe you'd forgotten...so much can happen in a year.

WOODROW: So much can happen in a day.

LIBBY: I suppose so...were you surprised when they nominated you for mayor?

WOODROW: Surprised isn't the word for it.

Libby pats his hand then snatches her hand back in her lap.

LIBBY: Excuse me.

WOODROW: That's all right.

LIBBY: Did you ever think of me in Guadalcanal?

WOODROW: (Dully)
No.

LIBBY: (Slightly hurt)
Oh, I guess that was a pretty busy place.

WOODROW: I guess so. I thought of you in other places though.

(Continued)

D-24 (Cont'd)

LIBBY: Where?

WOODROW: Just other places.

LIBBY: I'm so glad...even though it can only be a memory now...do you remember when you cut our initials in the tree?

WOODROW: Naturally.

LIBBY: (Pointing to them)
There they are...they'll be there always.

WOODROW: Unless something happens to the tree.

LIBBY: I would never allow that.

WOODROW: You'd be better off to chop the tree down and forget me for good...that's why I'm so glad you're going to marry Forrest...why it's such a load off my mind there's no hope for Mom she'll just have to leave town but at least you can say you suspected it all along and that's why you broke off with me and married Forrest, who's all right if you like people like that, and then you won't be hurt, see?... because outside of Mom you're the only thing in the world I care for, the only thing that matters. And now that it's over, I can tell you that letter I wrote you was the hardest thing I ever did in my life...and I've thought about you every night...and every morning... and every afternoon...and every girl I saw reminded me of you...and every flower, I wanted to send you...that's why I'm so happy see? Because you had such a narrow escape.

LIBBY: I think you're a little bit feverish, dear.

WOODROW: Who me? I'm a little bit phony, that's all...a little!

LIBBY: (Tenderly)
You a phony

WOODROW: That's right...you don't have to tell anybody, they'll find out soon enough...but I'm never going to be mayor or anything else, you understand? And I was never in Guadalcanal or anyplace else and I never got any medals and I wasn't even in the Marines... you understand?

(Continued)

D-24 (Cont'd)

LIBBY: (Gently)
You've had a very hard day, dear.
(She looks around as if for help)

WOODROW: (Prophetically)
Yes, but wait 'till tomorrow comes.

LIBBY: I don't think you're feeling very well.

WOODROW: Me? I never felt better in my life except I never felt worse.

LIBBY: You'll be all right, dear.

WOODROW: I suppose you despise me now?

LIBBY: Despise you! How can you despise anybody you love...even if you are engaged to.... another man. I'll love you as long as I live, Woodrow and I might as well tell you so now while we still have a few moments... a last few moments...together.

WOODROW: I don't think you understood what I said: I'm a phony, I'm a faker, I'm a...

LIBBY: (Weeping)
I know...you're just saying that to make me feel better but I'm never going to feel any better...I'm just broken-hearted Woodrow I, I, I,...

WOODROW: Now wait a minute...
(He takes her in his arms and starts patting her on the back)
Now wait a minute, will you?
(He looks around to see if anybody is listening and gives a double-take to the gate)

CUT TO:

D-25 THE GATE (NIGHT)

The Sergeant stands here.

SERGEANT: (After a soft whistle)
Here he is.

Now he comes through the gate followed presently by the other Marines.

(Continued)

D-25 (Cont'd)

SERGEANT: I almost thought you took it on the lam for a minute...oh excuse me.

CUT TO:

D-26 WOODROW AND LIBBY - (NIGHT)

WOODROW: Come here.

Then as the Sergeant comes into the SHOT.

WOODROW: Will you tell Libby I've never been in Guadalcanal or any place else, that I'm just a phony?

Libby looks up at the Sergeant tearfully.

SERGEANT: Sure, he's never been in Guadalcal. He's never been no place...none of us have...we're all phonies, see 'specially after a hard day, only sometimes we're more phony than others, you get me?

LIBBY: I understand.

SERGEANT: He aint runnin' for mayor or nothing, you understand...he just needs a good night's sleep.

WOODROW: (Indignantly)
What are you trying to...

SERGEANT: (Clamping a heavy arm around his shoulders)
A good night's rest.

WOODROW: Will you take your arm...

CORPORAL: (Putting his arm around Woodrow)
You outta see me in a thunderstorm.

LIBBY: Good night, Woodrow.

She kisses him quickly and runs into the house.

SERGEANT: What are you tryin' to do, make a sucker out of the Marine Corps?

WOODROW: (Violently)
Let go of me.

To cover this the Sergeant starts to sing.

(Continued)

D-26 (Cont'd)

SERGEANT: (With a look to the others)
"We Want Woodrow"

The others pick it up as Woodrow is turned around and marched out of the gate.

CUT TO:

D-27 LIBBY - LOOKING AFTER THEM

This is from the back door of her house. She looks very miserable.

DISSOLVE TO:

D-28 THE BAND AND THE CROWD GOING DOWN A STREET (NIGHT)

This should be just outside the Noble Chair Company. They sing and play "We Want Woodrow". They are carrying torches.

CUT TO:

D-29 MR. NOBLE'S OFFICE - IN THE NOBLE CHAIR COMPANY

Here we see Mr. Noble, the Boss and four or five of his minions. The Boss is talking to these latter but we do not hear what is said because of the deafening noise of the parade. Possibly we see some of the flickering of passing torches and possibly it would not show in the lighted office. Mr. Noble's untouched dinner sits on a tray on the desk. Mr. Noble himself is tossing a Bromo-Seltzer from glass to glass. Now he tosses it down his gullet and nearly strangles. The Boss pounds him on the back then sends his minions away.

THE BOSS: Feel better?

MR. NOBLE: Thank you...brrwulp...of all the cheezy songs I ever heard...that one certainly takes the crackers...brrrwulp.

THE BOSS: Why don't you eat your dinner?

THE NOBLE: How can you think of food at a moment like this?

THE BOSS: (Picking up a piece of cheese)
You gotta live.

MR. NOBLE: It would turn to Russian dressing in my stomach.
(He shakes his head at the thought, then jerking a thumb toward the departed minions)
What did they say?

(Continued)

D-29 (Cont'd)

THE BOSS: They said it looks very good...

MR. NOBLE: (Quickly)
They did?

THE BOSS: ...for Woodrow.

MR. NOBLE: Oh.
(He gives the Boss a dirty look, then paces up and down)
Don't eat with your mouth open...do you mind?...I'm just a little bit irritable.

THE BOSS: I don't blame you.

He picks up a wedge of pie and contemplates it.

MR. NOBLE: (After staring hypnotized)
Well are you going to eat it or aren't you?

The Boss bites the end off the pie. Mr. Noble walks down to the end of the room and back.

MR. NOBLE: I mean to say why did he have to come back at a moment like this? I mean to say if he had to come back why couldn't he have come back after the election...I mean to say I don't want to s ound unpatriotic or anything but I mean to say a man like that BELONGS in ... Guadaloupe.

THE BOSS: Guadalcanal.

MR. NOBLE: Guadalcanal...I mean to say in a war like this -
(Mr. Noble is slapping the desk at the proper places)
every man must do what he does best and what he does best he does in...Guadal... canal.

THE BOSS: (With his mouth full)
Shave your voish, Evvy.

MR. NOBLE: What?

The Boss makes a gesture that it doesn't matter anyway.

MR. NOBLE: I mean to say a boy like that needs exercise and violent physical conflict to keep him fit...he'll be lost in a town liek this...the quiet will kill him.

(Continued)

D-29 (Cont'd)

THE BOSS: (Swallowing it)
Save your throat, Evvy, you don't have to persuade me.

MR. NOBLE: What I'm trying to say is...

THE BOSS: I know what you're trying to say, I've been listening to you long enough.

He picks up a chop and contemplates it.

MR. NOBLE: Do you always eat backwards?

THE BOSS: (Biting into the chop)
Hunh?

MR. NOBLE: I mean to say I don't even think he wants to be Mayor!

The Boss, having a full mouth, waves this down.

MR. NOBLE: (Mimicking his waving)
What does that mean?

THE BOSS: (After swallowing with difficulty)
Everybody wants to be Mayor...that's human nature.

MR. NOBLE: (Slapping the desk)
Everybody but me! With me it's just civic pride...shy don't you look what you're doing?

He picks up a napkin and stuffs it in the Boss's vest.

THE BOSS: (Looking down at his vest)
Thanks.

MR. NOBLE: (Walking up and down)

I mean to say soldiers coming back at moments like this can upset a political balance that has taken years to adjust.

THE BOSS: You're telling me.

He does something with the food.

MR. NOBLE: I mean to say they take on an importance that, that, that I mean to say that completely overshadows the, the, the...I mean to say if you took all the seats I'm building for the Army and the Navy.

(Continued)

D-29 (Cont'd)

MR. NOBLE: and the Marine Corps and sat them side by side they'd probably stretch from here to the the the...Halls of Montezuma...but I can't wear one around my neck or pinned on my bosom with a purple ribbon...you notice they don't bring MacArthur back on the eve of a National election.

THE BOSS: (Putting salt and pepper on the second chop)
I wonder if he really _is_ a hero?

MR. NOBLE: (Hopefully)
Who, MacArthur?

NOTE: make protection close-up without reference to MacArthur.

MR. NOBLE: (Down again)
Why certainly he's a hero, they're all heroes and if I didn't happen to have got stuck in the Quartermaster Corps during the last war I'd probably have more stuff on me than you could hang on a Christmas tree.

THE BOSS: How do you know he's a hero?

MR. NOBLE: (Tapping his chest)
Because I saw the, the...the stuff.

THE BOSS: That don't make it official.

MR. NOBLE: What are you talking about! Don't go chasing moonbeams...there're some things you have to accept on faith...value... face value and one of them is a hero... you can't ask him for his...union card.

THE BOSS: Then why do you suppose he took off his uniform? That ain't natural.

MR. NOBLE: Because he's home...because he's been... dismissed...or whatever you call it.

THE BOSS: What for?

MR. NOBLE: (Angrily)
How do I know what for?...maybe he has corns or, or pyorrhoea...how do I know?

THE BOSS: (Taking the phone off the hook)
It ain't natural to take off a uniform in war time...it's just the other way around.

(Continued)

D-29 (Cont'd)

MR. NOBLE: (Pointing to the phone)
What are you doing there anyway?

THE BOSS: Get me Western Union...I'm just gonna wire the Marine Base in San Diego and check up on our local hero.

MR. NOBLE: (Upset)
What's the matter with you? Are you trying to kill me politically <u>forever</u>?

THE BOSS: Save your throat, Evvy.

MR. NOBLE: You leave me out of this you understand... I don't want to be mixed up with this in any shape, form, connection or even by innuendo.

THE BOSS: I'm waiting for Western Union.

MR. NOBLE: If you send this it is entirely at your own risk and peril. I challenge his fitness as mayor but the one thing that I do <u>not</u> challenge, question or doubt is the fact that he is a hero. I want that definitely....

THE BOSS: Shut up, will ya. Hello Western Union, I want to send a night letter.

DISSOLVE TO:

D-30 WOODROW - <u>IN HIS BEDROOM</u>

He is sleeping fitfully in just enough moonlight to register on the film.

WOODROW: (Thickly at first)
Here they come, boys, here they come!.. they're sneaking through the palm trees, they're coming through the palm trees, here they come, boys, there's thousands of them...man the guns...LET 'EM HAVE IT...CHARGE.

He makes a wild movement and falls out of bed on the floor.

CUT TO:

D-31 <u>THE DOORWAY OF WOODROW'S ROOM</u>

BUGSY: (Coming in)
What's the matter?

(Continued)

D-31 (Cont'd)

He crosses and helps Woodrow back into bed.

WOODROW: I must have had a nightmare I guess.

BUGSY: You're lucky.

WOODROW: Hunh?

BUGSY: You're lucky you don't have them all the time....like some guys.

He laughs, goes out and closes the door. Now Woodrow swings his feet out of bed, turns on the light, and starts to dress with great determination. After pulling on his pants he tiptoes to the door and peeks out.

CUT TO:

D-32 THE UPPER HALL

Woodrow suddenly sees Bugsy arranged on two chairs, a magazine in his lap.

BUGSY: You want some more hot milk or somethin'?

WOODROW: I'm all right. You gonna stay there all night?

BUGSY: I don't care much about sleeping at night.

Woodrow goes back into his room.

CUT TO:

D-33 WOODROW - IN HIS ROOM

He closes the door, looks sourly at it then crosses to the window and looks down.

CUT TO:

D-34 JONESY - STANDING GUARD BELOW (NIGHT)

JONESY: Was you looking for somethin'?

CUT TO:

D-35 WOODROW - IN HIS ROOM

He pulls his head back into the room, goes slowly to his bed and sits down on it. Suddenly he scowls at something on the wall.

CUT TO:

D-36 INSERT - THE BEAUTIFUL EMBROIDERED 'SEMPER FIDELIS'

CUT TO:

D-37 WOODROW - ON THE BED

He starts taking off his pants.

FADE OUT:

END OF SEQUENCE "D"

SEQUENCE "E"

FADE IN:

E-1 THE STATUE OF GENERAL ZABRISKI - (AT SUNRISE)

Around it and on it the birds are chirping merrily.

DISSOLVE TO:

E-2 WOODROW PACING UP AND DOWN - IN HIS ROOM - (SUNRISE)

The tails of his nightshirt flop against his legs. Now he sits dejectedly on the bed. Slowly a ray of sun comes down on his head as it did on the head of General Zabriski.

WOODROW: (Suddenly)
I've got it! OH BOY.

He does a little dance around the room, then opens the door and sticks his head out.

CUT TO:

E-3 THE UPPER HALL OF WOODROW'S HOUSE

Juke is dozing in the chair formerly occupied by Bugsy.

WOODROW: (Ecstatically, as he sticks his head out)
I've got it...everything is all right.

JUKE: Hunh?

WOODROW: It came to me with the sunrise.

Juke scratches his head and looks after him as Woodrow disappears.

CUT TO:

E-4 WOODROW - IN HIS ROOM

WOODROW: (Happily)
Oh boy.

He hops into his bed, pulls the covers up and with a sigh of relief prepares for sleep.

WOODROW: (Drowsily)
Oh boy.

7-6-43

E-5 A SMALL STEAM ROLLER - (FULL SUNLIGHT)

It is actually the type run by gasoline although, I think, still called a steam roller. It is parked in front of the local painter, paperhanger and interior decorator's store. Against the store the painter and his assistants are preparing banners. The steam roller is receiving the personal attention of the Chairman and Mr. Schultz. The banner across it reads: "Help Us Flatten Noble." The big wheel has been filled with a disk sign which reads: "Up With Woodrow" and then when it turns upside down: "Down with Noble." The Leader of the Progressive Band stands in the SHOT waiting to talk to the Chairman, who, with the assistance of Mr. Schultz is tying bunting to all the protuberances of the stéam roller.

PROGRESSIVE BAND LEADER: Now we start with "Win With Woodrow"...

CHAIRMAN: That's right.

PROGRESSIVE BAND LEADER: Then we modulate into "The Halls Of Montezuma."

CHAIRMAN: That's right.

PROGRESSIVE BAND LEADER: Then we modulate into...

MR. SCHULTZ: Why do you always have to modulate into everything? If you want to go into "The Halls of Montezuma" why don't you just walk in?

PROGRESSIVE BAND LEADER: Why don't you mind your own business? You handle the meat, I'll handle the music.

MR. SCHULTZ: Look, you floor flusher, if I couldn't play a better E Flat Cornet as you...

CHAIRMAN: Gentlemen, gentlemen, please...no dissension within the party lines.

PROGRESSIVE BAND LEADER: Then I modulate into "There'll Be A Hot Time in The Old Town Tonight."

MR. SCHULTZ: Then you modulate out of it.

CHAIRMAN: That's absolutely correct, Ed. Now Ewald...

PROGRESSIVE BAND LEADER: (Exiting) The name is Ned if it's all the same to you.

MR. SCHULTZ: It could be Shpitzenvogel and it would be all the same to us.

CHAIRMAN: Please, Ewald...don't tie your end so tight... make the bows lighter...airier...with more zoom.

(Continued)

E-5 (Cont'd)

MR. SCHULTZ: (Crossly)
Look, when you've tied up as many veal roasts as I have...

CHAIRMAN: That's just it, Ewald, it's bad enough that it still looks like a steam roller without its looking like a veal roast... or even a pork roast...

MR. SCHULTZ: You handle the breast, I'll handle the rump.

CHAIRMAN: By the way you don't happen to have a pork roast do you? I'm drooling for one.

MR. SCHULTZ: With fried apples, smashed potatoes and brown gravy?...

CHAIRMAN: (Drooling)
That's right.

MR. SCHULTZ: NO.

CHAIRMAN: (Crestfallen)
Oh.

MR. SCHULTZ: But if Woodrow wins...maybe.

CHAIRMAN: Then I practically have my teeth in it.

The Judge and Doc Bissell drive into the SHOT.

JUDGE: Everything ready?

DOC BISSELL: Zero hour is at ten.

CHAIRMAN: Everything is ding how.

DOC BISSELL: What?

CHAIRMAN: That's leatherneck for okey.

JUDGE DENNIS: Oh. Then: Up High Street, down Main. Then we go around into Oak Street...

MR. SCHULTZ: We modulate into Oak Street.

JUDGE DENNIS: What?

DOC BISSELL: Is that some more leatherneck?

CHAIRMAN: Pay no attention...we go around into Oak Street...

JUDGE DENNIS: And pick him up.

(Continued)

E-5 (Cont'd)

CHAIRMAN: Right.

DOC BISSELL: Right.

JUDGE DENNIS: Right.

MR. SCHULTZ: Left.

JUDGE DENNIS: What?

CHAIRMAN: (Laughing)
He's just contrary this morning.

JUDGE DENNIS: Oh...well come on.

He drags Doc Bissell away.

DISSOLVE TO:

E-6 SOME FLAP-JACKS SIZZLING ON A GRIDDLE

Woodrow's Mother's hand adds them to a pile on a plate and as she walks to the table with them we discover ourselves in her kitchen. The Marines are eating hungrily. Only one is missing: Juke.

CORPORAL: Oh boy.

CUT TO:

E-7 WOODROW - COMING DOWN THE STAIRS

He looks spick and span and very happy. He is whistling, "We Want Woodrow." Now he sings the third line:

WOODROW: 'We want Woodrow for our mayor.'

As he adjusts his cravat, now the CAMERA PANS him into the kitchen.

WOODROW: (Happily)
Good morning all...good morning, Mama.
(He kisses her, then looks around)
I hope you all had a good night...how about a stack of your famous flannel cakes, Mama? Light as a feather and put together by fairy hands...taste their crunchy, brunchy munchiness...ask your grocer!

During the last of this we have

CUT TO:

7-6-43

E-8 THE SERGEANT - NEXT TO AN EMPTY SEAT AT THE TABLE

He watches Woodrow very suspiciously, as the latter comes into the shot and slaps him on the back before sitting down.

WOODROW: (Happily)
Good morning, Sergeant Heffelfinger...is every body happy...I trust your conscience didn't keep you awake during the night...you know there's nothing like a housebroken conscience ...now you take the conscience in its wild or native form...when first trapped let us say...

The Sergeant leans over and smells his breath.

WOODROW: What's the matter, am I unpleasant? Ah! Is the reason for my unpopularity at last revealed as in a vision?

SERGEANT: I was wondering if you'd been guzzling some more of that cooking wine.

WOODROW: (Shocked)
Guzzling! At this hour of the morning, Sergeant...you offend me.

SERGEANT: What happened, did somebody leave you some dough or something?

WOODROW: You mean because I'm happy? Wouldn't you be happy if you were about to become mayor of this fair city? Not large, mind you, but fascinating...lives there a man with soul so dead who never to himself hath said...good morning, Libby, won't you join us in a stack of collision mats as we say in the good old Marine Corps...and a cup of Jamoke?

CUT TO:

E-9 LIBBY - IN THE DOORWAY

LIBBY: Good morning, Good morning, Woodrow...I'm glad you're feeling better.

She comes into the room.

WOODROW: (Helping her to a chair)
Just call me, Mr. Mayor...I never felt better in my life.

Libby catches the Sergeant's eye who looks back at her very dubiously then shrugs his shoulders.

LIBBY: You got over all that nonsense then?

WOODROW: What nonsense was that?

(Continued)

E-9 (Cont'd)

LIBBY: (Making sure his mother isn't listening)
I mean about...never having been in...
you know...Guadalcanal?...and all that stuff.

WOODROW: (Astounded)
I said such a thing?

LIBBY: Well I certainly understood you to...

WOODROW: (Interrupting)
But how could I?

He looks from one Marine to another.

WOODROW: I'm a great hero...people run when they see me coming...I kill Nips with a wave of the hand...I blow them down...
(He blows through his lips)
I shoot them from all angles, backwards, forwards, while looking in mirrors...I swim into the water and drown them like rats...
I pick up machine guns...

SERGEANT: I got it.

WOODROW: (Severely)
You got what?

SERGEANT: He's gonna play Screwloose from Toulouse.

WOODROW: (Waving no, no, no)
Oh no I'm not...I invite an investigation...
I'm as sane as a Dane...and I'm going to be the mayor.

LIBBY: Are you sure you feel all right, Woodrow?

WOODROW'S MOTHER: (Coming into the SHOT with a stack of wheat cakes for Libby)
What are you talking about, dear?

WOODROW: Well I'll tell you one thing...I certainly feel a lot better than I did yesterday...

THE PHONE RINGS.

WOODROW: Ah.

He looks at the Sergeant with amusement

WOODROW'S MOTHER: I'll get it dear.

She hurries out of the SHOT.

(Continued)

E-9 (Cont'd)

SERGEANT: What are you trying to pull?

WOODROW: (Amiably)
You'll find out.

CUT TO:

E-10 THE TELEPHONE - IN THE HALL

Woodrow's Mother comes into the SHOT and picks up the receiver. Judge Dennis and Doc Bissell come into the house and stand near her.

WOODROW'S MOTHER: Yes...yes he's here...the what...oh yes.
(She turns and looks into the kitchen)
Woodrow, the Marine Base in San Diego wants to talk to you.

CUT TO:

E-11 WOODROW WITH THE MARINES AND LIBBY

WOODROW: (Very innocently)
To me! Why whatever could the Marine Base in San Diego want to talk to me about?

He looks brightly from the Sorgeant to Libby. The Sergeant looks very worried indeed as he exchanges a look with the Corporal.

WOODROW: I'd better find out...good morning, Judge, good morning, Doc Bissell...I'll be with you in a moment.

He crosses to the telephone and the CAMERA PANS him over.

WOODROW: (Into the telephone)
Hello...yes, this is Corporal Truesmith... who is it...yes sir, Colonel...

CUT TO:

E-12 THE SERGEANT AND THE OTHERS

SERGEANT: Know about what?

CUT TO:

E-13 WOODROW - AT THE TELEPHONE

Judge Dennis and Doc Bissell come forward, a little worried.

7-7-43 (Continued)

E-13 (Cont'd)

WOODROW: They've taken me back in the Marine Corps for limited service. I'll have to leave for San Diego at once.

The band outside the house starts PLAYING "We Want Woodrow." Doc Bissell checks the time on his wrist watch.

JUDGE DENNIS: But the parade! The rally! The mayoralty! Aren't you going to be our mayor?

WOODROW: I'm sorry Judge, the United States comes first.

CUT TO:

E-14 A TELEPHONE BOOTH - IN THE LOCAL DRUGSTORE

The door opens, Juke sticks his head out, looks around like a conspirator to see if he is observed and leaps away from the phone booth, relaxes and walks out of the drug store whistling "We Want Woodrow."

CUT TO:

E-15 WOODROW AND THE OTHERS - IN THE KITCHEN

Everybody looks greatly depressed except Woodrow, who is bearing the news with great fortitude.

WOODROW'S MOTHER: (With her arm around her son)
They won't be sending you anywhere dangerous anymore?

LIBBY: (Indignantly)
Well I should hope not after what he's been through.

WOODROW: (To his Mother)
You don't have a thing to worry about, Mama. It'll probably just be, you know, like clerical work or maybe some kind of work in a shipyard or maybe an airplane factory...you know, guarding things.

JUDGE DENNIS: (Indignantly)
Then why don't they leave you here?... where we need you.

DOC BISSELL: That is one of the weaknesses of the military viewpoint...it does not always recognize the importance of civilians in war time.

7-7-43 (Continued)

E-15 (Cont'd)

JUDGE DENNIS: (Almost tearfully)
He could do so much more good here.

DOC BISSELL: I suppose it's natural in a world surrendered to the sword.

WOODROW: I hope you win, Doc.

DOC BISSELL: I'm afraid my chances are very slender... but thank you.

JUDGE DENNIS: You were our only hope, Woodrow.

WOODROW: I'm terribly sorry, Judge, but when duty calls...
(He pauses to look at the Sergeant)

CUT TO:

E-16 THE SERGEANT

He is looking at Woodrow sourly.

CUT TO:

E-17 WOODROW

WOODROW: ...duty calls.
(He looks at Bugsy)

CUT TO:

E-18 BUGSY

He is looking at Woodrow with a very cold expression indeed.

CUT TO:

E-19 WOODROW, HIS MOTHER AND LIBBY

WOODROW'S MOTHER: Do you have to leave today, dear?

WOODROW: I'm afraid so.

LIBBY: You won't even be here for my...wedding?

WOODROW: Well to tell you the truth that's one thing I don't mind missing...although I certainly wish you all the happiness in the world.

7-7-43 (Continued)

E-19 (Cont'd)

LIBBY: I know you do.

JUDGE DENNIS: Woodrow.

WOODROW: Yes sir.

JUDGE DENNIS: You'll ride in the parade anyway, won't you...now that it's all dolled up and everything?

WOODROW: (Not too anxiously)
Well...sure if you want me to but what good will it do?...When you gotta go you gotta go.

JUDGE DENNIS: It might do some good...we won't tell them anything about your bad news... until you get to the town hall, then you can tell them you have to leave suddenly and maybe swing some of your.... enormous popularity to the Doc here.

DOC BISSELL: Not that I want it for myself personally you understand...but I think it would be good for the town.

WOODROW: I know it would.

JUDGE DENNIS: Just your endorsement would mean a great deal.

WOODROW: I certainly can't refuse that.

JUDGE DENNIS: (Starting out)
Then I'll see if everything's ready.

DOC BISSELL: It's going to be more like a funeral march.

He goes out also.

LIBBY: Can I ride in the parade with you, Woodrow...just this last time?

WOODROW: Well sure...if you think it's all right.

LIBBY: Of course it's all right...I have the right to say goodbye to you.

Woodrow's Mother turns away and her shoulders start to shake.

WOODROW: I'm sorry, Mama...I can't do anything about it I...

7-7-43 (Continued)

E-19 (Cont'd)

WOODROW'S
MOTHER: It will be so lonely without you.

Woodrow makes a helpless gesture then catches Bugsy's eye.

CUT TO:

E-20 BUGSY

The Sergeant stands behind him. Bugsy makes a slight move as if to come forward. The sergeant drops a hand on his shoulder to restrain him and gives a double-take at the new arrival in the doorway.

SERGEANT: Where have you been?

CUT TO:

E-21 JUKE - IN THE DOORWAY

JUKE: (With exaggerated innocence)
Who me?...Oh I was just taking a little walk.

CUT TO:

E-22 THE SERGEANT AND BUGSY

SERGEANT: Since when do you forget to have breakfast?

CUT TO:

E-23 CLOSE SHOT - JUKE - IN THE DOORWAY

JUKE: Well I...just a...

Now THE CAMERA PANS off Juke onto the wall phone.

CUT TO:

E-24 THE SERGEANT AND BUGSY

SERGEANT: Oh...you were just making a little phone call...to that dame in San Diego ...I got you Colonel.

CUT TO:

7-7-43

E-25 JUKE

He smiles a kind of a sickly smile.

JUKE: Well...you know.

CUT TO:

E-26 THE SERGEANT AND BUGSY

Bugsy comes from behind the Sergeant like a bat out of hell. As he flashes past the CAMERA:

SERGEANT: (Making a dive after him)
Hey.

Now the Corporal and the others jump to their feet and also hurry PAST THE CAMERA. Woodrow, his mother and Libby try to get out in the hall also.

BILL: We're very sorry...it's nothing... there's just a little ill feeling there...

He holds his arms out to keep them out of the trouble. Quickly Woodrow forces his way by.

CUT TO:

E-27 THE STRUGGLING MARINES - AT THE FOOT OF THE STAIRS

We HEAR mostly panting and dull thuds.

SERGEANT: (Quietly)
Lay off, will ya...you can settle it later.

With the assistance of the big Corporal he pulls Bugsy off Juke. Juke, slightly dazed, sits on the stairs. His left eye is closed and his mouth is bleeding.

JUKE: What's the big idea?

Bugsy struggles to get at him again. Now Woodrow forces his way into the SHOT. He looks at Juke then confronts Bugsy. During the following scene the men keep their voices very low so's not to be heard by the women. Outside the band MODULATES into "Hail The Conquering Hero Comes."

WOODROW: (Through clenched teeth)
You meant that for me, didn't you?

BUGSY: What about it?

7-7-43 (Continued)

E-27 (Cont'd)

WOODROW: You think I'm afraid, hunh?

BUGSY: (Sneeringly)
Well, I'm glad I wasn't never in a fox hole with you.

He laughs bitterly.

WOODROW: Let him go.

BUGSY: You yellow bellied...

WOODROW: (Nearly crying with rage)
Let him go I tell you!

Bugsy laughs in his face and Woodrow hits him a terrible punch in the mouth. The Corporal and the Sergeant exchange a glance, then drop Bugsy's arms. Bugsy looks at Woodrow for a moment, spits some blood out of his mouth, then speaks:

BUGSY: Go find a woman to fight with...that's all you know how to hurt.

Now he leans over and helps Juke to his feet.

BUGSY: Come on, kid.

The two Marines start up the stairs.

CUT TO:

E-28 CLOSE SHOT - WOODROW

He massages the knuckles of his right hand. Now his lips tremble and a couple of tears run down his cheek. The Hero MUSIC outside gets louder.

DISSOLVE TO:

E-29 THE PARADE IN FULL SWING - (MORNING)

A double banner is carried in front of it. It reads: "Follow Us To The Big Rally, Everybody Welcome." Behind this comes the steam roller with the Chairman running it, assisted by Mr. Schultz' advice. They are having a terrible time. Now comes a sign which reads: "Free Seats, Free Speech, Free Food." Behind this a much larger sign which says "Free Drinks." After this: "Win With Woodrow." Then: "Honor The Hero - Make Him 'His Honor'". Then: "Honor And Courage." Then: "Come and Meet The Mayor." Now the Progressive Party Band followed by the car containing Woodrow, his mother and Libby in the back seat and Judge Dennis and Doc Bissell in the

7-7-43 (Continued)

E-29 (Cont'd)

front seat. The five Marines walk alongside as a guard of honor. Behind the car there appears a banner which reads: "A Warrior for War Time". Behind this another car containing the Sheriff, the Rev. Doctor Upperman and the town painter and the other members of the Bissell delegation.

CUT TO:

E-30 CLOSE SHOT - WOODROW, HIS MOTHER AND LIBBY

All three look quite depressed, though they try to smile in answer to the hoorays. Now Woodrow scowls out of the SHOT.

CUT TO:

E-31 AUTOMOBILE SHOT - OF THE CROWD WALKING DOWN THE SIDEWALK AS IT FOLLOWS THE PARADE

Bugsy is leaning against a lamp post which parts the crowd. He is chewing gum. Apart from this his face has neither movement nor expression.

CUT TO:

E-32 WOODROW, HIS MOTHER AND LIBBY

Woodrow looks very sore. The CAMERA PANS AROUND as Woodrow's car goes by and we see the parade, with the church in the background, turning the corner.

DISSOLVE TO:

E-33 EXT. NOBLE CHAIR COMPANY (DAY)

Mr. Noble's followers increase in number on the sidewalk, as the music of the parade approaches. Now Mrs. Noble comes out and looks down the street delightedly.

MRS. NOBLE: (Clapping her hands)
Oh isn't it exciting? I love a parade.

CUT TO:

E-34 MR. NOBLE, THE BOSS AND FORREST - IN THE PRIVATE OFFICE

The music of the parade drifts in faintly.

MR. NOBLE: Parades...statues...burning mortgages...

THE BOSS: I subscribed to that.

MR. NOBLE: So did I for that matter but I mean to say...

(Continued)

E-34 (Cont'd)

THE BOSS: Save your voice, Evvy.

MR. NOBLE: For what? I mean to say I have nothing against the boy personally, a hero is a fine thing...IN ITS PLACE.

FORREST: You mean in a park.

MR. NOBLE: I don't mean that at all...I don't wish this young man anything but, ahem, success IN WHAT HE CAN DO BEST BUT WHAT CAN HE DO BEST?

FORREST: Well...

MR. NOBLE: (Cutting him off instantly)
That is our problem. I speak, not as your candidate for mayor but as the most humble voter.
(He turns to his son)
Get me a glass of water, will you?

THE BOSS: Why don't you save...

MR. NOBLE: Why don't you shut up?
(He puts a cough drop in his mouth)
I mean to say this problem is not local... it is national...In a few years, if this war goes on, heaven forbid, you won't be able to swing a cat without knocking down a couple of heroes...now: are we to be governed by young men, very young men, however, well meaning and patriotic they may be, whose principal talent consists in hopping in and out of wolf holes, or...

THE BOSS: Fox holes.

MR. NOBLE: What?

THE BOSS: They're called fox holes.

MR. NOBLE: (Running all the words together)
Oh...who'sprincipaltalentconsistsofhopping-inandoutof...FOXHOLES, and killing hundreds of enemies with one swoop of the sword, or are we going to be governed by respectable civic leaders of mature age who do

(Continued)

E-34 (Cont'd)

MR. NOBLE: (Cont'd) not seek the appointment but to accept it as a civic duty? I refer to men like...well... myself. I did not...wait a minute: did they take out a permit to hold this parade?

FORREST: (Appearing with a glass of water)
What does it matter?

MR. NOBLE: (After taking a sip of water)
What does it matter, what does it matter?... that's the trouble with the American viewpoint...it matters very much indeed.

He starts out of the office and the others follow him...

MR. NOBLE: (Cont'd) This country is run by permits, that is to say laws, and just because it's wartime these soldiers think they can they can...

CUT TO:

E-35 EXT. THE NOBLE CHAIR COMPANY (DAY)

Mr. Noble comes out followed by the Boss and Forrest.

MR. NOBLE: They'll find out whether it matters or not...

MRS. NOBLE: Isn't it exciting, Everett...they make a handsome couple, don't they...oh I'm sorry, Forrest.

Mr. Noble starts forward.

THE BOSS: Hold your horses.

MR. NOBLE: What's the matter now?

We see the little old Western Union man coming through the crowd. THE CAMERA PANS him in the SHOT with Mr. Noble.

THE WESTERN UNION BOY: Howdy, Mr. Mayor...I got a telegram for ya if I can just remember where I put it.

MR. NOBLE: What kind of a telegram?

THE BOSS: Can you remember where it came from?

THE WESTERN UNION BOY: Now let me see...
(He takes off his cap to scratch his head)
San Diego I think.

At this the telegram falls to the sidewalk. Mr. Noble and The Boss make a dive for it, bump their heads, pick up the telegram at the same time and tear it in two as they straighten up.

MR. NOBLE: (Severely)
You're a big help.

(Continued)

E-35 (Cont'd)

Now they read the two halves of the telegram.

CUT TO:

E-36 INSERT

We read: "Marine Headquarters, San Diego, California

Private Woodrow L.P. Truesmith medically
discharged one year ago.

Reason: Chronic Hayfever.

A. B. Hilton, Major U.S.M.C.
Adj. to C.O.

SLOW DISSOLVE TO:

E-37 MR. NOBLE, THE BOSS, FORREST AND MRS. NOBLE - LOOKING OVER THEIR SHOULDERS

MR. NOBLE: (Deeply puzzled)
But then how could he have been
in a...Guadal...canal?

THE BOSS: (Amused)
That's just it...he wasn't.

MR. NOBLE: (Indignantly)
But then he's a fraud, a faker, a,a,a
why he ought to be tarred and feathered.
(Now he beams)
Oh boy.

FORREST; Oh.

MRS. NOBLE: Who's a fraud and a faker?

MR. NOBLE: (Pointing)
Right there, look at him.

CUT TO:

E-38 THE PARADE

Woodrow is just going by.

CUT TO:

E-39 MR. NOBLE, THE BOSS, FORREST AND MRS. NOBLE.

MRS. NOBLE: I don't believe it.

MR. NOBLE: You don't believe it. Well, he laughs
last who laughs, laughs. Hah.

(Continued)

E-39 (Cont'd)

He puts the halves of the telegram in the hands of his son who is glaring at something else.

MR. NOBLE: Here...glue this together for me and hurry up about it.

As Forrest does not answer, Mr. Noble follows his gaze.

MRS. NOBLE: I'm sure you're mistaken, Everett. Remember, your impulses are always wrong, dear.

CUT TO:

E-40 CLOSE SHOT - LIBBY - IN THE OFFICIAL CAR

She smiles sweetly to Noble.

CUT TO:

E-41 MR. NOBLE, FORREST, THE BOSS AND MRS. NOBLE

MR. NOBLE: (Taking back the telegram)
Never mind...we'll wipe that smile off her face, too...personally I wouldn't marry her for that.

MRS. NOBLE: Please, Evvy, you talk such nonsense.

Now he starts after the parade.

MR. NOBLE: Come on.

THE BOSS: (Holding him back)
Where are you going?

MR. NOBLE: It says, 'Everybody Welcome' doesn't it?

THE BOSS: Be careful, you're fooling with dynamite.

MR. NOBLE: You watch my smoke.

MRS. NOBLE: Evvy, all my intuitions tell me....

He hurries out of the SHOT followed by Mrs. Noble and the Boss. Forrest follows slowly, ignoring the hat request. Now Bugsy walks into the SHOT. The CAMERA PANS after him onto the statue of General Zabriski, the town hall, the halted parade and the crowd.

DISSOLVE TO:

E-42 SHOT DOWN THE STEPS OF THE TOWN HALL

Woodrow comes up toward us. Half way up the steps Libby sees Forrest and Woodrow sees Bugsy.

(Continued)

E-42 (Cont'd)

As Woodrow, his mother and Libby go PAST THE CAMERA, Mr. & Mrs. Noble and the Boss come up to the door.

MR. NOBLE: (Happily)
After you.

THE BOSS: No, no, after you.

MRS. NOBLE: (Pushing Noble through)
Age before beauty.

They go in. Now Forrest comes up and after him Bugsy.

CUT TO:

E-43 INT. OF THE TOWN HALL - (DAY)

The band is PLAYING its usual tunes. Shooting toward the entrance from the side we pick up Mr. Noble and the Boss and Mrs. Noble. PAN them around to the back seats. This brings them face to face with the FREE LUNCH table.

MR. NOBLE: Ah.
(He exchanges a look with the Boss)
I wonder if this would be rubbing it in?

THE BOSS: (Pointing to the sign)
It says: "Help Yourself."

MR. NOBLE: Well...there's plenty of time.

MRS. NOBLE: Everett, I just have a feeling you're going to make an ass of yourself...I'm just going to pretend I don't know you.

She goes on. He makes himself a little sandwich; the Boss takes a sour pickle and they move down to some empty seats just in front of Mrs. Noble. THE CAMERA FOLLOWS them, thusly PANNING OVER three sides of the set. The town hall is decorated with bunting, flags, "We Want Woodrow" signs and other banners.

CUT TO:

E-44 FORREST - COMING IN

He sits down in the last row. Now Bugsy comes in and walks down front. THE CAMERA TRUCKS ALONGSIDE him so that we shoot across the long rows of people. Bugsy takes a seat in the second row and in a little.

CUT TO:

E-45 BOOM SHOT - THE PLATFORM - FROM APPROXIMATELY BUGSY'S POSITION

There is a speaker's table with ice water in front and behind this a row of chairs for notables. On these sit the elders of the Bissell delegation, the Sheriff, Reverend Doctor Upperman, the Town Painter, Mr. Schultz, Judge Dennis, Doc Bissell, Woodrow, his mother, Libby and the five Marines.

(Continued)

E-45 (Cont'd)

The Chairman is leading the band on one side of the platform. Now Judge Dennis gets up and comes forward to the speaker's table. The Chairman brings the band to a STOP and goes over and sits down.

JUDGE DENNIS: Yesterday morning seven Marines got off the Northbound.

There is a hooray from the crowd.

JUDGE DENNIS: Six of them were strangers to us...one a local boy who had made good.

There is a wild hooray from the crowd interspersed with "We Want Woodrow."

CUT TO:

E-46 CLOSE SHOT - WOODROW

He smiles wanly at the audience, waves his hand a little, then scowls at Bugsy.

CUT TO:

E-47 BUGSY - IN THE AUDIENCE

He looks at Woodrow.

CUT TO:

E-48 JUDGE DENNIS AND THE OTHERS - BOOM SHOT

JUDGE DENNIS: Yesterday afternoon we asked this local boy to cast his lot with ours, you might call us the "unvested" or shirtsleeve interests of the town, and lead us to victory.

There is a wild hooray from the crowd and the band starts to play "We Want Woodrow."

CUT TO:

E-49 MR. NOBLE AND THE BOSS

Mr. Noble is busy eating his sandwich. He pantomimes to the Boss that it is very tasty. Mrs. Noble does: "SH."

CUT TO:

E-50 THE JUDGE AND THE OTHERS - BOOM SHOT

JUDGE DENNIS: (Motioning for silence) I'm going to ask Woodrow himself to tell you the rest of the story.

(Continued)

E-50 (Cont'd)

The crowd goes wild and the band plays "We Want Woodrow" again, as Woodrow gets to his feet and comes forward.

CUT TO:

E-51 WOODROW'S MOTHER AND LIBBY

Woodrow's Mother cries a little. Libby watches Woodrow proudly.

CUT TO:

E-52 FORREST

He watches all of this with some displeasure.

CUT TO:

E-53 CLOSE SHOT - WOODROW

CUT TO:

E-54 CLOSE SHOT - WOODROW - LOOKING AT BUGSY

CUT TO:

E-55 CLOSE SHOT - THE SERGEANT - LOOKING AT BUGSY

CUT TO:

E-56 WOODROW

Behind him the Judge waves for silence.

CUT TO:

E-57 MR. NOBLE AND THE BOSS

MR. NOBLE: (Fingering the telegram)
Shall we do it now or let him linger?

THE BOSS: Let him have his moment.

Mrs. Noble behind them shushes them. Mr. Noble turns and gives her a dirty look.

CUT TO:

E-58 CLOSE SHOT - WOODROW

WOODROW: I came here this morning to say good-bye to you.

CUT TO:

E-59 THE CROWD

They look at each other and murmur their displeasure.

CUT TO:

E-60 MR. NOBLE AND THE BOSS

Mr. Noble turns to the Boss in astonishment, then looks back at Woodrow.

MRS. NOBLE: You see?

CUT TO:

E-61 BUGSY

He takes a toothpick out of his pocket and starts chewing on it.

CUT TO:

E-62 WOODROW

WOODROW: I came here to tell you that I had been called back into the Marine Corps for limited service and that for that reason I would not be able to run for mayor.

There is a murmur of distress again.

WOODROW: Well...I'M NOT GOING TO DO IT.
(He looks straight at Bugsy as he says this)

There is a wild hooray from the crowd.

CUT TO:

E-63 BUGSY

He looks puzzled.

CUT TO:

E-64 MR. NOBLE AND THE BOSS

Mr. Noble looks utterly bewildered. He starts to pull the telegram out of his pocket but the Boss motions him to put it back in.

MRS. NOBLE: You see what I told you?

CUT TO:

E-65 THE SERGEANT

Perplexedly he looks at the Judge.

CUT TO:

E-66 THE JUDGE

He looks hopefully at Woodrow's Mother and Libby.

CUT TO:

E-67 WOODROW'S MOTHER, LIBBY AND DOC BISSELL

Libby looks hopefully at Doc Bissell, who does not understand at all.

CUT TO:

E-68 WOODROW - MOTIONING FOR SILENCE

WOODROW: You'd better save your hoorays for somebody else...for somebody who deserves them ...like Doc Bissell here...who has tried for so long to serve you...only you didn't know a good man when you saw one...so you always elected a phony instead.
(He nods toward Mr. Noble)

CUT TO:

E-69 MR. NOBLE AND THE BOSS

The crowd laughs.

MR. NOBLE: (Getting to his feet)
Oh I am, am I...well let me tell you something, young man.
(He starts to reach for the telegram)

There are yells of "quiet" and "sit down!" The Boss, helped by Mrs. Noble, pulls Mr. Noble down. Mr. Noble sits down muttering "You'll find out."

MRS. NOBLE: Everett, you're making a spectacle of yourself.

CUT TO:

E-70 WOODROW

WOODROW: Until a still bigger phony came along... then you naturally wanted him.

The Sergeant gets up in the background, walks up to Woodrow and taps him on the shoulder.

WOODROW: (Quietly)
Sit down, Sergeant.

SERGEANT: Now wait a minute...

There are calls of "sit down" and "quiet" from the audience.

(Continued)

E-70 (Cont'd)

WOODROW: This should have been the happiest day of my life...it could have been...instead it is the bitterest...It says in the Bible "my cup runneth over"...Well my cup runneth over...with gall. This is the last act... the farce is over, the lying is finished... and the coward is at least cured of his fear.

SERGEANT: (Hurrying up)
Ladies and gentlemen I think this whole thing had better be called off, he don't feel very good in the head sometimes.

There are yells of "quiet" and "sit down."

CUT TO:

E-71 LIBBY - LOOKING AT WOODROW ANXIOUSLY

The Sergeant sits down beside her.

LIBBY: It's the same thing that happened to him last night.

SERGEANT: Yeh, only a lot worse.

CUT TO:

E-72 WOODROW

He looks back from the Sergeant.

WOODROW: I was born in this town...my father was born here. Most of the town is on my grandfather's homestead...his well was just about where I'm standing and it leaks into the cellar sometimes...they've had quite a lot of trouble with it...

There is a nervous laugh which Woodrow ignores.

WOODROW: My grandfather was an honorable man. So was my father...I've sold papers on the street to most of you who are here this morning...I've known you all my life. Your affection means a great deal to me and now that I've lost the chance forever I want you to know how much it would have meant to me to be the mayor...or the city clerk, or the assistant city clerk...or the dog catcher ...of this town which was my grandfather's farm...by the same token I would gladly have given my life to have earned just one of the many ribbons you see on these brave men's chests...if I could have reached as high as my father's shoestrings, my whole life would

(Continued)

E-72 (Cont'd)

WOODROW: (Cont'd)
be justified and I would stand here proudly before you...instead of as the thief and coward that I am.

There is a hubbub of voices and for the first time Woodrow speaks with authority.

WOODROW:
Quiet...a coward because I postponed until now what I should have told you a year ago when I was discharged from the Marine Corps for medical unfitness...a coward because I didn't want my mother to know...well, it wasn't to save her it was to save me.

CUT TO:

E-73 WOODROW'S MOTHER AND LIBBY

Woodrow's Mother lowers her head. Libby looks rigidly at Woodrow...a look of compassion on her face.

CUT TO:

E-74 THE SERGEANT

He looks around nervously, then his gaze fixes to something at one side of the stage.

CUT TO:

E-75 THE EXIT SIGN - OVER THE BACK DOOR OF THE TOWN HALL

CUT TO:

E-76 WOODROW

WOODROW:
A thief because I stole your admiration, I stole the ribbons I wore, I stole this nomination.

CUT TO:

E-77 BUGSY

During the preceding speech he has got up from his seat, walked around onto the platform and taken his place beside the other Marines.

CUT TO:

E-78 WOODROW

WOODROW: I have never been in Guadalcanal or any place else...I've been working in a shipyard for the last year. I've never received a medal of any description...naturally, since I've never fought. Two days ago I decided to come home. Since I'd written to my Mother I was overseas I had to come home as a soldier...I had to have some ribbons so Iya bought them in a hock shop. When I was all dressed up I met some real Marines...I brought them home with me to make things look better...I fooled them as much as I did the rest of you, not that I really wanted to fool any of you...I just wanted to come home.

SERGEANT: (Getting to his feet)
That's as dirty a lie as...

There are YELLS of "quiet" and "sit down."

WOODROW: I've told you all this because too many men have bled and died for you...and for me... to live this lie any longer...I guess that's why I told you...I certainly didn't mean to when I came in...I'm gonna pack my things now so this will probably be my last chance to say good-bye to you. I know my Mother will give you back the mortgage...and I hope you won't hold it against her that her son didn't...quite come through...there's no use telling you I'm sorry because I wish I was dead. I -- that's all.

He turns and looks toward his mother, then walks toward the back door with squeaking shoes.

CUT TO:

E-79 MR. NOBLE AND THE BOSS

MR. NOBLE: (Confidentially)
I need some air.

He pinches his nose. They rise and start out. After a moment Mrs. Noble goes out, wiping away a tear.

CUT TO:

E-80 WOODROW'S MOTHER AND LIBBY

They get up and start out. At a gesture from the Sergeant, the five Marines surround them and escort them toward the door.

JUDGE DENNIS: If everybody will please keep their seat.

(Continued)

E-80 (Cont'd)

Now the Sergeant turns and comes up to the table beside Judge Dennis.

SERGEANT: I just wanta tell you one thing, see...I seen a lot of brave men in my life...that's my business...but what that kid just done... took real courage...and now that he's shot his mouth off you might as well hear the rest of it...in fact you'd better hear it... there's six of us see, and we got fifteen cents between us...and we're from Guadalcanal AND NO FOOLIN' what I mean...

DISSOLVE TO:

E-81 TRUCKING SHOT - BESIDE WOODROW

At first he walks with his hands in his pockets and his head down. Presently he holds his head high. After awhile he takes his hands out of his pockets and holds his head still higher. We leave him striding along quite manfully. Way in the background we see Woodrow's Mother, Libby and the five Marines.

CUT TO:

E-82 CLOSE SHOT - WOODROW'S MOTHER, LIBBY AND THE MARINES

LIBBY: (Taking her departure)
I'll be over in a few minutes.

WOODROW'S MOTHER: You'd better not, dear...you've got yourself in enough trouble.

LIBBY: I'll be over in a few minutes.

THE CAMERA PANS HER over to the Noble Chair Company as Woodrow's Mother and the Marines start down the street. As Libby goes in the Chair Company -

CUT TO:

E-83 MR. NOBLE'S PRIVATE OFFICE

Here we see Mr. Noble, the Boss and Forrest.

MR. NOBLE: Pitiful, pitiful...there you see one of the fallacies, I wouldn't want this to go any further you understand, of the Democratic principal: They can vote for anybody they like. I was never deceived for an instant, but the poor misguided voters, without a brain to bless themselves with, without a cerebellum to the carload. Make a note of that one, Forrest, I'll use it...

THE BOSS: I wouldn't. (Continued)

E-83 (Cont'd)

MR. NOBLE: ...open wide their arms to...oh, there you are.

CUT TO:

E-84 LIBBY - IN THE DOORWAY

LIBBY: (Quite placidly)
Hello.

She comes forward and THE CAMERA PANS HER into the group with others. Mrs. Noble hurries in after her.

MRS. NOBLE: I'm so sorry, dear, my heart bled for you.

MR. NOBLE: You have the effrontery to return?

LIBBY: What?

MRS. NOBLE: Oh shut up, Evvy. Don't pay any attention to him, Libby.

MR. NOBLE: What do you think of your hero now?

FORREST: Don't rub it in, Father, she probably feels badly enough.

MR. NOBLE: (Crossly)
Well she should feel badly and if you ask my advice...

FORREST: Which I don't.

MRS. NOBLE: You heard him.

MR. NOBLE: You're a sucker if you even consider going through with...

THE BOSS: (Taking a quick powder)
I want to see somebody outside.

MRS. NOBLE: I don't blame you.

The Boss exits.

LIBBY: But I don't feel badly at all.

MR. NOBLE: You don't?

MRS. NOBLE: Good for you.

FORREST: Father, I wish you'd keep your nose out of my affairs...this is a matter entirely between Libby and myself.

LIBBY: ...and Woodrow.

(Continued)

E-84 (Cont'd)

FORREST: And Woodrow!

MRS. NOBLE: Naturally.

MR. NOBLE: What do you mean "naturally"?

FORREST: You don't mean to tell me that after that disgraceful exhibition you still have any...interest...in the "hero"?

LIBBY: I guess women feel a little differently than men do about these things, Forrest... so if you'll please forgive me and...not think too harshly of me...

(She starts to take the engagement ring off her finger)

(Continued)

E-84 (Cont'd)

MRS. NOBLE: You see what I told you? You walked right into it.

DISSOLVE TO:

E-85 THE FIVE MARINES - ON THE PORCH OF WOODROW'S HOUSE

Nobody seems to have much to say. One is rolling a cigarette, another is whittling.

BILL: What time is the train?

JONESY: Who's got the dough?

CORPORAL: If I could just find a good crap game.

Bugsy spits over the rail.

DISSOLVE TO:

E-86 WOODROW AND HIS MOTHER - IN HIS ROOM

She is sitting on the edge of the bed. He is packing the suitcase on the top of his dresser.

WOODROW'S MOTHER: Why couldn't you stay here?

WOODROW: Who's gonna give me a job?

WOODROW'S MOTHER: Well...

WOODROW: I'll tell you what I'll do, Mama, if I can find a nice place, I'll send for you and...

Woodrow's Mother comes behind him and kisses him.

WOODROW'S MOTHER: I know you meant it for the best, dear, I know you meant it for me no matter what anyone else might think.

Her lips tremble as she turns and leaves the room. As she does so Libby appears in the background. She comes into the room.

WOODROW: Hello.

LIBBY: Can I help you?

WOODROW: I'll manage all right.

(Continued)

E-87 LIBBY AND WOODROW - CLOSE SHOT - IN HIS ROOM

NOTE: This will require a small piece of set matching scene E-86. Before putting this set up check with Stu. Gilmore to see if CLOSE UP of E-89 can be tie

LIBBY: (After kissing him)
Of course I'm going with you, I've never loved anybody but you and you've never loved anybody but me and...
(She starts to weep a little)
you can't say it's because you're a hero I'm running after you, can you? OH, Woodrow, when I think I almost lost you, stupid, stupid, stupid...
(She kisses him)

WOODROW: (Interrupting the kiss)
You're crazy, honey.

LIBBY: Then I'm crazy.
(She kisses him again)

DISSOLVE TO:

E-88 THE HANDS OF THE STATION MASTER

To the MUSIC of "Mademoiselle from Armentierres" the hands ARE STAMPING TICKETS. The music had better be in a Minor

CUT TO:

E-89 WOODROW'S MOTHER AND BUGSY - NEAR THE TICKET WINDOW (Stage

He pats her on the shoulder, then looks away. The CAMERA PANS over the other Marines onto Libby and Woodrow as the latter turns from the ticket window. Libby has an overcoa over her arm. Woodrow's suitcases are at his feet. He starts to pick them up, but the Marines do it for him.

WOODROW: (To the station master - Robert Dudley)
Is she on time, Mr. Kennedy?

STATION MASTER: (A little hard of hearing)
How was that?

WOODROW: Is the South Bound on time?

STATION MASTER: Be here in four and a quarter minutes. Where you goin'..I thought you was runnin for Mayor?

WOODROW: I changed my mind.

(Continued)

STATION
MASTER: Oh...that's very unusual.

WOODROW: Well, this was an unusual case.

STATION
MASTER: I said it's very unusual.

WOODROW: You said it.

CORPORAL: How about the Sarge?

WOODROW: (Looking at his watch)
Well...

JUKE: I told him where you were.

CORPORAL: Go look for him.

Juke starts out.

CORPORAL: He'll be here...he don't never miss nothin'.

CUT TO:

E-90 SHOT - DOWN THE MAIN STREET - (DAY) - (RANCH)

The Sergeant, followed apparently by the entire town, is coming toward us. The MUSIC (Already recorded) is very grim.

CUT TO:

E-91 CLOSE - BOOM SHOT - (RANCH)

We see the Sergeant and the elders of the town walking along. We also spot the political boss (Al Bridge).

CUT TO:

E-92 JUKE - LOOKING OUT THE DOOR OF THE STATION - (RANCH)

He reacts to the oncoming mob and hurries away.

CUT TO:

E-93 LONG SHOT - THE MOB COMING TOWARD US - (RANCH)

CUT TO:

E-94 WOODROW, LIBBY, WOODROW'S MOTHER, BUGSY, THE CORPORAL, BILL AND JONESY. - ON THE STATION PLATFORM - (RANCH)

Juke hurries into the SHOT.

(Continued)

E-94 (Cont'd)

JUKE: (Excitedly)
Cheese it, the whole town is coming.

WOODROW: What is it...A lynching?

CORPORAL: (Very hard)
With us here.

He makes a gesture to the other Marines.

CORPORAL: We'll just kind of surround you, see?

WOODROW: Yea, you were gonna do that before.

His mother and Libby step close to him.

CUT TO:

E-95 THE APPROACHING MOB - FROM THE FRONT OF THE STATION (RANCH)

We let quite a few of them go under the CAMERA.

CUT TO:

E-96 MOVING BOOM SHOT - ON THE STATION PLATFORM (STAGE 4)

We pick up the Sergeant and the leaders of the mob. We bring them into position opposite Woodrow and the Marines, then PAN once around Woodrow's group, to show the platform filling up, then back on to the leaders over Woodrow's shoulder.

SERGEANT: Leave a little room there...quiet!

As quiet is established we hear the distant WHISTLE of the South Bound. The Sergeant moves to his place with the other Marines.

JUDGE DENNIS: We had quite a talk after you left, Woodrow. The Sergeant told us a few things.

MR. SCHULTZ: Quite a few things.

CHAIRMAN: (Severely)
That you had forgotten to mention.

JUDGE DENNIS: Naturally the nomination went back to Doc Bissell, but he got up and said...

MR. SCHULTZ: "Ladies and Gents..."

DOC BISSELL: Don't misquote me.

JUDGE DENNIS: What?

(Continued)

E-96 (Cont'd)

DOC BISSELL: I said, "Ladies and Gentlemen."

CHAIRMAN: Of course you did.

DOC BISSELL: I said, "Ladies and Gentlemen, in all the years that I have been unsuccessfully mixed into politics this is the first and only time that I have seen a candidate for office given an opportunity to prove publicly, permanently and beyond peradventure of a doubt that he was honest, courageous and veracious."

JUDGE DENNIS: That means truthful...he likes those big words.

DOC BISSELL: And I said further that if to act out a little lie to save one's mother humiliation was a fault...in other words if tenderness toward and consideration of one's mother was a fault, it was a fault any man might be proud of.

DOC UPPERMAN: Hear, hear.

A VOICE AMONG THE SPECTATORS: Hooray.

DOC BISSELL: Thank you. I made a very good speech on your behalf...better than I have ever made for myself.

JUDGE DENNIS: It was a wonderful speech, Woodrow.

SERGEANT: The guy had us all blubbering.

DOC BISSELL: I meant every word of it straight from the heart, Woodrow, I concluded by pointing out that if this town really wanted an honest, courageous and veracious mayor...

JUDGE DENNIS: That means truthful.

DOC BISSELL: They had better catch you before you caught the Southbound and got away.

JUDGE DENNIS: So we come right over...That's why we're here.

CUT TO:

E-97 WOODROW, HIS MOTHER, LIBBY AND THE SERGEANT

WOODROW: I'm a little dizzy. I guess I don't quite understand what you mean.

LIBBY: I think they mean they want you as mayor, Woodrow.

(Continued)

E-97 (Cont'd)

WOODROW: They want me as mayor?

SERGEANT: That's right.

WOODROW'S MOTHER: They want you as mayor?

WOODROW: No, no.

CUT TO:

E-98 THE JUDGE AND THE OTHERS

JUDGE DENNIS: We're all a little dizzy, Woodrow, but that's what we mean...we want you for mayor.

We hear the train pulling into the station and see its shadow.

CUT TO:

E-99 WOODROW AND THE OTHERS

WOODROW: You mean you still want me?

CUT TO:

E-100 THE JUDGE AND THE OTHERS

JUDGE DENNIS: We still want you...very much.

MR. SCHULTZ: What do we want a soldier for, anyway?

DOC BISSELL: Politics is a very peculiar thing, Woodrow... if they want you, they want you...they don't need reasons any more...they find their own reasons...just like when a girl wants a man...

LIBBY: That's right...you don't need reasons, although they're probably there.

CUT TO:

E-101 THE CONDUCTOR OF THE TRAIN (Harry Tyler)

THE CAMERA PANS him over to the group.

CONDUCTOR: (Sarcastically) Pardon me for intruding, but is anybody here interested in getting on this train...or is this the Democratic National Convention?

(Continued)

E-101 (Cont'd)

WOODROW: (Still thunderstruck)
Oh....well...

LIBBY: Of course you're not going.

WOODROW'S MOTHER: Of course you're not.

JUDGE DENNIS: (To the Conductor)
We won't detain you any longer...
nobody's leaving...thank you very much.

CONDUCTOR: O.K. all aboard.

SERGEANT: Just a minute, Mac.
(Then to Woodrow)
Gimme six of them tickets, will ya...we
still got a little work to do...in our own
line...So Long, kid, see youse in church.

WOODROW: Will ya come back?

SERGEANT: Well, we always come back before...so long
everybody...come on there, rookies.

As they move toward the train

CUT TO:

E-102 THE BOSS - COMING IN TO MR. NOBLE'S OFFICE (ALREADY SHOT)

THE BOSS: (Coming in)
Save your voice, Evvy, they've just
renominated Woodrow.

MRS. NOBLE: (Hurrying in)
Oh isn't it exciting, Evvy...Now the
battle is on again.

MR. NOBLE: (Horrified)
Shut up! What on?

THE BOSS: I don't know...but I think it's a
vindication campaign.

Mr. Noble rolls his eyes up and FALLS FLAT OUT OF THE SHOT.

FORREST: Look out.

He hurries to pick up his father.

DISSOLVE TO:

E-103 DOWN SHOT - ON WOODROW AND THE GANG - Stage 4

WOODROW: So long, gang.

CONDUCTOR'S VOICE: All aboard.

WOODROW: I don't know how to...

CUT TO:

E-104 THE MARINES - ON THE OBSERVATION CAR

SERGEANT: Don't say it...it was a pleasure.. anything for the son of an old friend.

We hear the bumping of the couplers up ahead as the train starts to move.

CUT TO:

E-105 WOODROW AND THE GANG AROUND HIM

WOODROW: I knew the Marines could do almost anything but I never knew they could do anything like this.

CUT TO:

E-106 OBSERVATION PLATFORM - PULLING AWAY

BUGSY: You got no idea.

He laughs a little and raises his hand in farewell. The other Marines do likewise. The band starts to play "From The Halls of Montezuma To The Shores of Tripoli".

CUT TO:

E-107 SHOT OF WOODROW AND THE GANG - AS THE TRAIN PULLS AWAY FROM THEM DOWN THE STATION PLATFORM

CUT TO:

E-108 CLOSE SHOT - WOODROW

Just audibly he says:

WOODROW: Semper Fidelis.

CUT TO:

E-109 THE MARINES - PULLING AWAY

Their arms are raised high in salute. The music gets faster and faster and the United States Marine Emblem DISSOLVE IN.

THE END